King Ted's

A biography of King Edward VII School Sheffield 1905-2005

BAH 93

By John Cornwell

Published by King Edward VII School
Glossop Road
Sheffield, S10 2PW

KES E-Mail address is: office@kes.sheffield.sch.uk

First Edition Published October 2005

ISBN Number 0-9526484-1-5

Printed by DS Print, Design & Publishing
286 South Road
Walkley
Sheffield
S6 3TE
Tel: 0114 2854050
Email: info@dspad.co.uk
Website: www.dspad.co.uk

The cover design is by Andrew Holmes, a KES Y13 Sixth Form student in 2005.

The title page from a watercolour by Ben Marston (KES 1984-90), painted in 1993.

CONTENTS

FOREWORD

By MICHAEL LEWIS

Headteacher of King Edward VII School

King Edward VII School! KES! King Ted's! The various names of the school resonate with Sheffielders of all generations. For a hundred years the School has occupied a central role in the educational life of the City of Sheffield.

When I tentatively approached John Cornwell three years ago with the suggestion that he might like to consider writing a history of the School to celebrate its impending centenary, I hardly imagined that a volume of such significance would emerge. Neither could I foresee the labour of love combined with a real taste for scholarship and original research which my innocuous question had set in motion.

This work is a unique chronicle. Throughout the troubled twentieth century King Edward VII School has evolved and adapted. It has survived and flourished. It has lived through and reflected the dramas of the times at home and abroad, in good times and bad.

John Cornwell weaves a fascinating narrative, drawing on many original and hitherto unpublished sources, to portray the journey of the School from the imperial post Victorian era to the dawn of the globalised and multi-cultural Twenty-First Century. He finds themes of permanence and continuity in a period of change which would have bewildered the Methodist founders of the original Wesley College in whose magnificent building the contemporary school still thrives. He records with forensic thoroughness the cut and thrust of local politics which shaped the destiny of the School in this most political of cities. He traces the emergence of this most diverse and successful co-educational comprehensive school from its origins as a small fee-paying Edwardian Boys' Grammar School with public school pretensions, and in the process captures the pivotal moments in the School's history.

Yet this remarkable book is much more than a constitutional history of the English education system. John Cornwell brings to life with great affection and generosity the many characters who have graced the School and left their mark on it. He recalls anecdotes, achievements and rivalries. His pages are animated by the sport, music and theatrical aspirations of the staff and students of the School, set in the context of their time.

King Ted's: a Biography of King Edward VII School does honour to a great school. There is much in this book to appeal to the widest readership; whether you have personal memories of the School as a pupil or as a member of staff or a passionate interest in the vicissitudes of Sheffield politics or whether you have just wondered all those years what actually happens behind the imposing façade which looks out on Clarkehouse Road, you will find something to surprise and delight you in John Cornwell's history.

September 2005

ACKNOWLEDGEMENTS

When I was asked to write the history of King Edward VII School, I was delighted to accept because I have long been fascinated by the extraordinary changes, events and achievements that have defined the history of this remarkable school during the last one hundred years. I particularly wanted to get a proper understanding of the major constitutional crises that faced the school in 1926-7, 1944-5, 1965-69 and 1985-86, and also discover just how Wesley College and the Royal Grammar School were fused into the new entity that became King Edward VII School in 1905.

It soon became apparent that there were two histories of KES. One that explores the symbiotic relationship of the school with the City Council and the manner with which the school coped with the education legislation introduced by successive governments, the other that is the "family" history of the over 15,000 Old Edwardians and over 1000 staff members who have studied or taught at the school since 1905. The first is to be found in the minutes of the meetings of the Governors and the Education Committee, in letters and reports written by Headmasters and Council Officers, in local press articles and in discussions with former senior Councillors and Education Department Officers. The latter was revealed in the school magazines, in concert and play programmes, photos of sports teams, old school rules and in the numerous personal recollections of Old Edwardians, staff members and friends of the school.

I am neither an Old Edwardian nor a former teacher at the school, and so, through a hundred or so interviews during 2003 and 2004, I tried to gain an understanding of life at the school as former pupils and staff remembered it. For most of them their memories revolve around celebrated teachers and notable pupils, familiar rooms and freezing playing fields, scout troops and sports teams, concerts, plays and societies and always the omniscient presence of the Headmaster of the day.

I am very much aware that only a few of the people who have gone through the school have been able to contribute their personal reminiscences, and that, therefore, this history is certain to be incomplete, because every person's story reveals some new aspect of life at KES. However, if you are mentioned and I have got it wrong, I apologise. If you have been left out and feel an injustice, please chalk it up to the need for selectivity or the final book would be of unmanageable proportions.

When my own school celebrated its centenary over a decade ago, they also produced a history of the school. My main interest was to read about "my" era and I was underwhelmed by the lack of detail on offer. On the other hand I found later decades appeared to have far too much information (although they were in reality no longer) and I would have settled for a briefer outline of the major themes and events. In this book I have tried to write a reasonably full account of all the different periods of KES history, so that the book reflects the memories and opinions of those involved in all the decades, whilst also serving as a formal record of the school's progress over the last century. At the same time I have attempted to maintain a popular touch to avoid overly turgid and tedious chapters.

I have used some abbreviations and initials throughout the book for convenience sake. It does not seem unreasonable to use KES for King Edward VII School, as the school has used that form throughout its history. Similarly SRGS (for Sheffield Royal Grammar School) and LEA (for Local Education Authority), although with the latter I have sometimes referred to the Education Committee or Department, or the City Council, and even the Labour Group, depending on whether a decision was taken by councillors, officers or the majority party members on the Council. I have also used Oxbridge throughout when speaking of Oxford and Cambridge Universities. I appreciate this raises hackles in some quarters, but to write out these two universities' names in full every time seemed an unnecessary imposition.

I am particularly beholden to the two living Headteachers of the school, Russell Sharrock and Michael Lewis, for their advice, support and the reading of the early drafts of the book. Dr. Peter Beeley O.E. has also been particularly helpful, especially with information on the periods when Ronald Gurner and Richard Graham were Headmaster. I am indebted to Prof. John Roach for his help with the chapters dealing with the Grammar School from 1604 to 1905 and to Chris Price for background information used in several chapters, especially the section dealing with comprehensive education in the Sixties. Dr. Don Nicolson, Secretary of the Old Edwardians' Association has unearthed vast amounts of extra information through his enthusiastic use of the internet, and Ann Smith, who first suggested the idea of a Centenary History, and then helped to shape the scope of the book in the early days of preparation. Ann was one of the key people, along with Peter Lawton, who produced the excellent history of the school in 1995 entitled "Tha'll never gerr in theer". We both agreed, along with the Headteacher, that this volume would be a more formal chronological history of KES to complement the earlier anecdotal ninetieth anniversary book.

I would like to thank my proof-readers, who also commented on the early drafts of the chapters. They include Gordon Cumming, David Anderson, Paul Allen and Robert Jackson, all Old Edwardians, and Patricia Waugh, Arthur Jackson, the former Deputy Head, and Dr. Karl Gehring, the present Chair of KES Governors. Dr. John Poyser O.E. has prepared the photographs for printing, often enhancing very dim ancient sepia photos into most respectable images, whilst Andrew Holmes, a current member of Y13, produced the design and the artwork for the front and rear covers.

Moira Meadows, the Headteacher's Secretary, and earlier Lorna Barton, have been extremely patient and helpful in meeting my constant requests for photocopying and secretarial support. The staff of the Local History Section of the Central Library, where so much relevant material on KES history is to be found, were also very helpful, as well as Keith Crawshaw, the City Librarian and a former KES Governor, who made available the three volume "Centenary History of Sheffield" which has been an invaluable source of reference. I also drew extensively on work done by former members of staff, Peter

Wallis, Valentine Wrigley and Edward Watling, who undertook considerable research into the pre-history of KES from 1604-1905. At a late stage, when I was on the fourth draft of the book, I came across a short history of the school from 1604 to 1950 written by Val Wrigley, still full of alterations and revisions, which he may have intended to publish but which never reached the printers. It did not contradict anything I had written but it added considerably to the story of the Free Grammar School of King James, and also included a note saying that this manuscript might be useful to anyone writing the history of the school in the future.

I also very much appreciate the help and support of the following, many of them staff members or Old Edwardians who submitted to interviews without which I could not have written the book.

Kenneth Arnold,	Eric Sivill G.M.,	Alan and Margaret Jowitt,
John Carter,	Frank Melling,	John Shaddock,
Eric Allsop,	Eric Kalman,	Dr. Peter Wells,
Robert Wall,	David Law,	Reg. Hobson,
David Kirkman,	David Gregory,	Sir Norman Adsetts,
Peter Fletcher,	Derek Platts,	Janet (Manners) Duffin,
Bill Duffin,	Frank Bland.	John Brierley,
Prof. Clyde Binfield,	David Holford,	Peter Holgate.
David Sheasby,	Terry Saunders,	David Tomlinson,
Anthony Clapton,	John H. Hemming	Nick Waite,
Peter Harrison,	Prof. Ted Wragg,	Prof. David Downes,
Richard Nosowski,	Keith Robinson,	Neil Newton,
Michael Curley,	John Bainbridge,	Rony Robinson,
Chris Meakin,	Paul Whyman,	Prof. Rod Nicolson,
Gordon Adam,	Arthur Jones,	Peter Munn,
Robert Williams,	Dr. William Hall.	
Peter Horton,	Michael Harrison,	David Heslop,
David Waxman,	Sir Irvine Patnick,	Joan Barton,
Rt. Hon. David Blunkett,	Brian Goodwin,	Ken Mathews,
Sir Robert Kerslake,	Jonathon Crossley-Holland,	Sid Cordle.
Alan Powell,	Sheila (Jackson) Cole	Arnold Lawson,
Eileen Langsley,	Catherine (Ball) Pratley.	John Phillips
Rod Auton,	Eric Ruding,	Ray Stittle,
Jonathon Stittle,	Dorothy Hall,	Mike Russell,
Peter Kay,	David Dunn,	Kathryn Sheldon,
David Corker,	Martin Johnson,	Nick Thatcher,
Jean (Nelson) Poyser,	Jane Simm	Gladys Manifield,
Philip Skinner,	David Pollard,	Julian Harrison.

Mike Denial, Kay Madden, Nick Jones,
Roger Watkin, Chris Phipps, Prof. Julian Kinderlerer,
Prof. Mike Blackburn, Peter Moulson, Emily Maitlis,
Lydia (McLean) Cook, Shelagh Marston, Alan Eost,
Eileen Battersby, Ian Rodgers, Mary Sharrock,
Sue Rogers, Julie Fimusanmi, Angela Cooper,
Dr. David Marcer, Dr. Ben Jackson, Dr. Dennis Brown,
Aileen Gamble (T.L.Hanna High School USA).

John Gallacher, Trudi Gehring, Kath Auton,
Hannah Lavery, Hock-Ann Chia, Alan Friggens,
John Saddler, Paul Desgranges, Mohammed Ackram,
Dr. Rebecca Carpenter, Ben Barker, David Kirkup,
Eva Lamb

My thanks also to Barry Darling, City of London School, John Sharples, Headteacher, and Michael Dickinson, Archivist, of Sir Thomas Boteler C. of E. High School, Warrington, Tony Money of Radley College, Rev. Les Slow, Deputy Headmaster, Bradford G.S., all of whom sent information and, in three cases, the published history of their school.

Paul Scarrott of DS Publishing has also been most helpful, always willing to meet last minute requests for changes to the grammar, spelling and the text.

Finally I would like to record my appreciation of the support I have received in publishing this centenary history of the school from the Headteacher and the current Staff at KES, the Governors and the Old Edwardian Association.

J.C.C. *Nether Edge, September 2005.*

CHAPTER ONE

TOM SMITH'S LEGACY

Within the completely recast school buildings, from now on to be called King Edward VII School, an expectant audience waited in the newly created Assembly Hall for the Opening Ceremony to begin. They included not only the leading figures in the city's political, industrial and religious life but also several important visitors, while presiding over the events of that afternoon on 2nd. November 1906 was the leader of the Liberal Party on the City Council, Alderman William Clegg. To all intents and purposes William Clegg, soon to be Sir William, was the founder of KES; for he was not only the Chairman of the City Council's new Education Committee, he was also the Chairman of the new school's Governors and this was definitely his, and the Council's day of triumph, as the flagship project in their ambitious plans for educating the young people of Sheffield was launched.

Promptly at 3.00 p.m. Clegg got the proceedings under way and the Sheffield Morning Telegraph, reporting at some considerable length on what their reporter termed this *"charming ceremony"*, was impressed with the way he maintained the tempo of the speeches – there were ten altogether — so that the whole event was completed in ninety minutes. The first speaker was the key visitor who officially opened King Edward VII School. Sir Augustine Birrell, K.C. M.P., the President of the Board of Education, was the cabinet member in Campbell-Bannerman's relatively new Liberal Government responsible for bringing coherence to the many loose ends of the British educational system that had been bequeathed to the Twentieth Century by the Victorians. He began his speech by declaring the school open and wishing it well, before going on to give his thoughts on what he believed constituted a good, sound education. The eighth speaker, as if to emphasize this was not the teaching professionals' day, was the Headmaster, James Hichens, who had been running KES for just over a year in temporary premises.

The School had opened its doors, or at least the doors of the former Firth College in Leopold Street, in September 1905. The refurbishing of Wesley College, which had cost the City Council £22,000, had not been completed in time for the first year's intake of pupils. So Hichens, newly arrived from his last post as Headmaster of Wolverhampton Royal Grammar School, had to organise his school in a number of buildings in the city centre, including St. James Chambers on Church St. overlooking the Cutlers Hall and the city's Parish Church – later to become a Cathedral when the Diocese of Sheffield was created in May 1914. The main body of the school was based in the buildings in Leopold Street that already housed the offices of the new LEA and had formerly been occupied, since 1879, by the Sheffield School Board. The complex also was home to the Central School, founded in 1880 and later High Storrs G.S., and had until very recently been the home of the University College, originally Firth College when it was opened in 1879. King Edward VII School took over these latter buildings, their former occupants having just decamped up to Western Bank to become the University of Sheffield. The King had come to Sheffield to open the University and if KES's re-built school could have been ready in time, he might very well have been persuaded to travel the short distance up Glossop Road to open the school that bears his name. As there would be no way a ruling monarch would visit a northern industrial city a second time in two years, Augustine Birrell was persuaded to leave the *"stormy atmosphere"* of Parliament, where his Education Bill was just about to founder in the Lords, and perform these opening formalities in Sheffield instead.

It would not be lost on any of the civic leaders present, or on the parents and the pupils, (only half of the school's 317 boys could get a place in the hall) that the significance of this occasion was not just the establishing of a new school, which the Council intended would be in the forefront of the great day public and grammar schools of the country, but it was the end of the independent existence of its two predecessors, the Sheffield Royal Grammar School and Wesley College. It would also have been made clear to James Hichens, as he struggled to amalgamate the two traditions, that in starting the school's life near Campo Lane and Townhead St. the School was, in fact, coming back to its earliest roots. Even earlier the clergy of the parish church, then named the Trinity Church, would at various times in the middle ages have given instruction in understanding the Latin service and prayers to some of the choristers and brighter boys of their congregation, and, therefore, a school of sorts could be said to exist in medieval times at the parish church. Indeed Peter Wallis, a master at KES after the Second World War, claimed in a booklet he co-produced on Yorkshire Grammar Schools that a school in Sheffield could be traced back to 1275. That would make it the third oldest school in the three Ridings after St. Peter's, York and Beverley G.S. both of which were originally based at their minsters. The evidence for Wallis's claim is, that when the grandson of Thomas de Furnival, the Lord of the Manor of Sheffield, was christened in that year, it is reported that a boy, Thomas Wood, left his school in Sheffield and walked some considerable distance to the christening at Whiston.

The first written evidence of the school's continued existence dates from 1564 in the records of the Church Burgesses. This significant body in the ecclesiastical and civic life of Sheffield for the next three centuries had been established in 1554 during Mary 1st's reign and survived the second reformation under Elizabeth. At varying times they made small amounts of money available to help poor scholars as well as fund a master and occasionally an usher. The Grammar School buildings at Townhead were in existence in Elizabeth's reign and the first master in 1564 was William Swyfte, whilst one of the first pupils educated there, Robert Sanderson, went up to Caius College, Cambridge and later was a member of Lincoln's Inn. The Master, in 1581, was paid 5 marks a quarter, (approximately £13.33 p.a.) by the Earl of Shrewsbury, the Lord of Hallamshire, and by 1594 there were 40 boys at the school. However it is possible that the school failed to continue this progress and the buildings may have fallen into disrepair, or even been abandoned, by the end of the sixteenth century.

Enter Thomas Smith an Attorney at Law living at Crowland, a small village just inside Lincolnshire's southern border, six miles north of Peterborough. Thomas Smith had originally come from Sheffield and had at one time had a law practice in Wisbech, fifteen miles to the east of Crowland. He died in 1603, the year that James 1st became the King of England, and in his will of 2nd July 1603 he remembered his home town and made the following bequest:

"Thirtye pounds a yeare as longe as the world will endure for the finding of two sufficiently learned men to teache and bringe up the young children there in godlinesse and learninge."

The rest of his will instructed the distribution of his other monies to family members, one of whom was his cousin, William Slack, a Sheffield blacksmith, who the Church Burgesses appointed to be one of the twelve governors of the new school they founded with the legacy of Thomas Smith. Granting bequests to aid or found schools was, of course, not uncommon at that time and many of to-days' most famous schools started in unpretentious circumstances in the Sixteenth Century, or Jacobean times, with finance from private sources. To-day, a latter day Thomas Smith might leave his money to help finance a hospital wing or a university department's buildings, but in his time, on the revenues of a reasonably modest acreage of land, you could help found a school that would grow over the centuries into a formidable institution.

THE FREE GRAMMAR SCHOOL OF JAMES, KING OF ENGLAND

By the end of 1603 the Church Burgesses, who owned the Grammar School building, had petitioned the King to obtain a charter for their proposed new school. The King issued to them the Letters Patent, dated 4th May 1604, which stipulated that the school should be called, *"the ffree Grammar School of James, King of England within the Town of Sheffield in the County of York"* and defined the type of instruction that should be given and the qualifications that the Master and his deputy, the Usher, should possess. It also detailed the requirement for the nomination of thirteen *"discreet and honest men"* who would be the Governors of the school responsible for its *"Goods, Possessions and Revenues",* clarified their duties and the method of selection of their successors.

Among the new Governors alongside William Slack, kinsman of Thomas Smith, was the fiery puritan Vicar of Sheffield, Thomas Toller. The Vicar of Sheffield was to become an ex-officio appointment and Toller's successors would almost always be members of the Governing Body. This would, of course, seem obvious to people in the 17th century, where the connection between education and the church was taken for granted and at a time when the protestant succession was never entirely secure. Catesby's plot to assassinate the King by blowing up Parliament was foiled the following year and Guido Fawkes, an old boy of another Yorkshire school, has become one of the most infamous men in British history because of his role in the conspiracy.

The executor of Thomas Smith's will made over to the Governors £200 in cash and the ownership of land at Leverington in Cambridgeshire, which produced £21 in rent per annum. With the interest from the cash lump sum and the rent payments the Governors had an income of £30 p.a. with which to pay the Master and the Usher. However, there was no extra money (Free Grammar School meant free tuition for the pupils) for repairing and refurbishing the dilapidated buildings at the junction of Townhead St. and Campo Lane and so an assessment was levied on all the householders in *"Sheffeild, Hallom, Brightsyde, Ecklesall, Atterclyffe and Darnoll"* which produced £103 18s 3d. and was described by James Wrigley, in his article on the Grammar School in the Hunter Archaeological Society's Transactions, as Sheffield's first Education Rate. Some of this money went to pay the legal costs of acquiring the Letters Patent and the rest was used to restore the old school building. There was also a nominal rent to pay for the building as the Church Burgesses charged the Governors one shilling a year. In 1619 they granted them a lease for 800 years at the same rental for what is to-day a prime city centre site. At the same time they conveyed to the Governors, the school house and the croft which ran down the hill towards West Bar Green, approximately where Tenter St. now stands.

The school designed a badge displaying a schoolboy of the time holding a bible with the twelve arrows crossed in a saltaire behind him. It was incorporated into King Edward VII School's new arms in 1905 and is still there to-day. The device was surrounded by the school motto:

Verbum Tuum Lucerna Pedibus Meis

The twelve arrows in saltaire represent the twelve Church Burgesses, and in time this device became the Arms of Sheffield and is included in the City's Coat of Arms today. It is believed the background was red and the schoolboy stands on a green field. The saltaire represents a sheaf of arrows and is probably a pun on Sheffield's name. The motto translates as "Your word is a lamp to my feet".

Badge of the Free Grammar School of St. James.

The First Teaching Staff

The first master, appointed in 1604, was John Smith who was paid £20 on 1st August as his first year's salary. He was paid directly by the executor of Thomas Smith's will and there may be a case of early 17th century nepotism in his appointment as he is only one of two "Headmasters" in the history of the Grammar School who did not possess a degree. However a town involved in the cutlery and metalworking business is likely to have a number of people called Smith amongst it's citizens and he may have had no connection whatsoever with the founder of the school. John Smith did not survive long in the post of Master and in 1606 he was replaced by Henry Saxton, a Derbyshire born BA from Queens' College, Cambridge who took his MA in 1607 and became ordained as a priest in September 1610. The first Usher, who was paid £10 p.a., was the only other member of the teaching staff. The first holder of this post was John Hancock, a graduate of St. John's College Cambridge, and he would replace Saxton as the Master at Christmas 1608. He had already been ordained a priest in August of 1608 and again it would have been seen as quite normal, if not obligatory, for a cleric to be the headmaster of a grammar school. It is probable that, up to the creation of King Edward VII School in 1905, almost all the headmasters of the Grammar School were ordained Anglican Priests.

The three masters that followed Hancock, when he left and became the Vicar of Ashover, all served for short periods until Thomas Rawson became the Master in 1625. He remained in office for nearly twenty years and ended his career at the school in a most dramatic way. He was a stalwart supporter of the Parliamentary cause in the Civil War but unfortunately for him the Royalists under the Earl of Newcastle took the town in May 1643, establishing themselves in the castle. Rawson decided the most prudent cause for such an outspoken critic of the King was to flee the town and hide in the Derbyshire countryside, while the Royalists were in control. In August of the following year, when Parliamentary forces had re-taken Sheffield after a siege of the castle, Rawson returned and demanded his back pay. The Governors were none too impressed with his request, seeing no reason why they should pay a teacher who had manifestly not done any teaching during the year. Furthermore they needed to use the money saved to make repairs to the school house which, either through Rawson's neglect or perhaps the damage caused by soldiers billeted in the town, had become uninhabitable. Rawson appealed to General Fairfax and the Governors made a counter appeal, but it appears Fairfax found for Rawson; although there is no record in the accounts that he was ever paid. They also had no intention of re-instating Rawson and William Young was appointed in early 1645 in his place.

Re-building the school 1645-51

The school had to move into temporary premises down the hill in the town's Workhouse on West Bar Green. They would stay there for five and a half years. Opened in 1632 the Workhouse had considerable spare capacity and for an annual rental of £1. 3s. 6d. they were pleased to accommodate the Grammar School. To make their schoolroom at the Workhouse fit to teach in, the Governors had to find another 16s. 10d. before lessons

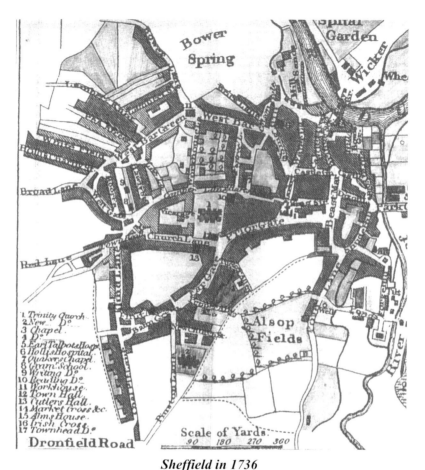

1 Trinity Church.
2 New Do.
3 Chapel.
4 Do.
5 Earl Talbot Hosp.
6 Hollis Hospital.
7 Quakers Chapel.
8 Gram. School.
9 Writing Do.
10 Reading Do.
11 Workhouse.
12 Town Hall.
13 Cutlers Hall.
14 Market Cross &c.
15 Alms House.
16 Irish Cross.
17 Townhead Do.

Scale of Yards.
90   180   270   360

Sheffield in 1736
The Grammar School is numbered 8, the Trinity Church, now the
Cathedral (1) and St. Paul's Church, now the Peace Gardens (2)

could start and they continued to have repair bills, such as the 14s. 3d they had to pay in 1650 for windows broken by the boys. The rebuilding of the Grammar School itself did not commence until 1648 because the Governors had to set about raising the necessary capital as they had no financial reserves. They even borrowed from the new Master, William Young, who lent £40 and was finally paid off in 1651 when he had already moved on, after struggling with these difficult teaching circumstances at West Bar Green for three years. The Church Burgesses chipped in with a £100 loan in 1645 and they only received their first repayment nine years later. Work on rebuilding the school at Townhead got under way in 1648 and it is popularly assumed that stone from the castle, demolished in 1649, was used in the reconstruction. It is more than probable that such a useful source of building materials might well have been used on the school site, especially as it was a stone built edifice with a steep pitched slate roof. Certainly there is evidence that some of the timbers used in the re-building came from the castle.

The school now had a main classroom facing south onto Campo Lane that was some feet below the level of the street. The smaller room used for writing ran at right angles on the western side forming an L shaped building. The floor was stone and the furniture low oak benches that ran the length of the schoolroom in parallel lines with a broad gangway in the centre. This linked the Master's seat, that must have resembled a throne with its seven foot high sides, with the Usher's seat at the other end of the building where the junior pupils sat. The poor light through the leaded panes of the stone mullion windows created a dingy interior which could be very cold in winter, with only one central fire to warm the pupils. Through the porch, with the date 1648 carved over the door, the boys could get out into the walled school yard which one former pupil commemorated in verse as;

"The wall encircled court that day withstood
Low sunk, in which our noisy prison stood"

For recreation the boys could use the school yard, or the croft, or even play football on the open field where Paradise Square was laid out in the 18th Century. To reach these fields boys would have to walk the short distance along Campo Lane, hence the street's Italian name.

It is also recorded in the accounts for re-building the school 1648-51 that; "Drinkeing moneys given to the workmen att sevrall times" came to 13s 10p (roughly 70p) and no doubt eased the burden of their labours.

The school prospered in the second half of the 17th Century under their long-serving Master, Thomas Balguy. He was Master from 1664-1696 and only three headmasters served longer in any of the family of schools to which King Edward VII School belongs. During his thirty two years at the school, twenty three pupils went up to Cambridge, usually to St. John's, Magdalene or Sidney Sussex Colleges. This was just over half the number of Sheffield Grammar School pupils who went to University in the 17th Century, and the records, painstakingly researched by Mr. G.C. Moore-Smith for the Hunter Archaeological Society in 1932, suggest that they all went to Cambridge, which seemingly served the north of England, for none were undergraduates at the "other place". Balquy, who was born in London, probably of Huguenot descent, was a graduate of St. John's himself. A dedicated teacher, he served the school well and died in post in 1696. Cambridge entry is not the only way to assess a school's performance, although at least three of the Headmasters at KES placed the highest premium on Oxbridge success, but in 1676 and 1677 the Grammar School achieved three Cambridge successes each year, enough for an honours board to have been commissioned and placed on the school wall.

Early in the next century, in 1709, work was started on a house next door to the school for the use of the Master and his family. It was completed in 1710 when William Humpton

(1709-1720) was the Headmaster and it cost £120, with most of it found from public subscription as only £23 came from the school's own funds. Later in the century in 1776, another subscription from the inhabitants of Sheffield for the repair of the master's house, and the main schoolhouse next door, raised £805, with the Duke of Norfolk, the district's biggest landowner, contributing £100. The renovated buildings would now last until the Grammar School finally left the centre of town and moved to St. George's Square in 1825, when further subscriptions would have to be raised to build that school.

The old Grammar School never again reached the heights of Balguy's time although they did send 30 pupils to Cambridge between 1701 and 1824. Schools, in general, in 18th Century England had lost much of their earnest endeavour to advance and their strict classical curriculum (Sheffield G.S. had always taught Greek as well as Latin) was being questioned by the people of the new century, where industrialisation and overseas commerce already played a larger part in the nation's economic and social life. In response to this dissatisfaction, Charles Chadwick (Master 1776-1809) modified the curriculum and very daringly introduced English language lessons, while later still, in 1818, the school adopted the Madras, or monitorial, system of instruction that was currently in vogue, and judged a success at some leading schools like Edinburgh High School and Charterhouse.

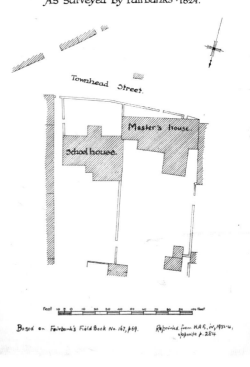

SHEFFIELD GRAMMAR SCHOOL.

As surveyed by Fairbanks · 1824.

Based on Fairbanks's Field Book No. 167, p69.   Reprinted from H.A.S. iv, 1932-4, s/johsn/e p. 284

A couple of characters

Rev. Charles Chadwick, Master 1776-1809, was also the Vicar of Tinsley, then a hamlet some way outside the boundaries of Sheffield. The stipend from this living added to his parsimonious master's salary of £60 pa. He always wore a clergyman's three cornered hat, carried a gold-tipped walking stick and rode out on his horse to take services at Tinsley. He kept order at the school with the help of a strap, he somewhat mysteriously called "his Custard".

He was followed by Rev. Joseph Wilson (1810-18) who had a bad leg and always travelled in a sedan chair. He is believed to be the last man in Sheffield to use this peculiar form of transport. His period as Master ended with his suicide in the Master's House, adjacent to the school.

The school was described in 1818 in a book entitled, "*A Concise Description of the Endowed Grammar Schools of England and Wales*", as a school open to all boys inhabiting the Town and neighbourhood of Sheffield, although the right of admission lay with the Governors. The Master was paid £60 p.a. and he had responsibility for 40 pupils, half of them on Foundation Scholarships. The pupils used the Eton Grammars for their Latin and Greek classes, which were still the overwhelming part of their daily classroom instruction, but did not have the advantage of any closed Exhibitions, or any other specific university awards, to help them get into higher education. In fact, Moore-Smith's records show that very few boys were now proceeding to Cambridge and that was one of the reasons why the rising middle class of the town supported the new Collegiate School when it asked for purchasers of £25 shares to invest in a new institution in Broomhall Park. They now increasingly preferred to send their sons to this new school and, if they were nonconformists, they had another option after 1838, when the Wesley Proprietary Grammar School (later Wesley College) was opened in Broomhill.

The new Grammar School building at St. George's Square, 1825 - 1884

CHAPTER TWO

THE TAKEOVER

The Grammar School received a new lease of life when it moved, in August 1825, into new buildings on the east side of St. George's Square, on what was then the edge of town. Later in the century Jessop's Hospital would be built on the opposite side of the square. Another subscription had been raised from the townspeople in 1824 and had realised £1400, enough to erect a new Grammar School in the gothic style to complement the existing St. George's Church in the middle of the square. From the square, pupils entered the building through a stone archway into the yard, passing the small caretaker's house on the left. Through a porch, the main door opened straight onto the classroom and the layout of that room, although considerably larger, was not very different from the old school at Townhead.

At one end of the stone flagged schoolroom was the Headmaster's high seat, topped with an imposing canopy, now raised up on a two-step platform. Around this dais was a circle of stools where the boys would gather for their instruction and their desks, carved and cut with all kinds of initials and designs, were positioned around the outside of the room. Each boy had a desk and a school-box in which he kept his books along with the junk of schooldays; marbles, conkers and catapults and some even kept "*new born white mice tethered in the feet of ladies' stockings and bartered at dinner time for cash.*" The second master sat at the opposite end of the room on a smaller chair with his class around him and now there was a third master as well. In the Master's desk was the instrument of justice nicknamed "the Spanker". It resembled an old barber's razor strop and was used freely for most of the perceived indiscretions and errors of the pupils. There was an alternative of detention and fifty lines but most boys, perhaps through bravado, took the option of the Spanker. The only other room in the building was the Head's "sanctum" which he sometimes used as a classroom but where he also kept books, ink and candles. These "halfpenny dips" were brought out in the late afternoon in winter and affixed to the desks with their own wax, so that pupils could still see to work. Again the school was very cold in winter as it only had one central fireplace, so boys used to place red-hot cinders on their writing slates for a modicum of extra warmth.

The Grammar School had moved to St. George's Square during the period when the Headmaster was William White (1818-1830), who had been appointed on the condition that he introduced the monitorial system. He was followed by the long serving Percival Bowen, and then by the redoubtable Dr. Joseph Jackson (1863 – 1884), known to his pupils as the "All Highest". It was Jackson who in 1869 introduced the Annual Sports Days which were held at Bramall Lane and the annual trip into Derbyshire in horse buses pulled by four horses each. Once there the boys would have to climb Kinder Scout, or some equally forbidding moor, and if the heavens opened up they just got wet.

Getting Athletic Equipment

"We decided we needed to practise putting the shot before the athletic sports, but the school had no shots. A bright idea struck us that we could get some cannonballs from the Artillery range at Whyming Brook. Eluding the keepers we took a couple of balls and started trundling them back the five or six miles to St. George's Square. We set them rolling down the gutters of Manchester Rd. and then Glossop Rd. and so got our shots back to the school.

The Athletic Sports had by now become a big occasion in the school calendar, with a military band who didn't guess where the shots had come from."

The Franco-Prussian War 1870-71

"We fixed up two small armies, one German and one French. We armed ourselves with catapults and small shot ammunition. It was a dangerous game as some of us got nasty wounds in our "famous" attacks and retreats.

It all ended when the Head on entering the school yard got a stray shot in the cheek. He ordered us to empty our pockets and surrender all our weapons. Into the stove they went and for us the "war" of 1870 was over."

Two stories related by James Figorski (pupil 1868-74) and featured in the school magazine in 1948 when he was 89 years old.

Dr. Jackson ran an efficient school but shortly after he left the school was inspected, in 1865, by Sir Joshua Fitch on behalf of the Royal Commission (1864-68) that was inquiring into the state of schools in England and Wales. Sir Joshua Fitch concluded that the Grammar School, which then had 122 pupils, provided a good education for the children of the commercial classes of the town who intended to remain in trade in Sheffield, but it wasn't capable of providing for those boys who wanted to go on to university, partly because it didn't have any closed exhibitions. Dismissively he wrote *"the general character of the institution was that of a secondary or commercial school of a high class rather than a purely grammar school"*. The school, he felt, that offered the Sheffield middle class the best chance for Oxbridge success was the Collegiate School, founded 29 years earlier.

THE SHEFFIELD COLLEGIATE SCHOOL

Dominus Illuminatio Mea

It was a group of Anglicans, notwithstanding the Grammar School's long connection with the Trinity Parish Church, who raised the £3000 necessary finance to construct and meet the running expenses of the Collegiate School, which opened its doors in July1836. Supporters took out £25 shares for the new venture in Broomhall Park; idyllic surroundings for a school. To the south was the country road leading to Hunter's Bar and

The motto was cribbed from Oxford University whose motto is "Dominus Illuminatio Mea"

Ecclesall along which would pass horsemen and the carriages of the well-to-do, and beyond this road, on a wooded hillside, was the new cemetery, opened in the same year and entered by a classical portico. Viewed from Ecclesall Rd. the gothic schoolhouse with its three prominent gables stood back from the outer wall behind a charming sunken playing field. The Principal's House was nearer to the road and it not only served as a family residence but was spacious enough to take a few boarders and overflow classes as well. Behind the school was the large empty expanse of Crookes Moor, although within a very short period after the opening, the boys of the school would have been able to hear the construction work going on below the Glossop Rd., as the Wesleyan Proprietary Grammar School was being completed. The suburb of Sheffield, that has become the home to so many key educational institutions, had started to take shape and to add to the interest of the area, the Botanic Gardens had also been opened in 1836.

The aim of the founders was to create a day school on the lines of the reformed public schools like Rugby and Uppingham. Whilst classics would still dominate the syllabus, there were also classes in mathematics, science, literature, ancient and modern history, geography, French, German and drawing. The school was designed to cater for 120 pupils and at its opening some of the more able boys at the Grammar School migrated to the Collegiate School, which very early on established a fund for four Exhibitions at Oxford and Cambridge ensuring their connection with those universities was sustained. It became the practice for the more promising Grammar School boys, who intended to try for university, to finish their studies at Collegiate. Despite this it took some time to build up their numbers, but after a decade reached 100 pupils on roll during the period when Rev. George Jacob (1843-52) was the Principal. Like the Grammar School all seven Principals of the Collegiate School were ordained Anglican clergymen and in the new high-minded atmosphere of the mid-century, the school's teaching would strongly emphasize moral and religious learning, all in conformity with the principles of the Church of England.

So popular and successful was Jacob that he was presented with £110 by friends of the school to complete his divinity doctorate. Having achieved this, he promptly left to become the Headmaster of Christ's Hospital. This promotion indicates how high was the reputation of the Collegiate School, but the achilles heel of proprietary schools was finance and however well they were performing academically, they were perennially in debt. There was a rescue mounted in 1853, when the school was mortgaged and the original shareholders were bought out, thereby securing the immediate future of Collegiate, although in the early Sixties the school was in difficulties again. The creation of so many boarding schools (now more easily accessible by the extensive railway network), and the reformation of many of the older public schools, meant that the wealthier beneficiaries of Sheffield's industrial prosperity could be choosy about where they sent their sons to be educated. At a top public school their boys could rub shoulders with the children of the aristocracy, as well as the political and social establishment of the country. Sheffield Collegiate School and the Grammar School could not offer them such attractions.

The Rev. George Atkinson (Principal 1861-71) further advanced the reputation of Collegiate in the 1860s. He played his part in the educational life of the city where he was a keen advocate of technical teaching and the education of engineers. He even wrote a pamphlet entitled "Establishing a School of Practical Science" with the intention that such a school would be a branch of the Collegiate School. Unlike the Grammar School, Atkinson got high praise from Fitch in 1864 when investigating for the Royal Commission. He concluded that; *"Few proprietary schools in my district in the North aim so high, or achieve so much as the Collegiate."* In Atkinson's time science was introduced onto the syllabus, a choir was formed and the school contributed to the community by allowing their hall to be used for night classes in technical education for engineers, and also, on other occasions, made available to amateur music societies for their practices. External examiners had been introduced before Atkinson's time in 1852 and dons from Oxford and Cambridge visited annually to examine the pupils. Occasionally, when examining a specialist area, a master from another school might join them, as a teacher at Liverpool Collegiate Institution did in 1852. The Collegiate, again modelling itself on the reformed public schools, emphasised the importance of organised games and former Collegiate pupils played their part in the formation in 1857 of the Sheffield F.C., the oldest Association Football club in the world. There is also evidence to suggest the school made an important contribution to the developing rules of the game in this period and former pupils also set up the Collegiate Cricket Club in 1881, who still play at the top level in the Yorkshire League.

Another major financial crisis in 1871 saw the school put up for auction. Henry Wilson, who had helped out in an earlier crisis now bought the school outright and replaced Atkinson with an old boy, the Rev. James Cardwell. He increased the number of pupils almost to the maximum and, in co-operation with the Sheffield School Board, he agreed to accept boys from elementary schools in the city on scholarships organised by the School Board. Thus began the free educational ladder for bright boys of whatever social

Sheffield Collegiate School

Sheffield Collegiate School from Ecclesall Rd.
Both the main school building and the Principal's house still exist.

background. Over the next 100 years thousands of Sheffield children would take advantage of this initiative, which started so modestly in 1871 with the Collegiate, and the Grammar School sharing the scholarships awarded annually. One of the first scholarship boys was Maurice Jacobs, son of the Sheffield Rabbi. After six years at Collegiate, he went to Wadham College, Oxford and later was a member of the Jewish Board of Deputies.

Another important initiative of the School Board was to establish a "higher grade school" offering in essence secondary education on the rates. The Central School which opened in 1880 was so successful that it had a serious adverse effect on the numbers of pupils at Collegiate and at the Grammar School. In 1884 Collegiate was down to 40 pupils whilst the Grammar School had 84. Despite its educational achievements and an impressive list of alumni, which included Sir Robert Hadfield and Col. Tom Vickers, two of Sheffield's most important steel magnates, as well as Dr. H.C. Sorby, the internationally renowned microscopist, the Collegiate School was sinking and was no longer financially viable. The Grammar School however, thanks to the original bequest of Thomas Smith in 1603, had regular revenues from its land investments in Walkley, bought with the money obtained when the Cambridgeshire lands were sold in the 17th Century. What the Grammar School did not have was adequate buildings and they must have regarded with envy their rival school's buildings only half a mile away, while perhaps experiencing a little "*schadenfreude*" at their financial predicament.

In 1884 Collegiate was sold to the Grammar School Governors for £7000 and ceased to exist. It wasn't a union or an amalgamation, it was a takeover and to-day all that remains to mark its existence, apart from the cricket club and a street name, are the buildings. The main school building eventually became part of the new Training College in 1905 and is now used by Sheffield Hallam University as part of its "Collegiate" campus.

S.R.G.S. 1885-1905

At the same time as the Collegiate School was closing in the summer of 1884, the Grammar School got a new Headmaster, the Rev. Edward Senior, who would guide the fortunes of the reformed and re-sited grammar school until the end of the century. Another public subscription was organised and all the familiar names of Sheffield's establishment,— Firth, Mappin, Jessop, Osborn,— were contributors. The Town Trustees gave £2000 and the sale of the old grammar school in St George's Square brought in another £1944. After considerable work had been done to the old Collegiate buildings, the Grammar School was ready to move to Broomhall Park at Easter 1885. The new premises, after internal refurbishment and equipping requiring another £2000, served a larger community of boys (about 180) than before. There were now six classrooms, a laboratory that had 13 double benches, well supplied with chemistry and physics equipment, a workshop and in the improved playground, a fives court. In the early Nineties a west wing was added in the same gothic style that included rooms for woodwork and singing. The old buildings in St. Georges Square became the Technical School, which in turn became part of the University College in 1897 and finally was demolished in 1912, to make way for the present Dept. of Applied Science buildings of the University, constructed on the same site.

The badge and motto of SRGS was just an updated version of the one used in the 17th Century

With the exception of some old honours boards (which still exist in KES's lower corridor near the dining room) the fact that this had been the Collegiate School for 48 years was totally ignored. The name now adopted by the Grammar School, confirmed in the scheme of governance approved by the Endowed School Commissioners in 1888, was the Sheffield Royal Grammar School. The old Grammar

School badge and motto were also adopted and although the title King James 1st Grammar School was dropped, it had never been used in common parlance. Everyone involved with the new positioning of the school took it for granted that this was the same school whose founder was Thomas Smith and that in no way was it a new partnership with the Collegiate School.

There were, however, some very significant changes now the School had moved to Broomhall Park. The 1888 Scheme confirmed that the Governors would no longer be drawn from the Church Burgesses, but would now be a fully representative body. The Town Council would have three representatives, the School Board two, Firth College two, and there would be six co-opted members thereby allowing the Governing Body to bring on leading figures in the city, like Sir John Brown. The Vicar of the Parish Church was still an ex-officio member and usually acted as the Chairman of the Governors. The result of these changes was to bind the SRGS more closely to the city's political and industrial leaders and ensure they would consider the Grammar School to be their favoured child, both in terms of public funds and in supporting its general interests.

The new school offered a much wider syllabus than the school at St. George's Square. Ironically it was closer to the syllabus available at the Collegiate School, and Edward Senior in his 1888 Report delighted in all the opportunities now open to pupils at the school. Apart from classics and science, there were *English Subjects* which included history and geography as well as English grammar. The Modern Languages taught included French and German, and students were also examined in drawing, scripture, and vocal music and could access instruction in several instruments. A course of physical training formed a regular part of the school curriculum, with classes run by a retired Army sergeant who also organised drill practices. The Headmaster was particularly pleased that the Grammar School at last had its own scholarships tenable at Oxbridge, or even Durham and Trinity College, Dublin. These scholarships were made available by the Town Trustees and they were worth £50 for three years. There was only one scholarship a year and it was awarded on the results of the summer external examinations with the Head having the final say. They were most valuable, because even for middle class families £50 could go some considerable way to keeping an undergraduate out of debt and concentrating on his studies. To meet their obligation to the bright child whose parents couldn't afford the fees, there were Foundation Scholarships for boys from the town's elementary schools. It wasn't an over-generous provision because the number of scholarships could not exceed 15 in all the school, with a further restriction limiting the awards to only three pupils in any one year group.

S.R.G.S.

1888

158 pupils on roll
Eight Full Time Teachers (+ the Head)

Fees are £12 per annum, £4 due each term
Entrance fee One Guinea (£1.05)
Boarding fees £45 per annum (10% reduction for brothers)
School Dinner £3. 5s (£3.25) per term. Room available for packed lunches.

School year has three terms named Winter, Spring, and Summer.
Seven Weeks' holiday in summer, four at Christmas and two at Easter.
School Hours: 9am-12.15pm and 2-4pm. Except Wednesday and Saturday
9am-12.30pm

The School plays Football, Cricket and Athletics
Fives and Swimming (Summer) Gymnastics (Winter)
The games programme is run by a committee of Masters and Boys.

The Nineties

Under Senior the school grew slowly in numbers during the next decade, although it never reached 200 pupils. This size was not unusual for a prestigious secondary school at that time and it meant that the school was a close-knit community with the staff knowing all the boys quite well. Meanwhile, in comparison, the Central School on its Leopold St. site, had exceeded 1000 pupils, half of them girls, and its name had become synonymous with the "Central Schools" model throughout the country. Many of the institutions and activities that would seem familiar to boys at KES in the first decade of the next century, had already been introduced by Senior at the Royal Grammar School. There was a Preparatory Department for boys under 12 run by Mr. Pode, a Dickensian name that matched his Dickensian appearance. Edward Pode had been at Winchester and Exeter College, Oxford but he was universally known as "Humpty Dumpty". A kindly man whose mere possession of the cane was enough to ensure order, he inculcated in his young charges a love of cricket and he himself was a good batsman wafting away the bowling, rather like the sports superstar of the day, W.G. Grace. A proper school magazine, with five editions a year, was first produced in 1889, replacing the Annual Report that was more of a yearbook than a magazine. Like all school magazines its editors were constantly demanding to know what its readers thought should be included to brighten its pages. They often seem to assume that more poetry will encourage sales and in one edition there was a wonderful parody on the leading poets of the century. Someone, perhaps a master, had created cricket poems in the style of Macauley,

Tennyson, Burns, Longfellow and Wordsworth. The briefest was a parody on Robert Southey; it read.

You are old Father William, the young man cried,
One would think you too feeble to play;
Yet you smacked a slow donkey drop out of the ground-
Now tell me the reason I pray?

In the days of my youth Father William replied,
I was reckoned a dab at the game:
I punished slow bowling and now I am old,
I still go on doing the same.

In 1890 a Debating Society was started, later linked to the Literary Society, and eventually amalgamated with the Scientific Society. In the way of school societies, these groups ran out of support and finally re-emerged as the Natural History Society. The presence of these societies had helped to initiate a proper school library and even a small scientific museum at the school, displaying pupils' collections and their findings from their nature rambles around Derbyshire. In 1895 the first school play was performed by the new Dramatic Society, there was a Musical Society, Glee Club, Chess Club and a Scripture Union, who, in the best evangelical tradition aimed at nothing less than getting every boy in the school to join them.

At the end of the Eighties an Old Boys' Association had been formed enabling former pupils to keep a connection and, when needed, give their financial or moral support to the School. Individually they were colloquially known as O.B.s and they never acquired a more specific name as the Old Edwardians did later. They seemed more interested in having O.B. Dinners and setting up cricket clubs but their activities were reported at length in the school magazine. At the first of the O.B.s Dinners they were reminded that this was not the first such reunion occasion, because former scholars of the old Grammar School had met at the Tontine Inn in 1790 to celebrate themselves and the school. The O.B.s at university commenced sending Oxford and Cambridge Letters to the magazine editors, although, because they were so few in numbers, the letters concentrated on events at the university rather than the O.B. s own nefarious activities. By 1895 the O.B.s at Cambridge numbered seven and founded their own SRGS Cantab Association, inviting Dr. H. Jackson, a don at Trinity, who had been at the Collegiate School, to be their President. Meanwhile at Oxford there was the S.O.S. (Sheffield Oxford Society) which O.B.s joined, but was open to any student with a Sheffield connection.

SRGS appears to have been a happy school and there seems to have been genuine affection for the two Heads and for most of the staff. Caning was not unknown but more common was the use of detentions immediately after school at 4.15p.m run by the Drill Sergeant. He would put the defaulters through extra drill and P.T. using dumb-bells and the intensity of it was such that it was not considered a soft option. These old soldiers, like Sgt. Bell formerly of the Connaught Rangers, acted in the manner of an "Orderly Sergeant" around the school and the grounds, apprehending misbehaving pupils. Bell lived in a lodge by the main gate, (still there to-day) and he was also well placed to encourage unwelcome visitors to leave the premises. Peer group ragging and bullying were however prevalent and one O.B., Mr. J.G.Williams, writing sixty years later, told how fights were arranged for you if you were not malevolent enough to instigate your own. He claims he arrived at school one day in the 1890s and found he was scheduled to scrap with the members of the Smith family over a number of days in the preferred venue for these contests, the large cloakroom. There could be fisticuffs with local youths who often yelled out "School Bugs" as SRGS boys passed through the town, and set-piece fracas with Wesley College students in adjacent streets were also not infrequent.

Correspondence from the School Magazine April 1898

Sirs, —— Will you allow me to draw to your attention the prevalent practice of boys, or their parents, giving away their school caps to poor children when they cease to have any use for them. The Headmaster asked us to make sure caps were destroyed when finished and not given away. It is, at any rate, possible to remove the school's distinctive features, namely the School arms and the red stripes and still leave a perfectly good cap.

I am sirs, —— Yours truly J.G.C.

On the sports field however Wesley College reigned supreme. At football they were well nigh unbeatable often getting double-digit goal tallies against SRGS. One match in 1891 was lost to the College by 23-0, bad enough, but Wesley College claimed the score was actually 29-0. Perhaps it was the extra training that a boarding school could achieve, but it must have been very embarrassing to lose so regularly in a city that placed such a high value on Association Football. There was one glorious year in 1894-95 season when the worm turned and SRGS recorded a well-won 3-0 victory. Years later elderly men's eyes would water at the very thought of that outstanding victory when the College XI was finally brought to earth. It didn't happen often. SRGS played most of their matches against adults, or scratch sides, until 1900 when they developed their fixture list to include the local grammar schools, Rotherham, Retford, Chesterfield and Doncaster. They still played the Bankers, Medicals, Firth (later University) College and the clergy. At football they could beat their ordained opponents; at cricket it was a different matter. The match against the Clergy was the great match of the season. Unusually it started in the morning, and was a two innings affair played in front of the school with a large number of the boys as spectators. Many Anglican clergymen, at that time, regarded prowess at cricket as almost part of their pastoral duties and they could turn out a very useful side. The school rarely beat them and appropriately the very last match that SRGS played in the summer of 1905 was against the clergy. It was also appropriate that they recorded a huge final win by an innings and 16 runs. This reflected SRGS improvement at cricket in its twilight years. In 1904 they had thrashed Wesley College, getting them all out for 26, and in the following game against Worksop College, Dodson (141) and Maples (55) put on 179 for the first wicket, a record for the school and unbeaten at KES.

To strengthen their sporting challenge to other schools and to give coherence to the organisation of virtually compulsory games, houses were introduced in the early Nineties at SRGS.

Town,   Sharrow,
Hallam,   Park.

A boy joined the House representing his side of town and this no doubt increased the rivalry between the houses when they competed in their annual fixtures. The houses were purely a device for organising games and had no pastoral or tutorial significance, and this was normal at most day schools, including KES when it was established.

Haslam, the 29th and Last Headmaster

In 1899 Rev. Edward Senior retired as Headmaster after considerable absence through ill health during the preceding year. His illness was incurable and he died in 1902. His fifteen years in charge of the school were fondly remembered and appreciated and, as a mark of their respect, the O.B.s organised a subscription for a brass plate to commemorate his memory that was hung in the school hall. It was transferred in 1905 to KES and can still be seen in the lower corridor at Upper School. The reputation of the school was so high that there were just over a hundred applicants for the vacant post. The Governors however chose the man who had been second master since 1890, Rev. Arthur Brooke Haslam, one time Head Boy and Captain of the XV at Rugby School, and he seems to have been a popular choice. Haslam had been the Headmaster at Ripon G.S. (1879-90) before he arrived at SRGS and he is credited with raising the level of the classics teaching at the school, with the result that some of the Grammar School's most impressive academic achievements were in classics. Gilbert Norwood, at St. John's Cambridge, won two Gold Medals in classics and the Porson Prize, ending up as Professor of Classics at the University of California, whilst Kenneth Kirk, who was the first Sheffield pupil to win the coveted Akroyd Scholarship, became the Bishop of Oxford and would keep in touch with KES till the end of his life.

Haslam had other ambitions for his school and planned to make part of the Upper School an *"Organised School of Science"*, whilst on the Commercial Side he wanted *"sound English, with French, German and possibly Spanish, along with a knowledge of book-keeping and shorthand, to form the bulk of the work."*

He did introduce a Junior Class for very young pupils and appointed an experienced lady teacher to be in charge. She was the first lady in the history of the Grammar School to be on the permanent staff of the school and the class was held in the Head's own house.

In reality the school that Haslam took over was perhaps rather complacent and not as efficient as it might have been. The Royal Commission, who reported in 1895, sent A.P. Laurie to inspect the secondary schools of the West Riding and he was not altogether complimentary about SRGS. He commented on the small size of the school and specifically on the inadequate size of the sixth form. He felt that poor use was being made

The whole school photograph of SRGS circa 1895.

of the physics laboratory, and that there was scarcely any physics teaching at all before pupils reached the sixth form. This was despite a successful application by the school, in 1891, for a considerable grant (£600 p.a.) for science teaching from the Sheffield Technical Instruction Board, who in return were offered two places on the Governors. These places were taken by Ald. William Clegg and Sir Henry Stephenson, two very useful, and influential, additions to the Governing Body. Although Haslam increased the number of pupils to 198 by 1904, these criticisms of SRGS would be reflected in the Sadler Report of 1903 that was the catalyst for the creation of King Edward VII School. Yet a great deal of time and effort during Haslam's six years as Head would be taken up in managing a school that was going to be abolished in its present form, only to be re-established as a new entity in the buildings of the struggling Wesley College. Any serious hopes Haslam had of new additional premises — a gymnasium and a swimming pool had long been on the wish list — or new initiatives in the curriculum, were blighted and put on hold by the larger strategic political developments taking place which would bring to an end the Grammar School's 300 year existence.

One project that was brought to fruition was the purchase of Whiteley Woods playing fields in 1901. The Lord Mayor had launched an appeal in 1900 for the £2000 needed to purchase the land. Neither its situation nor its topography were ideal, but the school was desperately short of playing fields. Broomhall Park, which had provided a most attractive setting for the Collegiate buildings and extra space for sports, had now been developed with graceful Victorian villas that rather hemmed in the Grammar School. So when the Lord Mayor opened the new fields in November 1901, and was presented with a silver referee's whistle engraved with the school's crest and the city's coat of arms, it solved the problem of insufficient sports facilities. An even more impressive visitor, Dr. Temple, the Archbishop of Canterbury, spoke and distributed the prizes at Speech Day in the same year. Something of a "coup" for Haslam, who had been a pupil of Temple's when he was Headmaster at Rugby.

Meanwhile boys followed the Imperial fortunes in the Boer War and in 1902 were saddened to hear of the death from enteric fever of an O.B., Harry Longbotham, who was living in South Africa when war broke out. He had joined up in the South African Light Horse and had been captured at Colenso. Escaping to fight again, he succumbed, like so many British soldiers, to disease rather than combat, and unfortunately his death was only the first of many old boys who would die on the battlefields of the new century. Enthusiasm for the war led to the formation of a "*Military Drill and Rifle Shooting Corps*" under the instruction of Sgt. Bell. The whole school took drill practice on Saturday mornings and Bell, a former musketry expert, was prepared to instruct small firing parties, for any boys over the age of twelve years, in the use of the Lee-Enfield. Whether, or not, the stress of controlling his charges was too much for him, Sgt. Bell suddenly dropped dead from a heart attack at school one morning in February 1905. He was buried at Intake and as a mark of the regard in which he was held a very large number of boys attended the funeral.

Already in 1903 the new City Council LEA had commissioned Sir Michael Sadler to produce a report on the future of Sheffield's Secondary Education. The main recommendation in his published Report was that SRGS should be amalgamated with Wesley College and move to their premises. When the City Council accepted this proposal, the fate of Grammar School, that had started life in Campo Lane in the 16th Century, was sealed. There was no place for Haslam in the new re-organisation and he was paid off with an annual pension of £300, which he continued to enjoy until his death in 1941. Rather poignantly, the school magazine, after a plea for the final settlement of subscription arrears, ended its last edition in July 1905 with the words;

"And so farewell to all!"

S.R.G.S. – O.B. – O.70 S.

In 1953 a group of Old Boys of SRGS who were at the school between 1890 and 1900 met and formed an O.B.s Over 70 Society. It was the visit of one of their founder members, Ludwig Glauert, who was then the Director of the Western Australian Museum in Perth, that led to a re-union at Cambridge and then to the formation of the society, which flourished for several years. They were a distinguished bunch including bishops, university professors, numerous clergymen and at least one knight of the realm. Mr. H.W. Middleton of Albany Rd., Sharrow was elected President by seniority and they deigned to make Prof. H.W. Turnbull (one of the school's most distinguished maths scholars) a temporary junior member because he was not yet seventy. Apart from re-unions, or symposiums as they preferred to term them, their rules required each member to send a card to every member having a birthday, and this they unfailingly did.

CHAPTER THREE

A PALACE FOR THE CHILDREN OF THE KING OF KINGS

SHEFFIELD WESLEYAN PROPRIETARY GRAMMAR SCHOOL
(1838-44)

WESLEY COLLEGE
(1844-1905)

"A palace for the children of the King of Kings!", was the compelling image conjured up by James Montgomery, poet, hymn writer, editor of the Sheffield Iris and one of the city's most famous sons, when he spoke at the opening of the new Wesleyan Proprietary Grammar School on 8th August 1838. In truth the 161 new pupils had only half a palace as only the central section, including the corridors to the left and right of the central block, had been completed at that date. The two wings, each with their four pillar portico, would be finished within the next two years, the east wing with its long school room on the first floor would be ready in 1839 but the chapel, two floors high at the west end, would not be completed till the following year.

Nevertheless, all present could congratulate themselves on a remarkable achievement for the Wesleyan Methodists, who, within two years from conception, had produced this magnificent palladian building, now standing pristine white in Sheffield's most fashionable new suburb. The key mover in the project, who also had his turn to speak at the opening ceremony, was a young 32 year old Wesleyan minister, a native of Burton on Trent in Staffordshire. The Rev. Samuel Dousland Waddy had arrived in Sheffield to join the circuit and then realised the city was fertile ground for another major project, the creation of a boarding school for the sons of Methodist laymen residing in the North and Midlands of England.

For a quarter of a century Waddy would labour, first, to create and then guide the school, which became Wesley College in 1844, when it was accepted, by Royal Warrant, as a university college of the University of London. That function ran concurrently with its continuing role as a grammar school, modelled to some extent on the new reformed public schools, but always keeping close to the principles of its Wesleyan foundation and the vision of education propounded by John Wesley himself, in the previous century. Much of Wesley's work had been among working-class neighbourhoods in the new industrial towns and pit villages, and between his first visit to Sheffield in 1742 and his last in 1788, he was not an infrequent visitor to the town of cutlers and little mesters. His twin themes of a more godly society and an educated populace, attracted massive support (sometimes upwards of 20,000 people would gather to hear him preach) and he reinforced the Dissenting tradition in Sheffield that had been growing in strength since the early 17th Century. So much so that by the early 19th Century the Wesleyans were the largest Free Church in the town and they were second only in size to the Anglicans who still formed the town's establishment. Their strength and confidence can be judged by their erection of the Carver St. Chapel in 1805, built to accommodate 1500 worshippers, which, during the 19th Century, provided sixteen Presidents of the Methodist Conference.

As a young man with limited clout in the Methodist Connexion in Sheffield, Waddy took up the key role of secretary to the Provisional Committee formed in 1836 to bring to fruition the great scheme to build and run a Wesleyan boarding school in the town. The more senior Rev. George Marsden was selected as Chairman, but it was Waddy who did the bulk of the work to raise the money and enthuse sceptical Wesleyans to become £50 proprietors and send their sons to this new secondary school. Wesley himself had founded Kingswood at Bristol, now in Bath, in 1748 but it had become a school almost entirely for the sons of Methodist ministers. Woodhouse Grove, founded in 1812 near Bradford, also exclusively served the Methodist ministry, whereas Waddy and the Sheffield Committee wanted their school to serve the lay members of the Wesleyan movement and, specifically, the new rising middle class (which included the Firths, the Osborns and the Cole Brothers) who were growing apace in the industrial towns of the North and the Midlands. This was not going to be a school for poor scholars. Waddy's plans envisioned a "democracy" of numerous well-off subscribers, all Wesleyans, who would become joint proprietors through purchasing a £50 share in the school, with no one person allowed to hold more than three shares.

By 1838 the Committee had secured 209 proprietors, of which only 57 were from Sheffield, with the others coming from towns all over the North and Midlands. Manchester provided 23, Leeds 13, Rotherham 12, Birmingham 5 whilst among the Sheffield names were Waddy himself and William Flockton, the brilliant young architect of the school, as well as Messrs Newton, Chambers, Cockayne, Ibbotson and Wolstenholm and other names familiar to Sheffielders to-day. By 1837 they had purchased an area of sloping land from Mr. William Newbould (a man commemorated since in the name of the road by the school) of five acres, two rods and twenty perches for £4374 and they managed to raise £13,000 towards that purchase and the cost of the building and its equipment.

After selecting William Flockton to design the new building, and approving his bold, impressive classical plans for a school building on the grand scale, they were ready to lay the foundation stone. This ceremony took place on 29th March 1837, and is regarded by some as the date of the foundation of Wesley P.G.S./Wesley College, although during that year the building was in construction and there were no pupils enrolled. Unlike later Methodist practice, the foundation stone was then buried deep within the building and as James Montgomery later pronounced; *"That stone was now buried in darkness with a magnificent pile above it. It should never be exposed to the light, till the beams of the Sun of Righteousness shone upon it, at the breaking up of all things, when the graves themselves must render up their dead. "* He would no doubt be pleased that the stone still lies buried and even the rebuilding of 1905, or the blitz of 1940, has not disturbed it.

The Dyarchy

There were 161 pupils registered for the school's first term, 90 of them boarding full time in the spacious dormitories (they were designed to take 235 beds) and they came from all over the North and the Midlands and even further afield. Only 29 came from Sheffield, more from the surrounding towns, whilst two came from Ireland and two more from Malta. The very first pupil to be registered was Waddy's son, also called Samuel Waddy, who had stayed overnight in the school with his father so that they could be the first to sign up when the registration process began. Samuel Waddy Junior would go on to be one of Wesley College's most famous pupils with a career that included becoming a Q.C., a Judge and Recorder of Sheffield, as well as representing Brigg in Parliament in the Eighties and Nineties.

The Governance of the school was split between the Governor/Chaplain and the Headmaster. The Governor, who was theoretically the more senior of the two, was responsible to the directors, the trustees and ultimately the Methodist Conference for the general direction, business, and staffing of the school as well as the religious education of the boys. As Chaplain he conducted the Chapel Services and ran the Divinity curriculum, whilst as Governor he had the authority to suspend masters, sack the non-teaching staff and prowl around the school "visiting" any of the school rooms, dormitories and other premises as he thought fit. It was laid down in the Deed of Settlement, that was in effect the constitution of the new school, that he must be a Wesleyan Minister, technically appointed by the Methodist Conference and to act as a powerful executive chairman responsible for making sure that the school ran efficiently but; *"to secure not only the religious but the decidedly Wesleyan character of the institution."*

Waddy was disappointed that the directors nominated Rev. John McLean as the first Governor, a nomination subsequently confirmed by the Methodist Conference. Waddy wanted this position to go to a dominant and energetic figure within the local Wesleyan ministry who had a clear vision of the school's educational and strategic social role. Instead they selected McLean who was a supernumerary within the circuit and suffering from indifferent health. He was the first of six Ministers who would hold the post until it fell into disuse in 1888, and he moved his family into the substantial apartments on the first floor. Meanwhile, the new Headmaster, John Manners MA, lived off the premises in his own home, even though a number of masters lived in the school and supervised the boarders' social life and their dormitories.

The Headmsaster's position must have been made very difficult by these curious constitutional arrangements. All Headmasters, unless they were the proprietor, were of course responsible to a chairman and a board of governors, but few would have had to suffer the claustrophobic arrangements that were set in place at Wesley P.G.S and continued at Wesley College. The Deed of Settlement laid down that the Headmaster had to be a graduate of Oxford or Cambridge (Manners' college was Corpus Christi, Cambridge) and if he was in Holy Orders he must not have any pastoral duties outside the school. Manners was a layman when the school started, unusual at the time when almost all headmasters of prestigious schools were clergymen (as was the case with the SRGS Headmasters), but even more surprising was that he was an Anglican, although as a Methodist he could not have taken a Cambridge degree at that time. In 1841 he was ordained and became the curate of Dronfield from 1841-43. We must assume that Wesley P.G.S. was aiming high and therefore prepared to waive their rule about other pastoral duties, and even accept an Anglican, to get a headmaster of the right calibre.

Manners was in sole charge of the education of the pupils and was; *"responsible for the good behaviour of the Masters and their regular attendance to their duties, not only in the school but at all times."* Although he had a right to be on any committee appointing or dismissing staff, the final authority for numbers, salary and engagement of masters lay with the Governor and the directors. In practice it would appear that Manners, by force of personality, acquired a dominance over Mclean, who moved on in 1842 and was replaced by the Rev. Isaac Keeling who, in turn, only lasted two years.

It is clear that not all was well with this dual control of the institution and Waddy, who had moved to Bath, circulated all the proprietors in 1843 with a proposal to clarify the roles and strengthen the position of the Governor. The upshot was that he returned to Sheffield and became the Governor himself in 1844, holding the position until 1862 when he retired. The school now entered a period of considerable success mirroring the Collegiate School less than a quarter of a mile away down the hill in Broomhall. The decision of the local Anglican community, dissatisfied with the education on offer at the Grammar School in St. George's Square, to set up their own institution in 1836, no doubt helped Waddy to galvanise the Wesleyan community to found their own school with a more modern approach to teaching, and a much wider curriculum than was usually on offer at the older established day or boarding schools. From the earliest days, pupils at Wesley P.G.S. could study mathematics, which included algebra, trigonometry, calculus, mechanics and *conic sections.* All pupils took Latin, with an option to do Greek and Hebrew, whilst other core subjects included History, Geography and English Literature, with French taught by a *native,* one Monsieur Henri Vully. If parents wished that their sons should study German or Italian, then competent tutors would be hired on a part-time basis to teach those languages, but all students could do music and drawing because there was a full-time music master and M. Vully was a qualified drawing master. With only five full-time staff, the Headmaster could offer parents a very impressive curriculum with the only obvious gap being science teaching. Occasional lectures on branches of *natural philosophy* had to suffice for instruction in Science, but there was a small science laboratory for experiments, which they claimed, was well equipped with *extensive and splendid apparatus.* For the less academically gifted pupil, who was pursuing a more practical course of study before joining the family firm, the Commercial Department offered ciphering, book-keeping, land surveying, mental arithmetic and *neat penmanship* under the tutelage of the writing master.

Religious instruction under the control of the Governor and Chaplain permeated every part of the day's routine. There were individual prayers every morning at 6.45 a.m. and every evening before bed, lectures once a week on the scriptures *with critical expositions,* one Divinity lesson a week in their separate classrooms, and a bible class at seven o'clock every morning that appears to have been voluntary. On Sunday the regime was, of course, intensified with boarders and day boys attending a morning service at one of the Wesleyan chapels in the town before returning to school for *Conference Catechisms.* Then in the evening they had to attend the service in the school's own chapel when the Governor would preach at length to an uplifting text of his own choosing.

For some pupils even this regular affirmation of their faith does not seem to be enough, and in the mid-Forties a group of senior pupils, including the young Waddy, believing that their fellows were backsliding and straying from the paths of righteousness, started their own "Great Revival" movement. Boys were encouraged by their peers to *"give their hearts to God"* and attend to their religious duties with true diligence forsaking the casual observance that was common practice among them. As if the official programme of services was not enough, they organised Saturday night prayer meetings that went on for hours and gained no little fame in the district, drawing in not only almost all the boys in the college, but also the domestic staff and people from the neighbouring hamlet of Crookes. No doubt over the sixty seven years of its existence, Wesley P.G.S./College had its fair share of unenthusiastic nominal Christians, even agnostics, but it did produce a substantial number of Wesleyan Ministers, many lecturers at Methodist theological colleges and three Presidents of the Methodist Conference.

FLOCKTON'S MASTERPIECE

The school building, completed in 1840, from its front and side elevations looks exactly the same to-day as it did one hundred and sixty five years ago. Then it was dazzlingly clean unlike the gun metal grime that now covers the walls and the magnificent sixteen Corinthian pillars. The main palladian staircase and the two commanding wings, whose white cupolas can still be seen from two miles away across the Sheaf valley, were all part of William Flockton's original design and are still in place to-day.

William Flockton (1804-1864), the son of a builder and carpenter, had founded his own architect's practice in 1833 when 29 years old. Almost immediately he was given the commission to design The Mount, the prestigious town house development at Broomhill, also built on land belonging to Newbould. Called "Flockton's Folly" because cynics thought that it was too far out of town to attract "quality" people, its success was assured when James Montgomery took one of the eight apartments in 1835. Not only did the Mount then flourish, but Broomhill, and points west to Ranmoor, became Sheffield's most exclusive suburb.

The Provisional Committee inspired by this building decided to take a chance on the young, and essentially inexperienced Flockton, and in 1837 asked him to design their new school. The Mount, with its six column central portico, could be a scale model for the finished exterior of the school, albeit in the Ionic style rather than the Corinthian of Wesley P.G.S. However when work began, the residents of The Mount, including James Montgomery, realised that their glorious view across the valley was now to be impeded by the bigger building going up just across the Glossop Rd., and like most householders in a similar position, they were not greatly pleased.

457 Glossop Road, as the school was always referred to in the census and other official documents, was completed in 1840 at a total cost of £24,000 (exclusive of the purchase price of the site) a quarter of which covered the cost of furnishing the building. Waddy's fundraising only raised half this total cost and so from the beginning the school was heavily mortgaged and never cleared these debts. However for the moment there was all-round praise for Flockton's achievement even if as one critic said, "the building could not claim originality, but in appropriateness to its situation and in the boldness with which it soared above the common level, the school is remarkable for a confident ambition amounting almost to genius."

Flockton left his signature on the architecture of his native city. The new Workhouse on Union Rd. at Nether Edge (later the hospital, more recently exclusive apartments) was designed by him in 1844. This "palace for the children (and parents) of the indigenous poor" was also built on the grand scale but in the Elizabethan Style. It gives one an inkling of what Wesley College might have looked like if Flockton had been asked to design the school a decade later, after the pure classical style had gone out of fashion.

His son Thomas J. Flockton (1823-99) joined him in the practice at 13 years of age and arguably made an even bigger impact on Sheffield than his father. Flockton Junior's work includes the Leopold St. complex of the Central School, the Education Offices and Firth College. He also designed the Cutler's Banqueting Hall, the Mappin Art Gallery, St. John's Ranmoor and some of the great steelmasters' houses, like Endcliffe Hall and Oakbrook built for the Browns and the Firths respectively.

In 1905 it was their firm, Flockton and Gibbs, who rebuilt the interior of the school that had become King Edward VII School

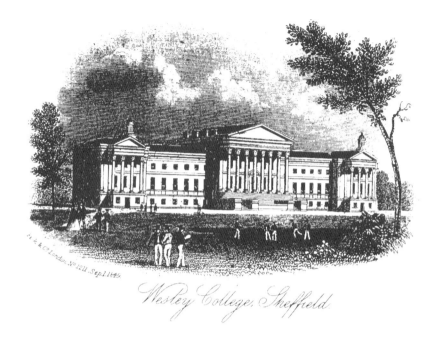

Wesley College, Sheffield

A Different Interior

Students at KES today would be quite lost in Wesley College, whether the year was 1838 or 1900. There were, for a start, no wide corridors well lit by high windows, instead on the first and second floors one passed along corridors that were dingy and narrow with classrooms or dormitories on either side.

On the ground floor until 1876, when the Junior Department was created, there were just two large empty wings to the building. To the east, on the town side, there was the covered playground occupying the whole space. In effect it was a simple sports hall, that recognised that British weather was often inclement and that boys needed somewhere to let off steam. Pick-up games of cricket and football could easily be accommodated and no doubt it was the venue for a number of quarrels that were settled in the time-honoured way of young boys. On the other side of the central crypt where the kitchen and laundry were sited (now the dining hall) was another large empty space called the cloisters. This area was for study and quiet contemplation and probably looked much the same as the covered playground except for a few uplifting prints and texts, a few benches and writing tables. Later, after 1876, this whole area would be transformed into the Junior School with benches and desks and partitions that could create separate classrooms if they were required.

The first floor had four individual classrooms to the east and the dining room to the west and in the main Entrance Hall , the Headmaster had his room where the office now is and the office, perversely, was where the Headteacher's room now stands. The Entrance Hall would be the only part of the building recognisable by to-day's students, including the staircase going off to the left, then the school's only stairs, and the marble table which may have originally been in the chapel. The chapel occupied the whole of the west wing and its exterior access door is still there, but sealed and unused in present times. The chapel was the grandest part of the complex, two floors high, with a balcony accessed from the first floor; it had a magnificent high double pulpit, stained glass windows and a brass lectern that was returned to KES in 1922 and still stands on the platform in the Assembly Hall today. The body of the chapel was filled with box pews and every boy had his own place which his parents had to purchase, as they would expect to do as wealthy patrons of their own chapel.

The Chapel of Wesley College during Harvest Festival

The second floor housed the living and sleeping quarters of the boys, the teaching staff and the Governor and his family. The latter could be quite an extensive brood. Waddy had ten children and they all lived in at the college, but after 1888 it was the Headmaster, Joseph Findlay, who took over these apartments and the Governor's post was discontinued. For extra payment *"boys of a higher class"* could have their own study bedrooms, but most pupils had to put up with a communal dormitory over the Schoolroom or the Chapel. Later, in Findlay's time, these became the basis for the two houses for the boarders. If your Dormitory was over the Chapel, or you had an adjacent study, you were in Chapel House and if over the Schoolroom, you were in School House. The Schoolroom on the first floor, where the library is today, served as an open plan, multi-use work area on the traditional pattern. The Headmaster would often preside on his raised "throne" and masters would tutor their groups in different corners of the room.

The more detailed teaching went on in the separate, but adjacent classrooms, and this would have been something of an innovation in 1838.

The top floor behind the classical pediment was the servants' quarters and dormitories for the very youngest boys. Here Matron presided over a small army of women who ran the domestic arrangements of the school. Never less than 14 female staff (many of them local, unmarried women in their twenties), enough for a sizeable country house, served as servants, doing the cooking, the laundering and the cleaning as well as administering to the sick and unwell until the college doctor could visit. Finally, outside were two facilities that many Old Edwardians would remember. The outside "privies" were in the same position as they remained until the 1970s, although, of course, they were earth toilets at first, and the Open Air Swimming Pool, a very advanced facility for the first half of the 19th Century, was soon added at the lower south east end of the Close where the covered pool stands today.

We are a College now!!

Samuel Waddy's arrival at the school brought immediate changes as the school applied for a Royal Warrant to become a university college of the University of London. In 1844 the University granted this privilege and the school to mark its change in status changed its name to Wesley College, the name by which it was known for the rest of its history. The college could now offer courses, to a relatively small number of its brightest pupils, to study for the Batchelor of Arts and the Batchelor of Laws degrees of the University of London, at that time one of only four universities in England. The college always claimed, in its prospectus, that graduates could then go on to do an M.A. or a Doctorate of Laws, but very few seem to have followed this course while residing at the college. Until the Eighties the college maintained a "University Division" of its most able students, some of whom were already following the undergraduate Pass and Honours courses of the University as laid down in the University Calendar. This "Division" also included those younger pupils who were preparing to undertake the degree courses when they had matriculated.

These University Division pupils lived in the college into their early twenties, wore gowns to signify their academic status and only went up to the parent University in London when they were sitting their degree examinations. The success of Wesley College was for the moment assured. Its progress was followed by other Wesleyan institutions, including the West of England Proprietary Grammar School in Somerset, founded in 1843, which also became a university college of London University. This school is now known as Queen's College, Taunton, a change of name made to celebrate Queen Victoria's Golden Jubilee in 1887, which was a decision of their then Headmaster, J.J.Findlay, who shortly afterwards became the third Headmaster of Wesley College.

The long reign of Dr. Shera

Samuel Waddy settled in for a long tenure at the college. Nicknamed the "Bulldog" for his ferocious demeanour when castigating a miscreant, he none the less ran a liberal regime, compared to the brutal punishments common at many boarding schools. It is to the Wesleyans' credit that they believed pupils could be reasoned with rather than beaten to maintain discipline and impart understanding. The prospectus of the college explained the school's philosophy on discipline thus: —

> *"Discipline is enforced by uniting firmness with kindness; by creating the feeling that it is better to be orderly than disorderly, that it tends essentially to their own comfort and happiness and promotes their own improvement. Should anyone decide to be refractory, he is taken into an adjoining room and reasoned with on the impropriety of his conduct."*

In December1853 John Manners retired, having established a good academic reputation for the college, and the directors appointed an Irishman, Dr. Henry McEffer Shera MA. LLD. They waived aside the requirement that the Headmaster had to be an Oxbridge graduate, to allow Shera, a graduate of the protestant Trinity College, Dublin, to become the Headmaster and he remained at Wesley College for thirty four years, the longest serving Headmaster at any of the schools that make up the KES family tree. A genial leader, who invariably wore his academic hood as well as his gown and mortar board, he was described in the school prospectus as a man of *"the broadest and most universal character"* who conducted systematic weekly examinations of all pupils on his regular rounds of inspection. He was a keen sportsman who built up the college's intimidating reputation for success in Cricket and Football and was clearly the life and soul of the social life of the school as well as driving its academic progress. It is recorded that he was often challenged by the boys to perform his "party piece", kicking a football right over the school building and then throwing a cricket ball over for good measure.

Waddy served for eighteen years as Governor (1844-62), almost nine of them working alongside Shera. In 1859 he was elected as the President of the Methodist Conference a singular honour for the

Dr Henry Shera
Headmaster 1854-88, Died 1892

45

College as well as for Waddy himself. He was followed by four more Governors, the Rev. John James in the Sixties, a Rev. John Harvard and the Rev. William Jessop in the Seventies and finally by the Rev. William Dallinger F.R.S. from 1879–88. The balance of power between the two positions, and how they co-operated, depended on their respective personalities, but it is clear that a legendary headmaster like Shera became the dominant force in the relationship after Waddy had retired from the post. In fact when Jessop retired in 1879 the directors had some difficulty in filling the post, but Rev. Dr. Dallinger, who was a distinguished and nationally recognised biologist, accepted the position only on the understanding that he could teach his subject as well as be the Governor and Chaplain. He was, in effect, one of Shera's staff as well as being technically his superior officer: a situation that, at best, required careful handling and at worst could lead to divided responsibility and organisational chaos.

The years when Shera and Waddy shared control were perhaps the College's most successful period. Certainly numbers on the roll went up and by the 1861 census there were 147 boarders in residence with a total population of 236, most probably the maximum that was ever achieved. The College continued to serve the Wesleyan communities of the North and Midlands, although it was never an exclusive sectarian school, and some of its boarders came from far away. In 1861 there were three boys from Dublin, another three from Belfast and one all the way from New Zealand. Perhaps the most intriguing pupil was 17 year old A.E. Davis from Jamaica who was possibly the first black pupil at the college, for there certainly were black pupils at the College later in the century, as they appear on the house and class photographs. One thing is certain, they either came from wealthy families or they had wealthy backers because Wesley College was not cheap.

TERMS PER ANNUM
Circa 1850

BOARDERS

Pupils 9-11 years; £35. Pupils 11-15; £45. Pupils over 15; £55

A student with a room to himself and taking breakfast, tea, dinner and supper with the Governor and masters; £85.
Two brothers occupying the same room but with separate beds; £75

DAY BOYS

Under 15 years ; £10. Over 15 years £18
(more than KES charged 50 years later in 1905)

Each pupil was expected to find for himself;

A Bible and Hymn Book, three suits of clothes, six shirts, three nightshirts, six pairs of stockings, four pairs of shoes and six pocket handkerchiefs all to be clearly marked with the pupil's name in full.

THE SCHOOL UNIFORM

In the first decade boys wore the short jacket (inelegantly nicknamed bumfreezers) and white trousers with a small mortarboard for their headwear.

In the second half of the century they would dress in a suit, much like public school boys today. For headgear they would wear a boater with the school band around it, or a school cap. In the Eighties this cap was a soft pillar-box affair but was replaced in the Nineties by a cap with white piping that looks remarkably like the cap worn at KES until the 1950s. Bowler hats seem to have been permissible in Dr. Shera's time.

The Dispute of 1888

Somewhere along the line in Shera's long period as Headmaster, the College's reputation began to slip. The school struggled to maintain its numbers and therefore its financial viability, the perennial problem of 19th Century private educational establishments. The Collegiate School down the hill had a fine academic record but it was regularly beset by financial crises and finally gave up the fight in 1884 when it sold out to the Grammar School. By 1871 Wesley College was down to 84 boarders and although it had risen to 96 by 1881, the College was beginning to feel the competition of numerous newly founded boarding schools, many admitted to the Headmasters' Conference. The Methodists themselves had established the Leys in Cambridge in 1875, Truro School in 1879 and Rydal in North Wales was opened in 1885. Wesley College was beginning to struggle to keep itself attractive to its potential market, even though there was a steady advance in the curriculum on offer.

The school was divided into three divisions with the B Division aimed at those pupils who were "*intended for mercantile pursuits*". The A Division in the words of an 1870's prospectus consists of those; "*who are designed (sic) for the Learned Professions, and those of whose wealth, rank or tastes make it desirable that they receive a more complete education.*" Finally there was the University Division that included those taking London degrees and those studying to matriculate at that University. The syllabus now included more Science, with weekly lectures in Chemistry as well as "*Natural Philosophy*" and there were now regular classes in Elementary Science. The core staff was still only six or seven, but tutors were hired to teach the more arcane courses, like Hebrew and Syriac, although one wonders how many Sheffield lads, or even Boarders, really wanted to do an ancient Aramaic dialect from Syria. "*Accomplished foreigners*" still taught German and French and ex-drill sergeants took compulsory classes in drilling and gymnastics, now firmly part of an English school's routine. Successful students might qualify for the twelve or so internal scholarships, tenable for a year and worth between ten and twenty guineas, or be rewarded by the presentation of a gown, or a gold or silver medal. One of these medals turned up in Hong Kong shortly after World War Two and was bought by a sailor in the U.S. Navy. He took the trouble to return it to KES, who then passed it on to a living relative of the boy who had won it for proficiency in Modern Languages in the summer of 1880.

There were other important changes by which Shera tried to keep his school abreast of the competition and maintain the school's attractiveness to potential recruits. Young boys, some as young as eight or nine had always been welcomed at Wesley College, but in 1876 their education was put on a proper formal basis. A discrete Junior Division (initially called the Lower School) was created for boys under 13 years of age, with masters in charge who had experience of teaching younger boys. Wesley College now had established its own prep. school and in 1881 there were 16 boarders in the Junior School, one as young as nine, and an unspecified number of day boys. The cloisters on the ground floor were converted into a schoolroom for the junior boys and their numbers were swollen by recently arrived older pupils whose early education was judged to be deficient.

The JUNIOR SCHOOL on the Lower Ground Floor

In the late Seventies under the instruction of one George Jennings, *"the eminent Sanitary Engineer to the Board of Ordnance",* a modern sewer and drainage system was installed at the College, which included putting water closets in the outdoor toilets. This was trumpeted in the prospectus as a far-sighted move, as indeed it was, and for the rest of the century the College could boast, and did, that it had had no serious outbreaks of any infectious disease. The toilets stayed in place for almost a century and were regarded less affectionately by their Twentieth Century patrons, who knew them as the "Backs".

To encourage the corporate life of the school, Shera also introduced a school magazine, The Wesley College Journal (first published1885) and the Mutual Improvement Society. The latter founded in the middle Eighties was an all purpose school society that, mainly through the medium of lectures, debates and readings, introduced pupils to a very wide range of topics of interest. There were all-school trips out into Derbyshire, Ashopton on the River Derwent (now lying under Ladybower reservoir) being a favourite venue and in 1888, in Shera's last term, a day's holiday was granted for his birthday. On another occasion in that last term, permission was given for a group of favoured pupils to see the Australian touring team play Yorkshire at Bramall Lane.

However storm clouds were gathering and about to break for Shera and Dallinger. The minutes of the directors' meetings, now unfortunately lost to posterity, talked of furious rows, inquiries and investigations, confidential reports and extraordinary meetings; not the best way to celebrate the first fifty years of the school. It is not exactly clear what was at the bottom of the disputes that wracked the college and caused the resignation, not just of the Headmaster, but also Dallinger, the Governor, and in a clear gesture of solidarity with Shera, all the teaching staff. Whether it was another financial crisis, or the continual drop in the number of boarders, or a clash between Governor and Headmaster, or the failure to keep up with the style and academic progress of similar schools, is not now clear. It was probably a combination of all of these problems, plus the age and longevity in the post of Shera himself. Even in the 19th Century, thirty four years was a long time to keep an effective control of one's school and, although much loved, Shera may well have just got too old for the post. A fund to give him a testimonial was started immediately by his supporters, and Shera, along with Waddy, are the only two people connected with Wesley College who were honoured with a bronze plaque in the Entrance Hall; plaques that are still there to this day.

The New Young Broom

If Shera's age, possible inflexibility and resistance to change was the main problem, then the directors administered some strong medicine to cure the patient. Joseph John Findlay MA was a young man in a hurry. After Wadham College, Oxford, where he obtained a First in Mathematics and also in History, he had then taught at Rugby and at the amazingly young age of 24, he was appointed to turn around a Wesleyan school in Somerset which he re-named, rather in the fashion of a modern "makeover", Queen's College, Taunton. So impressive was his work there that it resounded throughout the Methodist community and the Sheffield Directors decided he was just the man for them. He was only 28 when he arrived and only stayed three years, but the College was changed, if not out of all recognition, then quite substantially both in its organisation and in its style.

Firstly, there was to be no sharing executive power with a Governor, although the Rev. Valentine Pearson did agree, if a little reluctantly, to take on the position of Chaplain. Findlay now moved into the Governor's considerable apartments at the College, the first Headmaster to live on the premises, and the Governor's position was quietly abandoned.

Findlay didn't feel the College needed a new name to create a new image, but he gave it a coat of arms which surprisingly it had not enjoyed before.

Manliness, a very English 19th Century concept, religion and learning were very much the ethos of the advancing successful public schools, and it was their model that Findlay, who had been inspired by his period of teaching at Rugby, wanted to follow as closely as possible in Sheffield. He introduced the House system, re-named the school magazine "the Sheaf", although its general style did not alter very much and in 1890 he established the school cadet corps.

He believed in compulsory games, added Lacrosse to the games played at the college and introduced colours for sustained performance during the season. These were worn on a pupil's cap and took the form of a small replica of the school's badge. He introduced prefects to support the staff and encourage the responsibility of senior boys, and through them, more self-reliance amongst the general body of pupils. He also started a register of the College's Old Boys as a catalyst to build up an Old Boys' Association.

Coat of Arms of Wesley College
The shield displays the quartering of the arms of the town of Sheffield, with those of the University of London and the Wesley family.(Cross and shells sable on a field argent). The motto, which was in use earlier in the College's history was:
Virtus Religio Doctrina - This translates as Manliness, Religion and Learning

The New Houses

The Boarders
CHAPEL HOUSE (Light Blue) for those whose dormitories were over the Chapel.
SCHOOL HOUSE (Claret) those with Dormitories over the Schoolroom
The Day Boys.
NORTH TOWN HOUSE (Dark Blue) for those who lived North of the school,
SOUTH TOWN HOUSE (Chocolate) for those from the south of the town
The Juniors
Had a house of their own and their colour was Cerise.

The houses not only served to create competition in sport but were also active in providing entertainment through house concerts and socials

There was also a renaissance in the music life of the College, that just pre-dated Finlay's arrival but was much encouraged by him. Mr. H. Clough, the new music master, also from Queen's College, Taunton, was a most energetic teacher who improved the Music lessons, strengthened the singing, pianoforte and organ instruction, and introduced a special singing practice on Sunday afternoon for practising the hymns and anthems to be played and sung in the Chapel Service. Under his prompting the College was alive with music as houses and classes all ran their own concerts as well as staging public and "sacred" concerts. He produced a programme of organ voluntaries to be played at each service on Sundays in which Mendelsohn, Bach, Beethoven and Schubert competed with the Organ Sonata by Sir F.A. Gore-Ouseley.

Because all the teaching staff had rather gallantly, or perhaps foolishly, resigned, Findlay only took back those he felt he could work with. So, fortunately for him, any opposition to change which an existing staff's inertia, or sheer opposition, might mount had been eliminated by their own actions, leaving him free to mould the school in the way he wanted. He realised the College would have to rely more on recruiting larger numbers of day-boys. Therefore it would have to abandon its rather aloof attitude towards Sheffield, and recognise the popular need for commercial, and, increasingly, technical, education. Findlay laid particular stress on teaching Technical Drawing and he enlisted the services of the Head of the Sheffield School of Art to give every boy, up to 15 years of age, technical drawing lessons every week. Furthermore, he arranged that boys who had completed their studies at the College could remain as boarders, while receiving instruction in all branches of engineering and mechanics at the Technical School. This institution, based in the old buildings of the Grammar School in St. George's Square, had developed a high reputation and in 1897 it joined with Firth College to form the University College, subsequently becoming the University of Sheffield in 1905. In this way Findlay, and Pearson who soon followed him, kept a direct link with higher education after the relationship with London University seems to have withered away.

Findlay's "public school" ideas did not suit everyone connected with the College but there was a general agreement that he made many positive changes, marginally increased the number of pupils and left the school on a firmer footing. He resigned in 1891 and devoted the rest of his career to educational theory, being particularly prominent in pioneering the teaching of modern languages and the systematic training of teachers. He ended his career as Professor of Education at Manchester University (a post held earlier by Michael Sadler), and died at Torquay in June 1940.

The Happy Last Lap

In the spring of 1891 the Rev. Valentine Ward Pearson wished to tender his resignation as Chaplain of the College. He was persuaded to stay on and then found himself offered the Headmaster's position when Findlay left suddenly in the summer. A Lancastrian, born and educated in Manchester, he was only 34 years old when he became the last Headmaster of Wesley College. He was to enjoy a happy and successful fourteen years in the post and all reports of Pearson suggest that he proved to be the right man for the job. A

London BA graduate from Owens College, he had impressed as an eloquent preacher when Chaplain, but was also regarded as a very effective teacher who now took on direct responsibility for the education of the senior pupils in the Sixth Form. An accomplished sportsman, he turned out for the College at cricket and football when they played men's teams, played golf at Sandygate, fished for trout at Yorkshire Bridge, was an excellent ice skater, and his fine voice augmented the choir at the concerts. He had the social graces that Findlay lacked, was well respected by his staff and extremely popular with the boys.

He took over a school that had just gone through a difficult transition period and he benefited from the reforms that Findlay had put in place. One of the first fruits of the reforms was the creation of a new and better equipped science laboratory, that was moved from its position under the Schoolroom and re-sited on the

The Rev. V.W. Pearson, Headmaster 1891-1905

second floor, where the gallery and the atrium of the Assembly Hall are today. The vacated area was turned into a gymnasium and with a little alteration is still in situ today.

Academically the school had never been stronger, with virtually all pupils taking outside examinations and a larger than usual number staying on into the sixth form. They were however a small school, their numbers never rising above 200, and therefore it was only a trickle of pupils who went on to University; perhaps no more than six or seven each year, with one or two going to Oxbridge, some to Durham and the majority to Firth College, or London University itself. At sixteen most boys took the Junior Level of the Oxford Local Examination, (the "O" Level of its day), those doing commercial studies sat the Examinations of the College of Preceptors and those who wanted a Science qualification sat the "South Kensington" examinations. In 1899 the College's hubris over its examination results led it to claim that it had the best results amongst all the Methodist independent schools; no mean feat because there were fifteen of them and they included girls' schools, like Queenswood in North London.

A group of senior boys including pupils from the West Indies. Circa 1898

Virtually invincible!

Perhaps because of its policy of compulsory games, the College was well nigh unbeatable, at its main sports, by any other school in the Nineties. The number of matches lost by the Football Team in that decade does not reach double figures and many opponents were well and truly thrashed, especially SRGS, losers by 29-0 goals in 1891. So successful was the College, that Pearson had to publicly deny at a prize-giving ceremony that sport was the College's top priority, and stress that this success at games was not at the expense of the boys' academic study. At both cricket and football the College had an impressive fixture list, playing all the prestigious schools in the area, including Manchester and Leeds Grammar Schools, Mount St. Mary's, Woodhouse Grove, QEGS Wakefield and Nottingham H.S. It was a cut above the schools the Grammar School played, and it was the College's fixture list that was taken over by KES when they started to play inter-school matches in 1906. The two main team sports were played on the Close, in front of the school, on a pitch that sloped badly towards the swimming pool and was always too small for comfort; even worse after a four yard strip of the school grounds were sold to the Council in 1891 to enable them to widen Clakehouse Rd. The Football Team was, however, alarmed by a F.A. rule change in 1892 that stopped one of their most effective tactics. It was no longer permissible to barge the goalkeeper unless he held the ball, and they bemoaned this change saying, "*Our favourite dodge of one man centring the ball while another charges the goalkeeper will now render us liable for a free kick!*"

There were other sports available to the boys. The annual swimming sports were held at Glossop Road Baths, a house shooting competition at the R.E.'s Glossop Road Drill Hall and there were now a couple of Fives courts against the eastern boundary wall for Fives and Racquets. The open air pool was available for swimming instruction and it is known that on hot summers' nights, some daring boys would sneak down from their dormitory windows and take a cooling swim, whilst in the winter, when the pool froze over, it served as a skating rink.

Wesley College Staff in HM's garden in 1893. James Shearer is on the extreme left and Rev. Valentine Pearson, the Headmaster, (second from right back row)

The staff, never more than ten permanent masters, also found time for relaxation. Mr. S.A. Richards, a Modern Languages Master from 1896-1901, recalls; "*There were numerous invitations to whist drives, dinners and dances in the winter, and in the summer, cycle runs out to Fox House and Hathersage with lady friends, followed by bounteous "Yorkshire" high teas on their return.*" They were even allowed to practice their golf swing in the Close in their dinner hours, whilst the photographic skills of James Shearer, Second Master and later KES Registrar, rather usefully captured forms, house groups and teams on camera, producing a fine visual record, some of which we still have today.

Sold out!

With the advent of the Twentieth Century, Wesley College became increasingly vulnerable. On the surface Pearson was running a successful school with all the trappings of a minor public school, but the 1902 Education Act, which cleared the legal way for Council's to run their own grammar schools subsidised by the rates, put small schools

The Cadet Corps

Founded in 1891 the Cadet Corps was attached to the 1st West Yorkshire (Volunteer) Royal Engineers and wore their uniform of scarlet tunic and dark blue trousers with a thin red stripe. The pill box hat they wore, now only worn by the Gurkhas, was standard headgear for many regiments and corps at the time. A member of staff supervised their activities and boys were promoted to NCO rank, the most senior being Sergeants, whilst a regular Sgt-Major of the Engineers came up to the school once a week to supervise the parades. The corps was voluntary and never numbered more than fifty, but that was at least a third of those who were old enough to join. The Corps held annual camps but they were usually in the vicinity, one was at Lydgate, another at Rivelin, both areas which were then in the countryside. When the Sheffield Volunteers returned from the Boer War, the Wesley College Corps was invited to be part of the celebratory parade as it marched past the Town Hall. The special "Victory" edition of a Sheffield paper caught them on camera and with unconscious irony captioned the photograph "preparing for the next war!"

like Wesley College in jeopardy. Increasingly the College was relying on Sheffield day-boys to fill its ranks (by 1903 it was down to only thirty boarders) and a fair number of them were not Methodists. Partly as a way of encouraging recruitment, Pearson always fully supported the Junior School and was prepared to take boys as young as seven in the Junior Forms. After 1902 the Master in Charge of the Junior School was F.T.Savage, who, in 1905, was one of the few Wesley College masters offered a position at KES, where he became a school legend. Junior School pupils were now almost exclusively

Wesley College Form Group - Circa 1896

local boys, but the College was never embraced by the city in the way that the SRGS, or the Central Schools, were. It always remained something of an outsider and had few supporters among the city's ruling élite.

There were those who still saw a future for the College. Judge Samuel Waddy Jnr. was now Recorder of Sheffield and as keen as ever for the school to prosper, and there were others like Angus Holden M.P., an Old Boy who had won the Buckrose Division of Yorkshire in the 1892 elections, and Samuel Cocker, a wealthy local Old Boy who led fund-raising drives with substantial donations of his own. In 1897, to celebrate the Diamond Jubilee of Queen Victoria, Cocker gave an individual engraved bible to every master, pupil and household staff member at the College, almost two hundred in all. He also replaced the school's "Union Jack", which had always been flown on the first day of term to "celebrate" the pupils' return to their lessons after the freedom of the holidays.

Some of the Directors hoped that the continuing financial difficulties would be solved by the Methodist Conference taking over the school. They had not been able to persuade the Sheffield Technical Instruction Board to give them the sort of annual grant aid that the SRGS enjoyed, ostensibly because they were a proprietary company whose shareholders might therefore benefit from public funds. However, the Wesley College shareholders were well aware that the Methodists had set up a national development fund (the

Twentieth Century Fund) as a springboard for expansion in the new century, and they also knew that moves were afoot, in 1903, to use part of this fund (£70,000) to create an umbrella organisation to oversee and support the existing prestigious Methodist boarding schools. The upshot of this initiative was that Wesley College, along with three other Methodist boarding schools, was sold to the Twentieth Century Fund in early 1903. The Funds' Committee were in the process of establishing a "Board of Management for Methodist Residential Schools" (created in 1904) and it was assumed that Wesley College would be included on their list of schools that would be supported in the future. Instead when they received the proposal of Sheffield City Council to buy out the College and amalgamate it with SRGS to form a new "superior" school, the Wesleyans in London moved with almost indecent haste to accept the offer.

Perhaps it was because of the College's continuing mortgage and other debts, perhaps because it was rapidly becoming a day school in all but name (how those thirty boys must have rattled around in dormitories designed for seven or eight times the number), or because it was increasingly serving the general public, not just the Wesleyan community. However by 1904 the College had been sold to the City Council and the new LEA ran it for its final year. Everything and everyone remained in place, outwardly it was still Wesley College with Pearson still the Headmaster, and the same staff continuing teaching the same courses. Pearson himself was very positive about the change, there was to be no rearguard action to save the College led by him. At the College's last Prize Giving Ceremony on 20th July 1905 Pearson, in commending the new venture to the parents and the boys, said; "*This new school was going to be the finest day school in the country, through noble environment, ample equipment, adequate (sic) staff and municipal sympathy.*" His audience was not entirely convinced. Perhaps, because Pearson, who had already had a two month leave of absence to study teacher training methods in North America, had already accepted, from the Council's Education Committee, the new position of Principal of Sheffield City Training College, who were about to start life in the buildings soon to be vacated by the SRGS on Collegiate Crescent.

CHAPTER FOUR

MICHAEL SADLER'S MARRIAGE PROPOSAL

There is a view, popular among Old Edwardians and friends of the school, that King Edward VII School was an independent school until the 1944 Education Act turned it into a maintained grammar school. Moreover, that during the forty years of independent existence, it had enjoyed the status of a public school, although it always had a close, if undefined, relationship with the City Council. The truth is that KES was a total creation of the City Council, who financed the buy-out of Wesley College and the Royal Grammar School, fused them into one institution and controlled their governance and their finances from the very beginning in 1905. To achieve this the Council used the provisions of Robert Morant's 1902 Education Act, which set up the LEAs and allowed County Boroughs, like Sheffield, along with County Councils, to provide grammar schools and other secondary schools on the rates.

The leading Liberal and Conservative Councillors on the new Education Committee enthusiastically embraced this new legislation. Fired by a fierce civic pride, they had a vision to create a secondary education sector to match the success of the old School Board's elementary provision for the city. One of their earliest acts, after the Education Committee was established in April 1903, was to invite Professor Michael Sadler of Manchester University to review the existing secondary and higher education provision for the city, with a view to making radical recommendations for new and improved institutions. His remit included the University College and the training of teachers, as well as considering improved public library provision. The key concern of the councillors, and many of their middle class electorate, was the need for a prestigious boys' day school to rival the old and successful institutions in the other great northern industrial towns. Wesley College and the Royal Grammar School may have had their successes and their Oxbridge honours but they were not in the same league as Bradford G.S., Leeds G.S. and, especially, Manchester G.S.

Michael Sadler, born into a Radical family in Barnsley, had only recently been appointed to the Chair of Education at Manchester's Victoria University, having served for a decade as one of the leading civil servants formulating education policy in London. He was the driving force behind the Bryce Commission of 1895, that grappled with the inadequacy of secondary school provision in Britain and the concerns that the nation was falling behind the Germans and the Americans, who were by now Britain's main trading rivals. It was Sadler's Department that investigated the educational systems of other countries, and he became convinced that there should be a new structure that would provide a secondary tier of education for able pupils, to allow them to continue their education after elementary school. Action became imperative after the infamous Cockerton legal judgement of 1899 declared all London School Board spending on secondary schools illegal. This decision placed at risk all the ad hoc arrangements, including the Sheffield Central Schools in Leopold St., put in place for secondary education by school boards across the country and the Government was now forced to act. Unfortunately for Sadler his thinking was not radical enough and his former assistant, Sir Robert Morant, took over and masterminded the 1902 Education Act. Sadler moved on to his new post at Manchester and in time would be Vice-Chancellor of Leeds University, and later Master of University College, Oxford.

Sadler began work in June 1903 and had his report on the desk of Sir Henry Stephenson, the Chairman of the Education Committee, by the 22nd July. He surveyed the situation he found in Sheffield and concluded that there had been much good, if not outstanding, work at the elementary level, but that the secondary provision was quite inadequate for a city of Sheffield's importance and size. He had praise however for the Central School and his second main recommendation set guidelines for the growth of that institution as a 12 -16 school for boys and girls. However his first and main recommendation concerned the two leading independent boy's schools in the city. He proposed that the Royal Grammar School and Wesley College should merge to form one school and be housed in the grand Palladian premises of Wesley College.

It is possible that this idea might have been put into his head by one or two leading councillors, because, in a speech he made at the official opening of the new school in November 1906, he mentions that three years earlier, when he was commissioned to write his report, at least one senior councillor had:

> *"instilled in my brain the revolutionary project for the establishment of this school by a combination of elements."*

Yet Sadler was under no illusions that to amalgamate an independent denominational boarding school, like Wesley College, with an ancient day Grammar School with strong Anglican connections and a close relationship with the City Council, might well be an undertaking that was mission impossible. However, his recommendation was that the only way to give the city a boys' school to match the provision for girls that the Girls' High School had provided since 1878, was to fuse the two institutions. In his report he wrote that this new school should:

> *"Be on the highest plane of intellectual efficiency, thoroughly well staffed, have long courses up to 18 or 19 and be accommodated in good buildings, well equipped with a library and apparatus."*

> *"School games should be carefully organised and other forms of school activity which develop esprit de corps, give good tone, and teach the virtues of corporate life."*

> *"Manual training should be encouraged throughout the school, as training of the hand helps to develop the brain."*

> *"Great care should be taken to make the most of the average boy but without sacrificing the interest of the specially clever pupils."*

Sadler admitted that, with help, both SRGS and Wesley College could separately be raised up to the level of excellence he described. However, he believed that the City Council would not be able to fund two such institutions and it would be better to start with a clean page after a union of these two schools had been achieved. He then went on to sketch out alternatives, but concluded that to give both institutions small amounts of financial support would be wasted money. If a choice between them had to be made, then, in his judgement, it should fall on the Grammar School; *"being an ancient local trust and public foundation."*

The Council's Response

Everything that Sadler had written about the proposed new school was music to the ears of the leading councillors. Ald. William Clegg, the Liberal Leader, and Ald. George Franklin, Leader of the Conservatives on the Council, along with Stephenson, now set the wheels in motion in the Education Committee to realise and flesh out this scheme that Sadler had proposed. He had given them the ammunition to overcome the opposition, which would assail them from several directions. Firstly there was opposition from people associated with the two schools. Staff whose posts were endangered, parents and former pupils all of whom would regret the passing of much loved institutions. The Sheffield Wesleyan community were especially determined that if a new school were to be formed it be non-sectarian, whilst many in their ranks bemoaned the loss of a specifically non-conformist education if the College were to lose its independence. The Governors of the Grammar School intended to finesse the situation, so that once again, as in 1885, they would in effect be making a takeover and the new school would be a continuation of the old Grammar School in a new and improved guise. As many of their Governing Body were members of the City Council they had considerable influence, whereas the non-representative governors of the private Wesley College had very little.

The enthusiasts for the new school also had to face a general reluctance from many Council members and ratepayers to undertake prestige municipal projects that would increase the rates. A penny rate in 1903 only produced £6,700 from a city of 425,000 inhabitants, and for a decade the Council had been building and supporting municipal projects, like Mountford's palatial Town Hall, to give themselves the trappings and the infrastructure commensurate with their new status as a large county borough. Opposition to *municipalisation* cut across party lines, but usually the party that was in power was willing to attempt to tackle some of the all too obvious social problems, whilst the party in opposition was obsessed with keeping down the rates. Finally there was that suspicious and cynical attitude to all things new and expensive that probably exists in all communities, but seems particularly prevalent in the hard-bitten steel city.

Wesley College sells out, 1903

Wesley College, which at first sight appeared to have the most to lose, capitulated almost immediately. For some considerable time they had been in financial difficulties, unable to cover their costs and meet a heavy mortgage, so in 1903 the college was sold to the national Methodist Church. By that time only 17% of their pupils were boarders and they were therefore no longer serving the northern and midlands Wesleyan community as they once did. The Council met the Westminster based Methodist Twentieth Century Fund Committee, who now owned Wesley College, and on the 15th October 1903 they wrote back and accepted the Council's general proposal to buy.

The letter read; *"We are glad to inform you that we will sell Wesley College to the City Council in order that one high class school in Sheffield, on an absolutely non-denominational basis, might be established."*

Later in the month three representatives of the Methodist Church from London met the Council and agreed a price of £18,500 for the sale of the buildings, contents, the swimming pool, and the Close. (The cost of building and furnishing the College in 1837-40 had been £24,000 and the purchase of the land another £4374). In almost indecent haste the London Methodists recouped their outstanding mortgage on Wesley College and, with the exception of some portraits, the lectern and the stained glass window from the chapel, they were prepared to hand the whole site over to the City Council. From 1904 the College, still under the charge of the Headmaster, the Rev. Valentine Pearson, was run as a council grammar school and thus became eligible for council and government funding which had eluded them in the past. In this somewhat inglorious manner Wesley College, opened in 1838, passed into history. Its existence had been almost coeval with the reign of Queen Victoria and its future would lie in a union under the name of her sometime wayward son, King Edward VII.

The crucial amendment of January 1904

The Royal Grammar School Governors had also been quick off the mark. In November 1903 they put forward their own proposals as to how the merger should be conducted. They proposed to buy Wesley College with their own considerable funds and sell their own buildings and grounds to the City Council. They also proposed the setting up of a joint scheme of management for the new school with the Council; each party having half the representatives on the new governing body. There was of course a great deal of overlap as the SRGS Governors included many councillors wearing two hats, including crucially Clegg and Stephenson, who were in favour of this proposal and agreed to send it to the Education Committee, where they intended to see it through. They also sent their proposal to the Board of Education for their approval, suggesting that all that was necessary were a few amendments to the SRGS's existing Scheme of Governance approved in 1888. At Westminster they relied on Samuel Roberts M.P., a member of their Governors, to see that it got the Government's approval.

If this proposal had been accepted by the City Council, then the new King Edward VIi School would have been an independent institution for the next forty years, albeit one heavily reliant on the Council's financial support. It would also have been in effect a reprise of the takeover of the Collegiate School in 1884, except that this time it would be Wesley College that would provide the cuckoo's nest and then be consigned to oblivion.

The Board of Education was largely prepared to go along with this scheme, although A.F. Leach, writing on their behalf, insisted that the City Council should have a clear majority on the new school's Governors. The Education Committee was divided on this issue but for the moment they agreed that there should be a joint management scheme with the Grammar School Governors, the exact proportions to be decided further down the track.

The councillors now retired for Christmas and the New Year celebrations but when they met again in January 1904 the division of opinion had become an open battle. The issue came to a dramatic head at the Education Committee meeting of 25th January when Ald. Robert Styring, who later would be Chairman of the Governors of KES for twenty years, introduced a crucial amendment that bound the new school completely to the City Council. He moved: —

> *"That the amalgamation of the Royal Grammar School and Wesley College be carried out under the direct control of this committee and the Council buy Wesley College for this purpose. If necessary the Council purchase Wesley College and create a Higher Grade School in the ownership of the Education Committee."*

The second part of his amendment was a direct challenge to Clegg and Stephenson and other supporters of the Grammar School proposal, that the Council would, if need be, by-pass SRGS and found a new school without them, along the lines that Sadler had recommended. The amendment was then put to the vote and carried by the narrowest of margins, 19-18 votes. Haslam, who was a co-opted member of the committee, abstained and Pearson, who also was a member of the committee, was absent in North America. The Liberals and the Tories were divided among themselves, but all the Education Committee members who were also Grammar School Governors voted against the amendment.

The Grammar School's independent proposal was now dropped and they concentrated their efforts on gaining adequate representation on the new Governing Body. The final agreement was that there should be 15 Governors, plus the Principal of the University College, and that a third of them should be chosen from the old Grammar School Governors. There was no representation reserved for the Wesley College Governors and the Council now went ahead and purchased their buildings for the agreed sum of £18,500. The new Governing Body, to emphasize its importance, included all the leading Education Committee members and Ald. William Clegg was elected as the first Chairman at their initial meeting. They would be treated as a sub-committee of the Education Committee and their minutes were reported to that committee in the same way as the Finance, or the Buildings, sub-committees would report their decisions for approval.

The "Founding" Fathers

**Alderman Sir William Clegg
(1852-1932)**

**Alderman Dr. Robert Styring
(1850-1944)**

Sir William Clegg was a member of a prominent family in Sheffield public life in the late 19th and early 20th Century. A lawyer, he unsuccessfully defended the notorious Sheffield murderer, Charlie Peace, and was a keen sportsman. He played for Sheffield Wednesday and twice represented England at Football in matches against Scotland and Wales, whilst his brother, Sir Charles Clegg, played in the first ever England – Scotland match in 1872 and was later a long serving President of the F.A. from 1890-1923. By 1905 William Clegg was Leader of the City Council, Leader of the Liberals, the Chairman of the Education Committee and the first Chairman of KES Governors. Knighted in 1906, he remained the dominant figure on the City Council, leading the new Citizens' Association (Lib-Con) coalition after 1920, until his Group was swept from power by the Labour Party in 1926.

Robert Styring was also a well-known solicitor in the city. He served on the City Council as a Liberal for forty years from 1886 –1926 and in 1907 he became the Chairman of KES Governors, a position he held until 1926. He was Lord Mayor in 1906-07 and lived at Brinkcliffe Tower, which he gave to the city and it is now a retirement home in Chelsea Park, Nether Edge. He set up the Styring Scholarships at Sheffield University in 1923 (which many O.E.s won) and in return they gave him an honorary doctorate the following year. In his autobiography he said of Clegg: "he never had an original thought himself in politics". After he was removed from the Aldermanic bench by Labour in 1926, he did return to the Education Committee in the Thirties as a useful co-opted member. He died in 1944 at ninety-four years of age.

Purchase of the Royal Grammar School, January 1905

Having made the decision, the Governors of the Royal Grammar School were keen to finalise the outstanding issues. They met the City Council and agreed a price of £12,000 for their School buildings, the Grounds, the Headmaster's House, the Porter's Lodge and the playing fields at Whiteley Woods. It was agreed that the Governors would keep this considerable sum of money and put it into an independent trust that could be used to benefit the new school. Along with its existing lands and endowments it was believed that would give them an annual income of £750. So was born the Sheffield Grammar School Exhibition Foundation that helped to pay for scholarships at the school and also for the four leaving Scholarships of £50 p.a. tenable at any British or Colonial University. It also paid the Rev. Haslam's pension of £300 p.a. and he retired to Grassington to enjoy it. The Foundation regularly helped projects at the school and many years later, in the 1950s, it made a considerable grant to help build and furnish a new Library. It is still aiding education in Sheffield today, although after King Edward VII became a comprehensive school its largesse was made available to any school, or pupil, in the city, although present day students at KES still take advantage of its grants. The sale of the Royal Grammar School was completed in January 1905 and the City Council, who now had new plans for those buildings as the core elements of their new City Training College, had finally put all the pieces in place and their new "élite" school could go ahead. Two days before Christmas in 1904 the Council received a communication from the Home Office. The Home Secretary informed them: —

"That the King has been graciously pleased to accede to your request, and commands that the School be styled - King Edward the Seventh School at Sheffield."

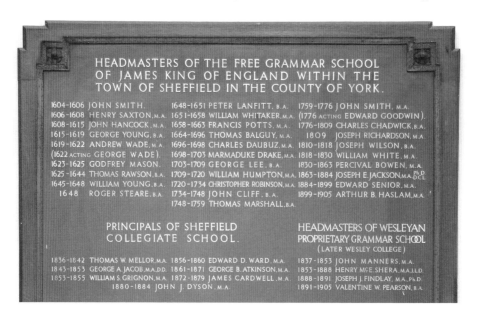

CHAPTER FIVE

"THE BOYS WILL WORK HARD"
1905-1914

James Harvey Hichens was appointed, from a shortlist of three, to the post of Headmaster of KES in March 1905. There were 54 applicants for the position, which had been first advertised in February, and Hichens was selected ahead of a Housemaster from Clifton and the Headmaster of Middlesborough High School. He was to be paid £800 per annum and the Council agreed to build him a house within the grounds of the school to compensate for the loss of residential facilities inside the school that the recent Headmasters of Wesley College had enjoyed. This 45 year old Cornishman already had nine years' experience as a headmaster at Wolverhampton R.G.S., where he had completely re-organised the school and developed a fine academic record. This successful experience appealed to the six Governors, all Education Committee members, who made the appointment and he would have been left in no doubt what type of school they wanted King Edward VII School to become. Hichens knew that they would be satisfied with nothing less than a school that would be among the best day schools in the country, the equal of Manchester G.S. or Bradford G.S. A school that, by invitation on to the Headmasters' Conference, would attain recognition as a public school at some date in the not too distant future. He was expected to provide a fee-paying school for the sons of the city's middle and "upper" middle class, the brightest to be able to win scholarships to the older universities, while others would strengthen the intake of the new civic university. At the same time the parents of the "average" boy, who didn't want the expense of sending their sons to expensive boarding schools in the middle of nowhere, expected the new school to provide a sound education to fit their boys for a career in the family firm in commerce, the professions or in industry. Robert Styring, then Lord Mayor, parodying Wellington, expressed these latter aspirations when he spoke at the first Speech Day in 1907, and asserted that; *"the commercial victories of Sheffield will be won within the walls of King Edward's."*

Hichens appointment broke the old tradition of SRGS, whose Headmasters had always been ordained. By the start of the Twentieth Century it had become not uncommon for laymen to be headmasters of public schools, but quite clearly KES had to signal to the nonconformist community that it was a non-denominational school, and so it was therefore imperative that Hichens should not be a clergyman. Having appointed Hichens, the Governors adopted an arms length attitude to his control of the school. He had the sole right to hire and dismiss his staff and it was also a written part of his terms of employment that he must have free access to his Chairman, always a very senior councillor, to enable his views on the running of the school to be heard and virtually always accepted. The Council had agreed an initial staffing level of fifteen teachers on three different salary levels and he had only four months to appoint his staff. The Second Master was to be paid £300 and Hichens overlooked the current deputy at the Royal Grammar School, John

Hodgetts, and appointed Rev. Henry Chaytor, from Merchant Taylors, Crosby, instead. Hodgetts was offered and accepted a post, as did four other teachers from SRGS. Three of these, Ben Cauldwell (1905-26), Harry Shorter (1905-34) and William Mease (1905-32) would have long and distinguished careers at the school and their presence would ensure that former SRGS boys coming to the new school would find familiar faces among a third of the staff. Wesley College teaching staff were largely ignored, with only two being appointed. John West, the music master, joined the staff but left within a year, but the other ex-Wesley College staff member became a legend at KES. He was Frederick "Toby" Saville (1905-40) and he would serve the school as the Master-in-Charge of Lynwood, the school's boarding house, Housemaster of Lynwood House, when it achieved that status in 1908, and the Master-in-Charge of the Junior School.

The Governors agreed that, under the direction of the Head, Saville could open a Boarding House in his own home at Lynwood, at that time in Collegiate Crescent. The approved fees would be £40 p.a. and it was hoped this facility would appeal to existing boarders at Wesley College and future pupils whose parents, for reasons of work or geography, needed to board their boys. Saville, who was on the lower salary level of £170, received no financial help from the school or the Council, and he ran the house as a private venture which became an integral, and very happy, part of the life of KES.

One other Wesley College teacher would be appointed, but not to the teaching staff. James Shearer was employed as Hichens' clerk for £100 and in 1906 his post was re-designated as the Registrar. He too would serve the school for many years and would establish an effective working relationship with Hichens, although he cannot have been much help to him in finding his way around the school buildings. The interior was about to be gutted, and during 1905 one former student described the "*mournful*" scene as if "*some Russian anarchist had brought off a highly successful performance in the cellar.*"

The architects for the refurbishment were the well known local firm of Gibb and Flockton, thereby continuing a link with the original architect of the building seventy years before. It took a year to complete the work and the final bill for the alterations and additions came to £16,969, with on-costs of £1270 for professional fees. The total bill for purchase, rebuilding, furniture and additional remedial work to the swimming pool, fives court, and asphalting the yard was a little over £49,000. The Governors had considered roofing the swimming pool, but they decided against spending more money on the school, and so three decades of Edwardians had to suffer the black, and often polluted waters, of that dubious facility. Plans to build a house within the grounds for the Headmaster — there were to be five bedrooms — were abandoned when they found that Mount View, a house built on the grand scale, on the corner of Newbould Lane and Glossop Road, was up for sale. The Council purchased it for £3000 and it served as the residence for three Headmasters, and was known to more recent Edwardians as Melbourne Annexe.

The original plan, to run the school and cope with the rebuilding during the first year, was to decant the staff and boys, and all their furniture and equipment, from one wing of the building to the other as the building work progressed. The architects and Hichens agreed that this was quite unsatisfactory and so the search for alternative premises began. The Senior School were quickly fixed up in the buildings the University College had just vacated in Leopold St. with additional premises obtained at St. James' Chambers, but there was more difficulty in obtaining suitable accommodation for the Junior School. Eventually a temporary home was found for them in the school rooms under Glossop Road Baptist Chapel (now the University Drama Studio), and Saville moved in there with his 79 pupils and his staff.

Hichens' task of starting his new school not only in temporary premises, but also with a split site, must have faced him with massive problems. He had to weld his staff, recruit his pupils, select the curriculum and establish syllabuses for forms serving 9 to 19 year olds, as well as choose his examination board and organise the Higher School and Lower School Certificate examinations. Furthermore, he had to establish the ethos of the school, along with the symbolic trappings and distinctive style of KES that parents and boys, as well as Governors, would be expecting. To start an organisation from scratch with not so much as a paper clip to your name is an exhilarating, hugely satisfying, yet exhausting, process. To have to do that with your school on three temporary sites, one of them a mile from the other two, is a very great achievement.

 Not surprisingly, when Hichens made his first report to the Governors in March 1906 he bemoaned.

> "The separation of portions of the school and the deficiencies of the temporary accommodation."

However he went on to report how these difficulties were being overcome and that the school was already functioning satisfactorily. The new school had attracted most of the 198 pupils at SRGS and the 168 at Wesley College, but they had only recruited 317 boys, instead of the 400 they were hoping would enrol. Some boys, in the former schools, would have left in the summer of 1905 in the normal course of events and some 19 who had been boarders decided to try elsewhere, but the new school certainly hadn't been oversubscribed and another 28 left during the first term. All the pupils at Wesley College and the SRGS had been offered a place at KES on exactly the same financial terms as they had enjoyed at their former school and most had accepted. Another 27 boys joined in the spring and by the end of the academic year the numbers were up to 323.

Hichens had a budget of £6605 voted by the Education Committee. They had estimated that the fees from 400 pupils, averaging £13. 10s. p.a., would bring them in £5400. They were led to expect that with those numbers they would receive a grant from the Board of Education of £810, leaving a shortfall for the ratepayers to pick up of only £395. Because the pupil numbers were only just over three quarters of what was estimated, they received less in fees and less from the Board of Education in grant, so that the final bill to be found by the Council in that first year was nearer to £1500. Alarm bells began ringing amongst the critics of the school and when they saw that the number of sixth formers taking their Higher Certificate was only nine, and that there was only one distinction, the doubters became more vocal. Hichens had decided that if the future academic performance of his ambitious school was to be judged by the highest standards, he must enter its pupils for the examinations of the prestigious Oxford and Cambridge Schools Examination Board, the Board preferred by 81 of the leading schools in the country. To enter the pupils for the Lower Certificate added another £47 to the budget, whilst the parents of boys taking the Higher Certificate had to find the fees from their own pockets.

THE FIRST BUDGET 1905-06

Revenue Expenditure.

- *Salaries* — *£4225*
- *Books, Apparatus, Stationery* — *£850*
- *Fuel and Light* — *£380*
- *Cleaning and Water* — *£400*
- *Repairs to Buildings/ Furniture* — *£280*
- *Rates and Insurance* — *£310*
- *Sundries, inc Exam Fees* — *£160*

TOTAL — *£6605*

All income, (fees, grants etc.) went straight to the City Treasurer.
The Council voted KES an annual budget for their expenditure.

The Revenue Expenditure in the approved 2005-2006 Budget is £7.6 million

---

Despite the difficulties of operating at the three sites, Hichens had laid down the essential framework of the school before they moved to the refurbished buildings in Glossop Road for the new academic year in September 1906. Pupils would enter the Upper School in Form 2 at 12 years of age. The preparatory, or Junior School, would have pupils from 9-12 in three year forms starting with Form J3 and, rather peculiarly, numbering downwards to the senior form, Form J1. There would be a common syllabus until the end of the fourth forms when the boys would be 14. At this age boys and girls in elementary schools in the city would leave school and start work. It was therefore a natural starting point for specialisation in a secondary school like King Edward VII. The boys had three options. The academically gifted would be encouraged to enter the Classical Side where they would be prepared for entry to the Universities and a professional career. Latin and Greek were a substantial part of the syllabus but there would also be advanced teaching in Maths and additional Maths, Science (still rather quaintly called Natural Philosophy by the Examining Board), French, and English Literature. Most pupils studied History and Scripture Knowledge, and there was a Geography and German option.

These were the high flyers who went into Transitus, (the Lower Sixth or later Y12) and then took their Higher Certificate in the Sixth Form (Y13). The boys who wanted a career in commerce, the professions or industrial management went on to the Modern Side. Here they had two more options. While there was a common syllabus in Maths, English Language and Science, one Division concentrated on languages, French and German as well as Latin, whilst the other Division offered Geography, History and English Literature, along with book-keeping and shorthand. The majority of boys on the Modern Side would not aspire to the Sixth Form but would probably leave at 15, whilst others would stay on and take their Lower Certificate the following year.

The symbolic features that filled in the colour and texture of the school were also selected. The school's superb coat of arms, which would have graced any Oxbridge College, was constructed from the badges of the three parent institutions, SRGS, Wesley College and the City Council. A school tie was designed in the new school colours of dark blue with single thin horizontal silver stripes and the Latin motto, *"Fac Recte Nil Time"*, chosen. Several school societies had got off the ground while the school was still camped out in the centre of town. The Debating Society, usually the flagship group, held their first debate in October 1905.

In the Chief are the arms of the City of Sheffield, On the dexter side are the arms of SRGS and on the sinister side the arms of the Wesley family and London University, which were part of Wesley College's arms.

The crest, with a rampant Lion holding a shield, emblazoned with a saltaire of arrows, on a mural crown, is the crest of Sheffield City Council and was chosen as the cap and blazer badge of KES.

The Motto — Fac Recte Nil Time (Act Honourably and Fear Naught) — was the motto of the Hichens' family and the Headmaster just adapted it as KES's new motto.

By 19 votes to 16 they decided that; *"If they were not English they would rather be German than French"* and later in the year they voted by a large majority (actually 20) that *"The barbarian is happier than modern man"* and that; *"Cricket is superior to Football"*, although only a majority of three on that occasion. By the Spring there already was a Literary Society, an Orchestral Society that numbered 15, twelve of them in the strings section, a Sketch Club and a Photographic and Botany Section of the Scientific Society, whose inaugural visit was to the Neepsend Gas Works, belonging to the Sheffield United Gas Light Co.

At the School's opening ceremony in November 1906, James Hichens drew attention in his speech to the number of Societies already established and flourishing at the school. He used that opportunity to spell out his personal vision for the school. He explained that; *"Whilst the teaching and standard of work will be of the highest order, there is perhaps (at KES) the atmosphere of the great public boarding school with a strong corporate life and loyalty of its members to it and one another. It is desirable that the boys' interests should centre in the school and I cannot emphasize enough how I wish to encourage them to play games and take part in the various school societies."* These sentiments, emphasizing the parallel importance of extra-curricular activities with the highest academic endeavours and standards, would be echoed in similar terms by all his six successors. For six days of the week the school would provide all the interests and activities that a boy should require. That was why day schools like King Edward VII operated a six day week, with Saturday morning teaching and two games afternoons on Wednesday and Saturday. Considerable amounts of homework would ensure that the school's requirements filled most of the boys' time at home in the evening and on Sunday. Most boys would accept this closed regime — some more willingly than others — for there was no teenage culture to offer an attractive alternative, whilst the continual contact with home and family in a Sheffield suburb injected an appreciation of the real world of everyday problems and issues.

When KES left the Leopold Street premises in July 1906 they also left an insurance claim for £97. 13s. for two unexplained fires that the Fire Brigade had been called in to put out.

The Tramways Committee of the City Council voted in March 1906 to allow KES boys to ride at half fare on all Sheffield Corporation Tramways. This gesture probably recognised that KES had pupils who travelled considerable distances across the city, whereas elementary school children would go to their local school.

To encourage the corporate spirit, especially on the games field, a house system was introduced as soon as the school re-assembled in their new premises for the new term in September 1906. For a school that aimed to be great, the houses would be named after the great country houses of the district.

Chatsworth, Clumber, Haddon, Welbeck and Wentworth.

The one geographical outsider was **Arundel**, the Sussex home of the 15th Duke of Norfolk, but he was closely associated with the city, having served as the first Lord Mayor in 1893, and he regularly visited and stayed at his house in Norfolk Park.

Lynwood was raised to the status of a house in late 1908. It's members would argue that they were the only "true house" because many of them lived in, as they did at public schools were the residential house system was an obvious way to encourage sporting and social competition. However, the KES houses never lacked the competitive spirit, nor the loyalty of their members, and they survived until the early Seventies when they finally ran out of support, and perhaps relevance, in the comprehensive system. **Sherwood,** in 1920**,** was the last house to be founded, to accommodate the increasing numbers in the school.

While many pupils over the years would take part in house matches in many sports, in the early years house matches only meant competition in Football, Cricket and Gymnastics. In the first year only Football was played at school representative level, with the first ever game against the Masters' XI at the beginning of October 1905. Although the match was played at Whiteley Woods this ground was not as yet designated for use by the school. There was much dissatisfaction with Whiteley Woods, which the Council now owned after purchasing it from the SRGS Governors. The Headmaster and the Governors looked at several possible grounds, including ones in Fulwood and Crosspool, before finally deciding in April 1906 that Whiteley Woods was after all the best ground that was available to them. The KES Football First XI, playing in the newly selected school strip of white shirts with dark blue shorts, had a winning first season (P12, W6, L 5, D1) including a 3-1 win in that first game against the Masters. The cricket season never materialised because part of the former Wesley College Close was being used as a store for building materials, although there was enough room for net practice. They only managed to play one game in the 1907 season as well, and this was away at Worksop College in June, but Hichens was determined that sport should be one of the pillars on which a boy's education would be constructed, and soon compulsory games, subject to parental consent, were introduced in 1908.

Prefects were instituted by Hichens in September of 1906, with a head boy entitled the Senior Prefect. One might have expected them to have been in post the year before, but perhaps the Headmaster wished to review the quality of his sixth formers before making a selection. Certainly, to a man steeped in the culture of the public schools (Hichens had gone to Epsom College and taught at Radley and Cheltenham), he would regard the prefectorial system as not only normal but crucial to the smooth running of his school. A remote figure to most of his pupils, James Hichens, every inch the Victorian gentleman, exuded authority and backed it up with a ferocious set of rules that were read to pupils in the Assembly Hall at the beginning of each term. Included amongst the offences was any buying, selling and lending, whilst the borrowing of bicycles was expressly forbidden. Each member of staff was handed the complete set on joining the staff. Dr. C.J. Magrath

(1908-49) recalled that one applicant for a post was shown the rules before his interview and promptly departed, declaring *"This must be a **b..... asylum**"*. To enforce his rules Hichens did use the cane, but corporal punishment was so institutionalised as the cornerstone of discipline in the English education system, that KES's more regular use of detentions (four detentions was the common sentence and equalled an hour in time after school) was probably the sign of a more moderate regime than in most of the city's schools. After the Rev. F.E. Brown, the Second Master, had left in 1911, Lloyd –Davies became the Second Master and he had a fearful reputation as a disciplinarian. Indeed it was part of the task of the Second Master to act as the RSM of the school disciplinary system and this role was continued by J.S."Old Nick" Nicholas after he succeeded Lloyd –Davies in 1926. For the next twenty-one years he would terrify pupils of all ages but he is, perhaps, the best remembered of all the KES staff, and invariably the first master who is recalled by Old Edwardians of his period.

Hichens was hard on those staff whom he felt would not make the grade. Of the first group of teachers appointed in 1905, four had left, three of them without working out their notice, by the start of the new academic year in 1906. Teaching staff had no training in how to handle a form of boys who would automatically test their ability to control the class from the very first day. As one teacher appointed in 1907 wrote later, *"For discipline you were left on your own, you either sank or swam. If you sank you left at the end of term."* Even a Mr. J. Bulley did not last more than a year in 1909, and even in the Twenties Hichens continued to make a large number of temporary appointments, presumably so that he could more properly judge staff members' academic and disciplinary competence. It was a harsh system, but a good school requires good teachers and a class in chaos is unlikely to be working efficiently. Hichens was under pressure to produce results quickly and for that he needed a calm, positive, teaching environment where new staff members, like Dr. (later Sir) Henry

Dr. James Harvey Hichens M.A. LLD (Hons)
(1859-1938)

Coward, already a legendary figure in the music community of Sheffield (he has a blue plaque on his former home in Sharrow), could flourish.

Dr. J.H. Hichens — Headmaster of KES 1905-26

Hichens was a Cornishman born into the gentry in Redruth in 1859. His father was a doctor and he expected the young James to follow him into medicine. Hichens was educated at Epsom College and Queen's College, Oxford, where he read Chemistry and graduated in 1886. Like many Oxford graduates he continued a close connection with his college, and the Provost of Queen's spoke at the school's opening ceremony. Shortly afterwards KES was added to the list of north country schools that were eligible for Lady Hastings Scholarships and Exhibitions.

Hichens taught at Radley and was later a Housemaster at Cheltenham before taking up an appointment as Headmaster of Wolverhampton Royal Grammar School in 1896, where he is reputed to have reorganised the school and doubled the number of scholars. He was appointed the first Headmaster of KES on a salary of £800 p.a. and the school became his life and love with "no detail too insignificant for his attention if it contributed to the growing efficiency and splendour of the school." His success attracted offers from famous schools to become their Headmasters, but few were surprised that he turned these offers down, because his dedication to KES was total and he did, "in twenty years turn a stunted, rather unwanted phoenix of a school into the Cock o' the North."

Physically, Hichens was of slight stature with a severe affliction of the eyes that required him to always wear smoked glasses. To preserve his sight he rarely read for pleasure, yet many Old Edwardians can attest to accuracy of his caning, one stroke never straying by even a millimetre from the mark of the previous one. Dressed in the formal attire of a Victorian gentleman — morning frock coat and silk top hat — he struck quite a figure both in the school and in Broomhill. Those older pupils who were taught by him in Sixth Form Chemistry lessons, or were invited to tea at his house at Mount View, can attest that he had a sense of humour and was more sensitive to pupil's needs than he chose to appear in his daily routines. Outwardly he was very correct, with a strong sense of justice, and a keen desire to prove himself and his school by examination success.

There is no doubt that Hichens was respected by his former pupils and the conferring of an honorary Doctor of Laws Degree by the University of Sheffield when he retired, demonstrates that this respect was felt throughout the civic and academic community in the city. He retired to Paignton and died on 12th September 1938.

The continuing concern about the criticism of the school and its expenditure surfaced in the speech of the Chairman, now Sir William Clegg, at the very first Speech Day on 31st July 1907. It is not so surprising that Hichens, in defence of the school, was only too willing to answer these concerns by talking up the examination successes and the scholarships won at Oxford and Cambridge. The school's first Oxbridge success came in the first year when M. Andrews won a scholarship at Jesus College, Oxford, but he had received virtually all his education at the old Grammar School. In the following year in the scholarship examinations in December 1906, R.G Maples won a Classics Scholarship at Queen's College, Oxford and E. Lipson won a History Exhibition at Trinity College, Cambridge. Maples, the School Football captain, would be the first Old Edwardian to win a blue and he played in all three varsity matches whilst he was up at the University. Ephraim Lipson, who is the first name on the school's honours boards, became a professor of Economic History and was one of the leading figures in the development of that particular academic discipline in Britain. The school had already become eligible in 1905 for Lady Hastings Scholarships and Exhibitions tenable at Hichens' own college, Queen's College, Oxford. The Hastings, open to fourteen leading north country schools, was a highly prestigious award, although a KES pupil did not win an award until S.W. Rawson secured one in 1908, followed by the remarkable E.A. Berrisford (later President of the O.U. Boat Club and within nine years a wartime Brigadier) who was successful in 1909. They would be followed by many Edwardians during the next sixty years who would go to Queen's College on a Hastings Scholarship or Exhibition and help develop a very close relationship with that ancient college. Even more prestigious was the Akroyd Scholarship open to all schools in Yorkshire. This was referred to as the "Blue Ribbon" award and was regarded almost as a "county championship" for the brightest pupil in Yorkshire. Considered much harder to win than an Oxbridge scholarship, the examinations were held at one of the participating schools and schools sent their most able pupils who sat papers in their chosen subjects. KES's first success came in 1909 when S.W.Rawson, already a Hastings Exhibitioner, was awarded the Akroyd Scholarship and they continued to triumph in this particular competition throughout Hichens' time as Headmaster and in later decades. Rawson, later Sir Stanley, had a good year because he won a number of scholarships aggregating £180 in value, which must have made him a popular chap when he went up to Queen's Oxford, where he eventually got a First in Classics. C.C. Bissett and H. Glauert won the Akroyd in the next two years, and this success alone ensured that the school was making its mark throughout education circles in Yorkshire and beyond.

KES was also achieving almost total success in securing the Sheffield Town Trust Scholarships during this period. There were four awarded annually, three of them tenable only at Sheffield University and two of them available to any Sheffield resident of either sex, and therefore they could be won by girls at Sheffield High School and boys at boarding schools. In the years 1905-1909 KES took all the scholarships except one and there were calls from other schools to change the regulations to give other schools a chance. This superiority did not necessarily make the school very popular, but it did confirm the claims of the Headmaster and senior councillors on the Governors, that the school was a success and was a real asset to the city. Hichens used the Speech Days to trumpet the success of boys in the Oxford and Cambridge Examining Board's Certificate Examinations. One feels he would have loved the league tables introduced by Mrs. Thatcher's Government at the end of the century, because he was continually making favourable comparisons between KES and the senior public schools. In 1909 he announced that only ten schools among the 81 taking the Higher Certificate had achieved more distinctions than KES. These ten included Eton, Rugby, Marlborough and Bradford G.S. and so by inference Hichens was positioning his new school alongside the most famous in the land. In 1910 he particularly drew attention to the number of Lower Certificates awarded to KES boys. They lay second in the total number of certificates awarded (25) and led all the other schools in the number of First Class passes (44) they achieved. In 1912, he enthusiastically detailed in the school magazine that only seven schools had more Higher Certificates than KES's 24, and only four had more distinctions than the 17 won by the school. Despite the triumphalist note it was a remarkable success story for a school that was only seven years old, silencing the critics who had felt the new venture would founder and the ratepayers would be lumbered with an expensive, but ordinary, grammar school.

STAFF

"The staff seemed split into two cliques, one headed by the three most senior masters and their followers, and the other containing all the rest. The meeting place of the first clique was the summer house at the top of the (Master's) garden, where Newbould Lane and Glossop Road met. Wet or fine they resorted to this retreat at break and exchanged rude ideas about their junior staff."

(Dr. C.J.Magrath, a staff member for forty one years.)

The first two Second Masters soon got their own Headmaster's posts. Rev. H.J. Chaytor (1905-08) became the Head of Plymouth College and Rev. F.E.Brown (1908-1911) became the Head of Preston Grammar School. Rev. Chaytor later became the Master of St. Catherine's College, Cambridge.

Not in our school!

Criticism now came from another quarter. In 1910 the Governors petitioned the Board of Education to allow them to make a compulsory charge for a number of school activities and costs, including games, the library, the magazine, stationery, equipment and apparatus. The Board refused this request and also a request to increase the fees to cover all these extra costs. In their reply the President of the Board of Education in Asquith's Liberal Government, observed that the school's fees of 16 guineas (£16.80) for the Senior School and ten guineas (£10.50) for the Junior School, were the highest in the country for a "Provided School", i.e. one that got a grant from the Government. This grant of £713 had not altered since 1906, whilst the annual budget for the school had almost doubled to £11, 924, with £4767 now coming from the rates to meet the shortfall.

Having been refused, the Governors, backed by the Education Committee, whose leading figures were to all intents and purposes the same people, found that they had opened up a political can of worms.

The Liberal Government, who had just battled through against aristocratic privilege to pass Lloyd George's People's Budget, and was in the process of taking on the House of Lords and limiting the power of the Upper Chamber, was in no mood to compromise with an exclusive grammar school in Sheffield. The President's letter to the Education Committee pointed out that KES was clearly in breach of the 1902 Education Act with regard to free places for pupils from Elementary Schools in the city. To qualify for a Government Grant at all they should be moving towards 25 % free places. However, as far as he could ascertain KES had only 5%, which equated to five free scholarships each year, although as often as not they only made four awards on the grounds of the insufficient quality of candidates. The Government now instructed them to immediately provide 10% of free places annually at the school, or their grant would be removed. If they complied they would receive another £665 p.a. to cover the costs of these extra pupils and the Government might allow them to raise their fees as well, to cover the extra costs they were so concerned about.

At the Education Committee meeting of July 1911 the Council, acting on a decision of the KES Governors, refused the Government's request resolving; *"that KES will be withdrawn from the list of schools recognised by the Board of Education as eligible to receive Government Grants."* By their deliberate decision they therefore lost the £716 already paid by the Board, not to mention the extra £665 they would have received, and instead agreed to add these costs to the rate contribution already being paid to the school. If this had been a purely financial issue the row would have blown over in a day or two, but the issue went right to the heart of the question of what sort of school KES was, and whom it was for. For some time the nascent Labour Party in the city had been very critical of KES, not just because of its great initial capital costs that finally reached almost £50,000, but because of the substantial contribution from the rates for a school that only catered for sons of the middle and "upper" middle class. In a period of industrial turbulence in the city, Labour, who had gained their first Council member in 1905 and their first Labour M.P. (Joseph Pointer elected for Attercliffe in a 1909 by-election), was beginning to flex its muscles. A right to the best available education was one of their fundamental aims, and the issue of privileged entry to KES formed part of their 1911 election campaign. Whilst they had no wish to abolish KES, they did want to see it open to fair competition, so that the bright sons of the Sheffield working class could gain places on merit at the school.

This was not the view of the Governors at all. The speeches, in defence of their actions, by the leading Conservatives and Liberals are breathtaking in their defence of privilege and snobbery. Yet the arguments would be understood to-day by parents choosing private education, although it is certain they would be more discreet and circumspect in stating them. The minutes of the Education Committee of that meeting give a more dispassionate flavour of the views more raucously expressed by the council members.

"The Governors submitted that in carrying on this school (KES) they have to deal with facts as they are. The Sheffield Royal Grammar School and Wesley College in the past held high social positions and the children sent to them came as a rule from the upper middle classes. It was an undoubted fact that if the state of things suggested by the Board were brought into operation, the entire character of KES would very speedily change."

"The majority of parents who are now willing to pay the fees charged would certainly conclude that the object for which they make the expenditure had disappeared, inasmuch as the character of the school would approximate to that of the Central Secondary School to which parents may send their children at a cost of £2 p.a."

The Governors all felt that not only the ethos but the entire social fabric of the school would soon collapse, if working class boys from elementary schools were admitted to KES. Coun. John Derry went one further and suggested they already had great difficulty finding even five boys a year from the elementary schools who were of sufficient ability to warrant a scholarship to KES. They were robustly challenged by Daniel Evans, then the Labour candidate for Brightside Ward (later, in the Thirties, the Chairman of both the Education Committee and Secondary School Governors), who angrily protested; *"The class prejudice that such utterances reveal deceives nobody, least of all the working men of Sheffield. KES will continue to be a school for the middle class only, but all the citizens, of which the working class were the great majority, would have to continue to pay even more for it."*

Even more compelling were his comparisons with the highly successful Bradford G.S. which did take 25% of its pupils from the local elementary schools, and had 170 such pupils in a school of 550 at any one time. KES was built to accommodate a similar number, but it had only reached 400 pupils for the first time in 1909 and was only 398 strong in 1911, and therefore had the capacity to accommodate bright boys from the elementary schools in Sheffield. The Bradford experience also indicated that these "free" pupils won the majority of the honours, as, of course, KES's own later experience would show as well. In reality, KES already had 141 pupils in 1911 who had gained their early education at elementary schools, before their parents had sent them as fee-payers to KES at twelve years of age. Furthermore, most of the boys who won the five free scholarships came from modest middle class homes and from schools in the south west of the city, further exposing the nonsense of the Governors' objections.

The school would change its policy during the Great War and for most of the interwar years a quarter of the pupils at the school would be on free scholarships. If this later decision changed the school's ethos, or made it less popular with fee-paying parents, it was not obviously noticeable before 1944, when the old arguments would re-surface when the school was faced with new reforming legislation.

SOCIAL CLASS of KES PARENTS.
(From HMI's Reports)

Inspection Report Classes in life from which pupils are drawn:	1910 %	1914 %
Professional	29	56
Farmers	1	1
Wholesale Trades	25	1
Retail Trades and Contractors	16	20
Clerks and Commercial Agents	13	16
Public Servants	1	2
Domestic Service	0	0
Artisans	8	2
Labourers	0	1
No occupation given	7	1

Clearly KES served the middle class and increasingly those in the professions. The drop over four years in the number of pupils whose parents worked in the wholesale trade may indicate that wealthier families were sending their sons to more exclusive boarding schools. On the other hand the number of children whose fathers were skilled working men declined sharply from an already low base.

THE JUNIOR SCHOOL

While staff and parents would have been closely watching the row between the Governors, the Council and the Government, the boys in the school were unaffected and the even tenor of the school activities continued to develop and flourish. There had been a very successful Inspection of the school in 1910 by five Board of Education Inspectors who, after a week of intense investigation into every aspect of the school's life, had been fulsome in their praise for the school when they reported to the Governors. The Junior School had also received its fair share of praise and "Toby" Saville's work in establishing the junior department was fully recognised. The Junior School in the first few years was housed on the ground floor of the main building where there was so much spare capacity. They started with 79 boys in 1905 and their numbers did not increase very much in the period up to 1914. However, when the total numbers in the school increased to over 500, the Governors then looked for new adjacent premises in 1916, and found them in a large house virtually opposite the school entrance on Newbould Lane.

By 1914 almost half the boys in the Senior School had come up from the Junior School. This was the preferred route for pupils coming into the school, where they could get a good foundation education linked to the curriculum in the Senior School. The syllabus included French, geometry, algebra and arithmetic, along with English Literature, history, scripture and geography, and there was also time in the week for drawing, recreation and modelling in clay and cardboard for which there were graded positions on a pupil's report. Surprisingly there was at that time no science, although they did do nature study, nor were there any Latin classes. They were taught in small forms, around 20 pupils each, that numbered from J3 for the nine year olds, to J2a and J2b with the eldest forms starting at 11 years of age numbered J1a and J1b. All the boys were fee-payers, but the ten guineas (£10.50) fee required, was considerably less than the fees of their seniors, and they were eligible for an "Open" Scholarship at the end of their period in the Junior School, which would pay for half their tuition in the Senior School. Two of these scholarships were awarded annually by the Council, and though they were available to elementary school boys, they always seem to have been won by pupils in the Junior School.

The Junior School had its own sporting calendar with cricket and football matches against long departed prep. schools like Montgomery College and Derwent House, Bamford, and they also played the boarders of Lynwood House and the local prep. school, Birkdale. Their academic programme was lightened by country walks in Derbyshire and paper chases each term starting from the King's Head on Manchester Rd. and then run across open countryside and farms in the Rivelin Valley. Regular visits to Glossop Road Baths on what were termed "clean water days" and full participation in the Athletic Sports and the school's cross-country run, completed their sporting calendar. Before 1912 football and cricket matches were played between forms, but invariably the senior forms won and so the Junior School's own house system was introduced to encourage more even competition. The houses were named;

ANGLES (Dark Blue) ;   **BRITONS (Green) ;**
SAXONS (Light Blue);   **NORMANS (Red) ;**

After school on Friday the Juniors had lantern slide lectures, or "socials", that could include recitations, readings, piano and violin solos or just a good old communal sing song, and they always had a good attendance at Saville's Summer Camp at Winchelsea in August.

KES By The Sea

Until the start of the Second World War one of the most famous of KES's institutions was the summer camp organised by "Toby" Saville in a farmer's field at Dog's Hill, a couple of miles outside Winchelsea on the Sussex coast. Saville was a native of the area, knew all the locals and had begun these camps in 1903 when he was a new master at Wesley College. He continued them for KES pupils in 1906 and they provided a boys' own paradise for Edwardians for a couple of weeks during the summer holidays. Many pupils stayed on for four weeks while others came and went, but for many boys it would be the only out of town holiday they would get. Even middle class families did not necessarily go away for a fortnight at the seaside in the Edwardian period, and this idyllic period under canvas in bell tents must have been a wonderful alternative for the boys. It cost their parents 25 shillings (£1.25) a week, including the excursions, and they slept up to twelve to a tent, with a master sharing their accommodation and keeping general order.

Before 1914 the numbers varied between 30 and 50 boys, but for those who stayed the whole month the school was essentially catering for all their leisure needs for almost every week during the year. Games were the staple diet of camp life, especially cricket, and teams were organised every year to play local schools and clubs. The cricket professional, J.W. Smith, started to attend after 1909 and he was in charge of the stores and equipment, as well as coaching the scratch KES team on "tour" in Sussex. Their regular field where they pitched their tents was close to the beach and there was bathing in the sea and boating on the Rivers Rother and Brede, even the use of a motor launch to sail to towns up the river. Excursions to Dungeness, Hastings, and the truly beautiful Bodiam Castle also became part of a time-honoured routine. If the weather was bad, and some weeks it was appalling, boys having fun scarcely noticed it, as they delighted in their own company and just being young.

F.T. Saville

LYNWOOD

F.T.Saville's third great contribution to the life of the new school was the boarding house he ran at his home, Lynwood. Firstly in Collegiate Crescent, and then, in January 1911, at "Broombank" on Clarkehouse Road in the splendid house, immediately re-named Lynwood, that was still in the school's use until 1990. Later it was sold and ingloriously turned into a modern public house rejoicing under the name of the Aunt Sally. Saville was the proprietor and the Master in Charge under the Headmaster's general supervision and he attempted to create an enjoyable experience for the boys who boarded there. They might not always have appreciated getting up and walking down to Glossop Road Baths at 6.30a.m. three times a week, although the alternative, even during the winter, was a cold bath in the best public school tradition. However, under Saville's enthusiastic guidance Lynwood boys got plenty of encouragement to play in school teams and take part in house matches and school sports like fives, shooting and gymnastics. As one of the school's official houses they were involved in the house football and cricket competitions, but because of their extra leisure time they fixed up matches for the younger boarders against the local prep schools.

Lynwood

Every year in early December, after considerable rehearsal, they presented the "Lynwood Entertainment" that combined musical virtuoso performances with amusing dramatic vignettes in an event that marked the start of the school's Christmas preparations. There were evenings of lantern slide talks, an annual billiard competition, which every boy had to enter, and a cycle club that made excursions out into the Peak District, often covering 30-40 miles on a Sunday, or shorter journeys on a summer evening to Hathersage or Grindleford. In the winter they would skate and sledge down neighbouring Broomhill roads and organise snow fights in the Close after everyone else had gone home. Cross country runs might very well be followed by a musical evening in Lynwood's dining room and they were encouraged to play the fullest part in school societies and the O.T.C. Behind all the activities was the driving force of "Toby" Saville who ran his house with firm discipline, but tried to ensure that all the pupils' needs were met, including making quiet space available to those who were studying for their school certificates or Oxbridge scholarships.

His moods could be uncertain, but he retained the affection of the young charges entrusted to his care, and in later life many a successful man felt their time at Lynwood had been the making of them, and that was "the Man's" most satisfying epitaph. He finally retired in 1941 and went back to the south coast where he died in 1942. Boarding was discontinued during the Second World War, although Lynwood continued as one of the eight school houses until the 1970s.

Almost a Public School

Within five years of the school having moved into the Glossop Rd. premises, the essential features of school life were all in place and they were flourishing. Hichens, and the Governors, grew increasingly confident that their, once much criticised, new school was going to be a great success. They increasingly referred to themselves as a public school, although technically this was incorrect as they had not yet been invited on to the Headmasters' Conference. The public schools served as the model for KES, as they did for almost every grammar school and secondary school in England. Although there was a growing awareness of the strengths of the German and American school systems, a public school education was universally regarded in England as the finest and most balanced that a school could aspire to. Hichens, and most of his staff, were products of public schools and it would have been automatic for them to recreate at KES the institutions of the schools with which they were so familiar – Speech Days, houses, boarders, prefects, compulsory games, a wide range of extra-curricular activities and societies, school magazines (which among other regular features included varsity letters), entering pupils for the prestigious Oxford and Cambridge Boards' examinations and, the epitome of the style, having an OTC.

The OTC was started in 1907 as the school's cadet corps attached to the 1st West Riding R.E. Volunteers based at their barracks on West St. In 1908 they became the Officers' Training Corps and, although never compulsory at KES, they were a major part of school life until 1927. More than any other institution in the school they stressed the special élite role of schools like KES, and when the corps went on field days or to their annual camp, they were accepted as peers by the contingents from other schools, almost all of which were Headmasters' Conference schools.

On Speech Days, Lord Mayors, councillors and visiting speakers referred to the school as a public school and Hichens continued to emphasise the success of KES scholars by reference to other public schools. At the 1913 Speech Day there was a vintage crop of fine school certificate results to report and the Headmaster eagerly pointed out that only four schools, Oundle, Rugby, Clifton and Bradford G.S., could claim better results in the Higher School Certificate Exams, and that the Akroyd Scholarship, won that year by W.P.Taylor, was now virtually the sole preserve of King Edward VII School. Not surprisingly he talked of his school as being in the front rank of academic standards among the most prestigious schools of the country. Amongst the Akroyd Scholarship winners was Herman Glauert, a member of an Anglo-German family in Sheffield (his brothers had had very successful careers at SRGS), who became a Wrangler at Cambridge in 1913 and would later become a Fellow of the Royal Society, an honour also bestowed on E.C.Titchmarsh, who won an Open Scholarship to Balliol in 1916. Stanley Rawson, the first Akroyd Scholarship winner, was elected to a Fellowship at All Souls in December 1914, at the age of twenty four, and every Speech Day the printed programme would contain a list of Old Boys who had graduated, often with First Class Honours at Oxford and Cambridge or the University of Sheffield. These were virtually the only destinations for Edwardians going on to a university education. Old Boys of the school won four Mappin Gold Medals at Sheffield University during this period, including C.C.Bissett, another Akroyd Scholarship winner, and those boys who chose medicine invariably did their degrees at the local university, as well as those whose primary interest was metallurgy or engineering.

The Magazine

The school magazine, with its sombre grey cover and often surprisingly chaotic ordering of reports, (the second edition in July 1906 began with three pages on the happenings of the Microscopical Society) chronicled the everyday life of school activities. It was never given an original name, unlike Wesley College's magazine *"The Sheaf",* and huge amounts of print were given to long forgotten football and cricket matches. Cricket reports gave the full score sheet and the Athletic Sports and gymnastic matches were reported in detail event by event. Society reports filled many of the pages, pride of place always going to the Debating Society, even though turnouts were a fraction of the school's population. However it enables a later generation to get some idea of the boys' attitudes to the major issues of the day, although many of the debates were designed essentially for intellectual gymnastics. We find that in 1911, the year of the big row over free places, a motion disapproving of the introduction of old age pensions by the Liberal Government was only carried by two votes, whereas a proposal that "The introduction of socialism is necessary for the welfare of the state" was well defeated by 21-5 votes. In a debate on whether "Women of the 20th Century are inferior to their predecessors," the house voted in favour of the modern miss, but only by a miserable 6-3 votes, whilst later in the year a debate on whether the house preferred Cricket to Football produced a vote of confidence for football by 12-5 votes. A mock election was held by the Debating Society in 1911, and the Conservatives and Socialists (never called Labour at schools like KES) tied for the "seat" with 14 votes each, with eight voters favouring the Liberals. If the purpose of the Debating Society was to train for public speaking and fit boys for a parliamentary career, then it was singularly unsuccessful in the latter case. Very surprisingly, when you consider how many old boys rose to positions of eminence in so many fields, only two Old Edwardians have ever been elected to the House of Commons, and both of those were in the last two decades of the century.

What is clear from the magazines is that a thriving network of societies was in existence by the end of the school's first decade. Often they only attracted a small minority of boys and some would fold when enthusiasts left, but they satisfied the Headmaster's requirement that the school should provide for all a boy's interests and that his education could be enhanced and extended by a fuller participation in this aspect of the school's life. There was a Model Aero Club set up in 1909 encouraged by a visit of boys to the Doncaster Aviation Meeting, and a Meteorological Society, membership of which mainly entailed being part of a rota to check the rainfall gauges and the barometer. A Choral Society was established in 1910, partly to offer the opportunity to have a good sing but also to provide a chorus for the school concerts, which still relied heavily on staff members and even their wives and daughters. A Shakespeare Society was formed in 1912 and there was always a society that visited industrial factories and the public utilities — never a brewery; sometimes it was called the Scientific Society, sometimes the Industrial, or even the Field, Society. The Natural History Society also made many excursions into what are now Sheffield's western outer suburbs, or further afield into the glorious Derbyshire countryside.

The magazine came out once a term and cost each pupil 1s 6d (7.5p). It was rather forced on to pupils who tended only to appreciate it if they themselves were mentioned. Each copy contained an Oxford Letter and, less regularly, a Cambridge one. This rather reflected the number of old boys up at the two senior universities. Throughout its history KES sent more boys to Oxford than Cambridge and undergraduates from KES at the colleges in Cambridge sometimes felt they were treated as second class. It was in one of these Oxford letters in 1908 that the term Edwardian was used for the first time to describe old boys. Until 1913 former pupils were still referred to as O.B's; after that date they had become Old Edwardians, or O.E.s, and the name became permanent. The Old Edwardian Association however was not formed until after the First World War and the magazine never took the name "Edwardian" for its title, which was a very common practice among KES's contemporaries.

At the Speech Day of July 1914 the Headmaster could once again report on a very successful year, which included six Open Scholarships at Sheffield University. The school and the university were both celebrating their ninth year and Old Edwardians continued to play a prominent part in the academic and social life of the University. In 1914 the editor of the University magazine, "Floreamus", and the Secretary of the Students' Representative Council were both O.E.s and others were prominent in the dramatic society and the football and cricket teams. Hichens also reported that the school now had 448 pupils on roll, indicating the continuing popularity of the school, and he seemed to think that was its optimum number, even though there was space for at least another hundred boys. The Bishop of Sheffield, when presenting the prizes, said he looked forward to the continued progress of the school in the immediate years to come and the whole occasion was wrapped up, as was the custom, with an oration and a short dramatic excerpt. D.S. Thornton gave the oration and F.M.Marrs, G.Holmes and C.L.M. Battersby performed three hundred lines from an Aristophanes play in the original Greek. Three of them would win Open Scholarships (two at Oxford, one at Cambridge) and one would win a prize cadetship at Sandhurst. None of them would survive the war.

CHAPTER SIX

SO MANY

There are ninety-two names on the bronze plaque commemorating the school's dead of the Great War of 1914 –1918. Ninety of them are old boys and two, Capt. A. Hardman and Lt. J.C. Scott, were masters at the school when war broke out. For a school that had been open for only nine years in August 1914 the numbers of fatalities are truly incredible. Many of those killed in the four year conflict had been at school when the war started, and by a rough calculation the numbers of Old Edwardians who had gone through the school from 1905 to 1918 was only about 750. By the end of hostilities 12% of all Old Edwardians had been killed in a war in which the major combatants had fought each other with all their industrial might, creating a stalemate of murderous defences that even the most able generals found impossible to breach. That unlucky generation of youth paid the price for the stupidity and vanity of Kaisers, Tsars and parliamentary governments who stumbled into a war they did not have the imagination, foresight or comprehension to avoid.

In the first few months of war, life at the school seems hardly to have been disturbed. Everyone was caught up in the jingoism of the early months, expecting quick victories as in the last major European war of 1870-71. The city and the school were in no danger from attack, unlike Scarborough and other coastal ports which were subject to sneak raids by German Navy squadrons, and the routine of school life quite naturally continued. External examinations were still held, house matches played and inter-school fixtures still fulfilled. The first debate of the new term in October 1914 discussed the world shattering issue of whether prefects should be abolished and another debate considered whether the OTC should have a regimental mascot. The camp at Winchelsea had run its course in August and with the fine weather had been particularly successful. The camp would continue to be run, as usual, throughout the war in the same south coast location, although the War Office confusingly refused to allow the school to use their tents, insisting that they find other accommodation, which they did in coastguards' cottages and farmers' outhouses. Sixth Formers continued to win scholarships to Oxford, Cambridge and Sheffield and in many cases they went up to the University and started their courses. Others decided, on leaving school, to join up in the new armies of volunteers that Kitchener was raising to support Britain's regular army. An army that was superb at battalion level, but untrained and woefully weak in the numbers needed to fight a major land war on the European continent.

Many Old Edwardians joined the new City of Sheffield Battalion, the 12th Battalion of the York and Lancaster Regiment, which despite its name recruited solely in South Yorkshire. This battalion was one of the "Pals" battalions and encouraged recruitment amongst middle class young men, making it particularly attractive to Old Edwardians and students at Sheffield University to join up as private soldiers. They were billeted at Redmires camp and when they marched into Sheffield, boys working in classes at the school could hear their school song being whistled or sung by O.E.s as they passed by on Glossop Road. Like most of Kitchener's army they would not see action until 1916, and life at Redmires must have seemed like a continuation of the fun and comradeship they had enjoyed at the OTC camps, for many of them were former members of the Corps.

The school made some concessions to the war. The School Lecture, an institution started in 1910 by the Headmaster and intended to be a prestigious and edifying occasion, was given by H.A.L. Fisher, the Vice-Chancellor of the University and one of the country's leading historians. In November of 1914 he came to the school and spoke on the "Causes and Issues of the War" in which, after a general survey of Germany's perfidiousness, he concentrated on the specifics of her invasion of Belgium and Britain's necessary and traditional response to protect her interests on the opposite shore of the North Sea.

Another lecture that same term, given by an Old Edwardian, F.C. Thompson, a leading authority on armaments, compared the merits of British and German guns, shells, torpedoes and armour, concluding that Sheffield's, and therefore Britain's, products were superior in all cases. Later in the term the lectures reverted back to type, when a classics professor lectured the audience on Knossos and Delphi and followed this up with a lecture on the ancient Olympic Games.

Although Britain had ostensibly joined the conflict to protect and deliver Belgium, they had of course done no such thing. Hemmed in around Ypres, in the south west corner of Flanders, they would slug it out for four years in the battlefields of the Salient, that would become all too distressingly familiar to far too many Old Edwardians as the war progressed. Belgium, however, was quite rightly perceived as the gallant victim of German frightfulness, and Belgian refugees arriving in the city in late 1914 evoked massive sympathy from the Sheffield public. Here was an opportunity for KES to do something positive for the war effort, so a fund was set up by the boys of the school to raise money to educate seven Belgian boys at KES. Five of them became boarders at Lynwood, and the fund-raising was so successful that the treasurer, in 1915, had to call a halt to the money coming in, because half the money raised was surplus to immediate requirements.

BELGIUM

On came the aggressor in full panoply;
With fire and reeking sword he spread alarm,
And in a country guiltless, thrifty, calm,
Dethroned good, exalted devilry.
Yet quenched he not the flame of liberty
Which burned more brightly for the grievous harm
Those heroes suffered, who now hold the palm
Of truth, self sacrifice and loyalty.

C.K.Wright, Sixth Form 1914, Later Classics Scholar at Jesus College, Oxford.

Perhaps surprisingly the school flourished during the war. The numbers at the school went up, passing 500 for the first time at the end of 1915, whilst the Higher and Lower School Certificate results just got better and better. In the 1915 Higher School Certificate Examinations KES achieved the most distinctions (36) of any school taking the Oxford and Cambridge Board Exams and in 1916 they had more certificates and distinctions than any other school. In W.P. Taylor, who had won the Junior University Mathematical Exhibition at Oxford, the school had produced the second best mathematician in that university, and in Stanley Rawson, they now had a Fellow of All Souls. Moreover, in 1915, KES Sixth Formers gained five scholarships at Oxford, one at Cambridge and three at Sheffield University, whilst the Akroyd Scholarship was won again, the sixth time since KES first competed for it nine years previously.

1915 marked the first ten years of the school and the Sheffield Independent commented in its leader:

"We could imagine an ambitious headmaster might wake up one morning after a particularly pleasant dream, in which he dreamt that all the successes that King Edwards announced at their Speech Day had actually happened to his school."

There was, however, now another honours roll that the school mentioned with pride on Speech Day. By the end of 1914 ninety-five Old Boys had joined the forces. Nineteen of them were already commissioned, the majority of them former members of the OTC. In the magazine their names were proudly displayed under the heading "Roll Of Honour", which at that time innocently meant that they had joined up to do their bit, although only one of the volunteers, 2nd Lt. Robert Skeggs, serving with the Rifle Brigade, had actually seen action at the front in France during the first autumn of the war. Skeggs, who the following year won the newly instituted Military Cross, would survive the war and in the aftermath would be the leading figure in starting up the Old Edwardians' Association.

The first fatalities came in early 1915 when 2nd Lt. Donald Henderson was killed in January whilst serving with the Kings Royal Rifle Corps in France. Nearer to home in February, Charles Hanforth , serving with the City of Sheffield Battalion at Redmires, caught influenza and died without having left Yorkshire. In contrast Leonard Bennett of the Australian Imperial Expeditionary Force had emigrated down under only to return to the very tip of Europe, to be killed in action in a bayonet charge at Anzac Cove, Gallipoli in May 1915. The Headmaster at the 1916 Speech Day in July read out all their names, nine in all. He was not to know that four days previously the greatest loss of life of Old Edwardians on any one day had just happened near the ruined village of Serre in the Department of the Somme. The City Battalion of the York and Lancs. Regt. had taken part in the "First Day" of the Battle of the Somme at the northern end of the line of advance and had suffered devastating casualties. Over half its strength were either dead, wounded or captured by the end of the day on 1st July. James Shearer, the school's registrar serving with the battalion, recorded years later that the saddest day of his life was spent on the afternoon of the attack, covering with earth the bodies of a number of Old Edwardians who had been killed that morning on the devastated slopes outside Serre.

After the war the City Council built the Sheffield War Memorial at Serre to commemorate not just the York and Lancaster Regiment's dead, but all of their citizens who were lost in the war. The site was chosen because it marked the most tragic day in the history of the local regiment. Local pride was a cornerstone of the British county regimental tradition and many Old Edwardians recognised this by joining battalions of the York and Lancs. Thirty-five of the school's dead were serving in the regiment when they were killed in action, or died on active service. They were a part of the final roll call of 8,814 officers and men of the regiment who lost their lives in the Great War, and who are commemorated by the regimental memorial in Weston Park.

There were to be no more Speech Days after 1916. In 1915, and again in 1916, the Headmaster had attempted to capture the optimistic and patriotic mood of the country in the content and organisation of Speech Day. On each occasion, after the prizes had been distributed and the formalities concluded, the whole assembly ended the proceedings by singing the national anthems of all the allies. Whether or not it was because Hichens could not face intoning lists of the dead that might number thirty or more a year, or possibly because he felt a congratulatory occasion like Speech Day was inappropriate in wartime, they were discontinued until 1919. He also banned major concerts and dramatic productions that would have brought large numbers of parents into the school in the evening. There was now a genuine concern that a Zeppelin raid might catch them unawares, so school events were scaled down and took place immediately after school. This enabled boys to concentrate on their schoolwork and may be one explanation why examination results improved year on year from their already high standard.

 In response to a Government request to reduce travel to a minimum, football and cricket matches against schools outside Sheffield ceased. A few scratch matches were arranged against army units in the area, but largely KES sportsmen were thrown back on their own resources and house matches assumed a far greater importance than usual. They were often watched by considerable numbers of convalescing soldiers from the hospital in Whiteley Woods, and their presence must have further emphasised to boys about to be called up what the true nature of the war was really like. Whiteley Woods playing fields themselves also made a contribution to the war effort, when a sizeable section was dug up by pupils of the school and planted with potatoes. Old Boys on leave regularly visited the school. Perhaps such visits provided them with solace for they were so young and the school had been such a large part of their lives, now so fragile and uncertain. One such visitor was Lt. R.C. Maples who had emigrated to Canada to practice at the Canadian Bar and returned with the Canadian Army to fight in France. He had been the school's first sporting hero, winning not only a football Blue but playing for England in an amateur international match against France in 1910. The Headmaster talked him into giving one of the School Lectures and he drew an amusing and bracing picture of army training in Ontario, whilst living in tents during a penetrating Canadian winter.

The Headmaster tried to keep in touch with as many Old Edwardians as possible. Most of those in the forces were serving in France or Flanders and the vast majority were in the infantry, where their experiences of war in the trenches were not very dissimilar from each other. However, there were old boys in almost all theatres of the conflict and in all branches of the services. Some were in Mesopotamia fighting the Turks and helping to capture Baghdad, a number fought at Gallipoli in 1915, and others served in various ships of the Royal Navy. Several old boys were pilots in the Royal Naval Air Service and others joined the Royal Flying Corps, transferring to the newly created RAF in 1918.

Unlike the Second World War, the main front was the Western Front and the British Army played a larger and more significant part in the war after 1916, and by the summer of 1918 the decisive part. These were the great killing fields of the 1914 –18 War and it was here, often during the major British offensives at Ypres, Arras, or on the Somme, that many Old Edwardians lost their lives. Amongst them were the four Head Prefects from 1912 –1916, W.P.Taylor (1912-13), G. Holmes (1913-14), D.S. Thornton (1914-15) and B.O. Robinson (1915-16). If anyone can epitomise the sacrifice and the waste of talent of this generation then it is these four brilliant young men.

William Taylor (Head Prefect 1912-13)

George Holmes (Head Prefect 1913-14)

He was one of the first intake of KES pupils in September 1905, an Akroyd Scholar, a Hastings Exhibitioner, and after a brilliant first year at Queen's College, Oxford, he was commissioned into the York and Lancs. Regt. in 1915. He found himself, in 1917, leading his platoon in an assault on the German front line of trenches. Wounded in the chest during the attack, he stayed on to organise his defensive area before going back to the rear, but was shot dead by a sniper crossing no man's land on his way to an aid post. He would have been one of the foremost mathematicians of his day, and who knows what positions he would have held in later life. In 1921 his mother and sister established a memorial mathematics prize to be awarded annually to the best mathematician in the school. In 2005 it is still awarded and it is his enduring memorial.

Holmes was commissioned into the regular 1st Bn. East Yorkshire Regiment and met his death at the Battle of the Scarpe near Arras in April 1917. Having breached the Hindenburg Line he was struck by a shell and died instantaneously. He had been the goalkeeper and wicket keeper in both school XI's and took up his Classical Exhibition at Magdalen College, Oxford, for a term in 1914 before deciding he ought to volunteer for the army. His original wooden grave marker still hangs on the wall of the nave of Hathersage Parish Church, with his name and regiment stamped out on an attached metal strip.

D.S. Thornton (Head Prefect 1914-15)

Bernard Robinson
(Head Prefect 1915-16)

Thornton was a boarder at Lynwood and Head of that House. When his death was announced it caused profound shock amongst all the boarders. He had only left in the summer of 1915 and was known and well liked by the entire house. "The one death we had most feared hearing about;" wrote his Housemaster in the Lynwood notes in the school magazine. Champion Athlete of the school, he played a full part in every aspect of the school's life and had won an Open Maths Demyship at Magdalen College, Oxford, which he intended to take up after the war. Serving as a 2nd Lt. in the 11th Bn. Sherwood Foresters he went to France in July 1916 and was killed by a sniper, having just captured a German trench at Le Sars, in October of that year.

"The best Head Prefect I ever had:" wrote Hichens of this young man. His C.O. in the Hallamshires wrote to the family and said. "He was a particularly capable and hard-working officer whose men would follow him anywhere. We never had a better subaltern". Another Champion Athlete of the School, he was intending to return after the war to Queen's College, Oxford and take up his Hastings Scholarship and read Mathematics. He had only been commissioned into the 4th (Hallamshire) Bn. York & Lancs Regt. in March 1917 and was killed in hand to hand fighting in the third line of the German trenches at Passchendaele early in the morning of the 9th October 1917. He was just twenty years of age.

The loss of lives continued during 1918, when the German Offensive started in March. Planned to split the Allies and push the British back to the Channel before American Forces could have any significant bearing on the outcome of the war. It got as far as Amiens before the great British counter-attack of August 1918 drove the Germans back, and then breached their lines and sent them into irreversible retreat. The final crop of Old Edwardian dead was caused by these offensives and they included nineteen year olds, just out of school, like 2nd. Lt. T. C. Cummins, 7th Bn. York & Lancs, killed in the March retreat, Pte. J.F. Frank, 15th Bn. West Yorks, and 2nd. Lt. F.H. Burton of the Sherwood Foresters, another Hastings Scholarship winner who would never have the chance to take up his award. He was killed as late as 15th October as British troops finally took Menin, when the German Army was forced to evacuate the Salient.

It was later recorded by one member of the staff, that late on the afternoon of Armistice Day when everyone had gone home, James Hichens stood for an hour at the top of the front steps under the great Corinthian pillars, looking silently and directly into the middle distance across the valley of the Porter. From the town came the continuous racket of the spontaneous celebrations, while smaller groups of revellers might have disturbed his gaze as they passed noisily along Clarkehouse Road. He has left no record of his thoughts but we can all easily guess. A school is finally judged by the quality of the pupils who pass through it. In another generation he could have expected the outstanding success of his school in its first decade to have continued peaceably, reaching a plateau of achievement at a comfortable high level. Instead, like all Headmasters in all the combatant countries, he had been forced to lead his school through the most unimaginable tragedy. His "family" had lost ninety members, including many of the most successful and those with the brightest prospects. Some Headmasters in some schools never got over the trauma of those years but Hichens, who was now 58, was made of stern stuff; he was well known for his ability to overcome any problem and he just carried on.

He was no doubt comforted by the many returning Old Edwardians who had survived. In a particular twist of irony, Thomas Peace and three other O.E.s had found themselves working, or studying, in Germany when the war broke out and had spent four years in the appropriately named Ruheleben internment camp, near Berlin. The Headmaster recorded for the Governors that many O.E.s (roughly 10% of those in the forces) had been decorated or mentioned in despatches. They included E. A. Berrisford R.E., who had finished up as a twenty–eight year old acting Brigadier with the DSO and the M.C., and was now continuing his studies at Oxford before going into the church. The Military Medal was won by five old boys, Cpl. A.E. Budd of the Royal Engineers, Sgt. A.G. Fauvel of the Queens Own Yorkshire Dragoons, Pte. H.C. Arridge, of the York & Lancs, who was later commissioned and transferred to the Indian Army, and two Gunners, H. Mellor and H.E. Allen. Altogether the school had won twenty-two Military Crosses, including Lieut. J.C. Sterndale Bennett R.N. who won the M.C. with the Royal Naval Division and would later go into the Diplomatic Service and end up as a KCMG and Head of the Foreign Office's Far Eastern Department. Capt. R. Oxspring M.C. and two bars of the K.O.Y.L.I. won an unbelievable three M.C.'s and yet survived the war. For his part in aerial combat over Lille in 1918 Capt., now Flt. Lt., S. Turner R.A.F. was a winner of the brand new Distinguished Flying Cross, whilst Capt.A.S.Wiles R.A.M.C. was awarded the Croix de Guerre by the French for his work with his ambulance team at Verdun and in the Argonne.

In a unique moment of the school's life, a Memorial Service was held in the Cathedral on 8th April 1919. Each death had been an immense personal, and often irreparable, tragedy for the parents and the families of the dead Old Edwardians. This was their occasion, supported by the returning servicemen who had lost the friends of their childhood years, as their names were slowly read out one by one without any reference to rank, for all were equal in their sacrifice. All the staff and boys presently at the school were there, most of whom would have lost at least one member of their own family as well. The Ven. Archdeacon Gresford Jones, a member of the school governors, in giving the address said:

> *"See them, then, once again. As their names recall them to you, see them as you knew them and loved them so short a while ago: on the playing field, at home, in the class room, on some friendly walk. See them again so swiftly caught up into their country's service, patiently waiting the supreme moment. Yes, see them crossing that narrow line of Death, and hear now their voices from the other side."*

The school magazine reporting the service added:

> *"We heard their footsteps as we walked to the Cathedral and in the stillness of the hush of the Eleventh Hour, once again they take their places with us. They too have returned."*

CHAPTER SEVEN

THE HEADMASTERS' CONFERENCE

James Hichens' career at the school achieved its consummation in January 1922 when he was finally invited, in his capacity as Headmaster of King Edward VII School, to become a member of the Headmasters' Conference. After a decade and a half of posturing as a public school, KES's amazing academic success was recognised by the accolade of an official ranking as an HMC school. The status of the public schools had never been higher than in the period after the First World War and this encouraged several new boarding foundations, including Stowe in 1923 and Bryanston in 1928. At the same time the HMC was keen to head off arguments that they were too socially elitist. They were now prepared to bring into membership some of the more successful day schools, even if they were council financed grammar schools, provided they had their own Boards of Governors who had virtual *de facto* independence.

In all respects KES was well qualified to join the HMC and, as if to emphasize their claim, the school once again achieved the top ranking in the Higher Certificate Examinations that year. They had achieved this distinction for the first time in 1915 and for several years they had been second or third in the list, which now included forty of the top girls' public schools. When the new and highly prestigious State Scholarships were instituted in 1920 by the Board of Education, boys at the school were awarded four and would continue over the years to gain many of these scholarships (in 1955 they won 16 in one year). Former pupils were regularly picking up First Class Honours degrees at Oxbridge and at Sheffield University, and the school had established a strong link with Balliol, after several boys won scholarships at that college. The school had also performed well in the new School Certificate Examinations (introduced at KES in 1918 for boys in the fifth form), with only four schools out of 144 doing better than KES in the exams in 1922. In the same year the numbers on roll reached the accepted full capacity of 650 and there was a very buoyant spirit about the building. So much so that Hichens felt he could ask the Council and the Board of Education to approve an increase in fees to 17 guineas (£17.85) per annum. As if to symbolise the school's new confidence and status, the great brass eagle lectern, which had been given by the Osborn family to Wesley College and then taken back into the family's keeping in 1905, was presented once again to the school and it stands on the school platform to this day.

School numbers had passed the 600 mark before the end of the war and the Junior School had moved into its new premises in Newbould Lane to create extra teaching capacity for the Senior School. Although the numbers undertaking post-sixteen education had gone down dramatically in the last two years year of the war, reaching forty-eight in 1917, it soon began to pick up after the Armistice and by 1922 had reached 120, which was considered the capacity for the Sixth Form. The demand for places at the school meant that the entrance examination for fee-paying pupils became more competitive and over a quarter of candidates were rejected. Compare this to 1906 when no-one was turned away and the school was desperate to take anyone whose parents could stump up the fees. Hichens reported to the Governors that ; *"The difficulty of getting boys into KES is having a good effect on the city, for it is impressing on parents that it is necessary for boys to have a satisfactory grounding in their early years before coming to the school."*

SHERWOOD HOUSE

An extra house was formed in September 1920 to cope with the increase in numbers in the school. It was called Sherwood after the forest and also after the Notts and Derby Regiment, The Sherwood Foresters, in which many Old Edwardians had served during the war. It was the last house to be created until the amalgamations of the 1970s and for a start its membership only comprised new boys to the school, so as not to disturb the membership of the existing houses. Humphrey Watkins was the first housemaster and its colours, not inappropriately, were green and white.

Important changes had occurred to the school's entrance policy for elementary school pupils during the last year of the war. Having fought tooth and nail in 1911 against increasing the number of free places, and making themselves very unpopular as a result, they now accepted a decision of the City Council in July 1918 to accept 24 free place scholarship boys, or 25% of the intake, per annum. The change in attitude by the Governors and the Education Committee, still the same people as in 1911, was partly because the war had made a nonsense of such crude snobbery and partly because of a new initiative to increase the provision of secondary education in the city. In 1914 Michael Sadler had been brought back to Sheffield and asked to write a new report on the way forward to improve secondary school provision in the city. He recommended new secondary schools at Pitsmoor (Boys) and Abbeydale (Girls) and because KES was such a success, he suggested the City Council should offer to take over the Girls' High School and run it as a council school, along the same lines as KES across the road. Although council action was delayed by the war, the report was acted upon and in 1919 Pitsmoor School (later Firth Park Grammar School) and in 1920 Abbeydale Girls Secondary, opened their doors to their first pupils. After a close vote in the Education Committee, the Council agreed that these two schools, and the two Central Schools, should not charge fees to any pupil, and at the same time KES was told to admit more free place boys.

In September 1918 twenty-four twelve year old scholarship boys joined KES. The assumption, at the time, that twenty-four working class boys would now get entrance into KES every year, is not borne out by studying the background of scholarship winners in the 1920s. Of that initial entry in 1918, only four could be classed as working class by virtue of their father's job, and only three came from schools in the east end of Sheffield. The sons of teachers, managers, engineers and even a clergyman took the other twenty places and some elementary schools like Hunters Bar and Western Rd. very proudly accounted for about a third of the intake. As a result of this decision, KES had its Government Grant restored in 1918, and the Board of Education paid over £3455 p.a. to the City Council to offset the cost of running KES, and backdated it to September 1917 for good measure. They too were pleased with the progress the school was making, — there had been another successful inspection in 1915 – and, moreover, in 1919 they increased the amount of central government grant by £1000.

Nothing, however, in the world of Sheffield educational politics is ever stable for very long and in 1921, in response to the cuts to the education budget imposed by the "Geddes Axe" of that year, Percy Sharp, the Chief Education Officer, imposed his own means test on the free scholarships award system. The City Council had to find 150 free places each year at Firth Park G.S., similar numbers at the Central Schools and 80 at Abbeydale Girls Secondary, so he decided that those scholarship winners at KES whose fathers could afford the fees would only get "honorary" scholarships. Therefore in 1921 there were only 17 free places awarded at KES and by 1923 it was down to 10, with 7 honorary scholarships. Literally this latter group would receive the honour of a certificate but not get any money towards their fees. Gordon Cumming, later a teacher at the school (1937-1953), was one of these pupils when he won an "honorary scholarship" in 1923 and entered 2D, the Form that was reserved for scholarship boys in the first year of the Senior School. Forms 2A, 2B, and 2C were for fee-paying pupils, the majority of whom had already been in the Junior School. In the following year the forms were re-setted according to ability, and the boys of this "scholarship" class were re-distributed amongst the four 3rd Forms. Between 1918 and 1945 there never were more than 25% of the boys in the school on City Council scholarships. The practice of a special entrance class, 2D, for these boys continued until the 1944 Act, after which all the new pupils at the school had passed their 11+ examination and gained free tuition at KES.

Other changes had taken place during the war and they were now incorporated into KES's normal routine. The first women teachers had joined the staff in 1917 as more male staff were conscripted into the forces, although one reluctant warrior only went into the army after a tribunal had, much to his annoyance, pronounced him fit for military service. Five ladies now taught in the Junior School and were so successful that they were given permanent contracts after the war. They were an impressive group and the first two were Miss A.H.Burford, who had taught at Roedean, and she was soon followed by Miss E.G. Roper, who had been at Cheltenham Ladies College.

After the armistice eight members of staff got a quick release and returned, including Nicholas, Magrath, Lutley (who joined the OTC as one of its officers) and Watkins. The latter had been badly wounded but he once again entered enthusiastically into the work of the school, founding a branch of the Scripture Union that very quickly reached a membership of 230 boys. The curriculum had been enlarged by the introduction of Spanish, Economics and Civics and these subjects continued to be offered at the school in the Twenties. Of greater importance to the boys, a tuck shop was opened in 1921 where you could get a doughnut for a penny and minerals and ice cream were also available.

SCHOOL DRESS

Boys are required to wear:

- *A dark coat and waistcoat, not necessarily black.*
- *The school tie or a black tie*
- *The school cap with badge or the school boater with the school ribbon.*
- *Trousers, either of the same colour as the coat and waistcoat, or grey.*

Jerseys or tennis shirts are allowed.

White or blue "colours" blazers can only be worn for sporting occasions.

No boy is allowed to smoke while wearing his school cap.

Old Edwardians' Association Formed

One important feature of a public school was to have a flourishing old boys' association, where former pupils could keep in touch with the school, their friends from schooldays and benefit from the network of influence that such an association could generate. They could on a regular basis, or when there was a specific project, raise funds to help the old school as well as being the unofficial guardians of the school's progress and traditions.

The aftermath of the war provided the spur to form an Old Edwardians' Association in March 1920, after the idea was strongly canvassed at an old boys' reunion dinner held at the Grand Hotel, Barkers Pool, in February. It was a time when many ex-servicemen felt the need to retain a sense of belonging to organisations in which they had been proud to serve. Many joined their regimental association, but many also felt the same pride and nostalgia for their school and empathy with their fellow old boys who had survived the war.

Robert Skeggs M.C., now a retired major, was the first secretary of the association, and he threw himself into the task of getting the new organisation off the ground. Initial membership was ten shillings (50p) per annum, a not inconsiderable sum in the Twenties, and the planning group agreed to set up Football and Cricket sections along with an Entertainment section, who would run the Annual Dinner, whist drives, the Annual Dance at the Cutlers Hall and hopefully an annual play as well. In time all these events became firm institutions. The Association also planned to set up a "professional information bureau" which would aid the networking of old boys and give practical expression to the "old school tie". The Annual Dinner held in December was the main event, which O.E.s were expected to attend if at all possible, and it was advertised in the London Times as well as the Sheffield morning papers.

Skeggs sent out a letter eliciting membership to all the Old Edwardians with whom the school was in contact. His next priority was to establish a scheme to help O.E.s disabled in the war as part of a War Memorial Fund, that would also provide remembrance memorials of the war dead. It was suggested that another ten shillings should be each member's contribution to that fund, and it was, of course, very well subscribed. Skeggs also sought information from members, parents and staff to enable a full register of war service and a complete roll of honour to be compiled, so that no name should be missed from the plaque that would eventually be placed in the school.

The Headmaster agreed to be the President for the first year; after that the Rev. Edwin Berrisford, who was probably the most famous Old Edwardian at the time, held the post for several years. From the beginning the Association intended to find a clubroom in the centre of town, which the many O.E. s who worked there could use as a "gentleman's club". Eventually, in 1922, they rented premises in Devonshire Street and the club was open in the evening, with billiard matches arranged with the Athenaeum Club and a programme of evening activities, including whist and bridge, to create more use of their exclusive rooms.

The Association and the club room were also open to those who had been at Wesley College and at SRGS, many of whom held senior positions in the life of the city in the Twenties. They were all eligible to wear the new Old Edwardian tie, designed in the school colours of dark blue and white but with a third dark green stripe as well.

Despite this energetic progress only 130 out of an estimated possible total of 800 joined the association in the first year, although numbers did rise steadily in the next few years. The sports clubs began their fixtures during the next season and the Football team posted a reasonable set of results. The Cricket team, who had a 5-2 winning season, played teams of a good standard and many of that first fixture list, including Stainborough, Hathersage and Collegiate, would remain fixtures for the O.E.s during the entire century. Their opponents tended to be smart clubs with attractive village grounds, which made for most enjoyable matches, win or lose. By the following year both the Football and Cricket sections had very full fixture lists: the Cricket Club played 23 matches and won 14, with Fred Ambler, now the O.E.A. Secretary, scoring the club's first century. The Football Club had also gone well, with only seven defeats in 23 games, and both sections had attracted enough players to run second XI's. The clubroom meanwhile had soon been abandoned through lack of use.

The Unveiling

On a grey misty afternoon at the end of November 1921 the Old Edwardians unveiled their War Memorials and handed them over to the school for their safe keeping in perpetuity. The first part of the ceremony was held in the Assembly Hall, where the bronze plaque bearing the 92 names was unveiled. It was positioned above the platform in front of where the organ now stands. The more dramatic part of the ceremony took place outside, at the immaculately clean granite cross marked simply, as is the London Cenotaph, "1914-1918 — To our Glorious Dead."

No famous name had been invited, for this was a private, but intensely moving, ceremony with the whole school and many parents and friends standing silently in the yard. All the members of the OTC were on parade, encircling the memorial with their rifles at the

*Platform Party at the unveiling. In the centre is the Bishop of Sheffield.
On left (left to right); James Hichens and the Rev. Edwin Berrisford.
On the right in frock coat; Ald. Robert Styring.*

present. Then the Lord Mayor unveiled the cross by releasing the Union Flag and the dedication was performed by the Bishop of Sheffield. The bugles and drums of the Hallamshires sounded Last Post, then the quicker tempo of Reveille before the Rev. Edwin Berrisford, representing the O.E.A., gave a short address and handed over the memorial. It was accepted on behalf of the school by the Chairman of Governors, Ald. Robert Styring, whose family had one name on the school memorial, as did other members of the City Council.

Every year until the 1960s the whole school would meet on Armistice Day around this cross to remember the sacrifice of the Great War, and the even larger number of dead Old Edwardians from World War Two. It is not easy to-day to fully understand how devastated the nation was by the losses of 1914-18. Nothing comparable had happened in British history since the Civil War, or even back to the Black Death in the 14th Century. Trams stopped, traffic and pedestrians stood still, and people in offices, shops and factories stood to attention for the two silent minutes. No one, not even the youngest member of the Junior School, needed to be reminded what this national ceremony was about. This had been Britain's "Holocaust" and Old Edwardians had paid as full a price as anyone in the adversity of those years.

At Christmas 1925 Hichens announced that he would retire at the end of the summer term in 1926. He would be handing over to his successor a school that was now recognised as one of the top performing schools in Yorkshire and indeed its reputation was well known in education and academic circles throughout the country. He would be sixty-five in 1926 and he knew that the school needed new and more vigorous leadership if its remarkable progress was to continue. Between 1923 and 1926 several long established members of staff had died whilst still serving at the school. Robert Johnson, who had come from Pocklington School as one of the initial members of staff in 1905, died of pneumonia on the eve of his 58th birthday. He had been the Senior Classics master and was responsible for the many Open Scholarship successes in that subject that KES boys had achieved. A bachelor who lived in at Lynwood, he was a keen sportsman who had in his younger days turned out for Warwickshire Gentlemen and rarely missed a county match at Bramall Lane. He had also served as the school's librarian where it was rumoured that he would never loan a book to any boy, or master, he didn't like. Harry Hodgetts had been the second master at SRGS and came over to the new King Edward VII School in 1905 as an assistant master teaching maths and science. He had been a pupil at Wolverhampton R.G.S. but well before Hichens became the Headmaster of that school. In Sheffield he gave 35 years service to the two schools and then, after a lengthy illness, he died in the summer of 1925. Perhaps, for Hichens, the saddest loss was when Ben Caudwell died suddenly of pneumonia in February 1926. He had also been a teacher of mathematics at SRGS, and very many distinguished old boys at that school, and at KES, would attest that he was the finest teacher they ever had. He never really got over the loss of his elder son, killed at Cambrai in 1917, but like so many bereaved parents he had got on with his life, his work and his hobbies. He was a consummate player of the viola and a very good craftsman of fine cabinet work, and the loss of such a friend and colleague must have caused Hichens great sorrow in his final two terms. Arthur Haslam wrote from retirement in the Dales; *"As a headmaster, I need only say that my greatest refreshment was a twenty minute visit to his classroom to listen to one of his lessons."*

These deaths and others, like Frank Jelly, another brilliant mathematician, whose death took everyone by surprise in 1924, left large gaps in the staff room and must have hastened the feeling that a chapter in the life of the school was closing. G. Lloyd-Davies, the Second Master and Head of Modern Languages, chose to retire in the summer of 1926 at the same time as Hichens. He had joined the staff in 1907 and been selected as the Second Master in 1910, and at various times had been Housemaster of Clumber, Editor of the School Magazine and President of the Debating Society. As Second Master he was responsible for the school's discipline and his sharp Welsh accent could often be heard terrorising even the most hardened wrongdoers, who regularly ended the day in detention. The Old Edwardians arranged a special farewell dinner at the Grand Hotel in July for both of them, when many of their former pupils came long distances to be present.

There were to be many farewells and valedictories for James Hichens that summer, but he wasn't prepared to let Speech Day pass without adding a word or two of his own. The final crop of Higher School Certificates had been one of the best ever. Not only had KES gained more distinctions (27) than any other school, but its nearest rival, Rugby, had only 23, whilst the best day schools, Bradford G.S. and City of London School, had only 13. (Ironically both of those schools would be led one day by a couple of his successors as Headmaster of KES). In his time, KES had won 11 Akroyd Scholarships out of the twenty awarded and there were now four Old Edwardians who were Fellows of Oxbridge Colleges, with twelve of the most prestigious Prizes and Scholarships those two universities had to offer having been won by old boys. He had even totted up the total value (£59,000) of the 280 scholarships and exhibitions won by boys of the school during his period as Headmaster.

He was aware that some critics felt he dwelt too much on these élite performances and did not give enough attention to the average boy. It was a charge that would be levelled against several of his successors as well, and he attempted to answer it, at one Speech Day, by highlighting the success of two old boys in their early twenties who did not go into the sixth form, or go to university. W.R. Allen had made a successful career for himself in the Public Works Board of India, and C.F.N. Wade had become the Chief of the Wireless Service in the colony of North Borneo. There he was on a salary of £650 p.a., more than Lloyd-Davies earned as Second Master, and Wade had considerable emoluments on top of this. He might have added that the professions, commerce and industry in Sheffield were full of successful O.E.s who, despite leaving the school at 15 or 16, now held important positions and also highly valued their time at the school.

One speaker, at one of the leaving functions, suggested that his epitaph might well be one he would be content with. It was a transposition of the comment he typed on so many reports. *"J.H.H. Very Satisfactory."*

Everyone, Governors, Old Edwardians, Staff and parents agreed it was the end of an era. Just how much of a change his parting would presage they had no idea, for the next four terms were to be some of the most tumultuous in the school's history.

THE OFFICERS' TRAINING CORPS

For twenty years KES had an OTC, the very epitome of a public school. There had been a cadet corps at Wesley College since 1888 and some form of military training had been instituted in the latter days of the SRGS, so it was expected that KES would continue with a corps. The King Edward VII Cadet Corps, however, began in a modest way in July 1907, when it was still attached to the West Yorks. Royal Engineers Volunteers, an important militia unit in a heavy engineering city. The corps was open to boys over thirteen and was never compulsory as it was at some schools. For a start the limit was 40 cadets, a number that was achieved straight away, but after that it was often struggling for numbers, except during the war. They were officered by masters and the NCOs were promoted from within their own ranks. The only staff member who was ex-regular army was the school's Sergeant /Instructor, who took the school's gymnastic classes as well as instructing in drill and musketry. Sgt. Thompson held this post for a start until his untimely death in 1909, and then Sgt. Major Costello succeeded him until the outbreak of the war.

No sooner had the corps been formed than a major change took place in the national organisation of school cadet forces. As part of the review of the army's reserves, the Territorial Army was formed in 1908 and school cadet forces were re-designated Officers' Training Corps. The clear intention was to put them on a more organised and better resourced footing, so that they would give preliminary military training to boys who could very quickly become junior officers in a national emergency. They were now kitted out in the army's new khaki uniforms, and wore them during lessons when they had a parade after school. Most school corps wore the cap badge of their local infantry regiment to which they were attached, but the KES contingent continued their connection with the Royal Engineers and wore their badge instead, although after the war they changed to wearing the school's badge on their cap.

The routine weekly parades included drill, map reading and shooting on the miniature range, but the highlights of the corps' year included the Annual Inspection by a regular officer of senior rank, visiting the Totley range to fire real .303 ammunition, providing a guard of honour on Speech Day, the Annual Camp and Field Days. Field Days were days out of school practicing manoeuvres and were highly popular. The contingent had a day off school, often travelling considerable distances to link up with other schools, almost always public schools. On arrival at some army training area they would effect a company attack or defence scheme, wildly firing off blank ammunition and executing basic fieldcraft. The Annual Camp, always referred to at KES as the Public School OTC camp, was a whole week and a half of the same. Run by a regular battalion — in 1910 it was the Guards Depot who organised it — they would join thirty or forty other school contingents and undergo a training regime not unlike the one regular Army recruits would undertake. Many at the camp would only be fourteen years old but, as at the school camp at Winchelsea, the tyro KES soldiers had the time of their young lives, living under canvas, enjoying sports matches and sing-songs in the evenings and playing at soldiers.

Yet despite having the corps, KES had no real military tradition. Unlike some older public schools like Marlborough, Wellington and Haileybury, very few boys went to Sandhurst, or to Woolwich, and then obtained commissions in the army. Although some Old Edwardians joined the merchant navy, no one had gone to R.N.C. Dartmouth before 1914, although city firms like Vickers made every conceivable part of a battleship and all other types of warship as well. One boy who did come from a military background was A.R. Carter. He had a couple of relatives who were admirals and he was the sixth generation to serve in the forces. He went up to R.M.A. Woolwich and was commissioned into the Royal Artillery just before the war. However, the KES cadets took their parades and duties seriously, and the more senior cadets went to Pontefract Depot and took the Certificate "A" Examination, whose possession would ensure a quick passage into the commissioned ranks when the war started in 1914. At that time the Certificate "A" was not an easy award to achieve and the corps only gained two or three a year.

The biggest day in the OTC's history before the Great War was on the occasion of the Coronation Review of the nation's cadet forces at Windsor in 1911 by the new sovereign, King George V. Forty-six KES cadets marched down to Midland Station and entrained for Windsor. After a night under canvas they joined thousands of other cadets in the Great Park and were formed into Battalions and Brigades then,

Thomas Peace (KES 1905-1912) was fourteen when this photo was taken in 1908. He was one of the first recruits into the OTC and is seen wearing the new pattern "Khaki" uniform that had been recently issued to the British Army. Ironically during World War One, Peace was interned in Germany for the duration, whilst all his closest friends at KES were killed in the Battle of the Somme in 1916.

led by a Guards band, they marched past the King in review order. It was almost a last hurrah for the days of the old empire and colourful displays of military glory, for many would not see out the decade and the two masters present, Captain Langton and Lt.(later Captain) Hardman, would both be killed on the Western Front.

Former OTC members were amongst the first Old Edwardians to volunteer for the New Armies and many joined the Sheffield City Battalion (12th Y& L.), whilst many others became subalterns in local infantry regiments in 1914 and 1915. More than a few fifteen and sixteen year olds tried to bluster their way past the recruiting sergeants and join up, but they all failed. They needn't have rushed, for many of the names on the school war memorial are those of boys who served in the OTC and many of them were still at school during the first two years of the war. However there were many other O.E.s who never joined the OTC who played just as courageous a part in the war: many were commissioned and more than a few were decorated. One can overestimate the contribution of cadet corps to the effectiveness of the army, especially the ranks of the junior officers, as no one before 1914 was prepared, or trained, for the attrition of trench warfare and the power of modern weapons of defence.

Nevertheless at the war's end each contingent received a letter from the War Office thanking them for their important contribution, and it was generally believed that the OTC had justified its formation in 1908 by the sterling performances of the boy officers of Haig's army. The armistice, however, saw a big drop in numbers of boys wanting to be in the corps. From a high figure of 100 during the war it slumped to 43 by 1920 and the school was in danger of losing its contingent. The War Office, who had seventy schools pressing them to start an OTC, had fixed a limit of 200 contingents but insisted that KES should have a corps that was 100 strong. This became a desperate situation by 1922 when Captain Proctor, who had been the OC during the war, left the school to become a "country gentleman" in the North Riding. The Headmaster now took a hand in the recruiting process. Having just been accepted as a Headmasters' Conference school he was not going to let the side down by having his OTC removed. A drum and fife band was started, new masters took over, and a Lewis Gun section and a signalling section were established. Within a year his persuasiveness had doubled the membership and KES passed the safety mark of 100 cadets in 1925.

Not all the staff and parents approved of the OTC. In the aftermath of the war the sight of so many young boys drilling in the quad, or marching imperiously around Broomhill and Ecclesall on their "marching out" parades, was not in tune with the spirit of the times. Rather unwisely, they were issued with the standard long blade bayonet for drill and manoeuvres and more than one cadet got an untimely poke from a careless or undersize colleague. At moments of potential civil strife, when there were national or local strikes, the army came and removed all the rifles from the school armoury, or on some occasions they just took the bolts. The school claimed that the corps taught leadership, co-operation and self discipline, as well as improving a boy's chances of a position in the civil service, and for those headed for the colonial service and the colonial police, a knowledge of elementary military procedure and competence with a rifle was thought to be very useful experience. It was point of honour in the OTC that cadets behaved in an exemplary manner in school and set a standard for courtesy and co-operation in lessons. More than any other school institution it stressed that boys at KES were an élite, and that they were destined to become the nation's leaders in war or peace when they finally left the school and went into the outside world.

By the start of the Autumn Term in 1926 the OTC had stabilised itself and appeared set to continue indefinitely, as it continued to do at all the other public schools. Then after twenty years existence, a political bombshell intervened to bring about its abolition in March 1927. The upshot was that not only did the master who was the O.C., Capt. C.E. Lutley, resign from KES, but it was one of the reasons why the new Headmaster, Ronald Gurner, himself a decorated war time officer, packed his bags and went back to London.

The entire contingent of the King Edward VII School OTC taken at their final parade in March 1927

CHAPTER EIGHT

WE'RE THE MASTERS NOW!

When a newly appointed Headmaster at a successful school starts applying for a new job before the year is out, then leaves after four terms, you can be fairly sure something rum has been taking place. Such a dramatic turn of events now unfolded at King Edward VII School between the summer of 1926 and Christmas 1927. Ronald Gurner, the new Headmaster, was appointed by a Governors' sub-committee where the influential voices were Sir William Clegg and Robert Styring, two of the Aldermen who had appointed Hichens twenty-one years before. Totally satisfied with Hichens' achievements, they were nevertheless looking for a much younger man who would bring fresh vision and enthusiasm to the school and would develop his ideas over a number of years. Gurner seemed the ideal appointment. A thirty-six year old high flyer who had come strongly recommended from a six year period as Headmaster of the Strand School in Brixton, south London. He was proud of the way he had taken this L.C.C. day school by the scruff of the neck and had in his own words, *"experimented and galvanised it"*, so that by 1926 he believed that they had had enough of him and that he needed a new challenge. Amongst his supporters who encouraged him to apply for the Sheffield post, were Dr., later Sir, Cyril Norwood, then Headmaster at Bristol G.S., and Ernest Barker of Kings College in the University of London, both of whom were leading educationalists of their day. They had no doubt marked the cards of the city fathers on the Governors and in March 1926 Gurner was offered the position at £1000 per annum, after they had originally tried to appoint him for less.

In some ways he was an odd choice for the Governors to make. They were looking for progress but not wholesale changes and Gurner, who was one of those returning wartime officers who had discovered the working class in the trenches, had become very critical of the class consciousness of the public schools and had made himself unpopular with many HMC schools. However, compared with the elderly and earnest James Hichens this tall, florid faced, bull of a man with an M.C. and a war hero's glamour, won them over and he arrived at the school in September as the proverbial fresh wind of change.

He was not in the least overawed by KES and its record over two decades. There was much he didn't like, starting with the Headmaster's residence at Mount View. Transplanted from a Wandsworth suburb, Gurner and his young wife were aghast at the "gaunt mausoleum" that they moved into. They didn't find the soot-black industrial city of Sheffield very appealing either and at times could be quite condescending about some of its inhabitants and the little mester tradition of much of its manufacturing industry. The new Headmaster recognised Hichens' integrity and achievements, but he looked askance at the emphasis put on examination successes and the unofficial league tables that Hichens delighted to quote on all occasions. He saw himself as representing a new social force to bring down the barriers of class and found the school, and especially the Governors and parents, full of *"petty municipal"* snobbery.

The November Council Elections 1926

One might then have thought that he would welcome the cataclysmic changes that happened to the City Council after the November Local Government Elections. Sheffield became the first large City Council in England to gain a Labour majority, after that party had continually increased their strength on the Council since 1919. Their Liberal and Conservative opponents, mirroring the national coalition of Lloyd George's Government, had formally joined forces in 1920 to form the Citizens' Association. Led by Clegg, it had a majority of Conservative councillors and its *raison d'être*, if not its total policy commitment, was twofold: to keep the socialists out of office and to keep the rates down. It neglected so many of the city's post war problems, including education, where two thirds of the 3000 children on the Manor estate still did not go to school at all, and where only 8% of the school age population went to secondary school. At the same time the Citizens' Association made sure that KES was adequately provided for and continued, even with reduced free places (only 12% by Gurner's time), to provide an excellent education for the middle class.

Farewell to the Founding Fathers

In one of the most famous occasions in the history of Sheffield City Council, the leadership of the Citizens' Association was voted off the Aldermanic Bench and literally picked up their papers and trooped off the dais, out of the Council Chamber and into political obscurity. The seven deposed aldermen included two men, who along with James Hichens, could rightly be said to be the founding fathers of King Edward VII School. Sir William Clegg, for a quarter of a century the Leader of the Liberal Party and then of the Citizens' Association, Chairman of the Education Committee and one of four or five genuine giants in Sheffield local government in the 20th Century, was followed out of the chamber on that November afternoon by Ald. Robert Styring, who for two decades had been the Chairman of KES Governors. For Clegg it was the last hurrah, but Styring did get back on to the Education Committee as a co-opted member, although he would never wield great influence again. Labour had won 29 seats in the 1926 elections against the Citizens' 18, and they used their majority amongst the councillors to rearrange the aldermanic bench and establish themselves in control of the Council for virtually every year till the end of the century. Ronald Gurner, just arrived from London, perhaps did not grasp immediately how this would affect his school, but he would have realised at once that he had lost two stalwart supporters. The new men were not only unproven but came from a social class whose real intentions, and competence to run the city, were unknown.

The crucial act that was to lead to confrontation between the Council and the school came almost immediately. In arranging the form and membership of the new committees, Labour abolished all the separate governing bodies of the secondary schools. Henceforth the Headteachers of the five council secondary schools would line up in the corridor of the LEA's Leopold St. offices on the day of the Higher Education Sub-Committee, then be wheeled in one by one to make a report, be cursorily questioned and then wheeled out again. One can assume the Headteachers of Firth Park G.S. and the Central School were not impressed by this treatment, but Gurner felt insulted and humiliated and in his own words *"settled into the trenches"* for a long battle. For KES the loss of the separate Governing Body —it had never really been independent, it just appeared so under Styring's rule – was of special significance. Without separate Governors, KES could not be a member of the Headmasters' Conference and would therefore lose its status as a public school. This was an unthinkable anathema to all involved with the school and Gurner had no difficulty in rallying parents and Old Edwardians to the school's defence. When he pressed the Councillors on whether or not it was their intention to change the status of the school, they were less than frank. Many amongst the school's staff and parents knew that KES had been a political football between the parties for almost all of its existence, with the play until now going all one way and Labour never scoring any goals. Now they were on the penalty spot and they were not going to miss their moment.

To make matters worse for Gurner, the Chairman of the sub-committee, now his de facto chairman, was not a leading politician as Styring and Clegg had been. He was the relatively new and junior member, Coun. R.H. Minshall, although the man pulling the strings, Coun. Ernest Rowlinson, now Leader of the Council and Chairman of the Education Committee, sat on that sub-committee and made sure Labour Group policy was carried out. Rowlinson was a remarkable man, the sort of Labour politician at another time that Gurner would have welcomed and worked with constructively. A railwayman turned union organiser, he had been an NCO in the trenches and would give

sound pragmatic leadership to Labour in Sheffield till his death in office in January 1941. He led a party that believed that municipal socialism was capable of making a big difference to working people's lives. Councils could achieve great changes in areas like housing and education and basic civic infrastructure, and in 1926, a few months after their "defeat" in the General Strike, Labour was eager to start. Maintaining a public school was not high on their agenda, but they had no real plans to change the status of the school they pejoratively called King Ted's. The route that KES parents feared they would travel was to turn the school into another all-free place secondary school like Central Boys School, or Firth Park G.S. Whilst this would have been politically logical, the Citizens' Association had left the incoming administration with large rates arrears, and Rowlinson and his Group needed to husband

Ernest Rowlinson in 1937 when he was Lord Mayor.

their resources to build new schools, not indulge themselves by reorganising KES. They could however indulge themselves in a little gesture politics that would cost the ratepayers nothing.

Abolition of the OTC

It had been part of Labour's Election Manifesto that if elected they would abolish King Edward's OTC and they announced that, as soon as possible, they would pass the necessary resolution to wind up the corps. They reflected the spirit of the times. The Locarno Treaty had just been signed in 1925, disillusionment with the League of Nations had not yet set in and they were a deeply pacifist Group, genuinely concerned that young boys should not be preparing for war. Gurner also soon found out that many councillors resented the snobbery that they felt was inherent in a corps for the training of potential officers. Here was an issue around which parents and old boys could rally. Meetings were held, letters and resolutions were sent to the Council, but this was one issue KES was never going to win. The Council's case was strengthened by some of Gurner's comments that the corps was in bad shape and needed considerable sharpening up. He was concerned about the casual attitude towards its financial records and asked the City Treasurer to institute an audit of the corps' accounts and, for good measure, because they also received public money, the Games, Library, and Magazine accounts as well. The latter three came out of the exercise with no problems but the corps accounts were a mess, nor could they account for all the equipment they had received from Northern Command. The new Headmaster, a former Major in the Rifle Brigade, was not impressed. In March 1927 the Education Committee formally abolished the OTC and insisted that every penny in the OTC account (Cadets had to pay 2/6d, the equivalent of 10.25p a year, to join) was paid back to the City Council.

The abolition of the OTC was not the issue that caused KES to be ejected from the Headmasters' Conference, but it was a high profile newspaper story that alerted other HMC schools to what was happening in Sheffield. Gurner dramatised his struggle with the Education Committee as one where the traditional "liberties" of a headmaster and his school were under flagrant arbitrary political attack for ideological purposes. The Council, in turn, argued that the school quite clearly belonged legally to them and they saw no reason why they should treat one school any differently from the rest. Gurner continued to browbeat the hapless Coun. Minshall, until the Council retaliated by passing a resolution that all future contact between headteachers and the Education Committee should be through Percy Sharp, the Chief Education Officer and not directly with the chairman of the sub-committee or the full Education Committee. Today that would not seem any great hardship and is in fact normal practice, but in the Twenties it was rightly interpreted as divorcing a headteacher from any direct say in the external affairs and even, when city-wide decisions were made, in the internal affairs of his school.

KES withdrawn from the HMC

Another Headmaster might have taken cover, waited for events to calm down and finessed a better solution for his school. Ronald Gurner was not such a man. He thrived on controversy and relished a scrap and he now fired off his heaviest salvoes. He wrote to the Headmasters' Conference and withdrew the school from membership. He must have been well beyond his authority to take such action unilaterally, but the HMC was one of those very English institutions that dealt theoretically with the person, i.e. the headmaster, rather than the school, and they replied with a very English response. He would be allowed to stay on the HMC in a personal capacity but the school would be removed from membership and future headmasters would not be invited to be members. He then arranged for questions to be asked in the House of Commons and this helped to create a mini *cause celebre* in the national press and arouse interest throughout the educational world. Cyril Norwood became the national spokesman for KES's cause and its wider implications. He was in effect sounding a clarion call against any future Labour controlled LEAs, led by working men with political agendas that did not sit easily with accepted practice about the independence of headmasters. The headmasters must also have felt a certain frisson that perhaps all big cities, in the highly charged political atmosphere of the mid-Twenties, would be won by socialists in the very near future.

Resignation.

In the summer term, fed up with the infighting or perhaps in a fit of pique, Gurner applied for the post of Headmaster of Whitgift School, the day public school in Croydon, and was appointed. He was well known and respected in south London because of his successful period at the Strand School. Moreover, his "principled" fight against "northern intransigence" had increased his reputation in London, rather than made them wary of his combative and restless nature. He had, of course, to work out his notice for another term, during which the Sheffield Education Committee would now have to find another Headmaster to take up the post at KES in January 1928.

"Blacked"

The battle though was not yet over. Whilst Gurner was taking his summer holidays in the Italian Alps, Norwood was continuing to lead the action inside the headmasters' own professional association. This resulted in KES being "blacklisted", which prevented any applications for the Head's position from amongst existing headteachers and deputies. This action must have seriously concerned the councillors because they would want to get the very best man for the post, and usually a school of KES's standing would expect to appoint a man who had already made a success of running another school. Whether that was their reason or not, in October the Education Committee reversed their decision on headmasters' access to the Sub-Committee Chairman, although they did not reconstitute the separate Governing Body until 1970, when KES had become a comprehensive school. Gurner claimed he had won a moral victory and his stand had defended the rights of headteachers everywhere. The Council now went ahead and appointed a new Headmaster who was currently an Assistant Master, thereby circumventing the blacklisting which the Headmasters' Association had imposed on the school.

Stanley Ronald Kershaw GURNER M.C. M.A. (1890-1939)
Headmaster of KES 1926-27

Ronald Gurner was the only Headmaster of KES who failed to complete at least a decade of service to the school. Despite serving only four terms as the Head, he did, however, make quite an impact, partly because of the dramatic events of that period and partly because of his complex personality.

Born in London, he was educated at Merchant Taylors' School, where he had an outstanding academic record, played three seasons for the First XV and was judged the best all round athlete in the school. Clearly he seemed at an early age to be someone who would make his mark in the world, and this promise was continued in his first two years at Oxford, where he was a classics scholar at St. Johns. He gained a First in Honour Moderations, won a University Latin Prize, but then suffered a severe depression in his final year and only ended up with an aegrotat degree.

This scuppered his chances of a post in the Indian Civil Service, and he took up part time teaching positions at Haileybury in 1912, before moving to Clifton in 1913. Some saw this breakdown at Oxford as evidence of a somewhat unstable character. Certainly, he seems to have been an impetuous man (he is reputed to have thrown out all of Hichens' files shortly after his arrival), who could be very domineering and radical in his actions, but who could be adversely affected by stress.

He gained a permanent post at Marlborough in September 1913 and returned there for a while after the war. In 1914 he was commissioned into the Rifle Brigade and served two years in the trenches before being wounded at Arras in 1917 by a sniper. He was shot through the brachial artery and was never expected to survive, but after six months' convalescence in England (when he wrote some war poems) he reported back for service and was sent to the Military Intelligence. There, amongst his other duties, he worked in the Propaganda Department, later serving as a Town Major in Belgium in 1918. He had won the M.C. at Arras, but he never returned to the front after his injuries and he suffered further severe depression as a result of his combat experience. In 1930 he wrote a novel, "Pass Guard at Ypres", which sold well and was a thinly disguised autobiography of his time as a junior officer in the Salient.

As if all this was not enough, he suffered the tragedy of his fiancée dying in the great influenza epidemic of 1918, and although he returned to Marlborough, he no longer found the exclusiveness of the "great" public schools congenial. He applied for the post of Headmaster of the Strand School, an L.C.C. school in Brixton, and at the age of thirty he was appointed. He also got married and soon his new wife gave birth to a son. He made quite a name for himself at the Strand School as a reformer, along with a reputation as a defender of day schools and a vocal critic of boarding schools, especially those of the extreme snobbish tendency. After six years he was ready for a move and was appointed to KES in spring 1926.

In the summer of 1927, after all the political controversy, he was approached by Cyril Norwood, now Headmaster at Harrow, to leave Sheffield and take up the vacant post at Whitgift School in Croydon. He was reluctant at first, but as he said in his autobiography, "I Chose Teaching", he had little sympathy for Sheffield and not much more for KES. He went to a school that was about to move into new premises at Haling Park, and appeared set up for the rest of his career in a prestigious boys' day school in his own city.

The story does not have a happy ending. He seems to have been regarded as a mixed blessing at best by his new colleagues, and later in the Thirties, during a severe depression brought on by a number of factors, including debt and drink, he took his own life in June 1939.

Gurner's life reads like the stuff of novels and indeed he wrote several himself. Apart from "Pass Guard at Ypres", he wrote a novel, "The Riven Pall", about a working class scholarship boy in a northern steel city called "Orechester", who went to a high-performing day school, then to Oxford, and ultimately gained success by inventing a new process that benefited the local steel and engineering industry. His other novels included, "The Day Boy" based on Strand School, "For the Sons of Gentlemen" (written under the pseudonym of Kerr-Shaw),and "Reconstruction" written in1937. All had a recurrent theme of educational progress and were vehicles for Gurner's current ideas on education.

Changes to school life

Whilst all the political excitement was filling much of Gurner's time, he was also overseeing a sea change in some of the internal institutions of the school. He had first of all to select a new second master and his choice fell on J.S. "Old Nick" Nicholas, the Senior Mathematics Master and a ferocious disciplinarian.

Gurner considered this appointment to be one of the best decisions he made during his time at KES. He could have looked for a replacement for Lloyd-Davies outside the school and brought in his own man, but he was certain enough of his own authority to appoint an insider who had been at the school since 1911, and who gave him total loyalty at what must have been a very difficult time.

Not only did he want to challenge the culture of examinations and tests that ran right through the school but he also wanted to devolve decision making where possible to staff members and to prefects. The latter were asked to sign up to the somewhat mawkish new Prefects' Pledge, while the former were all given the right to use the cane to enforce discipline. Gurner had little time for detentions, which were the usual punishment in Hichens' time, and preferred the quick administration of corporal punishment. He set out the regulations by which a master would send the offending boy to the school porter for the cane, then after logging the details in the punishment book he could administer the punishment with the porter, or another master, in attendance as a witness. To add to the banality of the occasion the porter often had a few practice swipes at a pillar in the Entrance Hall on his way to the classroom, and boys sometimes, with gallows humour, referred to the master who was the witness as the "referee".

THE PREFECTS' PLEDGE

Instituted by Ronald Gurner in the Autumn Term 1926
Administered on the platform at a morning assembly.

Headmaster: "Are you prepared, so far as in you lies, to serve this school, to promote its welfare by word and example, to strive for the preservation of its fair name and for its advancement, and to use your power and your influence among your fellows for this end?

Prefect to be: "I am."

Headmaster: "To you , who are now a prefect, a position of authority and trust is given. That you find to do right, do with all your might, using your power and influence for the sake of this your school, without favour and without fear."

Gurner found the boys conditioned to think that all their waking hours should be devoted either to work or games. He was on the side of those who thought a more reflective, spiritual, even more leisurely approach to education would produce the better rounded pupil, and he especially felt that the arts had only had a limited place in the life of the school in his predecessor's time. He helped to resurrect the school orchestra which had folded in 1914, and he encouraged a proper school play to be performed using only the boys as actors. Previously it was the practice to perform only excerpts from plays at Speech Day or on other school occasions, and the real dramatic productions in the school were undertaken by the Staff Dramatic Society. Short story prizes were instituted and more poems were encouraged in the restyled school magazine. In December 1927, the boys of the school produced an ambitious alternative Christmas edition of the school magazine, with fifty-two excellent pages of humour and parody, including short stories, poems, and caricatures in a style somewhere between Punch and P.G.Wodehouse. One could not imagine such a publication in Hichens' time and it further indicated how Gurner was relaxing the ethos and subtly changing the institutions of the school.

> ### An Extract from the Special 1927 Christmas Edition of the School Magazine
>
> *Sheffield Dec. 1927*
>
> *Sir*
>
> *I rejoice to hear that the Secondary Schools Sub-Committee have decided to put a stop to this terrible practice of allowing one school to make its own suet puddings. It has been the custom in the past to allow King Edward VII School to make suet puddings in its own kitchens, whereas the other secondary schools of our great city must have their puddings made in the kitchen of the Sub-Committee in Leopold St. It is time this class distinction was scrapped, and I hail this as a great advance in the progress of modern education.*
>
> *My only disappointment is that the School has not been put on a vegetarian diet and I hope this even greater blessing will follow with the establishment of vegetarianism as the creed of all the secondary schools of our City.*
>
> *Yours hopefully*
>
> *H.Clifford*

Gurner himself had written some poems during the war when convalescing and he was the author of several novels. One of them, *The Riven Pall*, based on the story of a boy at the school, contained his philosophy that talent from whatever social class should be given a chance. In this spirit he encouraged boys to go to the Duke of York's Camp in 1927, where public school boys could share camp life with boys from the slums already working in factories, and by sharing this experience class barriers somehow would be broken down. In a parallel move he encouraged former members of the OTC to join a new group called the Edwardian Service Corps; a group which ostensibly would undertake useful, if yet undefined, tasks in the less salubrious parts of the city. It survived beyond Gurner's period as Headmaster but never really got off the ground and it was the other major institution, the school's Scout Troop, which would fill that gap in the school's life created by the abolition of the OTC. Gurner had been very scornful of the suggestion, when it was first made in early 1927 by Labour councillors, that KES should replace the OTC with a scout group, but changed his mind when he lost the battle over the OTC and eventually, in June, encouraged the troop's formation under A.W. Gaskin, the Geography Master.

Like Hichens, who was awarded an honorary Doctor of Laws Degree by the University of Sheffield in 1927, Gurner regarded a lot of his young charges as rough diamonds, full of *Yorkshire grit,* but not known for their urbanity and grace, with some even outright uncouth *Tykes.* In his autobiography, *"I Chose Teaching",* he said that he was glad to leave Sheffield, but he honoured and respected the boys he had met at the school, especially those from poor backgrounds, often from families suffering from unemployment. Hard, tough and proud, they obviously left a permanent impression on him, and he acknowledged in his book that he learned more from them than he ever taught in return.

The boys of the school were genuinely sorry, if a little perplexed, to see him leave. Some of the changes he made were obvious improvements that all boys could see. He had got the Council to spend a mere £20 to make the swimming pool fit for use again, after being closed for most of the Twenties. He had acquired extra playing fields in Bents Green and he had shifted Speech Day to the Victoria Hall, so that every one of the 650 boys could be properly seated along with the staff and the parents and not be crowded on uncomfortable benches down the nearby corridors. They were also not likely to forget the morning assembly when, out of the blue, he devoted the whole proceedings to a detailed lecture on sex education, to the amazement of all and the acute embarrassment of many young innocents. All in all he had endeared himself to the boys of the school and almost all of them felt the keenness of the loss. He served eleven years as Headmaster at Whitgift, and then ended his life in tragic circumstances three months before the outbreak of the Second World War.

From the School Magazine.

THE SCHOLARD

A scholard was ther with his heyre brushd bak,
Of pomade and grece it noon did lack,
And al of his desyre and al his lust,
The Schole Certificate pass he must.
And al his langage was not Kinges English;
But slang wordes lyk bash and bysshe.
But strange to seyn at essays he was good,
Precis and paraphrase wel writ he could.
At cryket he excelled and at foot-bal;
In shouvelborde he was good with al.
Stoute he was and handsome it is soothe,
And ride upon a bike wel he kouthe.
Under his cote he wered gay and glad,
Though by his schole rules they were forbad.
But myrthe and jeste he set al biforn
And algat cleped was he Jones Minor.

H. C. H.   1927

CHAPTER NINE

THE RAMPANT LION

SPORT AT KING EDWARD VII SCHOOL 1905 –1939

By the time King Edward VII School was founded in 1905, organised games were so well established within the English educational framework that it would have been most unusual if KES had not embraced sport as a major element in the school's life. Almost all secondary schools followed the model of the oldest and most prestigious boarding schools. These schools during the previous one hundred years had moved from a position of hostility to casual and unauthorised recreation, played by boarders with too much time on their hands, to enthusiastic support of organised games. James Hichens, although no athlete himself, was a committed advocate of the cult of sport as one of the main pillars of the education and ethos of his new school. On several Speech Days he enlisted support from parents to encourage their sons, even when they showed no sporting aptitude whatsoever, to play one or more of the sports on offer at KES. In 1908 he finally made games compulsory in the school and only those boys with written permission from their parents to opt out of games could be excused.

Most parents would have been just as keen as the school for their boys to play sport. Apart from being an accepted part of middle class education, with all its claims for improving the manliness, character and physical well-being of the boys, Sheffield was a city with a great sporting tradition and it was a community that demanded achievement in sport. Yorkshire County Cricket Club had been formed in the Adelphi Hotel (approximately where the Crucible Theatre box office now stands) and Bramall Lane had remained the headquarters of the County Club until the end of the 19th Century, when it moved to Headingley. At the turn of the century United and Wednesday were amongst the leading football clubs in the country, with United having lifted the F.A. Cup in 1898 and 1902 and Wednesday winning the First Division Championship twice between 1902 and 1904.

More specifically relevant to KES was the success at sport enjoyed by Wesley College and SRGS. Wesley College, probably because they were a boarding school, were especially strong at football and cricket, rarely losing at either game to the local grammar schools. Perhaps though, an even stronger sporting antecedent of KES can be found in the Collegiate School, before their take-over in 1884. They eagerly embraced the new public school sporting ethos with great commitment and no little panache. It was Col. Sir Nathaniel Creswick, an old boy of this school, who was the founder of *The Sheffield Foot Ball Club* in 1857 and many of their early playing members were likewise Old Collegians. This club is the oldest football club in the world that still is in existence and in 1904, the year before KES was founded, had won the F.A. Amateur Cup at Bradford's Valley Parade ground. Some years later in 1881 a meeting of former pupils of the Collegiate School set up the Old Collegians' Cricket and Football Clubs. The Football Club went out of existence when they joined with the Sheffield Club in 1887 because they were competing for the same pool of players. However the Cricket Club, under its founder H.B. Willey, continued to prosper and, after playing at several grounds, settled down at Abbeydale Park in 1921 and became a member of the Yorkshire League. Ironically the Old Edwardians' C.C. moved to the same ground in the early Nineties and, with the numbers of players dwindling, amalgamated with Collegiate C.C. in 2001.

In the pre-1914 period KES were keen competitors but not world-beaters. The main winter sport was, of course, football. Always the association code at KES in the first half of the century, and the school's team was up and running within a month of the school's first term starting, despite being quartered at Leopold Street in the middle of town. On October 4th 1905 the School beat the Masters 3-1 and then three days later they beat Mr. Lewis's XI, probably the same set of masters, 5-2. Both games were played at Whiteley Woods where the SRGS had played their matches but which the school had not yet decided to adopt as their school grounds. Anyone familiar with that extraordinary playing field, which could accommodate five football pitches but had a cricket wicket that appeared to have been designed by Monty Python, can understand why they hesitated to move there until they had exhausted all other options. It was one of the school's continual problems that it had no vast expanse of playing fields immediately outside the building as Abbeydale, High Storrs or Ecclesfield schools had provided for them at a later date. The Close may have sufficed for Wesley College, and KES Juniors played their football and cricket matches there, but it was too narrow for serious football and had ridiculously short boundaries for cricket. After viewing alternatives, the school somewhat reluctantly agreed in 1907 to develop Whiteley Woods as their sports ground, and a Pavilion was built on site in 1908. It may have been an inconvenient, if attractive, location but at least it wasn't the glacial heights of Castledyke, where later generations of Edwardians were condemned to play some of their games.

The first football season ended with a narrow margin of wins over losses. Six wins, five losses and one draw, and a fixture list that suited the social pretensions of the new school. Out went the matches with the local grammar schools Retford G.S., Rotherham G.S. and Barnsley G.S. and in came Pocklington and Bootham, while ties were strengthened with other public schools like Mount St. Mary's, Worksop College and Nottingham High School. The latter school was the football powerhouse of its day and KES regularly took a beating home and away. In November 1907 the school found themselves 7-1 down at half time, but Nottingham had obviously not yet got into their stride because they added another thirteen goals in the second half to run out 20-1 winners. Good news then that Nottingham, like Pocklington, Worksop and Mount St. Mary's would sooner or later change to Rugby Union (as was the fashion amongst the public schools early in the Twentieth Century), as "Soccer" became increasingly dominated by working class players and supporters. KES continued to play the round ball game, as was appropriate in a city that had made such a large contribution to the association game. The number of men's teams that appeared on the fixture list, offering very competitive opposition, also strengthened their resolve. Apart from the regular fixtures against the Masters, eagerly

KES Football Team 1907-08 Season. The first season at Whiteley Woods.
L.C. Kirk Captain.

awaited by the bloodthirsty, was an Old Boys' match and games against the University, the Falcons, the Grasshoppers and the Sheffield Club.

Not that KES was without its stars. R.C. Maples, their centre forward in that first season, was a regular goal scorer and in the end of season pen pictures in the school magazine (which reported each match in the fullest detail) he was characterised as a player who was: *"The best forward, very fast. We hope to hear more of him in the future"* Prophetic words indeed because Maples soon was to get his Blue and play four seasons for Oxford, and twice represented England against France in an Amateur International match. Later, just for good measure, he picked up an M.C. fighting with the Canadians in the war. Not so lucky in the appraisal of his performance was Dufty, the team's left half. He was judged to be *"Very weak in tackling, kicking and feeding his forwards".* One wonders why he bothered to turn up, although he went on to Sheffield University and qualified as a doctor and perhaps put sporting achievements behind him. The best season in the pre-war period was 1911-12 when under the captaincy of G.I.Paine they posted a very good set of results. Eleven matches were won out of fourteen with only three defeats and, to add to it, the Second XI had a 100% winning record. They also defeated Nottingham H.S. for the first time and achieved it in some style when they won the home game by nine goals to nil. The one drawn match that season was a nine-all draw against the Municipal Officers; clearly in those early days defences had a great deal to learn about tactics and strategy. It was also the last season the school played in the old white strip with its rampant lion badge. From now on the school colours would be blue and white stripes of varying width, and the successful seasons immediately before the war demonstrated that KES football had come of age.

Cricket was slower getting started in the new school and there were no matches played against outside opposition until July 1907 when the KES team travelled to Worksop College and were outplayed. However in the peculiar manner of the summer game they managed a draw, holding out at 50 for 9 in reply to Worksop's 152 all out. A full set of fixtures was not arranged until 1908, when the team made a reasonable start, winning four out of nine games finished. The reason for the delay was simply because there was no wicket for them to play on. There had been net practice in the corner of the Close in 1906 when most of the area was still a builder's yard, but home matches had to wait until the Whiteley Woods wicket was bedded in and the pavilion finished. Cricket in that first decade of the century was the still the national game and still the main sport of the public schools. Although the Australians regularly deflated England's conceit, the game was

seen as quintessentially English and a reflection of the national character. In Yorkshire, of course, the game had mythical status as Lord Hawke still ruled the County Club, and the two best all-rounders in the world, Hirst and Rhodes, dominated their opponents in the county championship. Despite this Yorkshire pedigree some of KES's early efforts with the bat left much to be desired. In that first full season in 1908 they were regularly out for less than 60, but they did have their better days. L.C.Kirk, Captain of Cricket and Football, scored a couple of fifties and ended up with an average just under thirty, whilst G.F.Stones took 29 wickets in the season and scored 147 runs with the bat.

To improve performances the school took on a former professional cricketer as their coach and groundsman. J.W.Smith had played cricket for Kent and he was to become a well beloved, honoured and respected legend to

J.W. Smith - Cricket Coach and Groundsman 1907-35

the boys of KES who came under his tutelage in the next thirty years. Always referred to as Smith, he followed a well worn path of ex-professionals who found a quiet haven after their playing years were over at an accommodating school. There they could continue to participate in "*the noble game*" and get paid an adequate sum for a working man (KES paid £65 per annum for a start) and stay out of the mine, the factory or farm for the rest of their lives. Amongst his tasks was the upkeep of the horse that pulled the mower and cost KES £9 to buy, with £3 for its fodder during that first year. Smith also doubled as the football coach and referee and, although each team would have a master in charge, they would come and go, whilst he was the member of staff whose opinions really counted.

By the 1910 season the school was performing better against some formidable opponents. The fixture list included some of the major day schools in Yorkshire,

The KES Cricket Team, Season 1913.
*Back Row: J.C. Scott (Master i/c) **, W.P. Taylor **, A.E. Budd, R.H.B. Mathews **,*
*J.J.Kay, E.M.Carr **, A.E. Furness, J.W. Smith (Coach):*
*Sitting: F.M. Marrs **, G.B. Hill, F. Ambler (Capt.), H.M. Hibbert **:*
*In Front: A.E. Bagnall, C.L.M. Battersby ***
*** Denotes Killed in Action 1914-18 War.*

including Bradford G.S. and Leeds G.S., both of whom played Rugby Union in the winter season, and for the first time they beat the Masters, the Old Boys and the Sheffield Clergy, all of whom could field useful sides. To celebrate, the school designed a cricket blazer of blue flannel with broad white piping for those who had won their colours. They can be seen to this day in the old team photos in the entrance hall, the very essence of the casual, almost arrogant, confidence of the Edwardian "golden summer" sporting era. There could still be some bad days. In June 1912 the school was dismissed for 25 against Nottingham H.S. but in the next match ran up 142 against the Old Boys with Fred Ambler, their best batsman, later a stalwart member of the Old Edwardians' C.C., scoring 53. The following year Ambler scored 96 against Nottingham as KES took its revenge for the previous season's debacle, but it was not until the 1915 season that a boy scored the first century for the school. He was F.M. Marrs, another all rounder who was Captain of Football as well as Captain of Cricket. He scored 106 not out against Nottingham H.S. and ended the shortened season with an average of 77. It was to be his last season of cricket, because, like so many of the young KES sportsmen, 2nd Lt. Marrs, of the R.M.C. Sandhurst and the Worcestershire Regt., was killed in action in 1917.

Gymnastics

Gymnastics held a more important position in the sporting life of the school in the decade before 1914 than it would do in later years. It was in effect the school's third sport after cricket and football. The gymnastic tradition had developed out of drill and fitness instruction which public schools championed at the end of the 19th Century. Both Wesley College and SRGS had drill instructors who were retired sergeants, the only qualified experts available in Britain who could instruct schoolboys in P.T. and Gymnastics. King Edward's first sergeant instructor was Sgt. Thompson, who had endeared himself to his charges until his long illness and death in April 1909. He had set the foundations for P.T. on the curriculum and competitive gymnastics for the enthusiasts after school.

The first house competition was held in March 1907 and Haddon were the winners, with the competitors tested on the horizontal bar, the rings, the ladder, the parallel bars, the vaulting horse and the ropes. It was to the credit of each of the six houses that they could turn out a team of eight intrepid boys with enough skill and pluck to represent them. The first inter-school match was in March 1908 when Pocklington sent a team of eight gymnasts to compete against KES in the school's gymnasium. Unfortunately the East Riding school was too experienced for KES on that day and ran out winners by 516 to 400 points.

The school's gymnastic team was transformed when, in 1909, Sgt. James Costello, a warm-hearted, hot tempered Irishman, late of the Hampshire Regiment, who had instructed for five years at Marlborough, took over from Thompson. Like J.W. Smith he became something of a school institution, and matches now took place on an annual basis against Leeds G.S. and Bradford G.S. as well as Pocklington. By 1910 they were defeating all three schools, with J.G.Twigg, who was also the school Football Captain, the star of these teams, regularly gaining the highest individual score in an inter-school match. The gym was particularly popular amongst younger boys and this encouraged Costello to branch out by offering boxing instruction as well. After initial enthusiasm with forty aspiring boxers signing up, the *"noble art"* waned in popularity, as it did in later years when attempts were made to resurrect it. "Wally" Mease, the master who was responsible for safety in the gym, was amazed at how Costello could coax boys into *"the most adventurous gymnastic performances, hurtling through space over a lengthwise horse with a double somersault for good measure"*. The school eight would always be on display when there were visitors, or open days, and the exercises were breathtaking and would have done justice to professional acrobats.

After winning eight consecutive inter-school matches over three years they were finally beaten by Leeds G.S. in 1913. Although KES always had some good individual gymnasts, the house competition paradoxically declined as the school eight strengthened, and there was always a shortage of suitable replacements when star performers left the school. Costello himself left in 1914 and rejoined the army, despite being over fifty. The army was desperate for P.T. instructors and he was promoted to Sgt. Major, served at Aldershot throughout the war and was awarded the MSM. He returned in 1919 and was made a full member of staff, paid on the new Burnham scale, before retiring in 1926 and dying, much mourned, two years later. How he would have rejoiced to know that in the 1970s the school produced two gymnasts who competed for Britain in the European Championships. He would have been even more amazed to discover they were both girls.

Other sports

Four new fives courts were built for the new school in 1907 to replace the derelict ones left by Wesley College and were very well used on a casual basis by boys at the school. Two of the courts were built to the simple Rugby fives pattern and two were designed with the buttress and steps that were the essential feature of the Eton game. Fives, probably so called because of five fingers on the hand, was another quintessential public school game that started as a casual hand ball game using the wall of the school buildings and then developed accepted rules. Fast and skilful, the brave player played without a protective glove, and house matches and a school open championship were quickly arranged and both flourished in the period up to 1914. KES never found anyone with whom they could play competitive matches before the war, even though invitations were sent out to the clergy and officers' messes in the area, until eventually in 1911 the masters got up a team of four to play the school. The first inter-school matches had to wait until 1927 when KES lost to both Retford G.S. and Nottingham H.S.

Competitive swimming matches were, however, arranged with Worksop College but always at their open air pool, never at home despite the existence of KES's own algae covered swimming baths, also inherited from Wesley College but not upgraded. The first inter-school match was in July 1907, with KES winning the swimming races 5-1 but losing the water polo by one goal to nil. That remained the pattern for this one annual fixture until the war, with KES only once managing a victory at water polo but never losing in the races. It was not easy to commandeer the Glossop Road Baths, for a formal organised Swimming Sports, so those occasions had to wait until the end of the Twenties, when it would become one of the main events on the school's sporting calendar. However they could find enough time and space at the Baths to have a house knockout competition once the war had started.

One major sporting cum social event was the Annual School Athletic Sports. These were first held in April 1908 and usually at the end of the Lent term, when they often experienced indifferent weather. A track was marked out at Whiteley Woods and a full competitive track and field programme was held very much along the pattern that had been established at SRGS and Wesley College. Marquees were set up and the band of the Yorkshire Dragoons gave a carnival air to the occasion, whilst the final prize-giving, always by a lady, usually the Lady Mayoress or the Mistress Cutler, was an occasion for no little ceremony. L.C. Kirk was the first champion athlete and amongst his triumphs that day was the open 100 yards in $11\frac{2}{5}^{th}$ seconds, whilst H.E. Truelove completed the mile in 5 minutes 11 seconds, fair performances on a grass track. The occasion had its lighter side with sack and wheelbarrow races, throwing the cricket ball and races for members of the choir, the OTC and the Old Boys. The band members were also invited to take part in a Band 220 yard race, which usually attracted no more than two competitors. The whole programme was rounded off by a house tug of war, a big event in the first half of the Twentieth Century but one that is rarely seen today.

The school produced some competitive athletes and in 1912 sent a representative team to the Public School Sports Meeting held at Chelsea's ground at Stamford Bridge. Here G.I. Paine won the quarter mile in 55 seconds and came second in the long jump, whilst H. Burkett came second in the half mile with a time of 2 minutes 7 seconds. They were both school champion athletes, Paine, who was the Senior Prefect and Captain of Football, won the title in 1912 and Burkett won it in 1913 when he was the individual winner of the Open 100 and 220yards, the quarter mile and the long jump.

There were no competitive inter-school matches before 1914 in athletics, but many of the star performers also turned out for the annual cross country match against Worksop College. Situated in the foothills of the Pennines, Whiteley Woods invited cross country running along the Mayfield Valley, up to Ringinglow or, if you were particularly unfortunate, on to the moors towards Stanage. The first match against Worksop was on their territory in 1911, when the hosts won easily in the gentler byways of the Dukeries. In the return match in 1912 they found the steep valley and moorland course a new and difficult experience, and KES triumphed, as they would continue to do in both the home and away fixtures. Cross country running over the years was one sport at which KES was pre-eminent. From 1907, when Haddon won the first House Cross Country event, both the juniors, with their paper chase hare and hounds races, and the seniors, running for their houses, would become very familiar with the wild western outskirts of the city built on the seven hills.

For those who wanted more sport, there was croquet for the boarders on the lawns at Lynwood and the OTC fielded a shooting eight, which in 1913 trounced the University's team and later, in the same year, came seventh out of fifty schools in the Country Life Schools' Shooting Competition. The suggestion that the school should play Lacrosse was, perhaps not surprisingly, turned down by the Games Committee because the sporting calendar had become too crowded.

THE TWENTIES

Sport at the school was administered and controlled by the Games Committee. This all-powerful body was always chaired by the Headmaster, who could veto anything of which he disapproved. The membership included masters such as Humphrey Watkins who ran senior teams, "Toby" Saville representing the Junior School and boys who were school captains and house representatives. They decided what KES should play and, more importantly, whom they should not play. In the early 1920s they turned down invitations to play cricket from works teams at Firth's and T.W.Ward's, but agreed to play the local grammar schools at Soccer after so many of their original "posh" opponents had opted for Rugby Union. So it was that by 1922 matches were arranged with Retford G.S., Chesterfield G.S. and Central School. Rotherham G.S. were offered a Second XI game for a start and surprisingly they accepted this patronising indignity, before proving they were worthy opponents and being translated to full 1st XI matches at Football and Cricket. Fixtures against Firth Park G.S. followed later in the decade, and also Doncaster G.S. before they too turned to Rugby Union.

The Games Committee had a variable remit and among its decisions there were ones to create and name the new Sherwood House, turn down a request in 1922 by A.W. Gaskin to form a scout troop and, during the war, decide to send £50 from the games fund to Sheffield POWs in Germany. They also scrubbed all outside matches during 1917 and 1918 as a war economy measure and also rationed the teas at Whiteley Woods as a small contribution to the allied victory.

At Cricket and Football the school first XI's in the Twenties usually posted a reasonable set of results. If they had been in a league they would have almost always ended up in the middle of the table for most seasons in that decade. KES sides were not invincible but they usually had the better of the results against school sides. About a third of their fixtures were against adult sides and these they found more difficult. The season at both sports started with matches against XIs selected by "Toby" Saville and usually these teams were much too good for the school. So also were the Old Edwardians, whose sides often included some of the very best footballers and cricketers who had recently been at the school. On the other hand the School usually beat the masters at both games and shared honours with the University and the local football clubs.

There were of course some vintage years when enough old colours stayed on, promising youngsters came through and the school sides flourished. In the 1923 –24 Football Season the school was unbeaten in all their inter-school matches, sustaining only one defeat, against the Falcons F.C., whom they beat in the return match. The final tally was thirteen matches won, one lost and four drawn including the two games against Central

School, already playing their games at High Storrs, although it would be another decade before their new buildings would be completed on the same site. These games were real derby matches and it was reported to the Games Committee that feelings had run high both on and off the pitch and that many spectators from both schools had been guilty of unseemly behaviour during the match. Other difficulties that season included two burglaries at the Whiteley Wood pavilion and a cancelled match against Bootham School at York because of the railway strike. Amongst the stars of that season was a fifth former who was to play for the school for three years. H.W. Thompson was a centre half of commanding presence who later got a Blue at Oxford, founded Pegasus F.C. after the 1939-45 War and later, as Prof. Harold Thompson FRS, became the Chairman of the Football Association in 1976.

1924 was a better than average year at cricket as well. Nine wins were recorded, with only three defeats and two drawn games. However the most impressive performance of those years was the batting of L. Burdekin, the school cricket captain in 1925. Opening the batting, he scored over five hundred runs in twelve innings and these included two centuries against the University and Collegiate C.C. and an 87 against the masters. To score a century in school cricket is quite an achievement; to get a couple in a season was quite remarkable and no one achieved it at KES again.

The improved reputation of the school's football team after the 1923-24 season brought the acceptance of a fixture in the November 1924 against Repton, arguably the most élite public school in the north midlands. Colonel Morgan Owen, a former international who was in charge of Repton football, extended the invitation to KES but only offered them a second team fixture. Instead of rejecting it out of self-respect the school eagerly took up the offer. They won that first game at Repton by two goals to nil but over the next two decades they would rarely defeat their illustrious, albeit "A" team, opponents. The fixture demonstrated the gulf there still was on the sports field between a top ranking boarding school, with superb sports facilities and limitless practice time, and an ambitious day school. KES players were also amazed to see at the post match tea that their opponents had changed back into frock coats and white ties, which was still the code of dress at Repton until the Second World War.

For the rest of the decade school teams at both games won at least half their matches every year. Occasionally there would be an extraordinary result, as there was in October 1926 when centre forward Stuart Parker scored 14 goals in a 17-3 win over the Bankers' XI. Altogether he scored 60 goals that season and set a school record that seemed unlikely to be beaten, before he went up to Cambridge and gained a Football Blue. In December 1928 Parker, playing at centre forward for Cambridge, faced Thompson the Oxford centre half whose job it was to mark him out of the game. It was the first time KES had had an O.E. on opposite sides in the Varsity match, although quite a few old boys had represented both Universities at football. Perhaps the most famous of them at that time was Alec Russell, the huge goalkeeper who played for Cambridge, who not only was also a Half Blue for swimming but was selected to represent England Amateurs at Football in 1925 and was awarded an Amateur International Cap. It was a feature of sport at KES in the first two decades that some of the best players were also amongst the school's leading scholars, and their appearance in Oxbridge teams in the Twenties meant that they were playing in a very high standard of sport. The Rugby Union and Cricket sides of both universities competed with first class club or county opposition and were regarded as part of the top echelons of English sport, whilst the Football team played a number of professional league sides and could compete at that level. However, no Old Edwardian ever gained a Cricket Blue or played in a Varsity team that regularly supplied some of the best batsmen to the England Test sides.

There were many Old Edwardians in the sports teams of Sheffield University, still virtually the only other university that old boys attended. Apart from regular contributions to the football and cricket teams, KES supplied the University Captains of Hockey (S.E.Bain), Rifle Shooting (R.E.Ward) and Harriers (W.M.Rees) at varying times in the 1920s. As happened at Oxbridge, some O.E.s tried other sports when they went up to their university that they had been unable to play at school. S.Newsam played Rugby Union for Sheffield and Williams-Gardner got a county trial for Yorkshire at Hockey, but perhaps the most famous O.E. sportsman of this post-war period was the redoubtable Rev. Edwin Berrisford DSO, M.C. Like many freshmen at Oxbridge, he tried his hand at rowing and soon after leaving school in 1910 was stroking the Queen's College boat. On returning to Oxford from the war, he became the President of the O.U. Boat Club, the most prestigious sporting position in the University. At a time when the University Boat Race was as important to the national sporting calendar as the F.A. Cup Final or the Grand National, Berrisford was poised to stroke the Oxford Eight in the 1920 Boat Race. He became nationally famous when he stepped down and selected in his place another student whom he judged to be a better oarsman. His self-sacrifice was eulogised in a leader in the Times and one cannot help feeling that the whole story of his early life is just waiting for a British director, and a Hollywood producer, to give us a sequel to the film "Chariots of Fire".

A couple of dozen boys in 1923 found a very productive way of avoiding the "tyranny" of compulsory Wednesday afternoon games. For eight months they excavated the cloisters of Beauchief Abbey which had been recently purchased by the father of a boy at the school. What Henry VIII had put asunder the KES amateur archaeologists resurrected from under the ground and their excavations caused no little interest amongst the archaeological fraternity. Photographs of their work appeared in the London papers and the Hunter Society visited their site and pronounced their gratitude and congratulations. In typical KES fashion they took away some of the medieval cement found in the diggings and put it through analysis to ascertain its component parts. Then, not just content with exhuming the cloister walls, the boys involved also uncovered the altar and the tomb of Robert Fitzranulph, the founder of the Abbey in 1183, when they excavated the eastern end of the chancel.

Beauchief Abbey, or at least its adjacent Golf Course, was the venue three years later for a one-off school sporting event that might have become a permanent fixture if Ronald Gurner had remained at the school. In the spring of 1927 seven boys challenged the masters, augmented by Mrs. Gurner, to match-play over 18 holes. The match was halved when the Headmaster himself, coming in last, produced sparkling form on the back nine holes to halve his game and square the match. It was surprising that KES did not run a golf team to play the usual opponents. Although very few schools owned their own course like Ampleforth, enough boys with a low handicap must have played regularly on their fathers' courses to run a useful school team.

There was however plenty of sporting activity and the new Headmaster, Richard Graham, was an accomplished alpine climber and regularly supported school teams from the boundary or the touchline. The Athletic Sports continued to be one of the major events of the year, now under the direction of Sydney Carter who would be in charge for over thirty years. In 1929 he brought the Sports back to the Close, where the sprint races were run on asphalt and longer distances partly on grass. The sun uncharacteristically shone on the event and performances matched other years, but within seven years they were back at Whiteley Woods and there the event remained until athletes demanded proper facilities, like Woodbourn or the Don Valley Stadium.

Cartoon of KES Personalities - Athletics Day 1930

That same year saw the first Swimming Sports held in October 1929 at Heeley Baths. There had been house competitions fitted in with general swimming at Glossop Road Baths but here was a proper sports event that soon became a major fixture and would in seven years time be held in the superb new baths in the south east corner of the Close. In fact the promise that the baths would be built had become a regular litany of councillors at Speech Days in the early Thirties. Given the severity of the depression, the council's delivery of the pool in 1936, albeit not for KES's exclusive use, is nothing short of amazing and shows how relations with the Labour controlled Council had improved under Richard Graham.

Whilst neither the football nor the cricket team was invincible in the second half of the decade, the cricket team tended to post better seasonal results than the football team. The outstanding sportsman of that period was a boy who had been a boarder at Tewkesbury from the age of four until he joined KES when he was 16. C.R. "Bob" Wall was Captain of Football and Captain of Cricket and was a major contributor to the success of both those teams at the end of the Twenties. Relatively short in stature, he first played for the school in 1926 as a fiercely competitive half back, moving to full back in later seasons. As an opening bat he almost always got the school off to a good start and although he never achieved a century at school he knocked up quite a few fifties. During the Thirties he became a Yorkshire swimming champion and was occasionally twelfth man for Yorkshire C.C.C. If the county team had not been so strong under the captaincy of A.B. Sellers, he could very well have been a regular member of the Yorkshire side in the years immediately before the war.

THE THIRTIES

The Thirties were the best decade yet for sport at KES. The school teams were very competitive in all the sports they played at inter-school level and more boys were involved in playing, or competing, for their house teams than ever before. At football, the school had periods in the Thirties when they were invincible in matches against school opponents, and this high standard was backed up by a house football competition that included three teams per house playing in three leagues. The Games Committee still set the framework for the sports curriculum, still deciding who and what would be played, but under the chairmanship of the Headmaster, they were led by a relatively young man who was not only keen on sport but still a very competent performer. In 1932 he scored a stylish 52 runs in the School v Staff match and in 1937, at the age of 44, he turned out at right half in the Staff football team which beat the School 4-1. In swimming, the school had one outstanding performer, Michael Taylor, who before the decade was out would represent his country at the Empire Games and the World Student Games and who would win Yorkshire men's titles whilst still at school. All O.E.s of that generation remember another group of outstanding school footballers, cricketers and athletes, the Gray brothers, the three Sivils, Frank Melling, the Fulford brothers and Jimmy Settle, who overlapped with each other to produce such strong KES teams between 1933 and 1938.

The decade opened with the football and cricket teams performing much as before, producing results that usually left them with a winning season without having achieved anything too remarkable overall. True, there were some outstanding individual performances, such as the century scored by H.T.Bateman in 1930, for which achievement he was awarded a new bat by the Games Committee, a regular practice for outstanding performances. Douglas Parker, following the family tradition, scored 40 goals from the centre forward position in the 1930-31 season and then, like his brother, W. Stuart Parker, he went on to get a Blue for Cambridge. There were days when everything went right and the opposition was beaten out of sight, like the 9-0 win over Central School in the 1932-33 football season, or G.Tuft's captain's knock of 92 against new opponents QEGS Wakefield, who were one of the most formidable Rugby Union schools in the county, but who were regularly overwhelmed at cricket by KES.

The Athletic Sports, now regularly held in the inspiring, if cramped, setting of the Close were dominated by N.L. "Taffy" Evans of Sherwood House, who was the Champion Athlete for three years, 1930-32, and carried off all the distance titles from Quarter Mile to the Mile as well as some of the sprints. He was challenged in the track events by Gordon Nornable, who regularly won the 100 yards and vied with Evans for the 220 yards title. Evans went on to Jesus College, Oxford, on a Meyricke Exhibition, only open to boys of Welsh extraction, whilst Nornable went to work for the City Council and later would have a most daring, if unusual, war.

This was the period when Lynwood House dominated the Athletics Sports and almost everything else sporting as well. In the twenty years between 1928 and 1948 Lynwood won the Athletic Sports twelve times, with a run of three consecutive wins in the years 1932-34. At that time they also won the House Cricket League (1932), the Football Competition (1931-33), the Fives Championship (1932-33) and they won the Melling Cup for the House Swimming Relay four consecutive times from 1932 until 1935. Their victories in the Swimming Championships in the mid-Thirties were almost assured, because Michael Taylor swam for Lynwood and from the age of 14 he was outpacing all other swimmers in the school. In 1934 and 1935 he won every race for which he was entered and at the same time, whilst still at school, he was breaking the Yorkshire Men's Quarter Mile record and the Sheffield Men's 100 yards record. The school had little to do with this success because they didn't have a proper pool of their own at the time; instead Taylor did his training with local coaches at the city's swimming baths.

THE TROPHY CABINET

Such was Lynwood's domination of the other houses that consequently their trophy cabinet was full. The probably apocryphal story recalls that they asked trophy-impoverished houses if they could use their empty cabinets to display all their cups and shields.

These cabinets, one for each house, had been put up in the Assembly Hall on the instruction of the Games Committee in 1928. They stood in a row above the bronze plaque to the Great War dead, on the front of the balcony where the organ now stands, and every boy in the hall at Morning Assembly could take pride in his House's achievements or squirm in mortification if the cupboard was bare.

Their positioning underlines how seriously Houses and House sporting competitions were taken in former times at KES.

As for Lynwood's request, not surprisingly the other Houses did not readily appreciate it and Lynwood had to pack their trophies into their allotted space as best they could.

In time every House would have its day but Lynwood's success was largely due to the extra motivation that "the Man", F.T. Saville, inspired in his House.

THE INVINCIBLES (1933-36)

THE KES Football Team Season 1935-6

Between September 1933 and November 1936 the KES 1st Team were unbeaten against any school. This achievement was recognised in a rather unusual manner when the Ardath Tobacco Co. included the school team of 1935-36 in a pack of cigarette cards that they produced that year. The KES team, captained by Jimmy Settle, was card No. 60 in a pack that included the top teams of the day, Arsenal and Everton, the recent 1935 Cup-winners, Sheffield Wednesday, and the 1936 Cup runners-up, Sheffield United.

The most successful side of the Thirties was the 1933-34 team captained by Harold Pearson, who bettered the performance of the 1923-24 team and won 20 matches out of 21 played. Their only defeat was against a men's club side and they returned 13 wins out of 13 matches in their inter-school games. Amongst the 181 goals they scored were a record

63 by Bob Gray, who passed Stuart Parker's record of 60 goals in the 1926-27 season, and a captain's contribution of 45 goals from Pearson. The best win of the year was on Armistice Day when they finally defeated Repton 2nd XI again, by 3-1, and they went one better the following year and beat them 5-2. Nevertheless they had to wait until Dr. Barton's time in 1947 before they were accepted onto Repton's 1st team fixture list and the schools could play on equal terms. In such a season as 1933-34, Pearson's team had to rack up some big scores and Derby School took an 18-0 hammering and old local rivals, Central School were beaten 14-0 and 13-2 in home and away games.

This led Eric Simm, who was the master in charge of the 1st XI, to question in the Games Committee whether KES should, instead of home and away fixtures, play only one game a year against local schools, and thereby seek out more "glamorous" opponents. The move was deflected by a team member on the committee, whose father taught at Central School, who pointed out the importance of the "King Teds" fixture to local secondary schools and how such treatment would be resented within the city. Simm was a History teacher but he guided the successful football teams through these years, especially after he had introduced the KES defence to the revolutionary three back system pioneered by Arsenal. Another of his innovations was to bring in a professional coach, almost unheard of even at professional clubs, where training often included little more than a few laps of the pitch and a friendly practice game. Fred Spikesly was a former International left winger who had served Wednesday well. When he arrived at the school, in a bowler hat and his best suit, and was introduced to the team, he took off his bowler, placed it meticulously on the floor, and proceeded to demonstrate ball control using his hat. He was a considerable influence on the high standards of the KES team of those years and he brought the best out of some talented youngsters. Eric Sivil was one of the best full backs ever to play for the school and he recalls how the best behaviour on the field was expected from the KES sides. He remembers being hauled into the Headmaster's study on a Monday morning to answer for a particularly clumsy tackle the previous Saturday and he got the message that sport at the school was not just about winning. Frank Melling played inside left in these teams and he would go on to play for the Corinthian Casuals, score two goals for Wednesday in an 8-2 wartime "derby" defeat of United, and captain the UAU team after the war. More famous locally for his 21 years as a committee member of Yorkshire C.C.C., he also served for many years on the Board of the "Blades" and, until his recent death, was still involved with Sheffield United Cricket Club at Tinsley. When the key members of that team moved on in the summer of 1936, John Fulford, a free scoring centre forward, played an increasingly important role in the next season (he scored eight goals in the defeat of Huddersfield Amateurs) before leaving and also playing for the Corinthian Casuals. In 1940, whilst awaiting call-up, he was on the books of Sheffield United, one of the first O.E.s to play professional football, albeit during the wartime competition.

Athletics, Cross Country, Fives and Boxing

Whilst Cricket and Football were the school's major team sports, Athletics was taken very seriously in the school in the Thirties, although the competition was almost all internal, with no fixtures against other schools as in earlier years. The Champion Athletes in the middle and late Thirties were the same boys who performed so well at other sports. Bob Gray won the award in 1934 and 1935 and then John Fulford also held it for two years before leaving. His younger brother, David Fulford, carried on the family tradition and was Champion Athlete in 1938, before joining up in the peacetime RAF. The following year, when still under 16, Graham Parsons won all the main open track events from the 100 yards to the mile and he was subsequently entered for two events at the 1939 Public School Sports at the White City. He won the Champion's Award again in 1940, despite being only able to enter four events, under a new rule of the Games Committee designed to stop people like him dominating every track race. Nevertheless he won all his four events, including breaking the school's quarter mile record that had stood for 27 years.

The only outside threat to KES's reputation at Cross Country came from the Old Edwardians, as no school was brave enough to challenge KES in courses along the Mayfield Valley and up to Ringinglow. Similarly at Fives there were few schools who could regularly put out a competitive four to play KES. In 1931 the school won all their matches against Nottingham H.S., Retford G.S., Leeds University and Heath G.S., but after the departure of Stuart Whitehouse, to become the Headmaster of Wigan G.S., the number of inter-school matches declined until restored by Gordon Cumming when he returned as a master in 1937. Nonetheless, during the Thirties there was a flourishing house competition and an annual individual knockout competition, held always using the Rugby Fives courts. In 1935, Chesterfield G.S. challenged the school to a match at the more complicated Eton Fives. Hopes that this might be a regular fixture seem to have been dashed by the school suffering a whitewash by 12-0 games.

Boxing, which had had a brief popularity at KES before the Great War, reappeared as a school sport in 1934. This time it was Charles Unsworth, one of the History staff, who, seeing there was a considerable demand for the sport, set up sessions twice a week and then organised the school's first Boxing finals in July. This eight bout event drew a large audience and there were fights at all weights from fly-weight to light heavy, including three weights, beetle-weight, mosquito-weight and gnat-weight, that even if unknown to the British Boxing Board of Control, were fiercely competed for nonetheless. Peter Youens won the top of the bill fight and when he went up to Oxford he became KES's only Half Blue for Boxing. He was also the only O.E. to play regularly for the University RUFC, though he didn't play in the Varsity Match and therefore didn't get his Blue. His later life was equally dramatic. After a career in the Colonial Service in Africa, he was knighted and finally retired in 1994, having served as the confidant and chief adviser to Dr. Hastings Banda, the first President of the new state of Malawi, and later as an executive director of Tiny Rowland's Lonrho company. Surprisingly, after the success of the 1934 Boxing Finals, although there is no evidence that the Games Committee opposed the sport, Boxing seems to have withered away again at KES. This, despite the Thirties being a golden age of boxing, with major international sports figures like Joe Louis and "Homicide Hank" Armstrong, with Tommy Farr and others maintaining a large British interest in the sport.

The New Swimming Pool

Despite still using Glossop Road Baths for their curriculum and events swimming, KES swimmers keenly contested the Swimming Sports, with Houses competing furiously for the Dolphin Trophy and the Melling House Relay Cup. Almost all schools in Britain were in a similar position, having to use nearby corporation baths for all their swimming requirements, while envying those few schools that had their own facilities. To young eyes, to have your own pool bestowed a very special kind of prestige on a school, unless of course they were of the black sink variety that Wesley College had bequeathed to KES. In October 1936 all this changed and the City Council opened its long promised facility on the site of the old "al fresco" pool. The baths didn't belong to KES but the staff's line manager was Richard Graham, and everyone at the school and beyond thought of them as King Edward's Swimming Pool. (The name is still used today even though they have been run by a private trust since 1992).

To officially open the new pool, the Council invited one of Yorkshire C.C.C.'s most eminent former cricketers, Sir Stanley Jackson. This sometime captain of England (he won the series against Australia in 1905 in the school's first year of existence), went on to be an M.P., National Chairman of the Conservative Party and between 1927-32, the Governor of Bengal. The programme of events at the Official Opening was run by KES for KES. Michael Taylor, now an Old Boy, opened the programme with an attempt on the Yorkshire 150 yards backstroke record, which he duly broke. This was followed by an inter-school relay race which Bootham School won against KES, Leeds G.S. and Nottingham H.S. and an inter-house relay race which was won by Chatsworth. They even persuaded a couple of old boys of Leeds and Nottingham to take on Taylor in an Old Boys' race which not surprisingly the Old Edwardian won. Perhaps this was a fitting tribute to the Old Edwardians who had stumped up the extra money so that the building could be stone-clad in harmony with the main buildings, instead of the brick exterior which was the original intention.

The new pool encouraged more boys to learn to swim, more to do their bronze life saving medal and fostered the growth of Water Polo as a new school sport. In 1938, at the Swimming Sports, a demonstration Water Polo match was played by KES boys and by 1939 they were having competitive matches against the Technical School and the University. The Games Committee authorised a House Water Polo League and the first winners of the new shield, presented by the Wesley College Old Boys, were Wentworth. Finally, before the decade was out, the school found it had another high performing swimmer when Graham Foggitt broke two of Taylor's records at the 1939 Swimming Sports, yet only shared the Champion's Shield with J.S. Roycroft, who had swum outstanding races in the shorter events.

The Last Few Summers of Pre-War Cricket

KES cricketers could not quite match the standards of the school football team in the Thirties, although they usually had winning seasons and in 1936 they were unbeaten in all their matches. The most effective batsmen and bowlers were the same players who filled the key positions in the successful football teams during the winter and spring terms, but they had a tougher fixture list which included strong cricketing schools who played Rugby Union. In 1934 one of the most outstanding, sixteen-year old Bob Gray, scored 133 runs against QEGS Wakefield, which still stands as the highest score ever recorded by a player at the school. To mark his century he was awarded a rather special presentation bat that had been signed by all the 1934 Australian Tourists, including Bradman who had just completed his second triple test century at Headingley. Gray's century enabled the school to run up a total of 259 for 7 before dismissing Wakefield for 54 runs.

Gray was captain for the next two seasons and his period as skipper coincided with a major change in the cricketing life of the school. J.W.Smith finally retired as coach and groundsman and was replaced by Leslie Waghorn. Smith, much beloved and respected by all KES sportsmen since he first arrived in 1907, seemed irreplaceable, but there are few indispensable people and in Waghorn, "Wag" to future generations at KES, the school had found a very suitable successor. To mark his special contribution to the sporting life of the school the Games Committee decided to pay Smith a top-up pension of 12s.6d. a week from the games fund and it fell to John Carter, the son of the master, to cycle round with the money each week to Smith's house in Nether Green. Leslie Waghorn had been a promising left arm medium fast bowler who, at 29, had sustained a knee injury that finished his county career with Sussex. He was paid the princely sum of £3. 5s (£3.25p) per week, and apart from coaching, making teas and looking after a horse, he had to prepare seven cricket pitches at Whiteley Woods and five at Bents Green, on land where the LEA later built the Maud Maxfield School for the Deaf.

SMITH

Up with the dawn, before the world's awake,
He tends his pitches.   Having seen to that,
He hits us red-hot catches all the Break:
Patches a pad and binds a veteran bat.
Bowls at the Nets until the shadows fall,
Still with the same old cheerful courtesy
Showing us how to shape at every ball:
At long last snatches a belated tea;

Tracks down, collects and numbers all his gear;
Bestows it safely, making trip on trip;
Then, "Star" in hand, demonstrates how this year
Kent cannot fail to win the championship.
And while we sleep, still watching o'er our goods,
He nabs a thief or two in Whiteley Woods.

H.B.Watkins 1929

In the 1936 Season the school team had eight of the previous season's players returning and with this nucleus of talent, that included Bob Gray and Frank Melling among the batsmen and Scott Gray, Jimmy Settle and John Fulford leading a varied bowling attack which never conceded more than 118 runs to any school team. In his final term at the school Bob Gray ran riot at the crease, scoring two 70s and an 84 not out against Nottingham H.S. that included six boundaries off consecutive balls. He didn't get another century but he ended up with an average of 55.4 and, for good measure, he captained the side from the wicketkeeper position.

In 1937 KES gained a new fixture when they asked Hymers College for a match. The Hull side came to Whiteley Woods and were no doubt baffled to be playing on a steeply sloping pitch, where fielders had to be signalled when the ball was coming their way. They didn't bat very well, leaving KES with an easy total of 42 to get. However, the lads from the flatlands of the East Riding did better with the ball, and dismissed the last four KES batsmen for no runs to tie the match. Suitably abashed, KES recovered against the Training College the following week, when they dismissed their opponents for 9 all out.

One of the best ever KES bowlers made his debut for the 1st XI that season when he was only 15. Leslie Fletcher would play for the school for four seasons and he was a left arm slow bowler who had a lot of batsmen caught at forward short leg. In the 1939 season he broke the school record for wickets taken in a season when he dismissed 66 batsmen, and in his final season in 1940 he got another large haul of 59 wickets. He invariably opened the batting as well, and if the war hadn't intervened he might have added further cricketing honours when he went up to Oxford. His 5 wickets for 9 against Hymers ensured that KES took revenge for the tie in 1937, when they annihilated their opponents and shot them all out for 22 runs. His partner in opening the school's batting could not have had a more appropriate name. Ken Hutton scored 348 runs in that last season before the war, adding another 248 in the first wartime season when KES were again undefeated.

Cricket in the Thirties was still regarded as "the" national game, although football drew bigger crowds. Yorkshire dominated the County Championship, winning seven times between 1931 and 1939, and Test Matches between England and Australia were the most important international competition in any sport that England played. Therefore, it was important to a school like KES to have a successful cricket team and the players who represented the school in that era would have been amazed, and desperately disappointed, if they had known that within a half century there would not be any KES cricket teams at all for many years. However, in the new century, KES fledgling cricket sides have been formed, alongside the seventeen sports the school currently plays, and the school has won two national awards for its sport and P.E. programme

Postscript

Inter-school cricket continued during the war and the team still travelled out of town to play matches despite the exhortation screaming from poster sites *"Is your journey really necessary!"* The school even picked up some new fixtures, playing an RAF Barrage Balloon side, who were surprisingly quite good, as well as boarding schools like Repton, Trent and Worksop who could not travel across the country to play their regular matches. There were new stars at cricket and football like Tom Buckley, who captained the Football team and scored a not-out century against Collegiate C.C., and Philip Rhodes who captained Cambridge University at Football in 1941 and gained a wartime Blue along with Ross Gilfillan, whilst the Athletics and Swimming Sports continued as if there was no national emergency. The new Headmaster, Dr. Barton, even set up a staff squash club in Broomgrove House, across Clarkehouse Road, where senior boys could also play, but the club folded as the younger members of staff were called up and there were no players left to pay the rent on the lease.

KES 1st XI - Season 1935

R.Gray Captain. (Seated in centre), Leslie Waghorn Coach (extreme left back row).
The staff member on the right is Harry Starmer Smith. The white colours blazers had
originally been awarded for football. Cricket colours had traditionally worn a blue
blazer since before the Great War. However most player preferred the white blazer
because it had a distinctive look and a summer feel to it.

CHAPTER TEN

"THE LEAFY SUBURB" 1928-38

Richard Graham, the City Council's new choice as Headmaster, took over at the beginning of the Spring Term in January 1928. At 34 he was actually two years younger than Gurner had been when he was appointed two years before. Unlike Gurner he had not served as a Head; rather he had been the Senior Classics Master at the Quaker school, Leighton Park, in Reading. To some of the boys the quieter style of the new man was initially something of a disappointment after the strong, if not charismatic, character of the previous Head. In direct contrast to Ronald Gurner, Graham had not served in the forces during the war, but on leaving Magdalen College, Oxford he had gone straight into teaching and as a Quaker chose not to be involved in the conflict, even in the Friends' Ambulance Service where many Quakers served. He did have one claim to fame that would impress all the boys in the school. He had been invited to be a member of the 1924 Everest Expedition, probably the most famous expedition before 1952, when Mallory and Irvine lost their lives in an attempt on the summit, and left a legend that they might have succeeded and reached the top.

After the row over the OTC, the appointing sub-committee, led by Ernest Rowlinson, would have been impressed by Graham's pacifist credentials, while his Quaker faith would sit well with Labour councillors steeped in Methodism as much as Marxism. They were taking a chance on an untested, though very personable, young man who had never run any organisation larger than a small Classics Department. They did, nevertheless, make a happy choice, for the eleven years that Richard Graham stayed at KES were amongst some of the most contented and prosperous years in the history of the school. Graham believed he was taking over a successful school, which didn't require wholesale changes in its organisation or its personnel. He therefore had the luxury of finding his feet before effecting subtle organic alterations that would strengthen the quality of the education on offer at KES. He was aided by two crucial factors. After a temporary dip in numbers in 1928, dropping back almost to 600 pupils, the school's reputation amongst the new and growing middle class of Sheffield ensured the popularity of the school (KES passed the 700 mark in 1934). Moreover, this popularity raised almost £12,000 annually in fees that accrued to the council, sufficient to protect the school against any would-be abolitionists or reorganisers with which the next three Headmasters of KES had to contend. Secondly, the discipline of the school was in the firm hands of J.S. Nicholas, appointed by Gurner to the post of Second Master, who was the public face of authority within the school. Consequently some boys remember Graham as a shadowy, distant figure who spent much of his time in his room and he certainly was not the sort of Headmaster whose booming personality fills every corridor and every corner of the school buildings. That role was performed in Graham's time by Nicholas, and the security so provided allowed the Headmaster to distance himself from the role of martinet and develop a more positive and friendly relationship with the staff and the boys at KES.

Where Graham found inadequacies in the school bequeathed to him by Hichens, they were in the provision of the arts, in its religious life, its sporting achievements, and in its international outlook. Some of these issues had already been addressed by Gurner, who had re-founded the school orchestra and had challenged the notion that examination results and open scholarships were all-important. Richard Graham believed passionately that the purpose of education was to educate the whole person, *"to aid boys in the difficult and sometimes painful process of growing up, — to avoid the modern danger of over-emphasis on examination results, that will drive teaching along the lines of direct cramming which will improve statistics without improving the boy."* In the perennial dilemma of the schoolteacher, whether their priority should be examination results or a balanced education, Richard Graham was very firmly in the latter camp. He was, however, under less pressure than his predecessors, and also some of his successors, to demonstrate academic success, because these were more spacious days for KES and the examination results of their high flyers, from Higher School Certificate level to Oxbridge Firsts, seemed so impressive.

R.B. GRAHAM
HEADMASTER OF KES
1928-38

Richard Graham was born into a Lancashire Quaker family in Chorlton-cum-Hardy in October 1893. His father was a university lecturer, Liberal Party parliamentary candidate and author, who became Principal of Dalton Hall, Manchester. Graham was educated at Sidcot School in Somerset from 1904-06, then he was sent as a boarder to Bootham School, the Quaker School in York. He left there in 1910 to join the Sixth Form at Manchester G.S. and from there he gained a classics scholarship to Magdalen College, Oxford, where he obtained a Second Class in Honour Moderations and Literae Humaniores.

Richard Brockbank GRAHAM M.A.
(1893-1957)

In 1916, having graduated, he went straight into teaching when he became an assistant classics master at Bishop's Stortford College. At the end of the war he moved to the Quaker School, Leighton Park, in Reading as the Senior Classics Master and also the master in charge of Games. To this latter position he brought considerable experience of many sports, for he was a talented performer at both codes of football, cricket, lawn tennis, fives and squash. His main sporting enthusiasm was climbing, especially in the Alps and the Lake District, and he was invited to join the 1924 British Everest Expedition, although it is unclear whether or not he travelled with them.

At KES, where he started on a salary of £1000, he was the last Headmaster to live at Mount View, moving in with his wife and two young daughters in 1928. Apart from his impact on the school during the next decade, he played a prominent role in the community life of Sheffield. He was Clerk to the Sheffield Society of Friends, Chairman of the Hallam Branch of the League of Nations and also Chairman of the local Council of the Youth Hostels Association, three positions that reflected his personal philosophy and interests, namely the Quakers, international understanding and access and appreciation of the countryside. His peers also recognised his qualities by electing him as the Chairman of the Yorkshire Branch of the Incorporated Association of Headmasters in1934. Later, between 1945-47, he was a member of the Hobhouse Committee on National Parks, whose work led to the founding of the first national park, the Peak Park, in 1951.

He surprised everyone at KES when he accepted the post of Headmaster of Bradford G.S., partly because there were some who expected a KES Headmaster to stay at the school for the rest of their career, and felt slighted that Graham could consider a move to another school. Like Gurner at Whitgift, Graham joined a school that was about to move into new premises, but when they were ready in late 1940, the army commandeered them and the school only took possession in January1949.

Richard Graham stayed at Bradford until 1953, but he kept in touch with KES and was a regular visitor to the school right up to his death in January 1957.

A New Beginning with the Council

One of Graham's first tasks was to patch up relations with the City Council, where the Labour Party had strengthened their majority in the 1928 and 1929 local elections. This did not prove to be as easy as he might have expected, given that he had a genuine concern to work with the committee who in effect formed the governors of the school. He cannot have been helped by the smouldering guerrilla war between the Education Committee and the Sheffield Grammar School Exhibition Foundation, the residual body who had representation on the Governors between 1905 and 1926 and still controlled the sizeable funds that the SRGS governors had left to their trust. The Foundation continued throughout 1928 to assert that the Council could not legally abolish KES's own governing body without their approval, even though the decision to wind up their membership had been taken in 1922, long before Labour won the November 1926 elections. The issue though was not about representation, it was about saving the discrete Governing Body for KES, thereby keeping the school out of the "socialists" control and winning back public school status. Rowlinson, not surprisingly, was having none of it and through his Director of Education, Sir Percy Sharp, he fought off the Foundation's challenge, insisting that KES could only be treated like any other council secondary school. Nevertheless, as a fee-paying school it was an anomaly that could turn into an anachronism if it did not continually show it was a real benefit to the ratepayers of Sheffield.

Graham reported, along with the other Sheffield secondary headteachers, to the meetings of the Secondary Schools Sectional Committee, a sub-committee of a sub-committee of the Education Committee. Eventually, in November 1929, Graham's patience with the manner in which they were being treated boiled over and he wrote a firmly worded letter to Rowlinson, in his capacity as Chairman of the full Education Committee and Leader of the Council. Apart from the indignity of being kept waiting for considerable periods of time in the vestibule of the Education Offices, he was concerned that matters dealing with the internal business and curriculum of the school were being decided without any reference to him or any attempt to ascertain his views. One decision in particular concerned him when he discovered a council minute about the standardisation of scripture teaching throughout the secondary sector, something he had strong independent views about. He had also been censured for his conduct when he had insisted on interviewing a candidate for a teaching post at KES whilst in a nursing home in Reading, where he was recovering from an operation in the spring of 1929.

Rowlinson, publicly, chose to view this letter as a challenge to the authority of the Council to decide educational policy, though privately it does seem to have cleared the air and the school's relationship with the Council began to improve. At these monthly meetings each headteacher had to give a written and verbal report of the progress of his school, and Graham knew how to win the councillors support. He emphasised all the successes of the free place scholarship boys. These included Gordon Cumming and L.A. Ronksley who became Captains of Football, H.A. Hodges who left Oxford in 1929 and became Professor of Philosophy at Reading University, and E.L.Moore from Huntsman Gardens School in Attercliffe, who won a War Memorial Scholarship at Oriel College, Oxford, which was restricted to sons of fathers who had fallen in the war. The current free place scholars in 1930 included Graham's outstanding pupils of the period, Philip Allen and Head Boy Geofroy Tory, who both took Firsts at Cambridge and then went on to enjoy glittering careers in the public service. He also always reported on eminent visitors, like Norman Angel M.P., perhaps the best known pacifist of his day, as well as representatives of the League of Nations Union, who were due to speak at the school in a lecture instituted by the new Headmaster on "Peace Day", a Council initiative to encourage international understanding in its schools.

More important was his attitude to the free place scholarship boys. Still only ten or twelve a year in number in 1928 and 1929, Graham recognised that they were amongst the most gifted pupils in the school and that they rose to hold many of the senior positions as Head Boy, prefects, captains of teams and secretaries of societies. They were now referred to as school scholars and he wanted the Council to award more scholarships tenable at KES, in line with the earlier figure of 25 % of the first year intake. This finally happened in 1930, when 24 awards were made, and the figure remained the same throughout the Thirties, enabling a full class of scholarship boys, 2D, to be re-formed in the first year of the newly designated Middle School. Amongst these new eleven year old scholarship boys was Norman Siddall, who would later become the Chairman of the N.C.B., and, who some believe, might have avoided the 1984 Coal Strike if he had been kept on by Mrs.Thatcher, who preferred the controversial American, Ian McGregor. In the same year Jimmy Settle won a scholarship from Walkley Junior School and he was destined to be one of the school's legendary football players, and to captain the school team in 1935-36 season before going on to Sheffield University. The Council still operated the ad hoc system of honorary scholarship holders, but perhaps because of the depression there were fewer of these hybrid awards made. In the case of Gordon Cumming, who had originally been an honorary scholarship winner, he gained the full financial benefit of his scholarship when his father became temporarily unemployed and this enabled him to stay on in the Sixth Form. After that he gained entrance, with the help of other scholarships, to Sheffield University, where he took a First in History, eventually returning to the school as a master in 1937.

CIRCULAR 1421 AND THE MEANS TEST.

In 1932 MacDonald's National Government ordered all LEAs to prepare a scheme to abolish automatic free place scholarships at its secondary schools and introduce a means test whereby the better off parents would have to contribute financially to the education of their children. The information was contained in Circular 1421 and was vehemently opposed by the Labour members of the Council and the wider Trade Union and Labour Movement in the City. The new Municipal Progressive Party, which had superseded the Citizens' Association of Conservatives and Liberals, had little enthusiasm for it either, but they gained power in the Town Hall in 1933 and they then had to implement the changes.

It was feared it would have a major impact on working class pupils at the other secondary schools in the city, because at Central, Abbeydale, Firth Park and Nether Edge Schools all pupils had free education. Now, if their weekly household income was over £5, parents had to make a contribution, which rose in small amounts until it reached the maximum payment of £7.10s p.a. for those whose family earned £6.10s. per week or over.

Because so many people in Sheffield were unemployed at the time (there were 59,389 registered unemployed in Sheffield at the peak in August 1931) it had only a limited effect and its impact on the finances of the Council was minimal. It was estimated by the City Treasurer that it would only save the ratepayers of the city £375 in 1933, rising perhaps by the end of the decade to £2600.

The means test applied to KES as well, but they were on a different scale because their scheme had to equate with the existing fees of £18.18s p.a. Thus, if you gained a scholarship to KES and your family income was under £5 p.w. you received totally free education. On a sliding scale up to £8 weekly income, parents had to make a contribution and if they earned over £8 p.w. they had to pay the full fees of £18.18s. Because many KES scholarship winners came from middle class homes, a considerable number of them must have been caught in this trap and they became honorary scholarship winners.

On the other hand, a few KES Scholarship holders came from families that were so poor that they received an extra Maintenance Grant (up to a maximum of £22 p.a.) to help pay for their upkeep.

Strengthening the Classics

Shortly after taking over as Headmaster, Richard Graham was embarrassed to find that the Board of Education had communicated with the LEA concerning the small numbers of students taking Latin at KES after they had completed their School Certificate courses. This criticism came as something of a surprise to the school, which prided itself on the number and quality of its classical scholars over the years. As a classics scholar himself Graham moved quickly to try to remedy the situation. As far as he was concerned, instruction in the classics was the cornerstone of education in schools like KES. If pupils and parents could not see the intrinsic value of Latin, then he was quick to remind them that a School Certificate pass in the subject was a necessary requirement of entrance for any Oxbridge College for any subject, and to an Arts course at most provincial universities. Furthermore progress in a number of professions, including Medicine and the Law, would be barred without a qualification in Latin.

Latin was compulsory at KES for the first three years in the middle school and it occupied a huge part of the timetable with each pupil receiving six periods a week in the subject. By the time a boy reached the Fifth Form he could opt for Physics instead, but at least 40% of the boys remained in one of the two Latin sets preparing for the School Certificate. Enthusiastic classicists could choose Greek in the Fourth Form as an alternative to German or Spanish, and by 1933 eighteen pupils had chosen to do a second ancient language. At the time of the 1933 Inspection, the numbers on the Classical Transitus and the Sixth Form Advanced Course preparing for the Higher Certificate Examination had only risen to thirteen, even though they were taught by some of the most brilliant scholars on the staff, including Humphrey Watkins, the Head of the Department and E.F. "Marcus" Watling, both of whom were institutions in the life of KES, spanning a period between them from 1906 – 60.

The Speech Day Oration

Not content with setting classics teaching on a stronger footing, Graham wanted its influence to be seen throughout the life of the school. The school's name on the belt surrounding the school's badge was from now on invariably written in its Latin form, *Reg. Edvard VII Schola Escafeld,* and on Speech Day in 1930 there was a new innovation in the proceedings. Henceforth the guest speaker would be welcomed with a Latin oration delivered by the Head Boy and written by a boy in the Classical Sixth, supported by Edward Watling. Some felt it added considerable dignity to a great school occasion, whilst others thought it the height of pretentiousness, but it started a tradition that survived for over forty years.

Most guest speakers tried to affect an intelligent interest in their quite lengthy Latin welcome, whilst they clearly didn't understand a word that was being said. Occasionally the guest would be a classics scholar himself, who like Dr. William Temple, then Archbishop of York, and later a very influential war-time Primate, gently corrected one or two errors he perceived in the text. It says something for Graham's connections that he

All dressed up for the 1933 Speech Day, perhaps to celebrate the defeat of Labour in the November1932 Local Elections? Ald. Harold Jackson, (ex Wesley College) the new Leader of the Council, is on the left of the front row. The Head is in gown and hood and Ald. Sir Samuel Osborn, the benefactor of Clarke House, is at the extreme right of the second row.

managed to attract some very eminent speakers to Speech Day in the early Thirties, including the very popular author John Buchan and Lord Irwin, recently returned from a period as Viceroy of India, and later, as the Earl of Halifax, the man who nearly became Prime Minister in 1940 instead of Churchill. In the following years the text of the oration was printed in the programme, although only in Latin, and it became a point of some intellectual esteem for boys studying classics to laugh in the right places. When Geofroy Tory was Head Boy in 1931, he was faced with the task of finding a Latin translation for X-ray, as the guest that year, Sir William Bragg, had won international fame for his work with X-rays. Delivering the oration was a considerable ordeal for the Head Boy, and more than one who had to undertake it will tell you, that, even to-day, they can remember every word they had to deliver so many years ago.

To complete the symbolic Latin emblems of the school, Graham replaced the old school song in November 1937 with a new one in Latin written by Eric Tappe, the new Head of Classics. This remained the school song until, along with Speech Days, Latin Orations, Houses, corporal punishment and even school caps, ties and blazers, it became an anachronism in a local authority school and fell into disuse in the last quarter of the century. The teaching of Latin lasted quite a bit longer, and was only finally discontinued at KES in 1996. The school song is still sung by some Old Edwardians at their Annual Dinner on Maundy Thursday, but only unofficially and usually late on in the proceedings!

TERMS OF ENGAGEMENT

Corporal punishment up to a maximum of four strokes of the cane may be given by a member of staff under the following conditions. a. Another adult is present. b. It is reported in writing.

The offences for which corporal punishment seems to me most suitable are those which involve some degree of "Uppishness", or culpable negligence or an occasional outburst of animal spirit that has unfortunately to be suppressed.

Members of the Sixth Form are not to be punished without consulting me.

R.B. Graham, Headmaster, 24th September 1937

THE JUNIOR SCHOOL 1928-1936

One of the first staff decisions that Graham made was to formally recognise "Toby" Saville as the Master in Charge of the Junior School in 1928. He had carried out this "de facto" role since 1905 but without any official recognition and he was now brought more fully into the school's decision making process, with a special responsibility allowance of £48 p.a. in acknowledgement of his new position. The Junior School had always been a successful part of KES but it was now bursting at the seams, and some of the classes had come back into the main building because there was no room for them at No. 9 Newbould Lane.

Fortunately the adjoining house, No.7 Newbould Lane, came on to the market in 1928 and the City Council bought it and paid £425 to make the necessary alterations, creating classrooms out of two bedrooms, a first floor passage between the buildings and a ladies' staff toilet. Now with double the capacity the Junior School could expand and meet the increasing demand from Sheffield's middle class to get their sons into KES as soon as possible. This would ensure that their boy would be able to pass on to the Senior School unimpeded by entrance examinations or the shortage of available places. In 1933 only six boys entered the Senior School as fee-payers who had not been pupils at Newbould Lane.

Half the staff in the Junior School were women teachers, including the formidable Miss Copley (at KES 1918-47) who ran Form J 3, in effect the reception class. The curriculum had not altered from the 1900s and still did not include Science or Latin, but a start was made with the teaching of French, Algebra and Geometry in the last year when most boys were over 11 years of age. By 1931 there were 132 pupils in the Junior School, all, of course, paying fees. The classes were small, averaging about 17, and there were five forms in the final year, whose members provided the bulk of the boys in the Second Forms of the Senior School in the following year. Much of the rapid growth in numbers on the school roll in the early Thirties occurred in the Junior School, so by 1934 the Council began to consider purpose built facilities to house the Junior School, now 160 strong. The most likely site was between the open-air baths and the war memorial, exactly the same location as was chosen for the rather tasteful new building erected in 1995. The work was costed by council architects at £9000 and it was assumed its capacity would be for a Junior School of 200 pupils. The alternative proposal was to adapt the Headmaster's house at Mount View, which would only have cost £2500 to complete,

Clarke House

146

with the Headmaster and his young family being housed in more appropriate leased accommodation. Both schemes were short circuited when the family of Ald. Samuel Osborn, a keen supporter of the school, offered their home, Clarke House, to the Council as the new premises for the Junior School, which moved there in September 1936.

The Junior School held an Annual Open Day each summer, when the versatility of the formal and extra-curricular education was on display for parents and would-be entrants to see. The day's programme was something of a marathon, starting with a cricket match on the Close, sometimes against the parents but usually against Rotherham G.S., who also had a Junior School. This was followed by a house swimming competition in the cleaned up open-air baths and later in the afternoon a gymnastic display. Artwork and handicraft were on continual display in the school workshop and in the early evening, after refreshments in the Masters' Garden, the action shifted to the lawn at Lynwood where a full length play was performed. In 1932 the Juniors attempted "A Midsummer Night's Dream", quite a challenge for young actors who had been variously cricketers, swimmers and gymnasts during the afternoon. After 1936, Clarke House would provide a superb setting for the Open Day with much of the activity carried out on the lawns adjacent to the Botanical Gardens.

The four Houses still fiercely competed for sporting honours in cricket, football, swimming, cross-country and athletics. They still had the same names, **ANGLES (navy blue); NORMANS (maroon); SAXONS (light blue) and BRITONS (dark green)** and after 1936 they were joined by a fifth house **OSBORN (brown and white),** designed to cope with the greater numbers now enjoyed by the Junior School and named after the family who had owned Clarke House. The Juniors were also active in other areas of school life. Several of them were members of the school orchestra and they also had their own percussion band, and every morning they would all march over to the main school to be present at morning assembly, sitting at the rear of the gallery in the Assembly Hall.

The Many Mr. Chips and Also Short Term Staff

Richard Graham started with a permanent staff of 30 Assistant Masters and 4 Assistant Mistresses, the latter all teaching in the Junior School. It must have been quite a daunting challenge to the confidence and authority of a relatively young man, called upon to lead a staff that included so many long serving and brilliant teachers. Three members of staff, Saville, Shorter and Mease, had come from Wesley College or SRGS in 1905 to form the original staff and four others, Watkins, Magrath, Thompson and Nicholas had been appointed well before the First World War. These men gave continuity to the life of the school for they remained at KES for rest of their teaching careers, and they were joined after the war by ten others who would stay at the school for very long periods, including Joe Clay, the Senior English Master and A.W. Gaskin, the founder of the KES Scouts, whose first name was not even known to his closest colleagues.

The early Thirties were a good time for recruiting teachers of outstanding ability. Graduates had far fewer attractive alternative opportunities for employment during the depression. Going "east of Suez" was beginning to look less appealing to able men and there were only limited numbers of teaching vacancies at the relatively few universities in Britain. Graham used the opportunity to fill up the ranks of the staff with Oxford and Cambridge men and of the 56 appointments he made during his ten years at the school, 37 of the male staff were Oxbridge graduates and only eight from other universities, plus six Assistant Mistresses and five specialist teachers of P.T., Art and Music. Having a staff largely recruited from Oxbridge was very much part of the style and ethos of schools like KES, who although they were no longer technically a public school, continued to perceive themselves as one. The school prospectus of 1927 had a preamble which stated; *"the school is equal to other public schools of the highest type"*, while later prospectuses retained this sentence but just deleted the word *other* and any reference to membership of the Headmasters' Conference.

While many of the staff would remain at the school for twenty, thirty or even forty years, teaching more than one generation of the same family, just over half the appointments (29) were for very brief periods, whether the staff members involved were from ivy covered colleges or redbrick universities. Many of these temporary appointments were to cover genuine absences by staff, or to fill a gap whilst new permanent staff worked out their notice at their previous school, but mainly it seems the school operated a rather brutal form of probation, which was hard on the individual concerned but better for the boys and for the maintenance of the high standard of instruction at KES. Shape up or ship out, as the U.S. Navy would term it, seems to have been the code of practice at KES in Graham's time just as it was when Hichens was Headmaster. Graham did have one surprise in January 1937, when one young Oxford graduate turned the tables on him and failed to report for the new term. Noel Carritt, formerly of Oriel College Oxford, had taught for one term in the Junior School when he went absent without leave after Christmas. Enquiries into his disappearance discovered that he had gone to Spain to fight in the Civil War, and his contract was therefore deemed to have been terminated and he was never heard of at KES again.

The staff was full of characters, almost inevitable in a school where there were so many brilliant individual masters with virtual autonomy within their own classrooms. Harry Redston, nicknamed Trotsky because of a certain similarity of appearance, was the Senior Physics Master, who served over three decades of pupils. Admired for the quality of his teaching, he was also famed for stock phrases which were so predictable that boys could play "classroom soccer" using two equal lists of regular expressions ("You must always state your units" was one of them) and score a "goal" for "Wednesday" or "United" every time one was used. His nasal tone of voice was easy to impersonate yet he never raised his own voice and rarely smiled. Sydney Carter had joined the school in 1921 and he would leave as Deputy Head in 1958 after a distinguished career in the Mathematics Department. Organiser in chief of the Athletics Sports Day, he was also the first member of staff to drive to school in his own car, which he parked under the covered playground. Arnold "Long John" Thompson taught Chemistry and, to emphasize his disdain of the modern world, always wore a dark jacket that buttoned all the way up to the neck and was topped off with a high stiff collar.

"Billy" Effron had lived in Argentina and worked on the railways. His Geography or Spanish classes could always be diverted from the path of true learning to long reminiscences of blissful days on another continent. Each minute so detoured was regarded as a small victory for his devious class. Edward "Marcus" Watling, tall and scholarly, was another who survived for over three decades still teaching classics from his room at the top of the stairs. He had a major role in so many aspects of school life in the Thirties, producing school and staff plays and acting lead parts in the latter, whilst keeping an eye on the school magazine's youthful editors from his position of Honorary Secretary. Under his guidance the magazine in the Thirties was better displayed, included regular photographs, and contained a fair degree of good standard literary work. It also acquired a new cover design of a sharply stylised, virile rampant lion which would remain the cover layout for the next thirty years. In between all this extracurricular activity, Watling managed to translate Sophocles and other classical works for publication and for broadcasting on the BBC. Harry Scutt (At KES 1918-47) was Head of Modern Languages. Famed for his long fingernails, he operated a teaching incentive method whereby anyone failing to achieve 7 out of 10 for their vocabulary test got the cane. The one-eyed John Whitfield (1930-36) was in the same department and also believed a good slippering was a useful way to advance knowledge. More feared was a chunk of wood he referred to as a "morceau de bois" with which he also administered correction. Nicknamed "Twitters", he delighted in arriving late at Assembly when all had been hushed to a nervous silence and then tramping noisily and defiantly to his place in the gallery. Another brilliant scholar, he left in 1936 to become a lecturer in Italian at Oxford before setting up the Italian Department at Birmingham University in 1946. Active until the very end of his life, he produced a paper for his publisher on Palla Strozzi just a few weeks before he died in 1995, aged 88.

These staff characters formed a close knit society, enjoying a considerable social status as graduate teachers at a school of King Edward VII's reputation. A social round of staff plays, school orchestra and choir practices and concerts, playing in staff -school cricket matches, and lazing through Sunday afternoons at Lynwood at tennis parties, with the handful of boarders acting as ball boys and waiters. During school hours they could relax in the Masters' Garden situated in the north west corner of the school grounds and after lessons finished indulge their academic interests and hobbies by running the school societies. Many lived very close to the school and, apart from their normal family lives, the school was their existence. Several, including Redston, Carter, Shorter, Saville, Scutt and Nicholas, sent their own boys to the school but few Old Edwardians became permanent members of staff, although one or two did fill in a temporary gap when they came down from university. One who stayed was Stan Reyner, who had been a popular figure in the school in the mid Twenties, starring in the Football and Cricket XI before winning a scholarship to Jesus College, Oxford. He returned to teach Maths and Physics in 1929 and threw himself energetically into many aspects of school, staff and Old

Edwardian life. A welcome addition to staff teams and dramatic productions, he then rather surprisingly, when it looked as if he was going to be another member of staff who would loyally devote his life to the school, accepted a post at Ampleforth where he remained until the end of the Fifties.

A couple of staff members from this period made their considerable contribution to the school but are better known in sporting circles as the fathers of international players. Harry Starmer-Smith's son, Nigel, played for England at Rugby Union and Horace Brearley was the father of a future England Cricket Captain. If he had stayed at KES rather than move to the City of London School in 1946, then his son, Michael, would have learnt his cricket at the school and played for the KES team. Horace Brearley was a very good sportsman in his own right. The summer before he came to KES in 1937 he had played in a Roses match at Bramall Lane, in what was his only first team appearance for Yorkshire. He did, however, have two full seasons in the Colts from 1935 –37 but he could not play regular cricket when he joined the staff, although he did gain a regular place in the Yorkshire Hockey team and played for them up to the war.

Romance also blossomed in the staff room when the Misses Nancy Jones and Lucy Turner married Edgar Hickox, the new Senior Science Master, and John Michell respectively. Both ladies had been at KES since the Twenties and were very keen members of the Staff Dramatic Society. They both retired from teaching, as was the convention for middle class women at the time, when they got married. The Michells' marriage in 1936 was to be a short one, as John Michell succumbed to a long illness that was a legacy of his service in the Great War. Commissioned into the Royal Warwicks, he had won two M.C.s in 1916 and 1918 and in one bombardment he gave his gas mask to a married soldier who had a leaking one, causing one of his own lungs to be permanently damaged. This sense of duty and loyalty he brought to his work at KES, where he taught German and French, played cricket rather well and was a staunch member of the orchestra and the school choir, who turned out to sing at his funeral in Bradfield Parish Church.

The school staff's last direct link with SRGS was broken when first "Wally" Mease and then Harry Shorter retired. Mease went in 1932 after a teaching career spent mostly in the Junior School but his contribution to the school was much wider, for he had at various times been in charge of school football teams, run the Gymnastic Eight and served as an officer of the OTC. H.V.S. Shorter was from Bradford whose merits he was always advancing as superior to Sheffield, a point not always obvious or appreciated by his pupils. He had run the Science Department since 1905, initially in close co-operation with James Hichens who always took some sixth form classes. He ran the Scientific Society's numerous visits to works, factories and mines, refereed football matches and could still bowl out the school eleven when he was over fifty. He retired to Norfolk in 1934 expecting a contented retirement doing a little gardening and playing in the Cromer amateur orchestra, but he became ill and died the following year.

The death in 1934 of Humphrey Watkins when he was still only 54 was the loss that created the greatest sadness in the school. Richard Graham, who had obviously lost a friend as well as a close colleague and fellow classicist, wrote a four page obituary in the school magazine in honour of a man who had been at KES since 1906. Before the war he had worked indefatigably for the school teams, even though his own sporting prowess, like so many of the staff, was at Rugby Union and he also had a Half Blue for swimming. During the war he had served at the front as a subaltern in the Duke of Cornwall's Light Infantry and been badly wounded in the face. When he resumed teaching, with a visible steel plate holding his jaw together, he became a strong supporter of the fledgling Old Edwardians' Association and was ever in demand as a guest, or as a speaker, at their Sheffield or Oxford occasions. He took on the position of Senior Classics Master in 1926 but from 1930 onwards his work was interrupted by time in hospital, at first for heart disease and then for a virulent form of tuberculosis which eventually killed him. He was buried in his native Devon with his brother, the local vicar, conducting the service, whilst at the exact same time many members of the staff and school went to a memorial service at nearby St. Mark's, Broomhill. Graham wrote of him that; *"he was the best type of Christian gentleman whose watchwords were duty, faith and honour and the school and the boys he had taught owed him a debt that cannot be repaid."*

A section of the School long photograph of 1938
Staff members from left to right.
Messrs; Helliwell, Wright, Redston, Hickox, Gaskin, Tappe, Scutt, Nicholas, The
Headmaster, Saville, Clay, Magrath, Fletcher, Geo. Smith, Wheeler, Hunter.

The 1933 Inspection

Half way through Graham's period of office as Headmaster of KES, the HMIs gave the school its first major inspection since 1923. Whilst recognising the school's fine record in its post School Certificate work, the final report of the inspection delivered in June 1933 was not as fulsome in its praise of the school as were the later reports of 1997 and 2002. Whilst giving full marks to the teaching of English and History, the other departments came in for a certain amount of criticism. Perhaps the Inspectors felt that the school had become a little too complacent and that its record in the School Certificate Examinations in particular was not very impressive. Although, in the Thirties, there were no published league tables of results, the City Council kept their own record of the Sheffield Secondary Schools' performances in the public examinations, and the other secondary schools in the city seemed to perform better in the School Certificate Examinations.

The other schools took the Northern Universities Joint Board Examinations, while KES still did the Oxford and Cambridge Examination Board's papers, which were considered a harder test, but the Inspectors highlighted the four year course taken by most KES students as the core of the problem. They felt that too many boys of average ability were being rushed into their School Certificate when they were too young. 54.5% of the group taking the examination in 1932 had been under 16 at the time and they felt this accounted for a proportion of the failures. They also felt that the curriculum was weighted too much on the side of languages, thereby reducing the amount of time available for other subjects. They believed that the school should have more Science in the Middle School, more Music, Art, Handicraft and Physical Education throughout the school, that Trigonometry should begin earlier and that Biology teaching should be started in the school within the Science Department. Finally they concluded that Geography, at that time only taught to School Certificate Level, should be taught in Transitus and the Sixth Form and students prepared for Higher Certificate and University entry in that subject.

To find the time on the syllabus, the Inspectors suggested that the less able boys might only take one language and most probably drop Latin, a subject in which they felt that the School Certificate results were "*meagre*". They also argued that the pressure to get students to opt for a third language (Greek, Spanish or German) in the third year (i.e. Fourth Forms) of the Middle School was forcing many of them into wrong options and tying up the syllabus. Graham was not sympathetic to the main thrust of their argument. He was certainly not going to reduce the amount of Latin on the syllabus, and he thought it was totally wrong that a boy should leave school without studying at least two European languages. However he did introduce a more flexible system of choices which benefited German and Spanish, with only half of the fourth year (Fifth Form) henceforth taking a third language.

NOTES FROM THE INSPECTION

Based on figures available for the three years 1929- 1932

265 boys left the school in 1929-1932.
Average age of leaving 16 years 10 months

23% went to University
Oxford 16, Cambridge 4, Sheffield 41, London 1

21 Old Boys obtained First Class Honours.
3 Old Boys became University Professors.
37 boys entered the professions and 100 entered Business or Commerce.

There were 9 Boarders at the time of the Inspection and 640 Day Boys.

95% lived in Sheffield, 2% in the West Riding and 3% elsewhere in England.

Richard Graham was called to a special meeting of a sub-committee of the Education Committee in April 1934 to be vetted on the Inspectors' Report, and on any action that he had already instituted. The Report had also criticised the Council for not allowing a separate Governing Body for the school, but he made no headway on that point. On the other hand the Inspectors' concerns about overcrowding in the Junior School and the need for a covered swimming pool, did act as a catalyst for action and new facilities were provided for both by 1936. There had also been concern about the library, both its inadequate space and its very limited funding (£50 p.a. from the Grammar School Foundation), and the practice of devolving subject libraries to subject teachers' classrooms. This criticism did not produce any action and the creation of a new library had to wait seventeen years, when it was rebuilt in its present location over the gym. All in all the Inspection produced some organic changes to the curriculum, and KES's School Certificate Examination results began to improve in the latter part of the Thirties. Biology was introduced as a Sixth Form subject in 1936, when Walter Wheeler, was appointed and Trigonometry was introduced earlier in the Middle School. However, Geography courses leading to Higher Certificates and University Scholarships had to wait until 1948 before they were offered.

EXAMINATION RESULTS 1928-1938

School Certificate Examinations

- *KES did not perform very well in comparison with the other six Sheffield secondary schools (Abbeydale Girls; Central Boys and Central Girls (High Storrs); Firth Park; Nether Edge; and, after1933, City Secondary School.) at School Certificate level.*

- All the other Sheffield secondary schools took the Northern Universities Joint Board Examinations and KES may have been disadvantaged by taking the Oxford and Cambridge Board's Examinations (OCEB), which may have been more difficult, with some pupils taking them at an earlier age (15 or even 14).

- However, KES did not perform well against the OCEB's average pass rate either. Only once,in 1934, did they better the average and often they were well below it. (In 1928 they were 19% below and in 1932, 17.8% below)

- KES average percentage pass rate for gaining a School Certificate was only 53.4% for the years 1928-32. 1932, the year inspected by the HMIs, was a particularly poor one, with only 47% of the candidates gaining their Certificate. To be awarded a School Certificate you had to pass in at least five subjects and they had to include a language, English or a humanity, and Maths or a science.

- The Sheffield secondary schools, whose pupils were all Scholarship Free Place holders, averaged approximately a 73% pass rate and almost every year each of the other schools performed better than KES, who only had 25% of their pupils holding Free Place Scholarships.

- There was a marked improvement after 1933 when the KES average pass rate percentage moved up to 64.9%. However, the OCEB average also moved up to 71.5% so the school was still lagging behind. Only in 1934 did the school pass rate of 69.5% better the OCEB average of only 67.3%.

- Meanwhile the Sheffield schools, now including City Secondary School, formed from the old Pupil Teacher Centre at Leopold St., were still showing an average pass rate (1933-38) of approximately 77%.

Higher Certificate Results 1928-38

- KES performed with much more distinction at 6th Form level.

- Every year between 1928-38 they were well above the OCEB average pass rate. Over the eleven-year period their pass rate averaged 81.8%, with particularly good years in 1930 and 1933 when they averaged 90%. (The OCEB average for the same period was only 65.6%)

- KES also scored high on Distinctions gained. The average over the period was 15 with very good years in 1930 (24), 1933 (22) and 1937 (21).

- The only Sheffield secondary school that could compare with these results was Central Boys (High Storrs) School. They also took the OCEB papers and in several years did better than KES in pass rates and distinctions. The other Sheffield schools posted good results but presented a much smaller number of candidates and they all took the Northern Universities J.B. papers.

- The City Council from 1931 onwards also collected the statistics for the performance of KES's Free Place "Scholars" and the Fee Paying "Pupils" in the Higher Certificate Examinations. The Scholarship boys (usually 40% of the group) performed significantly better in every year 1931-38. In some years the gap was as wide as 20% and they also won the majority of the Distinctions. If KES had only entered Scholarship boys for the examinations the average pass rate would have been 89.8%.

THE SCHOOL HEADWEAR

The dark blue school cap was redesigned in the Thirties by adding white piping running from the crown to the four corners. The school crest, a rampant white lion, remained at the front of the cap. It was originally considered a mortal sin not to wear the cap at all times and boys in the Sixth Form found this particularly irksome.

One apparently serious suggestion was that sixth formers should be allowed to wear trilby hats in the appropriate school colour. Boaters, with the school ribbon, had been part of the authorised school uniform since the earliest days, but few boys ever wore one and they had become unfashionable by the Thirties. The trilby, by contrast, was then almost a badge of middle class respectability and was popular and very stylish among adults.

Writing in a letter to the next addition of the school magazine, one correspondent, we assume with tongue in cheek, suggested a school bowler instead. He maintained that a bowler with a ribbon in the school colours with the crest at the front would look more dignified and appropriate. For the prefects, he suggested they could attach a blue and white plume at the side to aid recognition of their status.

The Orchestra and the Arts

One of Richard Graham's early appointments to the staff was a new music master, Philip Baylis, in September 1929. Baylis, an ARCM graduate of the Guildhall School of Music, came to KES from a three-year spell at King's School, Canterbury and took over the fledgling school orchestra. He stayed at the school until just after the Second World War and became one of the major influences in developing KES's fine tradition of music. The orchestra was a rather scratchy affair in its earliest days and very short of equipment.

Baylis is reputed to have scoured the pawnbrokers for brass and woodwind instruments, as well as gratefully accepting anything that parents or old boys would donate.

The orchestra was a joint venture of masters and boys and might never have survived in the early years without the active involvement of a quite remarkable number of staff members, including Messrs Shorter, Magrath, Reyner, Whitehouse, Unsworth, Francis, Thomas, McKay, Michell, Hickox, Exton, Helliwell and Starmer-Smith, who were all capable musicians.

There had always been a Christmas School Concert at the end of the winter term but it had been largely choral work, small ensembles and solo performers. Now this event became the annual showcase for the talents of the orchestra. By 1930 they were getting bolder in their selection of works to perform. Beethoven's 8th, Grieg's *Peer Gynt suite* and selections from Gounod's *Faust* were attempted at that year's concert, finishing up with a spirited rendering of the popular tune, *Colonel Bogey*. The following year, having started with *HMS Pinafore,* they attempted Haydn's *London Symphony No.2,* more Grieg and concluded with Strauss's *Blue Danube*.

THE SCHOOL ORCHESTRA in 1933

As they gained in competence and ambition their reputation encouraged other staff involved in the growing artistic life of the school to call upon their support. They accompanied the Staff Play with selections from Lehar and on another occasion they performed Mozart's Don Giovanni. In a very ambitious departure the school's own Dramatic Society put on an operetta, *"Lionel and Clarissa"*, where Baylis combined with

"Marcus" Watling to successfully handle an intricate manuscript score. The Orchestra occasionally accompanied the Hymns at Morning Assembly and also became a regular feature of Speech Day, playing incidental music before proceedings began and performing their current work in the second half of the programme. They also arranged concerts at other times of the year, often to raise funds to buy instruments. One such concert in March 1933 performing Haydn's Oxford Symphony, was deemed to be a success when it raised £4, described as a useful sum to aid the orchestra's funds. When the School was inspected that year the Oxford Symphony was dragged out again for the Music Inspector, who commented favourably on how the orchestra had improved. In the main, though, the members of the orchestra just enjoyed their Thursday evenings in the Assembly Hall playing classical and light opera music and practising for their next important public appearance.

The orchestra came of age in June 1933 when they entered the National School Orchestra and Band Competition at the Queen's Hall in London. They acquitted themselves well, performing *"O say what Glory"* and *"Jerusalem"*, both of which had been arranged and scored by Philip Baylis. They came third in their class behind Westminster School and Beckenham G.S. and when they returned to school they claimed they were the third best school orchestra in the country, omitting to mention that there were a number of winners in more senior categories. Returning in 1934 they achieved second place, again to Westminster, and the adjudicator, who was the leader of the BBC Symphony Orchestra, praised their efforts.

In celebration of Handel's 250th Anniversary in 1935, an instrumental competition was inaugurated, with piano and violin solo prizes for under and over 14 years of age categories. This became a permanent feature of KES music, whilst the concert repertoire became more ambitious with work by Lully and Gluck and contemporary pieces like Eric Coates's *"Summer Day Suite"*. Stumped for a suitable musical play as the conclusion to the concert in 1936, Watling simply wrote an amusing plot in verse whilst Baylis composed the music for an operetta entitled *"Quid Pro Quo"*. In November 1937 the nascent BBC Television Service transmitted a performance of their production to their Home Counties viewers. KES had their own Lloyd-Webber and Tim Rice twenty-five years early.

That same year the school choir was finally established on a permanent footing by a newly arrived master, Walter Wheeler, working with Baylis. There had been choral singing at concerts in the past where solos, often by members of staff (in the Thirties no musical occasion passed by without at least one rousing aria from Bill Glister, later Headmaster of Chesterfield G.S.) were performed. This might appear unusual, or even embarrassing, to current students at KES in 2005, but the active participation of large numbers of staff in musical activities was taken for granted in the Thirties and no doubt contributed to a better relationship between masters and boys at the school. Amongst the works tackled by the choir and the orchestra in the next two years were *Iolanthe*, Holst's *"Turn Back, O Man"* and, somewhat incongruously, at Graham's final Speech Day in June 1938 they finished the proceedings with *Waltzing Matilda,* perhaps to cheer up Bradman's Australians who were touring England and losing the series.

The development of the School Dramatic Society in the Thirties mirrored the progress of the orchestra. Its antecedents had been one act performances at Speech Days or Christmas Concerts, until the formation in 1926 of the Literary and Dramatic Society heralded a new beginning. At first they were just a play reading society under E.F. Watling's guidance, but by December 1927 they were attempting more ambitious projects and there was a school production of Sheridan's *"The Rivals"* in the Assembly Hall, followed by *Twelfth Night* in 1928 and then in 1929 a play in French, *"Le voyage de M. Perrichon"*. The annual school play up to that time had meant the staff play, which drew a fair audience with the sort of plays where there was always a French window, a colonel, a dim-witted constable and a bright pretty daughter who was far too witty for the bumbling men-folk. Nearly a third of staff would act in these productions with lady teachers and wives of the staff playing the female roles. Add the lighting, scenery and front of house business helpers and at least half the staff were involved in their annual productions. Their society continued into the Thirties and was joined by an Old Edwardians' Dramatic Society, who also performed at the school.

Unlike the membership of the orchestra, the school's own plays would only draw on boys as members of the cast, with staff members directing and supporting behind the scenes. Watling again took a leading role, but two history masters, Wilfred Savage and Eric Simm, also directed plays during the Thirties with Harry Redston always organising the lighting and C.J. Magrath selling the tickets and collecting the finances. Younger boys, whose voices had not broken, played the female roles in the best Shakespearean tradition, and it would also seem impressive to present day Edwardians that an all-boy cast could be persuaded to perform, when currently in school plays the girls heavily outnumber boys in the cast. Unlike the drawing room whodunnits of the Staff and Old Edwardians' plays, the school dramatic society took on challenging work in the Thirties beginning with Moliere's *"The Imaginary Invalid"*, albeit in an English translation, and this set the pattern for the serious, even intellectually demanding, work for which KES Drama has become famous. Aristophanes' *"The Acharnians"* followed in 1932 directed by Watling, whilst Eric Simm produced *"Henry IV Part One"* the following year and there was another shot at Shakespeare in 1937, when G.D. Bolsover played the eponymous role in *"Hamlet"*. In between, the school had, equally ambitiously, put on Ben Jonson's *"The Alchemist"* and, like almost every school dramatic society, in 1934 they performed the iconic Western Front play, R.C. Sherriff's *"Journey's End"*.

The last production during Graham's time at the school was "Iolanthe", performed by the combined talents of the Dramatic Society and the Orchestra, with the local Elementary Schools invited to the performances as well as parents and boys at the school. Writing in the school magazine, the drama critic noted how this year; *"we did not have to pretend to be entertained because we could not help enjoying ourselves."* Certainly it appears to have been a very happy and highly competent production that underlined how the music and dramatic arts of the school had advanced during the previous decade, filling a large gap in the extracurricular education at KES.

When the school was inspected in 1933 the HMIs had reported that the teaching of Art had reached

"a good general level on formal lines, but the subject needs a full time Art Master with special qualifications to enable the school to provide an adequate course up to the end of the Fourth forms."

The appointment of Clarence Helliwell in 1936, who would stay at the school for the next thirty years, provided the impetus for the teaching of the Fine Arts and Art History that the school had hitherto lacked. Helliwell, from Penistone, had studied at Sheffield College of Art and at the Royal School of Art in South Kensington and was well qualified to raise the status and the standards of art teaching in the school. He also threw himself into the cultural life of the school, playing in the brass section of the orchestra and producing some brilliant sets for the school and staff plays.

CAST MEMBERS from the production of THE ACHARNIANS 1932.
Drawn by Harry Redston

The Thirties was a period of enlightenment for the arts at the school. The magazine included more poems and creative writing than it had done hitherto, and many of the poems were of a high standard. There was even a KES "Film Production Company", that filmed the scouts at camp in 1933 and in 1934 attempted a scripted film entitled "*The Year Dot*", using the scout hut as a film studio. They promised bigger things for 1935, but then seemed to have fizzled out until a new Film Society resurfaced after the war.

The Chapel Service

It was important to Richard Graham, a devout Christian who would have been at home in the company of some of his ordained 19th Century Headmaster predecessors, to strengthen the spiritual life of the school. When he first arrived at the school he introduced more solemn devotional hymns into the morning service, rather than the rousing tunes that had been the fare in Hichens' and Gurner's time. He took a part in the teaching of scripture along with fourteen other teachers in the Junior and Upper School and he took a close interest in the syllabus that was worked out in extensive detail. Every boy had one period of scripture a week (except in the Junior School and Form 2 where they had two), and there was an important emphasis on the historical dimension of the scriptures, with the involvement of all the history staff in the teaching of the scripture syllabus. Graham was so dissatisfied with the School Certificate syllabus in this subject that he prevailed upon the Oxford and Cambridge Board to allow him to design his own on the synoptic gospels, and KES pupils studied this syllabus from 1931 onwards.

Concerned that the spiritual values that he, and most of his staff, took for granted, were under assault from the growing, and attractive, secular culture of the time, he wanted to encourage devotional practice and inspire the spiritual well-being of the boys, without being overly sententious. His "Big Idea" was to institute a School Chapel Service along the lines of the regular Sunday chapel worship of the boarding public schools. He wrote to all parents in April 1933 indicating his intention of holding the first service on 7th May.

> *"The School Chapel plays an important part in the life of nearly all the greatest Schools of England, and I feel sure that these services (at KES), few as they are, will be of real value both to the corporate spirit of the school and to the boys themselves."*

Although he made it clear that these services, held on the first Sunday in each term, would be strictly undenominational and only for the boys of the school themselves, his new idea raised a storm of protest, not so much from the parents, but from the local Anglican Clergy. Notwithstanding that the Bishop of Sheffield had agreed to preach the sermon at the inaugural service, the Sheffield Diocesan Branch of the English Clergy Union sailed into the attack, led by the Rev. R.H.H. Duncan of Ulley. Without any discussions with Graham, they fired off a letter to the Board of Education demanding that they stop these services, claiming that they were in breach of a section of the 1921 Education Act, forbidding compulsory services outside normal school hours.

The thrust of their case was that Graham, in his enthusiasm to get all the boys of the school to attend his Chapel service, had demanded that, without a written letter of excuse from his parents, a boy would be expected to be in attendance. The clergy's real concern was that many members of their own congregations who were at KES would be missing from their own Matins services, and that perhaps KES might in the future hold a Chapel Service every Sunday. Graham was clearly stunned by the ferocity of the attack from the very group he thought might welcome his initiative. He came under pressure from the Board of Education and the LEA to call off the service until the charges had been investigated, and this he did. Initially, he replied to the Vicar of Ulley with scorn and no little sarcasm, but as the summer went on he moderated his opinion. He wrote again to parents clarifying the situation, making it clear that the service was purely voluntary and that there would be no requirement for any written permission for absence.

The first service now took place in October 1933 with the Bishop of Sheffield preaching the first sermon. During the next five years a succession of well known local churchmen of different denominations addressed the school at the Chapel Service, and Graham also prevailed on leading Christian Headmasters, including those of Bootham, the Leys, Rugby and Manchester G.S., to preach at KES as well. It was very fitting that at his last Chapel Service in September 1938, Richard Graham himself preached the sermon and used the opportunity to concentrate on the meaning and effectiveness of prayer. The Chapel Service was continued by the next Headmaster, although he replaced one of the services each year with a Commemoration Service to honour the founders and encourage an understanding of the history of the school. The Chapel Service was discontinued in the Fifties, but Graham would be even more disappointed if he knew that many Old Edwardians from his generation cannot even remember that there was a Chapel Service during the 1930s.

MORNING ASSEMBLY

The school's Morning Assembly had a ritual all of its own. Its primary purpose was to provide an undenominational Christian act of worship with a hymn and a lesson read by a prefect from the huge Wesley College bible placed on the brass eagle lectern. It also reinforced the corporate nature of the school community, bringing together all the school, including the Juniors who walked up from Clarke House, for the necessary notices and other school business.

The daily ceremony began with a drill that emphasised the hierarchy of the school. Boys would gather, form by form, in their own appointed places, coming to order as the prefects, the school's own Praetorian Guard, trooped in as a body and took up their places at the front of the hall. Now J.S. Nicholas would sweep in and mount the platform amid a fearful silence. The adjutant was now on parade and his eye searched the hall for the slightest sign of misconduct or indiscipline.

Finally the Headmaster, gown billowing with his mortarboard on his head, would enter the hall and all the staff and boys stood silently to attention as he took his place on the platform and commenced the service.

When the religious part of the Assembly was completed, boys who were Roman Catholics or Jews would slip in at the rear of the hall for the notices. Jewish boys were particularly envied, because not only did they miss most of the Assembly but they were also excused Saturday morning school because it was the Jewish Sabbath. There were also a small number of Asian boys at the school in the Thirties, sons of professional men in the city, who also missed the religious part of the Assembly unless they were Christians.

KES and the Wider World

It was during Graham's period as Headmaster that KES became more international in its outlook. While individual boys had been able to take family holidays in Europe and were encouraged to write them up in the school magazine, there had been no organised school visit to the continent until David Green took an official KES school party of thirteen boys to Paris in April 1928. His style was to ensure that all the boys should feel they were having a good holiday, touring all the famous sights, whilst their education appeared incidental. They were, of course, forced to use their rudimentary French because, in the Twenties, so few people whom they dealt with in Paris spoke English. The success of this visit encouraged Green to organise a French trip every year, until his untimely death in 1934. After a visit to Touraine and another trip to Paris, the annual KES French visit moved to the coast, firstly at Le Touquet and later, possibly because they found that sophisticated town a little too fast for the boys, they moved along the coast to Wimereux, three miles south of Boulogne. There the boys apparently frequented the casino on a regular basis, no doubt to better practise their language skills.

KES boys say farewell to Paris 1928

It was the contacts with German families, schools, and visitors that had the real appeal to KES boys in the inter-war period. These connections had an ulterior purpose beyond encouraging language skills and self reliance, and every boy who went to Germany, or received visitors here, could understand that they were playing a small role in helping to overcome the tragedies of the past, and help build a more co-operative future between the two countries. Graham developed a regular series of lectures in German, given by Germans currently in the city, usually at the University; there was even a visit in 1930 by a German touring company who put on a play in German at the school. The previous year three boys went on an exchange with three boys who were at an Oberrealschule at Harburg. This was the beginning of regular German exchanges up to 1938, and it was encouraged by the City Council, who arranged for a number of German boys to come to Sheffield during the summer holidays, and a group of 20 pupils from the city's secondary schools to go each year to Berlin. KES boys who joined these parties stayed in a holiday camp on an island at Birkenwirder on the outskirts of Berlin, and one year they were greeted on their arrival by their German hosts singing "God save the King". Their hosts also beat them 6-2 at football, and only lost by six runs in an exhibition game of cricket organised by the Sheffield boys.

These were optimistic days for Anglo-German relations, with the Weimar Republic appearing to be gradually getting back on to its feet after Germany had joined the League of Nations and accepted the Dawes Plan. Soon the economic collapse of the USA would send Germany spinning in a different direction, but for the moment so many people in both countries wanted to put old hatreds behind them and move on. Graham, a pacifist and an internationalist, was very much a man of this time and the school reflected his enthusiasm. In 1931 there was even a teacher exchange as "Billy" Effron went to teach for a year at a Berlin school and Herr Curtius came to teach at KES. Many of the initiatives for foreign visits came from enthusiastic members of the staff. When John Whitfield joined the staff in 1930, he immediately helped Green with the Paris trip and then later organised his own school visits to Italy, where the emphasis was cultural rather than analysing the Mussolini regime.

The school gave prominence to the annual Peace Day and played down the significance of Empire Day, which, although still given recognition on the school calendar, was usually marked by a talk on how the Empire was evolving towards its close, rather than trumpeting its glories. Some members of the school resented this change and wrote critical letters to the magazine. The editors still printed lengthy despatches from O.E.s playing their part in the far flung Empire, including some letters describing Old Boys running areas the size of the West Riding with only a swagger stick and creased shorts to back up their authority. Others articles from abroad took a more thoughtful look at how Ghandi was changing the political realities of the Raj, and there were talks by returning O.E.s who were missionaries, describing their ministry in the Sudan or in the Arctic. Other correspondents were soldiers or colonial policemen, one of whom, Gilbert Cole, an Indian Police Superintendent in the United Provinces, was later murdered in 1936, trying to arrest an armed man.

The creation of the KES Scouts, in Gurner's last year, also contributed to the opportunities for foreign travel and an international perspective It is unlikely that Graham would have applied for the post at KES if the school had still had an OTC, but a scout troop was very much in keeping with his philosophy and he welcomed its routine operations and the exotic locations of some of its foreign camps. Similarly he supported

KES students who went to the Summer School of the League of Nations in Geneva in 1935 and the Junior School members who had earlier formed a branch of the Junior Red Cross. The Debating Society in the early Thirties transformed itself into a mock parliament, where all boys attending were "M.P.s" and sat on the bench that suited their party loyalty. With a designated Prime Minister (Labour) — one of whom ironically was G.W. Tory — and Leaders of the Opposition Parties, they thrashed out some of the current national and overseas issues of the day, following parliamentary procedure. In October 1933 they defeated a motion congratulating "Herr Hitler" on the work he had done so far for Germany, but the KES Parliament lost its impetus, possibly because the McDonald Coalition Government had confused the battle lines, and it was replaced by a more orthodox debating society. This in turn was replaced in 1937 by a Discussion Group led by a new member of staff, History teacher Geoffrey Petter, which aimed to dig deeply into the chosen subject, and again National Socialism and Hitler's actions were probed by this new society.

It was the practice of the school librarians to review, in the school magazine, new books that had been donated or bought for the library. In the summer of 1933 a review appeared of "Mein Kampf", which had just been acquired. In the spirit of fairness the reviewer attempted a certain even-handedness but, in retrospect, he might well regret his last line, *"All will enjoy the sinewy strength of the thrusts he deals at Marxists, Internationalists and Jews."* However, as the book was in German its readership might well have been limited and later in the decade, when KES boys on exchange visits were faced with some of the visual reality of Nazi Germany, they appear on the whole to have been unimpressed. The exchange visits continued until 1938, after which the cantons of Switzerland were considered a less embarrassing venue for studying German. In 1935 the KES contingent had been shown around a political training college for boys and an "Arbeitsdienst" Camp near Halle, and in 1938 they witnessed Hitler's Birthday celebrations during their Easter holiday visit. The internationalism which had been one of the core values of the school during Richard Graham's term as Headmaster was being crushed by the realities of the Anschluss, Munich and Sudetenland and then, in March 1939, by the annexation of Czechoslovakia. The Editorial in the School Magazine for December 1938 reflects the school's anxious mood;

> *"The school was by no means exempt from the universal dismay manifested by the prospect of war. During the dark days of the (Munich) crisis boys no longer ran with gleeful faces through the corridors, but were strangely subdued, and changed their merriment for grave-eyed consternation."*

ARP buckets and equipment had been piled around the school during the Autumn; the happy decade at KES was almost over. The leafy suburbs of western Sheffield were preparing for one last Christmas before girding reluctantly and unenthusiastically for war. The Editorial continued:

> *"We who are young and will tomorrow be masters of our fate, must begin to shoulder our responsibilities - so we may devise saner solutions than those attempted by the modern world."*

Off to Bradford

The School was stunned when it returned from the Summer Holidays in 1938 to find that the Headmaster had been appointed as the new Headmaster of Bradford G.S. In Sheffield this was seen at best as a sideways move to another famous day school, albeit one with a much longer history and membership of the Headmasters' Conference. Graham, himself, most probably felt that his eleven years at KES had achieved all that he could expect to achieve; the school was thriving on all fronts and at 45 years of age he needed another challenge in an equally outstanding, high profile school. He had led the school's recovery from the complacency that had concerned the HMIs in their 1933 Report, reinvigorating many curriculum areas and improving the School Certificate, and even the Higher Certificate, results. In 1937 he had a vintage year of success at the Sixth Form level. KES achieved 14 scholarships to Universities, including eight Open Awards at Oxbridge, which he claimed was the best ever. In his last three years the school again carried off the Akroyd Scholarship after a gap of a few years, when C.K.Thornhill (1936), G.Chesham (1937) and T.G.Crookes (1938) were successful with other KES candidates running them close. In 1937 there were even three classicists gaining State Scholarships and the school was given a half-day holiday in July to celebrate all the achievements.

Graham had overseen two major building projects at the school. The Swimming Baths had been finally opened in October 1936 and, although they were owned by the Council and used by other schools, KES regarded them as theirs and they certainly got the most use out of this new facility. In the same term the Junior School had moved into its superb adapted buildings at Clarke House, had settled down well and was thriving. On the debit side, Saville had sold Lynwood in 1937 and moved into smaller and more appropriate premises, where he still accommodated the very few boarders left at the school. Losing Lynwood was the end of one particular era, although it would return to school use as extra classrooms in the Seventies, before finally being sold off by the Council when the new building, inside the Close, was opened in 1995.

If Richard Graham had had to suffer personal performance targets like a modern Headteacher, he would have come out of the exercise pretty well. He had been keen to widen the range of the educational experience for boys at KES and by the end of his time at the school he could point to an increased range of societies. The Natural History Society was formed in 1937 and the Gramophone Society, (which often listened to the records of works that would be performed in the forthcoming Halle Orchestra Concerts) in 1938, along with the Tuesday Club, a debating and book reading society for Second and Third Formers.

He had doubled the number of boys playing sport in house or school teams and a very high proportion of the school could now swim. As early as 1933 he had inaugurated a Parents' Evening for the Upper School, when parents could visit the school and sit down in turn with each master who taught their son and discuss his progress. This was a radical departure at that time, when parents were often seen by teachers as a barrier to real education, not as allies. At a time when very few Sheffielders went past Dover, he had wanted as many boys as possible to enjoy the experience of visiting a foreign country. By the end of the Thirties, eighty pupils a year spent some time abroad, often for three week periods, including about twenty in annual exchanges with Germany and many others through the Scouts. He gave support to school institutions like the very successful Scout Troop and visited their camps, even as far away as Peebles in the Lowlands. At the same time many of the boys were still enjoying an older summer tradition, travelling down to Sussex to enjoy a fortnight or a month at the Winchelsea camp. "Toby" Saville's programme rarely varied —its popularity with each new age group ensured it didn't need to — but his cricket fixture list seemed to grow each decade, with the KES team now calling themselves the Sheffield Ramblers.

Graham also gave support to the Old Edwardians' Association, making sure each new generation of leavers was fully encouraged to join the Association and, if staying in Sheffield and possessing the necessary skills, playing in one of the teams. At Oxford, always better populated by Edwardians than Cambridge, the O.E.s started a formal society called the Seventh Club in the Michaelmas Term 1930. Apart from its annual dinners, when the Headmaster would be the main guest and bring news of how the school was surviving without them, they met on a regular basis and kept contact between the new freshmen, seniors, research students and fellows who made up the sizeable Dark Blue O.E. community (there were 33 altogether in 1937).

At the end of the Thirties two significant chapters in the school's history occured. The first was when Old Boys of Wesley College celebrated the founding of their College in

The Two Cricket Teams representing the former pupils of Wesley College and the SRGS, July 1937.

1837. In June 1937 a large number of Old Boys from both Wesley College and from SRGS attended a very enjoyable open day where the central event, as befitted Yorkshiremen of that period, was the playing of a cricket match between the elderly gentlemen of the College and the Grammar School. Appropriately the match was a close draw, unlike former days when Wesley College usually thrashed their local rivals (the SRGS team were saved by one batsman, A.S. Furness, 75 not out, who got virtually all their runs). The Centenary Appeal to Wesley College O.B.s not only produced a plaque that was unveiled in 1938 and stills hangs in the Entrance Hall, but also instituted two annual prizes for English and for Natural Sciences, and an Inter-House Cup for Water Polo, the school's new fashionable sport.

WESLEY COLLEGE CENTENARY PLAQUE
unveiled in the Entrance Hall in 1938

The second event in the autumn of 1938 was the death in Paignton of Dr. James Hichens at the age of 79. He had kept in touch with the school where he was regarded as a legend. He must have been amazed that his immediate successor was leaving so abruptly, but content with the manner in which Richard Graham had conducted his stewardship. He may have felt that one decade was rather a short period to serve a school of KES's importance, and with war clouds so clearly gathering, a school needed continuity and tested leadership to face once again the loss of members of the "family" and even the possible destruction of the school buildings.

The School Song

Written by Eric Tappe, Head of Classics in November 1937

A new tune was written by Norman Barnes after he arrived at the school in 1947

Tempus est ut concinamus quicquid edvardensium,
Nunc adestis hoc sit omnes thema nostri carminis
Qualis est qui cuique nostrum semper aemulandus est.

Ille verus edvardensis quisquis humani nihil,
A sese alienum putabit usque consors ceteris.
Sive gaudebunt secundis, seu laborabunt malis.

Strenuus labore mentis, corporis non neglegens,
Omnium sententiarum perspicax inquisitor,
Semper artium bonarum pervicax videbitur.

(in English translation)

Now is the time for us to sing, Edwardians here today.
Let the whole theme of our song be this:
What kind of person is he whom each of us should constantly emulate?

A true Edwardian he, who shall not consider himself aloof
From any human affair, sharing ever with the rest,
Whether they rejoice in fair fortune, or are pressed by adversity.

He will show himself vigorous of mind and not negligent of body,
A keen examiner of all opinions,
and ever persistent in the good arts of life.

The first tune for the original Latin School Song which was in use before the First World War was one by Grafton, but by 1928 there appears to have been a new tune chosen by Ronald Gurner, whose composer was Duffell.

The SRGS used "Hearts of Oak", the march of the Royal Navy, as the tune to their school song which was written by Rev. Arthur Haslam in 1895.

CHAPTER ELEVEN

THE 167TH SHEFFIELD

For almost fifty years from 1927 until 1975 KES had a Scout Troop. In fact there were three troops for much of that period and a Rover Crew for Old Edwardians, who had left the school but had maintained the scouting "bug". Although, if the Council had not abolished the school's OTC, the scout troop — The 167th (King Edward VII Troop) Sheffield — might never have got off the ground. The prime mover in establishing the scout troop was A.W. Gaskin, and as we have seen he had pressed the Headmaster in the early Twenties for permission to start a troop and was rebuffed. James Hichens' priority was to build up the OTC, which he considered more manly and more appropriate for a school of KES's standing, believing that a scout troop would be a rival to the Corps and adversely affect recruitment. Ronald Gurner, initially, was also cool to the idea of school scouts, but changed his mind when he knew the battle over the OTC was lost.

So a school troop was founded in June 1927 and its formal Investiture, in front of the main school steps and in the presence of the County Commissioner, took place on 26th July 1927. Before that date the scouts had already had a number of weekend camps and selected their patrols. Each House had been asked to provide scout volunteers and within a few days they had twenty-two recruits and by the end of the year the troop numbered ninety members. The patrols were formed from members of each House and were given designated patrol colours as near to their house colours as possible. The green and white of Sherwood was replicated in the colours of the Peewits, and that became their patrol's name. For Clumber it was the Bulls, and Haddon members formed the Seals, whose red and black shoulder tabs were the closest to Haddon's colours.

Within days of the Investiture, the troop was under canvas at Sawdon, near Scarborough, which was to be a regular venue for the scouts in the early years. However, their ambitions did not just run to camps at Whit and for two weeks in August, for soon parties of KES scouts were visiting exotic locations abroad and becoming a real part of the phenomenon which was the worldwide Boy Scout Movement. In 1929 a party went to Lugano to join an International Camp there and, even more ambitiously, eighteen KES scouts went to a camp in Algeria in 1930 to join an international gathering organised by the "pied noirs", to mark the centenary of French colonial rule in that country. At Christmas another group was attempting skiing in Austria, and the following year a group of twelve scouts and two staff, who were scoutmasters, represented Britain at a Jamboree in Jamaica. Here was an opportunity to see a country that most Sheffield boys, at that time, would never have dreamed of being able to visit in the normal course of events, and for all of them it was their first contact with a multi-racial society, where Europeans were very much a minority.

Compared to all this, the OTC seemed suddenly rather sterile. Camping at weekends, building trestle or sheer bridges, constructing pioneer huts, participating in wide games and flag raids, or building up a formidable armful of badges, this was better than learning the parts of a Lee Enfield or drilling up and down the yard for no apparent end purpose. It is not always easy today to grasp how popular the scouts were in the first half of the Twentieth Century. Whilst having a superficial similarity to the cadet corps, they opened up a "boys' own" world of fun, friendship and adventure. Their internationalism, and their appeal to boys of all social classes, were very much part of the spirit of the times in the early Thirties, and the scouts' emphasis on outdoor activity, including huge long hikes (one year the KES scouts did a round walking tour of Devon), was very much in tune with the explosion of interest in the countryside as a popular leisure pursuit.

No-one at KES personified these values more than the Headmaster. When Graham, who became the Group Scoutmaster of the 167th, arrived at the school, he was delighted to see that the KES scouts, then only six months old, had chosen to wear the dark blue option for their uniform, thereby distancing themselves even more from the khaki of the OTC. Otherwise their uniform was as per normal, with the wide brimmed bush hat, nowadays only seen in official use in the U.S. and New Zealand, a neckerchief in the school colours of blue and white, thongs, cords and always, at that time, short trousers. Some scouts, in the best KES tradition, warmed to the badge and qualification culture that the scouts had created, and one of KES's first King's Scouts was Ted Flint, who won eighteen badges and was entitled to wear the "Gold Cords" and "Bushman's Thong" with his uniform.

By September 1929 the interest in the scouts was so great in the school that a second troop was formed. Now there were an "A" and a "B" Troop and they met on different days of the week and went to different locations for their regular and annual camps. Most convenient for weekend camps was the Grimbocar campsite, maintained by the Sheffield Scout Association in the Ashop Valley, near where Ladybower reservoir is today, and another favourite spot was Jaggers Clough near Edale. For their annual camps in the Thirties, the KES scouts visited every point of the compass in Britain, usually in the English counties, but there were memorable camps in Scotland in 1933 and 1938 and a couple in Sark in 1936 and 1938, as well as an International Jamboree in Holland in 1937. The Assistant Scoutmasters were members of staff, many whom had been scouts themselves in their youth, and their enthusiastic participation in the outdoor events, the weekly meetings and the annual camps, had a positive effect on staff-pupil relations through the more relaxed shared activities that the scouts offered, whereas in normal school time relations were very formal, if not confrontational. Apart from Gaskin — the dominant figure in the KES scouts until he retired in 1947 — Wilfred Savage, Eric Simm, Robert Exton, George Smith and Gordon Cumming (who had been amongst the first KES scouts in 1927) played particularly prominent roles in those years, but there were many others who, for longer or shorter periods, helped to sustain the life of the 167th.

Gaskin had hoped he would have a troop of about 100 scouts. In fact he usually exceeded that number and later in 1934 the troop was divided into five sections. Three of them were based on members from twinned Houses, with scouts from Arundel and Clumber having the numbers to form their own sections. Early on the scouts realised the necessity of having their own premises and so in 1930 they built their own hut, which served the troop until its disbandment in 1975. It was then used by the school for a number of purposes until the new building was constructed on that site in 1995. When the Rover crew was formed at the beginning of the Thirties, to serve those Old Edwardians who wanted to continue scouting in the Rover Scouts, they acquired the former groom's quarters in the upstairs room of the stables behind the Headmaster's house on Melbourne Avenue. This cosy "Den" was wood panelled and fitted out with a coal fire, easy chairs, a library and a table tennis table. Reached by a spiral staircase, it has only recently been demolished, although it is some years since the Rover Scouts, some of whom continued well into their twenties, occupied these premises.

Scouting continued during the War, with the troop initially limited to 96 members serving in only three sections. They still went camping and did their usual routines, but they also helped in the national defence effort, with scouts serving as ARP messengers on cycles, filling sand bags, helping at farming camps, and always collecting waste paper, which mysteriously was a vital requirement for a country at war. One Patrol leader, John Cotton, was awarded the Scout Gilt Cross for his coolness and bravery during the Sheffield Blitz of December 1940, and went down to the Scouts' Imperial Headquarters in London to receive his award. In 1941 when the school formed an A.T.C. unit, Gaskin was not prepared to be outflanked, and responded within a few weeks with the formation of an Air Scouts section, whose membership usually kept pace with the school's RAF Air Cadets. Their patrols took on the appropriate names of Skuas, Marlins and Kestrels and there were now new badges to be won, like the Spotter's badge for aircraft recognition.

Wartime shortages impinged on scouting as on all other activities. There was a shortage of scouters, because young staff members had been called up, and there were plaintive pleas for hand-me-down uniforms, belts, badges and hats because scarce clothing coupons had to be spent on more vital items. There was also the particularly sad news that came through, as former members of the troop, who had shared camps in far flung places, were now being killed and injured even further afield in the war that covered the globe. Many former scouts served in the forces and not a few found that skills learnt at Sawdon, Grimbocar or Jaggers Clough were more than useful to resilient servicemen in combat.

Altogether forty-three former scouts were killed in the Second World War, considerably more than a third of all the Old Edwardians whose names are recorded on the war memorial. They are commemorated in an exquisitely bound Book of Remembrance, which contains a photograph of every one of them, and includes their scout "history" as well as their war service details. Every year, during Remembrance Week, the book is displayed on an old school desk below the war memorials in the school's entrance hall. A number of today's generation of Edwardians take the time to leaf through it, the photographs of the former scouts a clearer reminder of the school's loss than even the many names on the bronze plaques above.

In 1942 the Scouts reverted to two Troops, "A" and "B", and then in the following year "C" Troop was founded. After the war "C" Troop held its meetings on Saturday afternoons whilst the other two met during the week. "A" troop even acquired its own den and "B" troop were the first to found a Senior Section in 1946 for scouts who were over 15years of age and therefore mainly in the Sixth Form. Although the Air Scouts had been disbanded after the War, the overall numbers continued to hold up in the post war period, even after A.W. Gaskin retired in 1947, when Gordon Cumming took over as the 167th Group's Scoutmaster.

The KES 167th Scout Group, May 1947
with Gordon Cumming and the Headmaster in the centre.

In the three post-war decades that the KES scouts survived, the pattern of activities that had delighted boys in the Thirties — hikes, wide games, camping, badge winning (KES scouts continued to become King's Scouts, and after 1952, Queen's Scouts) — continued to excite and enthuse new generations of KES pupils. There were great times at Whit camps at places like Newstead Abbey, and Summer camps in Cornwall, or the Lake District, where each patrol of around six scouts all shared one tent. The weekly activities still centred round the old scout hut, and as if to emphasise their comradeship, even their exclusivity, it was a long running joke amongst some KES scouts, *"that the Close would be ideal for scouting if it wasn't for that old building and all those kids who occupy so much space in the grounds of the scout hut."*

The 167th KES Sheffield Troop continued into the comprehensive era, finally running out of sufficient numbers to maintain a separate troop in 1974. It was given a year to see if the situation would rectify itself, but in 1975, with no change in the situation, the KES Scout Troop was disbanded. Keen KES scouts were now advised to join their local troops, indeed some Edwardians had always preferred to serve with their local scouts and never joined the school troop. David Marcer, who had tried to keep the troop going, now switched to running the Duke of Edinburgh's Award scheme, which was taken up enthusiastically and successfully by large numbers of boys and girls at the school. The Duke of Edinburgh's scheme was better suited to the temper of the times (scouts had become embarrassed about wearing their uniform about school, even if it did now feature long trousers, ties and berets), and, with so many of the activities of scouting to be found in the Duke's scheme, it can, perhaps, be said that the spirit, if not the exact form, of KES scouting, lives on at the school in the Twenty-First Century.

CHAPTER TWELVE

ACT HONOURABLY AND FEAR NAUGHT
1939-45

If you take the time to look at any village or town war memorial, you will be struck by how many more names there are for the dead of 1914-18, than there are for the Second World War. This is not the case with the two bronze plaques remembering the Old Edwardians who fell in the two world wars of the Twentieth Century. Despite the appalling losses suffered in World War One, when 90 Old Boys and two Masters were killed, KES fared even worse during the 1939-45 conflict losing 109 of its former pupils, and one boy still at the school. The reason for this is partly because the school had become much larger in numbers in the inter-war period, and partly because many were eager to become aircrew in the Royal Air Force. This turned out to be a fatal decision for so many, as over half the Old Edwardians killed in action, or killed on active service, were serving in the RAF.

At Easter 1939 Dr. A. W. Barton arrived to take up his position as Headmaster at the school, which for one term had been under the charge of J.S.Nicholas, the Second Master, after Richard Graham had left at Christmas to go to Bradford G.S. Dr. Barton was to have only one term of peace before the country was plunged into war, although after the German annexation of Czecho-Slovakia in March 1939, followed by Chamberlain's guarantee to Poland on the 31st March, it was clear that war was imminent. In normal circumstances when taking over a successful school that was running very efficiently, Barton would have taken a little time to play himself in and then set about strengthening areas of the school that he felt were under-performing. Instead he spent eighteen terms, almost half of his time at KES, running the school in the abnormal and highly stressful war time period, where the war had a much more direct impact on the school than had been the case in World War One.

Dr. Arthur Willoughby Barton's reputation had preceded him at KES when he arrived from Repton, where he had been Senior Physics Master. At Cambridge, after graduating with First Class Honours from Trinity College, he had worked as a demonstrator with Rutherford when he split the atom at the Cavendish Laboratories. After completing his PhD on radioactivity, he moved to Repton in 1925 where he wrote an important textbook on Heat and Light, which he quickly introduced at KES when he arrived. He was already known to some KES boys because he had refereed football matches between the two schools, and even better known as a Football League Referee who refereed First Division matches and had controlled an F.A. Cup Semi-Final. Tall, angular and impeccably dressed with the profile of a Roman pro-consul, he was the very model of a headmaster of the period and was regarded with respect, if not fear, by almost all of the boys in the school, who expected their Headmaster to be a severe and remote figure. Possessed of a brilliant intellect, he was also an effective teacher, whether taking senior boys for physics, where he initiated his top pupils into the "new alchemy" of the quantum theory, the fission of heavy elements and the counting of neutrons, or running a divinity class where he drew on his experience as a lay preacher. He was a dominating figure in the school in a way that Graham had not attempted to be, with the morning assemblies providing the forum where he could inspire and exhort the whole school. Sometimes sententious, often stimulating and energising, he had the strength of character and the leadership qualities to carry the school through the hard and critical days of the war.

Dr. Arthur Willoughby BARTON MA BSc PhD
1899-1976 (Headmaster of KES 1939-50)

Born 14th September 1899 in Nottingham. His father was the Professor of Physics at University College, Nottingham. Educated at Nottingham High School, where he was Captain of the School. Barton won an Exhibition in Natural Sciences to Trinity College, Cambridge in 1916, but did not go up to the University until 1919, after he had served as a subaltern in the Royal Engineers at the end of World War One. At Cambridge he took First Class Honours in Part I and Part II of the Natural Science Tripos in Physics and in 1922 completed a BSc at London University, where he again gained First Class Honours. From 1922-25 he was a Demonstrator at the Cavendish Laboratories working under Sir Ernest Rutherford, until he chose to become a schoolteacher rather than a University Don as he undoubtedly could have become.

Dr. Barton was appointed as the Senior Physics Master at Repton in 1925 and remained there until he became the Headmaster of KES in 1939. While at Repton he married Alison Mary Shaw but they never had any children. He also had a very active career as a First Class Football Referee, and the matches he controlled included a F.A. Cup Semi-Final, an Amateur Cup Final and the Austria- Poland 1936 Olympic Semi-Final. He also ran the line at the 1936 Wembley Cup Final when Sheffield United were beaten 1-0 by Arsenal; and later served on a FIFA panel of Referee Instructors.

Appointed Headmaster of KES by the City Council in late 1938, he took up the post in March 1939 and served at the school until the Summer of 1950. He moved to London when he was appointed Headmaster of the City of London School and became an active member of the Headmasters' Conference, something denied him at KES because of the events of 1926-27. He retired as Headmaster of the City of London School in 1965. He died in London on 24th August 1976.

At his first Speech Day in June 1939 Dr. Barton made this pledge to the City Councillors, the staff and boys at KES and their parents.

"I have no intention of trying to convert this school into a pale imitation of Repton or any other great boarding school. This school should become a great day school, second to none in the country. A school to which scholars would regard it as a privilege to be elected and one to which the best families in Sheffield would be proud to send their sons - a centre of true learning and culture."

"Such qualities as I have I will give freely to the school, and I know that whatever difficulties may lie ahead, I shall not fail if I remember that those qualities are not of my own making, but given to me by that Unseen Power which is the source of all true strength, to be dedicated to the service of others. I dedicate them to this School and to your sons."

Preparations for War

The school was on holiday when Chamberlain broadcast to the nation that we had declared war on Germany in order to save Poland from invasion, something that was quite clearly beyond the competence of Britain and France to achieve. The popular assumption was that death and destruction would rain down from the skies on the very first day and an industrial city like Sheffield would be battered and perhaps destroyed at a very early stage of the war. Official policy thought along similar lines and the belief that the bomber would always get through prompted urgent action to create defences for the public against aerial bombardment. While many boys would be helping to put up Anderson shelters, or more substantial concrete bunkers, in their own gardens or back yards, the City Council instituted three programmes designed to protect the schoolchildren of Sheffield.

Since May, the Chief Education Officer, H.S. Newton, had given priority to planning the evacuation of over 18,000 of the school population in the central and eastern industrial areas of the city. Evacuation was not considered necessary for the western suburbs but parents of KES boys could volunteer for it if they wished. Therefore on Saturday, 2nd September, under the supervision of Sydney Carter, a small number of Edwardians joined a larger group at Abbeydale Elementary School and, after being ticketed, were marched down to Heeley railway station and taken by a special train to Loughborough where they were billeted. Within two weeks they were all back home, although a member of KES staff, who had volunteered to be part of the teaching group for the evacuees, stayed on.

Before term started in September, the City Council had begun to dig trench shelters under the Close. They are there to this day lying undisturbed, forgotten but intact, in front of the school's main facade. The Council gave building priority for 23 schools outside the evacuation area and KES was amongst the first group of schools to have their shelters constructed. Approached through four brick entrances spaced at intervals in front of the school, they were in effect a linked series of zig-zagging underground concrete corridors with seats along the sides, which would have provided effective protection against most bombing. When they were completed by the beginning of December, boys undertook air raid practice in them, every one carrying his gas mask in its cardboard container as they did for every journey, including movement between classes inside the school. Occasionally during these practices young treble voices could be heard singing ditties like "We'll hang out the washing on the Siegfried Line", more to overcome the boredom than to maintain spirits in adversity.

The Parlour–School Period September to December 1939

Until the trench shelters were completed the Senior School could not use the school buildings because of the threat of the expected daylight raids. The Junior School at Clarke House was in a similar position but the solution for them was to turn the cellars of the building into reinforced shelters. They too had priority and so construction started for them at the same time as for the Senior School. In the meantime the City Council had evolved a scheme called "Home Service" whereby schools were divided into groups of 12 pupils of roughly the same age and farmed out to willing homes, who would allow them to take their lessons in a dining room or lounge, or even in some cases a billiard room or large bedroom. There they would be visited by their own teachers, who would carry on teaching the syllabus as best they could.

Each school organised its own arrangements within this general framework and KES divided the city into five "sub-school" districts, three of which were in the south west where the majority of the boys of the school lived. Each sub-school had a group of six masters or mistresses covering the main subject areas including one teacher covering the Junior School's curriculum. Within their district the staff travelled round from home to home by cycle, tram or on foot, giving hour-long lessons before moving on. Between visits the boys did set work usually supervised by the lady of the house, who invariably was a parent of one of the boys in the class. They were supposed to take on this somewhat onerous duty for only four weeks but some supervised the whole ten-week period, despite having to clear up chewing gum, paper planes and conkers amongst the other rubbish left in their homes. Meanwhile the Sixth and Transitus Forms were housed in rooms nearer the school and their lessons were much less disrupted as they managed to operate a fairly normal timetable. The Junior School shelters were finished first at the end of October and they moved back into Clarke House, but found they had to share their premises with the Central Day Commercial College.

All the Senior School returned to Glossop Rd. on Monday, 4th December to find the Close disfigured by brick shelter entrances, uncut grass and long lines of mud marking where the trenches had been dug for the shelters. During the school's absence an RAF Barrage Balloon unit had been training in the grounds and they added to the scruffy, untidy appearance of a school geared up for war time. The Luftwaffe, of course, never came during the period, nor would they ever attack Sheffield during the daytime because they would soon find out, like the RAF crews in Hampdens, Blenheims and Whitleys, that far from the bomber always getting through, it was highly vulnerable to the modern fighters each side now possessed.

The return did not however signal any return to full normality because the school now had to share its buildings with Nether Edge Boys School, whose shelters had not even been started. KES was not the only school so affected. City School had moved out from Leopold St. to be quartered with Central School, (soon to be renamed High Storrs in October 1940) whilst De La Salle School moved in with Firth Park G.S. In almost all cases the host school did the morning shift from 8.30 am – 12.15 pm and the visitors had the afternoon. This seriously affected school societies who had largely suspended their meetings during the period of Home Service and now couldn't easily restart because KES had to be out of their buildings by lunchtime. Partly because of this and partly because of the blackout and possible air raids there was plenty of time for homework and the library flourished with record borrowings. The long free afternoons did allow sport however to continue almost as normal, although regulations insisted that no more than twenty-five people should gather together for any game, or any other outside activity.

Normal School?

Not only did German air raids fail to materialise in the winter of 1939-40, there was no land war either. Both the Germans and the Allies had no plans for an offensive in the first eight months of the war, let alone a winter offensive, and so apart from the war in the Atlantic, which did start immediately war was declared, the nation continued its business as best it could in unreal and confusing circumstances. With most of the Staff still in post, KES therefore picked up the normal threads of the school year. Almost all of the usual curriculum was taught, with boys in the Fifth and Sixth Forms being prepared for external examinations in the summer and scholarship winners preparing to go up to their University in late September. The Dramatic Society managed to stage a school play in March but judged that "Charley's Aunt" would lighten the austerity of war-time better than a more challenging play. A Poetry Society was formed and the Scientific Society still visited local factories whose work was unconnected directly with the war. They went to a printers, a lace manufacturer in Nottingham and the Royal Crown Porcelain works in Derby, although they did pay a visit to the Central Fire Station in January to view war time preparations. The orchestra performed Beethoven's First Symphony and pupils were encouraged to go to the City Hall to hear Malcolm Sargent's Halle Concerts, including Haydn's Symphony No. 97, and piano solo performances by Myra Hess when she visited Sheffield. There was to be no nonsense in this war about listening to German music, but Barton did use assemblies to maintain a patriotic spirit within the school. He decided to once again celebrate Empire Day on 24th May, an occasion which had fallen into disuse in Graham's time, by flying the Union Jack from the school's masthead and giving an oration that was Churchillian in tone. All very much in keeping with the determined mood of a country which had just witnessed its Army outclassed in one of its worst ever defeats.

After Dunkirk it became more difficult to keep a school operating in normal circumstances, yet in June boys took their School Certificate Examinations, including the new subject of English Language, and later discovered that they had achieved a 76 % pass rate, better than previous years and above the national average for the first time. The Sixth Formers doing the Higher Certificate had a below average year for KES but who can blame 17 and 18 year olds for not fully concentrating on their studies when in a few weeks they could be in the services facing the prospect of invasion.

THE ANNUAL COMMEMORATION SERVICE

Dr. Barton created a new school institution, when on 28th April 1940 he inaugurated a Commemoration Service on one of the Sundays that had been reserved for the Chapel Service. It was in effect a founder's day occasion, which was very common at most public schools. The purpose was to remind the boys of their school's heritage and the date selected was the nearest to the 4th May, the date when the King James Grammar School's Charter had been granted in 1604. In the inaugural service the Headmaster stressed the debt to the Grammar School and Wesley College and to those that created and sustained the union of the two schools after 1905.

Barton was always keen to encourage the appreciation of the history of the school and would no doubt have instituted a Commemoration Service if it had been peacetime. However he was aware that at a time of grave national danger there was an added imperative to;

"make boys feel they belong to a Society which has deep roots in the past and which has seen and outlived many changes. This cannot but help them keep brave hearts and cool heads and distinguish right from wrong in these difficult times."

Old Edwardians Join Up

Already many Old Edwardians were in uniform with at least seventy having joined up by 1st December 1939 and this number was doubled by March. The School had begun to lose some of the younger staff members and when the call up age was raised to thirty in the summer of 1940, eleven masters left the school for the forces. The School Magazine from December 1939 till VJ day faithfully recorded in a "Roll of Service" all those Old Edwardians it had news of, who were in the services, been promoted or decorated. Soon the list would be headed with the names of the first casualties, those killed on active service as well as those wounded, missing, or known to be prisoners of war.

The first fatality in action was a ship's surgeon who had been at school in Dr. Hichens' time. Surgeon-Lieut. Frank Williams R.N. had served in the Navy before the war after being in general practice at Malin Bridge earlier. Ironically, he had already seen some action in China in 1938 when his ship, H.M.S. Cicala, had defied Japanese warnings and sailed 25 miles up the mine-littered Pearl River on a rescue mission. His luck ran out off the French coast when his ship was sunk, and although he was seen to get into one of the lifeboats, bad weather scattered them during the night and only one boat was rescued. For some weeks he was posted as missing, but by August the Admiralty was listing him as presumed drowned and his lifeboat was never found.

During the summer of 1940, because the war was being fought in the air, the O.E. casualties were all airmen. 24 year old Sgt. Percy Dryden had been one of the first school scouts in 1928 and after he left KES in 1933 he became articled as a chartered accountant. He opted to join the RAF in March 1939 when war seemed imminent and he trained as an observer. His bomber was brought down on the 20th July 1940 after he had undertaken many operations before and after Dunkirk. Sgt. Harry Bowmer (1933-37) was also an observer with Bomber Command and also 24 years old. He had done two months of operations when in August 1940 he was killed in an accident at RAF Scampton. Four years later his younger brother, F/O John Bowmer, (1933-38) was the pilot of an aircraft that failed to return from a 10 hour anti-submarine patrol over the North Atlantic between the Hebrides and Iceland. They were among four pairs of brothers who had been at KES in the Thirties and were killed in the war.

Two Old Edwardians fought in the Battle of Britain serving in Fighter Squadrons of 11and 12 Groups. Flying Officer Malcolm Ravenhill was shot down and killed in late September whilst serving with 229 Squadron and Sgt. Pilot, later F/O, David Fulford flew Spitfires with 19 and 64 Squadrons and survived until later in the war. The crucial importance of this battle, the first fought within Britain since Culloden almost two hundred years previously, is well understood even by people in this century. For the people at the time, including all those at the school, this victory, in a year of unrelenting gloom, meant the certain relief that Britain was not going to be invaded that year, even if, in reality, the nation now found itself in a military impasse. In the millennium year 2000, the Battle of Britain Historical Society presented a plague to the school commemorating the service of Ravenhill and Fulford in the battle. After an appropriate ceremony, attended by the Sixth Form, it was placed on the wall of the Entrance Hall adjacent to the War Memorial.

The Sheffield Blitz 12/13th and 15th December 1940

In the late autumn of 1940 the Luftwaffe changed its strategy to night bombing of Britain's industrial cities outside London. Although Sheffield had suffered the occasional raid since August, often by lone raiders, the expected onslaught came on the night of 12th and 13th of December. Almost 400 German bombers, mainly Heinkel 111's, flew virtually unmolested up the length of England from their bases near Chartres in Northern France. They attacked the city in waves throughout the night starting at 7.15pm in the evening when early arrivals bombed the inner suburbs marking a ring around the city centre for later planes to target. Broomhill, thought to be less vulnerable, was therefore in the thick of the bombing and although the school avoided structural damage, prompt action saved the building from damage by incendiaries. Gillman the Porter, was described by one member of staff as; "calmly putting out incendiaries in Room 71 at 4.00 am as if he had been doing it all his life." He was also responsible for saving the costumes that had been designed for a production of "Trial by Jury" due to take place the following night. The Junior School at Clarke House also escaped a direct hit. However, blast from nearby explosions blew out many of their windows and in the morning boys from the Senior School were drafted down the road to help with clearing up the glass.

Needless to say Gilbert and Sullivan was postponed, but the following morning the school had become a reception area for local families who had been bombed out of their homes. The Headmaster now ran the buildings as a residential hostel with beds and basic facilities in the hall, the gym and in many of the classrooms. The staff and senior boys gave up their holidays, which now started early, to help deal with unfamiliar duties and awkward organisational problems. The helpers worked on a two-shift system with the day shift under the Dr. Barton's supervision and Sydney Carter on duty at night. In the kitchens the redoubtable Mrs. Helstrop conjured up meals for all the new residents, a problem made

GORDON STRANGE (KES 1937-40)
In November 1940 whilst helping out as a member of the KES Scouts at the Sheffield War Weapons Week Exhibition in the foyer of the City Hall, Gordon Strange, a 14 year old boy who lived in Firth Park, was fatally injured by a round from an accidental discharge of a Boyes Anti-tank Rifle. A member of Form Va, he had already demonstrated that he was a brilliant scholar and would have gone into the Classical Sixth and probably gained an Oxbridge Scholarship. Although he was neither a serviceman nor been killed by enemy action, his name was included on the War Memorial, the youngest Edwardian to be so commemorated in either of the two World Wars.

more difficult by the fiddling regulations of ration books and cutting out of the coupons. Many of the families would spend Christmas and the New Year at the school and the start of the new term had to be postponed until 20th January when the school was ready to be returned to its normal state.

No boy at the school had been killed in the raid although many had had their homes damaged or even destroyed. Eric Allsop, of the Fifth Form, received a special commendation for his work that night, and later would be presented to the King and Queen when they came North to see the damage. One of several Edwardians who had trained as ARP messengers, he had continued delivering messages during the raid, helped put out fires for three hours using a stirrup pump and then when he returned home he found his own house in Nether Edge had been destroyed in the bombing.

The Luftwaffe returned two nights later but their target was the industrial east end and the school was not involved, although all their visitors were evacuated into the shelters after the sirens went. For the rest of the war KES boys, like everyone else in the city, had to get used to living amongst the debris of war. Familiar shops in the city centre had disappeared, the famous John St. stand at Bramall Lane was down, while nearer the school, St. Mark's Broomhill had been burned out and only the Tower survived when the church was rebuilt in the Fifties. The Luftwaffe raids on Sheffield, codenamed "Schmelztiegel" (Crucible) had killed 502 people in the first raid and 72 in the second one. 82,413 houses were damaged and almost 3000 destroyed, well over half the homes within the city boundaries. It was a particularly bitter winter that year and many homes were without windows, gas and water for some considerable time. The Luftwaffe recorded no lost aircraft on either night.

BLITZ

The horn in the night has risen.
Up from the mist of sleep, fear flames.

Here come the blind butchers,
Staggering in the darkness.

Sing while the chopper falls!
Sing! Sing! and drown the din!

Sing while the chopper falls!
Sing! Sing! and drown the din!

All over. There go the butchers,
Dipping their bloody hands in the East.

Dawn draws the bandage,
And the wounds of the City scream.

George MacBeth

This poem was written in 1949 when he was in the Fifth Form. His own father was killed in a sneak raid in 1941, close by the Botanical Garden entrance

1941 – The Year Defiant!

The systematic bombing of Britain's industrial cities, along with the victories in the Battle of Britain and over the Italian Fleet at Taranto and the Italian Army in Libya in November and December of 1940, put the nation in a defiant mood in the new year. KES shared in this new, if premature, optimistic spirit and it became a point of honour to work more conscientiously in the classroom and volunteer for activities that would help the war effort. For some senior boys this meant joining the Local Defence Volunteers, the LDV, who now became re-formed as the Home Guard. Others, as we have seen, became ARP messengers, whilst at the school a Fire–Watch rota was organised for Sixth Formers and Staff members. The Watch had a dual role; to observe the city from the Upper Floor of the school, looking out over the Corinthian pillars, and warn the ARP of any sign of fire and also being on hand to sound the alarm if the school was on fire and render some basic fire-fighting help. The boys on the rota slept in the Prefects' Room until it was their turn to patrol the building and climb up the spiral staircase to their observation post. Some discovered that even the most fearsome masters, the Second Master in particular, were really human and even humorous after all. It was a microcosm of how the country was pulling together and breaking down social barriers. Work in the summer on farm camps in Derbyshire and the support KES gave for Newhall Boys Club in Attercliffe, were all part of a new co-operative spirit that broadened the educational experience of KES boys as well.

In the summer of 1940 the Government had decided to reduce the school holidays by encouraging schoolchildren to return to school for three weeks in the middle of August. KES had dutifully opened its doors to almost all its pupils and they had enjoyed a programme of hobbies and recreational activities. With the Winchelsea Camp impossible to organise when the Sussex coast was the front line against invasion, this summer school offered KES boys some structured leisure activities. Similarly working on farms and living with your pals in huts at Bakewell and Grindleford was a healthy, even useful and enjoyable, alternative to a proper holiday. These farming camps would continue during the war years and Professor Adrian Horridge, who was at the school during the war and later became a leading neurobiologist in Australia, relates how he went each morning to pick up thirty German POWs who helped the KES boys with the farm work. He had to sign out for them and then march them to the fields to join in picking peas. They were paid at the same rate as the boys, 6d. (2.5p) a hour, and at the end of day he marched them all back to their camp and solemnly signed them off. He was only 15 years old at the time, and he had collected the prisoners and supervised them the whole day by himself.

Also, as part of the spirit of the times, the school became involved as a partner with Newhall Boys Club recently set up in Brightside in an old pub but later moving across the river to Attercliffe. Run by the local Anglican clergy and supported by the Headmaster, who later was Chairman of the Sheffield Boys Clubs' Association, the school mainly provided support by a regular cash collection (a penny a week) and also books and sports equipment, whilst some of the senior boys did get more directly involved in the activities at the club. Football matches were arranged at Whiteley Woods and Table Tennis games were arranged at both venues, while the lads from the club, most of whom were working, came across the city and used the swimming pool. The club flourished, with over sixty members providing enough players for three football teams; their First XI heading the Boys' Club League. There were films on Fridays, religious discussions on Sunday, canteen facilities and a snooker table and it no doubt served a very useful purpose in a deprived community. Towards the end of the war KES interest seems to have waned and the club's activities were no longer reported in the school magazine. In today's more cynical world such a partnership might be regarded as patronising and superficial, but it may well have been that more than one Edwardian got his first glimpse of the sheer scale of the poverty in the east end of the city through visiting the Newhall Boys Club.

Formation of an ATC Squadron 1941

The school, who had had their OTC abolished in 1927 by the City Council, found no such opposition in Spring 1941 when a new Squadron of the Air Training Corps was formed, recruiting directly from KES pupils over 16 and Old Edwardians awaiting call up. The school never attempted to re-form the army cadets, now re-named the Junior Training Corps (JTC), but there was a considerable demand from boys to join the RAF cadets of the ATC. Numbered No. 366 Squadron and commanded by S/L Ambrose Firth, the M/D of Firth Brown Engineering works, the school would eventually enrol over a hundred boys in the ATC

F/O Malcolm RAVENHILL (KES 1922-29)

Malcolm Ravenhill left KES after the Fifth Form and worked for Woolworths becoming a branch assistant manager in Glasgow. He joined the RAF before the war and trained in Egypt. He served with 229 Squadron and shot down three enemy planes over Dunkirk during the evacuation. He fought in the Battle of Britain and was forced to bale out himself in the middle of September over Kent. Ten days later in a dog fight over London he was shot down again and this time he did not escape. One of his hobbies was sketching and he had had a recent cartoon printed in Blighty, the services magazine. At 27 he was considerably older than most of the fighter pilots in 1940 and his body was brought back to Sheffield and buried in City Rd. cemetery.

SERGEANT PILOT John Michael FULFORD (KES 1927-37)

John Fulford was one of the best known sportsmen at KES during the Thirties. Champion Athlete in 1935 and 1936 and Cross Country winner in 1934, he had his colours for Football and Cricket and after leaving school he played for Corinthian Casuals and was the first O.E. to play professional football when he turned out for Sheffield United in 1940 whilst awaiting call up. The son of a former officer who was a pilot in the RFC, he intended to be a doctor and was studying medicine at Sheffield University before he joined up in the RAF in May 1940. By the end of the year he had his pilot's wings and after several operations across the Channel he was shot down and killed over Brittany in May 1941. He was only 22 years old and was buried by the Germans near Nantes

F/O David FULFORD DFC (KES 1928-38)

David Fulford was the younger brother of John Fulford and in 1937 he also was the school's Champion Athlete. He had joined the RAF when he left school and went to Cranwell and was serving as a Spitfire pilot with 64 Squadron at RAF Leconfield, near Beverley, when the Battle of Britain broke out. He moved south to join 19 Squadron at RAF Duxford and took part in the aerial battles of the summer of 1940. In 1941 he was awarded the DFC and in a documentary film about the battle called " The First of the Few", he flew a captured Heinkel 111, posing as a Luftwaffe pilot, before being posted out to Ceylon (Sri Lanka) in January 1942 to meet a possible Japanese threat in the Indian Ocean. He left a vivid record in the school magazine of his Hurricane squadron engaging Zeros and played their part in securing Ceylon from a possible Japanese invasion. Returning to England in September he joined 611 Squadron at RAF Biggin Hill, and shortly afterwards, in November 1942, he went down over the Channel after a routine sweep over the French coast.

undertaking pre-service training for the RAF and the Fleet Air Arm. They were given basic instruction in navigation, signals and wireless and aircraft recognition as well as drill, P.T and RAF Law and Regulations. Visits to operational stations were the highlights of the cadets' year, where, after seeing how pilots trained on Link trainers or how parachutes were packed, they were allowed to crawl along the fuselage of a Wellington bomber and handle the controls. Later in the war most cadets got the opportunity to fly some circuits when they made these visits, and others were accepted for courses of gliding instruction.

While not overwhelmed with volunteers, possibly because the KES Scouts had formed their own Air Scouts section, there were a sizeable number of boys at the school who had long set their hearts on flying and for whom the glamour of a pair of wings, an Irvine jacket and a chance to fly a Spitfire were a powerful seductive force. Many of them would fill the depleted ranks of the RAF Squadrons later in the war, although most of them would be assigned to Bomber Command, where the attrition rate was higher than in any other branch of the British armed services.

The Squadron's officers came mainly from the school and they included Sydney Carter, now an acting Flying Officer and Adjutant of the Squadron, although his own wartime service had been as an artillery subaltern in Italy in the First World War. Amongst the first keen recruits was Ross Gilfillan, the school Football Captain, who after leaving school spent a short period at Cambridge in 1942 awaiting call up. He qualified as a navigator in Bomber Command and was shot down on the night of 13/14th February 1945, the night of the Dresden raid.

In July 1942 all the school cadets were transferred to No. 364 Squadron where they constituted a separate "King Edward VII" Flight under the command of F/O A.P. Graham who had joined the school staff in 1940. No. 366 Squadron was now reorganised to compose only men over 18 who were already accepted for the RAF but deferred for education or work related reasons. The new KES Flight's routine training on Monday afternoon at 4.30 pm was now at the school, and this made it easier for new recruits to give the necessary time, with a further boost to recruitment coming in the summer when the entry age was dropped to fifteen. The specific purpose of the training was to enter cadets for the ATC Proficiency Award which would guarantee entry into the Air Force. This was a difficult examination which could be a passport to a short university course leading to a commission in RAF or one of the other services, and only twenty cadets achieved it whilst with the school's ATC flight.

By 1945 the Air Ministry began to consolidate the number of ATC Squadrons it supported, and so No. 364 Squadron was stood down and its members absorbed into No. 369 Squadron. By 1946 there no longer was a need for thousands of new aircrew and the ATC was drastically reduced in size. In the Spring Term 1946 the School Flight was disbanded and one of the school's main contributions to the war effort came to an end. Although there would now be no objection to a school cadet force at the school (most public schools continued their corps without interruption), KES reverted back to its pre-war policy of only encouraging membership of the school scouts, who were to enjoy another thirty years of existence.

KES – REVOLT AGAINST TYRAN(N)Y

Two ATC cadets, however, entered KES folklore for their role in the "revolt" in the closing weeks of the Winter Term 1941. At the end of November, five notices pinned up by the Headmaster on his notice board, were defaced by the addition of the letters NBG after Dr. Barton's own signature. At that time everyone understood the pejorative nature of those three letters, and they remained there through the first two days of the school week before the Porter removed them at the Headmaster's request. The following day there was more of the same, and another notice on a society notice board was scribbled on in a similar manner the day after that. Clearly the Headmaster had to act and, with the help of the prefects, a thorough investigation of all possible suspects was undertaken during the next six days. Many were questioned but no clear suspect emerged. This was not entirely surprising because the main culprit was an old boy, a member of the ATC now studying at the University, who had gained access to the school after an ATC parade at the week-end when the school was deserted.

Some Headteachers might have let the whole incident drop and enjoyed the joke with the rest of the school. Arthur Barton was not one of these men. Touchy about his dignity and virtually without a sense of humour, he set out to crack the case of these "scurrilous actions". Announcing to the full Assembly that if the culprit did not own up by 12.25 pm the following day the school would lose its Wednesday half day holiday, he dutifully invoked the punishment of extra classes when no one came forward to confess. This did the trick. Acting on information received, R.H.Maxfield, an Old Edwardian ATC member at Sheffield University, was summoned to the Headmaster's study and after some resistance owned up to his "crimes" and wrote out a full apology. In return Barton agreed not to report him to his Vice Chancellor but banned him from the school premises and grounds for five years. A further culprit, in the Fifth Form, refused to admit he too was involved and held out for a fortnight of interrogations until he could no longer deny the evidence that the Headteacher had marshalled against him. Barton suspended him and later welcomed his father's decision to send him to another school, but insisted that he paid the full fees for the next term.

Honour now satisfied, the Headmaster expected the school to settle down for the remainder of the term. However the most dramatic events were yet to come. Arriving at school on a Saturday morning a week later, staff and boys were welcomed by a large white sheet, flying from the masthead over the front portico, emblazoned with the misspelt words in red paint; "KES - REVOLT AGAINST TYRANY". The Porter was sent up aloft to remove this "revolutionary" standard, but this time the event was too public and it received column inches in the Daily Mail and soon the Education Committee wanted to know what was going on. In a four page hand written letter to Dr. William Alexander, the new Chief Education Officer, the Headmaster explained how the perpetrator, J. Meakin, another Old Edwardian ATC member at the University, had owned up the following day admitting he had done it partly in support of his friend, Maxfield, and partly as a practical joke. He too was banned from the school grounds and buildings for five years.

In the Assembly immediately following the removal of the flag, the word went round, "Don't sing the Hymn", and such was the emboldened and anticipatory mood of the assembled that when the first verse sounded Barton was left singing virtually on his own. He sang on, and then with superb sang froid at the end of the Assembly he announced that the hymn would now be sung again. The rebellion collapsed as everyone now mumbled their way through the verses and the "revolution" was over.

In January the LEA sub-committee, who were in effect the Governors of the school, received a report from Barton setting out the full chronology of the events and the action taken by him. The Governors gave him their full backing and re-iterated their confidence in him. He always argued publicly that the events were isolated incidents in no way indicative of the general feeling of the boys and parents. He may have been right, but every boy at the school at the time remembers the incident as if it was yesterday and the Headmaster must have been severely embarrassed, if not considerably chastened, by a clear challenge to his authoritarian regime.

The Changing Staff

The biggest, and continuous, problem facing Barton during the six years of war was the fundamental one of finding the right quality of staff to fill the posts left by those who were called up into the forces. He was ambitious to improve the school's academic record even beyond the levels achieved by Graham and Hichens and to do this he had to have highly qualified people who were very competent teachers as well. During the war Barton made sixty-seven teaching appointments, most of them temporary appointments because posts had to be kept open for the staff who would return when hostilities ceased, but others, like Gerry Claypole, who came to the school from Birkenhead School in 1941 to take up the new post of Senior English Master, were permanent appointments. Over one third (15) of Barton's male staff were called up, leaving him with an elderly male teaching staff and creating gaps he was increasingly unable to fill. Like his predecessors he would always prefer to appoint Oxbridge graduates if they applied for a position, but that was not so possible in wartime when recruitment of any suitably qualified masters became very difficult.

Not all the staff were called up at once, so in 1940 and early 1941 the Headmaster could still find suitable replacements like Alec Baker, a Cambridge Graduate who came from the Prep. School of Tonbridge School to replace Toby Saville, when he retired on health grounds in 1940. Baker not only ran the Junior School during the war but also took in some boarders at the new premises of Broomgrove House, immediately opposite the School on Clarkehouse Rd. For these extra responsibilities he got the usual Special Responsibility Allowance of £48, the same as the Heads of Departments, and he had a hard act to follow because Saville was, of course, a legend at the school with 37 years service, first at Wesley College and then continuing at the new KES after 1905.

The answer for Barton's staffing crisis was the same as it had been for Hichens and his Junior School staff in 1917. There were many very competent women teachers who were ready to come back into teaching and make their contribution to the war effort in that way. There had been a substantial minority of women teachers in the Junior School during the inter-war years and some like Miss J.W.M. Copley had been at KES since the First World War. When D.C.G. Sibley went off to join the forces in 1939 she was made the House Master (sic) of Norman House and very soon the majority of teachers in the Junior School were women. Lucy Michell (née Turner) had returned to teaching in 1938 after she was widowed, the LEA regulations allowing widows to teach but not young married women. When she got married again in 1944 and became Mrs. Goode, she had to get the authorisation of the LEA to carry on teaching, although such permission had by now become a formality. This particularly archaic convention, indeed regulation, whereby newly married women in the professions were not considered "respectable" if they worked, died out after the Second World War, although the practice of middle class wives staying at home as housewives, or supervising the "helps", lasted much longer.

In March 1941 the first woman teacher in the Senior School was appointed. Frances Daft was a graduate of London and Sheffield Universities and she was followed in September for the new academic year by several women teachers, including Mrs. Mona Nott (History), Miss Jean Knight (Classics) and Miss Barbara Steward in charge of the Art Department in Clarence Helliwell's absence serving in tanks in the Desert. They became permanent members of the staff although they all left as soon as the war was over. Others were on temporary contracts and filled in for shorter periods. Miss Daft taught Latin and English and gained the respect of the boys she taught, especially as she was prepared to administer some stinging slaps if she felt her authority was being challenged. Other women members of staff could not come to terms with the regime of corporal punishment that was normal in the school and it was understood that a male colleague would administer the cane on their behalf. Miss Janet Manners, later Mrs. Duffin, who joined the staff to teach Maths straight after she had left Durham University in 1944, was reluctant to punish any boy with a caning and could not even bring herself to be the official witness. She was only three years older than some of the sixth formers, as was Miss Doreen Horne who joined the school at the same time to teach Latin, and they were both paid only £12 per month.

By 1944 boys had become familiar with women teachers, some of whom were married, some who were spinsters but who were nearly all middle aged. The attractive Miss Manners and Miss Horne turned a few heads amongst the older boys, forced to spend their days in the monastic ambience of a six day a week boys school in war time. Janet Manners further impressed her Sixth Form set by providing the correct answer to an algebra problem that had defeated J.S. Nicholas and his top Maths set.

Although Barton appointed 21 women teachers during the war, including Miss J.K. Leslie who had been the Headmistress of the Coptic Girls College in Cairo, he still had difficulties in making up his losses of personnel. He persuaded Saville to return in 1941 and teach in the Senior School. At sixty-five it was probably too much for his frail health and he died in May 1942. A memorial service was held in the Assembly Hall and his dominating influence on four areas of the school's life, Lynwood House and its boarders, the Junior School, school sport and the Winchelsea Camp were fully chronicled . There were many of his former pupils who wished to be present but could not be there because they were serving in theatres of war all over the globe, and it was equally disappointing that his camps on the Sussex coast did not survive into the post war years as a tribute to his contribution to the school. Other staff left because they got promoted or moved nearer to their family homes. Wilfred Savage who had taught History and Geography since 1926 went back to teach at his old school, Plymouth College, in December 1940 and W.F. "Bert" Wheeler did the same in 1942 when he accepted a post of Senior Biology Master at Worcester R.G.S. where he had been a pupil. E.H.C. Hickox was offered the post of Senior Science Master at Ellesmere College on the Wirral, in April 1942, which he accepted, and then Joe Clay, now only the Senior History Master after the division of his department in 1941 (when Gerry Claypole came to KES and took over the new English Department), decided to retire because of severe ill health at Easter 1943. He had joined the staff just before the Armistice in 1918 and had served the school for quarter of a century. His "memorial" would include the long list of History scholars at Oxford and Cambridge whom he had prepared for their scholarship examinations. He was another of those long serving members of staff (there were now only three who had served longer) who appeared to be the "cornerstone of the building", and from Room 8 he had cast his benign spell upon hundreds of boys who passed through his classes, gaining their interest and friendship.

There were however a fair number of the key members of staff who carried on during the war and later some even had to get the Board of Education's permission to go on beyond retirement age. One was Harry Scutt, the Senior Languages Master, purveyor of the most dreadful puns often based on a pupil's name. If the boy retaliated in kind by saying "I'll scuttle along Sir!" or some such epithet, Scutt rarely saw the joke and caned them for insubordination. Another who served on past retirement age was J.S.Nicholas, whose teaching methods became even more eccentric with time. Boys recall having work set at the beginning of the period and then left to get on with it, whilst Nicholas scoured the building for boys running along the corridor, dropping litter or, best of all, parked outside a classroom from which they had been ejected for bad behaviour. It was even rumoured that he would nip into the staff room for a crafty smoke, before climbing back up the stairs to room 63 on the top floor. Protocol demanded that he coughed loudly near the top to allow boys to get back into their desks and resume work as if he had never been away.

Such eccentric behaviour was not just tolerated but almost encouraged as part of the rich patina of the traditions of the school, and if the master concerned continued to get boys to win Open Scholarships and gain good Higher Certificate results then who would wish to criticise.

Barton found a novel way to help him solve his staffing difficulties after the call up age for teachers had been raised to 35 in the Spring of 1941. He began to recruit German, Austrian and Jewish refugees who had come to this country before the war broke out to escape the Nazi regime. The men, not having been naturalised, found themselves rounded up in 1939 and interned in hotels behind barbed wire on the Isle of Man. They were kept there until 1941 when those who were considered no danger to Britain were classed as Category B Aliens and released. The idea to recruit some highly qualified teachers from this very well educated group may have come to the Headmaster after he appointed Eva Paneth, a refugee who had taken a BA degree at London University after arriving in this country. Eva Paneth, who was not interned because she was a woman, is well remembered by boys whom she taught. Many were confused that a German women could be teaching them German in the middle of a war against Germany but Fraulein Paneth was full of amazonian confidence, could exert forceful discipline and was clearly not a lady who would put up with insubordination. She was never given a permanent contract at KES but she stayed at the school until 1944 and her success encouraged Barton to employ some of the men now released from the Isle of Man. Some were highly qualified. Dr. Georg Sachs who came to teach Science had previously been a lecturer at the University of Vienna and Dr. Felix Behrend had been the Headmaster of the prestigious Kaiser Wilhelm Realgymnasium in Berlin and he too taught Science after he arrived at KES in the summer of 1942. He was not prepared for the traditional informal "warfare" of an English classroom, where any teacher who cannot exercise crude power over his charges, can find that their lives are a misery. Clearly at the Kaiser's school much greater deference to teachers was the order of the day and Dr. Behrend left in the following year. J.H.A.W. " Willy" Woellhardt arrived at the same time and he was taken onto the permanent staff to teach German and would remain at KES for many years, whilst Dr. Wolf Rosenberg stayed only for a year. He had used his time on the Isle of Man to teach Science at King William's College and he joined the Science Department at KES in January 1943 before leaving in December to become the Senior Science Master at King Edward VI School, Nuneaton.

It was not just the new staff members who had fled from Hitler: there were boys at the school who had arrived as refugees in England in 1939 and in time found themselves at KES. Eric Kalman (1941-50) had hidden for two years with his family in a flat in Frankfurt on Main before getting a place along with other Jewish children on a Kindertransport to Britain in Summer 1939. At the Dutch border the children thought they were going to be shot when they were twice stopped by SS Guards, who first robbed them and then deliberately humiliated them by making them polish their jackboots before letting them pass on their way. Kalman went to the home of an aunt in Hunters Bar and eventually when he was old enough moved on to KES. His father, meanwhile, had been arrested and sent to Dachau in 1939, from where amazingly he made his escape and managed to get to Britain just before the war started. Technically a stateless person, he was interned until 1941 on the Isle of Man, suffering the same indignities as the teachers who later joined the KES staff. Kalman settled in well at KES and enjoyed his time at the school, excelling in the school's swimming team amongst other activities. Today he is a leading member of the Jewish Community in Sheffield and a former President of the Sheffield Jewish Congregation.

It can have been no easy task for Barton to weld his team together and maintain an appropriate level of quality teaching with so many coming and goings during these wartime years. He was, however, a bleak and remote figure to his staff as well as to the boys, but he was well served by the "Old Guard", many of whom had seen service in World War One and understood how war time made heavy and unexpected demands on individuals and institutions. Nevertheless, he made little effort to promote any staff social life and was the first Headmaster of KES to live off-site in nearby Park Lane, rather than at Mount View in Melbourne Avenue. He also lost the services in 1943 of L.E.B. Warner, the school's Registrar, who had been a pupil at Wesley College. He had first served Hichens as his secretary before Graham appointed him Registrar, and who, since 1939, as an old soldier, had served in the evenings in the Home Guard. He had a 31year association with KES, longer with the building, and in war-time it was not easy to replace him. Barton made a temporary appointment and another small piece of history when the choice of Registrar fell on Miss Alice Mason, who was paid the extravagant sum of a mere £150 pa, considerably less then L.E.B. Warner had been receiving.

The Wider World at War

When Hitler launched Operation Barbarossa on 22nd June 1941 and then somewhat cavalierly declared war on the U.S.A. on 11th December in support of his Japanese ally, the war became a world war. For the British, prior to the summer of 1941, the war had become a stalemated conflict confined to the western European littoral, the Libyan/Egyptian border, the Mediterranean and the Atlantic. Old Edwardians in the services, who had been heavily involved in all these theatres of war, would now be called upon to play their part in the greatest conflict of arms in world history. It really was two barely related wars in different hemispheres and Britain, unlike most of the major combatants, was actively involved in both conflicts. The final roll call of the dead, from the Japanese invasion of China in 1937 to the use of two weapons of mass destruction in August 1945, dwarfed the losses of the First World War and may have been as high as 50 million people.

In the Great War, the experiences of most of the Old Edwardians who served at the front were very similar. Most soldiers were in the infantry, or their close support units, and they endured static trench warfare in France or Flanders for four years. The young men who had been at the school in the Twenties, Thirties and early Forties could now find themselves whisked off to fight on battlefields from Malaya to Norway and in very differing circumstances and formations. Peter Wheatley, who had been Head Boy for two years 1938-40 and had won a Hastings Scholarship to Queen's College, Oxford, could not in his wildest nightmares have guessed what would happen to him next. Joining up in the Royal Artillery in 1941 he was posted with his unit to the Far East just in time to be captured by the Japanese and spend three and a half years in their POW camps. Major Ken West, (1917-25) a company commander with the 4th "Hallamshire" Bn. York and Lancs Regt. went with 49th (West Riding) Division to Iceland in 1940 to deny the island to the Germans who had conquered Denmark. They remained there uninvited and barely tolerated by the Icelanders for two years before returning to Britain to prepare for D-Day. John Wollerton (1926-33) served in the same Battalion in Iceland and Normandy, ending his war at Arnhem (as a Major with the M.C.), when the British finally took the town in April 1945. They were unusual in choosing the Infantry. Only seven Old Edwardians who were killed in this war were in the infantry. Fathers who returned from France in 1918 had warned off their sons from risking involvement in another Somme or Passchendaele, especially as the prepared defences like the Maginot Line seemed even more murderously impregnable than the old trench systems.

In the Thirties the whole essence of the school under Richard Graham had been anti-war and internationalist in outlook. The school supported a scout troop not an OTC and very few old boys had taken up a military career before 1939. However almost a thousand Old Edwardians joined up during the war and their talents were now put to the task of defeating a very dangerous and genuinely evil enemy in Europe, whilst defending an old and uncertain Empire in South East Asia against the vigorous, expanding and totally ruthless Empire of Japan. Unlike the 1914-18 War when so many brilliant young men's lives were wasted in mass infantry assaults, many of this later generation of KES old boys found an opportunity to use the education they had received at the school, because modern warfare not only requires the traditional military virtues and a strong industrial base, but also highly educated servicemen and civilians if it is to be prosecuted successfully.

Geoffrey Turner, who had left school in 1921 and taken up a career in the family firm, was one of the very first to receive the George Cross for mine and bomb disposal work in 1941. This new award had been instituted in 1940 by King George VI to recognise the extreme heroism of servicemen and civilians not actively engaged directly with the enemy. Turner defused 15 land mines all over the North of England during the blitz of 1940-41, including one close to the Midland Station, and was wounded when one went off in his face at Southport. In most circumstances the George Cross, which officially is equal to the Victoria Cross, is awarded for saving life, and Lieut. G.G. Turner RNVR (later Commander) would be engaged in this harrowing work throughout the war, adding a George Medal to his G.C. in 1943.

Some Old Edwardians had the opportunity to play a more strategic role in the war. Edgar "Rabbit" Williams (1928-31) was a Fellow at Merton College, Oxford when the war broke out. He volunteered for service in the King's Dragoon Guards and as a callow Lieutenant served in the early Desert campaigns as an armoured car commander. Moving into Intelligence work he caught Montgomery's attention with the lucidity of his battlefield appraisals and his ability to read the mind of Rommel and other Axis commanders, partly through using "Ultra" to decipher their orders and battle plans. Montgomery credited Williams with playing a large part in winning Alamein and he kept him with him for the rest of the war.

He would be as useful to Eisenhower and the Joint Anglo-American Chiefs of Staff on and after D-Day and would end the war as a Brigadier showered with decorations.

Brigadier Sir Edgar Williams CB, CBE, DSO, and the U.S. Legion of Merit
Photos courtesy of the Imperial War Museum, London

Lionel Wigram had been one of the first scholarship boys in the expanded scholarship entry in 1918 and after KES he had gone on to Queen's College, Oxford in 1925, later becoming a solicitor in London. Commissioned into the Royal Fusiliers, and recognising the amateurism and vulnerability of British combat troops in the early part of the war, he played a major role in turning the Army into a sharply honed fighting force capable of taking on and defeating the Wehrmacht. He was selected to write the Official Manual of Infantry Battle Drill and was appointed Commandant of the first GHQ Battle School for the training of instructors. He rose to the rank of acting Lieut. Colonel but, after giving Montgomery the benefit of his critical advice on his handling of the Sicily campaign, he was bumped down to Major and packed off to Italy to organise partisans behind the German lines. In February 1944 he was killed leading a force of Italian irregulars against a German fortified village. Fifty years later his son created the Wigram Bequest in his father's memory, which makes annual awards to help present-day KES students.

The continuous Battle of the Atlantic, stretching from the coast of Norway to Cape Town and South America to Nova Scotia, was the longest struggle of the entire war on any front. From the very first days of the war in 1939 until the surviving U-boats surrendered themselves in May 1945, the desperate attrition of that unglamorous campaign continued claiming 37,000 Merchant Navy lives and the sinking of 784 U-Boats. Only a couple of score of Old Edwardians served in the Merchant Navy, perhaps not surprising for Britain's most inland city, but four of the Merchant Navy dead were old boys of KES. William Sadler (1924-30) was the Radio Officer on the tanker, San Demetrio, which was torpedoed in the Atlantic and its crew abandoned ship. As the fires seemed containable three of the ships life-boats returned to the vessel and managed to get her to Newfoundland. One of the boats, however, was swamped by the heavy seas and her crew were all drowned and William Sadler, who had been in the Merchant Navy for six years after leaving school, was in that boat. Later in the war a famous feature film was made about the incident and it is still available as a classic British war film of the time. Also torpedoed in the Atlantic was Signalman Edward Stringer (1932-37) who had just joined his new ship, HMS Egret, after having been torpedoed in the eastern Mediterranean only two months before. In August 1943 the Egret was torpedoed and sunk with the loss of all 203 hands. Geoffrey N. Arnold (1923-31) was a former Editor of the KES Magazine and was serving as a Sergeant in RAF Intelligence. He had gone to Oriel College, Oxford on a Kitchener Scholarship and as a language tutor had travelled widely in Germany before the war and knew the Third Reich from personal experience. He was in a convoy travelling to a new assignment when they were torpedoed in August 1941. He had been brought up by his mother because his father, Walter Arnold, had been killed in the First World War.

In 1942 Britain's main contribution to the defeat of Hitler on land was the campaign in North Africa. After the defeat of Rommel's German-Italian Army at El Alamein had turned into an unstoppable advance across Libya, Montgomery's Commonwealth forces entered Southern Tunisia after the very difficult battles at the Mareth Line and then Wadi Akarit. At the same time an Anglo-American Army landed in Algeria and advanced towards Tunis from the west. Amongst those British 1st Army troops was a battalion of the Duke of Wellington's Regiment, which included Lt. Leslie Denman (1931-38) commanding one of their platoons. He had spent a year at Sheffield University getting First Class Honours in his Intermediate B.A. in Languages before he joined up and was sent to North Africa. For particular bravery on a patrol in March and a platoon frontal attack in April he was awarded the M.C. He wrote home telling his parents of his decoration. His parents received the letter on the same day as they got a War Office Telegram saying that he had been killed in action in the last significant action before the Axis forces surrendered in Tunisia on 13th May 1943. He was 23 years old and had been recently married to a Flight Officer in the WAAF whom he had met at Sheffield University.

At the Speech Day in July 1943 the first item on the programme, once the platform party had taken up their places, was a minute's silence for the Old Edwardians killed in the present conflict. All their names were included in the Speech Day programme and at that stage of the war they already listed 53 old boys killed in action or on active service.

Mostly they had served in the RAF and they included several Sergeants who had died in training accidents. Two of them, Stephen Skerritt (1930-37) and Alec Oates (1929-38), were inseparable friends at school, and although they crashed within a month of each other whilst learning to fly, their accidents happened on different continents. Skerritt was killed in England, whilst Oates was on the Empire Pilot Training Scheme in South Africa. Their families arranged for a joint memorial service which was held at St. John's Ranmoor on June 27th 1941, the church where they had both continued in the 36th Scout Troop when they left KES. Also killed learning to fly in South Africa was one of the school's most successful bowlers, Sergeant/Cadet Leslie Fletcher (1933-40). In the two seasons 1939 and 1940 he achieved a record wicket haul of 115 wickets before going on to Brasenose College, Oxford to study for one year before the call up. He was just one of many Old Edwardian aircrew who would learn to fly in the comparative safety of Canada, Rhodesia or South Africa. Some, like Sgt. David Ditcher (1932-38), trained with the USAAF in Arizona or Florida and gained US wings as well as RAF ones before returning to England to fly with Bomber, Coastal or Transport Commands.

Regular Routine and a Different Kind of War.

For teenage boys at the school the war by the middle of 1943 was a distant event that did not affect their lives very directly, except that many had fathers and brothers on active service. Sheffield had not been bombed since October 1941 and was not to be attacked again during the war, and with the engineering industry working to capacity there was, consequently, full employment. Many boys kept maps on the wall at home and charted with pins and flags the now seemingly invincible progress of the Allies, but they had grown used to living in a city with a bombed out shopping centre and burned out houses in the suburbs. They had grown used to shortages, queues, black outs and rationing and so their school life just seemed a normal routine. It was in fact just that, and the school's academic performance improved quite considerably during the second half of the war. Barton now had the time to address the areas of weakness in the school and the main one was still the poor performance of so many boys, mainly fee-payers, in the School Certificate examinations.

Already in 1941 he had reduced the number of languages the "average boy" had to take in the Fourth and Fifth forms from three to two, thereby allowing them more time for Maths and Science. In September 1942 the Headmaster created a new class, the Fifth Remove, for boys who would take five years to prepare for their School Certificate and in future one class would be allowed to drop Latin in the Third Form. This class was now re-designated 3 R (Remove) and the "bottom" class would now be known as the Remove for each year group from the Third to the Fifth form, with its members on a different time scale and curriculum from the boys in the other three "higher" forms. By dropping Latin the assumption was that the boys in this form would not be going to university, but might spend more classroom time on Handicrafts and Art and eventually study only one language (French) and do more "practical" Geography.

The policy seemed to work because in the 1942 the school achieved a pass rate of 85% in the School Certificate Examinations well above the national average. Despite these results the C forms, the third "best" form, over a six year period could only manage a 30% pass rate which Barton felt was unimpressive and just not good enough. He could also see that the poor performance of so many fee-payers was an Achilles heel in the battle that would soon be engaged with the City Council and the Government. They would soon be asking why the ratepayer and the taxpayer should subsidise boys at a prestigious school who could not get past their first major academic hurdle. So from September 1944 onwards the C forms would also undertake a five-year period of preparation before taking their School Certificate.

While Barton was addressing areas of weakness in the school, others at a local and national level were giving serious consideration to what kind of education they wanted after the war. The Sheffield LEA had produced a report in 1942 which if acted upon would turn KES into an 11-16 Grammar School. Then the Conservative President of the Board of Education, R.A. Butler, produced a White Paper in 1943 on the future of British Education, which would eventually create the tri-partite secondary school system that pre-dated comprehensive education in Sheffield and almost all other LEAs in Britain. Barton now had a war of his own to fight and he mobilised all the support he could to oppose the provisions of the 1944 Education Act that would turn KES into "another" LEA all-free place scholarship grammar school.

At the same time the performance of the school's Sixth Form had never been better. The 1943 Higher Examination results had resulted in 18 Distinctions and in 1944 the school gained 16 Open Scholarships at Oxbridge the best performance by the school ever, eclipsing the vintage years of 1915 and 1931 and doubling the previous best year's total, eight scholarships in 1938. Barton was understandably ecstatic at Speech Day in 1944, when he echoed Dr. Hichens by declaring these results were better than anything Manchester G.S., St. Paul's or Marlborough had ever achieved. Added to that, boys at the school were awarded the Akroyd Scholarship in consecutive years from 1943 (J.H. Shaw) and 1944 (F. Fenton) until 1945 (M.P. Fanthom). It was a genuinely impressive record and although teaching circumstances may have been more difficult in other schools during wartime, it is a tribute to the academic leadership that Barton had given the school, working with a staff that included so many temporary appointments. It is also a tribute to the dedicated work of so many long serving Heads of Departments at KES, who personally prepared the Sixth Form boys for these external examinations and who carried so many extra responsibilities during the war years while their younger colleagues were away.

School teams played a fairly full fixture list despite the war. The football fixtures now included Manchester G.S., although most matches were against local grammar schools and there were inevitably fewer games against men's teams. The school had entered the Northern Public Schools Athletics Competition for the first time in 1941 and had performed quite adequately. They improved during the war and by 1945 they gained fourth place out of 25 schools participating. No one seemed to notice that they were not actually a public school, with Dr. Barton in charge they certainly looked like one. School societies recovered from the early days of the war and flourished. There were now one or two unusual ones. A Rhythm club was started in 1941 aiming at the serious study of Swing and Jazz, with their first meeting grappling with the challenge of defining what Swing actually was. There were Brains Trusts for the Sixth Form and the Middle School, modelled on the famous wartime BBC programme. Members of Staff usually provided the "brains" panel and they fielded questions, serious or otherwise, from the boys. Even more surprising given the Headmaster's right wing views was the formation in 1944 by *"progressive elements"* of a Socialist Society chaired by the Head of English, Gerry Claypole. Amongst their speakers was John Hynd the M.P. for Attercliffe and then having run out of Labour M.P's, they invited Roland Jennings the Conservative M.P. for Hallam to the next meeting to *"vindicate private enterprise"*. More acceptable to their low churchman Headmaster, who was also a member of the Diocesan Ordination Candidates Selection Committee, was the foundation of the Student Christian Movement in 1943 and later the rival Christian Union formed a branch at the school. Both these groups would thrive and continue into the Clapton era when a remarkably high number of the boys were regular churchgoers.

Two other school institutions flourished during war, the "Shout" and the Prefects' Dance. The "Shout" had begun in Gurner's time and was a burlesque concert held before the Christmas break, when, in best English tradition, the led were allowed to poke fun at their leaders. Often it was something of a rag bag of turns, some items falling flat, but others, especially sketches which were little more than a vehicle for impersonating the masters' eccentricities and mannerisms, were usually very well received even by the "victims" themselves. It was revived in 1942 after a lapse of a few years and it continued well into the post war period. The Prefects' Dance was the social event of the year. Much self-conscious preparation would take place to polish the Assembly Hall floor to a glassy sheen suitable for dancing, whilst coloured bulbs ensured a soft light and, despite wartime, the expensive 2/- (10p) tickets would enable the engagement of a suitable band. Then on the night, real girls would be welcomed into the school by awe struck young men, whose social confidence often collapsed when confronted with attractive young ladies in pretty dresses. Hospitality would be limited to the dancers gorging themselves on buns from Mrs. Helstrop and sipping their lemon squash, whilst some couples were even seen to slip away down a corridor, or sit out the dances in the balcony.

Normandy to Nagasaki

At dinner-time on the 6th June 1944, an excited C.J. Magrath rushed into the Dining Hall and demanded silence before announcing that he had just heard on the BBC that the Allies had at last landed in France. At that very same moment numerous Old Edwardians, in all three services, were taking part in the largest invasion in history, the start of a massive, crucial, two and a half month battle that compared in scale with the huge battles on the 1500 mile Eastern Front. When it ended, with the closing of the Falaise "Pocket" in August, the Wehrmacht had been routed in the west, and despite scattered strong points of resistance, would offer little real opposition until it retreated to the major rivers of the Low Countries.

Lt. Bob Mather (1929-37) was in the initial assault on Gold Beach on the British right flank. His battalion, the 6th Green Howards, was one of first units of the famous 50th (Northumbrian) Division who struggled ashore at zero hour. At the same time on Juno Beach where the Canadian Army landed, Eric Allsop (1935-40) of the R.E. Assault Engineers, who had performed with such calmness during the Sheffield Blitz, was defusing mines on the underwater obstacles that had been laid out in lines along the beach to impede Allied tanks. Later in the day he would meet up with another Old Edwardian on Juno Beach whom he had not met for years and never saw again. Geoffrey Holroyd (1933-39) was an Official War Artist and, while the mayhem of the landings was going on around him, was calmly sketching a record of the scene. Mather and his battalion forced their way inland, but he was fatally wounded four days later after taking part in some of the heaviest fighting of the whole Normandy campaign.

Amongst the naval personnel in Normandy was Lieut. Commander C. R. "Bob" Wall (1927-30) who was in command of Landing Ships and Petty Officer John Shaddock (1936-42) who put his Higher Certificate German to good effect and became an interpreter, as did many KES linguists in the latter years of the war. Serving in Combined Operations, he was on the extreme left flank of Sword Beach listening in to radio traffic from German E Boats based in Le Havre. Protecting the landings was a huge air armada of fighters who drove the Luftwaffe completely from the sky, whilst further inland Allied bombers carried out interdiction attacks against German transportation links to isolate their defenders opposing the beachhead. Whilst all the many other Old Edwardian aircrew involved in these operations returned safely, there was one fatality when F/O J.M.Wesley (1935-39) was shot down during an attack on Lisieux.

Also involved in stopping German reinforcements reaching Normandy were two old boys who were working with the French Resistance and other clandestine forces. Lt. Geoffrey Arnold (1924-28) serving with the Parachute Regiment was blowing up bridges in central France whilst leading a group of irregulars who had all been members of the International Brigade during the Spanish Civil War. Meanwhile, operating under the codename of "Guillaume Norman", Lt. Gordon Nornable (1926-32) had landed in the Ain Department in eastern France in July 1944 as part of S.O.E. joining up with a 5000 strong Maquis force led by British officers. It was his role to train new recruits and then lead them against sizeable German forces trying to escape via the Belfort Gap. For his actions over the next few months he was awarded the M.C., presented by the King himself, and the French Government added the Croix de Guerre.

Not infrequently during the war the Headmaster would announce from the platform at Morning Assembly, decorations and awards won by Old Edwardians. Altogether 48 old boys won 60 decorations between them with the first in 1940 going to Sqn Ldr. Douglas Parker DFC (1922-31) who had won a Blue at Cambridge for football during the Thirties. He was awarded a bar to his DFC in 1943. Another double DFC was P/O R.W.Bray (1930-37), whilst F/O A.C.F. Brown (1931-39) had already won the DFM, when he was awarded the DFC in 1943. Serving with the Fleet Air Arm, protecting convoys to Russia, and flying the obsolete, but oddly effective, Swordfish bi-plane, was Lieut. Gordon Bennett RNVR (1926-34) who won the DSC for sinking a U-boat in Arctic waters off Northern Norway. They were just four amongst many, and with the exception of David Fulford, Leslie Denman and P/O Donald Rollin DFC who was shot down over Berlin in December 1943, they all survived the war. Rollin (1931-38) had already flown 23 operations, three quarters of a full tour of 30 operations, as part of RAF Bomber Command's 1943 Heavy Bomber offensive against the Ruhr and Berlin, before the Lancaster he was piloting was lost. His first operation had been in May 1943, only seven and a half months earlier, and he had survived three times the average length of life (7 Operations) of bomber crews in World War Two.

Whilst the Allied armies were consolidating their hold on Normandy and then breaking out across France, Britain faced a new challenge from the air when V1 "Flying Bombs" were fired from sites in the Pas de Calais against London and the South East of England. No faster than the RAF fighters that chased them and also vulnerable to AA fire, a considerable number were shot down before they could reach their targets. It fell to Lt. (later Captain) Eric Sivil R.E. (1927-36) and his bomb disposal team to attend on the first V1 to come down and land intact. The Kent Police evacuated two thousand people from the village and Sivil got to work without any hard information on how to defuse a "Doodlebug". He eventually succeeded and the grateful villagers later presented him with a memento featuring a model V1 made from the wood of an apple tree that had been knocked down by the passage of the "Flying Bomb". He has it at his home in Broomhill to this day. He was also awarded the George Medal for this exploit, one of three won by Old Edwardians during the war.

Lieutenant – Commander
Charles Robert WALL D.S.C.

Bob Wall *had been one of the school's most distinguished sportsmen, captaining the First XI at Cricket and Football. In fact he was probably good enough to play cricket for Yorkshire C.C.C. He joined the Royal Navy when war broke out and commanded landing ships in the invasion of Sicily, at Salerno and on D-Day. He won the DSC at Walcheren in September 1944 when he commanded a flotilla of landing ships that suffered 80% losses. Nonetheless they put Commandoes and Canadians onto the island who freed the Scheldt estuary and opened up Antwerp's harbour. In private life he ran a successful sports shop and a specialised furniture business in Sheffield. He died in 1995.*

On leaving school in 1937 **Bob Mather** studied at Sheffield University and gained his Bachelor of Law degree in 1940. He then entered the army after serving in the University OTC and was commissioned in the Green Howards by the end of 1940. He went out with the 6th Battalion to North Africa as part of the 50th Division and saw action at Alamein and Wadi Akarit before taking part in the invasion of Sicily. Chosen for the initial assault on D-Day, his battalion landed at La Riviere on Gold beach at H (zero) Hour and after taking their beach they moved inland continually involved in heavy fighting. Four days later Bob Mather was seriously wounded and died on the 13th June. He is buried in a British Military Cemetery near Bayeux.

Lieutenant Robert Vivian MATHER.
6th Bn. The Green Howards.

Lieutenant Gordon NORNABLE,
M.C., Croix de Guerre.

Gordon Nornable served in the London Scottish and then the Gordon Highlanders before volunteering for S.O.E. work in France. A fluent French speaker he now trained as a parachutist, demolition and small arms expert and was sent to the Ain Department of France where he led a battalion of the Maquis against the Germans. At KES he was a leading footballer, cricketer and athlete winning the 100 yards event for three consecutive years. He went to work in the Sheffield City Council's Public Works Dept. on leaving school in 1932 and returned to the same job after the war. He never married and after retirement from the Council in 1975, he lived quietly in Norton until his death in November 2002.

Roy Hooper *had become a journalist on the Sheffield Independent when he left school in 1933, and in 1935 became the Sheffield representative for the News Chronicle before enlisting in the Royal Tank Regiment in October 1939. He moved to 5 Commando in 1940 when the commandoes were a newly formed unit before returning to tanks and serving in North Africa with the 7th Armoured Division (The Desert Rats). After service in Italy, he returned to England and took part in the invasion of Normandy and the breakout across France. As part of XXX Corps trying to relieve Arnhem in September 1944, his tank was hit and the crew baled out. However, his gunner was still trapped in his Sherman and in trying to free him Roy Hooper was hit and died instantly. He was one of seven Old Edwardians who were killed in action serving in tanks during the war.*

Lieutenant Wallace Roy HOOPER, Royal Tank Regiment.

During the First World War schools like KES provided so many of the junior officers for the army and to a lesser extent for the navy and the fledgling RAF. The position was the same in World War Two when the services looked to the Grammar Schools and the Public Schools to recruit the vastly increased numbers of officers required to lead the citizen armies. The fact that KES's OTC had been abolished seems to have had little effect on the number or quality of Old Edwardians who were commissioned during the war. The Headmaster calculated it was almost 40% of all who served who eventually took commissions in one or other of the armed services, and that figure would undoubtedly have been higher if many of the Sergeant-Pilots had not been killed in training or early in their tours of operations. Lt. Bob Gray M.C. (1931-36), the outstanding school sportsman of the Thirties, spent much of the war as a platoon sergeant with the local York and Lancs. Regiment, but in 1943 took a commission in the same regiment when serving in Italy where he won the Military Cross. 2nd Lt. R.J. Judge (1932-40) was a Corporal in the Duke of Wellington's "West Riding" Regiment when he took a "commission in the field" during the Normandy campaign, because his battalion had lost so many officers. He was later captured in October 1944 and spent six months as a POW before his release in May 1945. One old boy on being commissioned was advised by his C.O. to grow a moustache if he wanted to look the part, while another was surprised one day to bump into a friend from school days who had a recognisable German surname, but now thought it advisable to travel under the name of Lt. Powell. A considerable number of Old Edwardians were promoted to field rank during the war and there was quite a clutch of Lt. Colonels and Majors serving with the Indian Army, the second largest army in the Commonwealth, whilst there were others serving with Empire forces, including two Majors who served with African regiments and two subalterns with the Gurkhas.

When the war in Europe ended in May 1945, many servicemen assumed that they would be shipped out to the Far East to fight against Japan in a war that only seemed half won. Five Old Edwardians were killed in Burma between 1943 and the fall of Rangoon on the 3rd May 1945 and the last was Hedley Stagg serving as a Private in one of the four battalions of the York and Lancs. Regiment that fought in Burma. He was well known to boys still at the school, for he had only left in July 1943 and he had been a prefect, a stalwart member of the school orchestra and had an Open Scholarship at Jesus College, Cambridge waiting for him when he returned. He died from his wounds sustained defending his battalion H.Q. against a desperate Japanese attack in January 1945, the only Old Edwardian to be killed in the local regiment in the Second World War.

The two atomic bombs brought the war in South East Asia to an abrupt and quite unexpected halt and the highly disciplined Japanese co-operated in the post surrender arrangements in a remarkably efficient way. In some areas they were re-armed and under joint control of British and Japanese officers they kept order where there were no Allied troops to call upon. It also meant that Allied servicemen who had become their prisoners could now be accounted for. This was not a happy ending for many and the British have found it impossible in the years since 1945 to forgive Japan for the treatment of our POWs in Malaya and Thailand. Three Old Edwardians died in the work camps in Thailand after capture at the fall of Singapore in February 1942. Philip Browne (1931-36) who was a Corporal in the RAOC and worked on the "Death Railway" until he died of dysentery and malnutrition in October of 1943. LAC Joseph Rogerson RAF (1926-32), who before the war was one of the best known local amateur golfers in the Sheffield Union, also died at the end of 1943 and William Melling, (1920-27) who had emigrated to Australia in the Thirties and was part of the Australian Division that arrived at Singapore in 1942 in time to become POWs. All that his parents in Handsworth could find out was that he had died somewhere in the jungle after the prisoners had left Singapore Island in July 1942. They had just received word that their other son John Melling (1926-29) had died on active service in Italy in July 1945. Others survived the "death camps" and returned, amongst them Peter Wheatley who looked like a wraith to former school mates who met him back in Sheffield. He would recover and return to academic life, in time becoming a Fellow of Queens' College and a Senior Proctor at Cambridge University as well as a visiting professor at two American Universities.

Afterwards

Students and teachers to-day are often more comfortable discussing the First World War rather than the 1939-45 War with its echoes of triumphalism and military achievement. The devastating, pointless four year conflict of 1914-18, when there were victors but no winners, usually resonates better with modern attitudes to war than the fast moving, often intelligently fought, "morality play" that is World War Two.

Unlike the pathos and the anguish of First World War authors and poets, the Second World War, for twenty years or more, fuelled British films and popular literature with stories of bold action and amazing heroism; stories which still regularly occupy our television screens. It helped to define our national self-perception, as it did for the USA and the USSR, and helped us accept the loss of Empire and masked the reality of our comparative decline.

The British "citizen" servicemen who returned, including over 900 Old Edwardians, were for the most part modest about their achievements. Their medals, as often as not, stayed in the cardboard box that came through the post and they didn't "bore their grandchildren mightily" with tales of their extraordinary experiences of fifty years previously. Most of them have now died, but they deserve proper appreciation for the efforts and the sacrifices they made. The Old Edwardians who served had not planned to spend the first half of that decade fighting a war. They had intended to continue their careers as solicitors, engineers, businessmen, clergymen, teachers or university students; to have families and enjoy the growing suburban prosperity that was returning to the country in the late Thirties. In short, their contributions to the defeat of armed tyranny, along with millions of others in the forces of the Allies, did literally save civilisation and they deserve our recognition and respect.

CHAPTER THIRTEEN

BUTLER'S BRAHMINS
(1944-50)

While the British Army was fighting the bitter and critical battles of 1944-45 across North West Europe from Normandy to Schleswig-Holstein, Dr. Barton and his supporters were fighting a war of their own against the Sheffield City Council and the provisions of the 1944 Education Act. R.A. Butler, from 1941-45 the Conservative President of the Board of Education in Churchill's Coalition Government, had attempted to pull together all the ideas that had been current in education thinking since the Hadow Report of 1927, and produce one comprehensive, far reaching Act that would give a clear structure to secondary education in England and Wales. His legislative framework, which claimed a sound intellectual base, enabled County and County Borough Councils to establish the tri-partite structure of English education, where a small minority (approx 15%) would go to Grammar Schools, while the majority of children would now get a secondary education at Secondary Technical, or Secondary Modern Schools. Which type of school a boy or girl would go to would be decided by the scholarship examination taken by all primary school children in their 11th year. It was intended that this 11+ examination would be designed in such a way that it would indicate which pupils had academic ability, which had technical ability, while the rest, the great majority, should go to the new "Modern" schools because in the words of the 1943 Norwood Report *"they could deal more easily with concrete things rather than ideas."* This rather traditional, if not Platonic, way of looking at the educational abilities of schoolchildren now became the legacy of the landmark Butler Act, which was hailed at the time as one of the main pillars of the new post war society, where there would be equality of opportunity for all.

Although the three types of school (for most children it was only two types — grammar and modern) were supposed to have *"parity of esteem"* and were intended to best cater for each pupil's own *"aptitude and ability",* it was clear from the start which was the prestigious type of school and which was not. The Butler Act said that, unless the newly named Ministry of Education decided otherwise, all existing LEA grammar schools would automatically become "County" Grammar Schools on 1st April 1945 and they would be free to all pupils currently in the school and to all future pupils selected by the scholarship examination. For many existing grammar schools, including those in Sheffield, the changes would be positive even minimal, but to Dr. Barton and most KES parents, friends and political supporters the changes seemed cataclysmic. Their school would be reduced to being *"just another grammar school in Sheffield"* serving only their own "Western Division" of the city, unable to draw on the talents of scholarship boys and fee-payers from across Sheffield and from outside the city boundaries. Furthermore, they would lose their Junior School, with its fine building in Clarke House, as there would now be no legal powers available to the Council to allow them to run a prep. school at one of their grammar schools. Parents who could afford the current fees (still 18 guineas) would no longer be able to pay for their sons' education; instead, in the future, they would have to rely on their passing the 11+ examination, or send them to more expensive public schools outside Sheffield. More annoying, if not inexplicable to them, their daughters could still go as fee-payers to the Girls' High School across Newbould Lane; that was outside the LEA's control because they were a direct grant school, independent but grant aided directly by the Government, not run, owned and maintained by the City Council, as was the case with KES.

The bid to become a Direct Grant School.

A chance to escape from becoming a County Grammar School came from the most unlikely of sources, the City Council itself. Sheffield LEA, when they received the details of the 1944 Education Act, had to provide their response by the September Council Meeting; and their initial scheme provided KES with a lifeline by offering to let it become a direct grant school. This was a status the school had never enjoyed.

KES had been a "Public School" between 1922 and 1927 by virtue of James Hichens' membership of the Headmasters' Conference, but it had never been independent nor had it ever received a direct grant like the schools it considered its peers, including Manchester G.S. and Bradford G.S. Like many civic grammar schools it had been run by the Council but had been able to charge fees for the majority of its pupils. This was not uncommon before the 1944 Act, but it was one of the main anomalies that R.A. Butler was determined to end. If grammar schools were to be the preserve of those who were the intellectual élite, then they could not be diluted by pupils who bought their way in without passing the qualifying scholarship examination.

Spurred on by the 1942 Beveridge Report and driven by the need for the physical reconstruction of their blitzed city, the City Council had set up a Post War Reconstruction Committee of leading councillors to plan, not just the rebuilding of the city, but also produce a development plan for the future of education in Sheffield after the war. Even though the war was at an uncertain stage before the victories of Alamein, Stalingrad or Guadalcanal, the sub-committee on Post War Education in Sheffield produced its report in May 1942. It proposed that the school leaving age should be raised to 16, and supported the currently accepted formula of Modern, Technical and Grammar Schools from the age of 11-16. From 16-18 it proposed that all students who stayed on should be accommodated in "Junior Colleges", so that the LEA could give *"unity and parity"* to young peoples' full and part time education whether it was academic or vocational. KES was not mentioned by name in the report, but as an LEA maintained school it would presumably become one of these 11-16 Grammar Schools, because the report was quite clear that direct grant schools should not be included in the local structure and there should be no fees charged at any council-run school in Sheffield. Junior Colleges were not included in Butler's 1943 White Paper, nor in his 1944 Act, and the City Council publicly criticised this decision. Although they could not develop these "tertiary" colleges at that time, it was an idea that never went away in the local Labour Party, and would come back onto the political agenda in the 1980s in Sheffield.

The Education Committee were also critical of the White Paper because it had made no clear recommendations on the future of direct grant schools. So it was most surprising that in August 1944, the Director of Education, Dr. William Alexander, should propose, as his preferred option, that KES become a direct grant school outside the control of the LEA, with its own independent governors drawn initially from the existing trustees of the Royal Sheffield Grammar School Exhibition Fund. They had proposed a similar role for themselves in 1927, to stop the school losing its public school status, and had been vigorously rebuffed by Ernest Rowlinson and the Labour majority. Now the Labour Councillors, led by Alderman John Bingham, Chairman of the Education Committee, seemed prepared to float this idea as a possible solution to solve the anomalous position of KES within the LEA's family of grammar schools. They did however make it clear that they would not provide any free scholarship places at any re-designated KES and therefore the new "Governors" would have to find the cost of the necessary minimum of 25% free places from other sources. This was crucially important for without this minimum number of free places, the Minister could not award them direct grant status. Furthermore, the Council were unclear about who would own, or lease, the school buildings and what price, or rent, would be charged to any new governing body.

Alexander's alternative proposal for KES was that the school should become the boys' grammar school for the new "Western Division" of the city, offering a free education to all local pupils selected by the 11+ Examination. The school's organisation and governance would be the same as all the other grammar schools that were proposed for five geographical areas of Sheffield. Each of these Divisions would have either one co-educational, or a separate boys' and girls' grammar school, plus one girls' and one boys' technical school, whose pupils would be drawn exclusively from their own divisional catchment area. In their initial proposals the LEA indicated that where there was a surplus of existing grammar schools, one or more would become secondary technical schools, as was planned for the "South West Division", where High Storrs would remain a grammar school for boys and girls, while Abbeydale Girls G.S. would become a technical school. Where there were no grammar schools at present, as in the "North West" it was proposed City G.S. would move from the city centre to a site on Halifax Rd. (later Chaucer School), or in the "South East Division" where a new grammar school for boys and girls would have to be built.

Dr. Barton could scarcely believe the opportunity that KES had apparently been given, although one suspects he had helped to put the idea into Alexander's mind. The whole status of direct grant schools was unclear after the 1944 Act. The 1943 Fleming Report which had considered how the independent, public and direct grant schools could work closer with the "state" system had sent confusing messages to R.A. Butler on the future of direct grant schools. The chairman, Lord Fleming, found himself in the minority when he essentially recommended that the direct grant schools continue as before. The majority of his committee made up of a somewhat unholy alliance of left wing intellectuals, like G.D.H. Cole, and public school headmasters, like Birley of Eton, wanted direct grant schools to be assimilated into the local council education system with all fees abolished.

If Butler had accepted this recommendation, then it is difficult to see how direct grant schools would have been any different from LEA grammar schools in their organisation, if not in their performance. Butler dithered and never grasped this particular nettle, as he knew that the abolition of direct grant schools would have been extremely unpopular amongst suburban Conservatives. He therefore left a final decision for his successor, who turned out to be Ellen Wilkinson, the Labour Minister of Education, after the surprise Labour election victory of July 1945.

All Barton and his supporters could do was work on the assumption, right as it turned out, that direct grant schools would continue to exist, with their grant aid coming straight from the government in return for providing at least 25% free places for pupils from council primary schools. He tried at first to persuade the Labour Council to change their mind and agree to continue to send their scholarship boys to KES and therefore solve this problem at one stroke. This they refused to do, although the councils in several cities did decide to continue to pay to send scholarship boys to their direct grant schools, as at King Edward VI School, Birmingham, Leeds G.S. and Bradford G.S. While the Labour Group must have been divided over Alexander's proposal to let their most successful school leave LEA control, they said they would only consider such a move on two conditions. Firstly, the LEA would give no support whatsoever, including paying for free places, to this proposed "new" direct grant KES, and secondly, they would be able to finance the building of a new boys' grammar school in the Western Division for the scholarship winners in the area to attend. Having made clear those two important requirements, the Council let the supporters of KES attempt to obtain direct grant status for the school. How far the Council's position was decided by uncertainty within the majority group's own ranks as to the best way forward, how far it was a tactic to avoid an embarrassing political issue, is not now at all clear. Perhaps Bingham and the Labour Group were playing a long, if not cynical, hand because they guessed it would not be possible to establish a direct grant school without council financial support and, therefore, they only had to wait until 1st April 1945 for the school to automatically become a free place LEA grammar school.

The Proposal for "Independence"

The Council's proposals became public at the September Council meeting, and Barton immediately got to work to try and create a coherent plan that could be sent to the Minister of Education to enable him to award direct grant status to KES.

- *Firstly, he had to establish the reasons why KES should be treated as a special case, different and superior to the other grammar schools in the city. His arguments would have to be very compelling, because the Minister was reluctant to create new direct grant schools when their future was so unclear.*

- *Then he needed a group of capable people who were willing to take over the governance of an independent school with all the legal, financial and organisational responsibilities that would ensue.*

- *Working with these new governors, KES would have to establish a "business plan" which would convince the Minister that a new school would be financially viable.*

- *Finally Barton encouraged "friends of the school" to mobilise the public support of parents, Old Edwardians, the local press, sympathetic councillors and influential people outside the city, to sustain the pressure on the Council to allow KES to become a direct grant school, independent of their control in the future.*

He had little difficulty in identifying the group who would be prepared to step in and become the new governing body. The ready-made vehicle existed in the continuing presence of the Governors of the SRGS Exhibition Fund. They were willing to take on the role of Governors of an independent direct grant school. They had, of course, a clear historical connection with the foundation of the school and until the 1920s several of their members had been on the old KES Governing Body and they had been prepared to form the Governing Body in 1927 to save the school's public school status. They still administered the money from the old Grammar School endowments and these had often been used to support projects at KES, including regular financial aid to the library. Furthermore, under the chairmanship of Sir Samuel Osborn, they included amongst their numbers many of the great and the good of the city and therefore no-one could question their credentials to undertake the task. Through the battles of the next twelve months they never wavered in their support for the Headmaster and the school. Even in 1947 they were prepared to contemplate setting up a separate independent school in competition with the "maintained" KES, and failing that, at least, establish an independent preparatory school in what was about to become the redundant Junior School at Clarke House.

They reflected middle class opinion in the city that was enthusiastic for KES to escape from the "talons" of the Labour controlled Council, and continue as a fee-paying school independent of the vagaries of local politics. In fact most of the public, including many of the school's supporters, had assumed that the school was independent of the Council; that its status was the same as the Girls' High School and other prestigious day public schools in the other main Yorkshire cities. Although the Headmaster of KES had not been a member of the Headmasters' Conference since 1927, the school always acted as if it still was a public school. Barton very much encouraged this view, and in his correspondence during this period he often referred to the fact that KES had been "*run as a direct grant school since 1927*", meaning that in every way the style and ethos of the school were identical to other direct grant public schools in the North of England.

In preparing his case for re-designation as a direct grant school, he had no doubts that this would be the best way forward for the school. Educated himself at a day public school (Nottingham H.S.), then going up to Trinity College, Cambridge, before taking up a teaching post for fourteen years at Repton, he believed completely in the superiority of the public school system. He appears to have rejected at the start the possibility that, if KES became a maintained grammar school serving the wealthiest part of the city, the scholarship boys it received would not only be intellectually very able, but almost all middle class and that the ethos of the school would be "safe" in their hands. He already knew that the 25% of the boys in the school who were on LEA scholarships provided a much higher proportion of his academic high achievers and his open scholarship winners to Oxbridge than his fee-paying pupils, as well as a substantial number of his prefects, heads of the houses and the captains of sports teams. Another headmaster might have taken the view that the school's future might be even better served as a county grammar school, benefiting from a catchment area of approximately 100,000 population in a favoured area of a large city that had a university and a diverse industrial and social life.

Instead, he entered the campaign to gain direct grant status with his usual enthusiasm and intellectual vigour. He pointed out in a key memorandum of October 1944 that at the Sixth Form level KES had had a fine academic record over many years, whilst the recent achievement of 16 Open Scholarships to Oxbridge that year plus the regular success in the Akroyd Scholarship (seven times in the last nine years) marked it out from the other grammar schools in the city. In some of his correspondence to potential supporters, like Geoffrey Fisher, the new Archbishop of Canterbury who had been his Headmaster at Repton, he was more scathing of the standards of the other grammar schools. He feared that if the school became another divisional grammar school; " *the able boys who came to us from across the city would be distributed equally between the other schools and I believe that they will be so dispersed that they will be dragged down to the level of the mediocre material which will form the rest of those schools. The result will be that our standards will slowly but surely decline to that of the other schools of the city.*"

Barton also argued if KES was the only direct grant school for boys in the area, it would serve the whole of South Yorkshire and North Derbyshire as an independent fee-paying boys school in "*the same way as Manchester G.S. serves Lancashire*". He also stressed that the quality of education in the 180 strong, over subscribed, Junior School was far superior to that of the council's elementary schools and that also would be a loss to the city if KES became a maintained school and the Junior School had to be closed.

The first task of the "Governors" and the Headmaster was to try and convince the LEA (in reality convince the Labour Group) to rescind their decision not to send fee-paying pupils to KES. This would have secured the necessary financial underpinning and given a "de facto" vote of Council approval which would most likely persuade the Minister to approve direct grant status. To encourage Council sympathy and to overcome the oft-repeated objection that KES was "creaming" the city of so much of the best talent, they now proposed that the 25% free places at the school should be drawn only from the proposed "Western Division" of Sheffield. This was a considerable concession because Barton was reluctant to lose some of the very best pupils who came to the school from other parts of Sheffield, and it also compromised his argument that his élite school was serving the whole city and beyond.

The Labour Group, whose priority was about raising standards in all the city's grammar schools, indeed in all schools, found KES's claims to a superior position cut right across the fundamental direction of their policy. They therefore rejected this concession, forcing the "Governors" to accept that they would have to find the money themselves to fund the 25% free places, that would trigger the Government's Direct Grant. The "Governors" estimated, based on the Council's 1944-45 revenue budget for KES, that it would cost £30,000 p.a. at current prices to run the school and the present fees of 18 guineas (£18.90) would be nowhere near enough to meet the gap caused by the withdrawal of council funding. They proposed that the fees be increased to £30-£35 believing that could produce approximately £18,200 to support the school's budget. The Headmaster was confident, that even with fees at this level, there would be enough demand from parents in the area to send their sons to KES, to guarantee enough fee-paying pupils of the right quality. He based this on current demand for places (over 262 candidates for 100 places) and he foresaw that there might be post war economic difficulties that would encourage parents to send their sons to a fee-paying day school, rather than to a much more expensive boarding school.

The funding gap would be covered by the Direct Grant from the Government (they expected to receive an average of £9.10 shillings (£9.50) for each pupil) and support from the endowments of the SRGS Exhibition Fund. That fund only produced £2600 pa and would not be sufficient to cover the costs of 175 free places needed to qualify for the Government Grant. Therefore it was proposed to invite business firms or individuals to donate, what nowadays would be called, sponsorship packages. Seven scholarships to cover £35 tuition fees would be offered to sponsors/donors for £245 pa in perpetuity, and if the school could raise 25 such packages they could meet the cost of the required 175 free places.

At first glance this seemed to be a viable proposition, but it did not take into account the revenue consequences of any capital costs, such as buying the building from the Council, or paying the rent on an annual lease, not to mention the cost of buying or leasing all the school's equipment. The SRGS Governors hoped that the Council would sell or lease the buildings at a very modest cost or rent, or alternatively the Minister would make a capital grant available from Central Government funds to cover all the capital costs involved in the transfer. The buildings, playing fields and equipment were currently valued by the Council on their own books at a figure of £67,000 (they had cost £49,000 to acquire and re-furbish in 1905), added to this were outstanding loan charges on the school of £17,545. Any proper new valuation would certainly produce a much higher figure.

The SRGS "Governors" were therefore dependent on a benevolent City Council, or a benevolent Government, to overcome this financial obstacle and in the event they got neither. The Government, in early 1945, made it clear that they would not give a special capital grant and they also insisted that any sale or lease between the Council and the Governors should be based on a proper market value. By January 1945 the permanent officials at the Ministry of Education were beginning to be sceptical about the SRGS Trustees' ability to put together any credible financial plan. Their experience in the past of direct grant schools who did not have the support of an LEA, was that they usually failed to find the money for the free place pupils from other sources. However they didn't close the door on the KES initiative but they didn't give it much encouragement either.

De-graded

A letter of the 16th January from Sir Maurice Holmes, the Permanent Secretary at the new Ministry of Education, outlined all these reservations. He stated that the Minister was unlikely to award direct grant status if the LEA did not take up its free places, that any transfer of the buildings and premises would have to be on a strict commercial valuation by the District Valuer and then approved by the Minister. There would not be any support by way of a capital grant to help purchase the buildings, and he also thought it very unlikely that the Minister would sanction the building of a new boys' grammar school in the "Western Division" when the Council could avail themselves of places at KES, a school which they owned.

The Governors responded in late February by offering the Council 50% free places at the "new" KES, but there was no shift in the Council's position except to seek a meeting with the Permanent Secretary, which took place on 22nd March 1945. Holmes, acting on Butler's instructions, confirmed all the points he had made in his January letter and added the final crucial demand that the 25% free places would have to come from the LEA and not from any other source. He was in effect saying that unless the LEA would support the transfer of the school to the Governors by paying for scholarship winners, the Minister would not support direct grant status for KES.

Until this point all the manoeuvrings and proposals had been conducted in private although many people knew what was being proposed. Now the issue came into the public domain and it seemed that a decision on KES's future had to be made with indecent haste in a little over a week, if the 1st April deadline was to be met. The Education Committee met on 26th March and a ferocious debate took place on a motion of the Progressive Party (in reality the Conservatives), that the Council should allow KES to become a fee-paying direct grant school and take up 25% of the places for its "own" scholarship boys. Opening for the Progressives was Coun. F. H. Price, a member of the SRGS Trustees himself. He accused the Labour Party of "de-grading" KES back to an ordinary grammar school, whilst the Leader of the Progressives, Ald. Harold Jackson, ex Wesley College, current SRGS Trustee and long time supporter of the school, in a bitter speech censured the Labour members for, "*smothering the school in politics and carrying out an act of educational vandalism because of their fanatical hatred of the school—what the Socialists were doing to King Edwards was enough to make the angels weep.*" This kind of language was quite common in Council Meetings, but on this occasion the epithets that flew around the Council Chamber were not the usual sparring match polemics, but the deeply held convictions of very disappointed men. By comparison the Labour spokesmen, Ald. John Bingham and Coun. Albert Ballard, when outlining the Labour Groups' case, stressed that they were trying to raise standards for all secondary schools and that the policy of abolishing fees at all the city's schools had not been rushed through, but had been Council policy since the 1942 Education

Re-construction Report. They would not therefore send any scholarship pupils to a fee-paying school and furthermore, as the Conservative Minister would not let them build a new boys' grammar school in the west of the city, they now needed KES to be the grammar school to serve those suburbs; areas ironically represented only by members of the opposition on the Council. When the vote was finally taken the Progressives resolution was lost by 19 votes to 12 and, despite a considerable public campaign to continue the fight to gain direct grant status for KES, its future was decided. KES would become a maintained all-scholarship grammar school from 1st April 1945 until 1969.

An important concession

The result of this vote was greeted by outrage among parents of the school, Old Edwardians (including many abroad still fighting a war), and among most of the boys at the school. Eleven prefects, led by Jack Rollin, the Head Boy, signed a letter sent to the Sheffield Daily Telegraph in March 1945 arguing that if KES was not made a direct grant school then, *" the whole object of the 1944 Education Act would be defeated because a clever boy without private means would not be able to obtain an education worthy of his abilities."* This letter was one of many to the Telegraph and Star denouncing, often in quite bilious language, the decision of the Education Committee. The Sheffield Daily Telegraph was particularly hostile to the Council's decision and ran the banner headline the following morning, " HISTORIC KING EDWARD VII SCHOOL IS NOW DE-GRADED." They supported the Progressives' case and denounced the "Socialists" for not enabling KES to become independent. The Star was more balanced and gave more prominence to letters from readers who had become quite weary of KES parents trumpeting the superior merits of their school. One, from an Old Centralian, pointed out that High Storrs Boys G.S. had also produced fine scholars and successful old boys who had distinguished themselves in medicine, the law, academia and the civil service. Indeed, one Old Centralian diplomat had handed the Declaration of War to the German Ambassador on 3rd September 1939 and others had served with distinction as commissioned officers in the war.

Anger was strongest among the parents and the Old Edwardians. The parents called a well attended meeting at the school on 5th April and set up a Committee, chaired by Mr. W.I. Goff, which asked all supporters to pledge two guineas to a "Fighting Fund". They agreed a resolution opposing the "de-grading" of KES and sent it to R.A.Butler asking him to intervene and reverse the Council's decision. The Old Edwardians met the following night and they passed a similar resolution, also sent to the Minister. They stressed that their fee-paying school had produced a thousand old boys who had served their country well over the last six years with over a hundred giving their lives, and this sacrifice should be considered when a decision was made to change the status of their old school. The Seventh Club at Oxford weighed in with a letter from their President, Peter Wills of St. Edmund Hall. They too complained of the "de-grading" of their old school, but they concentrated their fire on the new provision that would only allow boys from the western area of the city to attend, rather than having a school of proven excellence available to all the city. This proved to be the one area where concessions were possible and where the Minister was prepared to agree some changes to the Sheffield Scheme.

In the meantime, the parents' committee continued its barrage of letters to the press and at a later meeting agreed to stage a mass protest at the next meeting of the Education Committee. When it was held in April they were all ejected from the gallery of the Council Chamber for their partisan comments during the debate. For many this was the final indignity, as a "Socialist" Chairman ordered the middle class KES parents out of the Town Hall because of their "unseemly" behaviour. The incident caused another rush of letters to the Telegraph which kept the issue of KES's angry concerns in the public eye. At the same time, parents were informed by letter that not only could their sons continue in the school until the end of their education, but they would now no longer have to pay any fees. The Junior School would not be closed immediately, but boys already in the Junior School would be able to continue at Clarke House until all existing pupils had completed their education there by July 1947. However, there would be no new eight year olds enrolled and any boy moving up into the Senior School would have to pass the 11+ scholarship, or go to another school.

Barton was still working behind the scenes to get the best deal he could for the school, but he felt as a "servant " of the Council it would be "*improper*" to be seen publicly opposing their position (he even had to seek permission from the Education Committee when invited to address the meeting of the Old Edwardians on 6[th]April). He continued to elicit support from those he felt well placed to help, but got no help from his own professional association, the Incorporated Association of Head Masters. Their secretary, L.W.Taylor, suggested that direct grant schools did not necessarily have a rosy future, as Labour Councils up and down the country may well take a similar view to Sheffield and, if there was a Labour Government after the July General Election, a Labour Minister of Education might well abolish their independence at an early date.

By March, when Barton realised that the Council was not going to budge and the Government was not going to challenge them, he began to look for other posts. He had shown an interest in vacant headmasters' positions at Brentwood School in Essex and at Manchester G.S. and he now sent off applications. He was interviewed for the post at Mill Hill School but he was unsuccessful, and after 1st April he left the battle largely to the councillors, editors and parents and concentrated on preparing for the new kind of school KES was to become.

The resolutions and the public campaign along with the pressure from the local Conservative M.P. for Hallam, Roland Jennings, did eventually produce a result when R.A.Butler asked the Sheffield City Council to send a delegation to discuss the situation of KES. This meeting took place on 26th April in London and Butler insisted that Ald. Jackson accompany Bingham along with the new Director of Education, Stanley Moffat. Although Butler recommended no main changes to the Sheffield Scheme, he did, as a way of meeting some of the complaints and recognising KES's particular concerns, strongly suggest that the LEA abandon their zoning system and open their grammar schools to pupils from any part of the city, and also give each grammar school its own governing body. These were two very important concessions that Butler knew would benefit KES and go a long way to easing the transition to an all-scholarship school. The Labour Group discussed these proposals in private for a month and it was not until the end of May that they were formally agreed by the Education Committee. KES gained its own Governors, although it had to share them with Marlcliffe Secondary Modern School in Hillsborough, although there must have been a rearguard action against this decision in the Labour Group, because the governing bodies of the six grammar schools were not appointed until November 1947. The abolition of zoning was, of course, very important to the future of the school. It allowed some of the most able boys from all over Sheffield to come to KES and consequently, during the next two decades, the parents of many boys of real ability chose KES in preference to their local grammar school. To a considerable extent KES was therefore allowed by these proposals of R.A. Butler to "cream" the city of talent, enabling the new KES to produce academic results even better than those of the school that Dr. Barton had fought so hard to maintain.

The "battle " lost

Any hopes of the parents that the decision over direct grant status could be reversed in the near future were finally dashed by the political changes at Westminster and by the November Council Elections in Sheffield. Goff, and the parents' committee, kept up the fight during the early summer of 1945 with a barrage of letters to the press and a great petition that they sent to the Council and the Minister. Their best hope was for the Progressives to regain power in the November elections, for they already had a public pledge from Ald. Jackson that, if elected, his party would overturn the decision on KES and make it possible for the school to become a direct grant school. Jackson, and most of the parents, assumed without question that the July General Election would be won by Churchill, and then a Conservative Government might appoint a new, and bolder, Minister of Education who might be more sympathetic to the KES situation.

Instead, Labour's overwhelming election victory in July, brought Ellen Wilkinson into the Ministry of Education, and among her other problems she had to make a decision on the future of direct grant schools. Unlike Nye Bevan, who fought to bring all the Hospitals into the N.H.S., Ellen Wilkinson eventually allowed direct grant schools to continue and almost all have remained independent to this day and are often amongst our highest performing schools. Wilkinson's decision gave a glimmer of hope to the KES campaigners, although it is unlikely she would ever have been persuaded to create a new direct grant school in Sheffield.

What finally finished off the hopes of the KES parents and supporters was the increased majority the Labour Party won on the City Council in November. No local or parliamentary elections had taken place during the war, so the City Council had remained unchanged, apart from deaths and resignations, since 1938. The Labour vote in Sheffield at that time had not fully recovered from the effects of the formation of the National Government by MacDonald in 1931, and so the Labour majority on the Council during the war was not as large as it subsequently was in the post war period. Yet, after Attlee's stunning General Election victory, the Labour Party in Sheffield expected to perform very well in the 1945 local elections. In the event they only gained 5 seats from the Progressives, but it gave them a comfortable overall majority of 18, out of a hundred council members. Ald. Jackson and his party would not therefore be overturning any decisions on KES, and in the following years Labour improved their majority, so that by 1947 the Labour majority had reached 36. It never fell below 34 until the mid 1960s and a long period of Labour Party hegemony in Sheffield was established.

Sheffield, in the next 50 years, was to be the only major town or city in England without a fee-paying boys' public school. A source of pride to the local Labour Party, especially as KES performed so well in comparison to the independent sector over the next twenty-five years. Ironically, council members, like Aldermen Bingham and Ballard, who in 1947 became the new Chairman and Deputy Chairman of the KES Governors, would bask in the reflected glory of their fully maintained grammar school, whose academic results stood comparison with the most famous schools in the country, and not a few Labour councillors and party members during the next two decades, were proud that their sons won scholarships to the school.

> *During the last few months of the war, Derek Platts (1942-47) missed the "voluntary" monthly Chapel Service. He was hauled up before Dr.Barton and asked why he had been absent. Platts, a scholarship boy from a council estate, replied that he had been looking after his ill mother whilst his father was on duty as a Special Constable. Dissatisfied with this excuse, Barton challenged him by asking,*
>
> **"Why couldn't your maid have looked after your mother?"**
>
> *It was only the second time Platts had spoken to the Headmaster. The other occasion was when he had gained an indifferent report and Barton summoned him and gave him a stern lecture, demanding that;*
>
> *"As a scholarship boy you owe it to the ratepayers of Sheffield, who are paying your fees, to do better!"*

What was it all about?

Whatever constitutional changes were happening to the school in 1945, the Headmaster and the Staff were determined that the ethos, the ambitions and the achievements of the school should not be changed, only enhanced. All the outward symbols of the school remained. No-one inside or outside the school wished to change the uniform, the coat of arms, the Latin school song, the wearing of gowns by the masters, the ritual of Morning Assembly, the regular calendar of events, the scouts, the numerous societies, the large choir and orchestra. These were all features that ambitious grammar schools aspired to develop for themselves, whereas KES already had a rich heritage reinforced by occasions such as Speech Day, with its Latin address of welcome, the Commemoration Service, the Chapel Service each term and its six day week which set the school apart in a very visible way from the other grammar schools in the city. There never seems to have been any pressure to add the word "Grammar" to the name of the school, and while the other grammar schools in Sheffield were proud to call themselves as such, King Edward VII School continued with its original name. It helped to strengthen the sense of continuity with the school of the period 1905-45 and it also helped to emphasize what it saw as its special position within the LEA maintained schools.

There was also little change in the social structure of the school, at least for the remainder of Barton's time at the school. In September 1945, all pupils in the school above the Second Forms had been at KES before that date and three-quarters of them had previously paid fees. When the new Second Form was selected, all the boys in the three classes 2A, 2B and 2C had come up from the Junior School and only 2D, as usual, were from the city's primary schools. All had passed their scholarship because as Barton had laid down in 1944, and the LEA had agreed, boys would only be allowed to pass from the Junior to the Senior School during the two year transitional phase providing they could demonstrate they were capable of passing the 11+ Examination. As the standard of KES's own entrance examination into the Junior School had got stiffer, the boys who passed it were also capable of satisfying the 11+ examiners and almost all of them moved up into the Senior School. One or two didn't make the grade and went elsewhere, and some parents did not like the new status of the school and now sent their sons to private schools. However, it was not till 1954 that all former fee-paying pupils had passed through the school, and therefore, for the remainder of Barton's time, most of the Senior School boys had been fee-payers when they first came to the school. It is also worth reflecting that if the school had become a fee-paying direct grant school, then at least two thirds of the boys who did attend KES between 1945 and 1969 would have been denied a place at the school.

Goodbye to the Junior School

The LEA arranged for the Junior School to wind down and then close in July 1947. In the meantime, they now fully funded the cost of the Junior School, as there was no longer any income from fees. When, in the Summer term of 1945, the mother of one of the boys in the Junior School, arrived at the school ready to pay the fees in cash, she was told, much to her surprise, that the Junior School was now free for the existing pupils. Her boy could now continue, without any payment, until the time came to take the 11+ examination, which would decide if he could remain at the school after J1. In September 1945, Form J3 was discontinued and some of the staff began to leave, including A.C. "Pop" Baker who resigned in December and took up an appointment at the City of London School in their Junior Department. He had been in charge of the Junior School since Saville's retirement in 1940 and he had served the school well, taking a role as a commissioned officer in the ATC during the war, as well as his work at Clarke House. He was replaced as Master in Charge by H.T. R. Twyford, just returned form war service with the RAF, who would supervise the run down of the Junior School and then join the Senior School staff. Others took the opportunity to leave, including some of the temporary female staff. Miss S.C. Parkes, who took J3B, and taught amongst other things a love of cricket to her charges moved on, whilst Lucy Goode finally left the school after a long career, first as Miss Turner and then as Mrs. Michell after her first husband so tragically died. She had come to KES in 1922 and enthused her pupils with an interest in silkworms and lizards as well as snails and frogs, often collected on nature study walks in the nearby Botanical Gardens. With nothing left for her at KES, she successfully applied for a post at QEGS Wakefield, which, as a direct grant school, still had its junior department.

A curious decision.

In September 1945 ten scholarship boys from the local elementary schools were admitted to the Junior School. One of them was Reg Hobson (1945-53), who recollects his Headteacher at Sharrow Lane School announcing that there was an opportunity for a handful of boys to win a free place at KES that Autumn. It meant nothing to Reg but his mother dashed down to the Education Offices when she heard of the scheme and filled in the application forms. Reg sat the examination and passed and entered Form J1C with nine other boys. The following year he sat, and passed the 11+ examination and moved up into the Senior School with almost all of his form. The Director of Education may well have felt that as the Council now had to cover the cost of the Junior School, it might as well get value for its money and send some able boys to KES ahead of the 11+ Examination.

The longest serving member of the Junior School staff did not leave immediately but was offered, and accepted for a couple of terms in 1947-48, a post in the Senior School. Miss J.W.M. Copley had joined the Junior School staff in the First World War and her understanding of small boys endeared her to at least two generations of Edwardians. She gained their respect in the classroom as well as on the sports field, where she would referee football matches and support teams from Norman House; the house she led as "Housemaster" during the war. One former pupil remembers how at eight years of age, as a new, timid and shy member of the class, he was introduced to the other class members as if he was Miss Copley's special friend and began immediately to feel at home. Another teacher who felt it was time to leave was Charles "Daddy" Wright, who had taught French and History to J1 classes and now retired to his imposing home at Eyam Hall, which had been in his family's ownership in the famous plague village since 1671.

The Junior School was held in high regard by the parents of KES boys. Before 1945 it had been difficult to gain entry as a fee-payer to the Senior School if you had not come up from the Juniors, and parents also supported the claim that it gave a much better foundation education than could be gained at any of the local elementary schools. In the short term KES would regard the loss of the Junior School as the real disaster of the imposed changes of 1945. The Senior School prospered in the next two decades, but the work done by Saville and his colleagues and their successors was lost. Barton made fulsome praise of their contribution to the school after they had finally closed in the summer of 1947. He stressed how the Junior School prepared boys for the courses in the Senior School, especially in French, Algebra and Geometry that were not taught at elementary schools. He added, that in 1947, as usual, two thirds of all the Open Scholarships were won by boys who had come up from the Junior School and they also shared, in roughly the same proportion, all the offices of the school open to boys. He paid tribute to the parents who supported the school up to the final day, to the cricket team which had only lost one match out of eight in their last season, and to Angles House who carried off the inter-house cricket championship in 1946 and 1947.

THE LAST JUNIOR SCHOOL CRICKET TEAM
Season 1947   P8 W5 D2 L1   Ian Mottershaw –Captain

There just remained the future of the buildings at Clarke House, which had provided such a handsome home for the Junior School for just eleven years. The LEA had built additions in 1936 to give the old house a proper Assembly Hall-cum-Gym, and they had even repainted the interior in 1945, so it was in fair condition. The LEA had already agreed to hand the building back to the Osborn family, who had made the original donation, although legally it was the Council's building. Sir Samuel Osborn was still the

219

Chairman of the SRGS Trustees and he and his fellow trustees considered a plan to run the building as an independent preparatory school in competition to Birkdale and Westbourne Prep. Schools. However, they needed Government approval to use their money in this way and the Labour Government refused them, and so the idea was dropped. Over the years Clarke House served as a nurses' home, and then in 1987 it was acquired by the expanding Birkdale School as their preparatory department. This is the continuing role of Clarke House to this day.

The changing of the old guard

With the end of hostilities staff members in the forces began returning to civilian life and to teaching at KES. Gordon Cumming and Clarence Helliwell were amongst some of the first to be "de-mobbed", and by the Autumn of 1946 all the staff who had served in the forces were back in civilian life. Some like Horace Brearley, who joined the staff of the City of London School, and Geoffrey Petter, who ultimately became an HMI, chose not to come back to Sheffield and their careers took them elsewhere. The return of these servicemen meant that the temporary staff members were phased out, so that all had left by 1947. Many of them were the women teachers who had played such an important part in staffing the school during the war; some of whom would no doubt have liked to have stayed on permanent contracts, whilst others were pleased to retire now the war was over. The effect of this, and the closure of the Junior School, was that KES staff became almost entirely male and by September 1948 there were only four women on the teaching staff at the school. Occasionally when the Headmaster was in a tight spot he would recall one of the former lady members of staff, as happened when Janet Manners was asked back to teach Maths, and Jean Knight also resumed teaching Classics at the end of the decade. Barton always followed a policy in his recruiting that was common to almost all leading boys' grammar schools; to appoint men unless there were no suitable candidates and appoint Oxbridge graduates where possible.

One of the arguments against the "de-grading" of KES in 1945 was that the school would become unattractive to well qualified teachers and especially to those who had been at Oxbridge colleges. There is no evidence to support this viewpoint amongst the crop of new teachers who were recruited in 1946 and 1947. They were nearly all graduates of Oxford and Cambridge Universities, and they included a group of young men who would have a quite considerable influence on the short and long-term future of the school. Some of them replaced some of the school's long serving legends. John Speight Nicholas finally retired, along with Harry Allison Scutt, the Senior Modern Languages Master, in the summer of 1947 having both had their careers extended beyond the normal retiring age. "Old Nick" had come to the school in 1911 and after becoming the Senior Maths Master, was promoted by Ronald Gurner to the position of Second Master in 1926. A terror to the boys, he had prowled around the school looking for wrong-doers wearing his trademark tattered and knotted gown, yet his sphinx-like exterior hid a man of some considerable humour, and his colleagues summed him up as a man who was as shrewd a judge of a boy, a fellow master or a situation as anyone who had ever served at KES. The

Headmaster thanked him publicly for his independent judgements and also his complete loyalty, not always the easiest of bedfellows, and suggested that the high standard of his teaching was exemplified by the appointment of two of his former pupils to become Fellows of the Royal Society.

Scutt returned briefly in 1949 when there was a temporary requirement for a Language teacher. Fluent in three European languages, he tried to teach his pupils a living language rather than they learn French or German from the written page. In the staff room he was missed as an expert at Bridge, the Listener crossword and the shove ha'penny board. Philip Baylis also moved on, although initially he went on secondment as a lecturer to Eastbourne Emergency Teaching College in December 1946; he never returned and he also became an HMI. Baylis had restored, if not created, the musical tradition at KES and he left an Orchestra that was 30 strong and a successful choir of 60 voices, enabling his successor, Norman Barnes, to take the standard of school music to new levels of performance.

The other long serving staff member who retired in the immediate post-war period was A.W. Gaskin who had arrived at the school in 1917 and completed 29 years service. He had long served as the Senior Geography Master but had failed to persuade two headmasters to elevate Geography to become a Sixth Form subject, as the 1933 Inspection Report had advised. His biggest contribution to the school was the formation of the King Edward VII No 167 (South Yorkshire) Scout Troop in 1927, after the school's OTC had been abolished by the Council. He had argued earlier in the Twenties for the creation of a scout troop at the school, but Hichens and the Games Committee, who decided these things, turned him down.

There were still enough long serving staff to continue to give a sense of continuity. The "father of the house", Charles J. Magrath, would soldier on until 1949 when he finally departed after 41 years service. Edward F. Watling was still teaching the classics, translating Greek authors for Penguin, producing the school plays and overseeing the production of the school magazine, now restored to its full glory. During the war as an economic measure the magazine had been reduced to the size of a paperback and produced without a cover. Now it was bigger and brighter with many more photos and a cover that, whilst it still retained the stylised rampant lion, was printed in a different colour for each addition.

Sydney Carter was appointed Second Master to replace Nicholas, and Peter Wallis came to the school in September 1947 as the Senior Maths Master. He was to play a prominent part in the life of the school, as master in charge of the 1st XI Football Team and as a keen enthusiast for the pre-history of the school. The present author is indebted to him for the research he did on the Sheffield Grammar School since the 17th Century, including undertaking interviews with former pupils who had been at the old Grammar School, both at St. George's Square and at Collegiate Crescent. He was highly regarded in the classroom by his pupils, never needing to resort to the cane, even if he was given to throwing the board rubber at boys he felt were not paying attention, or were not up to the mark. He was an enthusiastic socialist, even an apologist for Stalin's USSR at that time. In 1949 he staged a noisy walkout from Morning Assembly when Barton called on the school to pray for Cardinal Mindszenty, who had just been convicted of "treason" in Budapest and given life imprisonment by the Communist Government of Hungary.

He contemplated as early as 1948 writing a history of the school and, in the Magazine that year, trawled for information from past students. His main interest focussed on the centuries before 1905 and in his outline plan for the book he only allotted a couple of chapters to KES as such. He did start a draft of the early chapters, going into great detail on a school at the parish church in Sheffield in the Middle Ages and added firmer information on the Tudor school at Townhead. He got no further, however, because in 1953 he moved on to become the Headmaster of Henry Fanshawe School, Dronfield, and he worked on projects on the history of that school instead.

Valentine J. Wrigley, who came as the Senior History Master in September 1946, was also an enthusiast for researching the history of the school. Between them they arranged for a plaque to be mounted in the Entrance Hall in 1950, giving the names of all the Headmasters and Principals of the predecessor schools from 1604 up to 1905. Underneath the names there is a short précis of the pre-history of the school and the plaque still hangs in the same place close by the Headteacher's study. Barton who had inaugurated the Commemoration Service in 1940 and who enthusiastically continued it into the post war era, encouraged this work on the history of the school. Everything that could link the post-1945 KES with its long past and traditions, would help to strengthen the school's sense of importance and its special position in Sheffield. E.F. Watling also was a part-time unofficial archivist for the school, collecting and filing lists of old boys who had made good, as previously, during the war, he had faithfully recorded all the names, press cuttings and C.O.'s letters of Old Edwardians who had been killed.

This pride and awareness of the school's past was reinforced when, in 1947, the Beardsell family, who had lost two sons in the forces, presented to the school the original pulpit bible that had been used by Wesley College. From now on this huge and splendidly bound bible would be used by the prefects when reading the morning lesson, an ordeal made no less difficult because they had the responsibility themselves of selecting the passage to be read that day. At about the same time in 1947, a huge portrait of Edward VII when Prince of Wales, by A.W. Lumley Saville, was discovered in the props room of the Empire Theatre, Alfreton. It had mysteriously arrived there during the war from the ballroom of Rufford Abbey, and as the theatre had little use for a life size painting of this particular monarch, they offered it to KES for 40 guineas. It hangs to this day on the western staircase of the school.

The War Memorial Fund

The school also very much remembered its more recent history when in October 1946 the school held its Remembrance Service for its dead of the 1939-45 conflict. Unlike the service in 1919 this was not held in the Cathedral but in the Assembly Hall. In all other respects, however, it was an appropriate and solemn occasion with the sermon given to a large congregation by Rev. A.B. Swallow, who was an Old Edwardian himself and during the war had been a chaplain in the RAF. The following summer the Old Edwardians Association launched its War Memorial Appeal. Under the presidency of C.J. Magrath, with Michael Taylor as Secretary, the Appeal had five objectives. Firstly to add the inscription 1939-45 to the existing Cross in the Close, secondly, to provide a bronze tablet to include all the names of the war dead, in the same general style as the First World War plaque. The largest project of the five would be to provide an electric organ to be placed in the balcony behind the platform and be used in the morning and chapel services at the school. Finally, two educational projects that would encourage international understanding, the first to provide a section of books in the library dealing with world affairs and the second, to create a fund that would allow a travelling bursary for a boy at the school who would not otherwise have the funds, to make a visit abroad for a month during the school holidays. They estimated that they needed to raise £2500, although in the event this was an underestimate, the organ alone costing £2020, but they set about raising the money and the fund was well subscribed. Until the Memorial was unveiled in 1949, the names of the Old Edwardians who had been killed in the war were printed every year at the front of the Speech Day programme, and they were read out in full every 11th November when the school gathered outside at 11.00 am around the War Memorial Cross.

Some re-organisation and development.

With the war over and the arguments over grammar school status settled, it was time for Barton to consider administrative changes and curriculum developments that would take the school forward. Some changes were imposed upon him. The most important was the Council's decision that KES should operate a five-day week like all the other grammar schools. This challenged the school's sense of its own distinctive position. The Headmaster argued that the six-day week created an almost total school environment for the KES pupil, where their every interest could be served by the school and they did not need to resort to outside organisations or influences, other than the home and the church. He fought a rearguard action against the Council's policy, and it was not until September 1946 that Saturday morning school was abolished. It had taken a debate and a vote in the Education Committee to decide the issue, when the Progressives, in support of the Headmaster, narrowly lost an amendment to maintain the six day week at KES. As a result, the school now operated the same longer terms and shorter holidays that the other LEA schools kept; another blow to the traditionalists who enjoyed the extra weeks of holiday when other schools had already gone back for the new term. A less important issue, but also symbolic of the school's changed circumstances, happened when the old "Public School Hymn Books" the school had used during the last two decades needed replacing. The Education Committee, not unreasonably, insisted they use the same "Songs of Praise" hymn books that were provided for all the other schools from their central purchasing department.

The major new curriculum development was the creation in 1947 of the Economics Sixth Form Section. Barton had regularly applied himself to the concern that the school was not satisfying the needs of all its pupils. Now that all new boys were scholarship winners, and therefore obliged to stay at school till they were 16, he wanted to create the conditions where every boy could pursue a Sixth Form Course. This fourth Sixth Form Section, to stand alongside the Classical, Modern, and Science Sixth, was to comprise History and French and the two new subjects Geography and Economics. This first ever Geography Sixth Form course would be piloted through by Robert Towers, the new Senior Geography master, who had replaced Gaskin, while the responsibility of running the Economics Higher Certificate course was given to Gordon Cumming, universally known throughout the school as Cheese. Whilst KES was very much behind the times in not setting up a Geography Higher Certificate course previously, the Economics course was very much ahead of its time in grammar schools, as most schools would not offer Economics for another decade at least.

Barton did not expect that every boy in this section would go to University, nor did he believe they should, for he very much belonged to the school of thought that more meant worse when applied to University entrants. He feared, as many did, that the supposedly high standards of English Universities would be diluted and ruined by large increases in the student population. At the same time he welcomed the new and very generous LEA University Scholarships that were introduced in 1947 which paid all tuition fees and, depending on the parents own means to support their children, their maintenance expenses as well. By 1949, any KES boy who could gain a place at a University could apply successfully for one of these scholarships, which made possible the growth of student numbers at the existing universities and the creation of another generation of provincial universities. Open Scholarships now became a matter of prestige, while the LEA Scholarships made it possible for many children with parents of limited means to become the first generation of their family to be able to afford to go to university. They were also encouraged to get away from their home town and go to the university of their choice in another part of the country, and the maintenance element of the Scholarship grant made that possible.

There were changes at the other end of the school in 1948 when for the first time all the new boys in the year group were free place scholarship winners from primary schools. So all the classes were made an equal number of 30 pupils, as theoretically there was no need for smaller classes for weaker pupils and the classes were not streamed until the Third Forms. There is no existing reliable statistical data to indicate the social background of these new boys, and although Halsey and Floud in their classic study of grammar schools in South West Hertfordshire and Middlesborough in 1953 demonstrated that around half the places in those area's grammar schools went to working class children, anecdotal evidence suggests it was a much smaller percentage at KES. The geographic position of the school and the tradition of serving the city's professional classes, most probably ensured a considerable majority of middle class pupils coming into the school through the LEA's 11+ Examination, and while the social structure of the school undoubtedly became broader based, the middle class ethos of the school was so strong that, whatever your background, you were inevitably moulded into becoming a traditional Edwardian. This was of course the deliberate intention of the Headmaster and the staff, and few boys of whatever background challenged the school's assumptions of what were correct behaviour and manners, and the need for excellence in their work and sport.

Barton's relations with many of his staff were often rather tetchy. Some of the younger staff, many new to the school and often with wartime experience, set up a staff discussion group to informally consider new teaching methods and new ideas in education. The Headmaster viewed this, quite sizeable, group with some suspicion, so he invited himself and his deputy along to its meetings to make sure nothing too revolutionary was proposed. He had annoyed some staff during the discussions on Saturday morning school, when he had taken their support for granted when most of them preferred the five-day week. Virtually all the staff who had been in the services had been commissioned, and many had carried considerable responsibility and been through some cauterising experiences. These men did not take too kindly to Barton's authoritarian ways and they were irritated by his habit of putting numerous typed orders on the staff notice board, which they all had to initial to indicate they had been read.

TO ALL MEMBERS OF STAFF

SMOKING

It is the custom here for members of the Staff not to smoke in the School or the Close until 4.45 p.m. in the afternoon, or 1.30 p.m. when there is no afternoon school.

Members of staff may smoke in the Dining Hall after dinner and after tea, and at all times in the Common Room.

Members of the Administrative Staff may smoke between 1 and 2 p.m. in the office.

AWB Headmaster.   *September 1949*

He did though appoint some excellent staff and the level of scholarship amongst the masters was very high. In the latter part of the century, teachers with their qualifications, if they considered a teaching career at all, would most probably have become university lecturers. More than one obtained a Ph.D. whilst at the school. W.D. Hargreaves wrote a thesis on "Viscosity and Chemical Constitution" to gain his doctorate and Bill Duffin and Eric Tappe left to become university lecturers, Duffin at Hull University and Tappe as a lecturer in Roumanian at the School of Slavonic and East European Studies in the University of London. Four of his staff, Wallis, Wrigley, Harvey and Bradley became Headmasters themselves, but Barton was already facing the problem of shortage of staff in some subject areas. Maths and Science graduates were already aware that the economy offered a far wider range of careers than just teaching, and consequently schools were beginning to feel the pinch. The solution, as in war time, was to employ women staff, or re-employ them as in Janet Manners case. She stayed at KES until 1951 when she married Bill Duffin and later went to teach at Hymers College in Hull, a school which also found Maths staff difficult to recruit.

A great part of the problem was the appalling wages that teachers earned under the Burnham Scale. A salary of £450 p.a. for a master with a good honours degree and a responsibility allowance of £75 for a head of a subject department was desperately inadequate, even for the post war years of austerity. That was the allowance Victor Bramhall received when he took over from Harry Scutt as Senior Modern Languages Master in 1947. Known universally as "Spiv" because of his dapper appearance, his bow tie and most of all for his pencil thin moustache, much favoured by the wide boy fraternity at the time, he was one of an intake of remarkable teachers who came to the school in 1947. Norman Barnes was another who started that term, as did Denys " Bert" Harrison, the P.T. Master, who played a large part in widening the range of sports played at KES and Edwin Cumming, who came to teach History and sow a little confusion, at least on paper, because the History Department now had two masters named Cumming. Gordon Cumming had been known as Cheese since he first came to the school, so Edwin Cumming, a Scotsman, educated at Fettes before he went up to Hertford College, Oxford, inevitably became "Chalk".

Strengthening the House system.

One way of ensuring the traditions of the school carried over during this transitional period was to increase the importance of the House system. New boys still became members of one of the eight houses and seem to have developed a genuine loyalty, respect and enthusiasm for an institution that seems quite superfluous to modern school students. To Barton and the staff in 1947, the existence of houses was as valid as ever, if not even more important in helping to weld the "new" boys firmly into the KES community and accept its standards, rituals and routines. The houses were still basically a vehicle for organised, competitive games within the school, but they could have been a counselling institution as well. Barton introduced House Prayers once a week, when the boys would meet as Chatsworth or Haddon etc. and House Masters and Heads of House would have a public role relaying house messages and exhorting teams to gain victories. He arranged that houses would sit together at dinner to add to their sense of membership and loyalty and added more house competitions like Water Polo, and more teams so that there were third XIs at Football and Cricket as well as instituting the Standard Sports in 1948, that enabled every member of the house to contribute towards his house's athletics success. It fell far short of real social care supporting those who were faced with any emotional difficulties; boys were still expected to "pull themselves together" if experiencing any kind of personal crisis, whilst competitive sport was about being individually reliable and not letting the team down.

The Trinity of work, games and societies.

The school, in the immediate post war period, still demanded of its pupils that they aim to achieve the highest standards of excellence in the classroom and on the playing fields, and that they take an active part in as many school societies and activities out of school hours as they had the time and interest for. All the previous Headmasters would have signed up to the same creed, and like Barton would have added that the school also had a major role in creating a well mannered boy with a proper respect for the Christian religion. They would also all have said that examinations were not the be all and end all of education, but like all schools they made sure that their pupils did as well as was possible in the outside examinations and university scholarships.

KES had always judged itself on how well its Sixth Form did at the Higher Certificate Examinations, the number of Distinctions achieved and the number of Oxbridge Scholarships and Exhibitions it won in any one year. It had got used to winning the Akroyd Scholarship and gaining a few State Scholarships each academic year, and also to bask in the reflected glory of some of the Old Edwardians who did well at university and in later academic life. Barton was determined that the school should do just as well in all these areas now it was a maintained grammar school. Furthermore, although he was perceived by many who were not high flyers as being uninterested in the average boy, he set up structures within the school to improve the academic performance of all the pupils at KES. As a consequence the School Certificate results made a marked year on year improvement, with a record number of 36 Special Merits in 1946 and passing the 100 mark of successful candidates in 1947. From then on, until they were replaced in 1951 by the GCE Ordinary Level Examinations, KES would always be above the national average for School Certificate passes, something it had clearly failed to do in the past.

When Barton had taken over the school in 1939 there were 700 boys, including the Juniors, on roll at the school, with 90 in Transitus and the Sixth Form (now Y12 and Y13). When he left in 1950 the school numbered 680, all Seniors, with 181 in the two top years. The success at Higher Certificate reflected this increase with a new record of 56 certificates out of 60 candidates in 1948, overtaken by 68 successes in 1949. The Sixth Form, still composed only of boys who had come to the school before the 1944 Education Act, produced an increasing number of State Scholarships — there were 5 in 1946 and 7 the following year, when there were only 11 awarded to Sheffield grammar schools in total — and in every year after 1947, whilst Barton was the Headmaster, KES won at least ten Open Scholarships and Exhibitions at Oxbridge. They included an extraordinary sequence of Hastings Scholarships at Queen's College, Oxford (in 1947 they won 4 out of the 8 available for the fourteen northern schools who were eligible for the award) and added to these successes there were also more commoners going up to these two universities now the LEA's grant system could support many more undergraduates. So by 1949 the Seventh Club of Old Edwardians at Oxford numbered forty members, mainly undergraduates but some doing research and not a few Fellows. The Fellows included Brigadier E.T. Williams, back from a post with the United Nations in San Francisco, who became a Fellow of Balliol in 1947, Harold Thompson FRS at St. Johns, and Albert Goodwin who became Vice Principal of Jesus College in 1948.

The school also had many successes at Sheffield University as well. In 1948 it was still the only other university that Old Edwardians went to in any kind of numbers, and apart from a steady stream of First Class Honours Graduates, there were many former pupils who picked up prizes awarded by the University. In 1948 A.A. Belton won the Gold Medal for Pathology, J.E. Andrew the Mappin Medal for Engineering, M.S.Wang the Brunton Medal for Metallurgy, D.A.J.Tyrrell the Woodcock Prize for Physiology and G.R.B. Whittaker the Kay Prize for Mental Diseases. This was not a particularly atypical year for Old Edwardians at Sheffield, who pursued a range of courses with many opting to read for architecture, engineering and medical degrees.

Those pupils and Old Edwardians whose success Barton felt was of considerable significance were highlighted in his address on Speech Days and in his reports to the Education Committee. Mervyn Jones who had left in 1939 and after the war had gone back to Trinity, Barton's own college at Cambridge, won the Porson Prize for Classics in 1947 and went on to be a Fellow at Trinity, where the 1945 Akroyd Scholarship winner, M.P. Fanthom, became a Wrangler in the same year. The year before E.J. Lemmon had gained the 1st Demyship for Classics at Magdalen College, Oxford, even though he was only 16 years old and in 1949 F. Mandl, of Lincoln College, Oxford, gained his D. Phil for research on Atomic Physics.

Despite all these successes at the Universities, and there were an impressive 79 Oxbridge awards during Barton's time, the award the school most prized, as it had since 1905, was the Akroyd Scholarship. T.E. Kinsey won it in 1948 and Leonard Hunt in 1949 when Ralph Windle was the runner up, something that had happened on four other occasions since 1939. For one school to have won this highly valued, eminent award ten times in the previous fourteen years, seven of them during Barton's period at the school, was truly remarkable and a continuing tribute, not just to the successful boys, but to the quality of teaching in the Sixth Form.

Whom you play!

If there were any concerns that some of the schools KES traditionally played at cricket and other sports might shun them now that they were a maintained LEA grammar school, they were not to be realised. Rather the opposite occurred; as KES became involved in more competitive matches in Athletics, Swimming and Water Polo their fixture list became more glamorous, with fixtures against schools they would never expect to be invited to play at Cricket, and who did not play Football.

KES Football teams almost always had winning seasons after the war but they didn't quite rise to the heights of the teams in the mid-Thirties. Their fixture list was very similar to their pre-war one and they continued to have very competitive matches with the local grammar schools within the city and nearby. Chesterfield, Rotherham and Barnsley G.S. were always strong football schools and the matches with High Storrs were always keenly contested. They did play one or two public schools including Bootham and Manchester G.S., but the big match of the season was still the game against Repton. In 1948, after beating their 2nd XI three years on the run, they finally were offered a First Team fixture. Played at Repton in October, the school team hung on to a lead and gained a very satisfactory 4-3 victory. They may well have benefited from a two day visit to the school by Walter Winterbottom, the F.A. Director of Coaching and the first ever manager of the England team. Arranged through Barton's connections — he was a FIFA referees instructor— Winterbottom put the school team through pressure training, one–two football and short practice games, that were much appreciated, encouraging a better than usual turnout at training for the rest of the season and leading to the formation of a school 3rd XI.

The Cricket team continued to play the direct grant schools of Yorkshire and only normally played High Storrs and Barnsley G.S. among the local schools. After the war there were regular fixtures with Manchester G.S., Trent College and Repton 2nd XI. Nevertheless, despite this strong fixture list the KES Cricket Club had winning seasons almost every summer, and in 1948 C.B. Dawson, Peter Wreghitt and John Dickens played for Yorkshire Schools.

The new achievements in KES's competitive sporting reputation during the 1940s were in Athletics and later Swimming. They had first entered the Northern Public Schools Athletics Championship in 1940 and had always performed well in the events held in Manchester. In 1947 they came in 2nd place overall behind Barrow G.S. and then took two first places in events at the Public School Athletics Meeting at the White City. The

winner of the ¾ mile steeplechase was David Law, who was the finest KES track athlete of that, or probably any other, generation. He excelled for the school in all distance running including winning the Northern Schools Cross Country in 1949, the year when KES first won this championship (they won it again the following year when it was run at Ringinglow). Later, at Oxford, he was one of a small group of milers who have become sporting legends. Although he was not involved on the track when Bannister ran the first four minute mile, he was part of an Oxbridge Achilles relay team of Brasher, Chattaway, Bannister and himself that competed in the USA and Canada and he also ran in the Commonwealth

D.C. Law

Games in Vancouver in 1954. The previous year he had held the World Record for the 4 x 1500m relay along with Pirie, Dunkley and Nankeville, with a time of 15 mins 27.2 secs. He also took part in two World Student Games, in 1953 in Dortmund and in 1955 in San Sebastian, where he was the Great Britain Team Captain.

The school began a regular series of athletics matches with Repton and in 1949 they came a very close second to Shrewsbury in a tri-angular match at Repton. However it was at competitive swimming that the school was invincible. For five years up to 1950 they never lost a swimming match and they competed against some illustrious competitors, including annual matches against Leeds G.S., Bootham and King Edward V1 School, Birmingham, and then later against Rugby and Trent College. In 1950 they defeated the City of London School, who came up to Sheffield full of confidence and returned to the capital a beaten team. They also performed well at Water Polo even though they lost occasionally, but two of their players, J.E. Cooper and G.T. Edmunds, got Half Blues for the sport at Oxford, and Edmunds captained the Varsity team.

The 1949 Swimming Team with D. "Bert" Harrison middle of back row

Athletics and Swimming were now elevated to official school sports and full colours could be awarded to boys for excellence in these sports. However there were other sporting triumphs, including some that had little to do with the school. J. Sandy Bethell first played for England against Scotland Boys at Golf in 1947 and in 1948 he captained the successful English team in the same fixture before going on to reach the semi-final of the English Boys Open Golf Championship. A Table Tennis club had been started in 1946 and the school's first victory had been a resounding 12-0 win over the staff, although the temporary lighting they rigged up over the table tended to blow the fuses in the Library where they played. They did, however, receive recognition for one of their number when D.N.Tyler, a former Head Boy, became the Oxford University Table Tennis Captain in 1949. Rugby Fives was played again at the school, when the coke that had been stock piled in the fives courts throughout the war was cleared out in 1949, but the game found it difficult to compete with the counter attraction of the school's newest sport when a Tennis Club was started in 1949. Initially this club's membership was drawn just from the Sixth Form, Transitus and the staff, and they had to lease time at club premises because there were no courts at the school. After beating the staff by 3-2 rubbers, they found the club junior sides they challenged a little to strong for them, but the game would become a permanent part of the expanding sports programme and eventually tennis courts were built at the eastern end of the Close in 1959.

The growth of school societies

There were new societies too to interest boys after school. The most stimulating was the International Discussion Group (IDG) that filled the void previously covered by a debating society. It was Gordon Cumming's conception that got the new group started in 1946, with an informal agenda and a membership open to the Sixth Form and Transitus. Fifteen or so boys and a number of masters aimed to discus current international issues in more depth than could be achieved in a formal debate, and thereby encourage concern for the appalling difficulties faced by other countries in the post war world. Usually a boy or a master would lead off the discussion at their weekly meetings and members would then contribute their comments and analysis. Topics included some of the key issues of the day, where masters could contribute from first hand experience, including a talk on the reconstruction of Germany by Edwin Cumming who had been part of the Army's Occupation Government in the British Zone. Later papers on Czechoslovakia, Palestine and one on Indian Independence, led by an Indian boy at the school, continued the focus on the immediate crisis areas, but there were also discussions on Argentina, Egypt, Switzerland, the Soviet Baltic Republics, Sweden and other countries not usually considered by schools in the classroom or in debates.

By 1947 the IDG had formed a periodic link with the Girls' High School for joint discussion meetings, and KES routinely sent delegates, in the Easter and Christmas holidays, to Conferences in London run by the Council for Education in World Citizenship. In 1949, the CEWC held a conference in Geneva and several boys attended, with Gordon Cumming acting as one of the Wardens. Their meetings in the library may not have attracted large numbers, but the range of the issues and quality of the discussions must have fired the imagination of more than a few members of the group and encouraged a lifelong interest in international affairs.

The Ciné-Club, which had been founded near the end of the war, was still showing films to younger audiences that were either comedies of the Laurel and Hardy variety, or Government Information films or documentaries. They now developed a production unit which produced a documentary on school life in 1947 called "A Year in Celluloid". They gained considerable praise for their discriminating direction and photography, and their effective choice of background music, which ranged from Handel and Grieg to the Six Texas Hot Dogs. Thus emboldened, they ventured a wider canvass for their next production in 1949 when they attempted to capture the spirit of the whole city of Sheffield in a documentary entitled "Symphony of a City". In a well-composed 45 minute film, the Ciné-Club production team, mainly formed from Fifth Formers and under the direction of J.M.Dawson, portrayed the familiar activities of the city and its people. Even their blitz scene using burning matchboxes for houses did not stretch credulity too far, and in the second part of the film dealing with the city's industry, some of the camera work of G.S. Finlayson inside the giant steel works was almost of professional standard. He obviously felt he had found his vocation, because he left shortly afterwards to become a press photographer.

1949 was something of a seminal year for the Dramatic Society as well, when they took on the very real challenge of Maxwell Anderson's 1935 play "Winterset". After an acclaimed version of Journey's End the previous year, still a great favourite of school dramatic societies, it was a startling choice to attempt a play in verse that is not easy to produce with its mixture of poetry and New York underworld depravity. The well regarded local drama critic, L. du Garde Peach, came to see E.F. Watling's production and wrote;

> "Most school productions are beneath contempt except as fun and games for the pupils. This was a serious and highly intelligent production —— and it was both a pleasure and a privilege to see it."

The gamble in attempting this contemporary tragedy had paid off and the high standards of the Dramatic Society progressed.

CJM

One of the keenest supporters of all manner of extra curricular activity, whether it was brandishing the starter's gun at the Athletic Sports or selling tickets for a school play, finally came to the end of his time in July 1949. It would be superfluous to say he was a school institution, for Charles J. Magrath was the last link with the staff of the school's first decade. "Fatty" Magrath was a Channel Islander and a Wykehamist, whose uncle had been the Provost of Queen's College, Oxford, and he had a doctorate himself from Louvain University. He had been appointed by Hichens in 1908 to teach Languages and he inspired three generations of Edwardians in lessons in Room 68 on the top floor, where, it is said, that when Nicholas was caning boys across the corridor he was marking up the number of strokes on the blackboard. He also invented an unusual form of punishment himself when he "imprisoned" boys in the dark space below his desk and gave them the occasional prod with his shoe. A fount of good stories, a walking archive on the school's history, his unruffled calm and infectious laugh endeared him to his charges, especially the less able who were particularly grateful for the trouble he took with them. Somewhere along the line he acquired an OBE for work at Hillsborough Boys' Club, but he was prouder still to be chosen as the Vice-President of the Old Edwardians' Association. Despite passing the retirement age in 1947, the Education Committee had twice let him continue, until after 41 years at the school he eventually retired to his home in Rustlings Road.

The unofficial calendar

KES boys, like boys at most schools, operated a calendar of events of their own. Some events were affected by the seasons of the year, so that the conker season would start in the autumn and snowballing, of course, when snow fell, as it did in overwhelming abundance in the winter of early 1947.

To minimise possible damage to windows, the Headmaster issued a stern warning that all snowballing in the Close must be done; "from East to West and vice versa but never on a North – South axis".

Prefects were considered a legitimate target and even unwary staff members might take a hit. It is unlikely, however, that they would offer a temptation like an art master before World War One who ventured into the Close on a snowy day and had his top hat removed by a well aimed missile.

Other annual activities appeared on a whim without any warning. The annual "regatta" of paper planes depended on enough boys wanting to participate, although after a week or so their enthusiasm dried up until the following year. More sinister was the emergence in the late Forties of the plastic multiple firing water pistol that could soak a jacket, or part flood a corridor, and there were always ubiquitous games of mini-football in the quad, played with a tennis ball to arcane rules, using trees and even war memorials as goal posts.

Unveiling and Dedicating the War Memorial Tablet

The Old Edwardians' Association were finally ready to dedicate their War Memorial Tablet on 30th March 1949. With the families of those killed in the war given priority among a large congregation in the Assembly Hall that evening, the service was conducted by the Provost of Sheffield, with the address given by Rt. Rev. Kenneth Kirk, the Bishop of Oxford, himself an Old Boy of the SRGS and also the brother of a KES Head Prefect who was killed in the First World War. It fell to the Headmaster to read out 108 names that were recorded on the tablet placed in the Entrance Hall, below the memorial to the dead of 1914-18. This earlier memorial had recently been removed from its original position above the platform to make way for the new, and as yet undelivered, school organ, and the two tablets formed a uniform memorial to the school's war dead.

The lesson was read, most appropriately, by the former Headmaster, Richard Graham, for most of the Old Edwardians whose names were recorded had been boys at the school in his time. Then while the whole assembly stood in silence the platform party made their way to the Entrance Hall where Dr. Kirk performed the unveiling ceremony before closing with the National Anthem, "God save the King".

Within a year the names of two more Old Edwardians who had been killed in the war came to light. F/O Harold Stevenson (1934-39) was a Typhoon pilot who was shot down on Christmas Eve 1944 over Belgium and Lieut-Commander Arthur Troops R.D. RNR (1917-20), who had spent nearly thirty years at sea in the Merchant Navy, was killed in the Channel in June 1944, whilst serving as the Captain of H.M Cableship Monarch. Within a short time two bronze bars embossed with their names were fixed to the bottom of two of the columns on the memorial and all 110 Edwardians were appropriately remembered.

It wasn't quite the end of the story because in 1951 in the Korean War, Lt. John A.C. Milner (1937-42) formerly of Sandhurst and the Dorset Regiment, was killed in action serving with the Argylls as the Commonwealth Divisions strove to halt the onslaught of the Chinese Army after UN Forces had been pushed back from the Yalu River to the 38th Parallel.

He was the last Old Edwardian to be killed in war.

The Choir and Orchestra

When Norman Barnes MA, Mus Bach, and FRCO arrived at KES in September 1947 as the new Director of Music, he took over a strong choir and orchestra bequeathed to him by Philip Baylis and built on the existing tradition. By the time Barton resigned the choir was 110 strong and the orchestra had 40 players, with the potential to grow because 24 boys were learning to play the violin and five more were learning the viola. The SRGS Trustees had pitched in with a £400 grant to buy instruments and Barnes had established the tradition of putting on either Bach or Handel's Passion each Easter in either St. John's, Ranmoor, or at Ecclesall Parish Church.

As soon as Barnes arrived he re-instituted the live lunchtime concerts and breathed new life into the Music Club and the Gramophone Concerts and set up a Recorder Club. He used the prizes available under the Parents' Prizes Scheme (a re-direction of money raised for the redundant 1945 Fighting Fund) to set up competitions and awards for singers, instrumentalists and above all for composition. Barnes early concerts included a lot of works by English composers from Purcell to Vaughan Williams and by 1948 he felt confident enough for the Orchestra to attempt Elgar's Nimrod, that was judged at the time to be the most ambitious piece the KES Orchestra had ever tackled. In 1949 he formed a "Talent Team" of singers and instrumentalists who travelled round the city giving well appreciated concerts in community centres and church halls. Even though Barnes had only been at the school three years when Barton left, it was already clear that KES had

Norman Barnes with the Choir and Orchestra at St. John's Ranmoor in 1948

acquired a man of exceptional accomplishment to run its Music Department and the choir and orchestra.

Farewell to AWB

Characteristically, Barton provided his own valedictory at his final Speech Day in June 1950, when he reported at some length on his "stewardship" of the school since 1939. He had accepted a post as the Headmaster of the City of London School, then in its premises on the Embankment by Blackfriars Bridge and he remained there till his retirement in 1965. At 50 years of age he presumably felt, like his predecessor, that he had taken KES as far as he could and if he was to accept another challenge at another suitable school, he would miss the opportunity if he got any older.

There were few in the Assembly Hall that evening who did not appreciate what the Headmaster had achieved after he took over a successful school from his predecessor and immediately had to guide it through a World War; a war that literally came to the school's doorstep. Although he didn't mention it that evening, he regarded the one great failure of his tenure was not to have secured direct grant status for the school in 1945, and yet he must have realised five years on, that the essential spirit and progress of KES was not

235

Dr. A.W. Barton with his last group of Prefects in 1950. On his right is Sydney Carter, the Senior Master and on his left is Norman Adsetts, the Head Prefect.

going to be adversely altered by the decisions taken at that time. He had come to terms with his political "masters" and Ald. John Bingham, Chairman of the Education Committee and the School's Governors, sitting alongside him on the platform that evening, had become an enthusiastic supporter of the school and of its high minded Headmaster. What neither of them foresaw that day were the bitter arguments that would erupt in the Sixties over comprehensive education, and how KES would be once again in the forefront of the battle for the future of Sheffield's education. If the school had become a direct grant school at the end of the war, that particular battle would have bypassed KES.

The school Barton was leaving was in a confident mood. Since 1945 he could point to advancement in almost every aspect of the school's life and the presence on the platform of three distinguished Old Edwardians from three different periods and a Head Boy, Norman Adsetts, who later as Sir Norman Adsetts was destined to become a leading figure in the industrial and social life of the city, exemplified how the school was a continuum, despite the constitutional changes that buffeted it from time to time.

H. Keeble Hawson (1905-12) was the first Old Edwardian to be the Lord Mayor, and the first to be a Freeman of Sheffield as well, and later in the evening he gave a vote of thanks to the Speaker, Prof. Harold Thompson FRS (1917-25), who among other achievements yet to come in his life, would become Chairman of the Football Association. Seconding the vote of thanks was a leading skin specialist in the city, Dr. H.R. Vickers (1923-29) who while still in his thirties had recently been elected a Fellow of the Royal College of Physicians.

Within a month Barton had left the school and gone to his new post in London. There already were four former members of his old staff at Sheffield teaching at CLS, and it is rumoured that not all were happy with the turn of events. Amongst one of the first changes he made there was to institute a Commemoration Service, held in the rather grand surroundings of St. Paul's Cathedral, and he seems to have been well regarded at his new school even if they never saw him laugh or even smile.

His moving on had happened quite suddenly, as these things do, and his towering presence in the school had been so omnipresent that for a while it was difficult to imagine KES without him. All, but a very few, of his former pupils regard him with respect as a notable, even distinguished, Headmaster. The type of man you would want to have known as an adult, when your experience of the world and of people, would have given you more mature judgement with which to fully appraise Dr. Arthur W. Barton.

SIXTH FORM OPINION Circa 1949

The Sixth Form and Transitus were asked their opinions on burning issues of the day.

It was the first of a regular series of opinion polls of Sixth Formers' views during the next 20 years.

How would you vote if you were 21?
58% Conservative, 13% Labour, 2% Communist, 14% Others

Have you decided on your career?
58% yes. (52% Science Sixth. 6% Modern, Economics and Classics)

United or Wednesday?
40% Wednesday, 30% United, 30% No interest in Football.

Moral support?
51% Belts. 10% Braces, 20% Both, 19% Risk pants falling down.

Have you a girl friend?
50% Yes (50% go to work, 50% still at school), 15% Misogynists.

Shaving yet?
83% claimed to shave.

December 1949

CHAPTER FOURTEEN

BEST MAINTAINED
1950-65

In the decade and a half that Nathaniel Clapton was the Headmaster, King Edward VII School thought itself to be the best LEA maintained grammar school in the country. There were many outside the school who thought the same and when the Times Educational Supplement added its agreement, the accolade appeared to be confirmed. Yet it is noticeable that Old Edwardians of the Fifties and Sixties are far less sentimental about the school than their predecessors, and are more willing to criticise the teaching and the organisation of KES. Perhaps it is because the school was such a hard taskmaster, or that the achievements of its sixth formers gave the school such a robust and unchallengeable reputation, that they feel free to question whether the emphasis on Oxbridge Scholarships and GCE Examination successes, produced the best education for the élite group of boys selected by the city's Common Entrance 11+ Examination.

During Clapton's period as Headmaster, the more he believed the school was successful the more criticism, if not downright hostility, it attracted. Some was, no doubt, of the kind that is jealous of any successful institution. KES was, after all, known as " the snob school " to a whole generation of Sheffield schoolchildren who resented "King Teds" assumption of a superior position within the city. Others argued that the school's priority was to create a conveyor belt from the First Year Forms to Oxbridge for the able pupils and ignore the educational requirements of the less successful pupils, all of whom had not only been successful in the 11+ examination, but had gained a high place in the merit table. Clapton dismissed these assumptions, arguing that what he aimed to construct was a school environment where a very able group of pupils were given the opportunity to work to their maximum potential and gain the highest academic awards. He was in no doubt that the pinnacle of these honours was to gain entry to Oxford or Cambridge, preferably Oxford, and enjoy the life and the challenge of two of the world's leading universities. His aim, in this respect, was no different from any of his predecessors from Dr. Hichens to Dr. Barton. However, he had a greater opportunity than even they possessed, because the City Council each year handed to him some of the very brightest pupils in a city of half a million people, and he would have considered it a dereliction of duty to sell them short by not demanding the highest endeavour from them.

He had outlined his vision of how the school should progress to the leading councillors on the Education Committee when he was interviewed for the Headmaster's post in the summer of 1950. He understood better than most what a high performing boys' day school could achieve, for he had spent his teaching career in such schools after graduating with a First in Mathematics from Hertford College, Oxford, in the mid-Twenties. He had successively been Senior Maths Master at two prestigious day schools, firstly at Watford G.S. (which held a reputation in the home counties rather similar to KES's in the north of England) and then at Glasgow Academy, the leading day school in Glasgow. In 1940 he had become the Headmaster of Boteler G.S. in Warrington and it was from that school that he applied, and was appointed, to the post of Headmaster at KES. Some thought he was the council's man and would do their bidding; they could not have been more wrong. All those who knew N.L.Clapton agree about one thing; he was quite definitely his own man and he never courted popularity from politicians, the public, the press or even the parents. He said, and did, what he thought was correct and the staff, at least, found him straightforward and relatively approachable after Dr. Barton, whom some felt could be devious and who didn't communicate well with his assistant masters.

Clapton didn't make such an initial favourable impression with the boys of the school. After the imposing performances by his predecessor at morning assembly, he cut a much less impressive figure on the platform. Whilst Barton, always elegantly dressed, had lectured the school in ringing patrician tones, Clapton, dressed in an untidy manner, mumbling the prayers and messages seemed a poor replacement. He even sparked off some derision as boys observed his suits did not fit and his trousers were too short, yet he was continually chivvying them about their appearance at school and in public. The morning assembly was the only time most boys saw him regularly during their school career, because he spent most of his time working in his office, rarely walked the corridors and chose not to teach on the timetable. All previous Headmasters had done some classroom teaching, yet those who knew him at Watford and Glasgow attested to the fact that he was a very effective teacher. Nevertheless, at KES he saw his role as Headmaster as an administrative one, creating the structures and deciding the appropriate courses for each individual pupil to follow. It was a brave, self confident pupil who challenged the options that had been chosen for him as he moved up the school, whilst sixth formers were told which subjects they should read at university and which university they should apply for. Anyone he thought would have a remote chance of success at Oxbridge was packed off in the Autumn, or early Spring Terms, to take scholarship exams at distant colleges, and he worked his contacts at the colleges as best he could to gain acceptance for as many boys as possible. He would strongly deny that he was creating a conveyor belt for able boys to ride into university, for laziness was anathema to him, but he might have accepted that he was laying down tramlines where a boy, through diligence and hard work, could be driven to an appropriate undergraduate course or, as in many cases, win an open scholarship.

The New Broom

Clapton took up office on 1st November 1950 after Sydney Carter, the Senior Master, had run the school for the first half term of the new academic year. The new Headmaster soon showed he was no respecter of school traditions if he could find a better solution to a situation. Within a year he had re-arranged the calendar of major school events, so that Speech Day now was held in October, after the examination results were all available, and because the space in the Assembly Hall was quite clearly too small for this occasion, he moved the whole event back to Victoria Hall where it had last been held in 1928. After a particularly thin attendance at the Carol Concert he agreed that future concerts should be held at St. John's Ranmoor, and the main school concert usually held in early December was shifted into the early part of the Lent Term. As he was not a particularly religious person, unlike his two immediate predecessors, (Barton had surprised one new member of staff by telling him, "*It doesn't matter what you do in the classroom providing*

Nathaniel Langford CLAPTON MA
1903-1967, Headmaster of KES 1950-65

Born in 1903, the only son of a Worcester ironmonger, Nathaniel Clapton was educated at the Royal Grammar School, Worcester, before gaining a scholarship to Hertford College, Oxford, in 1921. He gained First Class Honours in Mathematical Moderations in 1923 and a First in the Final Honour School of Mathematics in 1925. However, he didn't like his college very much as he considered it "too full of minor public schoolboys", and encouraged KES pupils to give it a miss when applying to Oxford. After teaching at Watford G.S and Glasgow Academy, where he was the Senior Maths Master at both institutions, he accepted the post of Headmaster of Boteler G.S. in Warrington in September 1940 with the task of fusing an ancient Tudor grammar school, Boteler, with a relatively new technical school, Warrington Secondary School, on a new suburban site at Latchford. In his youth he had been interested in rock climbing and fell walking, but his main recreation in his time at KES was walking his dog in the countryside. He also had a considerable interest in the cinema and paid out of his own pocket for the films that were shown at the end of term at the school. In his youth he had been a member of the choir of Worcester Cathedral and it also would have surprised many pupils to know that he was a passionate lover of animals. So much so that in the Sixties he refused to allow a cull of pigeons, which were making an appalling mess of the front steps and portico, where they had taken up residence.

Clapton was married with two children. A daughter, born in 1926, and a son born the following year.

Such was the awe, if not fear, with which he was regarded by most pupils at KES, some considered that the school motto in his time should have read: "Fac Recte, NAT Time".

it is the will of God") he abolished the once a term Sunday Chapel Service that had been instituted by Richard Graham, although he did keep the Commemoration Service which celebrated the school's history because he could see some value in that event. He also abolished compulsory Saturday morning games, the last vestige of the time when there was Saturday morning school. School teams might play on Saturdays, but Clapton saw no reason why you should bring boys back at the weekend who had no particular skill at games, not to mention imposing on staff who had to supervise the matches, to satisfy a tradition that quite frankly had more to do with status than standards in sport.

If these changes were not too much for the traditionalists, the introduction of Rugby Union in 1951 challenged some people's perception of the school's true identity. The supporters of the different forms of football had long had an antipathy towards each other (the two codes of Rugby fought a bitter internecine war for over a century), but for some in the Association camp, introducing Rugby Union would only divide the football talent available to the school and therefore weaken the school XI. The Headmaster himself remarked that the decision had caused a *"little quiet opposition in some quarters"*, but whereas Clapton was not a sportsman himself, although it was rumoured he had enjoyed rock climbing in his youth, he saw no reason why a school of over 700 boys should not support a wide number of sports. By the time he retired in 1965 KES played twelve sports competitively at inter-school level, yet Association Football managed to survive as the main school sport.

N.L. CLAPTON with his Prefects in 1951 sitting next to him is the Senior Prefect, George MacBeth. Sydney Carter, the Senior Master is on his right.

The new Headmaster also strengthened the prefectorial system, creating a new rank of Sub-Prefect with an initial appointment of six boys but eventually raising the number to 12. Together with the Prefects, also a dozen, they served as a form of special constabulary backing up the authority of the staff and learning a little about taking responsibility within a hierarchical structure. Like all his predecessors, Clapton could not imagine how the general discipline of the school, especially around the building, in the Close and during meal times in the dining room, could be maintained without them. They were given a distinctive badge and later he agreed the design of dark blue blazer with light blue piping to mark their office. You had to apply in writing to become a sub prefect and full prefects still had to take the "Prefects Pledge" on the platform at Morning Assembly in front of the whole school. One of Clapton's first Head Prefects was George MacBeth, later one of the best known poets of his generation, who had already shown his extraordinary talent in the poems he had written for the school magazine as he progressed up the school. He had even on one occasion written the Table Tennis club's report in blank verse, a game at which the prefects were particularly well practised, because they had a table in their room.

Re-organising the Forms and the Curriculum

In September 1951 Clapton introduced the biggest and most far reaching change so far. He renumbered all the classes in the school in a logical sequence, and at the same time created a structure that would overcome some of the barriers posed by the new GCE "O" Level Examination, and give the flexibility to allow boys to study as wide a range of options as possible. The HMIs who came to inspect the school the following year were full of admiration for the mathematical precision of his construction, which they felt gave sound foundation to the continuous development of the courses from the First to the Sixth Forms. To Clapton's logical mind it seemed a nonsense to start the school in the 2nd Forms, another eccentric hangover from the days when there was a Junior School, and they were renamed the First Form. Out went Transitus, the first year of the Sixth Form with its idiosyncratic classical name, first introduced by Dr.Hichens in 1905 when the school began. This form was now absorbed into the new Fifth Forms along with the Remove classes, introduced for pupils who needed to take a longer route to their School Certificate Exams.

The First Forms, each of 30 pupils, were not streamed, as the school wished to see for themselves how able the boys were who had passed the 11+ examination, even though the Headmaster knew where they had all been placed on the LEA's merit list. That information is not available to us any longer. However, by common consent, we can assume that almost all the 120 new boys each year came from the top third of the 550 + boys in Sheffield who, in any one year, gained a grammar school place in the early Fifties. In the second year they were divided into two groups of two classes, each based on their examination results in English, Maths, French and Latin. Other subjects were not included in deciding the order that placed the most able boys into 2a and 2 alpha, with the less able in those four subjects going into 2b and 2 beta. It was not lost on the boys which subjects were regarded by the school as the most prestigious and most important.

The new Form structure introduced in September 1951

Age at start of year	Form Name
11	1(1) 1(2) 1(3) 1(4)
12	2a 2Alpha. / 2b 2Beta
13	3(1) 3(2) 3(3) 3(4)
14	4(1) 4(2) 4(3) 4(4)
15	5CMS 5Sci 5G1 5G2 (A Level) (0 Level)
16	6CMS 6Sci (1) (A Level)
17/18	6CMS 6Sci (2) (Open Scholarships, S Level, A Level)

It had long been the practice at KES for the majority of the pupils to take the School Certificate after four years in the middle school. The regulations for the new GCE "O" Level examination, when it was first examined in 1951, precluded any pupil from taking the examination before they were 16 years of age. This was an unacceptable situation for Clapton because it held up able boys from gaining their GCE Certificate at 15, as well as stopping them from progressing onto "A" Level courses, passing those examinations at 17, and then concentrating on gaining Oxbridge Scholarships.

His new Form structure was designed to overcome this problem. Boys would move into the Fifth Form and if they were deemed to be ready for Advanced Level work they would choose one of the combination of subjects available in the 5th Classical & Modern Studies Form or in the 5th Science Form. There they would start their three chosen A level subjects but would only take "O" Level in the other subjects which they would be dropping the following year. It provided a heavy workload for the boys taking up to ten subjects at different levels, but from the Headmaster's viewpoint it allowed a considerable number of able boys to get their A levels by the time they were 17 and keep the path clear for Open Scholarships preparation.

In 1953 the 16 year old restriction on "O" Level was dropped after pressure from schools, but Clapton kept his structure and boys in the 4th Forms took a number of "O" Levels (initially 4 or 5, but later in the Fifties 8 or even 10) at 15 and then they took more alongside their "A" Level courses in 5CMS or 5 Science. If they had any spare capacity there were "AO" Level examinations to attempt and boys could end up with fifteen "O" Levels, although they only needed five, provided they included English Language, Maths/Science and a Foreign Language for university entrance, and if they wanted to go to Oxbridge they also required Latin.

5 General

Those who did not take "A" Level courses in the 5th Form were accommodated in the two 5 General Forms, styled 5G1 and 5G2. The boys in these two classes made up 40% of the year group in the early Fifties and they only took the "O" Level examinations. They fell into two categories. These were the boys who had indicated that they wished to leave at the end of their fifth year in the school (Parents, or Guardians, had to sign an undertaking for the LEA when their son passed his 11+ examination, that they would not remove their boys at 15, the legal age for leaving school), and also the boys who were not considered academically mature enough to handle an "A" Level course at 15 years of age, but hoped to stay on in the Sixth Form. For both groups their core course included R.I., English, History, French, Geography, Maths, Physics and Chemistry but they could choose one extra option from German, Spanish, Latin, Music, Art, or Handicraft.

Some boys worked hard in these forms (reduced to only one 5G later in the Fifties) and started their "A" Level courses a year later with all their options still open to them. Many went on to university and one who followed this course, Neil Newton (1954-61), graduated from Leeds University and was later Chief Executive of Hammersmith and Fulham L.B. Council. The school only required four "O" Level passes to enter the Sixth Form, including the three subjects they had chosen for "A" Level and, if they had continued with Latin, they could still enter for Oxbridge Scholarships when they completed their "A" Levels.

The "controversial" group were those who chose to leave. They numbered around 30 at first, and some now believe that 5G had become a "sink" form where many pupils deliberately under-achieved, and where the most incorrigible boys ended up with consequent behaviour problems. At times Clapton acknowledged there were some discipline problems in this group, and in a school where status depended on academic ability many boys in these classes must have felt failures, even though they were among the most able pupils at any of the city's schools. It was not a phenomenon peculiar to KES. In every grammar school that streamed its pupils, the bottom set often felt rejected and inferior. The school believed it was giving them as much attention as its high flyers – many of them would disagree — but the academic success of so many others in their year group only served to make these early leavers feel worse. If KES, like other grammar schools, was losing or even wasting talent, it was happening in classes like 5G. Indeed, one of the compelling arguments for comprehensive education is that pupils of this ability range are well accommodated within the present structure at the school, and yet most of the boys in this form would eventually achieve successful careers in the professions, business and industry. One of them, Michael Curley (1954-61), founded, and still chairs, his own international conference and exhibition company, MICE Group, that is fully listed on the London Stock Exchange, has forty companies within the Group and an annual turnover in excess of £150 million.

THE NEW GCE EXAMINATIONS

The new GCE Ordinary level examination introduced in 1951 had three purposes.

- *To raise standards*
- *To meet the examination requirements of a five-year grammar school course.*
- *To give recognition to each subject passed*

The old School Certificate could only be acquired if you gained a formula of 5 passes that included English, Maths or Science and a Language. You could have many more passes but if you didn't fit the formula (e.g. could not pass in a language) you would not get a matriculation certificate and you would have no qualification to show for all your efforts during your school career.

The School Certificate pass mark was quite low and the new GCE "O" Level Pass was set at 50%, the equivalent of the old Credit Level. Now you either passed or failed as there were initially no other grades. To compensate for setting the more difficult pass grade and to create a coherent five-year course, a pupil could not take the examination until they were 16 years of age. This barrier was removed in 1953, but it had held up two thirds of the year group at KES, who would otherwise have taken the examination at 15 as usual. Clapton argued that there should be two "O" Level pass grades. A lower grade at 40% and a higher grade at 60%. This would give some indication to future employers of a boy's real level of ability and he also believed that many hardworking pupils just could not reach the new standard.

The transition from the Higher Certificate to GCE Advanced Level was a much more straightforward change, but again initially there were no grades. You either passed or failed, and pupils were not allowed to know how well they had done. This was changed in 1953 when the Distinction Grade was introduced and it was these Distinction Grades that determined whether or not a boy had won a State Scholarship.

The "O" Level examination survived until comprehensive education became the norm in England and Wales and then it was replaced by the GCSE which recognised levels of achievement below the "O" Level pass rate. The "A" Level Examination is still with us but under fire for being too specialised, whilst some believe standards have deteriorated, a view not shared by the present staff at the school.

245

The 1952 Inspection Report

For four days in late November 1952, eight HMIs visited the school and conducted the first official inspection since 1933. That inspection had barely managed two cheers for the school, this one could hardly have been more different. There was virtually no criticism at all of the subject departments, the teaching standards and the organisation of the school. They were clearly impressed by the new form structure, the school's academic record, Clapton's leadership and his *"shrewd grasp of the school's potentialities"*. In effect it was a report on his two years in charge of the school and he couldn't have been more delighted with their conclusions if he had written them himself.

In their final summary they concluded:

> *"This is a good school. It is well led, well served by its staff, efficiently administered and blessed with a sound and generous conception of a grammar school course. Not only is the school's reputation for work of high quality in the sixth form being well maintained, but similar high standards have now been attained in the lower forms. Emphasis is rightly laid on academic studies, but the importance of other subjects is receiving adequate attention. There is a healthy and vigorous corporate spirit and out of school activities are widening and developing. The school can feel a pride in its achievement."*

Unlike present day Ofsted Reports, this HMI's Report when it was published in February 1953 was a very confidential affair. Criticism of schools and their staff was something that was conducted in private in the Fifties, and even when the Report was discussed at the Education Committee, the minutes give no details of its contents. In presenting the Report, Clapton drew the councillors' attention to the criticism of some of the inadequate facilities at the school. Whilst noting that the school was about to get a new library and that a new wing was planned to create specialist art and handicraft rooms as well as extra laboratories, the Inspectors had stressed the need for a modern gymnasium block which would include adequate shower baths and changing rooms. Adverse comments were also made about the primitive toilet block where 732 boys were still served by outside toilets, open to the elements, and they were even less impressed when, during their visit, a cold snap had frozen all the lavatories, pipes and cisterns.

On neither issue did the Headmaster have any success with his political masters, and the KES Upper School still uses the same small gymnasium, although the balcony, which served as the firing position when the gym doubled as a "miniature" range before the First World War, is now the Sixth Form office. Nor were indoor toilets provided during Clapton's time, so boys still had to cross the rear quad in all weathers to use the "Backs" when nature called. The red brick outline of the old toilet block can still be seen on the school's stone curtain wall, although a mobile classroom now stands on the hallowed spot formerly occupied by the "Backs".

Clapton had more luck with the criticism in the report that the school was understaffed by four or five teachers. The LEA could afford more teachers but not capital works. Eventually in 1954 four new posts were created, including an extra specialist post in English that resulted directly from comments in the HMI's Report criticising the "*quality*" of the boys' speech. This particular post was filled by Philip May who, inspired himself by F.R. Leavis, similarly inspired many a boy in turn to appreciate poetry and good writing. This was his first appointment after graduating from Manchester University and he epitomises two aspects of the staff in the Fifties. Firstly, although over half the staff were still Oxbridge men many of the new appointments came from the provincial civic universities, and secondly the staff had a sizeable proportion of young masters. The HMIs had noted that out of 39 full time members of staff at the time of the report, eleven were under 30, another fifteen were under 40, with a regular turnover of 5 or 6 every year. Clapton had already made 11 new appointments by the time of the Inspection, and this rate continued throughout his time because KES staff regularly secured new appointments as heads of departments at LEA and public schools. Five of his staff became headmasters, and another five were eventually appointed as HM Inspectors themselves.

Finally, as if to answer some of the school's critics, the Inspectors included these comments on the standard of work in KES at that time.

> "*In general the standard of work throughout the school calls for commendation. In most subjects it is good and in none does it fall below a distinctly satisfactory level. Eight masters are teachers of distinction and several others are near that level. The vitality and responsiveness of the boys creates a good impression on the visitor. The objective of the external examinations loom large but not unduly so; the preparation for the examinations is not confined to narrow lines; there is real enlightenment in much of the teaching so that the boys achieve good examination results without strain and, at the same time, may claim to be educated.*"

Did they say that!!

Whilst the Inspectors seemed very satisfied with the overall standard of teaching in the school, much of it in retrospect can be seen to be pedestrian and uninspired. There was a great deal of reliance on "chalk and talk" and boys spent a lot of their time in class copying notes from the blackboard and taking dictated notes as well. This was the method of teaching in almost all grammar schools in England in the Fifties and providing a master did not cause serious discipline problems to spill out of the form room, or produce disastrous examination results, he was left to run his forms as he saw fit.

All boys at the school knew that there were some masters whose lessons were chaos and they were often the teachers who made some of the biggest contributions to the extra-curricular life of the school. Edward "Marcus" Watling had grown very deaf and when things got a bit too much for him he switched off his deaf aid and ignored the clandestine activities that were happening in his room. One form regularly took their hymn books into his lessons and practised hymn singing during his Latin lessons, whilst another, during periods in the library, organised steeplechase races over the high book stacks. Norman Barnes regarded his lessons as the space before the next lunchtime recital and then between lunch and the late afternoon orchestral practice. In their weekly music period, many boys can only remember singing popular English folk songs like Greensleeves, Drunken Sailor and his favourite, Admiral Benbow. They also learnt the Latin School Song, which could easily be sung to the tune of "Clementine", and it was not unknown for it to be practised on bewildered passengers on the Crosspool or Fulwood bus. However, if you were not in the choir or orchestra, — and by the Sixties a third of the school was — then you missed out on gaining a real appreciation of classical music, and the chance to learn to play an instrument while at school.

Clarence Helliwell's art classes also lacked real structure. You dabbled at a bit of painting or sketching and returned to it the following week to add a little more. When Helliwell had a pupil who wanted to study art seriously, like Chris Twyford, the son of the master, who went on to be the top of his diploma course at the Slade, then he demonstrated how imaginative a teacher he could be. He also gave thoughtful discursive lectures to the Art History Society on topics that included gothic architecture and post impressionist painters, but none of this was part of the normal art lesson, and if you didn't join one of these societies, then your education at KES could be quite philistine. This reflected the attitude of most boys, who felt that if they did not have to take an "O" level in the subject, then the school did not rate the subject too highly, so why should they.

A culture of intimidation

The school had always believed that firm discipline was one of the key factors in creating academic success and Clapton, no less than any of his predecessors, maintained a ferocious control of behaviour within the school. A terrifying figure to all, he ruled through fear, even though few boys had any daily contact with him. He did not use the cane very much himself — he did not need to — but he continued to defend its use at KES even though corporal punishment in schools was now beginning to be challenged by a section of the population (City G.S. abolished the cane in the early Fifties). The school still followed the guidelines laid down by Graham in 1937 and all official canings were logged in the punishment book, with four strokes remaining the maximum number, although as often as not only a couple were administered. Looking at that book now, what strikes the observer is how trivial the offences were, and one would have thought a school with so many motivated pupils could have found a different method to enforce its rules and behaviour. Each year Clapton added up the number of official canings there had been and it totalled 2131 over his fifteen years. There was a marked drop in the use of the cane after 1956 when the average number of boys caned dropped to 82 each year. Before that, from 1950-56, the average was 231 and then the Headmaster started to rein in some of the more arbitrary use of the cane after that date. One history teacher, who caned boys alphabetically at the end of the lesson, boasted that he had intended, and subsequently succeeded, to break his "record" with 13 canings during a recent First Form class. He left, and eventually became a Headmaster in Doncaster, but was last heard of teaching at a

Borstal. One science teacher was well known for caning boys who achieved three "Not Satisfactory" grades within a term, and this sort of behaviour became increasingly difficult to justify.

The real classroom discipline was kept not by the threat of the cane, but by the unofficial physical intimidation that was commonplace in many lessons. Although browbeating and bullying were so endemic in almost all schools in England, the Headmaster must be judged culpable of not rooting out physical punishment, often of a humiliating nature, that went on unchecked in the classroom. Throwing chalk, board rubbers and books at pupils – one member of staff once threw light bulbs—was accepted almost as an eccentric joke, but even in the Fifties this was clearly quite irresponsible behaviour and should have been firmly prohibited. It was not as if Clapton was not constantly sending the staff notices on how to enforce many of the school rules. He made it clear that he considered lines a wasteful form of punishment and was very precise that masters should set extra work that would be of some value, or issue detentions where, theoretically, improving work could be attempted. Despite this, some members of staff continued to inflict their own brand of corporal punishment well into the Sixties. At the same time other masters never resorted to the use of the cane and ran their classes in a civilised and friendly manner.

A LITTLE RETAIL THERAPY

To Thomas Hope Ltd.   8th January 1953
Manchester 4

Dear Sirs

I remember seeing in one of your catalogues the item – "canes". If you still supply these, I should be glad of a quotation for a number. This school is one where the staff can deal out punishment by the cane as necessary. Unfortunately we have now only one cane and I have no knowledge of where I can obtain others from, and it is quite a predicament.

Yours very truly
NLC   Headmaster

THOMAS HOPE LTD.
Contractors for School Materials
Manchester 4

Dear Headmaster

Thank you for your letter of the 8th inst. and your enquiry for a school cane. In view of the present day opinion our sale of punishment canes has deteriorated and we have only 10 in stock.

Yours faithfully
J.C.Saul

To Thomas Hope Ltd
Manchester 4

Dear Sir

I quite understand that in regard to present day opinion canes are becoming rare. While I do not subscribe to present day opinion particularly, I am definitely opposed to too frequent use of the implement. However, it is always wise to have "one in the cupboard", and it is with that intent I desire to have some in stock. If you are able, please supply a dozen, failing that, as many as possible.

Perhaps you will arrange that they are suitably disguised for transit.

Yours faithfully
NLC Headmaster.

A sea change in the staff

Within two years of the Inspection Report there was one of those sea changes that occur in any school from time to time when a number of leading, well-respected members of staff leave within a short time of each other, and a chapter in the school's history appears to close. In 1953 two Heads of Department left to become Headmasters at other schools. Peter Wallis, who had led the Maths Department since John Nicholas left in 1947 and who also coached the Football 1st XI, moved on to become the Headmaster of Henry Fanshawe's School, Dronfield. In the same year Barry Harvey, who had joined the staff just before the war and then been whisked off for service in the Royal Navy, resigned from his post as Senior Classics master and took up his new post as Headmaster of Dame Allen's, the Newcastle public school. They were replaced by Walter Birkinshaw and Dennis Henry, whilst Tom Cook eventually replaced V.J. Wrigley as Senior History Master, when he was appointed the Headmaster of a brand new grammar school, Apsley G.S. in Hemel Hempstead, in 1954.

When he left Wrigley wrote his impressions of his years at the school since he first arrived in 1946.

" I had never taught classes as good as the best ones at KES and it has remained a constant pleasure and stimulus to teach the abler boys here. What has been a disappointment for me has been the materialistic outlook of many boys when asked to take an interest in something beyond the syllabus. " Will it be of any use to me?" is their attitude, but say it will be useful for a Scholarship, or a General Paper, they will be immediately attentive."

"Nowhere is the popular view of a schoolmaster's easy life less true than at KES, but the compensation lies in the stimulus of teaching boys of a very high calibre. All who teach here must be very grateful!"

Later in the early Sixties it was reported that some students on teaching practice begged to be taken away from KES because they found the challenge a little too stimulating, and boys could be merciless with a student, or indeed a new member of staff, who did not *"know their stuff"*.

The redoubtable Jean Knight departed for the second time in 1952. She had been one of the wartime teachers who then returned in 1950 to help staff the Classics Department. Always neatly dressed in a suit, she preferred the boys to address her as "sir", and after leaving she went to live in Oxford where she coached a number of Old Edwardians through their Latin Prelims. In return, they made her an honorary member of the Seventh Club and she attended their dinners and functions. She was the last woman to teach at KES during the Clapton era, and for the first time since 1917 there would be no women on the teaching staff.

KES STAFF 1955
The Heads of Department on the front row (l to r) are; Barnes, Oppenheimer,
Wastnedge, Mackay, Redston, Carter, N.L.C., Claypole, Bramall, Towers,
Birkinshaw, Robinson, Cook.

By the end of 1953 both the Cummings were no longer at the school. Tragically E. C. "Chalk" Cumming died in May after being absent through illness for much of the previous twelve months. He was a scholarly and well read historian who had travelled widely in Italy, Germany and France as well as teaching for sixteen years in Belfast before the war. Edgar Vernon, the Chairman of the Staff Room Committee, wrote in the school magazine: *"Charles's untimely death has robbed the school of a loyal and conscientious master. A man without pettiness or intrigue and a very acute judge of a boy, who conscientiously persisted in his duty when his illness was weighing very heavily upon him."*

Gordon "Cheese" Cumming, on the other hand, surprised everyone by leaving school teaching altogether. He took up a post as Education Officer at Samuel Fox Engineering in Stocksbridge and so ended a career at the school which had started as a pupil as far back as 1923. In 1931, having held the positions of Second Prefect, Captain of Football and Head of Chatsworth House, he gained a Town Trust Scholarship and entered Sheffield University where he eventually took a First in History. Back as a master in 1936 he taught at the school until the war, and on his return from service with the Royal Signals, was asked to head up the new Economics course in the Sixth Form. Whether it was in the IDG or the Economics Society meetings, supporting the school scouts (he was an original member in 1927), or acting as the recruiting sergeant for the Old Edwardians' Association amongst those about to leave, he had played a very full part in the life of the school during the regimes of all the five headmasters from Dr. Hichens to Nathaniel Clapton. G.J.C. was to some extent, "Mr. KES", and the school seemed poorer for his departure.

Amongst the more interesting departures and arrivals were W.R. Fraser who went to New York in the summer of 1952 to work for the Quakers, who had official consultative status as a non-governmental organisation at the United Nations, whilst Geoffrey Ingham, who had served as 12th man for Yorkshire on a number of occasions, arrived from Leeds University to teach mathematics. C.H. "Curly" Harper was another member of staff who was well liked and who moved on at this time. He left in the summer of 1954 to go to Northallerton G.S., perhaps to be nearer to Ayresome Park, because he was a fanatical supporter of Middlesborough F.C. He was another master who had arrived at the war's end and been an inspiring science teacher, sharing the role of Sixth Science Form Master with George MacKay. He took over the coaching and running of the Football 1st XI from Wallis and ran the side for two seasons. The 141goals scored in 1951-52 Season was a record for that period, and that season (Wallis's last in charge) and 1952-53, were amongst the best Football seasons at KES between the war and the start of the comprehensive school in 1969. Harper, who had a reputation for being a little too scrupulously fair to the opposition when he refereed, couldn't repeat the success in his final season and the 1953-54 side could only manage seven victories in the entire season, but it is recorded that *"his sparkling wit never failed to raise a laugh after even the most ignominious of defeats"*.

The New Library and the Extension 1953-54

The first major alterations to the buildings since the opening of the school, were planned at the very start of Clapton's period as Headmaster. Apart from the Swimming Baths, which the Council had intended would be the first of a series of dual use facilities based at strategically placed schools around the city, (the war killed that programme and it was never re-activated except for the pool built at the new Rowlinson Technical School) there had been no building inside the Close, or any extensions to the main building, since 1906. The first project to be completed was the new Library, which was built at the east end of the main corridor in the room which had previously served as the Woodwork

Room. The Library had been in totally inadequate premises in the room that is now the Staff Room (some of the old book stacks still serve as shelves for the staff's books) and during the refurbishment of the new library, the Woodwork Dept. exchanged premises and moved in to the old library. Goodness knows how long the school would have had to wait for a library that matched its academic ambitions, if the SRGS Exhibition Fund, which had been supporting the library with regular donations to buy books since 1905, had not decided that their surpluses were just piling up for no good reason and it would be far better to use the money constructively for some major project at the school. Clapton, the Governors and the Education Committee were only too delighted to accept and they all agreed with the Trustees of the Fund that the library was the priority project. The City Architect's Department drew up the plans, the City Librarian gave welcome advice on design and restocking, before the Woodwork Room was cleared for a start in the Autumn Term of 1952. The Council's Works Department then took their time before commencing, but they had the new facility ready for the new academic year in September 1953. The structural works cost £1480, came in on budget, and the furnishings and fittings added another £2000. The SRGS fund covered the cost, and then generously added another couple of thousand pounds to add to the book stock. The following year the Old Edwardians, as part of their War Memorial Appeal, donated a substantial amount to buy books for the library's international section.

On 10th September the appropriate ceremonies took place. The Lord Mayor, Coun. Oliver Holmes, himself an Old Edwardian, opened the simple proceedings, and Geoffrey Chambers, Chairman of the SRGS Fund, who had been a boy at SRGS, unveiled the plaque and formally handed over the new library to the Headmaster. By way of counterpoint to the official enthusiasm, the reporter in the school magazine added a little sourly;

> "Will later generations see here an original style or one that dates from, say the 1920s? Are the filing cabinet, chairs and display stands good furniture or just "Design" in the hackneyed sense of the word? Does the whole room have that air of purpose and convenience that goes with the use of books."

Fifty years on, present day Edwardians still use the Library during lessons and in large numbers at lunchtime. Apparently the design still encourages study whilst satisfying the average aesthete's tastes.

There was no official opening for the "New Wing" and, as befits its utilitarian appearance, it slipped almost unheralded into the life of the school when it was opened for use a year later, at the beginning of the 1954 Autumn Term. The new extension on three floors did, however, significantly alter the teaching facilities available at the school. The Science Department now had two extra laboratories, one of them a specialist biology laboratory and this was a major contribution to easing the chronic overcrowding in science teaching. There were modern specialist rooms for art, along with well resourced woodwork and metalwork shops and two extra general classrooms. Although a very basic design, the buildings exterior was clad in local stone and tucked away behind the main building in a quiet corner of the grounds, where it did not give much offence to the architectural connoisseur. It did, however, reduce by a third the area which had always been the Masters' Garden, a rather pleasant haven of quiet behind the high walls of the north-west corner of the school site.

Designed by the City Architect and built by the Public Works Department, — as were all school buildings in those pre-Thatcherite days — it had taken two and a half years to complete since the first approval by the Council in February 1952. Once again the tender of £34,927 came in under budget and during the building operations the contractors had to create an entrance half way down Newbould Lane for their lorries to get onto the site. When the building work was completed this entrance was smartened up and remains in use to this day as one of the two vehicular entrances to the Close. The "New Wing" was the last significant building development at the school, apart from the indoor toilets and the ugly breeze block changing facilities, thrown up to cater for a co-educational school after 1969, until the rather graceful building in the Close was erected forty years later.

The Crowning Glory

At the 1956 Speech Day the Headmaster prefaced his report by remarking that the last academic year had been "a *good year but not remarkable in any way.*" He went on to stress his usual themes that boys should always demonstrate good manners and keep a smart personal appearance, two areas in which he was not an obvious role model. Clapton's cautious welcome of the school's most recent academic results was probably an honest reflection of his opinion, but there were many in the audience that night who were more readily prepared to be influenced by the raw figures. In 1956 the school had won 22 University Scholarships, 13 of them at Oxbridge with another 9 gaining entrance as commoners. Eight Scholarships had been won at other Universities and altogether 67 Edwardians would be entering University that year, or after their National Service. Of the 556 boys studying "A" Level courses in Sheffield grammar schools that year, 227 were at KES and the school's "A" Level candidates achieved 48 Distinctions and 8 State Scholarships, with a pass rate for "A" Level of 89.7%, whilst for "O" Level it was 74.3%.

The most remarkable thing about these results was that Clapton was right; there had been better years since he had arrived at the school. The previous year, as if to celebrate the school's first fifty years, the school had been awarded 16 State Scholarships (only Manchester G.S. did better that year) and its "A" Level pass rate had been 93% and the "O" Level pass rate 77%. For the first time ever over half the leavers between 15 and 19 years of age had gone on to University, an impressive figure for the Fifties — the HMIs had been pleasantly surprised in 1952 that this figure was 42% — and now they also went to a considerable number of universities. Until Clapton arrived at the school, as we have seen, Old Edwardians only went, in the main, to three universities, Oxford, Cambridge and Sheffield, with a handful studying at Durham or London colleges. Now boys were directed onto courses at all the major universities, with Nottingham being a popular choice, possibly because of its attractive campus and possibly because of its proximity. In the early Fifties boys occasionally went to the Slade, to RAF Cranwell and even to the

RNC Dartmouth. One boy went to St. Andrews and periodically someone would study at Edinburgh, but it was not common to go to a Scottish university.

The year that the HMIs inspected the school had been a poor year for Scholarships. Only three, all Hastings, had been won at Oxford and none anywhere else. Although many schools would have been justly proud of such an achievement, it was just a blip for KES and the school returned to its previous level of success the following year. Clapton, who had no doubts that anyone capable of entry to an Oxbridge College should do their utmost to be accepted, was just as keen to get boys onto courses at other universities. He commented at that same Speech Day in 1956 that "*the aim of every boy should be to have a university education and it is pleasing that so few of our boys of university calibre leave school for employment.*" Despite this he was realistic enough to realise that some pupils needed to be free of the constraints of formal education and would make their own way in the world of work, and as often as not would be successful.

The Headmaster's constant concern was that external factors would disturb the flow of Oxbridge Scholarships and indeed university places in general. Any problems caused by the introduction of the GCE Examinations in 1951 were soon overcome, but Clapton was obsessed by the possibility that youth clubs could divert boys from the academic straight and narrow. Today such clubs have a positive image, attempting to direct young people into worthwhile pursuits, often where they do not want to go. In the Fifties they represented the new teenage culture of skiffle, jazz and, dare one say it, rock and roll. There were girls and dancing, hair styles rather than hair cuts and outrageous cult dress fashions, and behind it all the inexorable advance of American popular culture which stood for everything the grammar and public schools of England were against.

The imposition of National Service, was a much more serious diversion that might weaken a boy's resolve to make that extra effort to gain a scholarship. The prospect of service in the forces might well de-motivate him, or they might become changed individuals after service in the RAF or Army, and perform unsatisfactorily at University when they returned. Students had a choice to do their two years in the military (raised from 18 months at the start of the Korean War) before they went to university, or have their service deferred for three years until they finished their degree. Those who served first either came out more mature individuals, better able to handle university life, or they may have imbibed too much of a culture of indolence, because for most National Servicemen, life after the initial "square-bashing" was one of utter boredom. A few got commissions, others got swept up onto Russian or Chinese language courses and then were stationed with the BAOR or in Hong Kong, monitoring Russian tanks or Chinese aircraft. A few unlucky souls might find their unit was sent to a real war in Korea, whilst others drew another short straw and served in Malaya, Suez or Cyprus. National Service was abolished in 1959 (although those already called up had to serve out their time), and it was therefore no longer a barrier to a continued education. No one had thought of gap years then. Most boys heading for university wanted to enjoy their three years, then graduate, get a good job in the real world and soon after get married and start a family.

Whatever difficulties were perceived by the school about outside distractions, examination changes or the sheer weight of competition as other schools acquired larger and successful sixth forms, they were all overcome in the last six years of Clapton's period as Headmaster. In 1959 the school had its best ever "O" Level results (87.1% Pass Rate) and in 1961 it recorded 55 Distinctions at "A" Level and its usual number of 8 State Scholarships. Clapton, cocking a snoop at the school's critics, described the 1961 results as our *"usual satisfactory production figures"* as he reported 14 scholarships at Oxbridge that year. Certainly at KES there could be tremendous pressure put on boys to succeed in these examinations at an early age. In the Classical 5th and 6th Form, regarded by most as the intellectual élite on the Arts side — Maths held an equivalent position amongst the Science subjects – boys could be taking their "A" Levels in Latin, Greek and Ancient History after one year and find themselves applying for University almost before they were 17. This happened to Terry Saunders (1950-56) who acquired his "A" Levels when he was still 16 and then went up to Merton College, Oxford and took a First in Jurisprudence, having decided the Law was a better future prospect than the Classics. Nick Waite (1949-56) found himself in a similar position, when as a seventeen-year-old he sat for, and was awarded, the Brackenbury Scholarship for History at Balliol. He had already won a place at another college, but the school had sent him back to "improve" on his award.

At Clapton's final Speech Day in October 1964 he announced another set of outstanding results in most of the areas that acted as the indices of academic success. The new "A" and "O" Level grades which had been introduced the previous year, made a better appraisal of the GCE results possible, and in 1964 the "A" Level results were the best yet, with 50% of the candidates getting the top two grades, although the "O" Level results were the poorest for a decade. Nevertheless, the school had won 16 Oxbridge awards, the same number as had been gained two years before in 1962, both of which equalled the previous record achieved during the war in 1944. Along with those who gained places at the colleges, KES was sending around 25 boys a year to the two senior universities, so that in the Sixties there were 80+ Old Edwardians at Oxford at any one time, and it was their boast that there was an O.E. in every college. Not always true, but near enough most years. The Seventh Club, apart from their traditional Annual Dinner when they invited the Headmaster and the Head Prefect, also organised a regular cricket and football match and in 1960 they even played the O.U. Women's Netball Team and finished up with an honourable 13-17 defeat.

By now the school fully recognised the value of the other universities. The success of Keith Robinson's Economics Sixth Form meant a number of students preferred to go to LSE rather than Oxbridge, although they were usually dragooned through the college scholarship examinations first. Clapton increasingly saw the value of some of the broader based courses at the new universities, like Sussex and Warwick, and he encouraged boys to consider applying to these institutions as well as the new Colleges of Advanced Technology. By 1964, 70% of all school leavers went into Higher Education, 63 boys went to university and 9 to colleges and this represented a rise of over 25 % since 1950 when he started at the school.

By Comparison ...... KES Examination Results 2003

2003 was an outstanding year for both the A Level and the GCSE results. Although it is difficult to compare like with like between the Grammar School results in the Sixties with those of the Comprehensive School to-day, especially when comparing the GCSE with the earlier "O" Level Examination, a study of the raw data gives some food for thought.

A Level

Since 1999 the A Level pass rate for grades A-E has been around 90%, but in 2002 it was 96.8%

In 2003 it was 97.8% with over 50% gaining A (25.3%) or B (25.1%) grades out of 534 individual entries.

GCSE

In 2003
99% of the 231 candidates achieved A-G Grades.
66.7% of candidates achieved 5 or more A-C grades.
30.5% of all grades were at A* or A grades.
33 students achieved 9 or more A* or A grades.

A-C Grades are usually regarded as a rough equivalent to an "O" Level Pass. All candidates were in Y11 i.e. they were in their 16th year Y11 is a fully unselected Year Group drawn from all over Sheffield and all social classes.

The Gathering Criticism

However successful the school was in its examination results and its scholarship awards, its critics continued to snipe at the school and its achievements. Clapton referred to KES as the *"most maligned grammar school in England"*. During the Fifties they were perhaps reflecting the traditional English habit of decrying the successful rather than celebrating a success, but by the Sixties the criticism had become sharper and, in no little way, politically motivated. The criticism of KES came from two directions. Firstly, that it was an élite institution that only served the middle class in the western suburbs; secondly, that it was also a sweat shop that force fed and closely directed its students, so that when they arrived at University they " burnt out" in the more self reliant and reflective culture of higher education, achieving poor results in their degree finals. Later, other critics, in retrospect, would claim that few Old Edwardians from the Clapton era achieved any positions of real eminence in later life.

By common consent when KES was a high performing grammar school during that period, its social structure was predominately middle class, as were most grammar schools in England. It is unlikely that there were ever more than thirty working class pupils in any one year at the school, although that was, of course, a big increase in numbers from the pre-1945 position. However the majority of boys winning the 11+ Scholarship did come from the south west of the city, and traditionally primary schools like Lydgate, Ecclesall, Dore and Abbey Lane were well represented amongst the new boys in the First Form. For almost all boys however, social class was not an issue inside the school. The "aristocracy" of the school was based on academic ability not parental wealth, position or postal address. In fact the school was not socially very exclusive, because the children of really prosperous Sheffielders went to boarding schools.

The median pupil was probably from a lower middle class background and regarded the school as classless. There were boys from the east end of the city who were considered streetwise and capable of looking after themselves, and no doubt they found KES a strange, intimidating place when they first arrived, but so too did many of the new entrants from middle class backgrounds. In the great majority, Edwardians were Yorkshire lads with local accents and few airs and graces; ability in examinations or at sport, not social pretensions, gained you the admiration of your peers, and if you came from a wealthy home it was best if you kept quiet about it.

No one would deny that KES drove its pupils hard. Some staff more than others embodied the regime of pushing pupils to their intellectual limit, none more so than Dennis Henry, the Senior Classics Master between 1953 and 1957, who left to become the Headmaster of Welwyn Garden City G.S. Members of his Sixth Form classes recall that after undertaking massive amounts of homework during the week, some boys had to spend Saturdays in the Central Library to enable them to finish a Latin verse composition one week or a Greek one the following week. For many the freer, more casual world of university had a liberating effect, none more so than in Oxbridge Colleges where an Old Edwardian might find himself amongst freshmen with a much wider range of interests, cultivated at schools who took a more leisured approach to education than KES. Some got involved in University clubs and societies; George MacBeth and Rony Robinson were involved in producing Cherwell – Robinson became the Editor — whilst others found the relaxed life highly seductive and they did not perform well in their finals. Despite this most KES undergraduates at Oxbridge gained Second Class degrees – no mean achievement at either institution – and Upper or Lower Seconds at the many other universities.

There were some extremely disappointing years at Oxford when Old Edwardians chalked up a considerable number of Third Class Degrees. In 1956 out of 12 students graduating, 4 got Thirds and one, a prominent university footballer, even managed a Fourth. By way of compensation three former KES pupils got Firsts that year, and at Cambridge the situation was quite reasonable with 4 First Class Honours and only 2 Thirds out of ten results. Worse was to follow in 1959 at Oxford, when old boys racked up 11 Third Class

Honours, a majority of the degrees awarded to Old Edwardians that year, whilst the position at Cambridge was more satisfactory.

However, many sixth formers going to other universities often found that the thorough grounding they had received in their "A" Level studies gave them a real advantage over their peers, at least in the initial stages of their course. Those who had studied "A" Level Economics under T.K. "Ticker" Robinson, thought by many to be one of the finest teachers in the school in Clapton's time, found that they had usually completed the first year's course work at school, and undergraduates taking other subjects experienced a similar position in varying degrees. It would though be wrong, and facile, to conclude that Old Edwardians did not on the whole succeed at their universities. In 1960 there were 12 First Class Honours degrees recorded, 3 at Oxford, 2 at Cambridge, 4 at Sheffield and 3 at Nottingham and during these years many former pupils stayed on for further degrees, with many becoming university lecturers and, not a few, ultimately professors. Those who left university with poor degrees, soon found that in later life no one cared what class of degree you had, just how good you were at your job, and so they too in the main prospered.

The Great and the Good?

The school's critics have also speculated that for all KES's vaunted superiority it produced remarkably few really famous men, and it is true that even before Clapton's time there were very few Old Edwardians who could be considered nationally known names. Unlike the City of London School, Dr. Barton's new school, who boasted of an old boy — Asquith was an Old Citizen— who had declared war on Germany on behalf of Great Britain and the Empire in 1914, KES did not have any Cabinet members, or even MPs, amongst all the talented boys educated at the school in its first fifty years. In retrospect the list of boys of the post 1945 meritocracy have also included few household names familiar to most people in the country. Hattersley and Blunkett in politics, Seb Coe and Michael Vaughan in sport, Michael Palin and Sean Bean in entertainment, all grew up in Sheffield but none of them went to KES. Nevertheless, if one looks more closely, one can see a legion of successful men from the Clapton era who have served the national and local community well in the last fifty years.

There are judges like John McNaught and David Bentley, whilst on the other hand there are some Old Edwardians who have been detained at Her Majesty's Pleasure. The school has produced too many professors to name, holding chairs at British and foreign universities, but in the world of education Ted Wragg of Exeter University is a revered figure as an education strategist and broadcaster. David Downes, now Emeritus Professor of Social Administration at the LSE, is one of a number of criminologists, one assumes coincidentally, produced by the school, while Sir John Beckman and Ian Roxburgh are leading figures in the area of astronomy and astro-physics. One old boy who did taste more than his share of fame was George MacBeth, who ranks among the major English poets of the century with his nineteen books of poetry, thirteen novels and seven anthologies. His work has been read world wide, and as a BBC producer and then freelance broadcaster he was listened to by millions in Britain and abroad.

If Lord Allen of Abbeydale, Permanent Under Secretary at the Home Office from 1966-72, represented an earlier generation, then Chris Brearley CB, Director General within the Department of Environment, Transport and the Regions and Giles Ecclestone, Clerk to the House of Commons and son of the famous "Red" Vicar of Darnall, are representatives of many from Clapton's time who served with distinction in the Civil Service. These include John Goulden at the Foreign Office, who has been the Ambassador to Turkey and, in the Nineties, Ambassador to NATO during the Bosnian crisis, and two of his contemporaries at school, Roland Smith and Jeremy Thorp, respectively Ambassadors to the Ukraine and Colombia. It may well be significant that so many of the most able pupils at KES went into one form or another of public service, including many levels of education; however there are also many who have had successful careers in the private sector of business and commerce.

Apart from Michael Curley, already mentioned, David Benyon was Chairman of ICI Europe, Chris Ball the Chief Executive of Unigate Foods, Martin Hall the Director General of the Leasing and Finance Association and Alan Wood Chief Executive of Siemens UK. Chris Meakin, after editing "Isis" when at Keble, became a senior financial journalist and later a Director of the CBI, and remarkably, the last two Executive Directors of Design for Ford Europe are both Old Edwardians. Peter Horbury has now moved on to be the Head of Design for Ford in North America and his recent replacement, Martin Smith, was previously Head of Design for Opel/Vauxhall. Another Old Edwardian from the Clapton "era" was the editor during the early Nineties of that great journal of record, the "Daily Sport".

Surprisingly, considering the importance of Sheffield as a political city, there have only been two M.Ps to date and both were at the school in Clapton's time. Roy Galley took the Halifax seat from Labour in the post Falklands election of 1983 and held it for one term, whilst Clive Betts won the Attercliffe seat in the 1992 Election and still represents that constituency. Betts can claim another first for an Old Edwardian. He is a former Leader of Sheffield City Council, succeeding David Blunkett in 1987 and serving till he was elected to parliament. He is almost unique, because he served as a Labour councillor, for whilst many O.E.s have been City Councillors (the school has produced three Lord Mayors and a former Council Leader, Sir Harold Jackson, Leader 1932-3, was at Wesley College) they have invariably been Conservatives with just a few in the Liberal ranks. There is, however, at least one major Trade Union figure amongst the school's alumni. Alan Jinkinson, a former General Secretary of NALGO, was at the school in the late Forties and Fifties and there are a number of old boys in TV and Broadcasting, including Roger Laughton, one time Head of the Meridian Television Consortium and before that a producer-director with the BBC.

Others decided after University, or after an initial period working away from South Yorkshire, to return to Sheffield and make their careers in their own city. Rony Robinson, the most familiar voice on BBC Radio Sheffield, is one whose personality helps to define the city, although he is still one of the most implacable critics of N.L. Clapton and his school in the Fifties. David Sheasby, Captain of the school Cross Country team for two seasons between 1956–58, has also worked in local radio as a producer and has written more than fifty plays for broadcasting on the radio. KES is well represented amongst the legal and teaching fraternity of Sheffield. Nick Waite and Terry Saunders, two of the school's most successful scholars came back into local law firms and like many others ended up as Senior Partners in their firms, whilst John Bainbridge, a Hastings and State Scholar, and Paul Allen, ex LSE, returned to teach in the city's comprehensive schools, as did David Tomlinson who also played a prominent part in organising Schools' Athletics and Cross Country during his career in teaching. Others pursued a teaching career outside the city, like Richard Nosowski, who retired in 2003 from his post as the Headteacher of Backwell School, a much admired Beacon School on the outskirts of Bristol. Those who have lived and worked throughout their adult lives in Sheffield, whether in industry, commerce, medicine or the myriad of service jobs created by our ever changing economy, are realising the dreams of the people who founded the school in 1905. It was always part of their strategy that a significant number of boys at the school would remain in the city, helping to ensure its progress, and it is a feature of Sheffield, perhaps to the surprise of those who do not know the city, that it retains many of the graduates of its two universities and welcomes back many who did their degrees in other towns.

A school, however, is better judged by the quality of those who play a useful, but largely anonymous role in both national and local life, than by the random success of a handful of individuals. It is unlikely that from Wath Comprehensive School there will ever emerge another Leader of the Conservative Party, whereas it is quite possible that any school in Sheffield, including KES, will produce an internationally famous rock star, as the Central Technical School did when it educated Joe Cocker in many things, but not pop music. His brother, Victor, meanwhile came to KES and became the Chief Executive of the Severn Trent Water Authority. It is certain that Old Edwardians, both men and women, will continue in the future to hold high positions in industry, commerce and the professions and may even become nationally famous, as Sir Norman Siddall of the NCB, and Sir Robert Scholey of British Steel were during the early Eighties.

The Occasions

Of all the major occasions on the well established school calendar, Speech Day, when the whole school celebrated together, applauded the prize-winners and absorbed the zeitgeist of the school, was the most important. Sydney Carter briefed those about to ascend the platform to walk with straight backs and look the Guest of Honour in the eye, whilst marshals, with identifying blue and white rosettes, ushered parents to their seats. The Victoria Hall hushed to hear the words of wisdom from guest speakers, the Latin Address and the readings in at least three, if not four, dead or modern languages. One year they even had a reading in Chaucerian English, as if to further emphasise the school's versatility, or perhaps its vanity. Occasionally a Guest Speaker would throw away the script, like E.T. "Rabbit" Williams, the former one man think tank at Montgomery's HQ and now, after a period at the UN, the Warden of Rhodes House at Oxford. " This is swot's night!" he told his audience, before declaring that Edwardians were classified into only two types, Wednesdayites and Unitedites, whilst the purpose of homework, as he saw it, was to escape the washing up.

The year before, in 1952, the guest speaker had been Sir Stanley Rous, President of the F.A. and of FIFA, and at that time the most famous name in world football. (Rous and Clapton had been colleagues on the staff of Watford G.S. in the Twenties). From then on Clapton invited mainly Old Edwardians to speak at Speech Day and the other major events, like the Commemoration Service and the Armistice Day. Old boys were a little flattered, and intrigued, to be invited to speak, and there were a considerable number of genuinely eminent ones available to fill each occasion. Sir John Sterndale-Bennett came in 1956 and spoke of his time in the Diplomatic Corps, which had included being present at the Locarno Conference of 1925 and accompanying Ernest Bevin to Moscow to negotiate with Stalin and Molotov. The Rt. Rev. Leslie Stradling came twice, once when he was the Bishop of Tanganyika and later on another occasion, after taking over from the Rt. Rev Ambrose Reeves, when he was Bishop of Johannesburg. Some of the most illustrious Old Edwardians from the school's first decade attended the Speech Days in the Fifties, including Sir Stanley Rawson, who had become a Fellow of All Souls in 1914 at the age of 24. Now the Vice- Chairman of John Brown Engineering, he spoke at the 1955 Speech Day and he was followed by Prof. E.C. Titchmarsh FRS, the Savillian Professor of Geometry at Oxford and then by Prof. Albert Goodwin, Professor of History at Manchester University. The message to the boys of the present generation could not have been clearer. These men sat in the same classrooms as you, walked the same corridors and have achieved outstanding success in their respective fields. Go forth therefore and do thou likewise! In the Sixties Clapton tapped in to a later generation of the school's *prominenti* for speakers at Speech Day. Sir Alan Dawtry had been at the school in the Thirties, and after war service that saw him rise to major and win an MBE, had entered local government and was now Town Clerk of Westminster City Council, one of a number of Old Edwardians who achieved that position in different county boroughs at that time. In 1961the speaker was Sir Philip Allen, then Second Secretary at the Treasury, who stressed the importance of the balanced education, one that was more than the accumulation of facts, but more about the acquiring of qualities of learning, clear thinking, good use of leisure and tolerance. These were the school's aims too but not all boys fully appreciated them when they were at school.

There were major anniversaries in the middle Fifties spread over three years. In 1954 the school celebrated the 350th Anniversary of the founding of the King James Grammar School in 1604, and invited Rt. Rev. Kenneth Kirk, Bishop of Oxford and Regis Professor of Theology, and more relevant to this anniversary, an Old Boy of SRGS, to give the sermon at the Commemoration Service. The previous year an Over Seventy Society of former Grammar School pupils was founded and they rejoiced under the acronym SRGSOBOSS and continued to have their "symposiums" every year, when they proposed the toast at their re-union dinners to *"King James the First, the wisest fool in Christendom — and the founder of the school."*

The following year, when it was the 50th Anniversary of the founding of King Edward VII School, the sermon at the Commemoration Service was given by the former Headmaster, Richard Graham, recently

Sir Philip Allen O.E. (later Lord Allen of Abbeydale) presents an award to Don Nicolson (later Dr. Nicolson, Secretary of the Old Edwardians' Association). Peter Points in background. Speech Day, 1961.

retired as Headmaster of Bradford G.S. Like Kirk the year before, Graham saw the anniversary in a strong religious context. That the school's creation in 1905 was part of a divine will for the people of Sheffield and he called on the present generation to be *"re-founders as well as heirs of the great patrimony that is this school."* Richard Graham had always kept in touch with his old school, even though he had, for fourteen years, been the Headmaster of the school that was KES's main academic rival in Yorkshire. Well liked and respected, the school was genuinely saddened, when after retiring to the Lake District he died suddenly in February 1957.

To complete the school's Jubilee Celebrations in 1956, Canon Rev. Edwin Berrisford DSO, M.C. gave the sermon in the Commemoration Service that year in the Cathedral. He was the most distinguished O.E. soldier of World War One, who after an academic career had entered the church and now took the opportunity to give a valedictory on the school's first fifty years. He even saw some good in the *"age long amicable antagonism between schoolmaster and boys"* and how in the future the boys would fully appreciate the debt they owed to teachers, so much so that *"masters would fleck memory's picture of our younger years with points of cheerful colour."* Perhaps not always in rosy colours, but love them or hate them, one's teachers would remain a crystal clear memory for the rest of one's life.

Every year on Armistice Day the school held a mid-morning assembly to coincide with the wreath laying at 11.00 am at the War Memorial. Ten years or so since the war this was still a very solemn occasion when each year Dr. Jack Burdekin, President of the Old Edwardians, read out all the names of the First War dead and Eric Sivil G.M., the Secretary, followed with all the names of the fallen of 1939-45. These two men had both played a big part in the revival of the Old Edwardians whose membership by the middle

Platform party before Commemoration Service 1955
(Back row) Rev. E.M. Turner O.E., Eric Sivil G.M. (Sec. O.E.A.) and the Headmaster
(Front row) Ald. Albert Ballard (Chairman of Governors), Richard Graham
(Headmaster 1928-38) and W.G. Ibberson (Master Cutler)

Fifties stood at over a thousand. Two Guineas could secure you life membership, with 1/6d a match if you played for the O.E. Football Club and 2/6d if you played for the Cricket team. The Football team dominated the South Yorkshire League, but when it sought promotion to a more senior league it was horrified to be rejected because its pitch at Whiteley Woods was not rectangular, and because of the topography the goal lines could not be made equal length. So they had to continue playing on their trapezoid in the South Yorkshire League.

1955 was the year of a General Election and KES became the "631st constituency" and conducted its own "mock election". Five candidates vied for the voters' favours and for a week posters, public meetings and the trappings of the hustings filled the school corridors. The seat was won by John Shillito, the Conservative candidate, but on a minority vote. The two independents came next, one of whom, Paul Swain, had originally run as the Prefects' Progressive Party candidate, but had been persuaded to drop this title as it had limited "market" appeal. Labour declined to run a candidate, or perhaps no one fancied losing their deposit, as happened to the Liberal candidate who saw his 2/6d go into the library fund. Eden won the other less important election in the other 630 constituencies.

In 1959 the candidates were persuaded to stand for recognised political parties but the Conservatives still won, this time with 49% of the vote. Held in pleasant autumn weather, many of the rallies were held "al fresco" with considerable use being made of the cricket roller whose shafts proved to be a convenient if precarious hustings platform. A.R. Williams won the seat for Harold MacMillan, whilst A. Rodgers came second for the "Socialists" with a mere 17%. Clearly the "never had it so good" society resonated with the KES voters and its appeal was still strong enough in 1964 when the Conservative candidate, A.Wiggett, held the seat with a reduced majority. I.S.White's Labour campaign for a "New Britain, full of white hot technology" with its clear appeal to the meritocracy, failed to appeal sufficiently to the KES voters.

School "Census" of 1955 and 1957
One of the school institutions in the Fifties and Sixties was the periodic opinion polls conducted amongst 'A' Level pupils. Called the "census" it had started in 1949

How would you vote?	*1955: Cons. 57% Lab. 18% Lib 6% Uncertain 20%.* *1957: Cons. 44% Lab. 22% Lib 8% Uncertain 26%*
Newspapers read?	*1955: S.Telegraph 48% Star 25% D.Express 21% Man. Guardian 15%* *1957: Star 26% Man. Guardian 22% S.Telegraph 20% D.Express 14%*
Wednesday or United?	*1955: Wed. 35% Utd. 26% 1957: Wed. 27% Utd. 32%*
Girl Friends?	*1955: Regular 54% 1957: Regular 51%*
Which sport?	*1955: Football 73% Rugby Union 18% Cricket 46% Tennis 46%* *1957: Football 49% Rugby Union 20% Cricket 41% Tennis 50%*
School Societies supported?	*1955: 2.3 1957: 2.3*
Religious Denomination?	*1955: C of E 54% Methodist 18% Baptist 3% Plymouth Brethren 2% "Eclectic" 3% None 13%* *1957: 79% Attend worship regularly*

Preferred career?	*44% had decided on their career in both years.*
	1957: Medicine 11% Engineering 10% Teaching 7%
	Clergy 1% Law 1% Civil Service 2%
Type of Music?	*1957: Classics 29% Jazz 28% Light 22% Pop 20%*
	Bagpipes 1%
Smoking?	*1955: Regular 2% Occasional 38% Non Smokers 60%*
Driving Test passed.	*1955: 4%*
Born in Sheffield.	*1955: 81% Been Abroad: 38%*
	1957: 83% Been Abroad: 38%

The Icons depart
Effron, Carter, Watling, Redston and also Claypole

Towards the end of Clapton's first decade at KES, a number of his longest serving staff members retired. They represented those teachers, who having put down roots in one congenial place, embody its spirit and remain to serve that school all their days. Four of them had taught for over thirty years at the school, two for nearly forty. The first to leave was G.H. "Billy" Effron, who had come to the school in 1917 when he was invalided out of the Army. Apart from a two year period at St. Georges, College in Buenos Aires between 1920-22 teaching the children of British settlers at the only public school on the continent, he had taught for 37 years at KES until he left in 1956. Each generation of Edwardians soon discovered that he could be de-railed from the syllabus, and in a "lively and discursive" way ramble on about Argentina, its railways and his experiences as a cowboy to a pleased, if unheeding, class. In retaliation he made unsatisfactory pupils stand on their seats, so that after a particularly unruly lesson half the form could be in this position, resembling nothing so much as a mini Manhattan.

Sydney "Sam" Carter on the other hand always kept to the task in hand and after joining the school as a Maths and Science master in 1921, following war service in Italy. He rose to be the Second Master for the last eleven years he was at KES. Earlier Edwardians would have known him as the organiser in chief of the Athletic Sports, as the father figure who, before 1945, guided the new scholarship boys of 2D through their first year in the school, encouraging them to realise their abilities while initiating them into the traditions of the school. During the war Carter had taken an RAF commission to enable him to help with the ATC, and along with other masters who were overage for military service, had helped Barton share the burden of running the school in war time. For two months in the Autumn Term of 1950 he was the acting Headmaster and handled his brief with characteristic efficiency. He retired in 1958 when he reached retirement age and the LEA insisted that his post was re-designated as Deputy Headmaster and that it must be advertised nationally. None of the current senior departmental masters fancied the new undefined position and so, for the first time since 1905, the position of No.2 on the staff went to an outsider. In September 1958, Arthur Jackson arrived from Mill Hill School to become the school's first Deputy Head, with an initial task of defining what the position was, without, he remembers, getting much guidance from Clapton or the outgoing S.V. Carter.

Staff Leavers in Summer 1958
Back Row (l to r) May, Turberfield, Hetherington, Wilson:
Front Row (l to r) Claypole, Carter, McKechnie:

Gerry Claypole also left that summer. He could not claim the same length of service at KES as his two colleagues but he had still chalked up seventeen years at the school, after arriving during the war as the first ever Senior English Master, the subject previously coming under the wing of the Senior History Master. Before he joined the staff at KES he was already a published poet of some sensitivity and style and he did his best to raise the status of poetry within the classroom and through the Poetry Society, which he founded. Amongst the grey suits of the staff room he stood out as the aesthete in more colourful attire. A light cotton jacket in summer, distinctive shirts in pastel shades, even purple trousers at times, but always the courteous gentleman who breathed enthusiasm for literature and who sparkled with puckish wit and infectious humour. He had taken over producing the school play from Watling in the Fifties and struggled, not unsuccessfully, to cope with the limitations of the Assembly Hall stage. He lived in a house full of his lifetime's collection of books, enjoying music and the fine arts, as well as displaying a passion for county cricket. His retirement, sadly, did not last long for he died in January of 1961.

At seventy years of age, C.A.P. Gillman the school porter decided to retire. He had been appointed by Graham in 1938 and seen through the war years with Barton. After nine years under his third Headmaster he left, taking up residence where all good Yorkshiremen dream of going when they retire – by the sea at Scarborough. Ever cheerful, always efficient in his many duties as befitted an old soldier, firm with the boys, courteous to the staff, he carried out his many duties, delivering messages to form rooms, compiling lists for action and, of course, heartily ringing the school bell. Except once, when during the war some boys removed the clapper and the unsuspecting Gillman narrowly avoided injury as he swung the empty and unresisting bell. During the Blitz of 1940 he developed a new skill, clearing incendiary bombs out of the building and rendering them harmless with a stirrup pump. So much was he part of the fabric of the school that some boys thought that, at KES, porters were called gillmen. A short while later Ivy Hutson retired from her position as the Headmaster's Secretary. She had outlasted all the older staff members having served for forty years and attended on all five Headmasters.

Mr. C.A.P. Gillman

Harry "Trotsky" Redston almost equalled her period of service. He had arrived at the school in 1921, and now managed to postpone his retirement for three years after he reached 65. This was partly because he was reluctant to leave, but also because Science teachers were becoming difficult to replace. He finally left at Easter 1960 having already handed over the position of Senior Physics Master a couple of years before. Nevertheless, his teaching had been as effective and stimulating as ever, and it is said that his sixth form notes were so highly regarded that they acquired a cash value at Universities, where O.E.s sold them to other undergraduates. For all of his 39 years at the school he had run the Scientific Society and played his part in out of school activities, especially when something electrical needed doing. It was Redston who fixed up the lights for the Dramatic Society's productions as well as using his skill as a caricaturist to record, in profile, the actors in numerous plays. At the Athletics Sports he was the timekeeper, he ran the chess club, and out of school hours, in the Thirties, he had been a champion ballroom dancer for the Midlands Region. Like Effron, Carter, and Watling he had already been honoured with life membership of the Old

268

Edwardians, a distinction not given lightly and then only to the staff members who were something of a legend to the old boys of the school.

Someone who would clearly qualify as a King Edward's legend also retired in the summer of 1960 after 36 years at the school. Arguably the most scholarly member of staff who ever graced the KES Staff Room (he had passed a classics examination at five years of age that would have tested a Sixth Former), Edward Fairchild Watling was undoubtedly the most celebrated among them because of his work in translating Sophocles plays for Penguin Classics Books. Certainly his Oxford College, University, thought so, as they ranked him amongst their most eminent alumni, even though they had only given him a Third Class Degree in Literae Humaniores in 1922.

At KES he never became the Senior Classics Master, even though they came and went with remarkable rapidity. Presumably the school was aware that his lessons were chaotic, and that they became even more of a shambles as he got older and deafer. He retired when only sixty, because he could see himself that he just could not carry on when he was nearly stone deaf. This condition only added to his detached, even at times aloof manner, yet he could surely, when younger, have had an academic life as a lecturer at a University. Perhaps he might have gone on the stage, because he was an accomplished actor, as well as a writer of penetrating critical reviews for the local press of productions at the Lyceum and the Playhouse. Instead, he chose teaching, initiating and then continuing to produce memorable and often challenging school plays for two decades. Housemaster of Haddon,

E.F.W. in 1960

Editor of the school magazine, his tall and distinguished figure could be seen on Speech Days announcing the prize-winners' names in his magnificent, resonant voice, having already usually written the Senior Prefect's Latin Address. His love for the school was such that he acted as an unofficial record keeper and archivist. During the war it was Watling who kept the Roll of Honour of all the dead Old Edwardians and he occasionally contributed articles to the school magazine on the pre-history of KES. For further relaxation he devised crosswords for the Listener, and he had published comic verse and dramatic sketches. Sheffield boys at KES would not meet such cultured and erudite men as Watling in their daily lives. Their parents and their family circle would be solid citizens, honest and fair-minded, who had the highest aspirations for their boys, but, with some exceptions, these same parents would have nothing of the cultural background of KES staff like Claypole and Watling. Through teachers like them, the children of the expanding middle class gained some access to the world of literature, fine art and poetry.

25! –Yes, 25 Societies!

Since the Thirties, KES had always enjoyed a thriving number of extra curricular societies; now in the Fifties and Sixties it expanded to quite amazing lengths. Never less than fifteen societies operated at any one time, and by the end of Clapton's time as Headmaster there were twenty-five, not including the Choir, the Orchestra, the Dramatic Society, the 150 strong Scout Group or any of the teams playing twelve official sports for the school. A fair size town would be delighted to have so much voluntary activity, so many societies with an intellectual purpose and such good quality of speakers and topics at their meetings.

Every lunchtime and every evening after school, rooms and halls would be in use for one or another group. Although the Headmaster played no part in any of these societies himself, he did use Speech Days and Assemblies to encourage participation, yet he was continually disappointed that despite the opportunities, most pupils were out of the school gate as soon as the final bell rang. Many who excelled at sport spent their out of school hours at practices, but at least in the Sixth Form the majority of boys belonged to at least two societies on average. This level of participation gave the lie to those who were trying to prove, for their own purposes, that KES was little more than an examination factory.

There was an even division between those societies which were an extension of the classroom subject, like the Classics Society or the History Society, and those societies which focussed on a hobby or an out of school interest. The great growth in the first category occurred when Junior and Middle School societies were set up catering for boys of all age groups. However, every year there were new groups formed, guided by a master and officered by a number of keen boys. "Spiv" Bramhall set up the Modern Languages Society in 1951. Among the topics at its early meetings, were talks on French Humour, Existentialism and the problems of an international language, whilst masters like Clarence Helliwell chipped in with a talk on Cezanne and "Joe" Oppenheimer led a discussion on Dürer. In 1954 Keith Robinson established the Economics Society, and a little later he organised the Northern Schools Economics Conference at Sheffield University, which was well attended by his Economics Sixth Form.

Some of the more intriguing societies lay in the second category. A Craft and Construction Society set up in 1952 aimed to help out with odd jobs needed by the Science, or indeed any department. To repair, paint, modify and occasionally invent any gadget or apparatus needed for lessons in the school were its aim. Amongst their early projects were an electrolyte dimmer system for stage lighting and a flicker photometer, while at all times always acknowledging their debt to their patron saint, the "blessed" Heath Robinson. The Photographic Society benefited from having a member of their group, called Mottershaw, and useful modern equipment found its way into their dark-room, whilst the new Radio Society produced a Cathode Ray Oscilloscope for the Physics Department. The Junior Astronomical Society, formed by Edgar Vernon in time to view the partial eclipse of the sun in 1954, was to be disappointed when ten/tenths cloud cover obscured the view, but the society flourished despite this and eventually a Senior Branch was formed.

There was schism in the school's Christian community, when the well supported SCM (the Student Christian Movement) found zealots chipping away at its hegemony by forming a Bible Study group, led by Olaf Johnson, and then later, in 1963, a new Scripture Searching Group further fragmented the faithful. Over half the boys at the school claimed to go regularly to church or chapel, so there were many potential recruits for the SCM but their numbers declined in the middle Sixties. Perhaps their mantle was picked up by Youth Action, formed in 1964 to do community service, including painting and decorating the houses of old and disabled people who lived near the school, and also by a Young Oxfam group who organised fund-raising events to aid Oxfam's work abroad. Both these groups were part of a wider Sheffield schools' initiative, perhaps indicative that KES was coming back into the fold, because apart from their Football fixtures they had only limited contact with the other secondary schools in Sheffield during the time Clapton was the Headmaster. One Secretary of the Cross Country team remembers only too well being told by the Headmaster not to arrange a fixture with Firth Park G.S., although running against High Storrs School does seem to have been acceptable.

A lively school also participates in outside events, competitions and opportunities and if there was any project on offer that was interesting, KES was usually amongst the takers. They had a rather curious twinning arrangement with a Merchant Navy vessel, the Blue Funnel Line's S.S. Hector, from 1951 onwards. Basically it was a pen pal scheme for bored members of the crew while they did their regular 10,000 mile trip to Brisbane. When the ship docked at Gladstone Dock, Liverpool, groups of younger boys would go over the Pennines to visit the Captain and his crew and spend an afternoon crawling over the ship. Presumably the British Ship Adoption Society, who had conjured up this scheme, hoped boys from grammar schools in inland cities would become the officers of the future in the Merchant Navy, then the biggest in the world and all still flying the Red Duster. A number of Old Edwardians had always been attracted to a life at sea and one of them J.Michael Bower (1941- 48), serving as the Third Officer on the liner R.M.S. Stratheden, lost his life when attempting to rescue Greek sailors in very heavy seas in the Mediterranean. For his brave action on that day in 1955 he was posthumously awarded the coveted Lloyds Silver Medal and the Greek Government recognised his action with the conferring of the Greek Nautical Medal 1st Class.

The school had recommenced its partnership with a German school, the Kreuzgasse Gymnasium in Cologne and parties of boys began to visit the Rhineland in the early

Fifties. The school was, of course, a new building on the best Bauhaus principles because, as the KES boys soon found out, most of Cologne had been flattened and much of it was still in ruins. They would all be familiar with the bomb damage down the Moor or in Fitzalan Square, but they had never seen devastation on this scale before and it was a sobering revelation, especially when they found out that a third of Cologne's citizens still lived in makeshift dwellings in cellars, in shelters, or in houses minus a wall or two. Each group that went was once again playing a small part in Anglo-German reconciliation, now much easier after the Berlin airlift and the election of the Adenauer Government, and they all returned full of admiration for the autobahns and for the German efforts to re-build their cities.

Boys went on trawlers in their Summer Holidays; one hardy soul, A. Rodgers, sailed from Hull, around the North Cape as far as the White Sea in north Russia. The Arctic Ocean can be a daunting place even in Summer, and fishing off Bear Island is a different proposition to a little gentle angling down by Tinsley Locks or on the Trent. Some went on Outward Bound courses in Eskdale or Aberdovey, whilst others took up the offer of nationalised industries like the NCB, British Rail and the Electricity Board, to do a short summer course staying at well appointed hotels. There was an unofficial CND Group at the school which sheltered under the wing of the International Discussion Group, many of whose members had been highly critical of the Suez invasion of 1956 and were concerned at the rhetoric and the very real danger posed by Cold War politics until after the Cuba missiles crisis.

Between 1960 and 1965 the school always won the British leg of the European Schools Essay Prize Competition and in 1962 Peter Bell, the Head Prefect, went on to win the Gold Medal awarded by the Council of Europe for the best essay in all twelve participating countries. The following year in 1963, along with D. Mingay, he gained second place in the Northern section of the Public Schools Debating Competition held at York after the school had only entered the event for the first time the year before.

Throughout these years the 167th Scout Group flourished as it had done so successfully since 1927. It celebrated its Silver Jubilee in 1952 with a pageant attended by the Lord Mayor, and they could all reflect on the happy choice that had been forced upon them when the new Labour Council of 1926 abolished the OTC. The School Scouts had given at least a thousand Edwardians immense pleasure and no little benefit during their time in one of the troops. The OTC were now called the Combined Cadet Force, and their association wrote to the LEA in 1954 and invited the Sheffield grammar schools to form an Army, Navy or RAF section. The Education Committee turned it down, but not before Ald. Harold Jackson and the Conservatives had demanded a vote – which as usual they lost. It mattered little, for the school and its Headmaster showed no interest in forming a cadet force; the scouts would do very nicely for KES for the present.

The Sound of Music

To the outsider three of the most extraordinary aspects of KES in the period 1950-65 were the number of undergraduates at Oxford, the number of societies, and the size and quality of the Choir and Orchestra. The music tradition had started with Philip Baylis in the Thirties, and when Norman Barnes arrived he had already shown in his three years at the school when Dr. Barton was the Headmaster, that he was capable of taking school music to unprecedented heights. Over the next fifteen years the strength of KES music grew exponentially in numbers and in excellence. Starting with a choir of 100 in 1950 and an orchestra of 43, they grew to include one third of all the boys in the school. By 1965 the choir numbered over 200 and the orchestra boasted 70 players. Barnes was helped by the number of boys who preferred classical music to popular music (29% according to the school's own census) and also by the numbers of regular church goers (about half the boys in the school), many of whom would be in their church choir and grow up in a tradition of church music, singing anthems, Te Deums and Magnificats. Nevertheless, he inspired many others to love music, to want to be members of the choir, and for some, to develop their skills at instruments that they might otherwise have discarded in their teens.

There was a regular pattern to the concert programme for the year. The first public performance was on Speech Day in November, followed by the Carol Concert in December and then the Main School Concert that initially was in January but later slipped into the Summer term. At Easter there was an Oratorio, and in between on any special school occasion like the Commemoration Service, school plays or Open Days, the choir and orchestra played a significant part. The venues had got more impressive too. After Clapton had moved Speech Day to the Victoria Hall, the concerts followed as well. When the choir got to over 200 members there were enough *"uncles, cousins and aunts"* to fill the Victoria Hall and over 1000 people would be at these magnificent events. The Carol Concert moved out of the Assembly Hall as well. Initially it was held at St. John's, Ranmoor, but then, in 1952, it transferred to the Cathedral, the original home of the earliest school in Sheffield. After the Jubilee Service of 1955, the Cathedral, now enlarged with its great new lantern tower at the west end, also hosted the Commemoration Service, and both these venues provided an inspiring setting for powerful performances, emphasising also that KES was part of the city, not a secretive enclave behind the high wall of the Close up in Broomhill.

There were particular magnificent nights when the music swelled and the audience was reduced to spellbound ecstatic admiration. In 1952 in their first performance at the Victoria Hall they took advantage of the superior acoustics and tackled Handel's Judas Maccabaeus, whose choruses gave full scope to the choir, achieving as the Sheffield Telegraph critic commented, *"A pleasing and often beautiful quality of tone, whilst the orchestra played exceptionally well evidencing good musicianship"*. In 1954, the verdict was that the choir and orchestra had surpassed themselves when they performed the Messiah with the soprano and contralto solos sung by small groups of younger boys. In the Jubilee Concert of May 1956 to celebrate the school's first fifty years, Barnes performed all his old favourite composers. Always true to British composers, the choir that night sang pieces by Vaughan Williams, Stanford and Thomas Wood, whilst the orchestra played Sullivan, Quilter and Armstrong Gibbs as well as the Sixth Chandos Anthem by that "Englishman by residence", Handel. However it was the 1965 Concert that Barnes thought was the best so far and led the local music critic to remark "*that music at KES was amongst the very best of any school in the North of England*". The greatest ovation of that night was reserved for NJB himself, for his choral arrangements of two spirituals and a "swingled" version of a Gavotte by Samuel Wesley. The Grand Finale was a stirring performance of Zadok the Priest sung with all the best northern fervour, with the opening, a succession of high F sharps and Gs, well sung in tune with excellent clarity.

Within the orchestra a number of sections and groups had been developed who were given the opportunity to perform individually at the concerts. Relying on a number of volunteer specialist teachers in the days before peripatetic music teachers, a small woodwind group of two oboes, a clarinet and a bassoon was started in 1954, and at the same time a small string group was established. From the choir a Madrigal Group was formed in 1956, and it grew in size and importance until it was almost the size of a medium sized choir itself. Then in 1958, under the guidance of Mr. Ralph Williams, a Brass Section was formed and he conducted it in the concert that year playing his own arrangement for Brass, Drums and Organ. The school organ, which had been formally unveiled at the Commemoration Service in 1951 and represented one of the elements of the remembrance of the school's Second World War dead, was used in choir and orchestra practices. However, it never really enjoyed its full glory supporting the great school concerts, because these events were moved out of the school buildings into bigger venues. Nevertheless, it did have an important role backing the hymn singing at the morning assemblies, giving some element of reverence to those occasions before the Headmaster got into his stride with the "*bollocking of the day*".

During the school lunchtime the Music Societies met and flourished. Both Senior and Junior would hear a live performance one week with a recording, perhaps, the next. In 1956 a Chamber Music Society was founded after a considerable number of the school's musicians had been on a summer course at Sherborne, and all the while the numbers of entries for the music competitions continued to rise until it reached over fifty. One Leader of the Orchestra, J. Buchan, in 1957, among his other roles in the school was also Captain of Football and a couple of Head Boys also played leading roles in the orchestra. Ivor Jones, led the cellists, and in 1954 was awarded an Organ Scholarship at Brasenose College, Oxford, (some years later he became the Principal of Wesley House, Cambridge) and Gordon Skidmore was the Leader of the Orchestra in 1964-65. Barnes was particularly proud of the boys who gained music scholarships and also two boys in the Sixties, C.M. Dolan and D.W. Williams, who became Associates of the Royal College of Organists whilst still at school. Similarly he would have liked more boys to have been selected for the National Youth Orchestra as he believed every boy in the Orchestra should aspire to this honour. Two of his musicians, J.P.Catchpole in 1957 and

J. Crawford in 1964, were invited to join the NYO and received instruction from the most eminent musicians including Walter Susskind and Yehudi Menhuin. Alternatively some of the musicians from the school orchestra put their training to good use during their National Service and joined their regimental bands, including A.L.Williams who played the bassoon in a Guards' Band.

The music tradition was now so strong that it challenged the primacy of sport as the main extra-curricular activity at KES. It was also strong enough to beat off the prevailing teenage counter culture at least within the school. In a parallel universe Edwardians, certainly by 1960, were forming rock bands and playing a different kind of music to the music as understood by the school. John Shillito wrote a serious article on Jazz for the school magazine and later achieved some local fame as "Kid" Shillito and his Band. He was amongst the first of a considerable number of young Old Edwardians who preferred a Fender to a French Horn. Even though Britain, quite improbably, had become the second fountainhead of popular music by the middle Sixties; Carnaby St., the Beatles, the Stones, and all the effervescent kitsch of "Swinging" England were kept absolutely extramural at KES, at least whilst Clapton ruled.

As for Norman Barnes his work at the school was not finished. He stayed on into the comprehensive era, making sure the music tradition continued and eventually retired in 1976. As W.D.L.Scobie wrote in the school magazine in 1964, "*A large school can produce performers and soloists, it can even produce an exciting programme, but unless the person is there to weld these elements together, the result will be chaos and cacophony and embarrassing misery for the audience. To NJB's credit none of these things ever happened at KES, and his concerts were always enjoyable and downright exciting.*"

Back to the Bard

Whilst Norman Barnes, as the Senior Music Master, provided continuity and direction with a sustained programme of regular concerts, the School Play depended on the enthusiasm of a non-specialist Master who was willing to take on the demanding annual task of producing. Edward Watling, the father of the school play, produced two more plays in the Fifties — Synge's Playboy of the Western World and J.B. Priestley's little known drama about the crew of a broken down tank, called Desert Highway —, but productions were always limited by the lack of a proper proscenium arch and the size of the Assembly Hall stage. Some producers in the Fifties tried to convince themselves that the Assembly Hall was not unlike an Elizabethan theatre interior, but the action always looked very crowded if there were more than half a dozen actors on the stage at any one time. Desert Highway had been chosen as the play in 1952 because it was only a six-hander, but that rather defeats the purpose of a school play whose aim is to involve as many actors of differing ages and give them, possibly for the only time in their lives, a chance to display their dramatic talents. The Dramatic Society hoped that after the school musicians' "coup" in gaining an organ, the next arts priority would be a purpose built stage, but it never happened. Later when the school acquired the Darwin Lane site, the school play moved there, where the hall had a proscenium arch or alternatively enough space to create theatre in the round or a thrust stage. In the Nineties the main school production of the year was held in the summer in the Crucible Studio, the Drama Department equivalent of school concerts at the Victoria Hall or the Cathedral.

There were also mutterings that Watling would not produce a Shakespeare play, and as the last one had been Hamlet in 1937 many felt it was high time this situation was remedied. So Gerry Claypole took over as the producer in 1954 and the Dramatic Society performed Macbeth, that was well received by the audience, especially on the night that Macbeth's severed head of papier mache rolled off the stage and down the aisle. The following year Claypole directed Shaw's Caesar and Cleopatra and continued the theme with Julius Caesar as his last production before he retired. In that play Ted Wragg played Brutus and three younger actors, Goulden, Thorp and Smith, were cast as extras. In later life, while "Brutus" became a well-known professor of education, the three erstwhile Roman soldiers all became H.M. Ambassadors. When Claypole left he paid especial tribute to all boys and staff, along with a considerable army of parents, who rallied round and did all the front of house and back stage work — including all the "fauvists" who caked on the make up — that made the plays possible. About sixty people, including the boys' mothers who did the costume design and creation, were involved in these productions, now fixed on the school calendar for the end of the Spring Term and running for at least three nights and at times, ambitiously, five nights in a week. Sometimes staff members were exasperated that more boys did not bother to support the events. " *This foolish and short-sighted indifference to the activities of the school"* thundered D. V. Henry in the school magazine of 1957. One wonders if he had more luck getting "posteriors on seats" at Welwyn Garden City G.S., where he was just about to become their new Headmaster.

1957 saw the return of the school revue; no longer called the "Shout" its ingredients were much the same in concept and execution. Boys ran sketches guying the staff and in return the staff, often showing not inconsiderable talent, displayed touches of comedy that were often a revelation to their charges. Called "Staff and Nonsense" it ran for four nights at the end of the Winter Term and a fair number of staff mucked in, some singing solos, some even tap dancing. It was repeated in 1963 but the energy was not there to make it a regular event on the calendar, even though it would have been much appreciated and good for relations between the boys and the staff which were still very formal.

There were years when no one could be found to produce a full school play but Bruce Chalmers, the Classics Master, produced four school plays during his short time at the school, including Henry IV, Part I, then St. Joan and finally Twelfth Night. The last two school plays of Clapton's time were produced by Peter Points who did Richard II, followed by Martin Axford, the new Senior English Master, who took on the challenge of the "Winter's Tale", the rarely performed late Shakespearean play that is a formidable challenge for a school company. Present day students are always amused to be told that in these plays women and girls' parts were played by boys, — in one play the leading lady had to be understudied one night because (s)he had badly sprained an ankle playing rugby during the day — but even more sobering is the revelation that in the plays, as well as the choir and orchestra, all the participants were boys, whereas today the large majority of performers in KES concerts and in school plays are girls, with boys noticeably thin on the ground.

Fourteen Sports

Competitive but not dominant, is the verdict on sports teams in the Clapton years, as it was in most decades at KES. The school played fourteen sports, if you include Chess — which the school defined as a sport — and there were house competitions in all of them, as well as regular inter-school matches in all except Athletics and Fives. After the well supported Athletics matches against public schools in Barton's time, it was surprising that Athletics declined in importance at KES, although there were several fine athletes who would have performed very creditably in a school team. Champion Athletes like Geoffrey Heritage in 1954, and Frank Parker and Richard Nosowski in the early Sixties, all went on to get Blues at Oxford, though not in Athletics but in Football. The 1955 Champion Athlete D.P. Allen twice represented Yorkshire (the whole county, not one of the four present day teams) in the English Schools Athletics Championship, the event in which all future Great Britain Olympic Athletes compete, and in 1955 he was joined in the Yorkshire team by John Shillito, who came 4th in the Mile, one of the glamour events at the two day Championship. It is one of the great regrets of KES sport in the Fifties that no member of staff was qualified, or interested enough, to take on the running of an Athletics squad, something that was not a problem in the 1990s when KES dominated Sheffield Schools Athletics.

The first ever KES RU XV. Season 1951-52 with the Headmaster and D.B. Harrison.

277

There were major new sports to compensate, with Rugby Union starting at the school in 1951, then Badminton and finally Hockey in the early Sixties. Rugby Union was the preferred sport of Bert Harrison, the P.E. Master, and once Barton had left he found the new Headmaster was prepared to give the green light to boys who wanted to try the oval ball game. Harrison was supported by "Bert" Towers, the Senior Geography Master, another member of staff who was keen to introduce rugby, but they found it very hard going to achieve any success on the pitch in the early seasons. When they played schools like Central Tech and City G.S., their first two opponents, they were defeated but not by too wide a margin. If they dared to play a rugby football school like Lady Manners at Bakewell or Doncaster G.S., then they were hammered and their ignorance of the arcane ways of the fifteen-a-side game were readily apparent. Occasionally they would venture north into the West Riding heartland of the other code, where QEGS Wakefield was all dominant, and whose 3rd XV could administer a thrashing to the fledgling KES side. Slowly though the team found its level and in the 1955-56 season they won half of their eight matches and then in 1958-59, under the captaincy of M.E.Sara, they posted KES's first winning season with 14 victories out of 17 games played. The school also gained its first representative honour in 1958 when Sara was selected to play for South Yorkshire Schools.

To enable this expansion of winter team sports to take place, the school had acquired the use of Castle Dyke Playing Fields above the snow line off Ringinglow Rd. Many schools along the edge of the Pennines have to put up with bleak, windswept facilities, but Castle Dyke was amongst the most grim and desolate of all of them. For three years boys had to survive without changing facilities until a squat utilitarian changing block, appropriately rather like a rescue shelter, was built on the hillside.

Fears that introducing Rugby Union would affect the school's Football Team's standards did not seem to be borne out in the first three seasons of the Fifties decade. As we have already discussed, the team under "Curly" Harper had successful seasons, followed then by something of a decline until the results picked up in the 1956-7 Season. However the best year in KES football during Clapton's time was the 1958-59 Season when the team was coached by Brian Arthur, later to become an HMI, and included, as a stalwart defender, Ted Powell, who went on to captain England's Amateur International side and play in the Tokyo Olympics in 1964. They only conceded 35 goals in 22 matches, winning 17, drawing 4 and losing only once when they came up against a strong Old Edwardian side. On top of this success the same team won the Sheffield and District Seven-a-Side Cup, defeating old rivals Ecclesfield G.S. by 17-2 in the final and they also reached the semi-finals of the Yorkshire Competition in Leeds.

The sides that followed this team could never do as well, but there were winning seasons, as in 1960-61, and on the whole KES maintained its usual level of satisfactory performance at soccer, without being a dominant force amongst the teams on its very strong fixture list. Nevertheless, the school produced some useful players who, although they didn't become household names, like some of their contemporaries — Howard Wilkinson at Abbeydale, or Bob Wilson in goal for Chesterfield G.S. — were good

278

enough to win Blues at Oxford and play in the Varsity Match at Wembley. The former Head Prefect, Peter Fletcher, played in the 1954 game, Ian Marshall in 1955 and G.R. Heritage in 1956. Then in the Sixties, Richard Nosowski played in two Varsity matches in 1962 and 1964, when he was joined in the Oxford team by Frank Parker who had also played in the 1963 match. Parker usually captained the Centaurs, the University Second Team, that at one time had six Old Edwardians playing for them. English Football in this period was going through a thorough reappraisal after the Hungarians had humiliated Billy Wright's team at Wembley in 1953, a reappraisal that culminated in probably the biggest triumph in English sporting history in 1966. So, while many Varsity Rugby Union players might very well still play for one of the Home Countries, Association Football now moved on to another level and grammar school boys who went to university infrequently became professional footballers.

Old Edwardians had other sporting successes at Oxford. Norman Adsetts captained the University Lacrosse team, and three O.E.s, Frank Parker, William Abbott and Barry Cheetham got their Half Blues for swimming against Cambridge in 1962, the year after they had left the school. Swimming was one sport in which KES's old dominance was maintained and they continued to have some undefeated seasons, even though attendance at their matches and even at the Swimming Sports, was declining. They had a limited number of fixtures (opponents had to have their own pools) but they were usually too strong for Trent, Leeds, Worksop, and Nottingham and also Rowlinson, the one Sheffield school they swam against, who had a community pool on its campus. Water Polo matches were on an "as and when" basis, and after winning all three games in 1953, the sport was largely played at House competition level. Similarly there were very few Fives fixtures, even though in 1953 the Eton courts were finally cleared of coke, and matches using those buttressed courts could begin again.

However, it was at cricket where a lack of success was most marked. Up to the war, cricket had probably enjoyed the status of the school's main game. Then it suited the school's image of itself as a public school in all but name: now in the Fifties, the game started to lose popularity to tennis. Although the England Team was thriving under the captaincy of Len Hutton and then P.B.H. May, and while the Yorkshire team contained some of the greatest players in its history, school cricket began to falter and begin the long if uneven decline that saw it extinguished altogether by the end of the century.

The best season of this period is at the beginning in 1953 when, under the captaincy of Ivor Jones, the school won 9 of their 17 matches and drew another 5. In 1954, and again in 1957, the team managed winning seasons but otherwise they usually ended up with more defeats than wins. In the 1963 season they achieved a sporting first for KES cricket when they failed to win a single match in 16 outings, despite John Linfoot scoring 114 not out against Ashville College, the highest score by any boy since the war. That match was part of the regular half term tour organised by Keith Robinson and John Hemming; enjoyable days that took them up to Newcastle one year, to East Anglia another, and were followed at the end of the season by a veritable cricket festival, when in the last week of term the school played six matches on consecutive days. KES was finding its fixture list a little too strong, as most of the schools they played had superb cricket grounds surrounding the school, whilst they had to play on their Pythonesque, if picturesque, square two miles away in Whiteley Woods. There Leslie Waghorn, "Wag" to each new generation of Edwardians, still dispensed his "flycatchers" –huge open jam sandwiches — and poured out the minute amount of cordial for his penny drinks (two pence would get you two minute doses, although it still tasted like coloured water), while he tended the pitches and in winter provided a large open fire that frozen football players could gather around to thaw out.

" Whiteley Woods, Bents Green,
Furnace Field and Ringinglow "—
Rain, hail, sleet or snow—
First to come and last to go.

"WAG"

Badminton started in the Fifties and school teams initially played University teams, Jessop's social club and sides from boys' clubs. There were almost fifty boys playing regularly and in 1963-64 they arranged 13 fixtures and won 9 of them. Hockey started as something of a lark with a game against Abbeydale Girls G.S. KES won by 2-1 goals and discovered that the game was no soft option and stick wielding amazons could be very worthy competitors. In the first season, 1962-63, they lost all five matches played, but they improved and by 1964 they won more matches than they lost. At Chess, the school was less successful than one would have imagined given the amount of intellectual fire-power around the building on Glossop Road. They played ten matches or so a year, but rarely enjoyed a winning season until the early Sixties, when they became virtually unbeatable.

The Tennis team competed for almost a decade before the school courts were finally laid down in 1959. Then ironically, because it was such a hot summer, the tarmac became too soft and the three courts in the Close could not be used immediately. After that the courts were well used and there was a new enthusiasm for tennis, partly sparked by the televising of the Wimbledon Championships which created new sporting heroes like the Australians Sedgeman, Hoad and Rosewall, along with "Little Mo" Connolly, becoming familiar to boys at the school. Tennis followed the pattern of other KES sports. Always competitive, the school could only manage winning seasons four times in the Fifties, and they were less successful after they got their own courts.

One sport where KES usually triumphed was Cross Country. Traditionally the KES teams were strong and when they ran at home their opponents found the Pennine foothills a nasty shock after their own relatively quiet byways. The final lap through the farmyard with the prevailing smell of pig manure could weaken the resolve of the strongest competitor. Amongst the Cross Country honours in the Fifties was that of John Shillito winning the individual trophy in the Northern Schools Cross Country, thereby helping the school gain a respectable sixth place. This was only the second time a KES boy had won the event, David Law having managed it in 1949 when KES won the team trophy. They did, however, come second in this same team event in 1964, running against 83 other schools and at varying times they posted good results in both the Yorkshire and North Midlands Schools Cross Country Events.

NLC

The school got the balance right with sport in the Fifties. Still a very important part of school life it no longer had the dominant position it had enjoyed in the period up to the Second World War. When Repton dropped the Football fixture in 1952, after KES had had the better of the five First XI encounters up to that date, Clapton was unconcerned. It did not matter to him whether or not a "posh" public school played KES or not. King Edward VII School was carving its own place in the educational world and its academic results were leaving boarding schools like Repton well behind. KES was not aiming to copy any other school; it believed it was leading the way and showing what a grammar school could achieve. Clapton was the complete meritocrat. The son of an ironmonger he had no room for social snobbery, but he had the highest regard for academic excellence and he believed his school should pass on as many of the boys as possible to the next stage of academic education. Leaving early, or not going to

John Shillito winning the 1957 Northern Schools Cross Country Championships.

university after the Sixth Form, appeared to him to be a failure. Not necessarily of the system, rather a failure of the boy himself, who had not taken the fullest advantage of the opportunities on offer at KES.

The Headmaster was also keen to make sure there was a balance between those who chose to become science and maths specialists, and those studying classics and arts subjects. To this end he supported the considerable growth of the Economics Department (Fifty "A" Level candidates a year by 1965) and he widened the curriculum by encouraging the introduction of new subjects. Russian was added to the three modern languages already studied, statistics in the maths courses, geology with geography and technical drawing in the handicraft department. Behind all the undoubted progress made in those years, unseen by the boys but clear enough to the senior staff, was the administrative skill of the Headmaster. Not all teachers move easily from the world of the classroom and the small-scale administration of a subject department, to running the complex organisation of a large secondary school with a staff of fifty. Clapton, however, possessed a passion for detail, an extraordinary ability to appear to know everything that was happening in the school — even though he rarely ventured from his study — and a phenomenal memory that maintained a precise mental dossier of all boys, staff and issues at the school. Every year, because KES masters were in such demand, he had to find suitable replacements for at least 10% of his teaching staff. Although some left because of retirement, the majority moved on to more senior posts, more often that not at public schools, and the consequent turnover most probably benefited the school by introducing people with new ideas and fresh enthusiasms. In the early Sixties there were four staff members with a PhD, at a time when a doctorate was still a relatively rare qualification, and five of Clapton's staff went directly to be Headmasters, while others achieved the position after a period at their next school.

Many of the staff had a respect for their Headmaster that was not just based on this vaunted efficiency. Many masters remember him as a man who could be most considerate of any illnesses or problems and whose decisiveness in making clear, and often efficacious decisions, was welcome and beneficial. It was Clapton who encouraged the staff to set up a Staff Room Committee, whose chairman, Edgar Vernon, would with appropriate deference relay their thoughts to the Head. Clapton welcomed many of their ideas and because his position in the school was so secure there was never any chance that this committee could be a challenge to his own authority. He did not however regard all his staff equally and clearly some went in mortal fear of him. Several Old Edwardians recall seeing masters in the queue outside his room, standing in a line of pupils waiting in turn to be summoned into his presence by the "traffic lights" outside his door. Some were clearly in a blue funk as they also waited to be dressed down for some inadequacy or indiscretion. David Tomlinson, when secretary of the Cross Country club, was surprised to be told by the Headmaster to make travel arrangements for the team himself, as Mr. X couldn't be relied on to get it done correctly.

If Clapton was an enigma to the staff, he made certain that the boys saw only one side of his character. To them he was always a stern, unsmiling and frankly unattractive figure, ready to hand out a personal or collective angry rebuke. He rarely praised even the most successful members of the school. Gerard Nosowski remembers that when he won a Hastings Exhibition in 1962, the drill was to place the letter of acceptance in the Headmaster's post box. A few days later it was returned by Clapton, marked with a tick and the single word, "noted!" Others did not get as much acknowledgement as that, yet he admired their "*innate Sheffield tenacity*" which he believed turned hardworking, motivated pupils into scholarship winners.

What they were largely unaware of was the toll that the death of his wife, in 1956, had taken on him. This was followed in 1958 by a serious accident when he fell down the attic stairs at his home and broke his leg. For a time he hobbled around the school and could not even mount the platform for morning prayers, instead conducting business from the side of the stage. This injury led to complications and he was never a fit man again. By the middle Sixties he was spending considerable periods in hospital. Characteristically he tried at first to run the school from his bed in the Royal Infirmary at Shalesmoor, with his secretary bringing him all the correspondence and school papers and returning to Glossop Rd. with his decisions. One such decision was to demote immediately two prefects, who, along with eleven other Sixth Formers, had sent a letter to the Star newspaper supporting the introduction of comprehensive education in the city. It fell to Arthur Jackson to take the flak as he announced this decision in the school assembly the following day, before publicly removing the prefect's badges from the " KES Two".

It soon became clear that the school could not be run from a hospital a mile away and Jackson took on the running of the school until Clapton was fit to return. It also became clear that Clapton was too ill to carry on as Headmaster and at the last moment in the summer of 1965 he handed in his resignation. Unloved, but respected as fair and highly competent by most of the boys at the school —although there are a sizeable number even today whose dislike of him is still strong and unabated — he was always a very private person who lived for his work at the school, often working past midnight and even on Boxing Day. He was the first Headmaster to choose to live at a distance from the school and even the Deputy Head was rarely invited to his home in Nether Edge, although in the Sixties he picked him up every morning in his car. Before that he had travelled in to school on the circular bus, that became very quiet once it had reached his bus stop.

He left as an embittered man, believing that his remarkable school was about to be destroyed by the actions of the Labour controlled City Council. Surprisingly he played no real part in the dispute over comprehensive education, partly because he was in ill health, but partly like Barton in 1945, he felt that as an employee of the Sheffield City Council it was inappropriate to lead opposition to the council's decisions in public. His action over the two prefects however make it very clear where his own views lay on the issue that would occasion the biggest change in the life of the school in its one hundred year history.

Clapton continued to live in Sheffield during his brief retirement. He never recovered his health and died a year and a half later in January 1967.

WHAT THOU SHALT WEAR!

Boys in the first three years must wear a School Blazer and grey flannels. It is strongly urged that this practice should continue as a boy passes into the Upper School. Gaudy shirts and pullovers should not be worn.

Boys in the First and Second Forms are to wear a School Cap and Junior Tie (Single silver horizontal stripes on a navy blue tie)).

Boys in the Third Forms are to wear a School Cap only during the Autumn and Spring terms and a School Tie (Triple silver diagonal stripes) throughout the year.

Boys in the Fourth Forms and above must wear a School Tie. Special Ties are available for Sixth Formers (Double silver diagonal stripes) and Prefects (Single silver diagonal stripes). Black ties are not to be worn unless necessary on account of mourning.

The wearing of rubber boots in school is also forbidden.

(Extract from the school rules 1964)

CHAPTER FIFTEEN

CREATING COMPREHENSIVES
1962-69

When the Labour Group on the Sheffield City Council in 1962, meeting in private at their regular monthly policy meeting, agreed that all the LEA secondary schools in Sheffield would become comprehensive schools within a decade, the fate of KES as a grammar school was sealed. Few people at the school at that time realised the full implications of this decision. Were they not the most successful LEA grammar school in the country? Hadn't a succession of leading Labour local politicians regularly trumpeted the success of the school at Speech Days? Had they not also taken every opportunity to tell members of other authorities how good were all their grammar schools, especially the one that regularly sent over twenty five boys a year to Oxford and Cambridge? Yet within seven years KES, and all the other grammar schools in the city, would be co-educational comprehensives. There would be a new Headmaster attempting to forge a continuum, building on the traditions and standards of two rather different schools, the sixty four year old King Edward VII School in Broomhill, and the new Crosspool School at Darwin Lane.

What happened during those seven years in Sheffield did not happen in a vacuum. The supporters of comprehensive education nationally had been pressing their case during the Fifties, indeed there had been some considerable pressure for comprehensive schools in London before the Second World War. By 1954 there were thirteen comprehensive schools in England and Wales, including Windermere and Anglesey and London's first comprehensive, Kidbrooke, was opened that year. The Conservative Government, whilst very much supporting the continuation of grammar schools, did allow the creation of some comprehensives, especially if they were in scattered rural areas or urban housing estates. So by 1965, the year when the crucial decisions on the future of KES were made by the City Council, there were already 195 comprehensive schools in the country and the new Labour Government's Education Minister, Tony Crosland, was pronouncing that; " *If it is the last thing I do, I'm going to destroy every grammar school in England".*

Sheffield, however, had not waited for his Circular 10/65 that made the creation of comprehensive schools government policy. They were by 1965 well down the road to finalising their own scheme, and already had several comprehensive schools up and running in the northern and eastern areas of the city. Although the staff and parents at KES had been largely unaware of any dissatisfaction with the tripartite system of education in Sheffield, a campaign for comprehensive education inside the local Labour Party had begun to bear fruit and led to the Labour Group decision of 1962. It was spearheaded by a number of young grammar school educated graduates, who had come to live in the city. Linking up with young councillors, some of whom were also grammar school educated, they overcame the opposition to change from the old guard led by the

Chairman of the Education Committee, and Chairman of KES Governors, Alderman Albert Ballard. In the aftermath of the Labour's defeat in the 1959 General Election, new ideas were pursued in the city. One, supported by the small, but influential, Socialist Medical Association, led to the creation of Sheffield's Clean Air Scheme, whilst the newly formed, and equally small, Socialist Education Association pressed for comprehensive education in the LEA's secondary schools.

This small group had some remarkable members including Martin Flannery, then a teacher but later M.P. for Hillsborough, Peter Horton, later Chairman of the Education Committee for 16 years, and Chris Price, later M.P. and Vice-Chancellor of Leeds Metropolitan University among his other positions. They found allies amongst Labour members on the Council including Roy Hattersley (ex City G.S.), Joe Ashton (a former pupil of High Storrs G.S. and later M.P.), Ron Ironmonger (who was educated at Firth Park G.S.), then the chief whip and later Leader of both Sheffield and South Yorkshire Councils and John Tomlinson, who came from the south, and later was an M.P., an M.E.P., and a member of the House of Lords. They were opposed in the Labour Group by most of the leadership of the Council, including Dame Grace Tebbut, the Council Leader, and by Ballard who took particular pride in "his" grammar schools, especially High Storrs and KES.

This group of younger, and leftish, councillors carried too many intellectual guns to be stopped and they had already achieved one victory when, in 1960, against the wishes of the Chief Education Officer, Stanley Moffat, Myers Grove was opened as a comprehensive school. Moffat had threatened to resign when his proposal that there should be three new schools on the one site was overruled. He was told by the councillors to put his resignation in writing, and when it was accepted he left and later was recruited to organise the tripartite system in Barbados. Meanwhile Ballard and some of his supporters, aware that they were losing the argument in the Group, circulated a proposal that the city could go comprehensive except for KES and High Storrs, which would remain as grammar schools outside the system. When he finally realised that this position was untenable he is reported as saying that; "*I shall go home and have a little weep for King Edward's and High Storrs.*"

Can they be stopped?

The issue, in 1962, that had brought the controlling Labour Group on the Council to a decision on comprehensive education, was the long standing proposal to build a girls grammar school in Longley Park, opposite Firth Park (Boys) G.S. As long ago as 1947 the Council had drawn up plans for new schools for the city, which included the provision of grammar school education for girls in the north of the city. When the plans for the Firth Park Girls G.S. came to the Labour Group, the members, on the initiative of Peter Horton, then a new backbench councillor, rejected the plans and followed this up by taking the momentous decision to introduce comprehensive education in all secondary schools in Sheffield. From that moment only four obstacles could stop it happening.

- That the Labour Movement (the Trades Unions and the Labour Party) turned against comprehensive education.
- That the scheme was unworkable in terms of the physical provision of appropriate buildings, or that the financial cost made it unviable.
- That the Conservatives gained control of the City Council and scrapped Labour's schemes.
- That a Conservative Government could be persuaded by local Conservatives members, backed by public support from actual, or potential, Conservative voters, that the scheme was not in their best political interests.

The first of these was not going to happen. Through the highly influential Trades and Labour Council, that represented the wider Labour Movement in Sheffield, there was massive support for comprehensive education in the city. Their opposition to the tripartite system was in the main centred around abolishing the 11+ Examination, which many people now believed was destroying their children's chances of a proper education and opportunities for gaining worthwhile careers. Any argument that KES was a special case because of its high academic record and its large number of scholarships to Oxbridge, cut very little ice in the Brightside and Attercliffe constituencies. By the Sixties most people with children at secondary modern schools saw them as the third best choice for their son's and daughter's education, at best doing an adequate job, at worst little more than child minding until their pupils were fifteen and could leave and go out to work. There was also only limited enthusiasm for secondary technical schools, which some on the left saw as a second class option, once again directing working class children into manual jobs. Others in the Labour Party saw the issue in strategic terms; that the nation was wasting much of its talent and that in an increasingly competitive world it no longer had the option of muddling through, but needed a major shake up of its industrial and educational life if Britain was to survive, let alone prosper, in the second half of the century. Labour embraced this new vision better than did Alec Douglas-Home's Conservatives in the early Sixties, and this led to Wilson's narrow election victory in 1964.

The second obstacle, adequate and appropriate buildings and facilities, was more of a challenge to the members and officers of the Education Committee. They chose to introduce comprehensive education by stages starting with the north of the city. Then they intended to progress to the eastern "region", before tackling the real areas of opposition to their scheme in the south and west of the city, where there were six of the city's eight grammar schools and two of its three secondary technical schools. Their opponents, including virtually all the staff at KES, accused them of introducing their proposals by stealth and creating a time table dictated by political expediency, because in the Labour strongholds of the north and east of the city there was only limited enthusiasm for grammar schools amongst the large working class communities, and the Conservatives were un-represented on the City Council.

Between 1962 and the municipal election of May 1967, Labour's hegemony on the City Council seemed unchallengeable. Labour held at least two thirds of the seats in the council chamber and the social "tectonic plates" that divided Sheffield, roughly along the line of the Don and Sheaf Rivers, ensured that there were very few marginals that could be won or lost at election time. Therefore it seemed that the Conservatives on the Council could only oppose, but not alter or divert any of Labour's comprehensive plans. Yet the unbelievable did happen and they gained control of the Council for one year in 1968, when they could have jettisoned the whole comprehensive scheme or, as in 1988, just leave the Hallam Constituency out of the plans. Six grammar schools, KES, High Storrs Boys and Girls, Abbeydale Boys and Girls and Grange G.S. would have then continued as selective schools, whilst Silverdale and Tapton would have remained as secondary moderns.

The final concern of the Labour Councillors was what the attitude of the Conservative Government would be, if their comprehensive scheme was vigorously opposed by middle class parents and Conservative party supporters in a section of the city. Although under Sir Edward Boyle, the Conservative Education Minister in the early Sixties, the Council felt fairly confident that they would be supported by the Government if their decision was seen to have broad public support. However, after Labour's victory in the 1964 Election and the party's conversion nationally to comprehensive education, the government became an ally and Sheffield was regarded as a model for other large cities to follow if they had not already produced their own schemes.

One of Boyle's lasting decisions was to agree to raise the school leaving age to 16, fixing 1971 as the date when it would come into force. That date initially was used as a marker for the Labour Council in Sheffield to have their comprehensive scheme fully in operation. Later it was moved forward to September 1969. If it had stayed at 1971 then the council would have found themselves dealing with a new Tory Education Minister, Mrs. Thatcher, who in her time in that office rejected 92 comprehensive schemes because they would have occasioned the demise of popular and successful grammar schools. It seems most likely that KES would have survived as a grammar school, at least till the return of the third Wilson Government in 1974, when Fred Mulley (Education Secretary and M.P. for Sheffield Park) took on the local authorities that had not introduced comprehensive education during the period of the Heath Government.

The Northern and Eastern Regions.

In 1963 the Comprehensive Plan for the Northern "Region" of the city was passed by the council. It envisaged four comprehensive schools based on existing schools and their recently completed additional buildings. The 1947 plan had recommended that where possible secondary modern schools be built in pairs, adjacent to each other on the same campus. They could then be used as single sex schools, or in the future the LEA might want to make them one large school, even create comprehensives. Now the new buildings at Hinde House, and at Chaucer, were combined with the existing schools, allowing Hinde House in 1963 to become the second comprehensive school in Sheffield, with Chaucer following in 1964. Myers Grove, under their charismatic and indefatigable Headteacher, William Hill, was making good progress and since 1960 had served as the model for the other schools in the north of the city to follow. So far the scheme was moving along well, with parents in this area assured that their children could either opt out of the 11+ examination if they wished, or continue to take it, and if successful, go to a grammar, or secondary technical school. Then, in 1964, the council made the first breach in the walls of the grammar schools when nineteen "unselected" boys, who had not passed their 11+, were admitted to Firth Park G.S. From then on the number of boys at Firth Park who had passed their 11+ scholarship declined, until it too had become a comprehensive school.

The plan also envisaged that the comprehensives schools in Sheffield would be 13-18 schools, and that "High" Schools, initially from 11-13, would act as an intermediate level between primary and comprehensive secondary schools. These were something of a temporary arrangement, because the Plowden Committee, which included Harold Tunn, Sheffield's Director of Education, was considering this very issue at the time and it was widely expected that they would recommend "Middle" Schools for 9-13, or possibly for 8-12, year olds. In the event, Plowden recommended 8-12 Middle Schools and Sheffield adopted these in 1967. Meanwhile as part of the re-organisation in the Northern "Region" of the city, a number of former secondary moderns were now designated as high schools, later becoming middle schools.

In 1964 the plan for the Eastern "Region" was passed and a similar scheme adopted in the area that was bounded in the north by Attercliffe Rd. and in the west by East Bank Rd. and Gleadless Rd. By 1967 comprehensive education in the north and east of Sheffield was well on its way to completion, and it was intended that it would be finally in place by 1970. So far there had been little opposition to the plans. Only two grammar schools were involved in the transition and one of them, City G.S., had just moved out from Leopold St. in the city centre to Stradbrooke, and therefore was already in a process of re-organisation, which now took a different form.

Hands off King Edwards!

However, only half the children in the city were affected by these changes, until it was the turn of the South-West "Region" to be subjected to the plans for change. Before January 1965, KES staff and parents had watched what was happening elsewhere in the city with some detachment. The city was so clearly delineated both socially and politically, that what went on in the terraced streets and large council estates of the north and east of the city, rarely rated any interest in the south western suburbs where the large majority of KES pupils lived. Suddenly the school found that its future, along with that of five other grammar schools and two technical schools, was under serious consideration and plans were near completion for the abolition of all these selective schools. They would then re-emerge as comprehensive schools, whilst most of the secondary moderns, including Silverdale, Tapton and Jordanthorpe, were destined to become 11-13 high schools.

One very great difficulty for the supporters of KES who wished to keep the school as a grammar school was that there was no one to stand up and declare the school's official position. If the school had been independent, then this would have been the role of the governors, but the KES governors (which they now shared with five secondary modern schools) were dominated by the leading members of the Labour Group. The Chairman of the Governors by tradition was always the Chairman of the Education Committee and Alderman Ballard was now supporting the drive towards comprehensive education. The Headmaster might have decided to step into this vacuum and fight the council behind the scenes as Dr. Barton had done in 1944-5 or, if necessary, in public. This is what happened in Liverpool, where the Headmaster of the Liverpool Institute (a school that was considered by many as second to KES as the "leading" LEA maintained school in the country) resigned his position and took on the Liverpool Labour Council in a public dog fight. He gave considerable prestige to their campaign because he was seen as the official voice of the school. Yet there is no evidence that Clapton played any real part in the uproar that was to come in the next few months. It is clear that he was desperately disappointed that the school he had helped to advance to new successes, was likely to be dismantled and replaced by an unselective school, no better, or no worse, than its peers in the area. He was, however, a sick man lying in hospital and could not play an active role. When he did resign in the summer of 1965, he only cited health grounds and made no gesture of defiance against the Labour controlled council. Arthur Jackson, the acting Headmaster, was placed in a very difficult position. He could not speak for the Headmaster and he could not take an independent leading position himself, so he played a dead straight bat to all the controversies that surrounded the school during the first half of 1965 and advised the staff to do the same.

The staff were almost entirely against the concept of comprehensive education. Some felt a change of function for KES was a personal *"breach of faith"* by the Education Committee. They reasoned that they had accepted the council's contract to teach boys of high ability in a top performing grammar school. Now they feared they would be asked to teach mixed ability children, and even worse go into a pool of teachers and be re-deployed to any secondary school in the city. Three scientists were amongst the leaders of the opposition in the staff room. Edgar Vernon, the Chairman of the Staff Room Committee (SRC), called a number of meetings in the next few weeks to review the situation, and it was his role to voice the opinions of the group. He made it clear that he would leave if the school went comprehensive, and several others claimed they would do likewise. George Mackay, who was another strongly against change, said in a full page newspaper article in the Star devoted to the views of KES staff; *" I have never wanted to teach anywhere else. It has been the ultimate pleasure to teach very intelligent boys and make them think for themselves. We cannot be humble, the teaching here is of the highest quality."* Dr. Bernard Knowles felt the secondary modern schools had not been a failure, and that the council should be putting more resources into them, enabling their children to take and pass "O" Level and then move on to the grammar school sixth forms. He was not alone amongst the staff members in believing that the so-called social evils of the tripartite system had been overestimated; that segregation happened in all walks of life and would in comprehensive schools. One master added, " *A future Balliol scholar would never mix with someone who couldn't read or write.*"

Some members of the council particularly incensed the staff. Alderman Sydney Dyson, for over forty years the resident bully on the City Council, had declared. "*I am not proud of King Teds, it is just a sweat shop*", and this had moved Jackson to break his silence and defend the school's tradition of a balanced education that also strove for academic excellence. However the councillor who really was anathema to the staff was the new Deputy Chairman of Education, Christopher Price. He had been the driving force on the Education Committee for change, after the Group had appointed him as Ballard's Deputy in 1963.

(This was a departure from Labour's practice, because Price was a West Riding C.C. teacher —Senior Classics Master at Ecclesfield G.S. — and the Group believed it was inappropriate to have the staff of other authorities on the committee, whilst their own teachers, of course, were forbidden by electoral law to even serve on the council. Their opponents claimed that this rubric was introduced so that no one who might have any understanding of education, would be involved in education committee business)

The 77 year old Ballard, who had left school at 13, and educated himself through the Co-op Movement , was the sort of Labour Councillor KES staff expected to deal with. Ballard was no-body's fool, but now they were faced by one of their own. It wasn't

Alderman Dr. Albert Ballard CBE photographed in his mayoral year

enough that Price was a grammar school teacher trying to abolish the grammar schools, he was also formerly at Queen's College, Oxford, exactly the sort of chap who might have been appointed to KES staff himself. Price, along with Peter Horton, who was not then on the Education Committee, were capable of answering any intellectual challenge that was mounted by the staff or by the parents, and when Price dared to utter the ultimate heresy "*That it was not necessary to send pupils to Oxbridge any more*", the staff room reaction was incredulity, derision and anxiety. If schools could be comprehensive, then all the expanding number of universities might achieve parity as well. Even if this didn't happen and Oxford and Cambridge retained their leading position and status, Price was articulating the view, that a whole city's education system could not be so organised for the principal purpose of sending twenty-five boys a year, from one of its schools, to Oxbridge.

Through their Union, the Assistant Masters Association, the KES staff tried to enter into a dialogue with the council to avert the comprehensive school scheme for the south west. Initially they expected that a reasonable solution would be found that would preserve the high performing grammar schools and run them parallel to the comprehensive schools in their area. Julius "Joe" Oppenheimer, the school librarian and languages master, was the press officer of the AMA in Sheffield but he soon found out that his union, which represented the male grammar school teachers, was largely frozen out of any discussions. Price had gained support from the Sheffield Teachers' Association (NUT), the Sheffield Schoolmasters' Association (NAS) and the Sheffield Headteachers' Association (representing Primary and Secondary Modern Heads) and their combined memberships formed the vast bulk of Sheffield's 2500 teachers. The KES staff were furious that they were virtually without a voice in the corridors of influence. One

Councillor C. PRICE.

Coun. Christopher Price, the 33 year old Deputy Chairman of the Education Committee (1963–66). Elected to Parliament for Birmingham Perry Barr in 1966, he was, ironically, related to "Toby" Saville, the founder of Lynwood House and KES staff member 1905-41.

staff member was reported in the Star as saying; "*It is as though in building a hospital you asked the advice of the porters rather than the specialists*", but they were beginning to realise that they had been outflanked. There were still many people in the city, even Labour voters, who, recognising the achievements of KES, High Storrs G.S. and Abbeydale G.S. were not certain about this leap in the dark into comprehensives, but it was developing an air of inevitability and, as in 1945, KES's demand for special treatment for an élite institution was falling on deaf ears.

Even inside the school not all were opposed to the change. A few staff members — Keith Robinson was one — were prepared to "consider" the change when they knew more information about the details. However, Robinson left in 1965 to take up a post at Jordanhill College, Glasgow. He later became a director of the Curriculum Council of Scotland and the Chairman, subsequently President, of the Economics Association.

Among the boys at the school there were quite a few who supported comprehensive education. One anonymous prefect, when interviewed by the Star, said, "*I know the masters are very worried, but we don't know what comprehensive schools will be like. I think both systems are evenly matched. If a bright lad wants to work he'll get on wherever he is*". Whilst another said "*I don't think it will be a disaster if KES closed. In this country anything out of the ordinary becomes a sort of legend. Add tradition and it becomes sacred*". Most boys, however, were not in favour of the changes although for many, as in 1944-45, the confrontation went over their heads. Many would agree with the senior boy who felt "*they did not like being experimented with*", whilst many knew it would not affect them personally because the changes seemed far into the future. Some boys, however, were very much involved in the campaign to save King Edward VII School, because their parents were active in the campaign that had its beginnings at a meeting in the Quaker Meeting House, Hartshead, on 14th January 1965.

Celebrating the Diamond Jubilee?

It was the reports of a one hour discussion on comprehensive education at the January Council Meeting, that suddenly alarmed supporters of the school that the Labour Council meant business and intended to introduce a scheme for the south and west of the city. The Sheffield Morning Telegraph had raised the spectre of the demise of KES as a grammar school in June of the previous year, but as it now rather peevishly said, no-one had seemed very interested at that time. They were now! Co-incidently on the same night as the Council debate, the Star published a letter from a Dr. Malcolm McCaig and his wife Dr. Phyllis McCaig who had two sons at KES and one at Silverdale. They were to be the leading figures in the campaign to save the school during the spring and summer of 1965. In their letter they called for a meeting to be held with a view to mounting opposition to the council's plans and their call was taken up by 60 people who met a week later in the Quaker Meeting House.

It was a very productive meeting and by the end they had elected a committee and sketched out a strategy to mount a campaign. They appreciated that, although almost all those present were KES parents, plus a few staff and Old Edwardian representatives, they would have to make a wider appeal to supporters of all the grammar schools, and to this end they named their new group, *The Sheffield Parents' Association for Secondary Education.* They also made it clear that they supported the continuation and improvement of the secondary modern schools, whilst not necessarily being against the existing comprehensive schools in the north of the city. These schools, they felt, could serve as a pilot to see if the new system could be sustained and achieve adequate standards, before being "prematurely" forced on the rest of the city to the detriment of grammar schools of proven worth like KES.

Dr. McCaig, a research physicist from Ringinglow became the Chairman, Mrs. Joyce Fowler, a former policewoman, became Secretary and another parent, Albert Main from Gleadless, who had already had letters in the Star defending KES, became the Press Officer. Their campaign followed the classic pressure group lines.

- They would try the frontal assault of lobbying councillors and M.P.'s.
- They would raise a huge petition. They aimed for 45,000 signatures to show the Council the strength of their support.
- In early February they would hold a large rally at the City Hall to start the petition and rally press and public support.
- They would link up with protest movements in Liverpool and Bristol and any other cities where there were similar concerns and opposition.
- They would mount a sustained letter writing campaign to the Star and the Sheffield Morning Telegraph.
- They would keep contact with the KES Staff and the Old Edwardians' Association and any supportive groups at the other Sheffield grammar schools.

In practice winning support from the councillors and the M.P.s meant getting help from the Conservatives. Although Labour councillors could be door-stopped and their arguments refuted, the Labour Group was now united in favour of comprehensives. Moreover, in those class conscious times, they perceived the Parents' Association as just a group of middle class KES parents living in the south west of the city, where all the seats were held by the Conservatives. The parents got more response from the Tories but they were of uncertain help. The Conservative Group on the City Council was divided about its attitude to the changes. Most wanted to keep some grammar schools, but even in their own wards they were aware that the majority of children went to secondary modern schools and their parents were not averse to the comprehensive idea. The local M.P. John Osborn was of more help. His position reflected the real view of most of his local party colleagues and voters. *"We are not against comprehensive schools as such"* he pronounced at a party meeting, *"but we want to keep the good grammar schools."* Everyone in the audience knew he meant KES, High Storrs and Abbeydale. One irreverent member of the audience asked him to name the "bad" grammar schools in Sheffield, and was promptly asked to leave.

Ignore its worth	*Not a word to a soul,*	*Slip in the knife,*
It's of Royal birth,	*No time for a poll,*	*Reach for its soul*
Level down,	*They might be apprehensive,*	*Something must die*
Quietly does it.	*At something comprehensive*	*For a doctrinaire lie*
Quietly does it.	*Quietly does it.*	*Quietly does it.*

Poem by G.W.P. in the press. Jan. 1965

However, helpful or uncertain, the Tories were out of power in Westminster as well as in Sheffield and they could not alter decisions in the short term. An appeal to the Liberals was even more pointless, because they had not had any council members for many years and scarcely troubled the political scene in the city at that time. The committee wanted the Headmaster to join them but he declined, although staff members kept in touch and voiced their support privately. They felt constrained to be seen publicly opposing their employing authority, although 38 of them (out of 44) did sign a letter to Star objecting to the failure of the council to have had any consultation with them whatsoever. One member, Ralph Braunholz, whilst supporting the need for the widest possible discussion and consultation did also write, perhaps rather bravely, and declare his support for comprehensive education in principle.

The McCaigs and Albert Main indefatigably bombarded the two local papers with letters defending the school. The McCaigs drew from their own family experience, to argue how a boy of reasonable ability will do well at a good secondary modern school, rather than be de-motivated by brighter boys in a grammar school. They challenged statistical evidence on comprehensive schools' progress put forward by no less an authority than Robin Pedley of Exeter University himself. Dr. Pedley was the "Guru" of the new system and he was known to have had a considerable influence on some of the younger Labour councillors who were driving the changes through the council. Main, as press officer, was equally active, firing off letters himself and encouraging sympathetic supporters to add their two pennyworths. One letter came from the retired former Senior Master, Sydney Carter, who, with some prescience, noted.

> *"KES appears to be faced every 20 years with a major cycle of change at the whim of the council. This cycle takes us to "1984" and then what policies will be enforced?"*

Old Edwardians wrote in from Oxford, Durham and other universities, one even from NSW, in Australia, but they were not all sympathetic to the cause and not a few supported comprehensive status for KES. The Sheffield Morning Telegraph, under its Old Edwardian editor Michael J. Finley, was an ardent supporter of keeping the grammar schools, whilst the Labour councillors felt the Star, which had a far larger readership, was more balanced with a series of very lucid articles by their Education Correspondent, Byron Rogers, which gave all sides a fair chance to put their arguments across. Throughout the Spring the volume of letters in both papers on this issue was quite remarkable, and when it appeared to plateau a new twist in the story resurrected interest.

That Letter

The parents' campaign was in danger of being temporarily derailed by the Headmaster's reaction to the letter, supporting comprehensive education, sent to the Star in late January by thirteen Sixth Form boys. Although the Star withheld the names, they soon came out and, when two were found to be prefects, Clapton's wrath descended on their heads and they were publicly sacked from office. One was a leading school sportsman. Ian Batty was currently the Football XI's leading goal scorer, and the previous season he had scored 27 goals and been the Champion Athlete, the other was Peter Woodhouse, who had been a Prefect for a longer period than Batty but was equally resentful of the charge;

"that their conduct was prejudicial to the good name of the school." Batty's father was unimpressed and demanded a full explanation and re-instatement, for what he considered a thoughtful letter, welcoming new possibilities but not *per se* criticising KES. There were many in the school, and in the city, that thought the same. Letters came flying in from all quarters condemning the Headmaster's action as a denial of free speech and the antithesis of an enquiring sixth form education. Whilst many were reluctant to write and challenge KES's academic record (an AMA survey of Oxbridge Open Scholarships from 1959-64 put the school in seventh position in the country, with their 73 Awards making them the top LEA school by many a mile), they were only too pleased to catch "King Ted's" with its metaphorical pants down. Old Edwardians wrote in from Universities to condemn the Headmaster, and many enjoyed the *schadenfreude,* as KES wriggled to minimise its embarrassment.

Dear Editor   *25 January 1965*

So far all the letters from parents and students at King Edward VII School, or from students themselves, seem to support the retention of the present educational system. This creates a false impression, because many of those immediately concerned are in favour of the comprehensive system.

The present system of deciding the form of a child's secondary education, by means of the 11+ examination, has two indefensible faults. Firstly the examination tends to measure the quality of a child's primary education and his social background, rather than his intelligence; King Edward's now receives a few pupils who do make the grade as a result of cramming at private schools.

Secondly the decision to send a child to grammar or secondary modern school is an irreversible one. If a child's intelligence improves it is extremely difficult for him to move to a higher level of education than that to which he was apparently suited at the age of 11. Supporters of the grammar schools seem to care little for the abandonment of the greater number of pupils who are sent to secondary modern schools.

Because of these faults the grammar school system must be replaced by a comprehensive one, in which everyone has a fair and equal chance, and King Edward's should be fully absorbed into this system because the changeover must be complete if it is to be successful.

The end of King Edward VII School in its present form, will mean the end of a long tradition, nothing else, and tradition must always take second place to progress and improvement.

Thirteen names
(They included; I.Batty, P.Woodhouse, P.Bradley, P.Cooper, R.Barker, I.Hogg, A.M.Dungworth, R.W. Flint, I.S. White, A. Pressby, A.E.Vaughan.)

Nine of the boys, excluding the two prefects, wrote a second letter in February to challenge claims that up to a hundred Sheffield pupils between the ages of 12-16, were currently moving up to grammar schools every year. They claimed they knew of no boy at KES who had left to go to a technical school, or of any secondary modern boy who had come to KES. This was the final letter on the subject in the Star for the moment, because the Editor closed the correspondence on the subject after such an avalanche of mail.

The big public meeting was held on 25th February in the Memorial Hall at the City Hall. It attracted two hundred people and the hall was packed, with the "World in Action" TV programme filming the event. The Parents' Association leaders spoke first, deploring the fact that the Labour Group had not seen fit to send Ballard, Price or another spokesman to address the meeting (they particularly felt betrayed by Ballard whom they had seen so often at Speech Days extolling the school's successes). Their main speaker was the Headmaster of the Liverpool Institute, Malcolm Smith, who had announced his resignation over turning his famous school into a comprehensive. Liverpool Institute was one of two high performing grammar schools in that city, and was already famous outside teaching circles as the place where the education of two Beatles (McCartney and Harrison) had been nurtured. Smith pulled no punches and warned that comprehensive "neighbourhood" schools would become ghettoes for socially deprived children of the working class, and comprehensives would only work in areas where *"they were allowed to grow fat on the carcasses of the dead grammar schools. They needed our children as a sort of educational fertilizer".* He went on to call for comprehensives and grammar schools to co-exist, a theme which played well with some of his audience, whilst others wanted resources put into secondary modern schools to raise their standards. Speakers in the hall picked up the theme that KES served all classes of people from all parts of the city, while comprehensives might very well be socially divisive between one area of the city and another.

As parents entered the hall, they passed a demonstration of 20 school children carrying banners supporting comprehensive education, saying "End Education Apartheid". Most were from Hinde House School, but at least one was a member of the KES 13 and he was unrepentant when interviewed by the press. Inside the hall a teacher from Hinde House challenged the speakers by defending comprehensive education, claiming that grammar schools took the cream of the talent and therefore had to go. He was shouted down by the audience, who were very largely KES parents and seemed uninterested in his viewpoint.

McCaig, in launching the petition, outlined the committee's alternative scheme for Sheffield. Parents could decide whether or not their children should take the 11+, there would be no compulsion, but all secondary moderns should have a GCE stream, so that they were in effect comprehensives and at 16 the children should move easily into an existing sixth form with whom the school had an arrangement. Those who opted to take the 11+, could go to grammar schools if they passed. However, if most parents in the future bypassed the 11+ and their children opted for "comprehensives", thereby creating little demand for grammar schools, and those schools could organically, over time, evolve into sixth form colleges.

In the next few weeks the Parents' Association busied itself with raising its petition and it was pretty successful. By the key debate in the Council Chamber in early April they had raised 15,000 signatures, and by the summer the number had risen to 20,000. Someone on the staff reminded the Association that this year, 1965, was the school's Diamond Jubilee and that a successful outcome to their campaign to save King Edward VII School as a grammar school would be a fitting celebration. When the Council finally received the petition, they referred it to the appropriate committee and then ignored it, as they did with all petitions that opposed agreed policy.

The Deed is done

The scheme for the re-organisation of secondary education in the south and west of Sheffield was finally debated at the Council Meeting of 7th April 1965. Under the plan there were to be seven 13-18 comprehensive secondary schools in the southern half of the city.

Abbeydale Grange (Boys and Girls)   High Storrs (Boys and Girls)
Newfield   Rowlinson
KES (Boys only)   King Ecbert

And finally the new school, now being built and known as Tapton II, would become a girls' comprehensive to complement KES boys' school.

Previously it had been assumed that this new building would serve an enlarged Tapton School, but under the new plan Tapton was to be an 11-13 high school along with Silverdale, Jordanthorpe and Gleadless.

In the immediate future Tapton II would be renamed Crosspool Secondary and take boys and girls from Western Road Secondary Modern School in Crookes, a school which was scheduled to be closed in July 1965, and the buildings wholly used for primary education and possibly for a middle school in the future.

The Conservatives, who had been strongly criticised in an editorial in the Sheffield Telegraph for their ineffective, indecisive, opposition to comprehensive education, launched a fierce attack on the proposals during a four and a half hour debate. Labour, secure behind an overwhelming majority, pointed out equally forcibly that despite all the "Tory" clamour and smart rhetoric they could produce no clear alternatives of their own. The Conservatives problem was that they were split on their attitude to comprehensive education. A minority of their members supported the thrust of Labour's policy. They knew that most parents, even in the "highlands" of south west Sheffield, were not averse to abolishing the 11+ examination, especially if they had suffered the "social stigma" of their child going to a secondary modern school, or worse if they had a divided family where one child went to grammar school and another did not. The Labour Group on the other hand were now 100 % behind the proposals and for once had a clear sense of purpose and direction. Coun. Peter Jackson, the shadow Conservative Education "Chairman", decide that the only tactic they could employ to unify their group was to move "reference back" of the whole Labour scheme. "Reference back" is local government speak for abandoning a proposal and sticking with the status quo, at least for a considerable period of time until a more acceptable way forward is found. Jackson, an elegant debater and a well known local solicitor, confined himself in his hour long speech to exacting the maximum embarrassment to Labour by dissecting the elements of the scheme which were still half formulated. He homed in on the areas of costs, building availability, the two year high schools concocted ahead of the Plowden Report (which was certain to introduce four year middle schools) and the re-ordering of financial priorities to the disadvantage of primary education. He finished by slipping in a low blow;

> "Why is Ald. Ballard now telling us that the system of education in this city is ineffective when for so long he has been saying it was par excellence?"

His father, the 83-year-old warhorse, Ald. Sir Harold Jackson, weighed in with a much more basic criticism of the whole theory of comprehensive education. He defended the tripartite system and, as on so many occasions in the last forty years, this former Wesley College pupil, defended KES against the "socialists" whose reforms always seemed to him to be inimical to the interests of the school. Labour, for their part, argued their case against all the points made, in a debate that neutral observers regarded as one of the best ever in the Council Chamber. Some claimed to see the bigger picture, where not only could futures be decided at 11, but where 81% of British schoolchildren left school at 15 years of age, whereas in the USA 80% stayed on till the end of high school at 18. They were looking to create real education opportunities for all the young people in the city and they looked forward to another "revolution" in the classroom, as teaching standards were raised and teaching methods became more imaginative and interesting. Ballard, speaking specifically about KES, said,

> "the school will not be destroyed, it will be enlarged. Melbourne Annexe will be vacated by the College of Commerce and the Annexe will be used by King Edward's. There is no reason why King Edward's should not be a very successful comprehensive school and it had an important part to play in the new education scheme."

When the Conservative amendment to refer the scheme back was put to the vote it was predictably lost by 48-17, and it now appeared certain that all Sheffield's LEA secondary schools would be comprehensive within six years.

Nothing personal, but we don't want you!

In early September 1965 the Education Committee appointed Russell Sharrock as the new Headteacher of KES. The full fury of the disappointed parents was now turned onto this 41 year old teacher who was currently the Deputy Head at Malory Comprehensive School in south east London. Infuriated that the Labour dominated committee had, not unreasonably, chosen a man who supported comprehensive education and who had direct experience running one of the relatively few comprehensive schools in the country, they believed that this appointment was the crucial nail in the coffin of KES as a grammar school. Even before the Secretary of State had finally approved the Sheffield scheme for the south and west of the city, they feared that the council was ensuring comprehensive education was a fait accompli by Sharrock's appointment, and also a little later by that of Tim Mardell, as the new Headteacher of High Storrs.

The Sheffield Parents for Secondary Education sent a letter to the Education Committee on the day of their September meeting, when they would be confirming Sharrock's appointment. They outlined their objections to his appointment and sent a copy to Sharrock with an extraordinary covering letter.

> "This Association's objection to your appointment was not intended to reflect on your personal qualities, but is part of our general opposition to the LEA's proposals for the re-organisation of secondary education in Sheffield. We feel you should be made aware of the opposition to these proposals and of the controversy that your own appointment has aroused."

The letter went on to say;

> "Indeed we have already been pressed by parents of boys at the school to convene a meeting of the Association to discuss the question of your appointment, and the possible dilution of academic standards that may ensue. We cannot help but feel that you will be a pawn - albeit unwillingly - in a political game."

Finally the letter added;

> "We trust that you will accept that this letter is not written in any spirit of personal animosity, but because we feel that it is only right that your attention should be drawn to the controversy in Sheffield of which you may well be unaware; no doubt however, if you seek further confirmation the local press will oblige."

If Sharrock was not aware of the ill feeling in Sheffield — he was now! He must very well have wondered what he had let himself in for. So he was pleased that the Star newspaper sent a reporter down to London to interview him at Malory School, thereby giving him the opportunity to start to defuse the anger and set some part of the record straight. The reporter soon found that the "ogre" was a benign and charming man with many years teaching experience in a very wide range of schools. No one on the staff at KES could match Russell Sharrock's teaching C.V., which included time spent in a secondary modern school, an HMC direct grant school, two LEA grammar schools and since 1962 his current position at a new, purpose built comprehensive school in Lewisham L.B, which had opened in 1958. Situated on a tough "overspill" housing estate that had taken people from Bermondsey, with two grammar schools in the area creaming off many of the brightest pupils, the reporter expected to find a co-educational St. Trinians. Instead, at the 1400 pupil school, he was struck by the quiet, calm atmosphere and the orderliness of the boys and the girls. There were uniforms, streaming and eight houses. The first batch of "A" level results had been most encouraging with 37 sixth formers, half of whom had failed their 11+ examinations, gaining a hundred passes. 37% of these passes had been at A or B grade and for those who took "O" level, seven passes was the average. The school operated a "tripartite" system within the same school with pupils graded according to their ability, but with great emphasis on children moving between levels when their "late development" or progress merited it.

Sharrock was calm in the face of the furore his appointment had caused back in South Yorkshire.

"I wish the parents in Sheffield could come down and look around here - it would really open their eyes. I understand how they feel - I used to share the same views myself. I went to a grammar school and taught in them for 13 years. When I get to Sheffield I shall run a grammar school for the first four years and then when the school goes comprehensive, I shall run a grammar school within a comprehensive for those pupils who can benefit from that kind of academic education. I know that this is what the Education Committee want to be done, to maintain the school's tradition of scholarships to Oxford and Cambridge and I hope that most of the staff will stay in order to make this possible."

Although Sharrock did not arrive at the school until January 1966, he had thrown down an olive branch to any hostile staff and parents. When he finally arrived at the school he took no time in reinforcing the same message of his vision of the kind of comprehensive school he wanted KES to become. The parents, who opposed his appointment, might have been further reassured if they had known that he had ruled himself out of one Headteacher's post in Crawley, when he refused to accept that the staff could be on first name terms with the pupils and that casual clothes would be worn in the school. He had also been offered the headship of one of his former schools, Sir Walton St. John in Battersea, where he had been Head of the Maths Department between 1958-62, and had an interview pending for the Headteacher's post at Shoreditch School, when somewhat to his surprise he was offered the KES position.

Like Clapton, he came from a modest social background and was a product of the local grammar school. He was a northerner whose sporting passion was Rugby League – he had grown up watching the great Wigan teams of the Thirties and Forties — and he was the first Headteacher at KES to be a graduate of a university other than Oxford or Cambridge. He had started a wartime degree in 1942 at Liverpool University reading Physics, but had broken off his studies to go as a research scientist at R.A.E. Farnborough during the years 1943-46. When he returned to Liverpool he changed his subject and eventually graduated in Mathematics. Some years later when teaching in the capital he took an external M.Sc. in the same subject, undertaking the three nights a week slog after school at Sir John Cass College, a far cry from the cloisters and ivy covered walls of Oxbridge. There were some on the staff at KES, where half the staff were still Oxbridge graduates, who were a bit sniffy about such matters, but Sharrock made it clear that KES was still in the business of getting as many pupils as possible into Oxbridge, and for the next decade or so the school was still chalking up the scholarship successes, even though they were no longer posted on the tall honours boards which remain frozen in time at 1965.

We won't stay and we won't wait!

Whilst Sharrock hoped that most of the staff would stay and share his vision of the new KES as a very successful comprehensive school, many of the 44 assistant masters were busily scanning the Times Educational Supplement to find a way out. By the time KES became a comprehensive school in September 1969, nine of the fifteen heads of departments had gone, and half the staff who were at the school in Clapton's last term in 1965, had left as well. The opponents of comprehensive education, both on the staff and among the parents, had forecast such an exodus and it is certain that the demise of the grammar school created itchy feet among many masters, some of whom would otherwise have been willing to see out their teaching days at KES.

Those who had been most outspoken against the " enforced" changes were among the first to leave, but KES had always had a large turnover of staff and almost every year during Clapton's time at least 10% of the staff gained new posts, often being promoted to head of department, or even to headships. So over the four years, 1965-69, the turnover was not all that much higher than previously, but there was now a restlessness in the staff room and KES teachers who sought interviews found that they were as much in demand as they had always been. If they applied for posts at other schools, they invariably gained an interview and in many cases they subsequently landed the position. Those remaining probably felt that if they were to leave it would be better sooner rather than later, because the number of grammar school posts was reducing all the time as more and more LEAs introduced comprehensive education.

Almost all staff leavers, who continued in secondary education, went to grammar schools, but increasingly a number of experienced masters were appointed to posts in university education departments, or in technical or F.E. colleges. Among the latter was Tom Cook, the Senior History Master since 1955, the Housemaster of Wentworth, Group Scoutmaster and the organiser of "Cook's tours" for members of the Junior Historical Society. He became a Lecturer in History at the University of Cambridge's Institute of Education at the beginning of 1966, whilst George Mackay, another Scot, who had been a forceful opponent of the council's plans, obtained a post in the Education Department of Sheffield University. He had been the Senior Science Master at the school since 1951; small of stature he radiated a big personality whose enthusiasms, which included at one time growing his own tobacco in the science prep room, were infectious and whose observations, regularly given, were invariably worth listening to. At one stage in his career at the school he had taught the Sixth Form for a whole week whilst wearing a bowler hat; the reasons for this decision now lost in the mists of time. "Joe" Oppenheimer left at the same time in the summer of 1966 and also went into higher education at Madeley College of Education, where he became Head of German. JO had been at the school for eighteen years and for almost all that time he had run the school library, as well as playing a fighting role in the AMA's campaign against abolishing the grammar schools. Alan Surguy, lately Housemaster of Chatsworth and the Head of Handicraft, who had built up an effective department since his arrival at the school in 1951, was seconded to the Institute of Education at Nottingham University, and although he was still on the school's establishment, he never returned to KES.

Seven leavers July 1966
Back Row (L to R) Messrs. Styring, Wild;
Front Row (L to R) Messrs. Slattery, Mackay, Oppenheimer, Surguy; Anderson.

The saddest departures were caused by the deaths of Clarence Helliwell in 1966 and Bert Harrison in 1967. Helliwell was the last master on the staff who had taught at the school before the war. Arriving in January 1936, he completed thirty years at KES, if one includes his period in tanks in the 8th Army in the North African desert during the war. Apart from his formal teaching, he would turn his hand to any job in the school that needed an artistic or practical touch and his stentorian voice singing hymns in assembly, or towering rages against malefactors that were soon replaced by gusts of laughter, marked him out as one of the school's most colourful characters. He lived in a house in the country, on whose gable end he had painted a very prominent bull, and at one time he was not averse to coming to school in a pony and trap if he felt the occasion warranted it. Shortly before his death in July he had taken a party down to the Royal Academy for a

Bonnard Exhibition and was even playing tennis with other staff members days before his death. Bert Harrison's death was quite unexpected by the staff and boys at the school. You don't expect the Head of P.E. to die of a heart attack at the age of 45, even though he himself had been concerned for his health because his father died at the same age in the same way. A keen rugby footballer himself, he had introduced the game to the school in 1951 and seen the teams grow in standard, one of them captained by his own son who was at the school. He had driven back to Sheffield from Spain in one long journey at the end of the summer holiday in 1967 and suffered a heart attack shortly after the start of term. It was a second heart attack that killed him in late September. At his funeral six of his colleagues acted as pall-bearers with the new Headmaster, for the second time in a year, leading the mourners.

Clarence Helliwell   *Bert Harrison*   *H.T.R. Twyford*

A little earlier another of the school's biggest personalities had left the stage. When he retired in December 1965, having reached his 65th birthday, Hector Thomas Rowley Twyford (H.T.R.T. to the school), was the longest serving member of staff having initially arrived as a supply teacher in the Spring of 1935. After that temporary appointment, he was invited back by Richard Graham to be a Form Teacher in the Junior School and teach maths. One of the first to join the forces on the very first day of the war in September 1939, he missed six years through service in the RAF, and on his return found himself propelled into the short term post of Head of the Junior School as it was run down. He then taught French and Maths in the "Senior" school for the next eighteen years, taking on the duties of Housemaster of Lynwood and being the corporeal spirit of Thursday afternoon games, refereeing matches in an old raincoat and rarely straying from the centre circle. On the last day of term, the Acting Headmaster, Arthur Jackson, in handing H.T.R.T his scroll of long service from the Education Committee, said with deliberate irony, "You will leave a large empty space when you go, you are a School Institution!"

The Interregnum

Jackson was the Acting Headmaster for the whole of the Autumn term and appears to have rather relished the role, although he publicly ruled himself out as a candidate for the vacant post after Clapton's last minute resignation in the Summer. In truth he had been doing the job for most of the year, but now he was in charge and with the help of Walter Birkinshaw as his No.2 and Edgar Vernon, who assisted with the routine administration of the school, they got on with the business of educating the boys in their charge after all the excitement of the earlier part of the year. Whether the controversy over comprehensive education had unsettled the school a little, both the "A" Level results (only an 80% average pass rate) and an "O" Level pass rate down to 75% (the poorest since 1956), were well below the usual high KES standards. In paying tribute to the professionalism of his colleagues in a very difficult year, Jackson commented, in his very full report at the Distribution of Prizes (the title Speech Day had been dropped earlier in the decade) at the Victoria Hall in October;

> *"Many of the Staff are profoundly disturbed, and disturbed for the most worthy and honourable of reasons. Their deep concern for the School, their understandable concern for their own futures, produced a mood of disquiet and restlessness which, whilst restrained with great professional dignity, must have affected their work during the year. The undue attention of Press, Radio and Television was an interesting experience but not helpful to smooth concentrated effort"*

Ald. Ballard sat a few paces from him must have felt a certain frisson at the implied criticism of his party's actions. However, this was England and good manners prevailed throughout the evening and extraordinarily at the end of the proceedings, Sir Harold Jackson moved a vote of thanks to Ballard as Chairman of the Governors. Albert Ballard CBE, LLD, had entered the lion's den and then been thanked for his "efforts" on behalf of the school, not only by the Acting Headmaster in his report, but also by his long time political adversary who had opposed him tooth and nail on all the changes in secondary education in the recent years.

Arthur Jackson, who in recent years had acquired the nickname "Flink", wanted to hand over a fully functioning and supportive school to the new Headmaster. KES had never had more pupils, 800 at the last count with almost 330 in the Sixth Form. 76 of these had left to do degree courses at 20 different universities or colleges, with 24 boys gaining entrance at Oxbridge. Jackson pointed out that this last figure, still meant that over $\frac{1}{5}^{th}$ of all the year group who had entered in the First Forms had gone on to the two "Ancient" Universities. That figure now inevitably slowly declined, even, in fact, while the school was still a selective school and in 1969 the last year when KES was a grammar school, only 15 KES boys went to Oxbridge, even though the total number leaving for degree courses was higher (97 at 44 different universities and colleges).

Jackson's interregnum left two other permanent features on the school's landscape. He renamed the second year Sixth as the 7th Form, thereby avoiding much confusion, and re-introduced Parents' Evenings. There had been Open Days and Parents' Evenings as long ago as the Twenties in Hichens' time but they had not become a regular part of the school calendar as they are to-day. Now, one was held for Fourth Form parents to discuss future options for their sons, whilst the first one, held in late October, was for the parents of boys in the First and Second Forms giving them the opportunity to meet subject teachers and check up on the veracity of the tales they were sometimes spun at home. Jackson had a secondary purpose, which was to reassure parents of boys new to the school that, though battered and disappointed by the "political" events of the year, KES, in its Diamond Jubilee Year, was still very much the school it had always been, with a staff dedicated to maintaining the expected high standards of this grammar school. As if to underline what sort of institution KES was, some of the younger boys performed a play by Sophocles, further emphasizing that, for the moment at least, it was business as usual.

Continuing Staff departures

One member of staff who epitomised the professional manner in which the staff continued to do their work, whilst at the same time making their own personal arrangements to leave, was Edgar Vernon. He had led the Common Room Committee during the comprehensive controversy, delivering their collective opinion to the authorities and when necessary to the press. He had made no secret of the fact that he would leave rather than teach in the "new" KES and so, in 1968 after 23 years at the school, he accepted a post as a part time member of the Education Department at Sheffield University where he joined George Mackay, another "exile" from the Science Department. In his later years at the school Vernon had gained an M.Sc. for a particularly well researched thesis and ended up as the Head of Chemistry. He saw his role to reinforce professional attitudes amongst staff members, and one younger member of staff remembers that when some criticism by him of the new headmaster seeped back into the school, Vernon hauled him over the coals for his unprofessional attitude.

Most of those who left the KES staff sought out, and were appointed to grammar school posts. John Pickup, who had been teaching Classics since 1963 moved to Manchester G.S. in 1965, but was most tragically killed in a climbing accident in the Lake District four years later. John Anderson became the Head of History at Queen Mary's G.S., Walsall, in 1966, and Mike Wild became Head of Biology at Lady Manners School at Bakewell. Two other scientists, Keith Bridgwater who had been at the school for ten years, left in 1967 to go to Churcher's College in Hampshire, and in the same year John Fordham, the Head of Biology took on a similar role at Yeovil School. Other staff who left and became heads of department at grammar schools, included Ian Cook who became the Senior English Master at Blandford School, and Malcolm Earl who accepted the post of Senior Maths Master at Skipton G.S. Finally, in KES's last term as a grammar school in 1969, Dr. Bernard Knowles left to become the Deputy Head of Batley G.S. where he remained for the rest of his teaching career, playing a key role in Yorkshire Schoolboy Cricket amongst his other interests. Meanwhile, Gerald Taylor , the Head of Classics, was appointed to the Deputy Headship at Bishop Wordsworth G.S., Salisbury, subsequently becoming the Headmaster of Skinner's School in Tunbridge Wells.

He was replaced as Head of Classics by Arthur Jones and new staff, who came to fill the vacant posts, would in time make just as large, if not larger, contribution to the life and teaching of the school. David Anderson, an Old Edwardian himself, arrived from Dronfield Henry Fanshawe School in September of 1967 to Head the Economics Department, after Trevor Nuttall moved on after two years service at KES. Anderson would, however, become one of the most respected members of staff and, like other new arrivals who would stake out their place in the history of KES, be eventually counted with the "legends" of the past. Sharrock, in 1966, also appointed the first woman to the staff for over two decades when Mrs. J. M. White, a Durham graduate, came to the school to teach French. Although she didn't stay long, her arrival signalled the end of the all-male staff that had prevailed since Jean Knight had left in 1952. Another unusual appointment was the arrival of Bruce Canning from Toronto, initially to fill in as P.E. master after the untimely death of Bert Harrison, until he was offered a permanent position in the English Department. Apart from introducing volleyball to the school and relating tales of teaching experience in Canadian and U.S. High Schools, he was horrified at the lack of equipment and facilities in British schools especially the Gym, once described as resembling a dungeon. He was used to a High School having two or three large sports halls and commented, when he saw the gym for the first time;

> *"I stood for ten or fifteen minutes trying to visualise how I was going to put a class in there and what I could do with them".*

He also could not quite grasp why British Rail could not keep their trains on time for such "short" journeys, or why the GPO had waiting lists for new telephone subscribers.

Staff Leavers 1967
(L to R) Wrigley, Vernon, Mrs. White, Scobie, Nuttall.

The reasons why some staff moved on, while others stayed were, as always, varied. J.A. Reaney, another Old Edwardian on the staff, left in 1965 to teach Physics in Nigeria, whilst Ralph Braunholtz, after revamping the school magazine, left to work for Oxfam. Bill Scobie, W.D.L.S. to all, took up a new post as Liberal Studies Lecturer at Liverpool Regional College of Art in 1967. He had only been at the school for five years, but he was one of the best-loved characters of that generation. Very much a larger than life character he came late to teaching after a career in the Civil Service, implausibly in the Income Tax Department, and his "Glaswegian" roar could terrify the indolent, as well as inspire and encourage his English classes. He involved himself in numerous aspects of the school life, taking on the Poetry Society, the Stamp Club, the Library and even launching an Origami Society. Most pupils, forty years on, however, remember best the daily excitement as another "W.D.L.S." tie of many hues was revealed to an anticipatory, if not wholly appreciative, school.

It's not over yet!

To those KES staff and parents who felt they had not been consulted over comprehensive re-organisation, Labour offered the old local government line – use the ballot box on Election Day. If this was the litmus test of the acceptability of the new comprehensive scheme, then Labour was vindicated by the 1965 and 1966 election results that saw their majority rise to 42 (71 Labour out of 100 seats on the Council), even though the popular vote was much closer. They had been having a changing of the guard themselves since the key decisions of April 1965. In 1966, Ald. Ron Ironmonger had become the new Leader of the Council, and a new Labour Group rule, pushed through by younger and more left wing councillors, barred Labour councillors who were over 75, from holding chairmanships of committees or other official positions. Amongst those displaced in this "coup" was Albert Ballard as Chairman of Education, and in 1967 he was replaced by Peter Horton, one of the keenest advocates of comprehensive education, who would hold this key position for 16 years until he retired in 1983.

Meanwhile Christopher Price, the man the KES staff regarded as the Svengali, or at least the Richelieu, behind the forthcoming demise of their grammar school, had been elected to Parliament for the Perry Barr constituency of Birmingham and was immediately snapped up by Tony Crosland as his PPS, because of his first hand knowledge of the issues and problems involving the introduction of LEA comprehensive schemes. He later became the Chairman of a Commons' Select Committee on Education and his interest in the strategic elements of education continue to this day. He never returned to live in Sheffield, although his sister, Helen Jackson, in due course became the M.P. for the Hillsborough Constituency.

Peter Horton soon found that he had new decisions to make. The Plowden Report came out in 1967 and recommended four year Middle Schools. Horton adopted this recommendation for Sheffield but decided on the 8-12 years option and then moved the whole timetable for comprehensive education forward by two years. Therefore, it was now intended that February 1968 would be the last time Sheffield pupils sat the 11+

Examination, and that the new comprehensive schools in the south and west of the city would begin operating with an unselected entry of pupils in September 1969. Although the education planners at Leopold St. worked overtime to create all the building and staffing changes, (one planner locked his door so that the Chairman couldn't pester him with numerous second thoughts and bright ideas) it became clear that it would be difficult to get all the Middle Schools up and running by September 1969. In the event most of the south west of the city did have a system of middle schools, while Silverdale, Tapton and Jordanthorpe now became 11 – 16 comprehensive schools, alongside the former grammar schools who continued with their sixth forms.

Horton's new plan created 35 comprehensive schools, and there was now a concern that some of them were too small to fully function as schools offering the necessary range of subjects at "O" level and CSE. The Education Committee asked the Chairman to look again at the options and he came up with a reduced formula of 31 secondary schools. Included in this reduction was a plan to amalgamate two schools in the west of the city that had been previously designated as single sex schools. In this somewhat belated, and exigent, manner the new mixed comprehensive school of KES and Crosspool was born, demonstrating once again to the staff and parents of both schools their inability to control events affecting their schools. Thomas Burnett, the Headteacher of Crosspool, had already seen the writing on the wall and resigned in the summer, and in January 1968 Russell Sharrock was named as the Headmaster-designate of the proposed new school.

The political bombshell came in May 1968 when the Conservatives won control of the City Council for the first time since 1932. The possibility of this amazing victory had been apparent since the previous year's election when Labour, after almost continuous control since 1926, had to rely on its majority of un-elected Aldermen to hang on to its control of the City Council. It wasn't the issue of comprehensive education that had caused this extraordinary situation but the dire unpopularity of the Wilson Government, especially amongst Labour voters, coupled with a rent rebate scheme which had turned every housing estate in Sheffield against its Labour Councillors. At the same time a considerable expansion of the city into Derbyshire and Parsons Cross, had necessitated "all out" elections rather than the "one third retiring" system that usually cushioned the party in power against any temporary electoral setbacks. In 1968 the "Tories" completed the rout, winning seats like Darnall, where Old Edwardian Michael Heath was successful, and brought onto the council an enthusiastic group of "Young Turks" who were going to show the "Socialists" and their jaded older colleagues just how to run a big city.

If KES staff and the Parents' Association believed the cavalry had arrived in the nick of time, they were to be sorely disappointed. Three years on from the heady days of early 1965, the comprehensive scheme had become accepted, if not virtually irreversible. It would have been easy enough for KES to have continued as a selective boys school, Russell Sharrock had, for two years, been running it as a grammar school pending the change in status, but elsewhere in the city the changes were far too advanced. Even a party with a clear resolution to reverse the old regime's decision would have found much professional, as well as general opposition, to such a policy. However, the Sheffield

Conservatives were still divided on the issue and Peter Jackson, now the Chairman of the Education Committee, was driven to distraction by the competing forces within his group, party and supporters. The Conservatives floated the idea that KES, High Storrs and Abbeydale might become sixth form colleges, thereby retaining a special academic status and dovetailing with the other schools in the comprehensive system that would all be 11-16 schools. The proposal had surfaced almost as afterthought in 1965 and been roundly condemned by all involved in the arguments at that time. It fared no better now, and in the new year, in Jackson's absence, the Deputy Chairman, Frank Adams, ironically an Old Edwardian himself and a supporter of comprehensive education, steered the Conservatives in the direction of accepting the Labour scheme with a little bit of tinkering at the edges. Parental choice was introduced as a sop to parents who feared they might have their children sent to local schools, which whilst equal in standard in theory, might not be so equal in practice.

Business as usual

The Conservative indecision on comprehensive education did not fester for too long. Totally against the trend of British politics, Labour won back control of the Council in May 1969 and the Conservatives fell from power, never to regain control again. Indeed, by the end of the century, they were well nigh wiped out as a party in the council chamber, as a resurgent Liberal Democrat Party gobbled up their seats and then ousted Labour for a while in 1999. In the six months before the 1969 Election, Labour stung by losing what they now considered their birthright, ran an amazing, and uncharacteristically energetic, campaign to win back their voters and mobilise them on Election Day. The Wilson Government, desperate for any good news, knighted Ironmonger, an honour usually given to civic leaders after years of public service. Sir Ron, who would soon justify his accolade and become one of the most respected Council Leaders in Sheffield's political history, now directed his Group, with a wafer thin majority and whipped as tight as any parliamentary party, to enthusiastically pick up their previous policies and put them back into action. Horton, returning as Chairman of Education, had under four months to complete the preparations for comprehensive education, if he was to meet the deadline of September 1969 as the vesting day.

He had four political decisions to make, and he needed the support of Adams and enough Conservatives to ensure smooth and speedy passage through committee and council.

Coun. Peter Horton Chair of the Education Committee 1967—83.

- To confirm that there would be no single sex comprehensives.
- All existing sixth forms (there were 13) would stay in place but there would be no others.
- Parental choice, desired by the Conservatives, was accepted and parents could make three choices of their preferred schools.
- All schools would have individual governors. The system set up in 1947 had been totally eroded and headteachers were treated in the bad old ways, hanging around in corridors waiting to make a perfunctory report on their school's progress.

Whilst KES expected Labour to put the comprehensive system back on track, staff had once again to come to terms with the prospect of being expected to travel over a mile, to take some of their forms in the buildings on Darwin Lane and also teach girls. While many boys at the school welcomed this latter change, there was much perusing of the TES by masters who, now, not only had to adjust to teaching pupils of a wide range of abilities, but who might be female as well!

As a final ritual all headteachers had to be confirmed in their new posts, for these were technically new schools. In an extraordinary hour and half, that must have seemed half cattle market, half old heads' reunion, thirty one headteachers trooped, one by one, into the offices in Leopold St. and were summarily appointed by the Chairman, Peter Horton, and Michael Harrison, the Chief Education Officer. When it was Russell Sharrock's turn he was offered the post of Headteacher of King Edward/Crosspool School and he accepted. Within seconds he was back in the corridor and someone else was getting the good news. Almost all existing postholders were re-appointed and the process, that now would be deemed to break every rule of personnel selection, went through without controversy.

CHAPTER SIXTEEN

THE FIVE SITE SAGA
(1969-1981)

Crosspool Secondary School's life was brief but quite a happy and successful one. For the start of the new term in September 1965 all the pupils, staff and movable equipment from Western Road Secondary School, moved up to the brand new buildings on Darwin Lane at Crosspool. Known as Tapton II during its period of construction, the new buildings might have been used for an enlarged Tapton School, but instead they became the home for this stopgap, co-educational, secondary modern school that always knew it had a very limited period of life. The plans for comprehensive education in the south-west of the city, published only a few months before its opening, marked Crosspool down to be a medium-sized girls-only comprehensive; then, when the plans were revised at the end of 1967, the staff found to their absolute consternation that they would be amalgamated with a boys' grammar school. Even more daunting was the realisation that the union would be with the nearest grammar school, the high-performing King Edward VII School a mile and a half down the road in Broomhill.

For the moment, in that first Autumn Term, all was novel and inspiring in the new school led by Tom Burnett, the veteran Headmaster from Western Rd. Burnett was very much a headmaster of the old school, formal, stern and imposing. He brought with him a small staff which included long-serving male teachers, like Norman Beatson and John North, both second world war returnees, with an equal number of women teachers, some of whom like Amy Perry had many years service at Western Rd. The pupils could not believe their luck. Here were modern facilities, all glass and light, with playing fields on two sides of a building that embodied all the current features of modern school architecture. Designed by the City Architect's Department it had two asymmetrical blocks at right angles to each other, linked by a bridge that housed some of the senior staff's rooms. Thought had gone into the design, with the communal areas of the assembly hall and the adjacent dining room creating a very useful space for major events when parents would be invited into the school for a play or a concert. Less than forty years on, its condition would so deteriorate that it was dismissed as *"a jerry-built construction of the Sixties glass and concrete era of public buildings"*, before suffering the final indignity of unceremonious demolition in 2001.

Crosspool never numbered more than 350 pupils, so they rattled around in a building designed for a third more. The fact that the corridors were rather narrow - some said a last minute economy measure during the construction to reduce the size of the buildings - didn't concern Burnett, whose first priority was to give the school its own identity and academic direction. He introduced a simple school uniform of grey clothes, white shirts and a plain red tie and this was enthusiastically accepted by his pupils, who were now introduced to courses leading to the new Certificate of Secondary Education (CSE), designed for aspirational secondary modern schools who wanted focus for their syllabus and paper qualifications for their pupils. Despite this, almost all of his pupils expected to leave at fifteen and get jobs in the local economy, and the advice they got from the school's careers teachers was very traditional, with boys directed into factories and offices and girls into the retail trade and nursing. To some extent the aspirations of the pupils were determined by their social background. Western Rd. School had served the still largely working class population of Crookes and Crookesmoor, but children from Lydgate Primary formed a significant number of Crosspool's intake and the new school probably was equally divided between working class and middle class children, as was the case with the new KES comprehensive school after 1969.

There were new teachers who started their teaching careers at Crosspool. One was Eileen Jepson, later Mrs. Langsley, who arrived at the school in that first term in 1965 to head up the Girls' P.E. Department. She recalls that as a secondary modern teacher one didn't apply to a particular school as a grammar school teacher would, you were instead appointed to the LEA and they sent you to a suitable vacancy. Eileen Jepson would go on to make a major contribution to girls' sport at Crosspool and KES, and other new young teachers included Sue Mappin, a former Wimbledon Junior Champion, who also stayed on when the school went comprehensive, before leaving in 1972 to pursue a professional career as a tennis player and represent Britain in the Wightman Cup.

Tom Burnett retired in 1967 when the plans for the combined comprehensive school were being formulated. He went down to live in Surrey, but like many long-serving teachers of that generation he died shortly afterwards in 1969. John North now took over as the Acting Headmaster, and it fell to him to steer a traumatised staff through the process of amalgamation with KES. Many of them were very unhappy at the prospect and several discreetly moved on before the new school started in 1969. Both Russell Sharrock and Arthur Jackson pay the highest compliment to "Jack" North for his co-operation and professionalism at this very difficult time. In a staff meeting at Crosspool, North spelt it out to a concerned staff familiar with a small 11-15 secondary modern intake of pupils. "*I don't like what is happening and you don't like it either, but we are going to make the best of it and we will make it work!*" he is reported as saying, and from then on the majority of the staff at Crosspool approached the new situation with a positive frame of mind.

For the ambitious staff member, the new comprehensive school might very well offer more opportunities for professional advancement than Crosspool ever could, although they all felt certain that all the head of department positions would go to existing KES graduate staff, whilst Crosspool teachers would become "second class citizens". One new teacher, who embraced the opportunities offered by the merger with KES, was Alan Powell. He had joined the Crosspool staff in September 1968, in the last year of the school's independent existence, and found himself the "de facto" Head of Boys P.E. as well as teaching History and English. After a distinguished teaching career of over 37 years, he is the only member of staff who taught at either school at that time, who is still in post in 2005.

Crosspool School
Became the KES Lower School from 1969-2001
From a 1966 painting by Ian Wasden, a pupil at Crosspool School

WESTERN ROAD SCHOOL 1901-1985

Western Road School, opened in May 1901, can claim along with the Royal Grammar School, the Collegiate School and Wesley College to be one of the parents, or grandparents, of the present day King Edward VII School. One of the last schools constructed by the old Sheffield School Board, it predated KES by four years and was built to serve the new and growing suburb on the north end of Crookesmoor. A substantial building of the traditional pattern, it had cost the School Board £15,000 to build, a third of the cost of the purchase and refurbishment of Wesley College in 1905, and it is still in use to-day a century later. When Jonathon Aitchison, the newly appointed Headteacher, started classes he had nine other members of staff; six women, all of course unmarried, and three men, with 447 pupils drawn from the local families of skilled working men, clerks and office workers. Until 1917, Western Rd. was a mixed elementary school, with pupils entering at five years of age in Standard I and leaving initially at twelve in Standard VII. For the first five years the boys and girls were taught in single sex classes before moving into mixed classes usually after Standard V, and they studied an impressively wide curriculum including Geography, History (which ended with the Hanoverians in Standard VII), Arithmetic and Mental Arithmetic, Domestic Economics for girls and Mechanics for boys, Science and BiblicalKnowledge. The latter was subject to an annual outside inspection and the inspecting official, usually a clergyman, had to write up his observations and conclusions in the school log. English language teaching was broken down into its constituent parts with classes spending whole lessons on spelling, recitation, writing and composition.

Because the syllabus did not necessarily appeal to all the pupils the school had a constant problem with truancy. On one day in July of their first year they had 112 pupils missing and the school log reports that; "parents are very apathetic in this matter." Nevertheless the school numbers quickly increased to their optimum of 700+ and Aitchison's staff increased to seventeen. In 1912 the school leaving age was raised to thirteen and a Standard VIII Class was created, and then, in 1917, the school was split with Standards V to VIII becoming a separate Senior Mixed County School, whilst the rest of the site at Western Rd. was re-designated as a Junior School.

If KES's great academic achievement for much of its history was gaining Oxbridge Scholarships, then Western Road School's equivalent was getting boys and girls to pass their scholarships to grammar school. Before the First World War this meant passing to gain a free exhibition at the Central School and in 1907 twenty-one 11 year old pupils in Standard VI were successful and went off to Leopold St. to the Central Boys' or the Central Girls' Schools. This was about the average pass rate for the school and placed Western Rd. amongst the more successful schools in the city. The first boy to win a scholarship to KES, who only offered local elementary schoolchildren about five per annum, was ten year old Herbert Hodges, who later, when only sixteen, won an Open Classics Scholarship to Balliol, thereafter becoming a very young Professor at the new University of Reading in the early Thirties. He was followed by two other boys, who won scholarships to KES in 1916 and 1917, whilst occasionally a girl would successfully win a free scholarship to the Girls' High School. After the war Western Road would continue to have a considerable reputation for success in the city's scholarship examinations with boys going to Firth Park and girls to Abbeydale, as well as the Central Schools. After 1918, when KES offered 25 scholarships a year, Western Road School was one of the most consistent winners of places at KES. In the first year of this widened opportunity, four boys won a place for free education at KES, with a record number of six in 1931. The year before, one of the school's pupils, who entered KES on a scholarship, was Norman Siddall, who fifty years later would be a nationally known figure as Chairman of the National Coal Board. Occasionally there were boys who passed the entrance examination and entered KES as fee-payers, but this was largely something outside the reach of the vast majority of parents in the Western Rd. School's catchment area.

Western Rd. School also took a real pride in those scholarship winners who went on to University and graduated with honours. The school log records seven such successes in 1917, six of them women, who had just graduated at Sheffield University and one former pupil who had gained a Maths Tripos at Newnham College, Cambridge. Many of the boys who had been at the school were at that time away fighting in France, and 64 of them were killed out of the 401 who joined up. When the armistice was signed the Headmaster, now William Cotton, brought all the children into the Hall and told them the news. However, as no holiday had been granted he sent them back to their lessons until later in the afternoon, when they reassembled and sang "patriotic songs, rendered recitations and had an enjoyable time together in commemorating the coming of the Great Peace."

In April 1919 they remembered their fallen former scholars. A tablet on the outside wall was unveiled which marked the planting of nearly a hundred plane and sycamore trees along Western Rd. and Gillott St. in memory of those from the school who had served in the war, including the former girl pupils who had been VADs and members of the auxiliary services. In the week preceding the ceremony boys and girls had been hard at work planting the trees and on the day some prominent visitors completed the work by planting a few more, before dedicating a large oak plaque containing the names of those who had been killed and the twelve old boys who had been decorated or mentioned in despatches.

After the Second World War, Western Rd. became a secondary modern school until 1965, when under its last Headteacher, Tom Burnett, it vacated its buildings and moved over the hill to the new school at Crosspool. The site was then taken over in its entirety by the Infant, Junior and Middle schools who were renamed as the Westways Schools in 1969. At that same time they became a feeder school to the new comprehensive King Edward VII School and remain so to this day.

A comprehensive challenge

Russell Sharrock, in September 1969, faced a more challenging situation than any of his immediate four predecessors. Even though two of them had faced major crises in the school's history in 1926-27 and 1944-45, they had all taken over a school that was in good heart and had a clear idea of its way forward. Not since James Hichens opened the doors of the new school in 1905 in temporary premises on a split site, facing a sceptical, if not hostile, public, had a Headmaster of KES had to wrestle with so many new and fundamental issues. The issue of the new school's identity was quickly solved. Any lingering ideas that the new school was a partnership between two schools was quickly settled. This was a takeover of Crosspool Secondary, like the takeover of the Collegiate

School by the Royal Grammar School in 1884, and there was no attempt to create the symbols of a new identity. The school would be called King Edward VII School, it would adopt its uniform, its arms and badge, school song and motto and Crosspool Secondary, along with memories of Western Road School, would be brushed from the school's history within a decade.

In practice any other solution would have been a deliberate attempt to be politically correct, whereas the course that Sharrock followed was the straightforward one, calculated to preserve as much as possible of the traditions and achievements of a successful grammar school yet offering to *"all the boys and girls in the neighbourhood a fuller experience, with the all-round opportunities which exist for personal advancement in a truly mixed society of this range and scope."* KES carried all the big guns and Crosspool just could not compete with it for recognition within the new school. Many Crosspool pupils were initially delighted that they too had got in to "King Ted's", although their parents, who had to buy new uniforms, were often less enthusiastic. It was Sharrock who persuaded the LEA not to include the word "Comprehensive" in the titles of the Sheffield secondary schools, as some councils like Rotherham did with pride. He wanted to emphasize that this was a continuum; that KES was continuing in a different form as it had done after 1945. Then the school, led by Barton and Clapton, had gone on to succeed so impressively in the next twenty-four years, so now Sharrock was determined that it would be a very successful comprehensive school. Not everyone was convinced, especially among the Old Edwardians and the parents who had fought to maintain the grammar school. The Old Edwardians' Association early in 1969 sent out a letter to all their members, which read:

OLD EDWARDIANS' ASSOCIATION

- Do you want the Old Edwardians' Association to continue, now the school is a mixed comprehensive school?
- Do you want membership of the O.E.A. in future to be confined only to boys who were at KES prior to July 1969?
- Do you want membership of the O. E. A. to be offered to all **BOYS** who leave the school in the future?

To their credit they did recommend the third option, if only because the Association would otherwise eventually die out, but they could not bring themselves to admit girls. They also asked for members' views on the council's intention to call the re-organised school, King Edward VII School, a decision that was causing some controversy among old boys, some of whom felt the "old" school should be decently laid to rest. Even to-day there are many who sigh for the "lost continent" of the grammar school, and consider the comprehensive school to be a usurper of the "former glories" of the school's first sixty four years. This can be very irritating, and even hurtful, to those engaged in making a success of the present day KES, whose task has not necessarily been as easy as some in the city assume. The Upper School of KES is unusually placed on the cusp of some of the most affluent suburbs in the North of England, while at the same time it is the nearest secondary school to the city centre. In some inner cities, former grammar schools with excellent reputations (Hackney Downs and Liverpool Institute are two in point) have been unable to cope with the change in their situation and have turned turtle and been closed. Whereas, initially in 1969, KES was more a middle class comprehensive school, by the middle Seventies the social profile had changed to include many more pupils from some of the most deprived areas in the city. This gave the school a distinctive pupil profile that continues to this day, with children from right across the social spectrum, some from very wealthy backgrounds while others came from the least well-off families in Sheffield.

The re-organisation priorities

Sharrock, working closely with Arthur Jackson, John North and John Hemming (who shared Middle School responsibilities on the two sites) and Eric Ruding, the new Head of Lower School, formed the management team that grappled with the numerous organisational problems. The strategic issues were;

- The split site. This created major organisational issues of staffing, pupil courses and extra-curricular activities.
- A short term requirement for "temporary" buildings, and the need for future LEA plans for new facilities and, preferably, a one site school..
- Whether to introduce streaming, banding or mixed ability teaching for the existing and the new unselected pupils.
- Running co-educational classes and the creation of a mixed Sixth Form.
- The system of pastoral care, a new concept for former grammar school staff and pupils.
- Maintaining academic standards, including the Oxbridge tradition, and reinforcing academic rigour throughout the school with the appropriate mix of GCE and CSE courses.
- Continuing with the remedial classes and preparing for the introduction of the raising of the school leaving age (ROSLA) in 1972.
- Maintaining and developing sporting excellence, including continuing the house system, with proper provision for girls' sport, and encouraging numerous extra-mural activities, including the scouts.

The split site created opportunities as well as facing the school with major organisational problems. From the beginning it was agreed that Darwin Lane (never Crosspool in KES idiom) would eventually become the exclusive home of the Lower School, comprising the first three year groups. At 14+ pupils would move to Glossop Road, now renamed Upper School, and they would become part of Middle School preparing for their GCE or CSE Examinations, before leaving or going into the Sixth Form.

In the meantime the split site was deliberately used to effect a slow organic merger of the two previous schools into one new comprehensive school. Sharrock took the decision that all boys who had started their school careers in the grammar school should continue to have all their lessons at Upper School, even if they were second or third formers. He was quite candid that the "political" outcry of sending boys who had passed their 11+ to "Crosspool" would have damaged the process of integration, and started the new school's life in a mire of hostile parental controversy. Lower School, therefore, for its first two years was split, with half the pupils on one site and half on the other and with only the new unselected First Form (all eight classes) completely based at Darwin Lane in September 1969. The other side of this coin was that former Crosspool students stayed on the Darwin Lane site, and many of them completed their school careers without having set foot in Upper School. Only a few former Crosspool students stayed on into the Sixth Form and, perhaps, more might have been encouraged to do so if they had become familiar with the ethos and requirements of Upper School at an earlier date.

There were however other practical imperatives why the former Crosspool pupils stayed at Darwin Lane. The Upper School had no basic facilities for accommodating girls. Until girls' toilets and changing rooms, as well as Domestic Science facilities were completed, the LEA would not allow girls, other than a small number, to be educated at Upper School. The timetable for change was therefore to some extent driven by how swiftly the city council could complete the new, unlovely, changing facilities (stuck like an ugly "carbuncle" on the eastern rear wall of Flockton's imposing Corinthian building), and alter prep rooms into girls' toilets. In the event they were not ready until September 1972 and so for the first three years of the comprehensive school's existence almost all pupils continued in an environment that was familiar and seemingly little changed. Former Crosspool pupils, despite the new dark blue uniforms, remained in the same building, largely taught by the same staff and doing the same CSE courses, intermittently visited by "King Ted's" teachers wearing gowns arriving by taxi, or car, from the direction of town. "Mr." North still seemed to be their "Supremo" at Darwin Lane, even if he was no longer officially called Headteacher, but if you were a boy, you now had to undertake a torturous bus journey across the valley to play games on woebegone fields swept by arctic blizzards, instead of using the fields immediately adjacent which were now reserved for girls' games only. One disillusioned boy wrote; *"Where is it written in the Ten Commandments that winter games must be played on the top of a hill?"*

If things seemed to be the same to pupils; they were not. Crosspool, as expected, had lost out in the appointments to the "new" Head of Department posts and also, initially, in the allocation of the new Year Tutors' posts. The first was inevitable, as the existing graduate Heads of Departments were confirmed in their positions. Only Eileen Langsley (Girls P.E.) and Jennifer Gelder (Domestic Science) from among the former Crosspool staff became subject H O Ds, whilst Amy Perry continued in charge of remedial education, all areas with which the former grammar school masters were unfamiliar. There were some jaundiced remarks in the Darwin Lane staff room at the way things had turned out, but

Sharrock was sensitive to these concerns and few could have been better at re-assuring bruised egos and settling ruffled feathers.

Some staff were therefore a little surprised to find that all the Year Tutor positions in that first year went to former KES staff and therefore all were men. This was remedied in 1970 when Gladys Manifield was made Year Tutor for the Second Year (now Y8) which had become, with the advent of the middle schools, the main reception year for the Lower School. From now on there would be two Year Tutors to every year group, one female and one male, and they offered a pastoral care that was new to the school and part of the new philosophy of comprehensive schools. The intention was to support pupils to achieve their potential and to survive the worries and traumas of teenage life, rather than the sink or swim approach that had sufficed heretofore.

The final key post that was occasioned by the re-organisation of 1969 was the appointment of Eric Ruding to the position of Head of Lower School. He had joined the KES staff from Rotherham G.S. in 1967 as Head of Biology and he now relinquished that position so that he could take on these new responsibilities. For the moment, his domain was split between two buildings, as half the Lower School in 1969 were former grammar school pupils who probably needed little guidance. Ruding had been selected, rather than a non-graduate teacher from Crosspool, to ensure that the courses for the new pupils at Darwin Lane were pursued with academic rigour and would bear the stamp of KES in terms of aspirations and achievements. Although he was based at Lower School, he shared the leadership responsibilities on that site with John North until 1972, when all the Middle School left the building and he was able to develop the distinctive profile and ethos of a detached Lower School, albeit one that was part of the whole KES family.

For thirty six years KES has argued the merits of the advantages and disadvantages of having Lower School on a separate site, but certainly in the early Seventies it was seen as an obstacle to the smooth working of the school. Firstly, there was the obvious inconvenience of staff having to travel between buildings, with resultant stress and lost teaching time. They were asked to travel at break or lunchtime, or were given extra free periods to allow travel between lessons, although teachers could use their own cars and claim expenses. However, many staff took advantage of a contracted taxi service, paid for by the LEA, that ensured that taxis were booked at regular times but could also be whistled up whenever an individual teacher needed to travel. Unfortunately their reliability varied and many a class was delayed awaiting its teacher because the taxi hadn't arrived. For most schools a split site means braving the elements to cross the playing fields to a classroom block, inconveniently placed a few hundred yards away. To KES staff, split site meant regular upheavals, carrying books, marking and teaching materials, then negotiating a major traffic bottleneck to drive to another campus of your own school over a mile away. In 1969, it seemed a most unsatisfactory imposition, and it is very much to the credit of succeeding teachers that they have coped with the inconvenience since that time.

The school nurtured the hope for a few years that the Middle School would also become accommodated in new buildings on the Darwin Lane site, leaving Upper School as the KES Sixth Form Centre. Sharrock made this plea publicly at several Prize Giving Evenings but it never appears to have been a starter for the Council. The extra buildings could have been physically accommodated at Darwin Lane in the position where the new school was built in 2001. However, it would have further reduced the amount of available playing-fields space, already totally inadequate for a secondary school (KES looked with genuine envy to other local schools like High Storrs, Abbeydale Grange and Ecclesfield, who had more fields than most exclusive independent schools would enjoy), and it was also felt that to place two large secondary schools side by side — Tapton's boundaries run cheek by jowl with KES Lower School — would be courting difficulties, if not "internecine warfare". The proposal caused rumours that the "wicked" Council was finally planning to sell off the historic home of King Edward VII School on Glossop Road, thereby completing, as one angry parent wrote to the press, *"the last act of the vandals, who having hung, drawn and quartered King Edward's were now going to throw the school to the wolves."*

This time it was not the Council who were proposing change, even though there was government money available for capital works to accommodate the expansion of schools caused by ROSLA (the raising of the school leaving age to 16). Sheffield City Council's building priorities were elsewhere in the city, and Sharrock still feels that the schools in the south west of the city were treated as poor relations. Instead, the Council offered adjacent premises and mobile classrooms to meet the ever increasing numbers of pupils as the school population rose from 1270 in 1969, to 1400 by 1972, and eventually, by the end of the decade to 1500. In 1971, in response to alarms that the Lower School could not cope with the numbers of extra pupils "delivered" by the catchment area, the Council temporarily removed Lydgate Middle School as a feeder school, with all the pupils going to Tapton. Although this decision was reversed in 1973, and even though Lydgate shared the Darwin Lane site with KES as well as Tapton, the number of pupils coming to the school from Lydgate never really recovered.

For KES, in 1969, having feeder schools and a catchment area was a new situation. When KES was a grammar school it proudly trumpeted that it served the whole city with its pupils coming from every ward (some seem to have convinced themselves that virtually every scholarship boy came from a family in straitened circumstances), now it would almost exclusively serve a segment of the city allocated by the council. Catchment areas and feeder schools are today one of the most sensitive issues in education politics and street-wise parents believe they can correctly judge the performance of a school by the social composition of the area it serves. Concerns about a "post code lottery" were not so prevalent in the early Seventies, but the council was aware that the shape of the catchment area would determine the school's social profile and believed here was an opportunity for a little social engineering to ensure that the former grammar schools in the south west of the city did not "cream off" all the middle class pupils. Informed by their feeder junior, or middle schools, the catchment areas of KES, High Storrs and Abbeydale

Grange were therefore drawn so that they included a wedge of the city's map radiating out from the centre to the south western suburbs, thereby including a fair cross-section of the city's population. KES Upper School lay on the south eastern edge of its catchment area that ran from Broomhall and Kelvin, via Walkley and Crookesmoor to Crosspool, Ranmoor and Nether Green. For a start the designated feeder schools were Crookes Endowed, St. Mary's Walkley, Westways (until 1969 known as Western Rd.) Lydgate and Nether Green. Most of them were currently being converted into 8-12 middle schools that passed on their pupils to KES at the age of 12+, while others, to add to the organisational difficulties, sent their pupils at 11.

In 1969 the first cohort of 11 year old KES pupils were mainly middle class and Sharrock believes 40% would have passed their 11+, or at least were capable of an "O" Level course. It was also possible to opt for the comprehensive school of your choice even though you came from another part of the city. This was not encouraged, and Mike Russell (1969-75), later the education correspondent of the Star and the Telegraph, recalls that as a boy living in Woodhouse, his Old Edwardian father had a real battle to get him into KES, even though such parental choices was official council policy. Later, in 1975, the Council included Burgoyne Rd., St. Stephens and Springfield Schools in the KES catchment area. This was to accommodate the children who lived on the new large council housing projects that had been erected on the edge of the city centre at Kelvin Flats and Broomhall, and this produced a social profile at KES that better reflected the city's population as a whole.

(EF) PQ / XYZ / HJK / ABC W / T / R (S)

It was the sheer size of the year group that so impressed the staff when the first intake of unselected first form pupils arrived at Darwin Lane in September 1969. Gathered altogether in the Assembly Hall, the first year group of eight forms (over two hundred and forty pupils) labelled in the KES manner forms 1.1 - 1.8, was a daunting sight, especially for the former Crosspool staff who had been teaching much smaller numbers in the same building for four years. Although an eight form entry school, with 230 pupils, is now the standard number for KES in 2005, and has been for several years, in 1969 it was just the thin edge of the wedge. In the following year there would be ten forms in the second form labelled PQ / XYZ / ABW / T/ R as extra pupils joined from the middle schools. If the numbers were intimidating for teachers, it was even more awe-inspiring for the children. Crosspool pupils especially regretted the loss of the intimacy of their small school where everybody knew everyone else, but for newly arrived 11 or 12 years olds they could feel as one said; *"like a worm in a million tons of earth"*. The first year classes were subject to limited streaming until the school had fully discovered the standards of the pupils, but in subsequent years a rigorous streaming regime was imposed.

It is difficult, thirty five years on, to track all the classes, as the naming of the forms was a movable alphabetical feast, but in the 1970-71 Form list for the 2nd Year, Forms P and Q were the highest flyers, taking Latin and already being groomed for four year "O" level courses, the Sixth Form and eventual Oxbridge Scholarships for some. The next band of XYZ were following courses that could lead to "O"Level in the pupils' strongest subjects, whilst they might be taking some CSE courses as well. ABWT children were considered pupils who would best benefit from CSE courses only. 2W, in future years usually named C, was a form that received all its intake of pupils from Westways Middle School, who had traditionally been in the same class when they had come up to Crosspool School and it was felt appropriate to continue this practice at least for the present. 2R was a small remedial class, a continuation of these classes at Crosspool School, although later it was re-designated S to make its status a little less obvious.

As the school population continued to expand in the Seventies the Lower and Middle School forms increased in size. At one stage there were twelve forms to a year group and new forms labelled H, J and K appeared in the middle band ability range. The school made no apology for streaming so emphatically, rather it saw it as a pragmatic way of delivering on its promise of offering a grammar school education to all those who were capable of coping with "O" Level courses. Sharrock was faced, like all comprehensive school headteachers, with the problem of meeting the educational needs and raising the standards of all the pupils, despite their widely varying levels of ability, while maintaining the opportunities for the brightest pupils to achieve the highest levels of academic success. He set out, in 1969, to run a "tri-partite" system within the school by streaming the forms within a banded framework. By this method it was hoped every pupil would find their own ability range, be brought on at their own pace, be recognised as full, equal and valuable members of the school community, and be given every chance to move between streams and bands by a thorough annual assessment exercise that involved all the staff teaching a particular year group.

This was the school's method of ensuring late developers were not left in the "wrong" form but could move up to join their learning peers. Thus the school sought to overcome the major criticism of the 11+ examination that it decided a pupil's level of education at an inappropriate age. Within a comprehensive school any changes in a boy's or girl's performance could be properly monitored and they could be then placed in the form best suited to their abilities. Certainly this process was taken very seriously at KES, where members of staff endured long meetings as fifty or sixty staff argued over proposals for promotion and demotion prepared by the Year Tutors and Heads of Lower and Middle School.

There was criticism of the manner in which KES dealt with streaming. One member of the Education Committee, later to be an M.E.P., officially raised concerns, which she claimed were also held by some of the staff, that the streaming regime at KES, rather than mixed ability classes with generous use of subject setting, was a negation of the whole principle of comprehensive education. KES made a nod towards mixed ability teaching but only in "safe" areas. P.E., Games, and Divinity were felt suitable subjects for pupils of different forms to join together for their instruction, but Sharrock did not deem it an unqualified success and there could be friction between boys and girls who for the rest of the time at school had little contact with each other.

He had hoped that vertical integration in the school could be achieved through an enhanced house system. He had seen this work at his previous school in south-east London, and he was keen to reinforce the houses and give them pastoral and social roles as well as being a vehicle for school games. KES had retained considerable enthusiasm for houses long after they had become an embarrassment to most schools. However, the split site thwarted his plans and it became impossible to run a pastoral system by houses, so the year tutor structure was adopted instead. In the early Seventies, as another exercise in inclusiveness, a School's Council was instituted with representatives from every form, but it didn't survive for long as interest in the idea petered out.

The "Crosspool" Fifth Form.

One of the immediate positive results of becoming a comprehensive school was the sizeable number of ex-Crosspool pupils who stayed on after the school leaving age of fifteen and went into the Fifth Form. Over twenty pupils took their CSE examinations in the Summer of 1970 and they were joined by ten girls and a boy from Greystones Secondary School, which had closed as part of the re-organisation. They were all made into Fifth Form Prefects and took all their classes at Darwin Lane, where they aided John North, and Eric Ruding, in running that part of the school. It was another aspect of the evolutionary approach to comprehensive education, with Neil Garner and Patricia Dronfield chosen as the Head Boy and Head Girl, positions they could have expected to have filled if Crosspool School had continued. There were also new staff who came across from Greystones. Gladys Manifield and Mona Harrison, who had been Senior Mistress at Greystones, were re-deployed to KES after interviews with Sharrock, and they helped to bring the Teaching Staff numbers up to 71. As few teachers had left from either school that year, most members of staff initially carried on teaching the same subjects to the same category of classes, until Heads of Departments could find their feet and produce a common syllabus with a single examination which could be accessed by all forms within the year group.

That first Fifth Form group taking CSE at KES did satisfactorily in the examinations. Almost all of them got seven or eight CSEs, but the school was interested in how many achieved Grade One, the "O" Level equivalent. Here the results were more patchy, but one girl got 6 grade one passes and another gained 5. They were both transferees from Greystones, and perhaps reflected the more confident attitude of pupils from that school, although their results would suggest that they should have been at a grammar school in the first place. In the following two years, double the number of former Crosspool pupils stayed on into the Fifth Form and the classes were moved up to the Upper School. Yet few went on to do "A" level, although some students went into the Form 6R and took some "O" levels to improve their qualifications, before going to F.E. Colleges for vocational training, or into art or teacher training colleges. In 1972, the school leaving age was raised to 16 and all pupils stayed on into the Fifth Form. Some were not well pleased by the government's decision!

Russell Sharrock M.Sc.
Headmaster 1966 - 1988

Born Wigan in 1924 the son of a plumber, Russell Sharrock won a scholarship to Wigan Grammar School and then in 1942 he went on to Liverpool University to start a degree in Physics. After one year he left to join the Royal Signals as a commissioned officer, but found himself directed to work as a research scientist at the Royal Aircraft Establishment at Farnborough until 1946, when he returned to Liverpool to complete his degree course. He graduated in 1947 and after gaining a Diploma of Education he went into teaching, in 1948, at Culcheth Secondary Modern School in Warrington.

During this period he obtained an external London Honours Degree in Mathematics through a correspondence course run by Wolsley Hall in Oxford. This enabled him, in 1950, to move to Lancaster R.G.S., an H.M.C. direct grant school, where he taught maths and it was there he married his wife Mary, the daughter of a Methodist Minister in the town, who was then teaching at the Lancaster Girls' Grammar School. Five years later they moved to London and Sharrock taught at the John Ruskin G.S. in Croydon before moving to Sir Walter St. John's School, Battersea, as Head of Maths in 1958. During this period he was studying in the evenings for a London University M.Sc. in maths at Sir John Cass College and after gaining his Master's Degree in 1962 he was offered the Deputy Headship of Malory School, a purpose built comprehensive school in Lewisham. In 1965, although he was offered the post of Headmaster of his previous school in Battersea, he applied for, and was selected to be, the new Headmaster of King Edward VII School and he took up his new post in January 1966.

His interests include Rugby League Football (what Wiganer isn't), the theatre and music, whilst after retiring he took up painting and had an exhibition of his geometric abstract paintings shown at a Sheffield gallery in 1993.

Meanwhile back at the ranch!

At Upper School, where two thirds of the school population resided, the comprehensive school had actually brought very little change. Every boy in every form was a scholarship winner, almost half the Heads of Departments had been at the school in Clapton's time, and the remainder were graduates who had arrived while the school was still a grammar school. For over half the boys in the school, Sharrock was the only headmaster they had known and for those who could remember his predecessor, there were many who preferred the present incumbent's more benign, approachable and relaxed style of leadership. He in return was determined to maintain the ethos, standards and symbols of the grammar school where they didn't clash with new imperatives; so in the academic year 1969-70, a boy at Upper School would notice little change. There were still the eight traditional houses and four types of ties (including the fag rag), S.G. Rider was "the" Head Prefect (they were unaware that there were fifth form prefects in another place) and he and his fellow prefects still wore special blazers with light blue piping. The scouts struggled on, although they were down to 25 members, the cane could still be used as the ultimate sanction of discipline, the "all-weather" toilets were still across the yard, and everyone attempted "O" levels after four years in the school. When the Prize Distribution was held in November 1969 it was purely an ex-grammar school affair, with former pupils of Crosspool not invited, as they were not involved. There was still a Latin Address of Welcome to the Chief Guest along with the Latin School Song, and the occasion was still held in the grandeur of the Oval Hall at the City Hall. Added to that, 1969-70, the first year as a comprehensive school, produced a better than average number of Oxbridge scholarships (9), with a further ten boys gaining a place at the two ancient universities. If Dr. Hichens, or Dr. Barton, had returned they would have recognised the old school as being little changed, and in the case of many textbooks, the latter would recognise many of the exact same volumes, because they had not been replaced since before the war.

Yet, there was one new experience, which achieved significance quite out of proportion to its numbers. Sharrock and Jackson had determined that there would be girls in the Sixth Form from the very start of KES's life as a comprehensive school. They could have waited for girls to work their way up to Upper School from Darwin Lane, and some Fifth Form girls did move up the following year to take their CSE examinations, but to the school's credit they wanted an academic tradition for girls to start straight away. In May 1969 the council gave permission for them to recruit twenty girls into the Sixth Form, providing separate basic facilities could be made available. In the event they only managed to find thirteen girls who were prepared to take the plunge and become the first female pupils ever in the Glossop Road buildings. They knew they were creating history, if only because the press came down and photographed them, and as one said at the time; *"for the first day or two we were treated like some objects from outer space, but soon things settled down and we are beginning to feel more at home."*

They came from three sources. Several were from Tapton, and followed a route that boys from that school had trodden for some time and would continue to do until they developed their own Sixth Form in the later part of the decade. Some were from private schools without sixth forms, like the Convent High School at Burngreave, and soon there would be a steady trickle of girls from the Girl's High School, as parents realised they could get an unparalleled sixth form education at KES without having to pay fees. The final group were girls whose parents had moved to the city and in some cases they joined their brothers at the school. The numbers did not grow very quickly in the first two or three years, but eventually they were reinforced by girls coming up through the school and they soon became an integral and established part of KES.

Many boys, who were not at all enthusiastic about finding themselves in a comprehensive school, almost unanimously welcomed the arrival of girls. Today, it is difficult to grasp what a disturbing episode it was for boys working alongside "real" girls for the first time — sisters didn't count — after spending their school lives in an all male environment. The former grammar school staff were even more apprehensive. They had mainly been educated in boys' schools, gone on to all-male colleges and then back to boys' schools. Many fitted the perfect stereotype, beloved of Europeans, of Englishmen totally ill at ease in female company and their union, the A.M.A., warned them not to be alone in a classroom with girl pupils. David Anderson, who had only arrived on the staff two years before but had taught at a co-educational school, was amused to find he was being sought out by long-serving members of staff for his advice on how to deal with this "phenomenon" that had descended upon them. Some boys observed that not only did the girls have a civilising effect on Sixth Form boys but they also had a softening effect on many of the teachers. Whereas there was still a classroom culture of enforcing discipline through sarcasm and a little light physical intimidation, this was not something you could apply to a girl in your class. The girls, many of whom also came from single sex schools, on the whole enjoyed the attention they had occasioned, but were often uneasy to find themselves addressed by their Christian names when everyone else in their class was called by their surnames only.

The Prefects of 1970-71. Margaret Kinsey (Head Girl) and Michael Jepson (Head Prefect) are third and fourth from left on front row. Note prefects blazer with light blue trim.

Some of that first group of girls went on to university and two gained entrance to Oxbridge. David Anderson, now the school "authority" on girls' education, was sent by Sharrock to meet Lady Warnock, the Principal of Girton, to discuss how girls should approach entrance to her college and indeed to Cambridge, although most colleges were still strictly men only. It was one of Anderson's Economics "A" Level pupils, Margaret Young, who was one of the first KES girls to win a place at Oxbridge, although she went to St.Hilda's at Oxford.

Within a year the school would have a Head Girl (Margaret Kinsey was the first to hold the position) as well as a Head Prefect (for some years always a boy), although Jean Nelson, Head Girl 1971-72, remembers being refused a place on the platform on Prize Distribution Evening, presumably because it was not yet thought appropriate. Nevertheless, the girls who joined the Sixth Form, and girls at Darwin Lane, all had to wear the newly

The new Sixth Form girls come to terms with the KES uniform.

designed girls' uniform, which was suggested by Mary Sharrock, the Headmaster's wife. A pink and white gingham blouse in winter, worn with a dark blue skirt but no tie, with a summer dress in similar pink and white striped colours. They were the colours of the Alexandra rose, named after the consort of King Edward VII, and therefore felt to be historically appropriate for a school bearing his name. Most felt happy with the choice of colours, although some believed that *"the striped dresses made us look like humbugs."* Later, dress regulations were relaxed for Sixth Form girls, as they were for Sixth Form boys, and the school never became overexcited about boys' fashionable long hair, which caused such discipline issues at some comprehensive schools, although embryonic moustaches were banned.

Settling Down.

All Sheffield comprehensive schools were supposed to have two Assistant Headteachers, one of whom had to be a woman. Yet, until 1973 the only Assistant Head at KES was Arthur Jackson, who preferred to call himself the Deputy Headmaster, and who concentrated his time on sixth form work and producing the school's increasingly complicated timetable. He thought of himself as " *the head of a sixth form centre*" and he organised the university entrance procedures, a role he had taken on when Clapton retired. Twice the school had started the process to advertise and appoint a second Assistant Head with a remit that would include overall supervision of girls' activities. However, they also wanted someone who would not be a "token" senior female figure busying herself only with the niceties of girls' uniforms, as happened at one Sheffield comprehensive school, but someone who could play a full part in the management team, as well as teach across the syllabus. On both occasions Sharrock and Jackson felt they could not appoint, so it was only in 1973 that the post was filled by Winifred Kinnear, who had been a Headmistress of a girls' secondary modern school in Glossop. That school, Silverlands, was combined with a girls' grammar school to form a large comprehensive and the other Headteacher was appointed to the new post, leaving Winnifred Kinnear free to apply for the post of Assistant Headteacher at KES.

In the same year the Council agreed that all their schools with Sixth Forms could have a third Assistant Headteacher. John Hemming was appointed to that position with a job description that was rather vague, his appointment being more on grounds of seniority, for he had served at the school since January 1946 after wartime service in the Royal Artillery where he reached the rank of captain. He had always been a key figure in the organisation of school teams and he continued this role, but as a local man, who had won a scholarship to the Central School when it was still at Leopold Street, and as a keen member of the Old Edwardians' Association, he helped in the reconciliation process between old boys, parents and the new comprehensive school.

Also playing a considerable role in helping to fuse the new staff into a united group, and defuse any remaining outside scepticism about the future progress of the school, was Mary Sharrock. Not since Graham's time, before the war, had the Headmaster's wife played such an active part in the social life of the staff and the school. Many female members of staff remember little kindnesses, and thoughtful considerations, when they were ill or had just given birth, and she could be the life and soul of staff socials. Pupils couldn't fail

John Hemming signals two leg byes in characteristic style.

329

to notice her regular support for school concerts, plays and the activities of societies, even turning up at athletics meetings in other towns to support KES athletes representing the city, or Yorkshire. She was, of course, a woman who enjoyed an active career of her own at Sheffield University, first working as a teaching supervisor in the Department of Education, then as Warden of Halifax Hall and a lecturer in English Literature in the Extra-Mural Department. For 29 years she sat on the Sheffield Bench as a magistrate and was active in the life of the city, not least in its theatre and music circles, serving on the Board of Sheffield Theatres later in her life.

Some members of staff, however, even to this day, never became reconciled to the demise of the grammar school but they were professional enough to put their feelings behind them and get on with the new challenge of teaching children of all abilities. Some rose well to the challenge, as intelligent people of goodwill always will. Others were hopeless with classes that required their attention to be constantly maintained, and their imaginations continually inspired, throughout every lesson. The pupils at Darwin Lane, across the whole ability range, were willing to learn but some graduate teachers could not cope with some of the more difficult classes. One teacher in particular had to be occasionally rescued from chaotic undisciplined classes by his former secondary modern colleagues, who enjoyed a little *schadenfreude* at his expense. On the other hand it had never been easy teaching the grammar school classes at KES, especially the Sixth Form. Nick Jones, later Head of Middle School, arriving at the school in 1974 still remembers that teachers needed to be totally on top of their subject if they were not to have a tottering time in the classroom. Teaching bright children was not always an easy option, and for the new teacher it often required considerable preparation to ensure a successful delivery of all the next day's lessons. Mutual respect was gradually established between colleagues who previously had never met, but now could recognise the dedication and specific skills of teachers with different professional experiences.

Nevertheless, there was a constant turnover of staff, some of them not easy to replace. Three mathematicians left in the summer of 1970, Messrs. Wilcox, Wilkie and Sharpe, the latter joining an examining board in Cambridge and their long-serving Head of Department, Walter Birkinshaw left at Christmas. He had arrived in 1953 from Boteler G.S., Clapton's old school in Warrington, and he was a teacher who always pursued excellence and high academic standards. His retirement unfortunately, like rather too many, was short-lived. Two years later when driving up the M1, he suddenly felt unwell, pulled over onto the hard shoulder and presently died. Martin Axford, the Head of the English Department, producer of school plays and the school magazine, also left to become an HMI in Scotland and as many as thirty four members of staff left between 1973 and 1975. Several became heads of departments and two, Clive Allen and Peter Wood, become deputy headteachers, with the latter moving on to be the Headteacher at Ikley G.S. Another, Old Edwardian David Meredith, gave up teaching French and Spanish, trained to be a solicitor and in time became the Recorder of Leicester.

One of those who closed his teaching career in 1974 was the Head of Modern Languages, Victor Bramhall, who had been at the school since 1947. A product of Barrow G.S. and

Sidney Sussex College, Cambridge, he was another member of staff who had served in the war, when his language skills had gained him a commission in the Intelligence Corps. Despite his fluency in French and Spanish he was posted off to join the Indian Army, although his French came in handy during British operations to secure Madagascar from the Vichy French. He had encouraged a love of all things French and Spanish for almost three decades of Edwardians, whilst rejoicing under the nickname "Spiv", because he bore a considerable resemblance, with his pencil thin moustache and his fastidious and dapper appearance, to the wide boys of the post-war era. He had begun to feel the strains imposed on him by the comprehensive re-organisation and after some absences through illness, he was advised by his doctor to retire.

New staff, of course, filled the vacant positions and as Arthur Jackson recalls, *" the school's reputation was such that it was always possible to get good quality people to replace those teachers who had left."* Amongst the replacement teachers in the early Seventies were many who came to the school because they believed in comprehensive education, and intended to sustain the advancement of KES as a comprehensive school. Arnold Lawson, who would teach at the school for thirty-one years, arrived in 1970 after his previous school, Hartley Brook, had been burnt down in a fire. He was appointed initially to be the Head of Lower School Science and co-ordinate science teaching at Darwin Lane, whilst Dorothy Hall came to teach History as a part-timer in 1971, one of the few women staff members based at Upper School at that time. She would later replace Jackson as the Head of the Sixth Form, and preside over the further growth of KES's very successful post-16 education programme. In 1973, Mike Denial left a new comprehensive school, near Glossop, to become the Head of Science, with a brief to create a coherent syllabus for Science across all the ability range throughout the school. He was graded as a Senior Teacher, one of four KES appointees to these new positions established by the Burnham Report of 1972, which had attempted to address the depressed salary levels and status of the teaching profession. When Jackson retired in 1981, Denial became an Assistant Headteacher in his place and had a considerable role in shaping the future of KES as a comprehensive school during the Eighties. With these new appointments, and others like Roger Watkin as the new Head of English, a critical mass of teachers was emerging by 1975 who had not taught at either of the two previous schools, and who only knew KES as a comprehensive school. At the same time the last pupils from the KES's grammar school period had finally passed through the school, and the comprehensive school had come of age.

KESMAG

Amongst the ecumenical forces helping to unite two schools, and then the two sites, was the school magazine. In 1970, after years without a distinctive name it was re-christened KESMAG, but the radical change in its format and presentation had started in 1968 before the school went comprehensive. Anticipating change in the school's status, the editors charged the old magazine with being " *a dry piece of establishment propaganda and whilst sound of content, visually dull."* In its place they intended to replace it with a magazine *"unstable of content but visually striking, an impressionist splurge of school life, a poetical bubble bath held together by a framework of iconoclastic photographs."* The school's great journal of record, founded in 1906 and so vitally useful to would-be historians of the school, had been replaced by a hybrid that was more tabloid than broadsheet. It mixed formal school news and literary offerings with articles, features, cartoons, numerous questionnaires and interviews (often with prominent staff members).

With a less crowded format of bold design and irreverent content, KESMAG aimed to reflect the interests of the "customers" from the first forms to the sixth, and, in 1969, made a real attempt to record the news and attitudes of former Crosspool pupils as well as those at KES. There were reports of Crosspool's last Athletics Sports in 1968, of staff departures and a report of a basketball match in November 1968 when Crosspool had beaten KES 11-8, with a team that included two girls. Not exactly a Lakers v Knicks scoreline, but a victory of some considerable importance and satisfaction to Crosspool at the time. Interviews took place with pupils on the Darwin Lane site and the front cover sported an imaginary board game by which, in twenty moves, you could reach Upper School from Darwin Lane whilst avoiding some familiar obstacles.

The magazine now came out only once a year, but it had a large editorial staff that included members of Lower School. There were KESQUIZes, of the select a, b, or c variety, and numerous KESTIONAIRES, including one on voting preferences in the 1974 Election. *(The staff opted for the Conservatives 42%, Labour 28%, Liberals 18% thereby giving lie to the rumour that they had been taken over by the "trendy" Left, whilst the Sixth Form also supported the Conservatives with 41% but with the Liberals (25%) ousting Labour (19%) into third place. Perhaps the magazine was capturing a moment of history as the Liberal revival in the Hallam Constituency may have started at KES.)* There were campaigning features, with KESACTION reporters interviewing all and sundry, on one occasion to obtain better pedestrian crossing facilities on Newbould Lane, and KESADS, where you could buy a guinea pig for 10p, or a Riley 1500 cc car, complete with a current MOT, for a mere £25. For only £2.50 you could purchase the entire Liverpool, Everton and Man. Utd. teams, but only in their Subbuteo manifestations.

In 1976 KESMAG was the runner up in the Sunday Times School Magazine Competition (there were 642 entries) but to their amazement, and consternation, their success was in the "Traditional" School Magazine category. Despite being unsure whether to feel honoured or insulted (they wondered what the non-traditional winner's magazine looked like), KESMAG deserved its recognition for it had made an honest, and at times inspired, attempt to capture the spirit, not just of official school events, but of the life of the school as lived and understood by the pupils. Some of the cartoon work was superb, including a parody of the Rake's Progress by Keith Ruttle in the 1972 Magazine, which paralleled Hogarth as it depicted the rise and fall of the "rake" at a school not unlike KES, who ended up rejected by five polytechnics. The Headmaster retained the final red pencil and articles got censored in part or in whole. One of the editors, now a working journalist, recalls how an article on the school's out of bounds secret places, including the water tank in the roof, was lost to posterity as the censor decided security, as well as decorum, was being compromised. The last properly produced magazine came out in 1983, after there had been a desperate bid to save flagging circulation in 1982 by getting it fully subsidised and making all copies free. A couple of type-written efforts appeared in the middle Eighties, but the days of the school magazine were over, and like several other KES institutions it became part of the footnotes of school history.

In the 1973 edition there were eleven pages of poetry including this one parodying Stanley Holloway.

There's a school by the name of King Edward
That's noted for hard work and fun,
So Mr. and Mrs. Ramsbottom
Requested that their only son
Partake of the culture and science,
The maths and the joys of P.E.
They paid their rates reg'lar tut council
And reckoned on getting it free.

They ascended the steps to the portal,
The Headmaster, tall, dignified,
Held open the door of the foyer
And ushered the trio inside.

"Opportunities here in abundance",
Spake the Head in a proud tone of voice,
"There's Oxford and Cambridge Externals,
And a dinner with freedom of choice.

Our sports hold a wide reputation,
The football will keep you in trim,
We still have a pool full of water
But now it's for those who can't swim

My qualified staff are devoted,
Tradition we never will lack.
"A wonderful thing's edycashun,"
Beamed dad as he gazed at a plaque.

The transfer was signed by agreement
The Sixth Form expanded by one
The pigeons continued gyrating
While KES just carried on.

Anon

Houses fall down

An early casualty of changed circumstances was the House system, which had enjoyed a robust life at KES long after it had fallen into decay at other schools. Even today, Old Boys will proudly recall the name and the colours of their house and yet, by 1971, the eight traditional houses had been reduced by amalgamation to four. In another two years they would have gone forever. This was not the wish of the Headmaster, who wanted the houses to be the vehicle by which he delivered the pastoral system and the vertical framework for unity among pupils from different academic and social backgrounds. Sharrock blames the split site for their failure. It proved impossible to maintain the "freemasonry" of belonging to these time-honoured congregations, when the link between house members of different age groups was severed by such a geographical divide. The mass resignation of six of the eight housemasters in 1969 cannot have helped to bridge the period of transition. One of them, Gerald Taylor, Housemaster of Wentworth, was leaving that summer but they had almost all been opposed to comprehensive education and for whatever reason they decided the new wider responsibilities were not for them. They may well have considered that new pupils from Crosspool Secondary would have no reason to feel any loyalty to these long established KES Houses and newcomers would not be properly inducted at Darwin Lane, where most of the staff had not been involved with the houses previously.

Perhaps for this reason Sharrock created four new houses in September 1971.

BOLSOVER,   CHANTRY,   MONTGOMERY,   SORBY

All named after famous 19th Century Sheffield worthies. Thomas Bolsover had created Sheffield Plate, Sir Francis Chantry was a well-known sculptor and artist, James Montgomery was a poet and writer who had lived at The Mount in Broomhill and had spoken at the opening of Wesley College and Dr. Henry Sorby was an internationally famous mineralogist who had been a pupil at the Collegiate School.

The Houses that were consigned to history included six that had been founded in1906, when the school moved up to its permanent home at the former Wesley College and two others, Lynwood (a "proper" house admitted in 1908, where some pupils actually boarded) and Sherwood, created in 1920, to meet an increase of pupils after World War One.

ARUNDEL founded 1906 Green Shirt *** CHATSWORTH 1906 Pale Blue
became Bolsover House

CLUMBER 1906 Cerise *** HADDON 1906   Red/Black
Became Chantry House

LYNWOOD 1908 Royal Blue/White *** SHERWOOD 1920 Green/White
Became Montgomery House

WELBECK 1906 Navy Blue *** WENTWORTH 1906 Brown
Became Sorby House.

Arundel won the last Athletics Sports Day in 1971 and Bolsover won the only two Athletics Championships of the new order in 1972 and 1973.

A Grammar School within a Comprehensive

"Our prime goal in this school is to get as many "O" levels as possible. People expect this school to do what it always has done and we try to do that. Every child who comes here takes external examinations."

Thus Russell Sharrock set out the academic priorities of KES as a comprehensive school, outlining his determination to maintain the intellectual traditions of the grammar school and give as many pupils as possible the opportunities formerly available only to scholarship winners. For those who could not reach the "O" Level standard, and pupils were given every opportunity to take them in their strongest subjects, then the school would embrace the CSE Examinations to the full, treating Grade One passes as GCE "O" Level equivalents and suitable qualification for "A" Level courses. Every girl and boy at KES would be challenged to do their best in the classroom, and examinations would provide the route for the delivery of their individual achievement.

No one expected that KES - the comprehensive school, would rack up the academic honours that KES - the grammar school, the apex of the city's academic selection pyramid, had regularly achieved. There were many in the Seventies who were waiting to sneer and gloat if, or when, KES's academic performance fell a long way below that of the days when Dr. Barton and Nathaniel Clapton were the Headmasters. In the event, the comprehensive school, with its unselected entry of boys and girls from all elements of the social spectrum, did not perform too badly at all.

Surprisingly, thirty years on, there are now few detailed records held by the school, or the LEA, of GCE and CSE examination results. Therefore it is not easy to compile a definitive comparison of how the school performed in the Seventies using the usual criteria of "O" Level, "A" Level, and CSE Examination results, as well as Oxbridge Open Awards and the numbers of Sixth Formers going on to Higher Education. However, in 1968-69, the last year of the grammar school, there was an 85% pass rate (all grades) at "O" Level, 20% better than the Oxford and Cambridge Examination Board average, whilst one form, 4L, gained a 97% pass rate and 75 boys got between seven and eleven subject passes each. At "A" Level, 14 boys achieved four subject passes, 56 got three and 80 got one or two passes each, thereby setting a rough bench mark to enable a comparison to be made with the following decade's results.

In 1972 when the majority of the last group of ex-grammar school pupils sat their "O" level examinations, 56 pupils, almost all boys, got seven or more "O" Level passes at all grades and then in 1974 when the same group took their "A" level examinations, two got four "A" Levels and 66 registered passes in three subjects. Not as good as 1969, but the number going to university, and other higher education institutions, from this year group was 107, the highest figure yet in the school's history. At the same time the number of pupils attempting the CSE Examination had risen exponentially. In 1974 191 pupils gained some CSEs and over half of them (112) had obtained six or more passes with most gaining at least one "O" level equivalent grade.

After the first five years as a comprehensive school the Headmaster and the staff could take some considerable satisfaction that, even if results were not quite as good as in the past, standards on the whole had been maintained. Moreover, in those first few years of the decade there had still been a sizeable number of sixth formers going to Oxbridge, certainly comparable with the latter days of the grammar school. 1970 was the high water mark with 19 places (nine exhibitions and scholarships and ten commoners); the following year it was 16 (five awards and another eleven places) and in 1972 there were

15 accepted, including six winning open awards. Thereafter the number of scholarships and exhibitions sharply declined (only eight between 1974 and 1978), though the number of Oxbridge places gained in the Seventies, averaged thirteen a year. During the Eighties, although the average annual number of places gained at Oxford and Cambridge was reduced to seven, there would still be many grammar schools in the country that would be envious of such a number of successes.

There were reasons advanced to explain this partial decline. Oxford and Cambridge themselves were widening their net and trying to attract more pupils from schools who did not have an Oxbridge tradition. The previously all male colleges were accepting girls for the first time in the Seventies, and whilst that would benefit KES in the long run, it worked to the disadvantage of the current, largely male, Sixth Form. Sixth formers themselves were less eager to go up to the two ancient universities than heretofore. Ivy covered cloisters were not so appealing to this non-conformist, even rebellious, generation who might well prefer the attractions of a campus in a big vibrant city. There was also a perception that Oxbridge had fallen behind the times in the Seventies, and the provincial universities were now offering more interesting and flexible courses, especially at the new and fashionable universities like Lancaster and York.

There were individual successes in the early Seventies. Mark Gore won the Akroyd Scholarship in 1972, the first Edwardian to win this award since Giles Ecclestone in 1955. At one time KES had appeared to have a monopoly on this prestigious Yorkshire Scholarship, but the school had largely ignored it since 1950 when Clapton became the Headmaster. Gore went on to Wadham College, Oxford and currently is the Deputy Director of Education for Warwickshire. There were successes for former Crosspool pupils like Jane Simm, who after achieving six Grade One CSE results went into the Sixth Form and embraced the opportunities that KES had to offer. Initially she went to a P.E. College but returned in 1973 to improve her "A" Levels, before becoming the first ex-pupil of Crosspool Secondary School to go to University. She went to the University of Wales at Swansea in 1974 and is now on the careers staff of Sheffield University.

The acid test of how sound were KES's academic standards now it was a comprehensive school, would come when the former grammar school pupils cleared the system by 1975. Some strategical preparation had been made by Sharrock and his management team to secure continued progress. In 1971 some of the first comprehensive intake of pupils were "promoted" to Upper School. They were third form high flyers, labelled 3E and 3F, who although technically Lower School and part of the first unselected comprehensive pupils group at KES in 1969, were seen as two forms capable of doing "O" Level, including Latin, in four years, then going into the Sixth Form at fifteen and becoming the Oxbridge scholarship candidates of future years. The rest of the third year and fourth years stayed at Darwin Lane and remained there until 1972, when the Middle School all moved up to Glossop Rd. allowing the three year groups of Lower School to finally be completely, and discretely, accommodated at Darwin Lane.

Two years later the decision was made to abandon the four year course to "O" Level. This had been the fast track by which you not only satisfied the intellectual capabilities of your most able pupils, but also enabled many of them to successfully sit Oxbridge scholarship examinations. It had also been regarded as a badge of intellectual superiority, something most grammar schools could not emulate, something that set KES aside from almost all of its peers. Soon after the ex-grammar school pupils had cleared the Middle School, the Headmaster standardised the system and all pupils took their "O" level examinations at 16 years of age. He argued that it allowed for a more discursive syllabus in the Middle School and an opportunity for candidates to gain more maturity in their subjects before taking their first external examinations. The decision was also driven by a realisation that there were less pupils in the school who could successfully attempt "O" level at fifteen years of age. Most pupils now came to the school at 12, and a three year course to "O" Level was not really a feasible option for all but a handful of students. Some pupils were still allowed to take up to two "O" Levels in the Fourth Form, usually in English Language and Mathematics and, in 1975, a couple of particularly able boys, one the son of a staff member and the other a professor's son, were allowed to join the year above them and sit their "O" Levels at fifteen.

*This changeover caused something of a dip in the "O" Level performance in 1975, but by 1979 there were 75 candidates, achieving seven or more passes (all at grades A-C), a figure that stands comparison with the results of the same group in the final year of the grammar school in 1969. In 1977, Sharrock could report that 32.7% of all the year group had achieved five or more passes at "O" Level, 13% better than the national average, with KES's Maths and English results almost twice as good as the national average. Furthermore by the end of the school's first decade as a comprehensive school, the CSE results had also considerably improved with 146 pupils in 1979 gaining six passes or more. They too had accepted the school's work ethic and were under the spell of **"the silent curriculum"**, as one former grammar school teacher termed the traditional demand of the school for academic achievement through examinations.*

The "A" Level results in the same period also gave much cause for optimism;

1975:   2 pupils gained four "A" Levels; 51 pupils gained three "A" Levels; 97 into Higher Education

1977:   7 pupils gained four "A" Levels; 62 pupils gained three "A" Levels; 100 into Higher Education

1979:   8 pupils gained four "A" Levels; 50 pupils gained three "A" Levels; 91 into Higher Education

Even the school's critics accepted that these results were *"very good for a comprehensive school"* and the Sixth Form, now with an 8th Form for scholarship candidates and pupils who wished to improve their "A" Level grades, had established its academic credentials and was serving as large a number of pupils as the Sixth Form before re-organisation. The 350 Sixth Formers comprised boys and, increasingly, girls who had entered from KES's Middle School, plus a sizeable number who came from 11-16 comprehensives and private schools (including Birkdale) who did not have a sixth form. Gradually during the Seventies almost all comprehensive schools in Sheffield started to run a few "A" Level courses and by the end of the decade Tapton and Silverdale had their own successful sixth forms up and running and had largely stopped sending their pupils to KES. However, the Sixth Form, under Arthur Jackson's guidance, continued to flourish; yet its very success made it vulnerable to those on the Council who wished to resurrect the plans for 11-16 schools and tertiary colleges. They were concerned that the imbalance between successful sixth forms, like KES, and those that were struggling, and frankly wasting teaching resources, at many other schools in the city, was distorting the comprehensive ideal, and that tertiary colleges would be a more equitable way to provide both academic and vocational post-16 education.

The ROSLA kids

There was one group of boys and girls in the middle Seventies not sharing in the general success of KES pupils and they were those who did not want to stay on at school after the age of fifteen. There had been a small "remedial" class each year at Crosspool and Amy Perry and Norman Beatson had continued to run these classes at Darwin Lane after 1969. However, as the school expanded this group of slow learners became much larger and eventually became two forms. With the school's emphasis on streaming, many in this group inevitably became unenthusiastic about school, and as they were housed in the bottom corridor of the four-storey building some of them might literally feel they were the "underclass". Nor did they thank the government for its benevolent addition of one extra year of schooling, when the school leaving age was finally raised to sixteen in 1972. Instead of escaping into the real world and getting jobs and wages, they were stuck in a school, which they felt showed little interest in them.

Behavioural problems really began to emerge when the Middle School groups moved up to Upper School in 1972. Designated 4M and 4C Forms, with the older group called 5M and 5C, they were shunted off to Melbourne Annexe, a decision that contributed to the problem and that all those involved now believe was wrong. For teachers who did not take these classes, Melbourne Annexe was a place you did not want to enter. Even for teachers like the young Rod Auton, newly arrived in 1974 with a sense of vocation to teach this difficult group, it could at times be a daunting, even shattering, experience when faced with almost total non co-operation from some of the boys and girls. He describes it as *"a state of apartheid"* and one which only improved when the M and C Forms were brought back into the main building and became part of the normal life of the school. These pupils took a two year leaver's course, which was much more vocational orientated than the usual CSE courses, although KES did not offer courses in commercial subjects such as shorthand, typing and office practice. Boys from these classes spent time with the redoubtable Alan Finch, reputed to be a former Rhodesian policeman, who ran the Motor Maintenance Department at the back of the school in the building which, before adaptation, had been the covered playground. He was a firm believer in strong discipline with experience of teaching at some of the toughest schools in the city. No one "messed" with Mr. Finch who enjoyed working with tough "kids" and would have liked to have given them more practical fieldwork so they did not have to spend all their time in the "purgatory" of a classroom. To this end he would have welcomed the school buying an old farmhouse, or a redundant railway station, or even a canal barge, that could be renovated by pupils and then used as an outdoor centre, especially by the pupils in the M and C Forms.

This episode of the "ROSLA" pupils at Melbourne Annexe is not one of the finest in the school's history. In the Seventies, the punishment book records that half of the official canings were given to members of these four forms and they responded by underachievement and hostility. By the late Seventies, when they moved out and the Economics and History Departments took over the building, Melbourne Annexe was in a dilapidated state and it never really recovered by the time KES departed in 1995. Today it forms part of the sprawling empire of the Girls' High School, although it did acquire one rather unexpected claim to fame in 1980, when the school was still in occupation. Thanks to a quick-witted constable, Peter Sutcliffe, infamous throughout the country as the Yorkshire Ripper, was apprehended in the adjacent grounds and his career as a serial killer was summarily terminated.

Melbourne Annexe in the Seventies
Formerly Mount View, home of three Headmasters 1905-1938

Prank of the Century

A different kind of challenge to the school's authority came at the end of the Easter term 1974, when the annual Distribution of Prizes had been moved to the school's Assembly Hall, because the City Hall was not available. Because of power cuts and the three day week in the final months of the Heath Government, the City Hall had been forced to cancel the school's normal January date for the event, and this change of venue allowed a plot to be laid that was as ingenious as it was memorable. The brain child of Philip Beet, along with a few sixth form accomplices, it intended a precision bombing of the Headmaster at an early stage of the proceedings, when he was speaking at the lectern. The missile was to be a deluge of flour dropped through a ventilation grate in the roof, which could be accessed from a cupboard in the Economics Room on the top floor of the building.

This daring, and outrageous jape, would have been amazing enough if it had involved perpetrators emptying the bags by hand at the appropriate moment, but Beet had planned that this would be a "sting" operation whereby the plotters would trigger the deluge by a time fuse mechanism, whilst calmly sitting in the hall enjoying the spectacle themselves. A box, containing several pounds of flour, was suspended by a twisted string over the grate, which as luck would have it was immediately above the lectern on the platform. As the proceedings in the hall were about to begin that afternoon, a candle was lit whose flame would eventually burn through the string, tipping the box and its contents into the abyss below.

The plan was worthy of the highest sixth form intellect, but the security was lax. The word had got out that something was going to happen, and at least one senior prefect knew precisely what was intended and sat wrestling with his conscience, trying to decide to whom he owed his loyalty in such a moment of truth. Fortunately for the plotters, unfortunately for the establishment, the platform party pressed on with the programme unaware of the suspended flour bag of Damocles, fifty feet above their heads.

The Headmaster made his "state of the union" speech at the lectern but the "bomb" failed to drop. He was replaced in the target zone by the Deputy Headmaster, Arthur Jackson, who began tolling the names of the prize-winners. At this point, after nearly twenty minutes, it seemed the candle flame must have gone out and therefore the plot had failed. Presently a huge column of flour fell from the roof and continued to pour down onto the head of the Deputy Head. Unaware that he was the victim of "collateral damage", he decided dignity was best served by standing immobile and receiving the full capacity of the flour bags. Covered in white, even the glasses in his hand acquired two perfect cones of flour on the upturned lens, he surveyed a hall shrieking with laughter. Many staff, including the Headmaster, could not repress involuntary laughter either, as one teacher, David Anderson, rushed up to the room above hoping to catch the culprits red-handed. He found, instead, that the tinder dry cupboard had been in danger of going up in flames, which could have added real tragedy to the afternoon's farce.

Later, after a suitable interval for calling of the roll in a vain attempt to identify suspects, and very much to Jackson's credit and imperturbability, the prize giving continued. The fun was not yet over because, against all gambling odds, the first boy to receive a prize after the re-start was called Whitehead and the laughter rolled around the hall again. The incident was so audacious, and so precisely executed, that it seemed churlish to prosecute the investigation too rigorously and Beet essentially got away with it. Unfortunately a year later he was involved in a road accident and was tragically killed.

Of the victims, intended and actual, there are no hard feelings now, but for those who witnessed the "Flour Bomb Incident" it will remain the abiding memory of their time at KES.

Mid-decade changes 1974-77

When Amy Perry was made the Head of Lower School in succession to Eric Ruding in 1974, her appointment symbolised two of the main changes in the school's life since re-organisation. The leadership of the school was now finely balanced with three members, John North, Winifred Kinnear and herself, with experience of secondary modern schools, whilst the other three members, Jackson, Hemming and the Headmaster himself, had been at KES when it was a grammar school. Her appointment, and also that of two Heads of Departments, Joyce Batty (Maths) and Stella Boon (Modern Languages), signalled that, although still in a considerable minority, this Headmaster welcomed women staff members as equal partners in the development and future of the school. Appropriately 1975 was the International Women's Year and from that time KES has always had a substantial number of women in senior posts in the school, and in the early Nineties all three Assistant Headteachers were women.

Amy Perry only stayed two years in the post and then along with two other long-serving staff, Hemming and Barnes, she retired in 1976. "Josh" Hemming who was the "Father of the House", having arrived at the school thirty years earlier, was one of a very few remaining members of staff who had served under Dr. Barton, whose death occurred that same year. Hemming, associated in the minds of most Edwardians with his huge contribution to school sport, especially cricket, had for many years served as a major in the T.A., after being called up as a "Z" Reservist during the Korean War. In retirement he became a KES Governor before eventually moving to Bridlington where he lived out his days on the bracing Yorkshire coast. Norman Barnes was another who enjoyed a long retirement, but he remained in Sheffield where he could continue as the organist and choir-master at St. John's Ranmoor and also serve as Vice-President of the Bach Society.

For his pivotal role in KES music, and his sustained contribution to music in the city generally, he was awarded the MBE in 1975, something that does not come the way of many schoolteachers and the first won by a member of KES staff since C.J. "Fatty" Magrath's award in the late Forties. Barnes had very much succeeded in keeping the musical traditions of the school going in the Seventies, although he found the split site a major problem, as it divided his choir and his orchestra. To overcome the latter difficulty he ran two orchestras, the First Orchestra was the senior one with the Second Orchestra catering for new musicians who were learning to play their instruments at Lower School. He took with him his well-worn jokes and left an understanding among hundreds of present and former pupils *"that to be a musician means you are never inactive or bored."*

There were other changes that signalled the end of old traditions and the beginning of the new. The Scouts finally "pulled up their tent pegs" and disbanded in 1975. They had suspended their operations the previous year hoping that new enthusiasts would fill the ranks and that members of staff would take on the role of scoutmasters; but it was not to be. The 167th King Edward VII Troop had lasted nearly fifty years and brought immeasurable satisfaction and enjoyment to hundreds of Edwardian scouts, but now the remaining few were encouraged to join their local troops and carry on the tradition in that way. Dr. David Marcer, who had been supervising the troop, now started the Duke of Edinburgh's Award Scheme at the school in 1975 and their programme appealed more to the temper of the times, yet it incorporated some of the activities that had made scouting so exciting to so many at the school since 1927.

Despite the Flour Bomb incident, or perhaps because of it, the Distribution of Prizes ceremony went back to the City Hall in November 1974 and passed off without incident. It was the last time the Latin Address of welcome was given. To the dismay of traditionalists, it was felt inappropriate in a school where only the top streams did Latin and at odds with a sense of parity and unity. Perhaps it was as well, because very few had been able to follow the Latin speech as it was delivered, even in the days when virtually all the boys had taken Classics. One year in the Seventies, the prefect giving the address, after a faultless first few sentences, completely forgot his lines but had the presence of mind to remember, and recite, a Latin prose composition he had recently done for homework. Only the Classics Department staff members noticed and he was applauded at the end, notwithstanding his "deception".

To compensate, the abbreviated Latin name of the school, "*Reg. Edward VII Schola, Escaf.*", was returned to the school coat of arms after some years of being written in English, but the Latin School Song fell into disuse. Gowns became an optional extra for staff, partly because they caused some friction between the graduates and the non-graduate teachers. There was increased embarrassment at the Prize Distribution evenings, when, not only were some staff without gowns, but the hall was awash with the rarely seen, multi-coloured, university hoods. One new member of staff recalls the City Hall looking like a production of "Joseph and the Technicolour Dreamcoat" and non-graduate members could feel somewhat *"below the salt"* on these public occasions.

A story doing the rounds at the time, concerned a very senior member of staff travelling in his gown from Upper School to Darwin Lane when he was involved in a minor traffic accident. Ever considerate, he got out of his car to assist the lady who had been driving the other vehicle. She was somewhat concussed, and as she slowly came round she found a tall figure looming over her, whose voluminous gown was blotting out all the light. Momentarily she thought she had died and this was the "angel of death" who had come to escort her to the other side.

There were changes that affected the status of the pupils, part of an attempt to make pupils feel they had a stake in the new community. After some stiff resistance, the Sixth Form gained a Common Room, in 1972, on the ground floor corridor opposite the Dining Room. No doubt a place for quiet contemplation in a busy day, but when a desperate shortage of rooms demanded that they move, they were offered the redundant scout hut as an alternative. Its run down furnishings and the black dust from the two coke burners made it an unsatisfactory venue, and low-level vandalism made it even less habitable. So in 1977 they were offered premises at Springvale, one of the school's new sites, inconveniently situated, but well away from the Upper School buildings and its vigilant staff.

In 1975, the LEA revised their regulations for the appointment of Governors and admitted two pupil governors to each secondary school governing body. Set up in 1970, the new, and separate, governing body of KES had LEA nominees (in reality local members of political parties) and also parents' and teachers' elected representatives. Its influential Chairman was Alderman Bill Owen, a leading figure in the Labour movement in Sheffield, who later had one of the main buildings at Hallam University named after him. The policy, at least in theory, was one of inclusion and transparency and Sheffield's initiative formed the model for the Taylor Commission's recommendations on school governance in the Seventies. One of the first pupil governors to be elected at KES, was Graham Fellows, who later would become one of the best known Old Edwardians of his generation. Under the stage name of John Shuttleworth, he not only had a hit record, "Jilted John", shortly after leaving school, but he was for a time part of the cast of Coronation Street, before establishing himself as a highly regarded alternative comedian.

New sites and old buildings

One institution that had to be replaced was the "Backs", the outdoor boys' toilets across the back yard. It seems incredible that even as late as the mid-Seventies such primitive facilities, dating from Wesley College's time could still be in service and, now the girls had been provided with new indoor toilets, action had to be taken by the Council to give the boys indoor facilities as well. A classroom on the lower corridor was converted to toilets, but for many Old Edwardians another nostalgic piece of the popular history of the school was lost. Surrounded by a halo of cigarette smoke and the home of secret drinkers of free school milk, they had been the scene, in recent years, of a small explosion using weedkiller and sugar, which blew off part of a door. They were later razed to the ground, leaving only their outline on the boundary wall until Archaeology "A" Level students excavated their foundations in 2004.

In 1976, to aid the continual pressure of pupil numbers, the school acquired its fourth teaching site. At least a good five minutes walk away from the main buildings. Springvale, a nearby LEA building, had recently housed a special needs school and was now re-furnished at a cost of £3000 and handed over to the Domestic Science Department. Situated in a pleasant dell below Lynwood, it was approached from Park Lane and it was this building that, a little later, also became the new home of the Sixth Form Common Room.

The Lynwood Stables

In 1978, the Art Department under Peter Jones, nationally famous for his railway paintings, moved into the stables behind Lynwood House, at the city end of Clarkehouse Rd. The stable block had been converted for the Art Department's use and now contained a painting studio, graphics and print room, a photographic studio, facilities for sculpture and a kiln and wheels for pottery. Finally in 1980 the city council persuaded the Polytechnic to vacate the main Lynwood House, which they had been using for residential accommodation for some of their students. It was handed over to KES, who moved in the Music and Textiles Departments and it remained in the school's use until 1990. No one on the staff could now remember the days when Lynwood had been the private home of F.T. Saville, who ran the building as the school's boarding house, but enough people knew the history of the place to appreciate the historical significance of returning to a building that had played such an important part in the life of the school between 1911 and 1938, when Saville had sold it.

So now the school was on five sites, in six buildings, and if you added in the two sports fields of Whiteley Woods and Castle Dyke, the school was running its curriculum across seven sites, three of them considerable distances from the Upper School and all of them across heavily trafficked roads. To organise the time-table for such a far-flung empire required a special level of ability and fortunately Arthur Jackson was very much up to the task. He recalls that a representative from one of the new computer firms asked if they could interest the school in one of their products to undertake the school timetable. When told that the school was on five sites they withdrew their offer, but another firm did attempt to programme the sixth form timetable only. Jackson delights to tell that he completed the post-16 time-table in a shorter time, and with fewer errors, than the computer.

Music Legends - Old and New

There were many who considered that if there were one school institution that would decline because the school had become a comprehensive school, it would be the school's music tradition. This didn't happen and school music has remained robust and vibrant till the present day. Much of the credit for managing the new situation and coping with having a geographically split orchestra and choir, must, of course, go to Norman Barnes who stayed on at the school in 1969 until his retirement seven years later.

> *"Our trebles and sopranos were at Darwin Lane and our tenors and basses at Upper School and for many concerts we could only get together for one or two rehearsals before the performance."*

Barnes often complained about the split site but he overcame the difficulties with no little panache. In the early Seventies there were over three hundred performers at the main summer concert, and Barnes was aided by the appointment of Ron Law in 1970 as a second music master, who taught mainly at Darwin Lane. When he left to become Head of Music at Silverdale in 1972, he was soon replaced by Alan Eost, who eventually became Head of the Music Department at KES himself. They were supported by the expert tuition that was given to pupils by the peripatetic teachers from the LEA's Music Service, who helped to establish guitar and recorder groups and later in the Seventies, a strong brass group.

To overcome the physical division of the school, the main orchestra of fifty-five musicians was based at Upper School and named the First Orchestra. Promising musicians at Lower School were bussed up to Glossop Rd. to join rehearsals, but for the many new pupils undergoing instrumental instruction at Lower School, a Second Orchestra was created to display their developing talents. The annual programme followed the same pattern as before, with a Christmas Concert in the Cathedral until 1974, when it moved to Ranmoor and then, two years later, to St. Mark's, Broomhill, where it is still held every year. In the Spring Term the Orchestra and Choir would perform at the latter end of the Prize Distribution Evening, but the major concert was in the summer at the City Hall. Julian Harrison, leader of the Orchestra in 1973, recalls the Leader of the BBC Northern Symphony Orchestra congratulating the KES musicians on putting on the best school concert he had ever heard. These concerts now, of course, featured girl musicians, not only in the Girls' Choir, but also adding immeasurably to the strength of the Orchestra and the full School Choir.

There were particularly gifted Edwardian musicians in this decade as there had been in preceding ones. Paul Webster won the Gold Medal of the Royal School of Music and was a prize-winning Associate of the Royal College of Organists, before leaving school with an Organ Scholarship at St. Catherine's College, Cambridge. Jayne Beeston played the clarinet in the National Youth Orchestra and at the same time, Brendon Clover, now Canon Clover, Precentor of Bristol Cathedral, played the trumpet in the British Youth Symphony Orchestra. Barnes's final parting remarks were modest as he recognised the need for new ideas, impetus and leadership from a younger Head of the Music Department. *"Someone who will bring a fresh mind to the problems of music in a split site comprehensive, with no purpose built accommodation for music and insufficient staffing."* When Norman Barnes died in 2000, a fitting tribute was organised by Shelagh Marston, a former Chair of the Governors, who launched an appeal to fund a Memorial Trust in Barnes' name, which gives annual grants to support musicians at the school and at St. John's Ranmoor.

There was however another musical tradition flourishing at KES in the Seventies that also brought fame to the school, even if most of the performances were outside of the school's curriculum and its official extra-curricular activities. Edwardians, in the Seventies, seem to have made a bigger contribution to the parallel teenage culture of rock and pop music than the pupils of most schools. There were several groups who lit up the local scene for a while and provided a little extra pocket money for their members playing in pubs, clubs and halls in the Sheffield area. "Blasé" were one such group of KES musicians. Founded in 1973, their core music was raunchy hard rock with the brothers, Dave and Martin Smith, as lead singers and songwriters. A little later Stuart Riley was the lead singer of a band called "Fassbender", Nick Hawnt lead vocalist of a heavy rock band called "Dynasty" and amongst other KES groups then in existence were "Wild Angel" and "Bruno Vishnu's Hippo Band".

The one rock musician who seemed to be heading for a professional career was Nick Battle, who along with his band "Rabat-Joie" even crossed the divide and performed in one of Barnes' last concerts at the City Hall. On leaving school, Battle joined a soft rock band, but it was to be three other Old Edwardians, who were at school in the Seventies, who became renowned stars of pop music. Phil Oakey became the lead singer of the "Human League", whilst Joe Elliot was the lead singer of "Def Lepard", two Sheffield bands that gave the city an international reputation for pop music. Paul Heaton, not to be outdone, was the lead singer for the Hull based band, "The Beautiful South", whilst their contemporary at KES, Mathew Bannister, went into broadcasting as a presenter and reporter and in 1993 was the man entrusted with resurrecting the fortunes of BBC Radio One, when he was appointed the Controller. One of his first actions was to sack two of the BBC's legendary DJs, Simon Bates and Dave Lee Travis, and bring in the irrepressible, Chris Evans. These bold moves signalled the new man was going to shake up the BBC's prestigious pop music channel and drive it in a new, and ultimately successful, direction.

Activities for all

Just as school music continued to thrive, so too did the intensity and variety of the school's extra-curricular activities with at least twenty-five different societies, clubs and groups operating during the Seventies. If there was a change in emphasis from the past, it is that there were now less subject-based societies and more communal activities in the new comprehensive school. It had long been common for some societies to have a short shelf life and fold as individual enthusiasts moved on, but many thrived throughout the Seventies in one guise or another, like the Debating Society. It was renamed Talkshop in 1972 and then the Political Debating Society in 1976, when it voted by 72-19 that the Labour Government should resign immediately, and could attract a hundred pupils to its debates in the LLR. Four hundred gathered in the Hall in 1978, when it was known as the Upper School Forum, to hear Martin Kelner, Radio Hallam's best known presenter, whilst speakers, or films, on the arms trade, factory farming, the Samaritans or the anti-smoking and anti-vivisection campaigns, attracted a usual audience of around fifty.

There was a Blues Society, a Writers' Club, a Craft Society — that tried its hand at jewellery and silverware — an Electronics Club, a Model Boat Club that sailed its creations on Wire Mill Dam, a Railway Society and for the cerebral a Bridge Club was established. Meanwhile, the Chess Club under the guidance of Gordon Adam, won the Sheffield Schools Chess League every year from 1965 –1972, and they excelled themselves in 1969 when they were the finalists in the National Schools Championship and followed this in 1971 and 1972 by becoming the Yorkshire Schools' Champions. Many of these activities were open to pupils from Upper and Lower School, but there were societies based at Darwin Lane, like the Lower School Art Club, that operated at lunchtime on that site and replicated clubs based primarily at Upper School.

One of the earliest societies ever formed at KES was the Natural History Society in 1905, and its successor in the Seventies flourished and even printed its own magazine, "KESTREL". They carried out field work in the Lower Loxley Valley and later in the decade, at the Lower School, the O.W.L. Club was formed, not to support Sheffield Wednesday, but to "observe wild life". Also working to improve the environment was a group of pupils, organised by Ray Stittle, who cleared a section of the River Loxley at Malin Bridge in 1973 and got themselves thoroughly wet into the bargain.

Youth Action could boast 90 members in the early Seventies and the volunteers helped out at Lodge Moor and Middlewood Hospitals, usually supporting the older patients but sometime leading play activities for younger children on the wards. It could be rewarding, if not disconcerting work, and one particular man in an iron lung made a considerable impression on the group with his cheerfulness, inquisitiveness and fortitude under the most desperate of circumstances. Girls played an increasingly significant role in all KES societies but particularly in Youth Action, though some today will admit they initially saw it as a way of "skiving off" games on a Wednesday afternoon.

For those who fancied something a little more strenuous there was the Fell Walking Club. Always popular in the Sheffield region with so many beautiful accessible hills and dramatic escarpment edges, it is not surprising that this club became well established in the Seventies. During school holidays the club tackled challenges like the Old Man of Coniston, or the Lyke Wake Walk from Osmotherley to the coast, although one Sixth Former's freedom to roam did not, it appears, mean freedom to smoke, and on returning one Monday morning he received the cane for his misdemeanour.

Some groups played an even more significant role in the life of the school and created a continuum to the present day. One was the group involved in the Duke of Edinburgh Award Scheme started by David Marcer in 1975. Appealing to both boys and girls, it required participants to attempt to gain a bronze, silver or gold award by undertaking an expedition, an interest, a design and a service. It was said that the idea was based on a similar scheme at the Duke of Edinburgh's old school, Gordonstoun, and in February 1977 two KES girls, Linda Edwards and Sarah Houghton went to the Palace to be presented with their Gold Award certificates by Prince Philip. They were the first KES pupils to achieve the Gold Award and they would be first of many (at least one in five

Linda Edwards and Sarah Houghton at Buckingham Palace in 1977

KES pupils on the scheme gained the Gold Award), while at least half the participants got their Bronze Award before dropping out. To recognise the progress of the KES group, the school was made an Award Centre in 1980, housed in the old scout hut, and much envied by other schools.

In 1978 David Anderson entered a KES team for the national Young Enterprise scheme. Initially named KESCO, the "company" had to design and manufacture a simple but useful product, (amongst these items were perspex picture frames, casserole stands, bird boxes, knee desks etc.) sell shares, organise marketing and sales and make a profit on its year long entrepreneurial skills. They had to keep company records, do VAT returns and establish a "Board of Directors" to co-ordinate the company's activities and finally produce a full company report. KES Economics students had been involved in three one-off competitions earlier, winning one in 1975 and another, a Sheffield Polytechnic's computer business game, in 1977. Now, participating in the Young Enterprise scheme, KES Sixth Formers would win at least one local award virtually every year. Four times they got to the finals, and although winning the national competition eluded them, they did come a very creditable second in the 1980-81 competition.

Anderson also organised the KES entries for the European Schools' Essay Writing Competition where KES candidates had regular success. KES had often won the British part of the competition in the early 1960s but now they were successful in successive years from 1967-75, and in 1975 John McCabe won the Gold Medal for the overall European winner, the second time the school had achieved this award.

Whilst most societies were well reported, they often only catered for a small number of pupils, but the school also encouraged communal activities which involved more pupils. The Lower School started its Annual Fairs in 1975, when the car park was a sea of stalls and apparently, among a plethora of objects sold, there was a great demand for back numbers of KESMAG which had plenty of remainders to sell off. In the same year the School Camp started, held under canvas at Thornbridge Hall, the City Council's Derbyshire "Chequers". To some extent this replaced the scout camps, but its greatest appeal was that it was held in term time and there was so much demand that a second week was booked to accommodate the numbers. It was the precursor of the residential weeks and it offered another opportunity to involve all pupils and strengthen staff-pupil understanding. Periodically in KES's history there have been variety shows usually just before the Christmas holidays (in the pre-war period they were known as the "Shout"). In 1976 they were resurrected and one of their features was a Miss KES competition, strictly male entrants, both pupils and staff, although one genuine "old" girl did feature as one of the first "Page Three" girls in the Sun newspaper around that time.

Jonson to Ayckbourn

Drama in the Seventies benefited from four new developments. Women's parts could now be played by KES's own girls rather than borrowing actresses from Grange Girls G.S., when young boys were no longer prepared to be cajoled into playing female parts. The new buildings at Darwin Lane had a purpose built proscenium arch stage in a hall with uninterrupted sight lines. A new teacher, Nick Jones, was designated as the teacher in charge of drama (although he was only informed of this at the time of the interview after he accepted the post of No.2 in the English Department), and Sheffield now had a producing theatre of national standing when the Crucible was opened in 1971.

In the 1970 production of Jonson's "Alchemist", KES girls took on the leading roles for the first time, with Margaret Young playing Doll Common and Caroline Wyke-Smith as Dame Pliant, in a quality production that defiantly staked out the intellectual high ground. The reviewer in KESMAG suggested that a goodly number of the audience may very well not grasp many of the nuances and topical allusions of an early 17th Century play, and a more modern choice might not go amiss. The following year "The Travails of Sancho Panza" was performed at Lower School thereby beginning the tradition of two plays a year, one at Upper School, mainly Sixth Formers, and a "Junior" play for the three Lower School years.

In 1973, the Upper School presented Gogol's "The Government Inspector" in a Yorkshire setting with local names, such as "Judge Fiddler" and "School Superintendent Lerner", replacing the Russian ones, and the eclectic nature of school productions was further advanced with a performance of "Hobson's Choice", Priestley's iconic North Country comedy also parodying the pompous inadequacies of councillors and their ilk. Was someone sending a message to the newly created councils like the new metropolitan county, who later rejoiced under the sobriquet of "the Socialist Republic of South Yorkshire"?

Nick Jones's first productions also picked up local themes by local playwrights. In 1974 the Lower School Play was Ayckbourn's " Ernie's Incredible Illucinations" and the School Play in 1976 was "Billy Liar", with Graham Fellows delivering a bravura performance in the eponymous leading role. Thereafter it was a return to Shakespeare in 1978, with "Taming of the Shrew" the choice for the first Shakespearean play since the school became comprehensive. In a play, not now necessarily the choice of feminists, the girls dominated the action with a strong performance by Jane Hill as Kate and some admirable cameo supporting roles from several girls. It was becoming clear that KES girls would play an ever increasing part in the development of school drama in the next three decades, as, indeed, they would do in virtually all aspects of school life.

Drama was not a curriculum subject for the Middle School, nor could you take "O" Levels or CSE examinations in the subject, but Nick Jones did run optional, "complementary time" lessons in drama for interested sixth formers, from which the 1977 production of "A Midsummer Evening" – an adaptation of "A Midsummer Night's Dream" – emerged. He also acknowledges that school drama was aided by the formation of the Sheffield Youth Theatre, in 1978, by Meg Jepson, the long serving LEA Drama Adviser. A score of KES pupils were members at that time, attending workshops in the holidays and performing at the delightful Merlin Theatre in Nether Edge.

Nick Jones passed on the production of the school play to Roger Watkin, who produced "Oh, What a Lovely War", in 1980, an evergreen production that utilises so many varied talents and is well suited to a school cast. Moreover, because of continual interest in the First World War, it always has a clear message for an audience from each new school generation. As an innovation the school borrowed some tiered "bleacher" seating for the hall and this improved both the audiences' view and the space available to the actors. It would be retained for almost all productions from then on.

Ahead of the pack

The Seventies, when the comprehensive school was finding its feet, was a "golden" period in KES sport. Not since the Thirties had so many KES teams had such success, with so many individuals gaining representative honours and performing in so many different sports. In one public speech, the Headmaster reported that the school had forty–five teams at all ages playing inter-school fixtures, and that he was particularly delighted at the strength of girls' sport, which had soon produced their own stars and whose teams were in no way overshadowed by the established boys' sports' teams. The particular success stories of boys' sport in that decade were the achievements of the Rugby Union teams and the school's athletes, whilst Football retained its premier position and school cricket had something of a revival.

Eileen Langsley, the Head of Girls P.E. was the driving force behind the remarkable growth of girls' sport at KES in that decade. Starting from a small base of ex-Crosspool pupils and building up teams in different sports from the Lower School forms, she developed a programme that at its height offered girls fourteen sporting options, with the school running 28 girls' teams. The major winter sports were Netball, Hockey, Badminton, Volleyball, Gymnastics and Cross Country and in the summer the emphasis turned to Tennis, Rounders, and Athletics, but there were also opportunities for Riding, Ice Skating and the development of a sizeable group performing Dance.

There were so many winning teams at all age groups that one cannot, in this chapter, pay them the recognition they deserve. However, there were some outstanding individual star athletes, players and performers who represented the city, the county and even Great Britain and who immeasurably raised the standards of the school teams. Amongst the first to be recognised were two girls who came up through Crosspool Secondary School, Wendy Theaker and Jane Simm. At Crosspool, Wendy Theaker had already been the Junior Girls Champion in 1969 but then she represented Sheffield in the Yorkshire Championships for three years (1971-73) in the Long Jump as well as the 400 metres. Jane Simm shared the Champion Girl Athlete's position with Wendy and whilst she too represented Sheffield at the Yorkshire Athletics Championships her real forte was in Cross Country, a new sport for most girls at the school in 1970. Whilst KES boys had long been pre-eminent at Cross Country, there were now some outstanding girl runners as well. Jane went on to represent Yorkshire at the English Schools National Cross Country Championships and later in the decade Sarah Bloor would emulate her achievements. Between 1974 and 1979 Sarah would represent Sheffield on the track, or at Cross Country, during every season and in 1979 along with two other KES girls would be in the South Yorkshire team at the E.S.A.A. Cross Country Championships. That same year saw Yvonne Hanson-Nortey win the Intermediate Shot at the E.S.A.A. Championship, and she went on to represent Great Britain at the Seoul Olympics in 1988 and win a Bronze Medal at the Commonwealth Games in Auckland in 1990. Yvonne can lay a fair claim to being KES's top athlete in any era, challenging the miler David Law, who at one time in 1953 held a world record for the 4 x 1500m Relay.

Yvonne Hanson-Nortey

Joanna Sime

Two girls who represented Great Britain while they were at school, were the Sime sisters. Inspired by Olga Korbut's performance at the 1972 Munich Olympics, KES started a very popular Gymnastics Club and very soon Katy and Joanna Sime emerged as two absolutely outstanding talents. By 1976 Katy was not only in the English Schools Team, but also became the Yorkshire Senior Champion and was selected for the National Senior Squad. She left school in 1977 and joined the London Contemporary Dance School to continue a career in Dance. Her younger sister, Joanna, went even further and when still in the Lower School she was the English National U14 Champion and already selected for the U18 National Squad, competing against Bulgaria, Poland, West Germany, Finland, and in the match against Sweden she was the overall winner. She left school in February 1978 to continue her training with an American coach in the USA but not before she had represented the British Senior Squad against Romania, Hungary, Poland and the Netherlands. Her school mates raised £400 to enable her to train in the USA and it is a tribute to both sisters that they could achieve such a standard with the limited facilities that were available in Sheffield.

Eileen Langsley left KES in 1980 to become a sports photographer. She was quite a sportswomen herself having represented South Yorkshire at Hockey and was an accomplished Alpine climber. She left a formidable legacy to her successors and in her last year, 1979/80, a year she considered the best yet, KES girls reached national school finals in four different sports. She had brought on some star performers like Debbie Bowles and Jackie Spence, who dominated Sheffield Girls' Badminton, and established

KES girls' teams as very serious competitors in all the sports in which the school participated.

KES Boys' Sport was equally as competitive, and ultimately as successful, as that of the KES Girls. There was a belief, fanned by some tabloid and broadsheet newspapers, that competitive sport died with comprehensive education, that competition was anathema to modern, "trendy" teachers and that team sport declined as a result. This notion took a firm hold in a good many people's minds, but if it was ever true it did not apply to Sheffield, and certainly not to KES. Boys' sport at KES had a long pedigree and in the Seventies its progress mirrored the girls' new achievements, with several outstanding team and individual performances.

For the first four years of the Seventies the Rugby Union Team was virtually unbeatable. In the four seasons from 1970-71 till 1973-4 they played 105 matches and won 94. In the two middle seasons they lost only one match in each season and although most of their fixtures were against schools whose main winter sport was Association Football, they did increasingly take on rugby schools, like Temple Moor in Leeds, Crossley and Porter in Halifax, Wath and a touring side from Penarth G.S. in Wales, and defeat them. Andrew Hall, gained the try scoring record with 35 tries in the 1971-72 season and the following year, when captain, he was selected, at centre, for the full Yorkshire side and played against Northumberland, a big achievement for a boy from a school where rugby was the second winter sport. John Phillips, a goal-kicking prop, was selected for the South Yorkshire side and he holds the record for the highest number of points (139) in a season. He was later a stalwart member of Sheffield RUFC at Abbeydale, and is currently President of the Old Edwardians' Association.

The staff, who had a very successful soccer team that was unbeaten in the early Seventies, challenged the school to a rugby match in 1974 but came off second best, going down 30-0. The match caused considerable interest, if only because it gave boys a legitimate reason to "scrag" their teachers, but in 1978 the staff managed an honourable 6-6 draw. There were always plenty of staff members who had played rugby in their own schooldays and often to a fair standard. Ian Reid, who coached the successful teams at the beginning of the Seventies was one in point. He was then the captain of Sheffield Tigers RUFC and a more than useful stand off or centre, but he left KES in 1971 and went into education administration ending his career as Director of Education for South Tyneside MBC. Among staff members supporting on the touchline was R.N. "Bert" Towers, the Head of Geography, who had helped launch the first KES Rugby Union teams in 1951, and could always be diverted in class when asked to demonstrate a proper tackling technique, or recount Obolensky's try that beat the 1936 All Blacks.

Rugby Union stayed strong in the Seventies, and in 1975-76 the team went through the season again with only one defeat, also providing five members of the South Yorkshire side. Yet the first team only had a small base of thirty to forty rugby players to call on, but in home matches they always had on their side *"the cold north wind to freeze unsuspecting opponents who ventured up to Castle Dyke"* (It was said that a game would only be cancelled if you could not knock a 6 inch nail into the pitch; if you could the game was on). Rugby Union had come of age at the school, with its annual dinners at the

George Hotel in Hathersage, its tours to Wales and Northumberland, and its reports now taking priority over Football in the school magazines. At the end of the Seventies the finest player of any KES generation began to play for the junior teams. Mark Reid, an outstanding lock forward, was later selected to play for England U19 Schools in 1983, the only boy from a comprehensive school amongst players from the most exclusive schools in the land. He later played for Leicester, arguably the best Union team of last quarter century, and also represented the Midlands. Yet despite all this success, Rugby Union in Sheffield schools would wither and die in the late Eighties and Rugby League, supported by the new Sheffield Eagles RLFC, would replace it in half the city's comprehensive schools, including KES, in the Nineties.

One might surmise from all this rugby progress that Association Football was taking a back seat, but you would be wrong. The 1970-71 side was probably the most successful football team the school ever fielded in its history to date. Out of 37 matches played, they won 33 and lost only 1. Captained by Mike Jepson, every regular member of the team scored including Wastnedge, the goalkeeper. For good measure they won the prestigious Yorkshire Seven-a-Side trophy and almost retained it the following year when they lost on penalties in the final. Steve Smith was selected for the Yorkshire Schools team in 1973, and when a separate South Yorkshire Team was created after the new metropolitan counties were established, KES boys regularly filled the ranks of the county team. One of those selected in 1976, Ian Froggatt, was probably destined to make the county side because he was the son of the Sheffield Wednesday legend, Redfearn Froggatt, though Nick Thatcher, who captained the team in the 1979-80 season, we understand was not related to you know who!

The KES TEAM Season 1970-71 Mike Jepson (Captain) J.C. Hemming at right rear. David Jinks at left rear.

Cricket teams on the whole did a little better in the Seventies than in the Sixties, although they still had as strong a fixture list that included a lot of traditional public school opponents, who took cricket very seriously. Cricket is the one sport that does not seem to have been in tune with comprehensive education and everywhere it struggled to survive. Nevertheless KES teams chalked up a fair number of wins and in 1973 they were unbeaten. They had retained virtually the same side from the previous year and it was Eddie Exley, the captain, who led this revival, scoring 102 runs against the staff, the first century at the school for just over a decade.

One school cricket legend who retired in 1971,was Leslie Waghorn, or "Wag" to three decades of Edwardians. He had been the groundsman, cum cricket coach, for longer than anyone could remember and his 36 years in the post outdid the length of service of his illustrious predecessor, J.W.Smith. He had played for Sussex, and was reputed to have bowled out Bradman, until a serious knee injury, sustained ironically playing football, had cut short his county cricket career. Arriving at Whiteley Woods in 1935 he had coached KES cricketers since the days when he prepared the grounds with a horse-drawn mower, and he also kept trespassers at bay with the help of a succession of fierce dogs. The last one of which was called Jasper, and the mere mention of its name could frighten off young intruders several years after it had in fact died. He coached bowlers by making them drop a good length ball onto a handerkerchief and it is said that on one occasion when the opposition failed to materialise, he took the 1st XI on by himself and beat them. His deputy, only ever known as Austin, took over.

"WAG"

In the 1977 and 1978 Seasons the school team was captained by Hamid Moghul, the first Asian boy to captain a school team (his brother, Abdul, had played for the First XV). Moghul, a stylish bat who had headed the batting averages in the two previous seasons 1975 and 1976, led the team to two fairly successful seasons, although both of them were badly disrupted by rain. He was followed as captain by Paul Barron, another consistent batsman, who gained a trial for the Yorkshire Schools XI.

The school ran boys' teams in thirteen sports in the Seventies, including Swimming, Water Polo (where they beat Manchester G.S. 9-0 in 1972), Biathlon (where Neil Marshall won the Sheffield Individual Title with 2100 points in 1970), Basketball, Badminton, Volleyball, Orienteering and Hockey. In 1973 Tony Hedley, who had joined the Sixth Form from King Edward VI School in Southampton, gained a place in the

England U19 Schools' Hockey team, after starring as a prolific goal-scoring forward for Yorkshire and the North of England. Unfortunately, just before the international match he broke his wrist and the opportunity to play for his country was lost. If he had played he would have been the first boy, in the history of the school, to gain international honours while still at the school.

Some of these sports were played as and when, but most had regular fixture lists and regularly produced strong individual competitors. In Tennis, Kevin Charlesworth and Ian McHale were triple winners in the Singles and the Doubles in the 1972 Sheffield and District Junior Tournament, with Ian McHale and Peter Shuttleworth winning four cups between them in the same tournament in 1974. Later, in 1976, Peter Shuttleworth won an Individual Snow Slalom Championship in the Cairngorms, and KES skiers began to benefit from visits of school parties to the Slovenian Alps and Italian Dolomites.

In Boy's Athletics the most successful athlete at the beginning of the Seventies was Peter Stacey, who, after helping the KES mixed team win the 1971 Sheffield Schools Championship, went on to win the Yorkshire 1500m steeplechase title. He then represented Yorkshire in the 1973 E.S.A.A. Championship in Cheshire, where he came third with a time of 4 mins. 28.4 seconds. He complained that whenever he ran, a certain Sebastian Coe, who considered joining the KES Sixth Form but preferred the wide open spaces of Abbeydale's playing fields for training, was always in the same event and usually beat him to the tape. At the end of the decade the school produced another star performer in Christian Bloor, whose success came in cross-country as well as athletics. Trained by Sheffield A.C. coaches, he gained county success at 1500m before stepping up to 3000m and winning the E.S.A.A. Intermediate Championship, thereby gaining selection for the 1978 English Schools team. In 1979 he was also selected to represent England against France in a Cross Country International fixture.

Sport at KES had not only survived comprehensive re-organisation — it had flourished, despite the disappearance of the house teams which now seemed an arcane irrelevance. Never before had the school produced so many top performers in so many sporting disciplines, but more important it had served to bind the school community together. It is often claimed by its defenders that sport unites communities and nations (not always obvious when England's Football team travels abroad), but in the strictly streamed regime of the Seventies at KES, pupils rarely had much contact with their peers in higher or lower streams, but they met in large numbers as equals, friends and team-mates in the school VIIs, XIs and XVs, bound by a common enthusiasm and skill that really does cross all social barriers.

On its legs and up and running

In 1978 the Sunday Telegraph ran a substantial two page article by a nationally renowned journalist, Graham Turner, comparing the fortunes of KES with those of Manchester Grammar School during the last decade. The Telegraph probably came with its own agenda about comprehensive education, but it claimed that the social cohesion of the school was limited, and that streamed classes, most likely reflecting the social background of the pupils, had produced social hurdles, even tensions, between different ability groups. Most pupils at the school at the time would agree. After all, the school had never disguised that it had set out in 1969 to preserve as much of the grammar school system as possible, using CSE courses to raise the standards of its other pupils while maintaining the maximum opportunity for pupils to progress and move easily between ability levels.

What Sharrock and his staff had done in the interim, was to address a large number of complex and difficult issues and find pragmatic solutions to them, so that at the end of the decade he could rightly say that he had set the new KES on its legs, and it was up and running as a comprehensive school. The huge number of pupils, almost twice the number of pupils there were in Clapton's time, would alone have created problems for cohesion and organisation, but when added to the task of fusing two different academic traditions, welcoming co-education and operating on five sites with two distant playing fields, then it is fair comment to say that the cautious approach to manage this change was the correct one, and an iconoclastic headteacher might well have come badly unstuck.

Furthermore, the Seventies had been a decade of profound change in young peoples' attitudes. Teenage lifestyles from boys' long hair and bizarre clothes, the availability of the pill and an increasingly strident pop culture, to protests over the Viet Nam war, student sit-ins, and even some school pupil activist groups like the National Union of School Students and the Students Action Union, could have been inimical to calm, constructive school work, and made the development of a new comprehensive school even more difficult to achieve.

Unlike the grammar schools, comprehensive schools were not part of a settled system of education, they were extremely complicated with everyone involved still feeling their way. Schools like KES were embarked on a continuous search to find the most effective way to engage, involve and raise the standards of all the pupils in their schools. It was no longer relevant whether KES had more Oxbridge scholarships than any other maintained school, or whether it was the "best" school in its city or county. It was not participating in a race with its contemporaries; its function now was to be part of the Sheffield LEA's family of schools, helping to provide the best education possible for the city's secondary school pupils.

At the beginning of the Eighties a new leadership group took over from Arthur Jackson, John North and Winifred Kinnear, and a number of other long-serving staff members retired around this time as well. In 1979, Robert Towers (Tim to the staff but Bert to the school) left after 33 years as Head of Geography. A former wartime naval officer and now the longest serving staff member at KES, his teaching suggested he had never become fully reconciled to the loss of the Empire. Fred Constadine also left, after 21 years teaching at Western Rd., Crosspool and latterly KES and a little later the flamboyant aesthete Charles Baker, the Head of Divinity, Stella Boon, the Head of Modern

Languages, Norman Beatson and then Gladys Manifield, the Deputy Head of the Lower School, retired or moved on.

It was, however, the retirement of Arthur Jackson and John North that marks the year 1981 as a seminal year in the history of the school. Jackson had been the guiding administrative force behind the new comprehensive school, as well as leading the Sixth Form, handling University Entrance requirements and doing the unbelievably complicated time-table. Sharrock said of him,

> *"He has been regarded as the doyen of Deputy Heads in Sheffield, and he committed himself fully, though not uncritically, to the new comprehensive school, even persuading two of his own daughters to come here. Stringently professional, loyal, painstaking in meticulous detail – he is the complete school master!"*

Unlike Arthur Jackson, who has enjoyed a long retirement, recently in a picturesque Derbyshire village, John North died within two years of leaving the school. North came from a farming background in the North Riding, but later joined the regular army and saw war service in France before Dunkirk and then in the Far East. He was captured by the Japanese in Burma and some believe

Arthur Jackson
(Deputy Head 1958-81)

John (Jack) North (Acting Head at Crosspool School 1967-69 and later Head of Middle School at KES)

never really recovered from that experience. He always looked to support the trier rather than the champion, and when he was President of Sheffield RUFC he would often be seen on the touchline of the 3rd or 4th XV urging them on, rather than watching the more glamorous senior teams. In the same spirit he served for 25 years as a voluntary leader of Grimesthorpe Boys' Club, where as a skilled cricketer, rugby player, athlete and angler he could enthuse another generation with a love of sport. He was replaced by

Nick Jones, as Head of Middle School, and his passing closed the chapter on the history of Crosspool Secondary School.

By 1981 the school knew that the drums of war were already sounding again in the Town Hall. Under the leadership of David Blunkett, the Council Leader since 1980, another far-reaching re-organisation was being planned. This appeared to have extreme consequences for KES; in fact it could well see the demise of the school and the end of the name. However, for the moment, KES under Russell Sharrock's direction, including its thriving Sixth From, had reached a successful plateau and Graham Turner's final comment in his 1978 article serves as a general comment on the Seventies at KES.

> *"Like so many of his staff, Sharrock is an honest, decent and dedicated person, who in difficult circumstances is producing remarkable results."*

CHAPTER SEVENTEEN

THE SIX THAT GOT AWAY!
1981-1988

In the Eighties, during the third phase of Russell Sharrock's period as Headmaster, King Edward VII School began to explore the paths that might lead to a more complete comprehensive system of education. The emphasis within the school, the city and indeed nationally, concentrated on engaging the interest of the less able, the bored and disillusioned pupil, and the minority whose rejection of the system could not only jeopardise their own futures, but also disturb the education of their peers. Although KES had always been very good at educating the able pupil, and the comprehensive school carried on this tradition, it was more uncertain about how successfully it provided for the education of the other half of its pupils. True, the CSE results for the average boy and girl had improved throughout the Seventies and the pass level stood at a satisfactory level, but in 1980 two thirds of the Fifth Form opted to leave after their examinations, most of them seeking jobs but with a significant number preferring to continue their education at an F.E. College. At the same time the number of Sixth Form pupils had dropped to 250, and although there were a number of reasons for this, it all helped to encourage a re-think of where KES was heading as a comprehensive school.

There was virtually a new senior team appointed in the years 1980 and 1981, and they came from a different generation. They had joined KES when it was a comprehensive school and they had an enthusiasm for extending the vision, and the reality, of what a comprehensive school could achieve. Kay Alcock (later, after 1995, Mrs. Madden) and Dorothy Hall were the first of these new appointments, when, in the summer of 1980, they became Assistant Headteacher and the Head of Sixth Form respectively. Kay Alcock had been Head of Biology at Cramlington H.S., a purpose built comprehensive school in Northumberland, before replacing Winifred Kinnear, whilst Dorothy Hall had taught part time, and latterly full time, at KES for a decade and now took over Arthur Jackson's Sixth Form responsibilities, two terms before he finally left. Another two key, internal, appointments followed them, when Mike Denial replaced Jackson as an Assistant Head, with Nick Jones taking over as Head of Middle School from the retiring John North. Only Sharrock, who was almost twenty years older than his new senior team members, and Bryan Gallagher, the Assistant Head and Head of Lower School, appointed in 1976, remained of the school's previous leadership group. Gallagher was a forceful personality, who had developed the Lower School character and spirit by taking advantage of the split site. He fully appreciated that the comprehensive experience at KES started in the Lower School at Darwin Lane, and he aimed to create a welcoming environment for new secondary school pupils who might well be overawed in a school of nearly 1500 pupils. Gallagher, who had taught at a variety of Sheffield schools, including Hartley Brook (before the fire) and Silverdale (where he was Head of History), was closer in age to the new senior members and shared their aspirations for the school. Sharrock, also, was more at ease with his new senior team. He too was ready to move the comprehensive school on, and he was keen to see a widening of opportunities for all the pupils and gave his support to the new proposals, when they were fully formulated.

In 1981, the KES staff were not fully aware of how dramatic a decade lay in front of them in the school, in the region, as well as nationally and internationally. They knew the new radical Conservative Government was intending to shake up most British institutions, and that education would become higher on the political agenda of the nation than at any time since 1944. They had already had the first of the Education Acts in 1980, relatively mild by the standards of the 1986 and 1988 Acts, and then in the long hot summer of 1981, they looked on aghast as the cities of Britain descended into riots, with destructive clashes between youths and the police, which in some neighbourhoods turned into race riots. The generation gap had turned very sour, even in Sheffield which was virtually untouched by the trouble (although the Police on more than one occasion were sufficiently concerned to remove all the guns from gunsmiths' shops and relocate them in secure places in the suburbs). The spotlight was turned on education to help solve this outrageous phenomenon of urban violence, that could literally tear society apart, and schools were encouraged to consider more inclusive teaching policies.

This youth violence, which surprisingly calmed down the following year, largely by-passed Sheffield, but the city, and the county of South Yorkshire, were in the "eye of the storm" for most of the major confrontations in the first half of the decade between the Thatcher Government and their political and industrial "enemies". Some of these "battles" impacted more on the school than others. The slow attrition of public sector cutbacks led to a school desperately short of money, so that, compared with many other industrial nations, our "state" schools were very much under-resourced, shabby and even dilapidated. The school got used to the poor condition of buildings, with leaking roofs, scuffed and peeling walls and annexes that were not fit to house lessons. These latter premises had to continue in use because the LEA, subject to rate-capping, could not possibly contemplate new building development within the Close, even if it would have wished the school to bring back the "diaspora" of the classes scattered around the neighbourhood.

The school, of course, as always, learnt to cope with these difficulties. They were after all nothing particularly new, unlike two of the challenges Sharrock and his senior team now had to face. The Teaching Unions, some of whose members perceived themselves as "demonised" by the Government, started an unprecedented "work to rule" that lasted for two years from 1984 until 1986, and had a profound impact on the nature of voluntary activities within the school, especially a long term effect on school sport. The other challenge was potentially far more significant than even the teachers' action. From early 1981, Sheffield City Council planned for another massive re-organisation of its secondary education. It intended to introduce tertiary colleges for all post-16 education and make all secondary schools, 11-16 schools. For the next five years KES believed it was going to be split into two institutions, one amalgamated with Tapton, to form a new 11-16 school at Darwin Lane, whilst Upper School would become a tertiary college.

Neither building would continue to have the King Edward VII name, and therefore the school, founded in 1905, would cease to exist.

A subtle change of culture

Mike Denial

Kay Alcock, (later Mrs. Kay Madden)
Photographed before her retirement in
2005

Mike Denial and Kay Alcock, the two new Assistant Headteachers, were the guiding hand behind many of the changes in the syllabus that were intended to strengthen the teaching for the less able pupils. They introduced a number of initiatives, which included making the banding more flexible so that a wider number of subjects could be taken by individual pupils. They wanted to ensure that pupils could attempt an easier mix of "O" Level and CSE subjects that suited their interests and their skill level, and avoid situations where early subject choices limit the opportunities for pupils later in their career, like access to a second foreign language or separate sciences. They encouraged subject departments to teach mixed ability classes and several took the plunge and tried this. This was the comprehensive enthusiast's dream, whereby, within the same class, unselected boys and girls would be equal in esteem, but working successfully at their own ability level. Roger Watkin ran mixed ability English forms, with Peter Corkill, the Head of the Geography Department, following suit for Geography. After a while Ray Stittle allowed the History classes to be run on the same basis and even French, at a later date, allowed mixed ability teaching in the second forms, although it was setted in later year groups. P.E. and R.E. were used to having an unselected group of pupils and they now continued to run these classes. Other subjects like Maths and the Sciences felt it was just not possible, whilst Craft, Design and Technology saw a real opportunity to recruit more of the academic high flyers onto its rejuvenated courses. On reflection, the "jury" was undecided about how successful the experiment had been with the academic subjects; it did not particularly improve standards, but neither did it weaken them.

One area where the school could ensure there were unselected classes was in the pupils' registration forms. There, at least, pupils of different abilities and backgrounds, would rub shoulders first thing in the morning, even if they went their different ways during most of the day. At the same time the subject choices available to pupils was expanded with an increase in those doing Spanish, Economics (in the Middle School), Personal and Social Education (PSE) run by Anthea Peers, Computer courses and Work Experience, which had a programme at that time, co-ordinated by Brian Crookes, for a relatively small number of pupils (about 30-40 per year) who were intending to leave and find work when they reached 16. Denial was also insistent that all teachers, however senior, taught across the full ability range and also spent some time teaching at Darwin Lane, to ensure that, to those making important departmental decisions, Lower School was not a far away, forgotten annexe.

The Dawn of the New Age

Computers first arrived at KES in September 1980, when the school acquired an Apple word processor and at the same time won a Commodore "Pet" that was stabled at Lower School. A modest article in KESMAG suggested that whilst not of "earth shattering significance" their arrival was likely to be of importance to the school in the future. They had not fully grasped that KES had joined a teaching revolution that is perhaps the most significant change in teaching during the last hundred years and whose full impact we have yet to realise. Ed Wilson, soon to be Head of Maths, guided those first classes in the use of the computer, until Chris Phipps arrived, in January 1982, to teach Maths and help to run the Computer Studies programme at the school.

When interviewed Phipps was asked, by the Headmaster, if he would be interested in running courses on computers, and he was so keen to come to KES that he willingly volunteered. Unbeknown to the interviewing panel, Phipps had never used a computer, but he spent the next few weeks before his arrival learning the rudimentary skills. He quickly found that, whilst, in the time-honoured way of newly qualified teachers, he could keep one lesson ahead of the novice pupils, those who had computers at home were keen to instruct him in these new and esoteric arts.

The following year, benefitting from a Government initiative, the school got ten BBC "Model A" computers and they were housed in Room 64, which became the computer suite. These were "primitive" machines, slow and unreliable, with everything loaded through a cassette, rather than a disk, and in September 1983 they were thankfully upgraded to Model B machines. By 1984, every pupil in

S3 (Y9) was taking a non-examination computer course, and there was an "O" Level and CSE option available for S4 and S5 pupils who wanted to try it.

Two years later there was a re-think, and it was decided instead to introduce ICT into as many subject syllabuses as possible, thereby creating practical uses for teaching and skills. The quality of printed material and graphics available to a class-room teacher was now also immeasurably improved, and the school could eventually say farewell to the poorly printed notes and examination papers, that had been squeezed out on the Banda or on inky stencils. Phipps became the man who co-ordinated this use of computers in the subject classes and in the absence of any technicians, he was in charge of maintenance as well. In 1989, the school decided to dispense with discrete computer courses and concentrate on subject based ICT work and this remained the school's policy until September 2004, when it was decided to run stand-alone computer courses again.

The office staff were not provided with word processors until the Nineties, and, of course, there was no Internet for the school to link up with in the Eighties.

Nick Jones, the new Head of Middle School, also wanted to introduce a pastoral regime that was less authoritarian and more caring than the one that had grown out of the traditions of the former grammar and secondary modern schools. He was guided by his experiences in 1979-80 when he was granted secondment to study for a Master's Degree in Education. He had made a study of pastoral care, with an especial interest in the dichotomy between the requirements of student support and the disciplinary role of the staff. He researched the practice in three Sheffield comprehensives, widely separated across the city and found that by and large they all got the balance right, although some of them had many more difficult pupils than KES had to deal with. When he returned to the school he advocated a more liberal ethos, with a more child centred approach to pastoral care, and now as Head of Middle School he could implement some of those ideas.

One immediate key decision, with the Headmaster's support, was to assume the sole right to cane in the Middle School. Before 1981 any member of staff could cane a pupil if they followed the correct procedure and in the Middle School that was still at a fairly high level of 70 canings a year, whilst the cane in the Lower School had fallen into disuse. Jones was concerned that a few members of staff used the cane too frequently and by taking the duty on himself, he could ensure that while corporal punishment existed at the school it would be fully controlled.

The demise of two "peculiar" English institutions

The whole issue of the use of corporal punishment in Sheffield schools was decided by the City Council in 1982. At the same time they took a unilateral decision to make the wearing of school uniform voluntary. In both cases they met much opposition, and some considerable hostility, from parents, school staffs and even from pupils themselves. While continental Europe and North America appeared to be able to run an education system without caning its pupils and without forcing them into uniforms, in Britain the continued survival of both institutions was seen, by many, as essential to a good education. Some, even now, appear to equate caning of school children with the maintenance of the wellbeing of the nation.

To Nick Jones, as Head of Middle School, both decisions helped to improve relations with his pupils. Caning was increasingly being resented by Fourth and Fifth Formers; the days when a boy would shake hands after a jolly good thrashing, and admit he deserved it, were no longer with us. School uniform presented a continual challenge to the school's authority. Pupils reluctance to wear clothes that seemed as ancient to them as Eton jackets and gymslips might seem to the adults, ensured a continual guerrilla war between teachers and those who constantly tested the boundaries of school uniform and dress codes. For teenage girls especially, the clothes they wore were very important to them, enabling them to show their individuality and demonstrate flair and imagination, and yet schools, in this instance, demanded unquestioning uniformity.

It is surprising that the City Council did not abolish corporal punishment earlier. Partly, it was because they did not want to upset schools and parents, in a matter that had largely been seen as the school's own business and partly because they guessed that they would receive a negative reply if they agreed to sound out parents' and staff opinion. KES parents were no more sympathetic to abolition than those of any other Sheffield school, but the Labour Council abolished it anyhow, citing its brutalising effect and its variance with the civilised values of our society. Many teachers are still not sure that outright abolition was the right course. Sharrock, himself, still believes it should be the final deterrent against the unrepentant bully and that it was quick, well understood and efficient in its application. Nevertheless, from September 1982 no pupil could be caned, or hit, in a Sheffield school and there were many who were bitterly dissatisfied with the Council's decision. However, the 1986 Education Act abolished corporal punishment in all maintained schools, brought Britain into line with other E.C. countries, and relegated the cane to a nostalgic, perhaps infamous, place in British educational history.

Whilst the Labour Group's actions over corporal punishment could well be justified as progressive thinking, and it is impossible to envisage that the cane will ever return, its arbitrary decision to make the wearing of school uniforms voluntary in its maintained schools caused it very great embarrassment. It is rumoured that the catalyst that brought the matter to a head, was the suspension of the daughter of a senior councillor from a comprehensive school in south Sheffield for not wearing the right shade of stockings. So confident were the councillors that children so disliked school uniform, and working class parents so disliked paying for updating their blazers, shirts and ties, that they assumed their decision to make the wearing of school uniform a voluntary matter would be a popular one. Only the Co-op Party delegates, for obvious motives, were against the move when it was debated, but Peter Horton, the Chair of Education, insisted that parents and schools must be consulted. So started a curious process, in which parents thought they were being asked if they wanted compulsory school uniforms, whilst the Labour controlled Council were in fact asking a rather arcane question about how their decision would be "implemented".

Coun. Joan Barton, then a relatively new councillor and Chair of the Schools' Sub Committee, now considers that the Labour Group handled it all very badly and they were politically very embarrassed. Parents and Staff, at every school, held meetings and ballots about the issue and all rejected the Council's decision. For good measure, pupils, when consulted, rather surprisingly voted to keep uniform too, adding to the Council's confusion and discomfort. At KES the parents, who responded to a questionnaire, voted 69% for compulsory wearing of uniform, 20% for voluntary with only 6% for abolition with 5% neutral or uncertain. The Governors, however, were largely sympathetic to the council's position, unanimously passing a face saving resolution that the issue of school uniform should be left to the discretion of school governing bodies, the position that exists in Sheffield schools today.

Notwithstanding all this overwhelming opposition to their policy, the Labour Group used its majority to push the decision through the September 1982 Council Meeting and reluctant schools were told, in no uncertain terms, that they had to comply. Nick Jones recalls how he announced at a subsequent Middle School Assembly (Sixth Formers had not been compelled to wear uniform for a decade, although prefects still wore their special blazers) that from tomorrow, the wearing of school uniform was voluntary. Came the morrow and there was not a uniform in sight. KES pupils had voted with their hearts and instead adopted the international, teenagers' "uniform" of sweater/shirt and jeans or slacks. KES introduced a very attractive royal blue sweater for sports purposes in the Nineties, but unlike most other Sheffield schools did not make it compulsory for wearing in lessons.

Left of centre Governors?

The Governors in the Eighties played a more than usually active role in the business of the school. When they were all present they formed a "mass" meeting of 27 men and women, with almost everyone represented who could stake a claim. Surprisingly, the Parent Governors, who often met privately to consider their representative view, formed a small minority of three, but they had an influence beyond their numbers (the next three Chairs of Governors were all Parent Governors). The Council retained a strong presence with nine LEA members, mainly from the Labour Party, and although there were no councillors on the Governors at that time, Mrs. Bobby Fleming, a much-respected Conservative nominated Governor, became a Councillor in the Nineties. The school was well represented with the Headmaster, three teaching and two non-teaching staff members and, until 1986, two pupil governors. Co-opted members and feeder school representatives made up the remaining governors, who included one or two former staff members, including Dave Meredith, who now was a solicitor in the city.

They were a very middle class group, with the university staff, the professions and graduates forming the majority of their members. The school might pride itself on representing all elements of the social spectrum in Sheffield, but the governors were more exclusive. They took their responsibilities very seriously and had a strong sense that they were on the Governing Body, not just to advance the school, but also to make the right decisions for Sheffield education in its totality, and sometimes these two priorities might very well appear to clash.

When Dr. Michael Blackburn, a lecturer at the University, took over the Chair, in 1982, from Mrs. Jean Mingay, the first woman "Chairperson" of KES Governors and herself a lecturer at the Polytechnic, the Governors began to play an even more intensive role in the governance of the school and the formulation of its policies. Dr. Julian Kinderlerer, the Vice-Chair and also Chair of Governors at High Storrs, recalls that there were numerous sub-committees, with the governors sometimes straying across that ill-defined line between making policy and involving themselves in management. Most governing bodies, like most committees or boards of directors, just coast along until they perceive a crisis. However, if there are strong, confident and knowledgeable personalities on a board, they can play a much larger role that might be most constructive, or alternatively might be destructive and divisive.

KES has had some considerable "intellectual firepower" on its Governing Body in the comprehensive era (three members of the Governors in the Eighties became Professors at the University, one of them became Pro Vice-Chancellor), and they had much to contribute to the continual debate about the nature and direction that comprehensive schools should follow. They were the official voice of KES and they spoke with a left of centre accent. Unusually for KES, the school, through its Governors, though not necessarily its staff, supported Sheffield's Labour Council on virtually all the major policy decisions of the Eighties, and whilst they had been forced to maintain a low profile on the issues of corporal punishment and uniforms, it was clear that they supported the council's decision. Later, in March 1984, the Governors, by an 18-1 majority, defended the council over rate-capping, despatching their resolution to the Secretary of State for the Environment. It read:

> "The Governors of KES express their strong support for the policy and action of Sheffield City Council in opposing the Government's rate capping legislation, and deplore the effect that such legislation would have on the City in general and on education in particular."

As rate-capping was the cornerstone of the Thatcher Government's policy of containing local government expenditure, it can only be guessed what the Secretary of State did with this resolution that arrived from a comprehensive school in the wilds of the "socialist" north. However, history records that rate-capping was introduced, despite the KES Governors' missive, and it did seriously affect the revenue and capital spending of the LEA and cause real financial hardship to Sheffield schools in the next decade.

The Governors could be just as forceful in defence of the school's interests, and at the same time as their foray into national politics they harangued the LEA over the *"disrepair of the school buildings and the lack of adequate facilities provided, that had reached such proportions as to seriously damage the morale, welfare and work of both the pupils and the staff of the school"*. However, throughout the early Eighties, no issue better illustrates their understanding of their governance role than their constant support for the Council over its plans for re-organisation of secondary education and the introduction of tertiary colleges. Most governing bodies would have automatically defended the status quo if their school was, in effect, being abolished. The KES Governors took the wider view, that the re-organisation was better for the school system in Sheffield as a whole, even if it meant the demise of a much-respected institution like KES. Russell Sharrock was always uncommitted on the tertiary issue, but even if he had been publicly opposed to KES's abolition, the Governors in the Eighties would have overruled him and continued their support of the re-organisation.

Reduced but most effective.

The school's Sixth Form had emerged intact from comprehensive re-organisation in the late Sixties and Arthur Jackson had successfully nursed it through the Seventies. So, although the school did not have as many academic high flyers as it had had during Clapton's time, the Sixth Form's record in the Seventies had been very commendable, so much so that a considerable number of pupils from other schools chose to complete their post-16 education at KES. In effect, the Sixth Form was still the "grammar school", because apart from pupils re-sitting "O" Levels and upgrading CSEs, all those in Forms S6, S7 and S8 were studying for "A" Levels and most went on to Universities or other places of Higher Education. Dorothy Hall took over a Sixth Form in 1980 that showed no drop in standard, but it did in numbers. In 1979 there were 302 pupils in the Sixth Form but by the following year it had dropped to 251, staying around that level till the middle of the decade when the numbers began to climb up again. This initial fall was not caused by a drop in pupil numbers across the city — the effect of the end of the baby boom would hit sixth forms later in the decade — but by the growth of other schools' sixth forms and by the popularity of courses at F.E.Colleges.

By 1980, Tapton and Silverdale had flourishing sixth forms and they were all set to grow in the Eighties. Tapton pupils, in particular, had largely gone on to do their "A" Levels at KES — the two schools were officially linked for this purpose — and KES had also taken in pupils from schools all over the city, who were now developing embryonic sixth form courses of their own. At the same time many Fifth Form students, including some who wanted to do "A" Level courses, opted to continue their education at one of the four F.E. Colleges in the city, where they could take vocational courses, like Ron Gains, who became an apprentice car mechanic, and Helen Newbould, who took a Medical Secretary's course at Richmond College. They both submitted to an interview in KESMAG, and stressed how they had no regrets about leaving KES at 16 and now felt more like independent adults, enjoying the college's freer atmosphere, unlike the more regulated life they had experienced at school. In 1980 the numbers leaving to go into work or F.E. Colleges could have rung alarm bells at KES, but there seems to have been a genuine desire to find the right courses, or satisfactory work placements, for Fifth Form leavers and not pressure them to stay on at KES.

KES still had the largest Sixth Form in the city, and so it has remained to this day, and Governors and Staff did not feel concerned that the pressure of numbers had eased off; some felt it would preserve the quality of the Sixth Form. It was not uncommon for older staff in particular to see all pre-16 education as a preparation for the Sixth Form, where "proper" education could begin and pupils could be treated like adults. It was these attitudes that helped to inform the debate about the creation of 11-16 secondary schools and tertiary colleges, because there was a view abroad that schools with successful sixth forms put too much emphasis, and too many resources, into this minority of pupils at the expense of the "common herd" in the early teenage years.

Whether or not this was so, the KES Sixth Form offered twenty different subjects in the Eighties with most subject groups averaging about 15 pupils. Some popular subjects, such as Economics, English, French and the three Sciences ran two or three groups in each year and Geography, in 1984/85, ran nine groups in both S6 (Y12) and S7 (Y13), a tribute to the work Peter Corkill had achieved since he arrived at the school. Some subjects struggled with numbers, among them Latin and R.E., with only two pupils to a year group, and Home Economics and Music with five were "sailing close to the wind" in a resource strapped school. The Latin Department, in particular, felt its position was being eroded by the decision in 1982 that Latin would be a voluntary subject for those taking "O" Level, and although a reasonable number still took Latin to "O" Level, very few pupils now wanted to make it one of their three "A" Level choices. The fact that entrance to Oxford and Cambridge Colleges no longer required an "O" Level qualification in Latin, also had a major effect on the popularity of the subject that had once attracted many of the school's intellectual élite. Ever practical minded, Edwardians shunned a subject that they judged to be of little use to them, despite pleas that they were ignoring both the school's, and western civilisation's, rich cultural heritage. Sharrock was keen to continue with Latin, but he did not feel he could make it compulsory for any class and so the Latin Department was further reduced to two teachers, Arthur Jones and Alan Sutton. When John Warkup, the staff room's Times crossword ace (always finished by Morning Assembly) who had come to the school in the late Sixties after a decade running a pub in Totley, left in 1981, he was not replaced by another classics teacher.

If the school maintained a wide choice of "A" Level courses, they also maintained a high pass rate. The Headmaster reported to Governors in 1984 that the "A" Level results for the last three years had been;

1982   A-E Pass Rate 84%,   A-B Grades 28%

1983   A-E Pass Rate 83%,   A-B Grades 35%

1984   A-E Pass Rate 76%,   A-B Grades 39%

All these results were well above the national averages and highly commendable at the time. Some pupils were outstanding and one of them, Richard Speed, of the Science Sixth, won the Akroyd Scholarship and joined a rather distinguished group of Edwardians who have won that "blue ribband" of Yorkshire Scholarships. He later went on to Worcester College, Oxford, and more recently he has become the Professor of Strategic Marketing and Associate Dean of the Business School at Melbourne University. Dorothy Hall encouraged pupils to try the Oxbridge Entrance examinations and organised visits to colleges, usually Queen's Oxford, where so many O.E.s had studied in the past. This enabled Sixth Form boys and girls to glimpse college life and perhaps overcome preconceptions that now often turned bright pupils away from these two ancient universities. This was partly a response to the situation in 1982, when only Rachel Perry, who went to Christ's College, Cambridge, to read History, was successful, but in other years there were several successful candidates, including 1986 when nine Edwardians won Oxbridge places.

Pupils still came to KES from around the city and links were formed with schools as far away as Stocksbridge and the Hope Valley, as well as the continual number of girls who came from the local independent schools, including Brantwood and the Girls' High School. Ben Jackson opted for KES Sixth Form, after he had completed his "O" Levels at Yewlands School, and he found a totally different atmosphere at KES from the one he had experienced at his former school in north Sheffield. Jackson recalls how, for six months, until he found his feet, he felt somewhat intimidated by the high standard of his KES peers, and it took a while for him to feel secure about his ability to succeed in the Sixth Form. Jackson, who was made a prefect, went on to gain a place at Pembroke College, Oxford to read engineering, before changing to medicine and returning to run a general practice in the Dearne Valley. By and large, the "incomers" fitted in well to the KES Sixth Form, and KES students were welcoming, appreciating the rejuvenating contribution newcomers could make to school life. Their social life revolved around the Sixth Form common room (by now in Melbourne Annexe, their fourth home in a decade) and this helped to break the ice and let all Sixth Formers, from whatever school, get to know each other.

A "mini" Inspection of the Sixth Form was conducted, in 1985, by H.M. Inspectors who thoroughly investigated the operation and subject teaching of the school's post-16 education. The timing of the week-long inspection may well have been directed by "political" imperatives surrounding the tertiary re-organisation, but the result was a most successful report. It was pleasing that the Inspectors were particularly impressed with the quality of the advice given to pupils about which courses to study, not only at the school, but later in Higher Education and also the manner in which newcomers to the Sixth Form were welcomed and integrated into their new school.

Staff –pupil relations were easy and relaxed, and the Sixth Form was a happy place, despite operating under an uncertain future, when the most likely scenario was that it was going to be abolished. Many pupils felt real affection for the school and there was a rise in the numbers joining the Old Edwardians' Association. David Anderson, a keen supporter of the O.E.A., played his part in this recruiting and also in getting the Association to drop its ban on female members. They also inaugurated a custom of inviting the Head Prefect to give the "School Speech" at their Annual Dinner and one of the first Head Prefects to speak was one of the KES girls. In the Twenty First Century, although there are no longer any Head Prefects, the custom of a senior pupil's speech continues, and they are invariably given by rather sophisticated young ladies, soon to take their "A" Levels and then head off on an intrepid "gap" year, before going on to university.

"They're at it again!"

In January 1981 the Chairman of the Education Committee, still Coun. Peter Horton, produced a paper for his colleagues entitled "Post-16 Education – The Longer Term". It was the starting gun for the Council to propose, and then implement, another massive re-organisation of secondary education in the city. As far as Horton was concerned, he was proposing the logical completion of the comprehensive system of Sheffield's post primary education, which had been left unfinished in the Sixties. From the start it was clear that the proposals would split KES into two separate institutions, and their Sixth Form would cease to exist, with its courses being subsumed into a new tertiary college.

Surprisingly this was the one battle that the School did not fight, unlike the bitter struggles of 1926, 1944 and 1965. Then, on all three of those occasions, KES had "lost", whereas this time the Governors and the Staff would support the Labour controlled council, and then see "victory" snatched from the "jaws of defeat" on their behalf, but without their involvement. This time there was a separate Governing Body for KES who could clearly determine the school's official position, and they supported the general principles of the tertiary re-organisation from the very beginning, saving their criticism for details of the scheme rather than the substance of the proposals.

Meanwhile the City Council was faced with some major problems that all the LEAs in the country had to address. Overshadowing all other considerations, there was the imminent massive fall in pupil numbers that would hit the secondary sector in the middle Eighties. Between 1977 and 1992 pupil numbers in Sheffield were forecast to be reduced by 41%, a greater reduction than virtually any other LEA in the country. The Sixth Form numbers across the city, which had been static for several years, were expected to reduce from a peak of 3700 in 1982 to 1800 in 1993, unless there was an unexpected increase in recruitment. The KES Sixth Form was forecast to be reduced to 170 pupils, still the biggest in the city, but even they would be struggling to provide the twenty "A" Level courses they currently offered. Only five other schools in the Nineties were expected to have a sixth form with over 100 pupils, and most would clearly be non-viable. Horton had lost the argument inside the Labour Group in 1975 when all secondary schools had been allowed to develop their sixth forms. It seemed then that Sheffield had turned its back on tertiary education, which they had first proposed as long ago as 1942, when planning the rebuilding of the city and its services after the Blitz. However the failure of many schools to build up a sustainable sixth form (Waltheof had 10 in the sixth form by 1985, whilst Herries had 9 and Norfolk 14 and only eleven schools had over 100 pupils) vindicated

Horton's concern that schools would remain unequal and inefficient, if they all tried to maintain sixth forms.

The solution he believed was to create tertiary colleges serving different areas of the city with each providing "A" Level, vocational, special needs and adult education courses on the same campus. Their size would mean that they could offer a very wide range of courses, including a full range of "A" Levels with minority subjects, or training, available at one or two of the colleges which had specialist departments. Existing F.E. Colleges would be subsumed into these new tertiary colleges, because the council was aware that they too had not been very successful in attracting school leavers to their courses. Although a substantial number of KES pupils had made the switch to the four F.E. Colleges, the overall numbers attending their courses were stuck at 11% of the age group.

The Tertiary and the 11-16 Schools' Plan

The Labour Group proposals, when they were firmed up, envisaged eight tertiary colleges, four based on the existing F.E. Colleges and four entirely new creations on the sites of existing secondary schools. They would cover all the council's post-16 education provision, except for the Sheffield Polytechnic, still at that time part of the LEA's huge empire. Twenty-seven of the remaining secondary schools would now become 11–16 schools, serving their local communities and then passing on their pupils, in the main, to the local tertiary college for their "A" Levels, or their City and Guilds etc. KES Upper School was selected to be the tertiary college for the "West Area" of the city, whilst the pupils of the Lower and Middle Schools of KES would all be located at Darwin Lane and amalgamated with Tapton to form a new 11-16 secondary school. The plan initially assumed nine schools would close, some to become tertiary colleges, like Rowlinson and Colley, while others would have their sites sold off, or used for other council purposes. These latter included Bradfield, which currently had a £500,000 building project in construction and Silverdale, which had already built up a considerable reputation and had a sixth form of 187. They were not well pleased to find that their pupils were being shunted off to High Storrs and that their buildings would be closed. Whatever assurances they were given, they felt Silverdale School was being abolished, and their governors, staff and parents decided they would not take this decision lying down.

The Planned Eight Tertiary Colleges were:

King Edward VII (Upper School) (W)
Abbeydale Grange (Bannerdale site) (SW)
Rowlinson (became NORTON) (S)
Richmond/Brook (became STRADBROOKE) (SE)
Granville College (became CASTLE) (E)
Stannington College (became LOXLEY) (NW)
Shirecliffe College (became PARKWOOD) (NE)
Colley/St. Peter's (became PARSON CROSS) (N)

KES Staff and Governors re-action.

The staff of the school were not initially in favour of change. Through the Staff Governors they presented a resolution to the Governors in November 1981 demanding that, *"KES remain an 11-18 school and continue to further extend its post-16 education"*. Many were concerned that the loss of sixth form teaching would not only be unacceptable to them personally, but would weaken the quality of teaching on offer at the school in the future, while the absence of older pupils would have an adverse effect on middle school pupils and on the general ethos of the school. The Governors rejected this resolution by a narrow majority and instead agreed to, *"accept the principle of tertiary education for the city and resolved that KES will play their full part in the process for change that will take place"*. The Governors believed they had a responsibility to find a solution that was best for the city, not necessarily one that was best for KES, which clearly could run a viable and successful sixth form. After that rebuff, staff opposition appears to have evaporated, many teachers at the school accepting, in a somewhat fatalistic manner, that another re-organisation was going to happen. The two pupil governors argued in favour of tertiary education, and many of the staff were sympathetic to the logic of the LEA's arguments about the drastic fall in pupil numbers and the need to encourage more than 50% of the school population of Sheffield to stay in full time education after 16 years of age.

The Council also consulted very widely, and Horton himself addressed meetings at the school of parents and staff and this also smoothed the way forward. Throughout the period from 1981-85 there were four phases of consultation with the public, governors, staff, and relevant institutions, the Council perhaps having learnt from the "mistakes" of the1960's re-organisation. To many the logic of their case was compelling, especially the strategic vision that the city, and indeed the nation, could ill afford a half-educated workforce and population, especially at a time when Sheffield's economy was taking such a battering, with 15% unemployment in the early Eighties. The city was in a desperate period of its history with the massive contraction of the steel and engineering industry, the Steel Strike of 1982 and the Miners' Strike of 1984-85. Indeed a genuine "battlefield" existed on the city boundary at Orgreave and there was a desperation abroad in the city, whose essence was later captured in the film "The Full Monty" set in this period. The city was beginning to realise it would have to re-invent itself and the proposals for the re-organisation of secondary and tertiary education were seen by many as a fundamental part of a revitalised infrastructure.

Early in 1982 the Council formally agreed to replace F.E.Colleges and Sixth Forms with tertiary colleges, initially indicating that 1985 would be the year for the implementation of the scheme. A blow to their plans occurred, when the Roman Catholic heirarchy in Sheffield decided to retain their two 11-18 schools, Notre Dame and All Saints, a move unanimously condemned by the KES Governors. The Governors, now with Dr. Michael Blackburn as the new Chairperson, whilst accepting the division of the school, were concerned about the numbers being proposed for the two institutions that would succeed KES. Many of the Governors, and the staff, considered that tertiary college status, with a very large proportion of "A" Level work, was not an inappropriate destination for the "Old Lady of Glossop Road" which had once run degree courses as Wesley College, and then become Yorkshire's leading LEA grammar school. However they doubted it could take 1100 students, even if you included the Lynwood and Melbourne Annexe sites. The Governors later, in 1984, even threatened to withdraw their support for the re-organisation if they could not get satisfactory assurances about building work at Darwin Lane, and they were horrified that the new 11-16 school there was being planned for 1540 pupils. They also found fault with the Council's costing of the refurbishment of Upper School, believing they had wildly underestimated the amount of work that needed to be done, and they challenged a similar lack of realism in the figures that were being considered for the new school at Darwin Lane. Early estimates by the council suggested the whole cost of the changes for the entire city might be only £11million, later revised upwards to £20 million, but still regarded by many as far too optimistic.

A serious row erupted when the governors found that the LEA was referring to the new school as the "new Tapton School". This caused a flurry of resolutions demanding that there must be a neutral name chosen that made no reference to either KES or Tapton; that this was an amalgamation of equals, not a takeover by Tapton, even if they were the larger school on the site at present. The Headteacher of Tapton, Graham Speed, was clearly pencilled in to become the new Headteacher of the new school and it was assumed by all that when the day came, Russell Sharrock, who would be over sixty, would retire with honour as the last Headmaster of KES. In the meantime the KES Governors, by way of a reminder to the LEA, now always referred to the new school as "Crosspool" in their minutes, which might very well have been its name if the plans had ever come to fruition.

By the time the Education Committee, under its new Chairman, Coun. Mike Bower, published its definitve plan in October 1985, both schools already regarded the changes as inevitable. After all this was a council, under the leadership of David Blunkett (Leader 1980-87), which was in the forefront of Local Government's battle with Mrs. Thatcher over rate-capping and public sector cutbacks. Sheffield City Council in the early 1980s was in a confident mood and led by some able councillors. Seven of them ended up in Parliament, including two Conservatives, and they provided a couple of MEPs as well for good measure, whilst Peter Horton had been a member of the McFarlane Commission, that investigated "16-19" Education in England and Wales and reported in 1980. Furthermore, the LEA, under the professional leadership of Michael Harrison (Chief Education Officer 1967-85), regarded itself as a leading authority in all of the main progressive initiatives taking place in "state" education at that time. They were unlikely to be diverted by protests from the relatively few dissenters among the parents and staffs at schools across the city, with the only organised objections coming from Silverdale School in the "Tory" heartland of Ecclesall Ward.

Sharrock and Speed now started a process whereby the KES and Tapton subject curriculum and syllabuses would be "harmonised", so that, in the near future, pupils who would attend the new amalgamated school would have been following similar courses before they began to study for "O" Level and CSE Examinations. The two schools were used to working together at Sixth Form level, and this co-operation was now extended by forming a joint advisory group, with equal representation from both schools and the LEA, to pilot through the necessary preparatory work to set up the new 11-16 school. Meanwhile, the KES Common Room Committee, in December 1984, had written to the Chief Education Officer confirming their support for tertiary colleges and the basic principles of re-organisation. Their concerns now were for their own futures and how smooth and secure would be the changeover, whilst still allowing the ambitious to apply for any posts in the new system. The Governors had already shown concern that the F.E.Colleges were "guaranteeing" that all their staff would be found places in the new tertiary colleges, and it was feared that school sixth form teachers would be largely ignored. The LEA, for its part, wanted as smooth a transfer as possible and in the 11-16 schools they hoped for the "minimum of disruption", which, in effect, meant "sitting tenants" would stay at their present school unless they indicated they wanted to apply elsewhere. Therefore KES staff who wanted to stay in the new "Crosspool" 11-16 school would almost certainly have been found a post at that school. Only the positions of responsibility would be subject to competition, if, for example, two existing heads of departments were applying for the same new post. For those who wanted to continue to teach "A" Level subjects at Upper School, now to be translated into a tertiary college, the position was less clear. Sheffield City Council operated a "no compulsory redundancy" policy in the Eighties, so every one would eventually get a job, but not necessarily in the Glossop Road building. However it is most likely that if the "West" Tertiary College had been established, a very large proportion of the KES Sixth Form staff would have become "lecturers" in that college, running the same "A" Level courses they had run previously at KES and probably in the same rooms.

A Very English Coup!

During 1986 the City Council waited for the approval of the Secretary of State, now Kenneth Baker, who until recently had been Minister of State at the Environment Department battling with intransigent left wing Labour Councils. His main battle had been with Ken Livingstone's GLC, which the Government was about to abolish, but Sheffield had not been far behind on the Thatcher Government's list of councils who needed to be taught a lesson. Having forced Sheffield to accept rate capping, Baker was in no mood to do the Council any favours and so he made no effort to rush his decision over the city's well thought out tertiary plans and secondary school re-organisation.

Moreover, he was being badgered by a vocal minority of dissenters, who had the total support of the Conservative Group on the City Council. The Sheffield Conservatives had never accepted the tertiary proposals in theory or in practice, so when Silverdale School governors, staff and parents publicly opposed the scheme, which would have "abolished" their school, the Conservatives rushed to their defence in a decisive and unified manner that they had not shown when KES parents were looking for support in 1965. The local Conservative councillor, Sid Cordle, a Shadow Chairman and also a Silverdale

Governor, organised the opposition to the closure of that school, and to the wider implications of the re-organisation plans, by chairing the "Save our Sixth Forms" campaign. Already, in September 1984, he had written a comprehensive alternative proposal for coping with the expected dramatic fall in pupil numbers. His scheme, which became the official position of the Conservative Opposition on the Council, rejected tertiary colleges completely and retained the distinction between 11-18 schools and F.E.Colleges.

To meet the problems of over capacity, he suggested that some schools should be amalgamated and seven schools should close. Amongst his proposals he accepted there was an overwhelming case for Tapton and KES to become merged as one 11-18 school on the Darwin Lane site, whilst the Upper School building at Glossop Road would be no longer required for school, or college purposes, and would be closed. Silverdale School, however, would continue as an 11-18 school, as would all the other schools in the south west of the city, with only King Edward VII School being abolished.

Cordle's plan was discussed in the Education Committee on the 19th September 1984 and inevitably rejected by the Labour majority. That is where the matter would have ended, if there had not been a Conservative Government. Mrs. Thatcher's radical Administration was unsympathetic to the pretensions of Local Authorities, determined to reduce their spending and their sense of independence, and downright hostile to those Labour Councils who opposed her policies and decisions. In this political climate the Sheffield Conservatives knew that the battle against tertiary re-organisation was not lost, and that a sympathetic minister could literally with the stroke of a pen reject it in whole or in part, provided he had some evidence on which to base his decision. Cordle mobilised his new "Save our Sixth Forms" campaign, which was joined by the Silverdale Parents Association, and together they aimed to build up public support and then convince the Minister that the Sheffield Scheme was flawed and needed to be rejected. It all looked like a re-run of 1965, but with the parents of another school leading the charge and the prospect that the Government might well answer the prayers of the dissenters.

Three times Sid Cordle went to London with delegations to meet Richard Dunn MP, the Minister of State dealing with the Sheffield Scheme. Known to the Labour Group as "Hissing Sid", Cordle relished confrontation with his Labour opponents and he now enthusiastically supported the representatives of the Silverdale Tertiary Opposition Plan (STOP) and the Association of Sheffield Parents, which included at least one KES Conservative Nominated Governor. A delegation of Conservative Councillors was joined by John Osborn, the M.P. for Hallam Constituency, and they found the minister was sympathetic, although he gave no clues as to any action he might take. It would appear that the presence of the local M.P. helped to focus Dunn's mind on a solution that would separate south west Sheffield from the rest of the city, whilst arguing that his proposal would preserve the schools with successful, and sizeable, sixth forms.

Baker's Half Dozen

Coun. David Heslop, the Leader of the Conservatives on the City Council, now faced the reality that his Group was not going to get all they wanted and he set about negotiating a compromise behind the scenes. He now proposed that the Sheffield Conservatives would not be opposed to the tertiary scheme per se, but they would argue that some schools, because of their outstanding record in recent years, should be exempt from the re-organisation scheme. His plan, backed up by supporting evidence and representations from sympathetic groups and individuals, envisaged six schools staying outside the tertiary system, whilst 11-16 secondary schools and seven tertiary colleges would serve the rest of the city. In his plan KES would be restored to a single 11-18 school, albeit still on the same split site, and High Storrs, Silverdale, Tapton and King Ecberts would also continue as before. The sixth school, included by Heslop, was not Abbeydale Grange but Myers Grove, which had a sixth form of 179 pupils, and was adjacent to the catchment areas of Tapton and KES. Abbeydale, which had a larger sixth form (194) than Myers Grove, was to remain as the one tertiary college in the south-west, although it would surely have been competing for pupils with its immediate neighbours, the three local sixth form schools. The loser in this scheme was Ecclesfield School (190 in the sixth form) on the north side of the city and therefore perhaps off the Conservatives' political "radar screen". Heslop could argue that he was following traditional Conservative values, preserving the proven successful schools whilst allowing choice between tertiary colleges and sixth form schools. He was enough of a politician to realise that he was defending sixth forms in the wards traditionally held by his party, but he was keen to include Myers Grove so it did not appear to be too crude a "political" solution benefitting only the Hallam Constituency, the only Conservative held seat in South Yorkshire.

Both Heslop, who was the National Vice Chairman of the Conservative Local Government Association and Irvine Patnick, soon to be an M.P. and the former opposition leader on the now abolished South Yorkshire County Council, were well known to Kenneth Baker through his involvement with local government issues in the middle Eighties. They lobbied him to support their proposal and reject the totality of the Sheffield Scheme. Heslop recalls meeting Baker in his room at the Commons and going over his report in considerable detail, fully believing that he had convinced him to accept it in total.

Meanwhile, the leading Labour Councillors, aware that a decision on their re-organisation scheme was being delayed, asked to see the minister. Michael Bower, along with Bill Walton, the new Chief Education Officer, visited London and met Baker on the morning of 13th October 1986 when they were quizzed in detail about their proposals. Baker gave no inkling that he was considering a compromise solution, and although Sheffield's relations with the Thatcher Government were severely strained, they expected the logic and thoroughness of their plans to be accepted, even if the Government were taking an unconscionable time in giving their approval.

Two weeks later they received the Secretary of State's decision. All the six schools in the Hallam Constituency would be excluded from the tertiary re-organisation and KES, High Storrs, Tapton, Silverdale, King Ecberts and Abbeydale Grange (but not Myers Grove), would continue as sixth form schools, whilst the two tertiary colleges planned for the south-west of the city would be abandoned. If the Council did not accept these amendments then the whole plan would be rejected. There was fury in the Labour ranks at what they perceived as a blatant "political" decision, that threw into turmoil all their careful planning to balance schools and colleges to accommodate the reduced numbers of secondary pupils.

The Labour Group met to decide whether it would settle for three quarters of a "tertiary cake" or abandon their scheme altogether. In December they decided to reluctantly accept the Secretary of State's decision, striking a defiant attitude and suggesting that the tertiary colleges would be so popular that most of the sixth forms in the south west would collapse as post-16 pupils voted with their feet. Only KES and High Storrs were felt to have a viable future as sixth form schools, and with some bravado, Coun. Bower committed the Council to seek to reverse the decision when a new Labour Government was returned at the forthcoming elections, expected in the middle of the next year.

The Chief Education Officer was hardly more circumspect in his language when he officially replied to Kenneth Baker.

> "The Secretary of State's decision has been met with dismay in five of the six schools involved, who understand that there will be too many secondary schools to serve the area and that the future viability of the post-16 provision is now problematic. The Secretary of State's attitude will bear hardest on the disadvantaged inner city margins of the west and south west areas, for whom the creation of tertiary colleges in their area gave the prospect of greater access to a wider range of educational opportunity."

Not to be outdone Michael Blackburn, on behalf of the KES Governors, wrote in a similar vein to the Secretary of State claiming;

> "Our general dismay caused by the short-sightedness of your response. KES Governors are wholly at a loss to comprehend your initiative which will create more problems in the south west and west of Sheffield than it can ever hope to solve."

There was, of course, no Labour victory in the 1987 General Election, nor in the 1992 one. It would be ten more years until there was a Labour Secretary of State for Education and then, by one of those neat ironic twists of history, the Secretary of State would be none other than David Blunkett himself. However, "New" Labour was no longer interested in yesterday's structural reform of the education system, preferring to put its considerable energies and increased finance behind the quality of the education inside the schools or colleges rather than creating uniform systems of secondary and tertiary institutions.

Two Groups of Six - Two futures!

Five of the six 11-18 schools "saved" by Kenneth Baker's decision, have, in the years since 1986, been very successful comprehensive schools. Their sixth forms did not wither but have increased considerably in size during the last two decades. The KES Sixth Form, always the largest in Sheffield, did not reduce to 170 pupils by 1990 as forecast, instead it had passed 350 in number by that time. Demand for places has continued to grow, so that now the school has been forced to introduce a maximum limit of 500 students in the Sixth Form, the vast majority of them doing "A" Level courses.

The six remaining tertiary colleges on the other hand, after opening in 1988, went through another re-organisation in 1992 when they were all amalgamated to form the independent Sheffield College, at the time the largest institution of its kind in Western Europe. No longer under the City Council's control, this huge institution has had a chequered history over the last decade and they have lost many potential post-16 "A" Level students to the thriving sixth form schools in the south and west of the city.

For the Conservatives on the City Council, 1986 was their "finest hour", when their backstairs "coup" reversed, albeit in part, a major project of the Labour controlled Council. They were to achieve another "coup" in 1988, when they persuaded the Thatcher Government to take the Attercliffe industrial corridor out of the City Council's control and set up an Urban Development Corporation to plan and administer the Don Valley. Yet, within a decade the Conservatives were virtually obliterated on the City Council, as all their traditional wards were taken by the resurgent Liberal Democrats. In 1997, they also lost the Parliamentary Constituency of Hallam, when Richard Allen, a KES Governor, won the seat for the Liberal Democrats.

Carrying on regardless!

In retrospect it seems difficult to fully understand how the school functioned so normally when major constitutional changes were being planned over a number of years. It had been the same in 1927, 1944 and again in 1965 and, of course, it is inevitable that it should be so, because pupils are, with a few exceptions, oblivious to these events and the professional staff, for the most part, tend to live from term to term. The Fell Walking Club still walked the Derbyshire Hills, the O.W.L. Club still sought out wild life and the Christian Union still discussed, in a non-denominational way, the relevance of their faith in the modern world. The Chess Club met at lunchtimes, a Model Club at Lower School and in the LLR, the Upper School Forum, run by Anthea Peers, still discussed the issues of the day and showed controversial films, like the "War Game"; Peter Watkins' work on the aftermath of a nuclear bomb attack, which had been banned from BBC TV screens.

Anthea Peers took time off in 1983 to do an M.A. in Peace Studies and when she returned she set up the PSE courses, which became such an integral part of the education of KES pupils. Ann Ritchie, one of the few survivors from the Crosspool staff, became the teacher in charge of Drama in 1981 and created a number of most enjoyable productions, while sharing the production of the Senior Play with English Department colleagues. In

1982 the Upper School play was the "Stirrings in Sheffield" a play that had surprisingly achieved iconic status within the Labour Movement in Sheffield, despite its anti-union message. There was also a very competent production of "Much Ado About Nothing", although the KESMAG critic, questioning the choice of a Shakespeare play, was unkind enough to point out that many seats were empty and the Hall was even emptier after the interval. He believed they would have preferred a musical like Oklahoma, an ambitious production by Ann Ritchie in 1988, in co-operation with Francis Wells and the Music Department, but only after another Shakespeare, "Mid-Summer Night's Dream" set in the late Thirties had been tackled. This had been produced by John Gallacher who arrived at KES in September 1984, and later he would become the first, and so far the only, Head of the Drama Department. One of his first productions was the farce "Black Comedy" by Peter Shaffer, first performed in London in 1965 with Derek Jacobi, Albert Finney and Maggie Smith in the leading roles. He was to mount many challenging productions in the next twenty years, when KES Drama became noted for its high intellectual quality, with many of the plays being performed in the Crucible Studio.

One outside venue long associated with great school occasions was the City Hall, where Speech Days, latterly called Prize Distribution Days, were held with all the considerable pomp and ceremony that a famous old school could muster. Early in the Eighties they were scaled down to a more modest presentation occasion in the Assembly Hall, perhaps in deference to a more egalitarian approach to success at school. Two of the last Speakers at the City Hall had been Jack Charlton, then manager of Sheffield Wednesday, and David Blunkett, then a new, and scarcely known, Leader of the Council, who, in trademark fashion, caught the mood of the evening and spoke good sense to the assembled pupils in a language that they could easily appreciate.

The school's major choral and orchestral concerts were also now held in the school Assembly Hall or at nearby St.Mark's, Broomhill. Alan Eost (1974-87) was promoted to the position of Director of Music in 1980 and he picked up the baton left by Norman Barnes, and more recently Dan Healey, adding to the laurels of the school's great music traditions. He was joined in a department of two by Francis Wells who put new life into the Junior Choir and the Second Orchestra and also formed a dozen strong Barber's Shop Group and a Recorder Consort to add to the flexibility of KES music. Eost inaugurated an annual Chamber Concert in 1981, held in the Hall at Darwin Lane, as a way of providing a performance opportunity for these new, or rejuvenated groups, many of whose performers were in the Lower School forms.

Soon the school began to pick up awards for its music. Under Healey, the First Orchestra had taken First Prize in its class at the 1980 Pontefract Music Festival and the Senior Choir gained second place, ahead of the renowned Dore Male Voice Choir, in the BBC Radio Sheffield Top Choir Competition and later was invited to perform live on BBC Radio Leeds. In 1981, at the Blackpool Festival, KES became the first school for 60 years to win the Mixed Voice Open Competition and, in 1983, surpassed even these achievements when they were invited to the Royal Albert Hall to perform in the

Sainsbury Festival of Choirs, the only comprehensive school from outside London to be invited to this festival of the top twenty choirs in Britain.

The quality of the orchestral and choral work that Eost was producing at KES could be heard in the major school concerts held at St. Mark's or in the Assembly Hall. In 1981 they performed Gabriel Faure's Requiem, followed in 1982 by two performances of Mozart's "Coronation" Mass. In a new departure in 1983, an ambitious St. John's Passion was given, with Michael Brewer, conductor of the British Youth Choir, and a professional orchestra supporting the young KES musicians. In 1985 the works chosen were Vaughan Williams's "Dona Nobis Pacem" and Bach's "Magnificat", and shortly afterwards, in a lighter mood, there was a concert entitled "Music for a Summer Evening", repeated the following February by "Music for a Winter Evening".

A select group of the choir, titled "The King Edward Singers", sang at that concert and later performed, with some considerable merit, at the Llangollen International Eisteddfod in July 1985. The selection for the major choral work in 1986 was Handel's oratorio "Jephtha", thought by some to contain some of his finest music, with Angela Bunting of the 7th Form taking her place alongside the highly experienced Principals. If this was not impressive enough, the Music Department was also a major partner in the production of two musicals, "Bugsy Malone", in 1985, and "Oklahoma", in 1988. Alan Eost left KES in the summer of 1987, but he has remained a leading figure within the music scene in Sheffield. Currently he is conductor of the Sheffield Oratorio Chorus, and undoubtedly, in the Eighties, he made a huge contribution to the continuing high standards of music at King Edward VII School.

A happy start!

Comment has already been made how, under Bryan Gallagher, the Head of Lower School exploited the advantages of having a school with a split site, creating a happy first three years of comprehensive education for pupils. Increasingly in the Eighties, they were drawn from all over the city and the First Year usually numbered only between 55 and 65 pupils, requiring only two forms of boys and girls who came from primary schools (especially the church schools) who moved their pupils on at eleven. The bulk of the Lower School pupils came at 12 years of age and the Second Year group numbered just over 300, until later in the decade when falling rolls across the city reduced it to nearer 200. This rather peculiar situation meant that the induction of pupils to the school happened twice for the same cohort of children, but under Gallagher's kindly and authoritative leadership, the school ran smoothly through this particular difficulty.

He was aided by many supportive, dedicated and competent staff and none more so than by his Deputies. Both could seemingly maintain effortless discipline. Gladys Manifield had the unquestioned authority of a very efficient RSM and could, with a disapproving glance, quell any incipient untoward behaviour at fifty paces. Her successor after 1983, and later Head of Lower School, Angela Cooper, was more likely to hug you to death, but if she uttered the warning "*I'll send for my handbag*", potential miscreants ceased their foolish ways because it was rumoured she kept a brick in it for extra velocity. Mrs. Cooper, to a generation of Lower School pupils, was everyone's idea of a favourite aunt, whom the pupils knew loved "kids" and would use humour to bring them into line. She had been a Form Tutor in the Middle School and taught in the History Department, and on her promotion she struck up a good partnership with Gallagher, from whom she readily admits she learnt a great deal about running what, in effect, was a medium sized school of nearly 700 pupils.

Bryan Gallagher

Angela Cooper

Whilst uncompromising academic standards were insisted upon, there was plenty of fun in the life of Lower School and Gallagher and Cooper were well placed to lead it. The Summer Fair had become a huge annual event. Held in the open air it resembled nothing so much as a successful car boot sale, but without the cars. One year there was an opportunity for visitors to try their hand at parascending, an activity more safely done at sea behind a speedboat, where accidents only result in an early bath.

Summer Fayre in the Eighties

Societies flourished at Lower School, even though the "tyranny" of the official school bus meant that children, especially on the east side of town, had to leave at the end of the school day or have a long journey home from Manchester Road. Ann Ritchie ran a Lower School Drama Group which formed the nucleus of the Lower School play. In 1982 she wrote a special play for the group entitled "Sea Change" but complained that she had *"28 Felicity Kendals but only a couple of Dustin Hoffmans"*. There was a Lower School Poetry Competition that year with prizes for all three age groups, a Gardening Club was started and the O.W.L. Club could muster 30 members. In 1983 there was a Lower School

Alan Finch with his Lower School Form in the early Eighties.

weekend visit to Boulogne and this became a regular trip in the calendar, whilst at the end of the Winter Term, Ann Ritchie organised the Lower School Pantomime. Suitably disguised with make up and costume, in time-honoured fashion the staff formed the cast and the pupils the audience, the latter eager to see their teachers making fools of themselves, but also become rather reassuringly normal at the same time.

Part of Lower School's success was in staying close to the parents. To this end, in 1987, the first Parent Teachers Association was formed at KES with its main locus at Lower School, where Angela Cooper played a large part in its organisation and a parent, Tony Booth, became the Chair. Parental support is always more obvious when children are younger, as parents later become more discreet in their appearances at the school, when their offspring reach their middle teens. So Lower School parents from all social backgrounds formed the bulk of the Association, joining in and focussing their efforts on fundraising, to help out departments that needed extras that the LEA would, or could, not supply.

Trouble at Mill!

Storm clouds began to disturb the "sunny skies" of KES in 1984, when unprecedented action by most of the teachers' unions, heralded three years of work to rule and short term strike action. This was not a protest against any actions of the school, but aimed at the Thatcher Government and their perceived unsympathetic attitude towards teachers. The "Teachers' Action" was, partly, a response to inadequate salaries, partly, perhaps, shadowing the climate of union "rebellion" all over the country (the NUM strike of 1984-85 could hardly be ignored in any school in South Yorkshire). Furthermore, the Government's policy of encouraging the private sector whilst cutting back the public sector, turned most teachers against the Conservatives at that time. Mrs. Thatcher, who once opened a meeting with a senior group of British Rail Executives by admonishing them with the words; *"if you lot were any good then you'd be working in the private sector!"*, sometimes appeared to have her opinion of teachers formed more by the lurid headlines of the tabloid press, than by the mundane reality of the everyday classroom.

At KES, like many schools, most teachers ceased doing their voluntary duties, although the AMMA, who were largely made up of the former grammar school teachers, would have no part in the action. The impact was felt most on supervisory duties at dinnertime, school bus departure queues, and voluntary societies (there was always a concern that concerts and plays would not be able to go ahead), and in inter-school sport where, traditionally, the small P.E. Department had been supplemented by an army of staff members who would coach a team in their own sport, or accompany a team to the away fixtures.

There were still a considerable number of KES staff who would help out with coaching and refereeing matches, but more "solid" action at other schools, meant that KES teams had no one to play and fixtures had to be cancelled. The members of the NUT and the NAS/UWT, who supported the action, where quick to retort that, *"these so-called normal extra-curricular duties are in fact voluntary and not part of any teacher's contract, and that P.E. staff would not be expected to mark their classes' homework, or assist in their lesson preparation"*. The "Action" threw a great, extra strain onto the senior staff. Many of the supervisory duties just had to be done or chaos would reign, and the three Assistant Heads along with the three Senior Teachers had to take on the extra burden. Angela Cooper, at Lower School, was doing five duties a day and recalls that; *"not only was it a sad and unhappy time, but it took the fun out of teaching"*.

Although the Headmaster and the Senior Staff took no precipitous action to inflame the situation, relations between colleagues were severely strained during this period. At times the action was intensified. At one time the NAS/UWT held a series of two period strikes without warning, at another the NUT organised a number of one day strikes in support of their pay claim. Cover for absent teachers was another flashpoint, and, in 1987, the unions raised the stakes by refusing to cover after one day of absence, whilst the LEA would not supply temporary teachers until three days had elapsed. On these occasions classes had to be sent home because there was no one to teach them, and KES suffered more from these tactics than most schools in Sheffield, because it was in the only Conservative held constituency in South Yorkshire.

Not only did the Headmaster and his management team keep calm in the face of these difficulties, taking the longer view that when the action was over, colleagues would need to heal any divisions that had arisen, but the Governors supported the teachers in their claims for better salaries and respected their right to take supportive action. A resolution of the Governors was sent to John Osborn, the lone Tory M.P. in this "red" neck of the woods asking him; *"to join us in supporting the long overdue pay award to teachers, who have the wholehearted support of the KES Governors."* There is no evidence that Osborn was converted to the teachers' cause by this missive, and the Government certainly had no sympathy for their unions' actions.

The new Secretary of State for Education, Kenneth Baker, fresh from his "victories" over Livingstone, ILEA, and Lambeth, responded with the 1986 Education Act. Amongst its other provisions was an attempt to turn the flank of the teachers and the LEAs, by promoting parent power on the one hand and strengthening the legal duties and powers of headteachers on the other. Baker, himself, said of the Act,

> *"Our Education Act radically changes the composition of school governing bodies and ends the dominance of the local authority and its political nominees. There will be more parent governors (for KES it was now four each for parents and LEA reps.) and the new style governing bodies will be answerable to an annual parents' meeting".*

Baker was placing his faith in the "consumers" whom he guessed (correctly in KES's case), would be represented by middle class governors, who, he further assumed, would most likely support the Conservatives and their general line of thought (wrong in the case of KES Governors).

The Grammarians depart!

Gordon Adam was one of those teachers who had always given more to the school than just his teaching in the classroom. A legend amongst linguists at KES for his phenomenal knowledge of many languages, he had run the very successful Chess Club and played the cello in the School Orchestra. One Assistant Head called him the "Master for Exotic Languages", because, although he modestly would only admit to being fluent in five languages, he could make a very creditable stab at many others. He had started the Russian courses at KES when first appointed by Clapton in 1959 and became the Head of German after "Joe" Oppenheimer left in 1966. He included Turkish among his languages and had taught for three years in Ankara after graduating from Cambridge. The teaching of Russian did not long survive him at KES, perhaps a reflection of how the pupils foresaw the future importance of the USSR.

He took early retirement in July 1985, when the LEA realised that it was going to have too many modern language teachers if the tertiary re-organisation proposals went through. Wilf Mace, who had been at KES for 38 years, and was Head of Physics throughout the comprehensive period, had already left at Easter. At the national level he was highly regarded, having helped to set up the Nuffield "A" Level courses in Physics, and he was later followed in the summer of 1988 by two other members of the Science Department, Geoff Paice (Head of Chemistry) and Alan Grace (Physics) who both left to join the staff of one of the new tertiary colleges. One wag suggested that the extremely thin, Wilf Mace, was KES's *"skeleton staff"*, and also that taken together, *Mace, Paice and Grace* sounded rather like a Dickensian firm of solicitors, but they were three more staff members who had survived from the grammar school days and were now moving on.

In 1987, Ray Stittle, the Head of History since 1965, decided to take advantage of the City Council's Early Retirement Scheme and leave KES after twenty two years service. For older teachers over fifty years of age, the Council was prepared to arrange for them to access their Teacher's Pension and then topped it up with up to ten years enhancement, permanently paid by the council. A teacher who was accepted for this scheme, therefore, in effect, got their full pension, and in retrospect it now appears a generous decision, driven by the Labour controlled Council's reluctance to make anyone compulsorily redundant. Unemployment was a major battleground between the political parties in the Eighties, and with so many thrown out of work in Sheffield because of the major restructuring of manufacturing industry, the Council was determined that they would not adopt similar wholesale sackings.

Ray Stittle, who recalls that his final "O" Level group in 1987 was one of the very best he ever taught, was only one of many teachers in the city who, given the chance to leave early, were only too willing to retire. Many had seen their elderly colleagues struggle on till 65 years of age, and then die shortly afterwards from the stress of trying to cope with teaching in large secondary schools with complex problems and continual changes of curriculum and organisation. One KES History teacher suddenly discovered that, come the next term, she would be teaching a Chinese History module covering several centuries from 500 B.C. to 1500 A.D., something not included in her university course-work. Little did they know that the workload, and the resultant pressure on teachers, was about to get much greater, and that on reflection the Eighties were still a time when you could still *"fly by the seat of your pants"* in many classes in many subjects.

The Sheffield Curriculum Initiative

When Bill Walton took over as the new Director of Education for Sheffield in 1985, the tertiary re-organisation appeared to be completed and only awaiting approval from the Secretary of State. He therefore switched the thrust of the LEA's reforming zeal to achieving a more dynamic and flexible curriculum for all the schools and colleges in Sheffield, in a brave attempt to solve the continual problem of alienation, boredom and underachievement of a substantial percentage of the school population. The result was the Sheffield Curriculum Initiative of 1986-89, whereby, through massive secondment of teachers from the city's schools (180 secondary and 30 primary teachers in the first year, with a maximum of five from any one school) new, exciting, relevant courses could be written up by groups of teachers, temporarily freed from classroom duties, who, in the language of the time, would have "ownership" of the syllabus.

The Government also encouraged new thinking about the curriculum in its drive to raise standards and gain value for money. Sir Keith Joseph, Secretary of State for Education before Baker, unleashed an unprecedented number of reports and publications mainly concentrating on raising achievement by new curriculum perspectives. These included H.M. Inspectorate publications in 1980, 1981and 1985 on curriculum initiatives, Reports of Committees like the Cockcroft Report on teaching Mathematics, the Rampton and the Swann Reports on the education of Ethnic Minority pupils and pilots like TVEI (Technical Vocational Education Initiative) and its related in-service training initiative (TRIST), both generously funded by the Government. Joseph produced a Green Paper in 1984, and a White Paper "Better Schools" in 1985, and the Conservatives then enshrined most of their current thinking on the organisation of schools in their Education Act of 1986.

In 1983 the Government, through Circular 8/83, charged LEAs to report on their progress with curriculum policy. The Sheffield Curriculum Initiative was a response to that circular, and also to the TVEI pilot that was run in three of the city's secondary schools. KES became involved when the Council in 1986, under a programme known as Schools' Focussed Secondment (SFS), seconded 180 secondary teachers, including four from KES, who were given two different, although related, targets. Firstly, to be instrumental in creating new syllabuses that encouraged active learning, cross curricular integration rather than rigid single subject segregation (Integrated Humanities was one of these courses, which 30 KES pupils subsequently studied at GCSE level in 1987-88), and modularisation of the courses, which would be then subject to continual assessment, with a consequent reduction in the emphasis placed on examinations. Secondly, these seconded teachers would work on specific projects that would benefit their own school and from this initiative came some permanent benefits to KES. Roger Watkin and John Sallabank used their secondment to construct the essentials of the "Residential Weeks" which became such an enjoyable and beneficial part of every KES student's time at the school. Their planning led to the first residential week at Cliffe College in July 1987, when a full year group was taken into Derbyshire for five days in term time, undertaking a full programme of activities, including adventure sports, the arts and drama. Alan Powell used his year's secondment to explore the transfer of pupils from primary to secondary schools across the city and specifically to assist the smooth transfer of pupils into KES, from, what were now, 40 different primary schools. Part of the lasting legacy of his work were the Induction Days, run for primary school children coming to KES in Y7, and the permanent liaison links with the feeder primary schools. David Marcer's secondment was focussed on developing a city-wide scheme for the Duke of Edinburgh's Award. After he had produced his report, he was offered the new position of Sheffield's Award Development Officer, and although he would be based at the school until 2003, and was later a parent governor, he resigned from the staff at the end of that year.

KES had an input into the working group designing the Records of Achievement Programme, which has enabled every pupil since then to record the totality of their successes and interests whilst at the school. So that at the end of their school career they have a portable record, not just of their examination results, but their accomplishments inside and outside the classroom, be it in sport, school societies, or activities undertaken outside school. In the Eighties, through the Record of Achievement, the LEA was aiming to give a more complete picture of the "whole person", increase a pupil's self confidence and self esteem, and encourage them to see education as positive and relevant, as well as possessing a record that would be regarded as valuable by potential employers, universities and colleges.

GCE + CSE = GCSE

As if these upheavals in the curriculum were not enough the University Examination Boards produced a major overhaul of the crucial 16 + external examination. The General Certificate of Education (GCE) "O" Level, which had replaced the old School Certificate in 1951, had remained the "gold standard" for 16+ school pupils in grammar schools and the top streams in comprehensive schools, and even most public schools were judged by fee-paying parents on their GCE results. For comprehensive schools the existence of two forms of external examination caused two serious problems. One was organisational, because the school had to run classes and courses for some pupils to attempt "O" Level and at least an equal number to do CSE courses, with a further complication at KES, where a considerable number of pupils "mixed and matched" between the two systems.

More importantly it divided the school, clearly delineating who was in the intellectual élite and who was not. In the spirit of all the other curriculum developments in the early and mid Eighties, the obvious course of action was to introduce an examination that could test pupils at different levels of ability, yet studying the same course and sitting the same examination. The courses for the new integrated examinations started in September 1986, and KES parents were introduced to the changes at a public meeting at the school, when a video entitled "A Revolution in the Classroom" was shown and questions answered. There was concern that standards would drop and that KES's success at "O" Level (the school averaged, for those who took the "O" Level Exam, a percentage pass rate in the high seventies, as against a national average of 60%, with the top 20% of the KES pupils gaining a pass rate in the middle nineties) would be reduced by a levelling down of course work, but proponents of the change defended the new examination by explaining how Grades A-C were the equivalent of an "O" Level pass, whilst Grades D-G were the equivalent of CSE Grades 2-5.

Not everyone was convinced then, or now, but the Governors supported the new proposals, whilst voicing their concern that insufficient resources appeared to be going into in-service training. The first pupils to sit GCSE Examinations did so in the summer of 1988, just before Sharrock left. In that first set of Examinations, where pupils were taking 23 subjects, including all the traditional subjects (16 took Latin) but also Media Studies, Computer Studies, Design & Realisation and Integrated Humanities, 54 % of the whole year group gained an A-C Grade, considerably better than the equivalent "O" Level passes in recent years, and with the boys outperforming the girls, something they would not do very often in the next two and a half decades.

The smack of firm government!

Frustrated by the teachers' work to rule and their unwillingness to agree a pay deal, Kenneth Baker introduced his 1987 Teachers Pay and Conditions Act, that abolished the negotiating procedures set up in 1965 and enabled him to impose pay levels and conditions himself, which he did until 1991. The 1986 Education Act had already begun to shift the balance of decision-making away from LEAs towards central government, but it was also aimed at weakening the influence of teachers, by strengthening the role of parents and headteachers. The Act also picked up a few of the concerns and disenchantments of the Tory Party faithful, abolishing "political indoctrination" in schools, (in practice this meant, in some other schools, an end to Peace Studies) and making sex education a clear responsibility of the Governors, who were expected to control any "inappropriate" information that might be imparted to pupils, who were becoming much more sexually "literate" than previous generations. KES Governors received two papers from Anthea Peers, who co-ordinated the PSE programme within which the school delivered its sex education, and after discussions in 1988 adopted the reports as its Sex Education Statement.

The White Paper of 1985 had recommended having a majority of parents on governing bodies, but Baker stopped short of that. LEA nominees were not always representatives of the "looney left", — in the shires and the suburbs they were usually Conservatives — but he did introduce, in the 1986 Act, the duty of the Governors to produce an Annual Report, followed by an Annual Meeting to give an account of their stewardship to parents. This procedure still applies, but in recent years the KES Governors present at the meeting considerably exceed the number of parents who turn up, and the whole business has become something of a waste of time, even a farce.

The Government also reined in all the new curriculum initiatives, some of which had been more successful than others. In Sheffield, some of the integrated cross-curricular courses lacked focus, and some teachers, who preferred their own subject disciplines, felt they were selling the pupils short with half prepared coursework on isolated topics. Baker seemed more prepared to be persuaded by the Black Report of 1988 which recommended a structure of a National Curriculum with regular testing and school league tables to enable parents to "shop around" to find the school of their choice. Baker's far-reaching Education Act of 1988, the most significant education legislation since 1944, incorporated these ideas and further strengthened the centre at the expense of LEAs and classroom teachers.

Sport - the victim of the time?

School sport at KES had been very strong in the Seventies and its success carried over into the Eighties. Yet by the second half of the decade inter-school team sports were in serious disarray with some sports at KES never recovering. While curriculum P.E. lessons could carry on as before, the teacher unions' action seriously affected the running of school teams. So many of the sides at different age levels depended on the voluntary support of non-specialist staff members who had an interest, or a real expertise, in coaching one or more sports. At KES many staff, especially those in AMMA, continued to run school teams, but they found, in the middle of the decade, that they had no-one to play, as the "Action" at other schools had virtually closed down their inter-school sports programme. However, there were other factors affecting school sport in the Eighties. The advent of tertiary colleges meant that most of the traditional sixth form fixture list with local comprehensive schools just disappeared, and the new tertiary colleges did not have the necessary degree of organisation to field teams of the right standard to take their place. The result was that inter-school sport for the Sixth Form, always regarded in the past as the school's senior teams, virtually ceased to exist. Rugby Union and Cricket, traditionally two of the school's main team sports, collapsed, although there is currently, in the last three years, a renaissance of King Edward VII cricket, whilst Rugby League later replaced Union as the preferred oval ball game at the school.

This crisis in school sport came at a time when, paradoxically, sport and leisure activities had moved high up the national political and social agenda. Under the umbrella banner of the "Leisure Revolution" many agencies were looking to sport, along with the arts, to fill the lives of a new generation now expected to be free from the drudgery of routine factory and office work. Sport was touted as the panacea for solving many social ills, crime, ill-health, unemployment etc., a role it had always claimed for itself but never, until now, taken very seriously by the key decision makers. In Sheffield, it was hoped sport would become the "philosopher's stone" by which an economically battered city would be re-generated and re-defined. It was therefore significant that the new "City Partnership" leadership in 1987 chose, as its flagship catalyst regeneration project, to hold the 1991

World Student Games, an event which involved many KES pupils as volunteer helpers when it was eventually held in the city.

The new Head of Girls P.E., Eileen Battersby, (1981-2004) epitomised this new enthusiasm for sport in schools and working with Ian Rodgers, the Head of Boys' P.E., who also served the school for over twenty years, they devised a detailed, and inclusive Physical Education programme. Battersby had herself competed as a sprint hurdler in the 1967 World Student Games in Tokyo, later playing Hockey for Derbyshire in the Seventies and she was keen to offer pupils as many sporting opportunities as could be catered for in school time. With two long P.E. periods a week, the core sports were Gymnastics/Dance, Netball/ Hockey and Tennis/Rounders for girls, while the boys shared their time between Gymnastics/Basketball, Rugby/ Soccer and in the summer,Tennis/Cricket. However the range of opportunities was now considerably widened especially for Sixth and Fifth formers, by using outside facilities like the YMCA for Trampoline, Badminton and Weight Training (including Girls' sessions) and the Ice Rink and Bowling Alley in the city, as well as Orienteering and Climbing among other outdoor activities. Swimming at the "school" baths was part of the P.E. curriculum and some disciplines were provided by outside coaches coming into school to take classes. This enabled KES to offer Tai Chi, Fencing and Step Aerobics, and Eagles' coaches, including International players Daryl Powell and Mark Aston, introduced Rugby League to the school in the Nineties.

Outside coaches were one way of overcoming a shortage of staff volunteer enthusiasts, and their use coincided with the decisions of the national ruling bodies of sports to establish their own structures for youth and junior development. This benefited school sport in a number of ways. Firstly, because these development officers or club instructors were properly trained and expert in their field, and, secondly, they enabled a number of KES pupils to achieve city, county and national recognition because of the extra coaching they gained through their own sport's training programme. Two of these top performers in the early Eighties were the swimmers Mathew Oxley and Lynne Brooks, the latter representing Great Britain and both competing in National Finals.

Mention has already been made of Yvonne Hanson –Nortey, who left in 1982 to go to Loughborough University and then on to the Seoul Olympics and the Christchurch Commonwealth Games. Another Loughborough student was Julie Fimusanmi, who by the Third Forms in 1984 was not only the City Champion for the Javelin but had amassed 350 medals, including 230 "Golds", for Judo and was training with the Great Britain Squad. At university she took up Rugby and became a dual-international, at a time when this was still "illegal" for Union players. She represented England Women at Union and then changed to League, where as a powerful hard running centre, or full back, she was selected as a member of the Great Britain Women's R.L. Squad.

Not to be outdone the 1983 KES Rugby Union Team boasted two full England Schoolboy internationals. Mark Reid has already been mentioned in the previous chapter, but playing above his age group at flanker was David Tether, who in the same season was selected for the England U16 team. In a sport very much dominated by the most expensive public schools in the land, the inclusion of two boys from a northern comprehensive whose main winter sport was soccer, must be almost unprecedented, especially as selection at the different qualifying levels was not always perceived as a model of objectivity.

In the same season, 1982-83, KES fielded one of its all-time successful Football teams which Ian Rodgers regards as the best team he ever coached at the school. Captained, for the second successive year, by Peter Moulson, who went on to captain both the England and the British Universities teams, later becoming a barrister in Leeds and serving as President of the Old Edwardians from 2001-2004. That team only lost one match (not a league game), and they provided ten of the Sheffield Schools' side and eight of the South Yorkshire team during that season. In an overconfident gesture they invited the superb KES side of 1971-2 to a challenge match. Dave Seal, captain of that side, managed to get his players together and they overcame their younger opponents, with Seal scoring a hat trick, in a 3-1 win for experience over youth.

In 1985 the U16 side won the Clegg Trophy for the first time ever. This is the oldest schools' football trophy in the world, established in 1888 by Sir Charles Clegg, brother of the school's "founding father", and a player, himself, in the first ever England–Scotland match. School teams competed for it in their last year of compulsory education and although KES never won the trophy again, they were runners up in the 1993-94 season. One player who was too young to play in that Clegg Trophy victory was Mathew Clarke who became one of the very few Old Edwardians to become a professional footballer. He has kept goal for Rotherham, Wednesday and Crystal Palace and played in the Premiership with Bradford City before retiring in 2004.

In a report to a concerned Governors' meeting in 1987, Rodgers and Battersby explained how the teachers' action had reduced the number of teams playing inter-school games from 37 Girls teams and 31 Boys teams to 3 Football, 3 Hockey (including a mixed side) and three Cross Country teams. Block fixtures on a Saturday morning with regular Sheffield opponents had been particularly hard hit, but it was not the KES way to accept an unacceptable situation. During the next decade school sport was rebuilt, and although there were some permanent casualties — Sixth Form sport for example — the school was awarded two prestigious Sportsmarks by the Sports Council in 1999, and again in 2002, for the quality of its P.E. and Sports' programme. They might have added that this was despite the appallingly inadequate indoor facilities before 2001, the inconveniencies of the split site, the loss of Whiteley Woods and the withdrawal from Castle Dyke.

The longest serving Headmaster

At the February 1988 meeting of the Governors, Russell Sharrock indicated his intention to retire in the summer. He had taken over a school in some turmoil after the decisions of 1965 had left such bitterness and foreboding and then, after 1969, he had led the new merged comprehensive school for almost a score of years. In 1969 he was re-assuring parents and staff that his intention was to maintain a grammar school within a comprehensive, nineteen years later he presided over a "very model" of a modern comprehensive school, even if, as one journalist wrote, it was difficult to appreciate at first sight, that behind its classical facade with its sixteen Corinthian pillars, this was a comprehensive school.

The old Upper School building had been a cause of great concern to the Headmaster. Many times before 1985 he had arrived very early at the school, in his customary manner, and spent the next half hour putting out buckets to catch the rain coming in through the roof in a number of well plotted locations. In 1985 the Public Works Department finally got round to fixing the roof, having swathed the school in scaffolding, and by the following year all was secure, at least for the present.

Not only did Sharrock make a point of arriving at school before the caretaker, and being one of the last to leave, in the Eighties he made himself more visibly accessible to staff and pupils by working in the Entrance Hall, at the marble desk that is believed to be the communion table from Wesley College's Chapel. His management style was described, by Mike Denial and Kay Alcock, as that of; *"a wise godfather, who didn't seek to dominate his team of senior staff advisers, but knew how to channel their more youthful enthusiasms and indeed cemented a strong management team. He was not confrontational, but receptive to new ideas even though he was coming to the end of a long career in a most demanding job in the most trying of times. However, in discussions he was quite capable of asking the killer question and if he remained unconvinced he would then dig his heels in hard."* Indeed, Sharrock spent a considerable portion of his time, before 1986, representing the school on committees dealing with tertiary education, whilst attending regular meetings of the secondary school headteachers with the LEA at Melbourne House. Added to these gatherings were Cluster meetings of the local secondary headteachers, Pyramid meetings with the heads of KES's feeder primary schools, and at one period, the Joint Working Party with Tapton.

The Council, once again, in February 1988, mooted the possibility of a merger with Tapton as a single 11-18 school. The decision of Keneth Baker to exclude Hallam Constituency from the tertiary re-organisation created, as expected, surplus capacity among the secondary schools in the west of the city. KES population in 1988 was only 1288 pupils, 251 less than it had been at the start of the decade, and the LEA was inevitably forced to consider closing schools somewhere in the system and re-deploy the staffs of those schools. KES Governors now showed no interest in a merger and the LEA went away and closed secondary schools in the east of the city.

The Sixth Form had recovered its numbers. In 1988 there were 314 pupils doing post-16 courses, a quarter of the school population, and with the advent of the tertiary colleges in 1988, the number jumped up to 349 for the start of the new term in September. The school in 1988 still ran 20 "A" Level courses, including four languages, although Ancient History and Economic and Social History had been lost through lack of takers, and some subjects like Technology, Home Economics, Music and Latin survived with very small groups.

The "A" Level results, and the percentage of pupils gaining the top two grades, stayed fairly constant during the later Eighties and, comfortably, 10% above the national average.

"A" Level Pass Rate	A-E	A-B
1986	78%	38%
1987	80%	31%
1988	79%	31%

When interviewed by the local press on his retirement, Sharrock had just received the news that eight of the "A" Level group of 1988 had been given places at Oxbridge and he told the reporter that; *"this is the best retirement present I could have had, it confirms what I have always said, that high flyers can succeed at comprehensive schools!"*.

He might have added that former pupils of his time at KES had gone on to success in later life in much the same way as their predecessors had done. KES still produced considerable numbers of lawyers, doctors and consultants, engineers, professors, lecturers and teachers, businessmen and people who found new opportunities in our changing economy. Mark Hudson, after reading Economics at Kings, Cambridge, wound up as the economic adviser to two states formerly in the USSR, Uzbekistan and, more recently, Georgia. David Pollard, who led the campaign for the Sixth Form to get their own common room, returned to Sheffield after Leicester University and founded his own P.R. business. He was selected to run the publicity for the World Student Games, an event Sheffield hosted in 1991, that still is very firmly remembered in the collective minds of its ratepayers. Over the years only a few Old Edwardians ever took up a military career, but Captain Philip Skinner of the 4th Royal Tank Regiment and Lieutenant Julian Harrison of the Royal Artillery saw service in Northern Ireland during the height of the "Troubles" in that Province. Skinner, now a successful international commodity trader based in Sheffield, went on to be President of the Old Edwardians between 1996 and 2001, whilst Harrison recalls, that in his schooldays, he had to cope with beginning every day passing the school sign outside the main gate, that included the name of the city's Director of Education, his father.

There now were Old "Edwardiennes" who would make their mark in the world. Emily Maitlis (1983-89) was headhunted in 2001 to become the main presenter of BBC "London News", the prime time nightly news programme, and was singled out by a leading national broadsheet as one of twenty "Women to Watch" who were going places in the not too distant future. One KES teacher of that generation saw this prophecy literally translated when a fifteen foot poster of Emily, on the back of a red London bus, blocked his view as he was negotiating the capital's traffic. Another "Star" on national TV is Julia Bradbury (at KES in the early Eighties) who is currently the presenter of the BBC's consumer programme "Watchdog". Also from that period is Lydia McClean (1984-1991), like Emily also a professor's daughter, who took holy orders after reading Theology at Balliol, becoming, at ordination, the youngest female curate in the Church of England. Lydia has at least one other claim to fame at KES. She believes she was the last person to play the school organ, which rather alarmingly gave off sparks before she closed it down and allowed it to lapse into its long coma.

When Sharrock left in July 1988, several senior staff members left at the same time to take up new posts at the tertiary colleges. One of them was Mike Denial, who, as much as anyone had guided KES into the paths of a real comprehensive school, now opted for a new challenge at Norton College, where he was to be in charge of student admissions and the "A" Level curriculum (running 40 "A" Level courses alongside vocational courses) until he retired in 1993. Some of the Governors attempted to persuade him to apply for the KES Headship but he was determined to make a new start in a brand new, and potentially, very stimulating teaching environment. Eileen Velarde, Head of Modern Languages, Ed Wilson, Head of Maths, and Geoff Paice, Head of Chemistry also went to the tertiary colleges. It had become unusual for KES to lose many staff in any one year, and certainly not so many senior teachers, because, in a happy and pleasant school, the percentage staff turnover was probably smaller than at any time in the school's history.

Russell Sharrock with his Management Team shortly before his retirement in 1988.
(L to R) Kay Alcock, Mike Denial, RS, and Bryan Gallagher.

Russell Sharrock, on taking his leave of the school, pointed out that not only was he the longest serving Headmaster of KES (having served the school for 22 years and 8 months — over a year and a half longer than Dr. James Hichens (1905-1926) — but that he was the fourth longest serving Headmaster of the Grammar School since 1604. Only Thomas Balguy (1664-1696), Charles Chadwick (1776-1809) and Percival Bowen (1830-1863) — whom the Governors nearly sacked because of his excessive appetite for corporal punishment — had served longer. He was always referred to as Headmaster, not the now familiar, Headteacher, and he was also the last member of staff to wear a gown, once, of course, commonplace at a grammar school. In fact after 1988 only one staff member, Arthur Jones, pre-dated him at the school and only two others had served briefly at KES when it was a grammar school.

Almost a hundred applications were received by the Governors for Sharrock's replacement and the whole Governing Body met to sift through the forms and references and draw up a long list, later reduced to a short list of five. Surprisingly, the five KES candidates were all men, including two headteachers from outside Sheffield and two local deputy heads. In May, a small sub-committee of three Governors, including the new Chair, Shelagh Marston, along with Bill Walton and two senior Councillors, made the unanimous choice of the Michael Lewis, an Oxford graduate, who was the Deputy Head, and currently the Acting Headteacher, of a school in Oxfordshire. He became the seventh Headteacher of King Edward VII School.

CHAPTER EIGHTEEN

CHALLENGES AND ACCOLADES
1988-2005

Nineteen eighty-eight, the year when Michael Lewis came north to take up the post of Headteacher, the first Head of KES to be so-called, was the most significant year in national educational politics since 1944. It was also a year of the most dramatic restructuring of secondary education within the City of Sheffield since 1969, and both the national and local changes set the agenda for most of the challenges that KES, and its new Headteacher, would face in the next decade. The 1988 Education Reform Act, colloquially referred to as the "Baker Act", after the combative and controversial Secretary of State who introduced it, was intended to complete the work of the Education Acts of the earlier Eighties. Taken together they were intended to meet the Conservative Government's objectives of raising standards by expanding parental choice, increasing accountability and securing value for money from the "state" education service. It also claimed to be giving increased powers to the schools and their governors, while at the same time taking more direct central government control over many aspects of education, including specifying in detail what was taught in all the classrooms of the country, something no previous British Government had ever contemplated. In the near future KES would be profoundly changed by the provisions of this act, which introduced:

- The National Curriculum
- Arrangements for Key Stage Testing at 11, 14, and 16
- Local Management of Schools' Finance (LMS)
- Publishing of "League Tables"
- Ofsted Inspectorate
- Increased powers for Governors
- Compulsory Christian Worship
- Grant Maintained Schools
- City Technology Colleges

In September of the same year the six tertiary colleges in Sheffield opened their doors to students for the first time, and this posed a more immediate problem for the new Headteacher, than the effects of the 1988 Education Act. Five KES Staff had joined the staff at the colleges, most of them at Norton College, and they included an Assistant Head, Mike Denial, and three Heads of Department; and Lewis had to fill these positions as soon as possible. So, before arriving at the school Lewis had been actively involved in recruiting and his decisions had already ruffled quite a few feathers. Firstly, he came under intense pressure from LEA officers to take a re-deployed teacher as Head of Mathematics but refused point blank to appoint him, later offering the post to another outside applicant, Petar Bavelja from Waltheof School, despite having two strong internal candidates. When he came to fill the Assistant (i.e. Deputy[1]) Head's post, which was ring fenced to Sheffield, he had thirty applicants, including six internal candidates and again chose an outside candidate, Kath Latham (later Mrs. Auton) from Newfield School. So before his first term had begun, Lewis had disappointed eight existing staff members and defied the LEA over the highly sensitive issue of re-deployment, caused by falling rolls and tertiary re-organisation.

Furthermore, although the decision of Kenneth Baker to leave the Hallam Constituency schools out of the tertiary re-organisation plan had been taken over two years previously, the political suspicion, if not downright hostility, resurfaced now the colleges had started their work. The Labour controlled Council made no secret of their disappointment that six schools had "escaped" from their citywide scheme and many councillors regarded the sixth form schools as the "illegitimate children" of the post-sixteen re-organisation.

The new Leader of the Council, Coun. Clive Betts, an Old Edwardian himself and a Cambridge graduate, made it clear that Labour would continue to press for the abolition of the sixth forms as soon as a sympathetic Labour Government was elected at Westminster, although that was at least three years in the future. Lewis, arriving in Sheffield that summer, found many of the LEA officers reflected this political thinking in their own attitude towards the sixth form schools. As the LEA still had a tight control over both revenue and capital spending, the school could expect few favours from them until the political smoke had cleared.

Lewis had deliberately sought out a post in Sheffield because it was a Labour authority, which, under Blunkett's leadership, had maintained a high profile in local government's resistance to the Thatcher Government's reforms. He had only made brief visits to the city before (on one of them he had to abandon his car in Crookes after overnight snow), and had never heard of King Edward VII School before replying to the advertisement for the Headteacher's post. He had, however, been educated at a school in Belfast in the Sixties that had a similar past to KES. Established by Presbyterians in 1810 it had, like Wesley College, been granted the right to prepare older students for degrees before Queen's University College, Belfast, was founded in 1849. It was a highly respected city centre HMC boys' grammar school, with a strong academic reputation and an obsessive tradition for sport, producing many Irish International Rugby Union players. After a "gap" year working in Hamburg, Lewis had gone to Lincoln College, Oxford, (Wesley's old college) and over a period of time had become more radical in his politics. He had been in Prague during the Russian invasion of 1968 and the events that year, as significant for the Twentieth Century as 1848 had

1   *Deputy Headteachers were always designated Assistant*
     Headteachers in Sheffield between 1969-2000, although their role
     was that of Deputy and other LEAs called them Deputy
     Headteachers.

been for the Nineteenth, confirmed his political move towards democratic socialism. By the time he arrived in Sheffield he had been a member of the Labour Party for almost twenty years, and had a teaching C.V. that reflected his political sympathies.

Lewis was the first Head of KES not to have taught at a public school, or even at a grammar school, for all his previous teaching experience had been at three comprehensive schools in the Midlands. They were three unusual comprehensives, for they were all "community" schools with a significant commitment to adult education and two of them were brand new when Lewis joined them. He rose quickly to positions of responsibility. A head of department at 26, a deputy head at 34 and finally in his last two terms before coming to Sheffield, the Acting Headteacher at Icknield School, in Oxfordshire, where he was considerably influenced by the radical thinking of the county's Chief Education Officer, Tim Brighouse, later the Chief Education Officer for Birmingham. When Lewis was appointed to the post at KES he was 38, professionally ready for the new responsibility, but aware that he had never taught at a comprehensive in a large city, nor in a multi-cultural school, or indeed one that had a strong sense of its own history, especially one with a past that might be oppressive as well as uplifting.

Like all his five predecessors, since Dr. Hichens retired in 1926, Lewis took over a school that was thriving and successful. Inevitably there were many who expected changes from a young and obviously vigorous, capable and reputedly radical new Headteacher, after such a long period under the previous incumbent. They certainly found when Lewis arrived in the Autumn Term 1988 that he was not going to accept time honoured working practices just because they were long established. He had little time for the deliberations of the Common Room Committee, set up by Clapton to give him a view of staff feelings. Instead Lewis set up a schedule of regular meetings on curriculum, pastoral and general issues. He enlarged the Management Team, by bringing into the regular formal meetings the Senior Teachers, Dorothy Hall and Nick Jones, respectively the teachers in charge of Sixth Form and Middle School, to join himself and the three Assistant Headteachers, Kay Alcock, Bryan Gallagher and, the newly appointed, Kath Latham. Bryan Gallagher unfortunately had to retire through ill health in 1990, and Lewis is fulsome in his praise for the tremendous support he personally received from Gallagher, especially in his role as Head of Lower School, where for 14 years he had inspired pupils new to the school and created a firm foundation for learning. Angela Cooper, his Deputy, moved up to be in charge of the Lower School and she also joined the Management Team.

The changes Lewis did introduce in the first year or two, were well thought out and beneficial to the school. He created five new positions, which all went to existing staff members, reinforcing areas of the school's organisation that he felt needed some priority. They included a cross-curricular co-ordinator for the development of information technology (Chris Phipps), two teachers who were responsible for the Upper and Lower School libraries (Tim Hutchinson and Val Beech) and a co-ordinator for the development of partnerships with business and employers, that was filled by Alan Powell. Powell was now encouraged to expand the limited work experience programme that had started in 1981 so that it would become a part of the educational experience of all Y10 pupils and soon he was finding placements for 240 students each Summer Term. Powell was also to be the school's link with new initiatives in the city aimed at strengthening co-operation between business and schools. Called the Sheffield Business and Education Partnership it aimed at improving training and educational opportunities for all school-leavers at 16, whilst its wider strategy was to help give substance to the new détente between the Labour Council and the business and industrial community.

From September 1989 the school instituted a Tutor Group system to enhance the pastoral care provision. On entry to the school each pupil would be assigned to one of a group of 25-30 pupils and would remain in that group, if possible, with the same tutor until they reached Y11 and took their GCSE. These pastoral care groups were deliberately composed of pupils of differing abilities, met twice a day for registration, and discussed issues of common concern, as well as allowing time for personal guidance. After an initial attempt to also use these periods to teach the social education curriculum, a separate specialised department was established to teach a challenging and widely recognised Personal Social Health Education (PSHE) curriculum to all Y7 -Y11 students. The existence of these Tutor Groups, which progressed vertically through the school, allowed the resurrection of a modified house system. Each Tutor Group was paired and then named after one of Sheffield's rivers **(Loxley, Porter, Rivelin, and Sheaf),** and as students now stayed in their Tutor Group for all of their Lower and Middle School career, the groups in each year with the same name could be linked up and form rudimentary houses. Although a house system never developed, the Tutor Groups remain as one of the key organisational structures of the school and they also serve for internal sporting competition as many students strongly identify with their group and its (L1, L2, P1, P2 etc.) designation.

There were other changes that perhaps concerned the traditionalists. The prefectorial system was abolished in 1989, by the simple expedient of not appointing any new ones, and another reminder of former grammar school days disappeared. KES had continued with prefects long after most comprehensive schools had found them redundant. It was now felt that giving older students "policing" authority over their Sixth Form peers and Middle School students did not sit very well with current notions of equality, and could lead to unnecessary friction between prefects and other students. Unfounded rumours of other changes that Lewis was supposedly contemplating, led more than one Old Edwardian to contact him to demand that he did not remove the wooden honours boards which cover almost all the public wall-spaces on the first floor. The Headteacher listened sympathetically to these requests, before informing the complainers that there had never been any suggestion of removing them in the first place. They remain in place to this day, a very clear symbol of the continuity of the history of KES.

Michael Hugh Arthur Lewis MA
Headteacher (1988 to the present)

Born in Belfast in October 1949, the elder son of parents who were refugees from Czechoslovakia. Both his father and his mother came from the town of Trutnov/Trautenau, which in the late Thirties was in an area known to the world as Sudetenland. Both his parents grew up in a German speaking community and came from assimilated Jewish families that were steeped in Austro/German culture. His father, who might have had an academic career (he was a graduate of Vienna Commercial University and had a Doctorate from the University of Florence), fled to Britain from Czechoslovakia just after Hitler invaded that country in March 1939. Because of some previous family connection with the linen industry, he found himself living and working in Belfast, the "linen capital of the world". His mother, who had studied at the German University of Prague and had trained as a teacher, dancer and choreographer, did not get away before the Second World War broke out, but after surviving the terrors and turmoils of continental Europe during the war years, she came to Britain and married Lewis's father in Belfast, where she still lives.

From the Royal Belfast Academical Institution, Lewis went to Lincoln College, Oxford (1968-72) and read Modern Languages and did his PGCE at York University (1972-3), which included a teaching practice at a tough comprehensive school in east Hull. His first teaching post was at the brand new community school, Belper High School, until1976, when he was appointed the Head of Modern Languages at Hind Leys, a 14 –18 Community College in Leicestershire, again a new foundation housed in modern buildings.

Eight years later Lewis was appointed the Deputy Headteacher at Icknield School in Watlington, Oxfordshire, another community school where his particular areas of responsibility were the community and the curriculum. Icknield was an 11-16 school, surrounded by neighbouring sixth form schools. This experience of competing for pupils with 11-18 schools gave Lewis an appreciation of the difficulties that might arise in Sheffield after 1988, when many people were not at all sure that the tertiary colleges might prove the more popular in the long run.

At Belper, Lewis had met and later married his wife, Petra, who comes from Germany and was teaching at that school at the time. Their two sons chose to go to KES when they moved up from primary school. A passionate supporter of the arts, Lewis in his youth, had acted at the Lyric Theatre, Belfast, and played the violin. He had also been a keen competitive front row forward and remains an ardent supporter of the Irish Rugby Union Team.

Because of the falling numbers throughout the city, the school that Lewis took over in September 1988 numbered 1260 students, the lowest number of students on roll since the school had become a comprehensive school in 1969. However, during the next decade and a half the school would slowly increase to its present size of 1676 because of its popularity. Pupils came from every ward in the city and even in 1988 there were already 40 primary schools represented among the school population. The Government's enthusiasm for parental preference certainly benefited KES, as demographic factors and increased university student accommodation in the area reduced the number of children living in the school's own catchment area. When, after the 1988 Education Act, examination "League Tables" were published the process was intensified and later the school's official "Standard Number" would have to be raised to accommodate students whose parents wished them to come to the school. Even then there were often many parents who were disappointed and many of them appealed (in one year as many as 57 appeals were heard) but the majority were disappointed, as the school was full. This could be a very sad process as parents desperate for their sons and daughters to come to KES pressed their case and extolled the school's virtues, but the Government's policy of promoting parental choice and "League Tables" inevitably led to some bitter disappointments. Popular schools on the western side of the city became oversubscribed, while secondary schools on the other side of Sheffield faced falling rolls (four had to close in the early Nineties), with some of their district's potentially most able pupils crossing the city every day to go to schools like Tapton, High Storrs and King Edward VII.

The Sixth Form benefited from the same phenomena, but until 2002 was able to cope with the number of students from 11-16 comprehensives who were suitably qualified and wanted to come to the school to take "A" Level, and later GNVQ, courses. In 1988 the Sixth Form numbered 347, the largest it had been in the Eighties, and it remained stable at this number until 1996 when it moved up to 400. The fears, or hopes, of some, that Sixth Forms would lose their appeal and students at sixteen would vote with their feet and take up courses at the new tertiary colleges did not materialise. Theoretically, both the sixth form schools and the six tertiary colleges formed Sheffield's "Unified Tertiary Provision", and the school honestly counselled sixteen year old students in Y11 about the courses available at the colleges that might be more beneficial to them. This resulted in about 40% of the year group staying on at KES at that time, while 20% decided one of the colleges would be best for them. The school was linked with Loxley College, which served the north west of the city, and some of its adult education evening classes did, for many years, take place at the school. To maintain links and aid co-operation, one co-opted place on the Governors was given to a college representative, and in 1991 Sheila Stevens, the Loxley College Principal, briefly took up that place, replacing Ken Marks, one of their lecturers.

Despite these formal connections the relationship between the sixth form schools and the colleges, (who were amalgamated into one huge Sheffield College in 1992, that claimed to be the largest college in Europe), has been a wary one. One College Principal did not help matters by loudly proclaiming that the future success of the college would *"see off the Sixth Forms"*. The college ran many "A" Level courses and the majority of students from the 11-16 schools on the north and east of the city who wished to take "A" Levels chose to go to the College, but a significant number opted for the sixth form schools and the demand has accelerated in recent years. KES in 2003 had, for the first time, to put a limit of 500 on the number of students in the Sixth Form, but despite this the KES Sixth Form still remains the largest in the city.

The School's "Aims", to give a *"broad, balanced and relevant educational experience"*, were set out by Lewis in the 1988-89 School Prospectus. To prepare and equip students for a complex and rapidly changing world, students would be offered a full range of subjects ranging from the intellectual to the physical and the practical, with balance achieved by avoiding early specialisation and trying to avoid restricting choices as much as possible. The "Aims" also recognised KES's continuing commitment to high intellectual endeavour and success in examinations and this was confirmed by the 1990 "A" Level results with its 88% pass rate, including 47% gaining grades A or B, at that time the best ever achieved by KES since becoming a comprehensive school. The following year in 1991, the GCSE results with a 97.7% Grades A-G pass rate and 49.2% Grades A-C pass rate, were another excellent achievement, and although since then there have been blips, the trend of success at "A" level and GCSE has been continually upward overall.

With the exception of the emphasis on "practical" education all the six previous Headmasters of KES would have echoed these values and aspirations, albeit with their own interpretation as befitted their school at the time. However, the school now recognised, in its newly published *"Aims and Values"* (which comprised a robust statement of its comprehensive principles) that the biggest social change in the school's population was the substantial increase in the number of students from an Ethnic Minority background. This trend had been occurring since the Seventies, when some of the first Black and Minority Ethnic (BME) students to join the school were the sons and daughters of Asian refugees from East Africa (one Old Edwardian from this period, Mukesh Savani had gone on to be a Labour Member of the City Council), but children from continental Asian and Afro-Caribbean families had started to come to the school during Sharrock's time as the ethnic population of Sheffield grew. Because the school did not collect ethnic statistics in the Seventies and Eighties, it is not possible to know how large were the BME numbers in the school, but Sharrock and his Assistant Heads believe it was roughly in proportion to the BME numbers in the city's overall population. By 1986 the LEA's response to the new situation was to establish SUMES, the Sheffield Unified Multicultural Education Service, and this organisation was beginning to work with KES before Sharrock retired. Early in 1988 a school working party had already produced an Equal Opportunities Policy, but the main emphasis in the document had been on gender issues, although there were important guidelines for racial equality as well. In the following years one of the school's main priorities has been to promote the cultural heritage of students from different cultural backgrounds (by 1991there were over

200 BME students who between them spoke fourteen different languages, other than English, in their home) and build on the rich diversity that exists within KES. In this way, and through the quality of teaching on offer to all students, a comprehensive school can make an important contribution to the progress of the Asian and Afro-Caribbean communities in Sheffield, and the Governors themselves were strengthened when Chandron Owen joined the Governors in 1988 (the first KES Asian Governor), and then shortly afterwards Mike Atkin, a well respected figure in Sheffield's Caribbean community, also accepted an invitation to join the Governing Body.

Housing the Arts

Michael Lewis inherited a strong arts tradition at KES, where the school had rightly become famous for the quality of its extra curricular music and its drama. To varying degrees all his predecessors had supported the development of the arts in the school, especially Russell Sharrock, but few had the personal commitment, appreciation and love of music, theatre, fine arts and literature that Lewis has. Not surprisingly then it became one of his priorities to extend the arts provision in the school, and make it as much as possible a part of the "entitlement" of every student at KES. While the school's cultural tradition might be strong, the facilities available for practice and performance were quite inadequate. The Art Department still housed in the stable block at Lynwood had to vacate those premises at a few hours notice in 1990 when they were declared unsafe and it was then housed in temporary mobile classrooms, until moved to other short term accommodation at Melbourne Annexe. One of the early decisions of the new Headteacher in 1989 had been to group Art with Craft, Design and Technology in a new ADT faculty, led by Bill Smiles, so when shortly afterwards all the buildings on the Lynwood site were lost because of their dangerous structural condition, the Governors were encouraged to press for better purpose built facilities within the Close. Surprisingly, in 1991 after sustained pressure, the LEA, although desperately strapped for capital monies, agreed in principle to a proposal from the Governors that a new three storey teaching block should be financed from the sale of the Lynwood and Melbourne sites, and built on the land lying between the old scout hut and the swimming baths. The Governors hoped it would be ready for September 1993 and the first proposals included generous provision for Art, Design and Technology. In the event the building, reduced in capacity, was not completed until September 1995 and was mainly used by other departments, with the Art Department finding a permanent home in the so-called New Wing, — new in 1954!

Janet Wright, became the new Head of the Music Department in 1991. Her new Department had just been ejected from Lynwood but in compensation they had gained new practice facilities in the old Caretaker's Cottage by the main gate in 1990, which are still in use today. They were eventually to find a permanent home in the new building when it was finally completed, where the main music room is not only effective for lessons and practice, but is also a useful space for concerts by small ensembles and modest audiences. Concerts and recitals were also tried in the main Entrance Hall, where music amid the Corinthian pillars proved an attractive success. The school's outstanding tradition in music has been well maintained in the last decade and annual concerts at St. Mark's still involve over 200 students performing in the two orchestras, the string, wind and brass sections, the two choirs, the barber shop ensemble, the madrigal, jazz and recorder groups. The withdrawal of the LEA's free Peripatetic Music Teachers' service did pose a real threat to school music in the Nineties, but the Governors found some money available from a very tight budget and most parents, from then on, had to make a financial contribution to allow instrumental tuition to continue.

The performance of a new work, by local composer Max Watson, of *"I have a Dream"*, based on the life of Martin Luther King, highlighted the maturity and competence of the school's musicians and there were, as always, outstanding individual performers within their ranks. Melody Cooper, in 1996, was a finalist in the *"Young Musician of the Year"* Competition, before making her international debut in St. Petersburg in Beethoven's Violin Concerto and more recently joining the BBC Philharmonia Orchestra. In 1998, the Alexandra Quartette was formed and two of its members, violinist Becky Pascoe and Harriet Mesher on the viola, went on to study at the Royal Academy of Music after graduating from Oxford. The superb standard of KES music was confirmed when an Octet, that included the members of the Alexandra Quartette, won their category at the national "Music for Youth" Competition held at the Royal Festival Hall in 2000, and in the following year another group of talented musicians, the Wesley Quartette, were invited to appear in the School Proms at the Royal Albert Hall.

The scale of music making continues to expand in range and quality and in the numbers of performers under the new Director of Music, Eleri Davies, who joined the school staff in 2002, while the high level of choral work is the responsibility of Fran Wells, the long serving member of KES Music Department who, in his spare time, is the Director of the famous Bolsterstone Male Voice Choir.

It was Drama, however, that received the biggest impetus and development in the 1990s, when firstly a Drama Department was established in 1990 and then given a permanent home at Upper School in 1991, when the LLR was turned into a Drama Studio. John Gallacher who had produced several school plays since he arrived in 1985, was made the first Head of the Drama Department and shortly afterwards was joined by Paul Desgranges, who had been working as the Education Officer attached to the 1991 World Student Games. Whilst there had long been Drama classes in the Lower School, Gallacher now started the GCSE course, Drama and Theatre Arts, in the Middle School and after 1992 when the first group of students passed their examinations, he began the Theatre Studies "A" Level course. Both courses have been successful and popular with two or three groups every year taking GCSE Drama course and usually two groups taking the "A" Level course. The students on these courses form the core of the casts that have performed a remarkable series of plays in the last fourteen years since Gallacher created the school's own production company in 1991. Named "The Blank Slate Theatre Company", it was his idea to give students a sense that they were part of a permanent theatre company rather than just coming together for a school play, however well they might perform on the night. The company has its own budgets, its own equipment and most of all a clear identity in the school and in the community. Members are responsible for all stage management, props, costumes, lighting as well as front of house and marketing activities, tasks once led by staff members. The ethos of the company is to be ready to tackle any play that professional actors can tackle and invite audiences to assess their work as they would any professional production. By this yardstick they have regularly succeeded and many members of the Blank Slate Company have gone on to university or professional drama schools to study Drama, and not a few have become professional actors themselves.

The Blank Slate Company has focussed on producing challenging drama, successfully attempting plays, like Aristophanes's "Lysistrata" and Brian Friel's "Dancing at Lughnasa", that many schools would not consider within their competence. They have put on over forty productions since 1991 and attempted every dramatic mode from Shakespeare to Steven Berkoff, including plays with a cast of fifty to two-handers. One of the latter was one of their undoubted successes, when in 1992 they performed "Not About Heroes" with Luke Enters as Siegfried Sassoon and Daniel Crowder as Wilfred Owen, both of whom have gone on to be professional actors. This play transferred to the Crucible and was featured in Radio 4's Arts Programme, "Kaleidescope". The Times Educational Supplement said *"rarely have I seen acting of such accomplishment"*, and later another critic, writing about "Dancing at Lughnasa", described the 2000 choice as, *"simply the best production of the play - amateur or professional - that I have ever seen".* The "Noh Mysteries", presenting the cycle of medieval mysteries in the style of a Japanese Noh play, was featured on YTV's Calendar programme, and along with "Ghost Dances", an original piece featuring Native American chant and song, demonstrates the versatility of the company. The latter production, at the Crucible, getting a standing ovation from members of the Lakota nation visiting from the USA.

Michael Lewis, no mean critic himself, says of KES Drama and Music, *"I have never seen work of such a high standard at any school; we have sustained an amazingly high level of achievement. At its heart is the quality of the curriculum, experienced day in, day out, by all our students and not just by the dedicated or particularly gifted."*

Bad News for Sport!

If some progress could be made in improving the school's arts' facilities in the first half of the Nineties, there was no such fortune for sport. No sooner had Lewis taken up his post at KES then the pavilion at Whiteley Woods was condemned as unsafe in early 1989. The Council estimated that the necessary remedial work would cost £60,000 and made it clear that in its present financial situation it was not prepared to find the money. Some of their critics felt that this was small change to keep a school playing field in operation, when compared to the millions already spoken for in the massive construction programme of facilities for the World Student Games. To provide for this huge sporting event, the "Flagship" project in the new Council-Business Partnership, three major, state of the art, international facilities were being built and two district sports hall, plus the refurbishment of the Lyceum Theatre — theoretically for the accompanying Cultural Festival. To provide these venues, which, arguably, a major European city of half a million people should have, the Council withdrew support from several smaller projects and Whiteley Woods was one of these. Without the pavilion, which contained all the showers and changing rooms, it was not possible to use the pitches for games, highlighting the disadvantage of not having the playing fields adjacent to the school. Ninety years of school sporting history went out with a whimper. The grounds so proudly opened by the Lord Mayor in 1901, as the playing fields of the SRGS, now fell into disuse until they were resurrected and had a brief life as the playing fields of the independent Birkdale School. They too moved on and KES's former grounds at Whiteley Woods now languish as just another rough pasture, where casual passers-by are oblivious to the memories of "golden goals" and "silky cover drives" that once seemed so important to generations of Old Edwardians, who coped with muddy pitches and those sloping outfields.

Whiteley Woods in earlier, and wetter, days.

To compensate, the LEA allowed KES more use of Castle Dyke and the P.E.Department negotiated greater use of the YMCA indoor facilities in Broomhall, but neither of these options was really satisfactory. Whilst it was, of course, impossible to increase the area of playing fields around either Upper and Lower School, the Governors were determined to get a sports hall built, and at that time it was assumed it would be at Upper School. The Council, who had just built a Sports Hall attached to Waltheof School (to meet the requirements of the World Student Games and then serve as a dual use facility for the school and the Manor Estate), felt it was in no position to build another one in the west of the city, especially as it had recently agreed to construct a new teaching block at KES. Some time previously, through the good offices of the Chair of Governors, Shelagh Marston, there did seem to be a possibility that the British Steel Company in South Wales might be able to supply the steel shell for a sports hall to be built where the old fives courts had been. However, the project still required a considerable input from the Council, who would have had to draft the plans and excavate the site and the opportunity was lost. It would be over ten years before the school finally got its much needed sports hall and then it would be on the Lower School site. In 1992 it also appeared that the Swimming Baths would be lost as well, when the Council, as part of its policy of the consolidation of facilities, was closing small pools, like King Edwards and Glossop Road, having just built Europe's biggest swimming centre at Ponds Forge. The pool, opened in 1936, had never actually belonged to the school and was always theoretically a public facility, but in recent years it had been run by the Council's Recreation Department as a small, district pool, while still, of course, convenient for the school to use. Faced with the loss of a popular suburban facility, a consortium of local business people and residents formed a trust and took over the pool. Amazingly, and very much to their credit, they have managed keep it open and it remains well used, especially by pensioners and mothers with young children.

Introducing the National Curriculum

The most fundamental change in the curriculum at KES came with the gradual introduction of the National Curriculum after 1989. In the next half decade the school would change over from its own syllabuses in ten main subjects, to those prescribed by the Government's official curriculum working parties, in which teachers had virtually no say and no involvement. A common curriculum for all schools in England and Wales, from the first year of primary school until students took their GCSE, was the Conservative Government's cornerstone initiative in an attempt to raise pupils' achievements by first creating uniform standards of teaching. Their critics argued that the curriculum was too prescriptive: it "Balkanised" subjects into rigid academic disciplines and allowed little time for minority subjects, or any of the cross-curricular work that had been very much part of the Sheffield Curriculum Initiative in the middle Eighties.

Concern about the massive increase in the teaching staff's workload, and the compulsory assessment through Standard Attainment Tests (SATS) was raised, but their full impact would not be felt until later. For the moment there were many teachers who feared the loss of control over their own subject syllabus and the abrupt curtailment of programmes that had enabled Sheffield teachers from different schools, and different disciplines, to work together to create new and imaginative courses. On the other hand the school welcomed the initial broad base of the National Curriculum which prescribed three Core Subjects and seven Foundation Subjects, which produced a range of subjects not dissimilar from those that the school had traditionally followed.

The Three Core Subjects were;
English, Mathematics and Science;

The Seven Foundation Subjects were;
History, Geography, A Modern Language, Art, Technology, Music, and P.E.

Other subjects like Latin, a second modern language or Economics, had to be squeezed into the 15-20% of teaching time that was not spoken for, although that time had to accommodate Religious Education, already theoretically compulsory for all but now reaffirmed. All year groups in English schools were designated the same, and the school's First Year became Y7 and the Sixth Form became Y12 and Y13. If schools still had romantically named forms like "Transitus" and the "Remove", as KES once had, these names were now removed. KES soon moved to a 25 period week to better deliver the requirements of the National Curriculum, which they began to introduce subject by subject over the next five years.

The first subject departments to undertake a **National Curriculum** *programme of study were Mathematics and Science for Y7 students in September 1989, and they continued into Y8 the following year. The third Core subject, English, started in September 1990, with the first Foundation subject, Technology, beginning in the same term. However the main curriculum change that year was when "Balanced" Science was introduced into Y10, which meant that all students in the school would study science for 20% of their time during the next two years. This placed a squeeze on other subjects, but it was important to KES to develop its own curriculum entitlement at 14-16, with full GCSE courses in the Humanities, Languages and Design and Technology, whilst protecting minority subjects and the ability to specialise, despite the extra demand for classroom time for Science. One by one the Foundation subjects were started, some ahead of the required date for their introduction. This huge project put much extra work onto the shoulders of the Senior Staff, especially the Assistant Headteacher, Kay Alcock (soon to be Mrs. Madden) who, along with Departmental Heads, was responsible for each subject's planning. It also added to the work-load of each member of staff who had to prepare the material needed for the new courses.*

Criticism of the new system, increasingly stridently heard, was about the details and practices of the National Curriculum rather than its general underlying principles. The subject working groups had overloaded the content in many of the subject syllabuses, with the result that the burden of extra work placed on teachers had become excessive, far beyond what would have been expected formerly when a change of syllabus took place. Moreover, it was relentless because there were constant syllabus revisions that appeared to have been taken by *"people operating in a vacuum"*, and often there was little or no training and inadequate resources to ease the teachers' heavy work-load. In 1992 KES had been a pilot school for the "trial" runs of the new SATS in Maths, Science and English at Key Stage Three (Y9), but by the following year the Governors, on the advice of the Management Team and aware of the Unions' opposition, declined to "administer" the SATS. The national concerns over the National Curriculum, underpinned by a testing regime which many felt was putting undue stress on young children, led to the Dearing Report of December 1993. This recommended a reduction and simplification of what should be taught, while the tests were judged to be too complex and Sir Ron Dearing recommended that they be simplified.

"The Magnificent Seven" and others.

While the school was implementing the National Curriculum, the number of students on roll continued to increase rapidly. By September 1991 numbers had passed the 1400 mark, due to the school's continued popularity, but during the following year they took an even larger jump to 1560 students, caused by an important change in Council policy. Faced with falling rolls across the city and a Government demand to prune the budget by reducing the number of schools, the Council set up its own Schools' Review Body, which reported in 1991and recommended that Middle Schools should be abolished and all children in the city should start their secondary education in Y7 at the traditional age of eleven. This was a great advantage to KES, and other Sheffield schools, who for twenty three years had welcomed a quarter of their pupils in Y7 and the majority of new pupils in Y8 when they were twelve. This altogether more logical approach was implemented in September 1992 and the school's population went up by 140 as a result. The Governors agreed that there would be a seven form entry into the Lower School that year and set a "Standard Number" for Y7 at 210 students, recognising that the immediate problem would be accommodation. The Governors looked to the LEA to meet this increase with at least some plans for extra permanent accommodation; instead they were given a massive recycled triple mobile classroom block, already in poor condition, which was sited adjacent to the west end of the Darwin Lane buildings. Whilst the Governors had been indefatigable in ensuring the LEA was fully briefed about Lower School's deficiencies, the Council, for all the usual reasons, did not produce any plans, or build any extensions at Lower School. Suddenly all that changed in 1998, when under the new Labour Government's Private Finance Initiative (PFI), they agreed to put KES Lower School on a list of four secondary schools who would be re-housed in entirely new premises.

The increase in student numbers meant an increase in staff, the school now having the full time equivalent of 96 teaching staff, indeed well over a hundred teachers if all the part-timers were counted in. Changes, of course, had been happening to the staff every year as teachers retired, or left for other posts, but there had been very sad occasions too. In 1989 Richard Cooper, the Head of Chemistry, had died at the untimely age of 38 after only just joining the staff, and in 1992 Chris Collier, the Head of Lower School Science, had sadly died aged only 32. When Bryan Gallagher was so unfortunately forced to retire through ill health, his position as Assistant Head was not filled immediately, partly because the school's financial position was so parlous, but also because the pause allowed Lewis to consider how best the Management Team could be strengthened. Then in September 1991, Liz Talmadge was appointed as the third Assistant Head with responsibilities for assessment. She soon settled into the school but then left after seven terms in December 1993, when she was appointed the Headteacher of Portland School, Worksop, where she stayed until she became the new Headteacher of High Storrs School in 1999.

Lewis also appointed a number of teachers who were being re-deployed, mainly caused by falling student numbers throughout the city. This could pose difficult problems for a Headteacher, who would want their school to play a part in helping colleagues find a suitable placement and avoid redundancy. However, it was always Lewis's policy to put the interests of the children first and he would not be pushed into appointing re-deployed staff who he did not feel were up to scratch. One risk he was prepared to take was to appoint a former National President of the NAS/UWT as the Head of History in 1992, after, she believes, she was sidelined at two other schools because of her union activities. Sue Rogers had taught at Jordanthorpe School (Meadowhead School since 1988) from 1978-91 when she was granted secondment by the LEA to be the President of her Union. When her year was over she joined the Sheffield teachers who were looking for re-deployment. She is grateful that Lewis took a chance on her appointment and for four years she played only a limited local role in her union's affairs. Subsequently she returned to the union's National Executive in 1996 and since 2001 she has been Treasurer of the NASUWT and a member of the General Council of the TUC. At that point she relinquished her post as Head of History and Politics to Sally Davies, although she continued teaching two days a week at KES.

The last two members of the Classics Department retired in the Nineties as the number of students prepared to take Latin continued to decline. For the first time the subject was not offered to Y9 pupils in 1994, and by 1996 Classics was no longer taught at the school. The significance of its passing may have been lost on many at the school, though it was not because Language teaching was not flourishing. The School had been offering Sixth Formers a course in Japanese between 1990-94, and from 1996 students could take Urdu GCSE and later Italian, as well as the three main European Languages that the school had traditionally offered. However, the loss of Latin, which the Governors hoped could be re-started if there was enough demand in the future, broke a link with the original purpose of the school when it was founded three hundred and ninety years previously. By definition, the King James Grammar School of 1604 was established to teach Latin grammar, which was then still the key to most learning and had obvious practical value to pupils at the time.

The Head of the Classics Department, Arthur Jones, the longest serving member of staff, retired in 1989 after thirty years service at the school. He was the only teacher left from the Clapton era. For two years he worked on a new translation of the Aeniad, until 1991 when he went to teach for a time at Birkdale School who were building up their Classics Department. Alan Sutton (1968-1996), the final survivor from the grammar school days at KES, was now the only Classics teacher on the staff and he continued running the GCSE Latin course until 1996. After retirement he accepted a part-time position at Silverdale School, where he still teaches Latin.

In the Summer of 1994, seven long serving members of staff left at the same time. There had been similar occasions before in the school's history when so many senior, well respected and familiar faces had departed at the end of one term that it seemed the school would never be the same again. These seven had almost 200 years of teaching between them, 148 of which had been at KES. Mike Paulson, who was a staff representative on the Governors, had taught for thirty years in Sheffield schools before replacing Richard Cooper as Head of Chemistry at KES in 1989. Marilyn Smith had joined the school as a young maths teacher when it first became a comprehensive school in 1969 and Bill Smith of the Technology Department had arrived in 1972 after a period working in industry. Ann Ritchie, who came as a part-time teacher of English to Crosspool School in 1967, had been at KES longer than all three of them and she was currently a Year Tutor. Perhaps she was best remembered by many Old Edwardians as the producer of school musicals, like "Oklahoma" and "Bugsy Malone", and the joyful mayhem of the Lower School Pantomime.

The "Seven" included two members of the school's management team, Angela Cooper and Dorothy Hall, both Heads of Section and both historians. Angela had 19 years service at the school, and for ten years had played a leading role at Darwin Lane, six as Deputy to Bryan Gallagher and then, since 1990, the Head of Lower School. Dorothy Hall, currently the Head of Post-16 Studies, had taken over that role from Arthur Jackson when he retired in 1981. She had then already been teaching History at KES for a decade and she later steered the Sixth Form through the difficult period after the tertiary colleges had been established, maintaining its high academic reputation and its position as the largest sixth form in the city. They were replaced by Kath Auton, the Assistant Headteacher, as Head of Lower School and by Sheila Basford, a Sixth Form Tutor, who now took over in charge of the Sixth Form, officially titled Senior Tutor for Post-16 Studies.

The final member of the "magnificent seven" was David Anderson, with 27 years service at KES, the longest serving member of the group. No member of staff could match his long connection with the school, which began in 1948 as a scholarship pupil from Crookes, until he went to University in 1955. He returned to the school as a teacher in 1967 when KES was in its last months as a grammar school and served the vast majority of his time as Head of Economics and Politics when KES was a comprehensive school. He carried on the successful Economics work of Gordon Cumming and Keith Robinson, and several hundred "A" Level students will always be reminded of the Law of Diminishing Returns whenever they bite into a Mars Bar. Many of Anderson's students studied Economics at University and went on to successful careers. Two are high officials of the International Monetary Fund in Washington and others are well placed in banking in the City of London.

David Anderson

Man and boy he had served under four of the school's seven Headmasters, only Gordon Cumming (pupil 1923 - 1931 and master 1936 - 1953) could claim a record like that.

A year before he retired David Anderson had been an exchange teacher at KES's new partner school, T.L.Hanna High School in Anderson, South Carolina. He found it interesting to compare teaching methods and curriculum content, but it was that school's enthusiasm for Football (the code with linebackers and wide receivers) that made one of the biggest impressions on him. In the Deep South, where Football is King, he found that all the school, including its marching band and its cheerleaders, turned out to watch the Friday night floodlit home games, displaying a remarkable corporate spirit as they enthusiastically rooted for the "Yellowjackets". These inter-school games could attract up to 4000 spectators, and his hosts assumed he was displaying typical British understatement when he told them that a school match involving the senior KES team might attract half a dozen spectators.

The Battle for Money

During the last seventeen years there have been no constitutional stand up fights with the City Council over re-organisation of the school, as there were in the Sixties and Eighties. Instead there was, throughout the Nineties, a long struggle of attrition over the financial resources available to the school. The Council, in its turn, believed it was caught in the middle, between an unprecedented squeeze on their budgets by the Conservative Government's policy and actions, and the demands of the LEA's schools just to maintain standards of funding, let alone reach the levels enjoyed by many other education authorities. Until 1991, the LEA in Sheffield controlled even the minutest details of KES's budget, and financial management was just not part of a headmaster's function. Michael Lewis recalls how in his first year in Sheffield he suggested transferring some money saved on an unfilled clerical post, to be spent on books and equipment at the school. He was met with incredulity by the council officers, who regarded such a request as heresy, as if, in any way, this money was the school's money. The only finance the school had discretion over was the "Capitation" allowance, about 2.5% of the budget, that could be used on textbooks, stationery, classroom equipment and office materials. In 1988 this amounted to a mere £43,000 (out of a budget of £1.9 million) and had reduced by over 10% from mid-Eighties.

The 1988 Education Act held out the promise of schools gaining more financial independence and organisational autonomy by establishing LMS, - the Local Management of Schools. In practice, although the Council would still decide the size of the total budget for all their schools, they would then, through a formula, share out to the individual schools their allocation and the schools would then have control over their own budget share to decide priorities. Unfortunately, during the Nineties, the money that was available to schools was often reduced in both actual and real terms, and with such a labour intensive operation (usually 80 to 85 % of the schools budget went on staff salaries) there was little room to manoeuvre in the harsh, stringent financial climate of that time.

Sheffield began to implement LMS in 1990, but KES was not one of the schools that piloted the programme, only coming on-stream the following year in April 1991. Under the old system the school's budget had risen to £2.2 million, but pleasingly, and surprisingly, under the new LMS formula the school was a considerable net gainer. In the first year of LMS the school's budget rose significantly by £500,000, so the school had the rare pleasure of being able to take on much needed teaching staff and effect some overdue repairs and maintenance. The following year there was another increase but this was entirely swallowed up by the requirements of funding the extra pupil and staffing costs of the Council's decision to abolish Middle Schools, and start all secondary school pupils in Y7.

If there had been a financial honeymoon for a few months, it was now over. The new grim reality was that both the Council and the schools were desperately short of money and would be until the end of the Nineties. The Governors recognised that the Council was "protecting" Education expenditure and that most of its other Departments were suffering even worse, but for KES and other schools, LMS, in reality, meant finding desperate ways of delivering quality teaching in the classroom, the school's core activity. The Governors and the Headteacher would not contemplate compulsory redundancies, especially at a time when the numbers of students were increasing. Instead, like most schools, they raided the repairs and maintenance budgets risking longer term difficulties, as well as looking to sensible marginal savings by better housekeeping, including not flushing the toilets during the night, replacing screw taps with levers and close control of heating and lighting.

The 1993-4 budget share from the LEA was a reduction in real terms and the following year it was cut again, this time in actual (£100,000 less) as well as in real terms (6.3%). Now the Governors were prepared to accept the loss of teaching posts if they did not involve sacking anyone. This was a line they were not prepared to cross, believing compulsory redundancy would seriously damage the ethos and morale of the staff. The taking of early retirement by the "Magnificent Seven" had helpful financial implications. They were all senior staff on comparatively high salaries and they could be replaced by younger teachers who would be less of a charge on the school's budget. Crude economics, but just acceptable in the circumstances. In 1996 for the first time KES did not have any Foreign Language Assistants at the school, and Governors asked parents if they might wish to contribute voluntarily to the cost of the peripatetic music teachers and the Library to maintain some up-to-date stock.

KES played a leading role in the local campaign to highlight the plight of schools, which they identified as the result of Government Policy and the Council's inability to protect them. Large protest meetings, mainly of teachers and governors from many Sheffield schools, were held in the school's Assembly Hall. The Headteacher exhorted parents in his Newsletter to write to Councillors and M.P.s and even join a demonstration in London in 1995 as part of the national FACE (Fight Against Cuts in Education) campaign to rally support for education (he even included the time and place of departure of the coach). It seemed to fall on deaf ears in Whitehall, but the Opposition noted the support and in 1997 when Blair took office his famous rallying call indicating his new Government's priorities was "Education! Education! Education!" Sceptics in education were prepared to wait and see if his new Government would deliver.

In 1996 the Governors, along with other Sheffield schools, sought out new battlegrounds over finance. If they had no realistic prospect of increasing the size of the "cake" they could demand more of the LEA's overall budget was spent on the schools. Currently the LEA retained 19% of its total schools' budget and passed the rest on to the schools, now they came under pressure to justify the amount they kept at the centre. This was spent on a wide range of functions, including a totally inadequate £3,000,000 for repairs and maintenance, top up payments for teachers who took early retirement, as well as small sums to groups, like the Sheffield and Rotherham Dance Project and a grant to the Sheffield Federation of School Sports. Gradually over the next few years, under the new Director of Education, the Council would reduce the amount of this money it kept at the centre to 7% and school budgets would gain some benefit.

Another front on which KES, and the other Sixth Form schools, challenged the LEA, was on the specific funding of Sixth Forms. Every pupil in a Sixth Form gained a school more financial support than a pupil at a Primary or 11-16 school, but the differential in Sheffield was amongst the lowest in the country. Despite the fact that, after 1992, the Sixth Form schools were the Council's only responsibility for Post-16 education (when the Sheffield College was created and taken out of the LEA's control), their funding was amongst the lowest of all the Metropolitan Districts, and below the average for even Yorkshire and Humberside, not the most generous region for funding in England. When they discovered that a similar sized school in Doncaster would receive several hundred more pounds per sixth former than one in Sheffield, the Sixth Form schools, all but one in the Hallam Constituency, were, not surprisingly, unimpressed with their treatment by the Council. After 1999, when the Liberal Democrats, whose councillors represented the south-west of the city, gained control of the City Council, small increases in sixth form funding occurred and this has continued on a larger scale after a new quango, the Learning and Skills Council, took over the responsibility for the levels of Post-16 funding in schools and colleges. Under their formula, KES's allocation was substantially increased, so that it is now closer to the national average.

By 1996-7 the last year of John Major's Conservative Government, the KES budget had only risen to £3.06 million and the school had been forced into a number of deficit budgets, including having to find the full cost of the teachers' pay award in 1995 without any new money at all to cover it from the Government. Since 1997 the monies available to the school have increased substantially. By 1999 the school budget was £4.5 million and to-day stands at £7.6 million although much of the increase is hypothecated for

415

Government programmes, like Excellence in Cities, Specialist Schools Status and the Training School Initiative and core activity funding is still tight.

GMS, No thanks!

One way the Governors could have alleviated the situation in the middle Nineties was to become a Grant Maintained School (GMS), leave the control of the LEA and enjoy a more generous funding regime, especially increased capital provision to renovate, repair and rebuild. GMS had been one of the main provisions of the 1988 Education Act, and the Government hoped that many schools would want to throw off the "yoke" of their local authority and obtain a regular annual "direct grant" from a Government supported quango. Between 1989 and 1993 many schools, especially in the Home Counties (in Hillingdon LBC all secondary schools went GM), took advantage of this provision. However, in Sheffield in that period, only Clifford C of E Primary School, which was faced with closure because of its small size, took the plunge and "opted out" of the LEA. Then in 1993 the two Roman Catholic secondary schools, Notre Dame and All Saints, did likewise, after strong encouragement from their Diocesan Director of Education.

Surprisingly not a single LEA comprehensive school in Sheffield opted out, although two, Silverdale and Tapton did go to a ballot of parents who, nevertheless, voted to stay with "the devil they knew". The Government was surprised that thriving comprehensive schools in middle class Conservative held wards did not jump at the chance to free themselves from Labour controlled LEAs, especially if they were former grammar schools in "one party states" like South Yorkshire. In theory KES should have been a prime candidate for opting out and becoming a GMS school. Yet despite being a former grammar school with a large middle class catchment area, the Governors, chaired at the time by Dr., later Professor, Tony Crook, rejected the possibility of even exploring GMS status, preferring to stay as part of the LEA family of schools despite all the turmoils of their relationship. For some Governors it was a straight political choice, for others they feared that GMS schools, (who could select 10% of their pupils) were the "thin edge of the wedge" of a return to selective schools and the abandonment of comprehensive education; generally they distrusted a Government who had made their school's life so difficult for over a decade.

Disappointed by the numbers of schools opting out nationally, the government insisted, by the 1993 Education Act, that each governing body should discuss the issue annually and report to parents. A governing body could not accept GMS status themselves, but if they were in favour they could initiate a ballot of all the parents and a simple majority for change would authorise their school becoming a GM school. Every year, until David Blunkett, the new Education Secretary in Blair's First Government, scrapped the GMS system, KES Governors voted on the issue and always rejected the option to ballot. Usually the Governors' vote against holding a ballot, and therefore against GMS status, was almost unanimous, with a lone secret voter registering their annual opposition.

Innovations, Interests and Achievements

KES in the Nineties gained a deserved reputation as a school that was prepared to be innovative, if the right project or idea was offered to the school. The school was in the forefront of new ideas and the City Council, especially under its new professional leadership of Bob Kerslake, from 1997 the new Chief Executive, and Jonathon Crossley-Holland, since December 1996 the Director of Education, encouraged KES to take up major long-term initiatives, like the Language College and the PFI re-build of Lower School, which subsequently led to the demolition of the old building, that had started life as Crosspool Secondary Modern.

The key date for both of these projects was 1998, but long before that KES had been chosen as a partner to run innovative schemes. In 1993 the school had taken up an offer from the University of Sheffield to become a centre for Initial Teacher Training for post graduate students, who now undertook their professional training at the school, initially in English, Geography, Languages and Science. Mary Aiston was designated an Associate University Tutor and led a team of several staff members closely involved with this work, later establishing similar links with Sheffield Hallam University to train Technology and P.E. student teachers. In 2000, KES was amongst the first group of schools to be designated as a "Training School", and the school continues to make an important contribution to professional development in the city and beyond.

The Work Experience Programme led by Alan Powell, as already noted, expanded after 1991to embrace all Y10 pupils and some Y11 ones. Now, instead of finding placements for 30+ students, he had to arrange for 229 students to find a two week experience at an office, business or factory, and since that date over 3000 students have been "placed", including one who undertook his placement in Majorca. Not surprisingly this work was heralded as an example of "good practice", and the school won the Master Cutler's "Tribute" Award in 1994, a joint award from Warwick University and the Post Office in 1997, as well as featuring in a two page article in the national magazine "Educational Computing and Technology" in 1996. Powell was then asked to visit a school with 2000+ students and speak to the faculty about the work at KES. He readily accepted – the school was in Plant City, Florida.

Other curriculum work that gained a high national reputation was the Sex Education Programme of the PSHE Department. In this sensitive and potentially difficult area, which was a legal requirement of all secondary schools after the 1986 Education Act, the KES programme won the coveted Pamela Sheridan Award, organised by the Family Planning Association. That was in 1996 when Anthea Peers and Dot Kesterton delivered the programme, and the Department was commended again by the FPA in 2004 when Kim Wilson was Head of PSHE.

KES pioneered another curriculum initiative when the school, in September 1994, introduced two of the new General National Vocational Qualification courses (GNVQ) into the Sixth Form. The two courses selected were Business and also Health and Social Care, both at the Advanced Level, and their significance was that they offered a wider choice of subjects to encourage more Post-16 students to stay on in the Sixth Form, when they might have left education altogether. Prior to 1994 the Sixth Form only offered examination courses to "A" Level, or as re-sits for GCSE, and in effect, post-16, KES resembled a grammar school. Now the comprehensive ideal was extended into the Sixth Form and the GNVQs, with their emphasis on course work, project work and regular assessment, gave a student who wanted a different style of learning the chance to gain a qualification that was equal to an "A" Level pass. Martin Shevill had led the preparatory work for these courses, but he left in 1994 to become a Deputy Headteacher at Honley High School in Kirklees, and Debbie McShane became the teacher in charge of the GNVQ work at the school. In 1996, after the successful introduction of the two year Advanced Level GNVQ courses, Intermediate GNVQ courses were introduced, giving some students a three year course to gain their higher GNVQ qualification.

There was some re-thinking of the Senior Management team after Liz Talmadge left at the end of 1993. Instead of appointing another third assistant headteacher, the Headteacher and the Governors agreed to appoint a Director of Administration to handle the increasingly complicated financial and non-teaching management of the school. KES now had a budget and staff the size of a medium range company and this appointment seemed a sensible way of using staff resources. In the event the move didn't work out and the Headteacher again took on the overall financial management of the budget, until the appointment of Debbie Bates as Bursar in 2002. The re-organisation allowed Lewis to bring two senior teachers into the management team, Richard Fone, whose brief included the increasingly important area of assessment, and Chris Phipps, who dealt with time-tabling and cover, as well as ICT. The school did not fill the position of a third "Deputy" until 2004.

This area of Information and Communication Technology, the single most important change in teaching methods in the Twentieth Century, one that five of the previous KES Headmasters could not even have imagined, was the one that suffered most from the restrictions on finance. While other industrial countries were finding extra resources for this expensive, but vital, new teaching resource, KES, like many other British schools, could only direct limited extra finance to ICT even though the Governors had identified it as a top priority for the school. They could however make a specific appointment of a Director of ICT to develop the school's ICT investment and programme, that was initially, in effect, a catching up process. However the school's ambitions were indicated by the completion of the school's first major network that was installed at Lower School in that same year.

There were new initiatives in communication inside and outside the school. The Headteacher's Newsletter started in 1992 and every term since it has offered a cogent topical report for parents and in 1997 it was joined by school's own "Green 'Un" , when the P.E. Department produced its green sports newsletter with stirring tales of team and individual successes. When Paul Desgranges was appointed to the staff in 1991, after secondment to the World Student Games, part of his duties were to act as the school's first Press Liaison Officer and present a fuller picture of the school's activities and achievements to the local press. The Year Planner, introduced in 1995 by Richard Fone, was much admired and copied by other schools. It was a Lower School equivalent of a University Calendar, giving basic information to new pupils as well as containing a diary in which to record progress and set work. It was continued into other years and became a permanent feature of a student's school life.

There was also an attempt in 1993 to resurrect the school magazine. "Kings" was closer in content to the teenage orientated KESMAG of the Seventies than the older journals of record of the grammar school era, but it did not have a prolonged life. Nor did a Lower School magazine, "Talk", which also bravely tried to test the school journalism waters. Much more successful was the American style Year Book introduced by Nick Jones in 1995, featuring Y11 Leavers in class group photos, alongside vox pop quotes and lists of the best and worst of him and hers. The Year Book has flourished and expanded to give students, at the end of their compulsory schooling, an attractive record of their years at the school. Jones also resurrected the long school photograph, so, now, every year, the whole of Y11, like its predecessors of the inter-war period, has an all-inclusive photo-shoot. The Lower School followed suit and they take a group photograph of all 700+ students once every three years. Sad to relate perhaps, modern technology has made it impossible for the pupil on one end to run round the back and appear at the other end, as happened in the past as the old cameras slowly traversed the group.

As always at KES there were numerous clubs and societies. Youth Action, Young Enterprise, who produced an attractive mug displaying the school crest for the Ninetieth Anniversary Celebrations in 1995, and the Duke of Edinburgh's Award, still turning out Gold Award winners, were all strongly supported in the Nineties. There was a Radio Club, a Bridge Club, that won the Regional Finals in 1992, a girls' soccer team that visited USA and played T.L.Hanna High School, a Christian Union group, and an Urdu Club. There were annual Oxfam Appeals, a "Cold Front" Appeal in 1993 to raise money for "Blankets for Bosnia", while others put their fundraising efforts into saving whales, or re-cycling tin cans to save the planet. One dumping ground for tin cans was found to be the old air raid shelters, hurriedly built in Autumn 1939 and now quietly hibernating unnoticed beneath the Close. Some teachers went "pot holing" in the school grounds and re-visited them in 1998, to find them intact but with little piles of drinks cans in corners where they had been shoved down the ventilation shafts. They also found that games of noughts and crosses, chalked on the walls of the shelters by boys during air raid practices, had survived for over fifty years.

However, the most dramatic success was probably that of the Young Engineers Club, founded in 1992 after running in an informal way for a decade. The main focus of their year was the Young Engineers' competition, where Sally Brook and Anna Cubison gained second place in the national awards in 1994 for their hard shell, secure beach bag named the "Soundaround", whilst Ben Barker, the Teacher who fired the imaginations of the club and classroom students alike, was named the first ever "Technology Teacher of the Year" in an award organised by the TES. KES Young Engineers visited Seattle, in Washington State, as guests of Boeing, had their work displayed at the Institute of

Electrical Engineers in London and also at the Engineering Employers Federation AGM in Sheffield. As if all this was not exciting enough, in March 1995, fifteen students were invited to represent the national Young Engineers and mount a three day display in the House of Commons, where they attracted the attention of many leading politicians, including the Education Secretary, Gillian Shephard and the new Leader of the Labour Party, one Tony Blair. To round off a memorable year the club also appeared on Blue Peter and a two Channel Four programmes and they reckon they covered 13,700 miles demonstrating their ideas and inventions in that one year alone.

KES pupils with Tony Blair at the House of Commons in 1995

There were also individuals and small groups whose work achieved unusual recognition. Sarah Mills had a prize-winning poem displayed on the local Sheffield buses, whilst several KES artists had their paintings displayed at the Chinese Embassy and then exhibited in the People's Republic. Lydia Mulholland, then in Y8, won the Silver Medal in 1996 Junior Mathematics "Olympiad", and a quintet of Y9 songwriters produced a song in French that beat 1500 other entries in an Alliance Française song writing competition. At the very end of the decade, a Sixth Form group produced a film "International School – International City" that was shown at one of the display features in the Millennium Dome at Greenwich in 2000. However, perhaps the most amazing experience of any Edwardian during that decade was the opportunity afforded to Kevin Slack of Y13, who accompanied the Prime Minister on an official visit to Japan in 1993. KES was asked to nominate a pupil because of its success in establishing Japanese

Studies and Kevin joined five others to spend a week with John Major in Kyoto and Tokyo, before returning to Britain and reading Law at Emmanuel College, Cambridge.

Celebrating an Anniversary 1995-96

The school chose to celebrate its 90th Anniversary in some style with a series of events that lasted a full year, marking not only the foundation of the school in 1905, but also the re-opening of the refurbished school building in September 1906. The Celebrations served a number of functions. Firstly, it was intrinsically worthwhile to mark the school's ninetieth year as a significant milestone in its history, but it was also, in such financially stringent times, a legitimate occasion to launch an appeal to raise funds for some crucial capital developments. The Anniversary was also a opportunity to draw a line under the divisions that still smouldered in some quarters, that the comprehensive school was not the true descendant of the pre-1969 grammar school. Through KES's continuing success, the school would be able to clearly demonstrate that there was a genuine continuum between the present school and the school of 1905 to 1969.

"The attractive new building, whose pillars complement Flockton's 1838 design for Upper School. It was designed by Sue Williams of the City Council's Architect's Department."

Somewhat fortuitously the Anniversary began with the opening of the new building in September 1995. Fortuitously, because it was originally hoped it would be ready two years earlier, but initial difficulties of finding a developer for the Lynwood site, and then planning objections from nearby residents, held up the financial planning and the construction work. The attractive curved building that finally emerged, the first new building in the Close (apart from the swimming pool) since 1838, was only a two storey building and no longer housing ADT specialist facilities as originally planned. The building opened by Norman Adsetts on 13th September 1995, was now to house the Modern Languages, History and Economic Departments with two purpose built music rooms for rehearsal and small concert work. Adsetts, later Sir Norman, opened his speech with the same Latin sentences he had last used when making the Head Boy's Latin Oration at Speech Day in 1950, and went on to say that what united the school of his day with that of 1995, was the same commitment to quality and the same desire to serve the people of Sheffield. The people of Sheffield, through their Council representatives, had found the finance needed to complete the £1.26 million scheme from the sale of the Lynwood and Melbourne Annexe sites, and this new building allowed all the teaching at Upper School to be accommodated on one site — there had been four in the 1970s. The Council also made £40,000 available, but disappointingly only as a loan, to enlarge the Library, house the Art Department in the "New" (1954) Wing and upgrade a number of classrooms at Upper and Lower School. The Girls' High School later welcomed the opportunity to add Melbourne Annexe to their collection of buildings and they own it to this day.

The Opening of the New Building. The speaker is Chris Goater Y13
representing the students currently at KES

In November 1995, the celebrations continued with the launch of an anecdotal history of the school that was the brainchild of Peter Lawton of the English Department. Over a thousand Old Edwardians and staff members were contacted and invited to contribute their memories of the school for inclusion in the book. At the same time a competition for students in thirty classes at KES, asked for short contributions so that the present generation could also be well represented in the book. As Lawton himself says, *"we had no comprehension of the wealth of material that would come flooding in",* and ninety pieces were finally included in the published book. Many of them were *"minor literary gems, others straightforward honest accounts"* with the oldest contributor, George Rayner, describing his experiences of the school in 1914. The title, *"Tha'll never gerr in theer",* cast in very best Sheffieldish, came from a contribution by Professor David Downes of LSE. It had been the instantaneous reaction of his schoolmates on Shiregreen when he announced he had been selected for "King Teds" by the 11+ Examination. Some contributions came from well known local personalities, like Bob Jackson and Rony Robinson, and some from national figures like Lord Allen of Abbeydale, formerly the Permanent Secretary at the Home Office. However, the continuity and changes in KES history were perhaps best caught by a comment of Dr. Peter Beeley, a Life Fellow of Leeds University, who wrote that when he left KES and considered the possibilities of his future, *"most wildly improbable of all was that I would one day have two grand daughters who would also go to KES and have their own memorable experiences of the school."*

The architect of the Anniversary programme was the Headteacher, with some advice from a small group of prominent Old Edwardians and the Chair of Governors. All would agree though that the real work in driving the different projects and undertaking all the organising and contacting was done by his indefatigable and resourceful secretary Ann Smith. Her enthusiasm for the whole year's programme turned it from idea to reality, and she would take on any job that required doing. Before the Grand Reunion that was held on the 21st September 1996 and brought the 90th Anniversary Year to a close, she had spent weeks washing and then polishing all the mottled and stained trophies that the school possessed and that had once meant so much to their young winners. She was also somewhat shocked to find that there were more plinths than cups, perhaps some far-off winners became a little too attached to their trophies, or maybe the natural processes of time just led to their disappearance.

Throughout the winter, from November 1995 to the following March, the school had arranged a series of six prestigious lectures mostly given by former governors or parents of children at the school. Professor Julian Kinderlerer, a former Vice-Chair of the Governors spoke on his work in Genetic Engineering, posing the issue "Was there a limit?", whilst a former Chair of Governors, Professor Tony Crook, talked on the less global topic of the past, present and future of Sheffield housing. The lectures were well attended, students appreciating the contents and the major issues discussed, but the speaker who pulled in the biggest audience was the current controller of BBC Radio One, the nation's touchstone pop music channel. Mathew Bannister, after leaving KES in the Seventies, had risen through the ranks of the BBC to a position were he could dismiss radio DJ's who were living icons, keep others, like "Status Quo", off the air waves and promote the careers of new men such as Chris Evans and other heroes of our times. He was listened to in something akin to reverence as he probed the subject of the "Future of Radio Broadcasting".

The Appeal, which aimed to raise £100,000, did not do too badly. It may have fallen short of its ambitious target but it still produced £70,000 towards some much-needed capital priorities. Half of the monies raised went to upgrading the Science Laboratories, which hadn't been improved for fifty years, and the Technology Department, the rest was divided between new ICT equipment and some important rescue work on the outside fabric of the building. The Governors had hoped that English Heritage might use some of their Lottery generated money to make a substantial grant to clean and renovate the school's exterior and were encouraged when a senior official of English Heritage visited and enthused about the glories of KES, a Grade II* Listed Building. After climbing all over the roof, accompanied by the Headteacher and the Chair of Governors, he blithely informed them, to their incredulity, that if they were a public, independent or grant maintained school he would be delighted to recommend KES for grant aid. However, as they were a LEA maintained school they were ineligible.

The Grand Reunion, held on a Saturday night almost ninety years since Sir William Clegg presided over the opening of the new school in the Autumn of 1906, was one of those landmark occasions in the history of a school. At an appropriate hour, speeches were made by the Lord Mayor, the Headteacher and then Wanda Adamczyk of Y13 addressed the different generations on behalf of the Class of 1996. However, the real enjoyment of the night for the visitors, was to meet up with old friends and former classmates of thirty or forty years previously, search for old so-and-so's room and notice how so much still seemed the same. Some ventured into the "Lions den" of the Head's study and felt the frisson and trepidation that a visit to that inscrutable chamber could still inspire. On the lower corridor a group of middle aged gentlemen were observed playing shove-ha'penny as they had done decades before, except they now used pound coins and credit cards as their equipment of choice. It was a very happy night that brought the year of anniversary celebrations to a close and showed past Edwardians, not a few who had travelled from abroad, how thriving, ambitious and

Russell Sharrock, Arthur Jackson and Kay Madden at the 1996 Reunion. Between them they spanned almost fifty years of service to the school.

optimistic their old school was, twenty seven years after it had become a comprehensive school.

"Very Popular, Truly Comprehensive and Successful"

The school's morale was further increased by the report in March 1997 of the OFSTED Inspectors who had made a week long visit of inspection in January. There was some trepidation and certainly no complacency, about the Inspectors' visit because under its current chief, the controversial Chris Woodhead, OFSTED's rigorous inspections and uncompromising reports had acquired a certain notoriety within the educational world, as they publicly "named and shamed" schools they did not feel were up to scratch.

How different it had all been in 1952, at the time of the last HMI's Inspection, when the findings of the report on KES were discussed in the deepest confidentiality. Not that the 1952 Report was anything but overwhelmingly congratulatory, almost too much some felt, although the Inspection Report of 1933 had come as a bit of a shock to a school that felt it represented only excellence in all its practices. In 1997 the Governors looked forward to the Inspectors' visit and their subsequent Report with some apprehension. They knew the school was performing well above the national average in all examinations, from "A" Level to Key Stage 3 SATs, but wondered if they too could have been guilty of complacency about much that was happening in the school, which they would not be aware of in the normal course of their formal meetings. Theoretically they welcomed the OFSTED Inspection to give them an informed outside judgement on just how good the school was performing; in practice, of course, they were as keen as any student and staff member to portray the school in the most positive light.

During the week of their Inspection the OFSTED team observed 224 lessons, conducted 70 formal discussions and had numerous interviews with students. Their overall conclusion could not have been more satisfying to the Headteacher, the staff, students, parents and Governors. It read;

> *"This is a very popular, truly comprehensive and successful school where pupils attain high standards and the very high degree of racial harmony is a strength"*

The Inspectors could not have been more fulsome in their praise and their comments on the courteous, tolerant and co-operative behaviour of students, their good relationships with the staff, the quality of the racial harmony in the school, and their recognition of the good teaching that went on in 95% of the classrooms visited. The Leadership of the school was especially singled out for praise, not just the Headteacher, for whom the report was a personal triumph, but also the whole Management Team, the Heads of Departments and the Year Tutors. Even the Governors got a little praise for their support and active involvement in the life and business of the school.

All Parents received a copy of the Official Summary of the Report and if they wished could buy the full Report. The Report was their guarantee that the school they, and their children, had chosen was delivering a fine education. Particularly gratifying was a questionnaire returned by 19% of the parents that indicated that only 3% of their children did not like the school, whilst an overwhelming 90% liked being at KES, not a result you would necessarily get at all schools.

The Inspectors raised six Key Issues for action, almost all of which were very helpful. The school took on board suggestions that there should be a systematic dissemination of good teaching practice within and between departments, and that KES should improve its development planning. The Governors were delighted that the Inspectors had added their influential voices to the demand for better funding for more teaching resources and improved accommodation, thereby giving them useful ammunition with which to challenge the LEA over sub-standard bulidings.

The final Key Issue was the demand that KES comply with the law on holding a daily collective act of Christian worship. The Thatcher Government had laid great store by the social benefits of old fashioned morning assemblies, with their non-denominational Christian hymns and prayers, and reinforced the 1944 law by including new duties in their 1988 Education Act. Whatever views one has about the religious efficacy of the traditional school Christian assembly, the law seemed oblivious to the fact that many comprehensive schools now had substantial numbers of pupils from other faiths. By the next OFSTED Inspection in 2002 the Governors had not managed to find a way of complying with this law and the Inspection Report of that year flagged up the issue again.

The Language College

The most significant recent change to the organisational structure of the school came in 1998 with the gaining of Language College status. It further defined what sort of comprehensive school KES would be, brought in substantial capital (£100,000 from the Government, with the school having to find private sponsorship to match that amount) and on-going revenue monies, and it even affected alterations to the school's coat of arms, unchanged since 1905.

KES was encouraged by the LEA to make a bid for specialist school status in late 1996 when the Conservative Government, who had pioneered Technology Specialist Schools, widened the number of specialist subject areas. This allowed schools to bid for increased resources that would enable them to offer enhanced teaching and services in other subject. Sheffield already had three Technology Specialist Schools (Notre Dame 1995, King Egberts and Yewlands both 1996), but now, as a pilot, KES was chosen to make a bid for one of the new subject areas. Specialist schools were controversial in some quarters, but the Governors supported the school's application to be a Language College, although initially there was a possibility that KES would make a bid to become a Performing Arts College instead.

The school failed in its first attempt in 1997. A successful applicant needed to have a business sponsor to put up a matching £100,000 to be viable and there were no takers amongst Sheffield firms, weary of sponsorship demands during the Nineties, and often only outposts of London, or foreign, head offices. KES was rescued the following year by the Technology Colleges Trust itself, which had a pool of money from corporate sponsors that they could direct to support worthy bids. KES's new, well-constructed application, worked up by Richard Fone, gained approval from the DfES in June 1998.

The capital monies gained were largely focussed on building a multi-media language centre with 30 work-stations, originally planned to be an addition to the Lower School building at Darwin Lane. However, this plan was superseded when the LEA also offered KES an opportunity to have a complete rebuild of Lower School, under the new Labour Government's Private Finance Initiative. As this building would not be completed for three years, the Language Centre was built at Upper School instead, at a cost of £150,000 and dovetailed seamlessly into the New Building. In January 1999 the new Director of the Language College took up her appointment, before completing the planning and preparation to enable the centre to begin work in September of that year. Eva Lamb, an Austrian by birth and a graduate of Salzburg University, had come to Britain as a languages assistant and stayed on to qualify as a teacher. No one could have embraced the concept and possibilities of the Language College with more enthusiasm and vision, whilst the Headteacher added the designation for the whole school as "The International Centre for Language Learning", in time for David Blunkett, for some time an enthusiast for KES, to officially open the new centre in February 2000.

The Language College was, of course, not confined to one purpose built room, nor did KES stop striving for excellence, and successful development, in all the other subjects taught at the school. Rather, the Language College's work involved both sites, and supported teaching in many other subjects across the whole school. Its aims were obviously to increase the opportunity for language learning in the school, so more pupils would study more languages, (the school had a target of 50% students studying two languages in Y10 and Y11) as well as increasing the number of languages taught at the school. The school already had a high reputation for its language teaching and its inclusive policy meant that all students learnt at least one language until they were 16, not the situation at many comprehensives. Apart from the

In 1999 a competition was held at the school to devise a new coat of arms for KES which would incorporate the logo and name of the new Language College. This design by Nick Marsh of Y11 was selected as the winner because it maintains all the bearings of the school's traditional arms with some relevant new additions.

three main western European languages, they could already take Urdu in curriculum time and Italian in their own study time. Now, Japanese was introduced to the Lower School, and it was possible for any student to study three foreign languages at Key Stage 3 and Key Stage 4 (14 -16 years). More recently NVQ Vocational Courses have linked language learning with ICT, as an option for some students in the Middle School, while there are cross curricular links at "A" Level with Art and Geography groups going to France and a History group visiting Germany. From September 2004 the school has 15 students who have taken up the offer to study Mandarin Chinese and contacts have been made with Qingdao No 1. School in north east China. To strengthen this connection, a group of four KES teachers visited Qingdao in February 2005 intending to develop educational and cultural links with other subjects, including History and Art and Design, while the Chinese students themselves are keen to improve their command of English through closer ties with a British school.

The Language College's role was, however, to be much wider than school coursework. A vital and substantial part of its remit is to provide a language learning facility for the community and encourage a wider appreciation of other countries and other cultures. To this end, KES has good supportive links with its five feeder primary schools and supports language teaching in a number of secondary schools by organising events for pupils and opportunities for teacher training (KES is an official Centre for Professional Development for Language Teachers). Around 300 adults a year take advantage of the courses run at the school in the evenings. Amongst the nine languages on offer are Mandarin Chinese, Urdu, Greek and Portuguese and would-be world travellers, business mangers and staff are among those taking these courses.

At the weekend the facilities, which includes the use of the full range of language classrooms in the new building as well as the multi-media room, are used by a number of Community Language Schools. Here members of different ethnic communities in Sheffield run their own language classes for their sons and daughters, many of whom have been born in Britain. They include both Cantonese and Mandarin Chinese, Sudanese community classes in Arabic, Chileans teaching Spanish and Farsi classes for Iranian children. The Language College helps these groups with administrative support, plus advice on access to funding and training, and this is a partnership that is much valued, both by the school and the communities involved.

After three years the Language College had to seek re-designation in 2001 and it successfully negotiated this hurdle and gained continued funding for another four years. In 2004 the school received £180,000 (2.5% of the school's overall budget) to enable it to run the Language College and all its successful outreach work. In Lewis's words, the Language College has *"made a real impact on the school and the community and given a real impetus to education in an International context."*

KES - International School.

In the 1930s, the then Headmaster of KES, Richard Graham, promoted the ideals of internationalism and encouraged pupil exchanges, especially with German Schools. During the next two or three decades international links were severed by the war, and then made difficult by the austerity of the times in Britain and in Europe. During Russell Sharrock's time as Headmaster, international travel became easier and he was committed to the same internationalism that had inspired Graham in the pre-war period. In the Nineties, however, the school actively sought out foreign partnerships to add to these links, like the French Intensive Residential Week in February half term in Cambrai and exchange visits to the Goethe-Schule in Bochum, which were established in 1989.

Increasingly these visits had a specific education purpose and were less and less just goodwill exchanges. In the early Nineties there were work experience and work shadowing exchanges with the Goethe-Schule and Lycée Fenelon in Cambrai, where KES pupils were found a range of placements in German and French offices and businesses, and the Sociology Department linked with two schools in Espergaerde and Sonderberg to study the social life of Denmark. Two Czech students spent the academic year 1995-96 at KES, supported by the British Council and the school for a period had strong links with the Biskupse Gymnasium in Ceske Budejovice, a town better known by its German name of Budweis, the original home of the beer.

From 1993 the school had sent small groups over to South Carolina to visit T.L.Hanna High School in Anderson. One year the successful KES Basketball Team visited them and were trounced 91-25 by the home side in front of 800 spectators, but benefited from coaching sessions from the school coach. Later, and on firmer ground, the Blank Slate Company took over a group of their actors from several year groups and performed a number of excerpts from their current productions, that were broadcast on the local TV cable network. Close relations have been maintained for many years with the Goethe-Schule, a Gymnasium in Sheffield's "partnerstadt" of Bochum, where, alongside the imaginative work experience links, there have been History Department exchanges, not the easiest of subject areas for Anglo-German discourses. There are partner schools also in St Valery-en-Caux, in Barcelona, and now Madrid, one in Pisa and more recently links with two schools in Japan, including one in Kyoto and the Morimura High School in Tokyo, who sent 180 pupils to visit KES in October 2004. Altogether, in 2005, there are now official links with 15 schools abroad.

If KES's international reputation rested solely on its outward looking programme of connections with partner schools it would have a perfectly valid claim to be an international school, but its formal links with schools in other continents was only part of the story. KES itself is an international community of 25-30 ethnic groups and at any one time more than 20 first languages are spoken by its students. In 2005, 26% of the student body are from ethnic backgrounds other than white European, including a substantial number of boys and girls with dual heritage. While some schools in the Nineties may have seen this as an issue or a problem, KES has consistently welcomed this diversity and developed a strong anti-racist ethos that runs from top to bottom of the school. This welcoming of the diversity of the students can be seen in the robust handling of racial issues in PSHE lessons and by the successful International Evenings that began in early Nineties and embrace cultural performances from different ethnic groups at the school. In a typical concert there could be African drummers, Chinese dancers, musicians from the sub-continent, African-Caribbean gospel singers or rap artists, all celebrating their different cultures with the evening topped off by a feast of diverse culinary offerings. The whole event rounding off an "International Week" of poetry, dance, cooking, talent concerts, art, music and even sumo wrestling. As one sixth former said; *"we chose to come to KES because it was multi-cultural, we know we will live in multi-cultural cities, even international cities like London, or we might very well live and work abroad in the future, and KES's society gives us a fair preparation for what is now the real world!"*

However support for Black and Minority Ethnic (BME) students also takes on a systematic form for those who require it. Many BME students are amongst the most able in the school and more than hold their own in mainstream classes and go on to university, but there are others, some of whom are amongst the 17% who have English as a second language, who require extra support and this is provided by the Community Liaison Team of teachers, drawn from the main communities who make up KES diverse cultural pattern. Set up in 1991 when five teachers from SUMES joined the staff with the specific purpose of supporting BME students who needed extra help. One of this first group was Singapore born Hock-Ann Chia, who came to Britain in1970 to do a Master's Degree at UMIST, and after a period in the pharmaceutical industry (he worked on Oil of Ulay and later, in 1984, was employed at Orgreave) he joined the first SUMES team at KES in 1991. Their role was to help students on an individual basis, take small groups withdrawn from some classes and also support their students in a normal classroom situation. In the early days they spent considerable amount of time on home visits and were closely involved in their own ethnic community in the city.

Hock-Ann Chia became the co-ordinator of this group until 2003, while John Saddler and Mohammed Ackram were early members of the team and are still on the KES staff. John Saddler was born in St.Kitts, gained degrees in Theology from Andrews University in Michigan, and became a Minister of Religion. Before coming to KES he qualified as an electronic engineer at Sheffield Hallam University and, after working with the SUMES team, he is now a mainstream science teacher at the school. Ackram, who set up the Urdu Club, has regularly organised Eid Parties for all the school, visits to the Mela at the NEC, or Wembley, and an Urdu exchange with a school in Birmingham. This also served as a substitute for the foreign visits most language students enjoy, because, until recently, school trips to Pakistan have been considered prohibitively expensive. Most prominent has been a large notice board displaying aspects of Asian life, fashions and culture, as well as religious information on Islam, Hinduism and Sikhism. Urdu as a GCSE and "A" Level subject was introduced at the school by Iffat Hamid, a graduate of Punjab University, a J.P. and a broadcaster on BBC Radio Sheffield, who qualified as a teacher through the school's Graduate Training Programme. Then in 1999, SUMES, which had been funded by a Home Office grant under Section 11, was replaced by EMAS (the Ethnic Minority Achievement Service) funded by a specific DfES grant to the school and the Community Liaison Team became mainstream subject teachers, spending a percentage of their time-table as departmental teachers as well as continuing their previous close support work.

The school is proud of its record in external examinations, where all BME groups usually perform well against the city average for all students. Some ethnic groups do outstandingly well, whilst some students may have only been in Britain for a short time and may have come from countries where there is civil war and administrative chaos. Some are still traumatised by their experiences, and in the Nineties, the Community Liaison Group supported students from Somalia who had never been to school, in one case had never used a pencil, and others from Kosovo who had witnessed unspeakable horrors against members of their own family. Some make rapid progress, like Lan-You, a Chinese girl who spoke virtually no English when she arrived in Britain before GCSE, then went on to gain a place at Cambridge. Similarly Nimao Bodleh from Somalia, who also arrived in Britain with no knowledge of English has recently graduated from Manchester Metropolitan University. Many foreign national pupils come to the school because their parents have taken up staff posts, or graduate courses, at the University, or in the Hospitals, and the school's high academic reputation, as well as its genuine welcome to overseas students, encourages many of them to choose to come to KES. Michael Lewis is keen to stress that raising the achievement of the BME students is not just the task of the Community Liaison Group but is a whole school objective. Therefore one of the most pleasing recent statistics is that the rate of progress of BME students between Key Stage 3 and Key Stage 4 is the highest of any students in the school; in modern jargon the best "added value" of all KES students.

A postscript to the internationalism of KES students occurred in 2003 when the Iraq War broke out. A substantial number of students walked out of school and joined demonstrations against Britain's participation in the fighting. The school, of course, did not approve or condone this "truancy", but it indicated how strongly many young people felt about the use of military action as an instrument of policy. Potentially the Iraq war was a divisive issue in the school. Some KES students were Iraqi nationals with family members in Baghdad and Basra, while others had family members in the Forces in the Gulf, and it says much for the mature way everyone approached this situation that differences of opinion could be aired and respected. Meanwhile, the Headteacher's sensitive handling of the situation, ensured that the unity of the school was maintained in what could have been a most difficult period.

PFI - Two Cheers!!

There was another exciting opportunity for the school in 1998, when after years of concern about the deterioration of the fabric and the interior of Lower School, the Governors were, quite out of the blue, offered the chance of a completely new school building. They had been selected, by the LEA, as one of six schools, four secondary (including next door Tapton) and two primary schools, for a complete re-build. It was made possible by the new Labour Government's Private Finance Initiative (PFI) that shifted the risk of financing the design, building and maintenance onto private consortiums of builders, architects, bankers and facility managers. Because the PFI schools were "owned" by the consortium, the cost of these new schools would not be included in the Government's PSBR, nor would it appear as part of the council's capital borrowing, instead the public purse would repay the consortium rather handsomely from revenue over the following twenty five years. If the Governors had any political, or philosophical, reservations about the method of financing (in 1998 they were not yet used to Labour's enthusiasm for partnerships with the private sector) they quickly realised they had little alternative and accepted the council's offer to build a new school by September 2001. At that point the old buildings, that had started life as Crosspool Secondary Modern in 1965, would be demolished.

The fact that the completed building has never had a formal opening (the Queen opened Fir Vale School, one of the four PFI secondary schools), speaks volumes for the difficulties that have occurred since the building was erected, although between 1998 and 2000, four Governors, and the Headteacher, regularly met with a working group at the Town Hall to detail specifications and then select the winning consortium. They were determined that the new building would not replicate the faults of the 1965 building, rather that it would be an attractive structure, that would be educationally viable, as well as innovative and imaginative in design. They were also determined not to let this opportunity slip to obtain, as an extra provision, a Sports Hall, that would complement the new replacement gymnasium.

By late 1999 the applicants had been whittled down to two consortia. One led by the builders Sir Robert McAlpine, and the other by Tilbury Douglas, who had completed a number of major projects in the city. They were to be judged not just on design, but on the financial, legal and facilities management deal that they could offer the Council. Tilbury Douglas emerged from this systematic vetting process as the overall winner, although the KES Governors preferred the McAlpine design that would have created a linear school building with a spacious, internal, glass roofed "street" running the length of the building. However the Tilbury Douglas design appeared to have much to commend it, with particularly appealing features such as the new Library, broad corridors and at last a purpose built Sports Hall. The latter had finally been conceded after a campaign of attrition by the Chair of Governors, who had sat in meeting after meeting repeating the mantra *"don't forget the King Edward's Sports Hall"*, until they had wearied and included it in the final plans.

Building work started in April 2000 and it was expected it would be completed by July the following year, at a cost of £8.4 million. This would allow a summer of transition from one building to the other. In the event, it was only through the Herculean efforts of the staff packing, and then unpacking, equipment by hand at the eleventh hour, that allowed the school to at least open on the Monday of the second week of the new Autumn term. Several Departments discovered that their rooms, or equipment, were just not available. The Technology Department and the Science Department could not function at all, and the Music Room and Drama Studio, conveniently placed next to each other, where unusable because sound travelled with little hindrance from one room to the other. Drama lessons were held in the Assembly Hall until adequate sound-proofing was installed. There were numerous smaller annoyances. The Science Department found that each of its 150 cupboards had a different key and no master key could be delivered till December. Rod Auton, who throughout the next four years would do sterling work engaging with the consortium to alleviate all the problems encountered (he did 39 tours of inspection), took three of the locks to a local locksmith, who produced a number of masters within the hour.

The New Lower School at Darwin Lane

Students and their parents were unaware of most of these difficulties and they delighted in an apparently splendid new building, but few were able to ignore the chaos that ensued in the Dining Room. The consortium, now called Interserve, having built the school, were now responsible for the maintenance, cleaning, the care-taker and security and the catering of Lower School. Under the PFI arrangements the school's educational provision was clearly under the control and direction of the Headteacher and Kath Auton, the Head of Lower School, but in return for a precept, deducted annually from the school budget, Interserve provided many of the key non-teaching services on the site. Frustratingly, Kath Auton and her staff could only complain and demand action, rather than take it, if there were problems. The biggest initial problem was catering, where it seemed to be beyond the capability of an international catering firm, who were a sub-contractor of the consortium, to serve the required number of dinners within the school's dinner time. Forty-five minutes were lost from the afternoon's teaching time on a regular basis, and a pre-paid card system, intended to speed up the process, was so universally disliked that eventually the students boycotted school lunch altogether. When this appeared in the local press, the consortium moved very quickly to abolish the scheme, change their caterers and eventually provide a satisfactory service.

The old Lower School was demolished in the Autumn term 2001 (the bridge with its offices, library and toilets was lifted out in one piece by a crane), and a sizeable floodlit all-weather pitch was built on the site were the old buildings and their car park had been. After four years the Lower School is running smoothly, although there are still major problems with acoustics, both reverberation and sound transference, and the drainage of some of the playing fields is a major problem in wet weather. However, if there is still frustration there is also pride in new facilities that are a considerable improvement on those that had gone before.

Main Entrance of the New Lower School

The PFI lasts for 25 years, after which time the ownership of the Lower School will revert back to the LEA, or their successor body if LEAs, or even councils, no longer exist. Payment for Interserve's management of the facilities has not been a great financial burden to KES so far, as the annual budget deduction was set at a fair level, and none of the consortium's services affect Upper School in any direct way. In that building the maintenance, catering, cleaning and the caretakers are all managed and funded in the same way as before, although most of the services since the early Nineties have been run by open tender contracts.

Over 500 - the Largest in the County!

KES has always had an outstanding Sixth Form, in fact one of the main purposes in creating the new school in 1905 was to establish a large Sixth Form with high quality teaching that would prepare boys for the universities. James Hichins, the first Headmaster, succeeded magnificently in this task, but he would be impressed to see that the current Sixth Form has 512 students (his entire school was only 317 pupils in 1905), who can choose from 26 "A" Level subjects and that 75-80% of them go on to University, including, on average, seven a year to Oxbridge.

Dr. Rebecca Carpenter, the newly appointed Assistant Headteacher in 2000, took over a successful Sixth Form which had grown in the later Nineties to just about 400 students under Sheila Basford, the retiring Head of Post-16 Studies. It was achieving very creditable "A" Level results and had widened its intake of students by offering two vocational GNVQ courses. In the last five years the Sixth Form has made another leap forward both in numbers and in external examination successes, while at the same time having to cope with major changes to the "A" Level courses and considerable semi-informed criticism of the standards and content of those same GCE examinations.

The introduction of Curriculum 2000 at the turn of the century, with its AS Level examinations in four subjects in Y12 (the first year of the Sixth Form) was intended to widen the number of subjects studied by Sixth Formers and avoid narrow specialisation. Students were encouraged to "mix and match", not just between sciences and arts subjects, but with vocational AVCE courses (which had superseded the GNVQs), but there was only a limited amount of subject "crossover" at KES. The first Year Group involved were unimpressed, partly because they had been the "guinea pigs" for the introduction of SATS in Key Stage 3 and the Key Stage 4 courses. They now found that the old relaxed and reflective year after GCSE, was abolished in favour of more examinations, in an education culture that had become over-preoccupied with exams. After completing their four "AS" Level Exams they could concentrate, as before, on just three subjects in their final "A2" year, although a significant proportion continued with all their subjects and subsequently succeeded.

Not only did the numbers in the Sixth Form increase so did the final "A2" Level results. In 2001 the overall pass rate was 95.2%, with 47.5% achieving A and B grades. By 2004 the pass rate was 98.1%, for the third consecutive year the school's highest ever pass rate, as well as averaging 50% A and B grades in all "A" Levels taken. Nineteen subjects had a 100% pass rate in 2004 and this in a school that is not selective, and only asked of its Sixth Form entrants that they had a minimum of five GCSE A-C Grades. It is not only KES students who have done well, for there is a national trend of success and it is frustrating to present-day students to find that the popular press, reflecting views of people — often forgetting how ordinary they were themselves at 18 years of age – who cast doubt on these successes. Instead of celebrating a remarkable achievement by today's young people, who have been asked to perform well in external examinations and have done so magnificently, they prefer to impugn the examination standards and belittle the Sixth Formers' accomplishments. How much better, however, it is to have the "problem" of these successes than what might have been, a feckless, uncommitted teenage population seduced away from education by all the glossy, if not tawdry, appeal of our imperfect popular culture.

By 2002 the numbers wanting to join the KES Sixth Form had reached over 250 per year and the Governors, realising that the school could not continue with an "Open Door" policy, fixed a limit of 500 pupils in the Sixth Form, with an annual admission limit of 140 "incomers" per annum. Since then, all the schools with sixth forms, in line with legislative requirements, have had to draw up criteria with the LEA, to maintain non-selective admission but on a demonstrably fair basis, comparable with the regulations governing admission to schools at Y1 and Y7. For thirty years the Sixth Form has been attractive to students at other schools who wanted to complete their post-16 education at KES and many sixteen year old students have come from all over the city, and also north Derbyshire, to join the Sixth Form. They have soon fitted into the KES community and perform as well in "A" Level Examinations, as do those students who have come up through the ranks from Y7.

The increase in Sixth Formers is partly because of the school's reputation, partly national pressure to encourage staying on and partly a recognition that good jobs available to 16 year old leavers have disappeared. Continuing in full time education was made more attractive for some, by the introduction of the means-tested Educational Maintenance Allowance, that can be worth £30 per week to students who qualify (more than 25% of KES Sixth Formers do), and the improvement in GCSE results has qualified more students to continue their education at KES. Some will be encouraged by the range of subjects available at "A" Level, where in 2005 there was a choice of 26 subjects including Psychology, Archaeology, Urdu, Photography and Philosophy as well as almost all the subjects that have traditionally been on offer at KES since 1905. Perhaps in the immediate future there may be a dip in Sixth Form numbers at the school, partly caused by a general demographic down-turn in numbers and partly by the new Longley Park Sixth Form College (opened in 2004) and the new Hillsborough Tertiary College (opened in 2005) getting into their stride. However, at present, the KES Sixth Form has never been more buoyant in numbers and morale. It is the largest Sixth Form in South Yorkshire and possibly the sixth largest in England and Wales, and has a very active Common Room Committee who organise social events, including a most sophisticated Leavers' Ball at Sheffield's top dining venue. Up to 80% of the students are involved in one of the popular extra-curricular activities on offer at the school, and Youth Action, Young Enterprise and the Duke of Edinburgh's Award Scheme are as well supported as they have been at any time over the last thirty years.

The effectiveness of the Sixth Form was highlighted by the school's second OFSTED report in 2002, which concentrated on the Post-16 work of the school. After praising the high standards of the school, especially its high degree of *"racial harmony"*, and noting how the school had moved on from its equally good OFSTED Report of 1997, they said of the Sixth Form;

"The Sixth Form is inclusive and very effective in meeting the learning needs of its students. Their progress is very good and they achieve high standards because the teaching is very good and the school sets high expectations. The Sixth Form is well managed, highly cost effective and creates an environment conducive to teaching and learning."

Two Sportsmarks 1999 and 2002

Of all the recognition of the school's achievements in the Nineties, none gave more pleasure than the award of Sport England's prestigious Sportsmark in 1999. Despite the meagre sports facilities at the school at that time, the Sportsmark recognised the thought and hard work that had gone into developing the school's holistic approach to sport and P.E., and the recovery from the difficulties of the late Eighties that had ravaged inter-school sport. Today, a century after the school was founded, there are 17 sports played at KES, nearly all of them on a cross-gender basis. So girls play Football and boys try their hand at Netball. The school now has indoor facilities and a floodlit all-weather pitch at Lower School, that can stand comparison with most schools. After years without a team, Cricket was re-established as an inter-school sport in 2003, partly because of the enthusiasm of Asian students who make up 60% of the team and in 2004 the KES Under 12's were the runners up in the Sheffield Schools' League. In 2005 the Y11 Rugby League XIII won the South West Yorkshire R.L. Cup for the fourth year running, demonstrating the progress the school is making at Rugby League Football that started at the school in 1995. KES are currently ranked second among the schools in the area.

Sixth Form sport has also made something of a recovery and the school once again fields an Open Age 1st XI Football team, but it is the Middle and Lower Schools that provide the players who gain city and county honours. One of their "stars", Tyrone Thompson, went on to play professional football for Sheffield United, the first Old Edwardian to play for either Sheffield club since the war. The new facilities at the Lower School, which include a state of the art weight training suite, have transformed the recreational programme that the school can now offer. No longer do large numbers of students go off-site to use outside facilities, like the dry ski slope or the skating rink, but most of the

The KES Y10 Rugby League Team. Winners of the 2004 South West Yorkshire R.L. Trophy.

seventeen sports can now be accommodated on the school premises, even if the number of grass pitches is still woefully inadequate for a school of 1676 students.

The school gained a second Sportsmark in 2002, after Alan Friggens, who has been a most effective member of the P.E. teaching team since 1995, had replaced Eileen Battersby as the Head of the Department. One of their most amazing records is the schools' success in Athletics. Since 1993 KES has won the Firth Vickers League Championship for Sheffield Schools in thirteen consecutive years, and regularly produce a number of individual Champions in the City Finals (in 1993 there were 14). Several athletes, like Katrina Buccieri, in 1996, and more recently Zara Hohn, in 2003 and 2004, represented South Yorkshire in the ESAA Championships, which have been held four times at the Don Valley Stadium since 1996, with a considerable contingent of KES students joining the volunteers who have run the event. The school's long tradition of success in Cross Country is still intact, with several runners representing the county, among them Nikki Squires who won the County Championship in 2003. One of the most impressive performances in recent years occurred when Sixth Former, Gareth Turner, a triple county cross country champion, was awarded the Sheffield Schools' Sports Personality of the Year Award in 2004, a trophy once held by Sebastian Coe.

In the Nineties KES produced at least a dozen international representatives, or national champions, in a bewildering range of sports. In 1995 Mathew Jenkins represented England in Nordic Skiing in Italy, Jonathon Cowie swam for Scotland in the Butterfly event in 1998, and in the same year Richard Gouldbourn was in the English Schools' Cycling Team competing in Holland. Richard Windle in 1993, Nat Cochrane in 1999 and Anthony Marsh in 2005, gained international honours for England at Basketball, and Cochrane was a member of the successful KES team that won a National Basketball Final in 2000, while Windle now plays professionally for the Sheffield Sharks. Another Basketball International was Frankie Morton, who, in 2001, was named as the English Women's Junior Basketball "Player of the Year". In the late Nineties, inspired by Richard Fone, before he left to become a Deputy Head at Brinsworth C.S. in Rotherham, the school had a very successful period in competitive weightlifting, a sport that had never featured at the school before. There were several individual champions at the North Eastern Counties Championships, including Zahaid Khan and Bryn Lucas who broke records when they lifted over 100% of their body weight in the 1999 competition. One weightlifter, Jordan Mitchell, entered for the "Britain's Strongest Youth" Competition and was the runner up; another first for KES. If all this was not enough, Adam Walker was a finalist in the Roller Blade National Champion, held at the NEC in 1998, Joanne Siddall, a Y9 girl, represented England at Karate, Daniel Tett represented his country at Orienteering in 2001, whilst three KES students qualified for the National Biathlon Championships in 2003.

Into the New Century

Five years into the Twenty-First century KES is in rude good health. 2002 was a particularly successful year when, apart from an excellent Ofsted Report and the award of a second Sportsmark, the school gained the European Award for Languages, one of only four given to UK schools that year by the European Union. The DfES chipped in with a second Achievement Award, which recognised the efforts of the staff in raising standards at the school year on year. This Government initiative only ran for three years, 2001-2003, and KES staff won the award in all three years. Apart from the usual certificate, £48,000 per annum was distributed equally amongst the 150 teaching and non- teaching staff, because this was an award to recognise the importance of teamwork, in schools that did significantly better than similar schools, mainly in their external examination results. There had been outstanding "A" Level and GCSE results in 2002, both of them all-time records for the school and both registering a pass rate of over 96% and there have been even better years since. To cap a successful year, David Bell, the Chief Ofsted Inspector, in his annual report to Parliament mentioned the school as having received *"an outstanding inspection report, and performed well in tests and examinations, given the circumstances of the school".* In recognition of these achievements, Michael Lewis was invited to a reception at Highgrove House hosted by H.R.H. The Prince of Wales, where, on a conducted tour of the gardens, he got soaked to the skin during a downpour of biblical proportions.

The then Chair of Governors, although he would be the first to admit that none of this success was due to him, decided now was the time to retire and was replaced by Dr. Karl Gehring, who had been a parent Governor and previously, before coming to Sheffield, a Fellow at two Oxford Colleges, Hertford and University. The 1988 Education Act had theoretically added many new duties to the Governing Body, but they worked in close partnership with the Headteacher and the school and saw themselves as practical supporters of a successful institution. The KES Governors, since their reconstitution in the early Seventies, have always contained some very able members, who have been encouraged to visits lessons and experience a normal day in the life of the school, not just attend evening meetings when all is silent and deserted. In the 1999 General Election two Governors, John Harthman (Cons) and Richard Allan (Lib Dems), fought each other for the Hallam Constituency. Allan won, thereby gaining the only seat in South Yorkshire to have changed hands in thirty-five years. In the 2005 General Election another recent governor, Coun. Angela Smith, was elected as the new Labour member for the Hillsborough Division.

There is, of course, another side to this story of the school's success in recent years. Comprehensive schools are subject to all kinds of dramas, and individual traumas, that can blow up at a moment's notice and take up disproportionate amount of staff time to resolve. Not for them the steady hum of the selective grammar school, rather KES, as a very large, city centre school, is subject to many of the problems that affect a modern LEA school. Yet it is the imperative duty of a comprehensive school, to offer the best education possible to students, even if they are reluctant to learn, or are confrontational and disruptive.

KES continues to have a student social profile that covers, in relatively equal proportions, the full spectrum of families in the city, from the very comfortable to the most deprived.

A successful comprehensive school is not judged just by its "A" Level results, its high ranking in the GCSE "League Tables", or even the numbers winning places at Oxbridge, but also how it strives to educate, not just the academically "weak yet willing", but those who appear to have no interest in formal education at all. KES like other comprehensives in the city, takes the unselected pupils who are allocated to it by the LEA. Catchment areas, "feeder" primary schools and parental choice clearly have a major influence on the kind of student that joins the school at eleven years of age, but a comprehensive school reflects its community, with all its imperfections, in a way a grammar, or independent, school does not. Adults who are on the fringes of society, even criminals and drug abusers, have children and they all go to one of their local comprehensive schools where they are entitled to as good an education as any other child. For some youngsters, KES is an *"oasis of calm, hope and achievement"* away from their chaotic, even violent and abusive, out-of-school environment.

Michael Lewis regards himself as *"a willing optimist, prepared to see the best in students and a belief that all have the capacity to change and develop"*. He refuses to take the easy cynical view that some children are beyond the help of the educational system, rather that during those *"complex teenage years amidst a complex society, KES should show a generosity of spirit and support, ensuring that the best the school has available is shared equally between all the students at the school."* Therefore at KES the best teachers, resources, opportunities, care and advice are available to the very difficult child, as well as the highest flyer. Recent Government policies on Inclusion only reflect what was already KES policy. A Student Inclusion Resource has been in place since 1999 and annually supports a number of vulnerable students, some of them with severe emotional and behavioural difficulties, and the third Deputy Headteacher post was re-created in 2004, when Robert Whittingham came from Myers Grove School to take up that position, with responsibility for Inclusion. The school is not naïve enough to believe it can solve all its problems, and teachers are only too well aware that indiscipline if not checked is a cancer that can destroy a school. The school is prepared to use temporary exclusions, but compared with most schools this runs at a fairly low level, while only two or three students (or .02%) a year are permanently excluded from KES, and only after every effort has been made to reconcile them with the requirements of the school.

Lewis also believes that comprehensive schools have yet to deliver their full potential. If he has any regrets about the seventeen years he has spent at KES so far, it is that like other comprehensives, the school has not sufficiently closed the achievement gap between middle class and working class students. As most of KES's ethnic minority students come from working class homes, there is also a gap between the average academic performance of the school's BME students and the overall school average, although some ethnic groups do remarkably well. Despite this, he believes that comprehensive education, far from having run its course, is one of the great social reforms of our time and among its really solid achievements to date, are the raising of standards and opportunities for so many, keeping our society unified and enjoying a more equal lifestyle.

The Leadership Team in 2005.
The Headteacher with the Deputy and Assistant Headteachers.
(L to R) Kath Auton, Kevin Drakely, Dr. Rebecca Carpenter, Kay Madden, Michael
Lewis, Rob Whittingham, Debbie Bates (Bursar), Chris Phipps, Tracy Tunbridge.
Photo by Karl Gehring

Lewis's great concern for the future is the perennial question of the quality and breadth of the curriculum. He believes strongly that; *"an enlightened, humane, relevant and intelligent education system has to have aspirations which go well beyond meeting the needs of the economy. The great challenge is to take the rhetoric of life long learning and make a reality of it in the day to day experience of all the school's students"*

There have always been competing demands for the "soul" of education, with employers looking for specific skills to benefit their businesses, while educational "purists" believe in pursuing knowledge for its own intrinsic worth. Perhaps KES's emphasis on Classics for much of its history is the best example of the latter view. Finding the right balance has never been higher on the political and educational agenda, and there is no doubt that at the beginning of KES's second century this crucial issue will have to be addressed at an early date.

In Retrospect!

When Dr. James Hichens died in 1938, KES was not much different from the school he had established in 1905. All the major institutions of the school were still intact, although

KES had lost its official public school status, the OTC had been replaced by the Scout Troop and the school was nowhere near as "philistine" as it had been, now there was a flourishing music and drama tradition. The numbers on roll had more than doubled since 1905, more boys were getting scholarships to Oxbridge on an annual basis and, although he had been an enthusiast for the sporting ethic in schools, there was considerably more success on the sports field than there had been in his time. While the main building was exactly the same, the school had acquired the use of a superb swimming pool, rather than the dank black hole bequeathed them by Wesley College, and the Junior School had found an elegant home in Clarke House, less than a quarter of a mile away.

If Hichens had been able to return in Nathaniel Clapton's final year, a quarter of a century later, he would still have felt instantly at home both in the building and in the classrooms. True, the boys wore dark blue blazers now rather than suits, the Junior School was long gone, incredibly the "backs" still remained, but the curriculum was little changed from his time. The staff, entirely male and predominately Oxbridge graduates, still strode the corridors in their gowns and in the main, used "chalk and talk" and note taking from the textbook and blackboard, as their preferred manner of teaching. Hichens, a keen collector of favourable statistics, would have been impressed, if not overwhelmed, by the Oxbridge successes of the early 1960s, and we can assume that he would have found the Council's recent decision to turn the school into a comprehensive school quite inexplicable. He was an élitist, but he might well have envied Clapton, whose school was composed of most of the city's young male intellectual élite, where examination success was almost guaranteed; unlike his own time when KES had quite a long "tail" of fee-paying boys of average talent.

If Hichens could walk through the Newbould Lane gates to-day from his house on the corner, as he did thousands of times in his twenty four years as Headmaster, would he recognise, or approve, of King Edward VII School a century after its foundation? The main building, of course, would be instantly recognisable, and he would no doubt find the new building quite acceptable, although he might be perplexed by the security measures of CCTV and entrance codes, introduced after the Head of Science, Arnold Lawson, confronted two intruders in 1997, one of whom threatened him with a revolver. He would expect change to have occurred over a hundred years – public schools in the early nineteenth century were brutal, often lawless and totally inefficient institutions (the militia was called out to quell a riot at Winchester) — so he might not be surprised that the school was now co-educational, after all he had appointed female staff members during the First World War to teach in the Junior School. He would, however, be surprised that half of the Deputy and Assistant Headteachers, and many of the Heads of Departments, were women and also that a quarter of the school consisted of students from the ethnic minorities.

Virtually all the institutions that defined his school, and were considered so vitally important for its effective progress, have all disappeared in the last forty years. Speech Days, formal Morning Assemblies of the whole school, Head Boys and Prefects, Uniforms, Houses, Corporal Punishment, School Magazines, Scouts, the teaching of

Classics and now, it would appear to him, most of the staff dressed not in gowns, but in casual clothes.

One would not expect him to be converted to comprehensive education, at least in the short term, but as a fair minded man he would appreciate how the modern KES was successfully educating so many pupils of such widely differing abilities and backgrounds. He would recognise that the school was achieving remarkable results despite a range of social and educational problems, that as the Headmaster of an exclusive boys' school he would not have been called upon to face, although poverty and deprivation were much worse in Edwardian society. Hichens might be a little overawed by the numbers in the school, at least five times the number in the Edwardian period (the present Sixth Form is as big as his whole school was when he left in 1926), with a budget well over a 1000 times larger and a teaching staff of over 100 rather than the 15 he had at the foundation of the school. If he wondered how all the 1670 + pupils were accommodated, he would discover that there was another building with nearly 700 students a mile and a half away, in what had been open fields in his day.

If there have been changes there is also much that is fundamental about the school that has not changed. Almost all the subjects that were on the curriculum in 1905, English, Maths, History, Geography, Science (now much extended), Foreign Languages, Music, Art, Wood and Metal work, Gym/P.E. and Divinity/R.E. still form the core of KES teaching in the Lower and Middle Schools. Only Classics is missing with its place as a major element of the curriculum taken by ICT. Perhaps it is appropriate that the medieval key to access knowledge, has been replaced by its modern successor.

Who knows where ICT will take us in the next few decades. It may even make formal teaching in school buildings redundant, as it has already affected the working situation for some. However, at present, almost all subjects are still taught in classroom groups, students sit at desks and teachers stand at the front using the board (now white not black) as their predecessors have done at KES throughout the century. The KES teaching staff themselves, as in 1905, are specialists not generalists, and almost all have degrees from British Universities, although very few Oxbridge graduates teach in comprehensive schools today. The senior students still specialise in a limited number of subjects when they enter the Sixth Form for their last two, or possibly three years, at the school, and their final external examination, whether the "A" Level of to-day, or the Higher School Certificate before 1952, is still a passport to university. To-day at least 50% of all the pupils who start at KES in Y7, will go on to University, and the percentage of to-day's Sixth Formers going to University stands comparison with any period in the school's history, and is, of course, much larger in actual numbers.

The pursuit of excellence is still very much a priority for KES in 2005, as it has been at all other times in the last century. James Hichens, and several of his successors, believed that this could be achieved, not only by good teaching, but also by a long litany of prescriptive rules that would be enforced by an omnipotent disciplinary code. A student entering KES to-day is more likely to be handed a list of the school's "Aims and Values" and reminded of their obligations, because a successful modern comprehensive school, reflecting our democratic society, runs, to a considerable extent, on the consent and co-operation of the student body. A "Code of Conduct" is, of course, still in place but, reflecting the world of 2005, makes reference to items and issues – drugs, weapons, homophobia, racism etc. – which a late Victorian like James Hichens, would have struggled to comprehend in a school context. Involving parents in their children's education and progress is now regarded as a right and a duty, as well as a practical advantage, unlike the attitude of one post-war Headmaster, for whom parents were, at best, a necessary evil. It is rumoured that this particular Head once frog-marched a parent out of the main entrance, because he had turned up to an interview without a jacket and tie.

Will there still be a King Edward VII School in 2105? - Probably not! Apart from the changes that are bound to be wrought on education by ICT, and other technological changes as yet undreamed of, education is certain to stay high on the political agenda of a nation that has to live by its wits in a world of ever accelerating change. Politicians, industry and commerce, the universities, the arts and sport, possibly the church and the mosque and even the military, will all have their ideas how education should be structured and what should be taught in the future. KES might well outlive the LEA, even the City Council, and the building designed by Flockton, one hundred and sixty seven years ago, will most probably still be standing, accidents and disasters notwithstanding. It might, however, be serving a totally different purpose (who would have expected the GLC to become a hotel and an aquarium) from that for which it was originally intended, although on balance, it is still likely to be a place of learning, as long as our society prizes education.

Few schools have seen as many dramatic changes as KES during the last one hundred years, yet through all these changes from fee-paying public school, to an all-scholarship boys' grammar school and finally a co-educational comprehensive, this remarkable school has continued to provide excellence in education and has served its community well. Maintenance of this achievement will provide the ability to respond to the opportunities ahead, and it is also its best defence against the vicissitudes of the future.

INDEX

It is regretted that it has only been possible to produce a limited index.

THE AUTHOR

John Cornwell is a former Chair of KES Governors (1994-2002) and is still a member of the Governing Body.

He was born in Hull in 1939 and educated at Hymers College, the London School of Economics and Sheffield University, before becoming a teacher. He taught History and Government for many years at Ecclesfield School and also taught abroad in Jamaica and Canada.

He divided his time between teaching and local politics and was the Deputy Leader of the South Yorkshire County Council and a sometime member of Sheffield City Council. He has held a number of national, regional and local positions including membership of the Arts Council of Great Britain (where he chaired the Touring Board and the Education Committee), Vice Chair of the Yorkshire and Humberside Sports Council (1974-86) and Vice Chair of Yorkshire Tourist Board. He chaired the Organising Committee for four English Schools' Athletics Championships between 1996 and 2003 and for a number of years was a member of the Football Trust. He was also a UN Observer at the 1994 South African Elections.

His interests include the theatre (he was the Chair of Sheffield Theatres – Crucible and Lyceum – from 1988 to 1996) and Rugby League Football, where he served as the Chair of the RFL Youth Commission. He has written the history of Sheffield Eagles RLFC and a number of poems that are strictly for family and friends only.